BAD ADVICE

BAD ADVICE

Bush's Lawyers in the
War on Terror

Harold H. Bruff

University Press of Kansas

Published by the University Press of Kansas (Lawrence, Kansas 66045),
which was organized by the Kansas Board of Regents and is operated
and funded by Emporia State University, Fort Hays State University,
Kansas State University, Pittsburg State University, the University of
Kansas, and Wichita State University

Library of Congress Cataloging-in-Publication Data

Bruff, Harold H., 1944–
Bad advice : Bush's lawyers in the war on terror / Harold H. Bruff.
p.   cm.
Includes bibliographical references and index.
ISBN 978-0-7006-1643-5 (cloth : alk. paper)
1. War and emergency powers—United States—History. 2. Government
attorneys—History. 3. War on Terrorism, 2001– I. Title.
KF5060.B78 2009
342.73′062—dc22
2008049820

British Library Cataloguing-in-Publication Data is available.
Printed in the United States of America

10 9 8 7 6 5 4 3 2 1

The paper used in this publication is recycled and contains 30 percent
postconsumer waste. It is acid free and meets the minimum requirements
of the American National Standard for Permanence of Paper for Printed
Library Materials Z39.48 1992.

BAD ADVICE

Bush's Lawyers in the War on Terror

Harold H. Bruff

University Press of Kansas

Published by the University Press of Kansas (Lawrence, Kansas 66045),
which was organized by the Kansas Board of Regents and is operated
and funded by Emporia State University, Fort Hays State University,
Kansas State University, Pittsburg State University, the University of
Kansas, and Wichita State University

Library of Congress Cataloging-in-Publication Data

Bruff, Harold H., 1944–
Bad advice : Bush's lawyers in the war on terror / Harold H. Bruff.
p.   cm.
Includes bibliographical references and index.
ISBN 978-0-7006-1643-5 (cloth : alk. paper)
1. War and emergency powers—United States—History. 2. Government
attorneys—History. 3. War on Terrorism, 2001– I. Title.
KF5060.B78 2009
342.73´062—dc22
2008049820

British Library Cataloguing-in-Publication Data is available.
Printed in the United States of America

10 9 8 7 6 5 4 3 2 1

The paper used in this publication is recycled and contains 30 percent
postconsumer waste. It is acid free and meets the minimum requirements
of the American National Standard for Permanence of Paper for Printed
Library Materials Z39.48 1992.

CONTENTS

ACKNOWLEDGMENTS

Authors get a lot of help, and I am no exception. Beginning this litany of thanks at home and moving outward, I send love and gratitude to my wife, Sherry, and daughter, Annie, who all too often let me disappear upstairs when a beautiful Colorado morning beckoned us all. At the University of Colorado Law School, Dean David Getches and the faculty and students graciously listened and responded when I developed some of the book's ideas in the school's Scott Lecture. Jane Thompson of the Wise Law Library unearthed many research nuggets. Colorado Law students Seaton Thedinger, Michael Levy, and Carly O'Connell provided expert research assistance. My faculty assistant, Cara Paddle, met every request with grace and skill.

The University Press of Kansas has been a joy to work with. Editor in Chief Michael Briggs, Assistant Director Susan Schott, and Production Editor Jennifer Dropkin have smoothed the path from manuscript to book. Copyeditor Melanie Stafford improved the flow and consistency of my prose. The press employed two outside readers, the thinly disguised Sandy Levinson and a still-anonymous reader, who critiqued the manuscript and helped me improve it materially in the late stages. Lou Fisher also supplied some crisp insights.

A group sometimes known as the Magnolias provided cures for incipient pomposity in locales ranging from Lucca, Italy, to Boston.

While in manuscript form, the book won the Roy C. Palmer Prize at the Chicago-Kent College of Law. The prize is for a work "exploring the tension between civil liberties and national security in contemporary American society," and that was certainly my topic. Many thanks to the generous and widely philanthropic donors of the prize, Roy and Susan Palmer, to Dean Hal Krent (who labors in the same vineyards I do), and to the faculty and students of Chicago-Kent, who welcomed me so graciously.

My final acknowledgment goes to the memory of Attorney General and Supreme Court Justice Robert Jackson, whose example guided me throughout this project. He would have understood—and lamented—the reason this book needed to be written. I like to think he would have shared some of its judgments. I dedicate the book to him.

Introduction

BAD ADVICE TO PRESIDENTS IS NEVER IN SHORT SUPPLY. Flooding in constantly from all quarters, policy advice ranges from brilliance to inanity. Good presidents adopt advice that history later regards as sound. Bad presidents entertain too many fools. But *legal* advice might be different. Because it has points of reference in the Constitution, statutes, and court precedents, it should be more objective and reliable. Law is not science, however, in part because it grades seamlessly into policy. Given the indeterminacy of law, how can we minimize the provision of bad legal advice to presidents? I write this book to address that question.

The stakes are certainly high. Debates about the limits of presidential power in perilous times involve collisions between basic values. The need to protect national security in the interests of all of us confronts the claims of individuals to their fundamental rights. I will argue that as presidents and their lawyers address these hard questions, they should follow some simple rules of behavior regarding their relationship. Failure to follow these rules has produced some unhappy episodes in U.S. history. I also believe that concepts of separation of powers furnish ways to ameliorate the clash between the imperatives of security and the rule of law. Hence I will state some substantive principles for assessing the legality of executive actions. Ignoring these principles has harmed our nation more than once. Throughout, I will try to advocate neither too much law to bind presidents, nor too little.

For good or ill, the Constitution provides few crisp answers to questions about executive power. Robert Jackson, a very able Supreme Court Justice (and former attorney general), eloquently captured the difficulties of interpretation:

> That comprehensive and undefined presidential powers hold both practical advantages and grave dangers for the country will impress anyone who has served as legal adviser to a President in time of transition and public anxiety. . . . A judge, like an executive adviser, may be surprised at the poverty of really useful and unambiguous authority applicable to concrete problems of executive power as they actually present themselves. Just what our forefathers did envision, or would have envisioned had they foreseen modern conditions, must be divined from materials almost as enigmatic as the dreams Joseph was called upon to interpret for Pharaoh. A century and a half of partisan debate and scholarly speculation yields no net result but only supplies more or less apt quotations

from respected sources on each side of any question. They largely cancel each other. And court decisions are indecisive because of the judicial practice of dealing with the largest questions in the most narrow way.[1]

These reflections might lead the reader to conclude that in matters of the constitutional separation of powers there is no law but only argument ruled by political preference. Such a conclusion would, however, ignore the fact that Justice Jackson, in the case before him, concluded that President Truman's seizure of the steel mills in wartime was forbidden by a statutory barrier that was only implicit and not explicit. For Jackson, the law had real content, even if it might be difficult to determine. Jackson's opinion in the *Steel Seizure* case is the greatest modern judicial opinion on separation of powers, one that provides a framework for analysis here. Today, the case stands for the bedrock principle that even presidents must obey statutory prohibitions. Presidents have usually conceded this principle in practice, if not always in their rhetoric. And presidents do always assert that they abide the Constitution.

The president's lawyers must translate the Delphic materials of the Constitution and the often opaque or conflicting statutes into real advice about the limits of law. This process is crucial to the operation of our government. In the realms of foreign policy and war, where the courts rarely intrude, the advice of the president's lawyers may well be final, in the sense that the executive action that implements it will not be reviewed by any court. Hence, whether the Constitution and statutes actually do bind the president is often a function of the relationship between the president and his or her lawyers. Accustomed as most Americans are to discovering what the law is from the pronouncements of the Supreme Court, it is unsettling to contemplate a law-deciding mechanism that exists mostly or wholly within the executive branch. Yet exist it does, and I probe it in these pages in several ways.

I begin by recounting some stories that epitomize the enduring nature of the dilemma of the executive adviser who wishes to honor both the ruler and the law. Drawn from English history, and resonant with the English legal traditions that underlie so much of our law, the stories provide some basic guidance for modern analysis. For the nature of human wisdom and folly is unchanging, although the centuries alter our garb and the particular issues we confront.

I then provide a necessarily selective outline of the history of executive advising in the United States. There is not space here to provide a comprehensive history of this function. Instead, my goals are more limited. I focus on some particularly revealing instances of the range of relationships involved. In every case, the president and his advisers considered important and difficult legal issues that lay at the edge of executive power. These stories should equip the reader to judge the executive's legal choices during the war on terrorism by showing what was unusual and what was not about those choices. The stories also contain particular lessons that pertain to today's problems and that merit remembering. Finally, I want to explain the institutional development of the advising function as our government has grown and matured.

With this background, I explain the substantive and ethical principles that should constrain executive advisers. Here the critical task is to distinguish the ways that these principles should provide constraints from the ways that they should support discretion. Happily, the principles are simple enough to be mastered as an everyday guide in a busy world, although that is not to say that it is easy to abide them under the pressure of crises.

The terrorist attacks of September 11, 2001, led to a series of controversial decisions made by President George W. Bush and supported by his lawyers. After examining the ways in which the Bush administration differed generally from its predecessors, I explore three extended case studies of legal advising in this time of crisis. These are authorization of warrantless surveillance by the National Security Agency (NSA), detention and trial of enemy combatants in the war on terrorism, and the choice of interrogation methods to be used for the detainees.[2]

In each of these instances, President Bush made broad and even unprecedented claims of unilateral executive power after a secret process of decision. In each of them, the President's lawyers endorsed the legality of the claimed power. In each of them, strong controversy arose after the nature of the decisions became public. And in each of them, the executive was forced to retreat from the broadest claims of power, because of pressure from Congress, the courts, and the public.

As a consequence of common characteristics in the advice given by the president's lawyers, these decisions in the war on terrorism involve similar issues of professional responsibility and separation of powers law. Therefore, it is feasible to propose a single set of ethical and substantive principles to address the problems that have arisen. Having once served as an executive adviser myself, albeit a quite junior one,[3] I am sympathetic to anyone who performs this task. If this book can help future executive advisers do their duty, and can help those of us outside the government to understand and appraise what they do, it will have succeeded.

PART I
Right and Conscience

May I with right and conscience make this claim?
—William Shakespeare, *Henry V*

I

The Dilemma of the Executive Adviser

FOR A VERY LONG TIME, powerful rulers have sought the support of their legal advisers for actions the rulers desire to take. The advisers feel pressure—and usually desire—to accede to the ruler's wishes, to support the claim of legal right to act. Yet the advisers may also feel the pressure of their legal knowledge and their conscience, which may counsel against acceding to the ruler. What should the legal advisers do? Consider the following examples, drawn from England in the fifteenth and sixteenth centuries.

AN ADVISER SUPPORTS THE KING'S DESIRES

In the opening scene of Shakespeare's *Henry V,* the Archbishop of Canterbury is a worried man. Parliament is considering a bill that would plunder the Catholic Church by taking many of its lands. Canterbury and the Bishop of Ely speculate about the new king's reaction to the bill. The two prelates consider Henry's transformation from the reckless Prince Hal to the very model of a young king. But what is Henry's position on the bill? Canterbury thinks the issue is in doubt, but finds the king "swaying more" toward the church's position of opposition. For the archbishop has made a suggestion to the king, "touching France," that could produce far more revenue than would the contested lands of the church. Henry's family has a venerable claim to the crown of France in addition to the English crown. While tantalizing Henry with this possibility in an earlier conversation, Canterbury was interrupted (as advisers so often are) and now awaits an opportunity to resume his efforts to divert his sovereign's gaze across the channel and away from the church. He does not have to wait long.

In the second scene, Canterbury and Ely are called before Henry and his council to elaborate the earlier suggestion. Before asking the archbishop's opinion, King Henry abjures him to speak honestly:

And God forbid, my dear and faithful lord,
That you should fashion, wrest, or bow your reading, . . .
For God doth know how many now in health

Shall drop their blood in approbation
Of what your reverence shall incite us to.[1]

The stakes could not be higher, Henry is telling Canterbury. He reiter-
ates that if Canterbury should "awake our sleeping sword of war," combat
between England and France is always attended by "much fall of blood."
The king concludes:

Under this conjuration speak, my lord,
For we will hear, note, and believe in heart
That what you speak is in your conscience washed
As pure as sin with baptism.[2]

Perhaps feeling a need to answer in great detail, Canterbury proceeds
to deliver a painfully tedious, pettifogging lecture. He is responding to the
anticipated argument from the French, which is that their "Salic law" bars
succession to the French crown through the female line, as Henry's claim
would run. After sixty lines of this, Henry interrupts: "May I with right and
conscience make this claim?"[3] That is the exactly correct question, posed
with Shakespearean economy. It calls for an assessment of technical legal
right, together with the adviser's assurance that the claim can be advanced
in good conscience. The king's interjection galvanizes Canterbury. Casting
aside all ambiguity, the archbishop confirms the claim of right and calls for
the king to "unwind your bloody flag." Other counselors join in to urge the
decision against France, with the archbishop noting that the clergy would
raise a "mighty sum" in aid of the effort. Henry, who shows no sign of needing much persuading, soon declares "now are we well resolved," and the
road to Agincourt and the crown of France stretches ahead.

Alas, dreams of empire do not always turn out well. In the view of another
great Englishman, Winston Churchill, "glory was, as always, dearly bought.
. . . When Henry V revived the English claims to France he opened the greatest tragedy in our medieval history. Agincourt was a glittering victory, but
the wasteful and useless campaigns that followed more than outweighed its
military and moral value, and the miserable, destroying century that ensued
casts its black shadow upon Henry's heroic triumph."[4]

Readers may draw their own modern parallels.[5] In Henry's case, the pity
is that he received the advice he wanted, instead of the advice he needed. The
legal advice Canterbury provided may have been correct, but focusing on it
distracted the group's attention from the policy question of the advisability
of the large foreign adventure in prospect. No one stepped forward to inject

a note of caution about that. Such advice would have been unwelcome and probably would have gone unheeded, but a good (and brave) counselor would have found a way to provide it.

Among the many joys of Shakespeare's plays is the range of interpretation they permit. There are two motion picture versions of *Henry V.* Sir Laurence Olivier produced and directed the first one during World War II, as an aid to morale in Britain.[6] In the role of Henry, Olivier exudes the heroic nobility that makes the king "this star of England," as the play's epilogue calls him. The scene with Canterbury is rendered as broad comedy. The windy archbishop and his foil the bishop blunder about the stage, dropping legal papers, searching the floor for them, and provoking the laughter of the audience in the Globe Theatre. Henry's impatience grows visibly. His interjection about right and conscience is delivered seriously and emphatically. Then it's off to war. The effects of treating the archbishop's advice as comedy are to deflect attention from the archbishop's interest in the outcome and to give the audience a moment's diversion before the serious business with France begins.

The later film, by Kenneth Branagh, is darker and treats the archbishop more seriously.[7] The extended lecture about the Salic law remains dry, but Henry (played by Branagh) and the council appear to be trying to listen. Henry's interjection occurs with the quiet intensity of a man both pressured and pressuring. He wants the answer upon which so much rides, and he wants it clearly stated. At the end of the first act, as Henry and the council exit to prepare for war, Branagh has the archbishop and the bishop exchange knowing glances and slight, secret smiles: it worked!

These competing interpretations of the first act of *Henry V* invite us to consider who is using whom in the play. Olivier's archbishop lacks the gravitas to sway Henry, try as he might. It is the king who decides. Branagh's cannier version of the archbishop appears to carry weight with Henry, although again it seems likely that the king already knew his own mind. Neither Olivier nor Branagh portrays Henry as having been manipulated successfully. Instead, he got the advice he wanted and needed.

But what does Shakespeare think, and why is the first act constructed as it is? In the first scene, he takes pains to reveal Canterbury's interest in war with France. Surely we should consider his advice in that light. Yet—isn't the king likely aware of the archbishop's interest? The play makes clear that Prince Hal's wild years were not without education in human nature. If so, perhaps the king is just waiting for the answer he knows Canterbury will give, and wants the council to hear it.

Why then does Shakespeare include the extended lecture on the Salic law, which badly interrupts the flow of the first act? It turns out that both *Henry V* in general and the lecture in particular closely follow the main history Shakespeare consulted, Holinshed's *Chronicles*.[8] This fact has led scholars to conclude that for the real King Henry, for Shakespeare, and for the play's Elizabethan audiences, the question of legal right to the French throne was a serious one that deserved full explanation.[9] For if Henry's claim was good, his war with France was just, and if it was not, the invasion was simple aggression, and hardly a shining example for English schoolchildren.[10] The passage in which Henry enjoins Canterbury to advise him soberly does not invite comedic interpretation of what follows, despite its length. Therefore, Branagh's interpretation seems closer to Shakespeare's intention than does Olivier's. The rest of the play treats Henry's claim as legitimate, and he plainly believes in it.

Consider the main possibilities raised by the legal advice King Henry received, and by his adoption of it. First, it may be that the claim was good in *both* right and conscience. That is, perhaps the claim to the throne of France was strong on its legal merits, and therefore Henry could advance it with an untroubled conscience. It is important to notice that there are *two* consciences at work here, those of the ruler and the adviser. Modern ethical notions would bar Canterbury from giving advice because of his direct interest in the outcome, with his emotions pushing him strongly toward a conclusion that could save the church in England. Still, someone else who knew a bit of Salic law might have concluded that the claim was so strong that *Henry* could adopt it.

Second, perhaps the claim was good in *neither* right nor conscience. Not surprisingly, the French thought it weak enough that they refused to surrender the crown without a fight. And Henry possessed a powerful personal interest of his own in believing in his claim to the French crown.[11] That may be why he relied on Canterbury's opinion—or seemed to—before asserting the claim. Third, perhaps the claim was good in either right *or* conscience, but not both. The claim might have been legally strong, but pressed for corrupt motives by Canterbury or accepted for self-interested reasons by the king. Or the claim could have been legally weak, but accepted for patriotic reasons by Canterbury, or Henry, or both of them.

Many features of this rich story recur today in the provision of advice to rulers. Each of the major players in the drama has his or her own complex set of interests and values. There is close attention to following the forms of law, if only as a fig leaf covering naked acts of power. The counselor's detachment disappears when the ruler reveals his or her own desires. And the claim of right, endorsed by the counselor, enables the action the ruler desires.

The legal advisers are not wholly responsible for the fateful final decision, but they cannot be absolved from complicity in it.

Clearly, there are threads to untangle before anyone can decide how heads of state and their advisers should behave.[12] Before beginning that effort, we must consider one more principal complexity. The first act of *Henry V* portrays a counselor giving advice that he wants to give and that he has reason to believe the king will welcome. Indeed, Henry's reaction is all that Canterbury could have desired. What happens, though, if the advice is contrary to the king's wishes, and if the adviser persists in it after the king has announced his objections? Where then do right and conscience lie? For an exploration, we must turn to another King Henry, the Eighth, and another adviser, Sir Thomas More.

AN ADVISER FRUSTRATES THE KING'S DESIRES

In Robert Bolt's fine play *A Man for All Seasons,* King Henry VIII is determined to assure the Tudor succession by divorcing his barren wife Catherine and marrying Anne Boleyn. The legality of this step is, to say the least, doubtful, but the volcanic Henry has little patience with quibbles. Still, he needs the support of his prelates and lawyers if the remarriage is to be presented as legitimate. Soon enough, almost everyone has fallen in line, with the notable exception of Sir Thomas More, then serving as Counselor of England. In the acclaimed motion picture version of the play, Paul Scofield as More is pressed to give his consent by Cardinal (and Chancellor) Wolsey, played by Orson Welles.[13] Wolsey, immense in his cardinal's red robes and with the chancellor's chain of office dangling from his neck, exudes a weary worldliness:

Wolsey: You're a constant regret to me, Thomas. If you could just see facts flat on, without that horrible moral squint; with just a little common sense, you could have been a statesman.

And later:

Wolsey: Now explain how you as Counselor of England can obstruct those measures for the sake of your own, private, conscience.
    More: Well . . . I believe, when statesmen forsake their own private conscience for the sake of their public duties . . . they lead their country by a short route to chaos.[14]

Thus, in response to Wolsey's realpolitick More asserts unbending principle, claiming that it best serves the nation. (It is often claimed that adherence
to principle has that advantage. It also has the tactical advantage of occupying the high ground.) Wolsey makes explicit the personal cost of opposition
to the king: More might someday wear the chancellor's chain of office if he
cooperates, and will earn the enmity of both Wolsey and the king if he does
not. Throughout the play, More is as impervious to the offers of high office
used to induce his assent as he is to the threats that eventually emerge. At
times, his dry asceticism irritates us, as when he lectures Wolsey, but what
saves him for us is his greatness of spirit—the intelligence and humanity that
animate him throughout.

More explains his view of the law in a famous exchange with his son-in-
law Roper, a naive young fool who cannot see why law should ever obstruct
just results:

> More: The law, Roper, the law. I know what's legal not what's right.
> And I'll stick to what's legal. . . .
>
>   Roper: So now you'd give the Devil benefit of Law!
>
>   More: Yes. What would you do? Cut a great road through the law
> to get after the Devil?
>
>   Roper: I'd cut down every law in England to do that!
>
>   More: Oh? And when the last law was down, and the Devil turned
> round on you—where would you hide, Roper, the laws all being flat?
> This country's planted thick with laws from coast to coast—man's laws,
> not God's—and if you cut them down—and you're just the man to do
> it—d'you really think you could stand upright in the winds that would
> blow then? Yes, I'd give the Devil benefit of law, for my own safety's
> sake.[15]

In the motion picture, More delivers these lines rapidly, with barely controlled fury. This exchange is a eulogy to the rule of law from a man who
will soon be cut down by the law's devices even as he continues to insist on
its sovereignty. Always More walks a fine line between courageous adherence to principle and self-righteous obstinacy. (The audience is left to decide
which one predominates.) And always More is the consummate lawyer. He
well understands that his client the king does not readily tolerate disagreement.[16] Therefore he seeks room to maneuver, so that he can serve both king
and conscience. When informed that an oath supporting the king's remarriage will be required of everyone, he immediately responds, "What is the
wording?"[17] He will take the oath if he can agree with the precise words it

uses. Alas, he cannot, and goes to the scaffold rather than "put his hand on an old black book and tell an ordinary lie."[18] This outcome reveals Robert Bolt's view of More, who "became for me a man with an adamantine sense of his own self. He knew where he began and left off, what area of himself he could yield to the encroachments of his enemies, and what to the encroachments of those he loved. . . . At length he was asked to retreat from that final area where he located his self. And there . . . he could no more be budged than a cliff."[19]

Thus More preserves his professional detachment from his client and from his own self-interest in his career as well. Because the latter is a lot to ask of anyone, we do not recuse advisers whose only apparent interest is in pleasing the ruler, with the advancement that may reward that behavior.

In life as in these two plays, executive advisers strive to accommodate their preferences to their principles. In modern times, shorn as we are of so many certainties, where does a lawyer's sense of self originate? Much of it surely forms antecedent to or outside of law school, in genetic heritage and in values instilled by family and community. Some of it comes from norms about the rule of law that law school and the practice of law inculcate. And some of it comes from influences as particular as the culture that surrounds those who work in particular institutions within the executive. In the end, though, there remain the mysteries about human behavior that the great playwrights plumb. For me, the stories of the two Henrys and their very different counselors establish an inescapable fact about the relationship between heads of state and their advisers: at bottom, these are personal relationships always vulnerable to the vagaries of human nature. Nonetheless, they can be assessed by tools for analyzing human behavior, not excluding common sense.

AN ADVISER'S CONSCIENCE

It may be that an executive adviser's pursuit of self-interest, correctly understood, can also serve the interests of the nation. Consider a final example from Shakespeare. In Act III of *Henry VIII,* Cardinal Wolsey has lost the king's favor despite the cardinal's constant attempts to please him, and now finds himself surrounded by the enemies he has accumulated in the king's service. Imagine Orson Welles again, this time stripped of the indicia of office. Plainly dressed—no red robe of the cardinal, no chain of the chancellor—he sits in a drab room, lost in reflection. When his faithful servant, the sniveling Cromwell, asks how he feels, the fallen magnate replies:

Never so truly happy, my good Cromwell.
I know myself now, and I feel within me
A peace above all earthly dignities,
A still and quiet conscience.[20]

And at the end,

Had I but served my God with half the zeal
I served my king, He would not in mine age
Have left me naked to mine enemies.[21]

At long last, Wolsey has learned that a bit more of that "horrible moral squint" might have better served both him and his king. Caught up in the daily desire to satisfy the king's whims, Wolsey had failed to try to call the king to his legal responsibilities. Wolsey had forgotten something that both King Henry VIII and his predecessor Henry V knew well: legal advisers can confer legitimacy on political actions. For the advice to have legitimating effect, however, it needs to be provided from a stance of professional detachment, not sycophancy. Wolsey lost his way by abdicating his duty to provide advice reflecting his own judgment of legal right and his own conscience. Thomas More never lost sight of that duty or of his adamantine sense of self. Wolsey came to regret his own failure to follow More's example more closely. If the king's legal advisers would not remind him of the law's requisites, no one else could be expected to do so. If the advisers did discharge this duty, the monarch might still act without right and conscience, but they would have done all they could to help the king meet his own duties to the law.

As the foregoing stories illustrate, executive advisers feel great pressure to make decisions that serve both the law and the nation. Sir Thomas More became a saint (Canterbury and Wolsey did not). It would not be prudent, however, to expect saintliness as a routine virtue among executive advisers or among the senior officials who are their clients. What behaviors, then, should we expect—and demand—of the lawyers as they serve their insistent clients? In considering this question, we can profit from more than two centuries of precedents concerning the relationships between U.S. presidents and their lawyers.

2

The President's Lawyers in the Formative Years

ALTHOUGH U.S. PRESIDENTS HAVE ALWAYS CONSULTED LEGAL ADVISERS, at the end of the day they have often been willing to make their own legal judgments. Over the years, the number of presidential advisers has grown along with our government. There have also been unofficial advisers hovering near presidents, offering advice of varying quality. From the formation of our government through the Civil War, the bureaucracy that directly served the president was very small (and would remain so until the New Deal in the twentieth century).[1] Therefore, the dialogue about legal questions between presidents and their advisers was usually direct, personal, and informal. In the formative years, no one could say presidents were remote from the administration of the government.

THE OFFICE OF THE ATTORNEY GENERAL TAKES SHAPE

Ever since 1789, the president's official legal adviser has been the attorney general of the United States.[2] Modern Americans think of the attorney general as a central figure in the executive branch, one closely tied to the president as the nation's chief legal officer. Surprisingly, the creation of the office was attended with enough ambiguity that it could have evolved quite differently than it has. Before long, though, some decisions by George Washington placed the attorney general at his side, there to remain.

Although the office of attorney general is mentioned nowhere in the Constitution or in the records of the Constitutional Convention, it had both colonial and British antecedents. The First Congress, in which many framers of the Constitution sat, performed the task of creating the new federal government. Within months, the Judiciary Act of 1789, after organizing and empowering the federal courts, created the attorney general.[3] From then until now, the attorney general has been required to "give his advice and opinion upon questions of law when required by the President of the United States" or by the heads of the executive departments.[4]

15

Notwithstanding this impressive statutory charge, early attorneys general were part-time officers, with no staff of their own and little prestige. It was not even clear whether they were exclusively executive officers or legal officers for the entire government who would report in one way or another to all three branches. The statutory duty to conduct federal litigation created a relationship with the courts, but one naturally constrained by the nature of the adversary process. Early attorneys general also appeared to feel some direct responsibility to Congress. They routinely responded to requests for legal advice from members of Congress, although the statute did not require them to do so. That practice stopped in the Monroe administration and has never resumed, thus clarifying the attorney general's reporting responsibilities.[5]

In separation of powers law, two fundamental ways to determine which branch an officer serves are to identify who appoints and who can remove the officer. The Judiciary Act did not say who would appoint the attorney general, and a draft of the bill that became the act would have assigned appointment authority to the Supreme Court.[6] This provision was deleted for reasons that are lost to history, leaving the identity of the appointing authority unspecified in the act. If the courts had retained the authority to appoint the attorney general, it is very unlikely that this officer would ever have become an intimate legal adviser to the president.

Modern conceptions of separation of powers define the principal functions of the attorney general as executive activities in the constitutional sense. Therefore, an officer who performs those functions must be appointed by the president, with confirmation by the Senate.[7] This conclusion results from a process of elimination. Congress may not appoint those who execute the laws, as attorneys general do when they decide what litigation to pursue and how federal law should be interpreted by executive officers. Nor may the courts appoint "principal" officers with responsibilities as broad as those of the attorney general.[8] That leaves the president, as now seems obvious to most observers (although much that seems obvious now did not seem so at the founding).

It does seem clear that the First Congress did not envision the attorney general as an instrument of the president's will, as the secretaries of state and war were to be. Congress expressly labeled the Departments of State and War (now Defense) as executive departments, and directed their secretaries to take orders from the president in performing their duties.[9] In 1789, no such clear subordination to the president attended formation of departments not related to the president's independent constitutional authority regarding foreign affairs and war. The Treasury Department, which would perform some functions linked to congressional powers of appropriating funds and other sensitive functions involving spending of those funds, was not described as an executive department and contained various officers who were clearly meant to operate free of plenary political authority.[10] The removal of executive officers was another issue of great interest to the First Congress, which understood that the power to remove an officer implied the power to direct his or her activities. Congress debated removability of the secretary of state and decided that the president would have that power.[11] The statutes creating both the State and War Departments specifically refer to presidential removal of the secretary without any stated limitations. By tradition, and probably by constitutional obligation, these officers have served at the pleasure of the president. Secretaries of state and defense who cannot follow the president's lead have been expected to depart the administration.[12] In contrast, the statute creating the Treasury Department said nothing about removal, implying a greater distance from the president. Overall, it does seem clear that in establishing the first three departments the First Congress thought the new administrative officers it was creating would have orbits of varying distance from the constitutional branches, depending on the functions the officers performed. Experience would then allow evolution of the new federal government. That process continues today.

The attorney general seemed an afterthought, tucked in at the end of the Judiciary Act and lacking any department to run. (The Department of Justice would not be created until 1870, in the aftermath of the Civil War.) The brief statutory provision in the Judiciary Act neither labeled the office "executive" nor instructed the attorney general to take orders from the president, nor addressed the removal issue. Did Congress intend that legal advice to the president and the heads of departments be provided from outside the direct executive chain of command to foster its objectivity? We cannot know. Over time, this question has become obscured as the attorney general has developed a direct relationship with the president. That process began—haltingly—in the Washington administration.

GEORGE WASHINGTON SEEKS LEGAL ADVICE
FROM HIS CABINET

As the first president, George Washington was acutely aware that his actions would form enduring precedents about the conduct of his office.[13] Happily for our nation's history, his judgment and administrative instincts were exceptionally sound. He soon asserted the power to appoint the attorney general by nominating Edmund Randolph to the office; the Senate acquiesced by confirming him. Ever since, the attorney general has been treated as a principal executive officer to be nominated and confirmed in accordance with Article II of the Constitution.

For the first attorney general, Washington selected Randolph, his personal attorney, who had been advising him without fee. The two men had been close since Randolph was on Washington's staff during the Revolutionary War.[14] Randolph had also served in Congress and as governor of Virginia prior to the Constitutional Convention. His lifelong tendency toward vacillation, which was undoubtedly well known to Washington, showed when he declined to sign the Constitution yet helped lead the ratification efforts in Virginia.[15] Nevertheless, Washington clearly trusted him. The selection of Randolph began a practice that has continued to the present: presidents ordinarily choose attorneys general from among their close personal and political supporters, obtaining the benefits of loyalty at the cost of bypassing the legal *eminence grises* who are always available.[16] This practice has tended to increase the likelihood that presidents will rely on the advice of their attorneys general and to diminish the likelihood that the advice will be dispassionate. (Especially in the wake of scandal, though, nomination of someone known for his or her independence may be necessary.)

Within the first administration, Randolph was outshone by the two brightest stars, Alexander Hamilton and Thomas Jefferson. In Washington's first term, the concept of a cabinet to provide group advice to the president was just forming. Attorney General Randolph did not attend these meetings until 1792: he was not only below the salt but out of the room![17] For routine issues, Washington usually dealt directly with the head of each department on subjects relating to it, asking the views of the secretary and then deciding.[18] Hence Randolph could expect legal issues to flow to him, and usually they did. Because Washington was "not a man of quick, intuitive judgments," his "invariable practice" was to ask the opinions of those he trusted.[19]

On issues of great importance, Washington, like most of his successors, was prepared to seek the best advice he could get, without worrying about departmental protocol. For the Judiciary Act did not obligate the president to ask the attorney general's advice; it just told the latter to provide it if requested. This fact has led to an enduring delicacy in the relationships between presidents and their attorneys general. The cabinet is never short of able and aggressive lawyers who head other departments, and who are quite ready to provide legal analysis supporting presidential initiatives if the attorney general should resist. The resulting pressure on the attorney general to be supportive is constant in our government.

The two greatest legal issues of the Washington administration, the constitutionality of a national bank and of a proclamation of neutrality, illustrate the competition for advice-giving. For both, the president outlined the issues to his cabinet and patiently elicited and considered the competing arguments. Then Washington decided each of the controversies in favor of Hamilton's position (and in line with his own natural inclinations), neither excluding nor relying on Randolph.[20]

When the bill to incorporate a national bank reached Washington, he was troubled that James Madison had opposed it in the House of Representatives as not "necessary and proper" to implement the enumerated powers of Congress.[21] This objection posed the great issue of the breadth of the implied powers of Congress. Washington first asked the opinion of Randolph, "in whose line it seemed more particularly to be."[22] Randolph produced two "rather rambling" and not very persuasive papers concluding that the incorporation of a bank would be unconstitutional.[23] Jefferson concurred. Washington then turned to Hamilton, who quickly produced a powerful forty-page opinion favoring a broad interpretation of the implied powers of Congress and supporting the bank bill.[24] Two days later, Washington signed the bill.[25]

This initial presidential legal decision had some remarkable aspects.[26] Washington, not himself a lawyer, had to resolve a spirited dispute among some of the finest lawyers of his or any other age. Apparently the president thought his constitutional duty faithfully to execute the laws charged him with deciding, whether he was comfortable doing so or not. More practically, the question urgently required an answer. In reaching his decision, Washington rejected the majority view of Madison, Jefferson, and Randolph in favor of Hamilton's opinion, with which he was more sympathetic. Thus, the nature of the opinions and not the number of the opiners appeared to control. Moreover, Washington was prepared to disregard his attorney general's official opinion in favor of another that suited him better. It would have been easy for a nonlawyer president to resolve these tensions via the bureaucratic excuse that the attorney general's opinion necessarily controlled. These characteristics of legal decisionmaking, new at the time, would reappear throughout U.S. history.

Attorney General Randolph's difficulty in opining persuasively about the bank bill stemmed both from his own cautious nature and from the presence of the very large issue of whether the Constitution should receive a broad or a narrow construction. There was much to be said for avoiding such a momentous question so near the nation's inception. Washington, however, was prepared to face and resolve it. Perhaps he thought that the question would need an answer sometime, and here it was in his inbox. By approving the bank bill, this president, who was so conscious of precedent, formed one of the most important ones in our history.

The neutrality issue arose in 1793, when revolutionary France declared itself a republic and went to war against Great Britain. On receiving reports of the war, Washington "inclined instantly toward neutrality."[27] He understood that the fledgling nation was in no position to go to war with one superpower under its existing alliance with the other. There was, however, nothing in the text or history of the Constitution that allowed the president to make general determinations of foreign policy. Congress had the power to declare war, but could the president declare peace? Washington asserted no power to override any decision Congress might later make, but until it acted with regard to neutrality, there was a need to advise Americans and others about the stance of the executive branch, which could affect various legal rights and duties.

Consulting the cabinet, Washington encountered a clash between the Anglophile Hamilton, who favored an immediate declaration of neutrality, and the Francophile Jefferson, who held back, arguing that only Congress could decide. Washington then decided on an immediate declaration and asked Randolph to draft the official proclamation, to allow Jefferson (who would normally be the author) to disclaim responsibility for it.[28] Here the attorney general, although sidelined in the legal debate over neutrality, served the function of the detached lawyer putting the president's views into official form.

In these two controversies, Randolph never dominated the process of providing legal advice to the president, but he did honorably discharge his statutory duty of availability. He was overshadowed by the force and energy of Hamilton, who was the nation's first great bureaucrat. By gaining the president's ear in both controversies and providing detailed and persuasive legal advice, Hamilton showed the potential of an aggressive and entrepreneurial lawyer to displace the formal primacy of the attorney general. It would not be the last time this occurred.

Washington's two great legal decisions were made with legal right and in good conscience. They created precedents legally sound enough to have endured at the core of our constitutional system. The first president sought and considered a range of legal opinions before making his judgments. It was a model performance, one that his successors would do well to emulate.

JEFFERSON BUYS LOUISIANA, NO QUESTIONS ASKED

Thomas Jefferson entered the presidency with developed views about the Constitution.[29] As a good Republican, he had espoused a theory of narrow interpretation of constitutional text since the fight over the bank in the Washington administration, in opposition to Hamilton and the freewheeling Federalists. Events would soon test—and overcome—his devotion to principle. Everything started out smoothly enough. For attorney general, Jefferson chose Levi Lincoln, who was a prominent Republican politician, an able lawyer, and a strict constructionist.

Attorney General Lincoln soon produced two opinions consistent with Republican orthodoxy. The first followed Jefferson's dispatch, without special statutory authority, of a naval squadron to guard U.S. ships against the Barbary pirates. Lincoln opined that the U.S. Navy could act defensively, repelling attacks by the pirates on its ships, but could not mount a general offensive against them.[30] Lincoln was trying to reconcile the Constitution's placement of the power to declare war in Congress with the framers' recognition that the president should nevertheless be allowed to repel attacks. Led by Treasury Secretary Albert Gallatin, the rest of the cabinet disagreed with this narrow interpretation of presidential war powers. Jefferson reacted strategically. He appeared to side with Lincoln by deferentially asking Congress to authorize offensive tactics against the pirates, although the orders he had already issued to the navy supported pursuit of the pirates.[31] Thus, an attorney general's opinion can provide a president political cover if he wishes to use its conclusions strategically.

Lincoln's second opinion took a position that would prove enduring: the executive branch has a power of constitutional interpretation independent of the other two branches. A legal controversy arose at the end of the quasiwar with France. An armed French ship, the *Schooner Peggy*, was captured by a U.S. privateer and claimed as a prize under a federal statute that awarded part of the value of such a ship to the captors. During the litigation to condemn the ship as a lawful prize and distribute the award, a treaty settled outstanding differences between the United States and France. The secretary of state asked Lincoln whether the treaty required restoration of the ship to its owners. While litigation of this question was pending in the Supreme Court, Lincoln advised the secretary of state that the capture was valid and had become final before the effective date of the treaty.[32]

A few days later, the Court ruled to the contrary.[33] Lincoln promptly wrote another opinion to the secretary.[34] He began by making it clear that he disagreed with the Court's legal reasoning. Conceding that the Court's decision was binding in the particular case, Lincoln denied it any broader effect, declaring that in other cases executive officers must obey "their own convictions of the meaning of the laws and Constitution of the United States, and their oaths to support them." President Jefferson emphatically agreed with this principle of independent interpretation.[35] So have many of his successors, as we shall see. It has a core of accuracy and serious problems of limits.

A momentous legal problem concerning the Louisiana Purchase provided an opportunity for both the president and Congress to interpret the Constitution. In doing so, they had no prior guidance from the courts and little expectation that the courts would review their actions afterward. News of the proposed treaty to buy Louisiana presented President Jefferson an acute dilemma. The Federalists opposed the Louisiana Treaty as unconstitutional, and Jefferson privately agreed: "The general government has no powers but such as the Constitution has given it, and it has not given it a power of holding foreign territory, and still less of incorporating it into the Union."[36] Attorney General Lincoln shared his doubts, but Treasury Secretary Albert Gallatin did not, arguing that the nation had an inherent right to acquire territory.[37] Jefferson dithered a bit and then went to work on a draft of a constitutional amendment to cure the problem.

This activity stopped abruptly on August 17, 1803, when urgent messages arrived from the U.S. negotiators in France, Robert Livingston and James Monroe. They warned that Napoleon Bonaparte was suffering seller's remorse and was looking for a pretext to undo the deal. They urged that Congress speedily and unconditionally ratify the treaty. Jefferson immediately reversed course and adopted a new strategy. He told Attorney General Lincoln, "The less that is said about any constitutional difficulty, the better; and . . . it will be desirable for Congress to do what is necessary, *in silence*."[38] In other words, be quiet and I will take the responsibility for this. Lincoln appears to have complied.

In September, anticipating the congressional session, Jefferson wrote Virginia Senator Wilson Cary Nicholas: "Whatever Congress shall think it necessary to do should be done with as little debate as possible, and particularly so far as respects the constitutional difficulty. . . . I had rather ask an enlargement of power from the nation, where it is found necessary, than to assume it by a construction which would make our powers boundless. Our peculiar security is in possession of a written Constitution. Let us not make it a blank paper by construction."[39]

Accordingly, Jefferson's annual message to Congress finessed the constitutional issue. Having the needed votes in the Senate, Jefferson saw "nothing to be gained, and much to be lost, by spinning dangerous webs of constitutional theory."[40] When Congress met in October, the Senate speedily ratified the treaty. The House, where appropriations to pay the price had to be sought, was less compliant. Jefferson's floor managers overcame opposition by making Hamiltonian arguments about the Necessary and Proper and General Welfare Clauses of the Constitution.[41] No wonder Jefferson wanted to remain silent.

Throughout the Louisiana episode, Jefferson showed high sensitivity to the precedent that *would* be generated by his actions and the precedent that *could* be generated by any theory he offered to justify them. He could not avoid the former kind of precedent and hoped to avoid the latter by suppressing debate. Jefferson tried to retain both Louisiana and his principles, but could not. He did not believe that legal right supported his claim. Many of his contemporaries disagreed on the merits, and U.S. history has ratified their judgment about the nation's power to acquire territory.[42] Jefferson himself, however, could not advance a claim of legal right in good conscience, as his silence implicitly admitted. Hence Jefferson desired neither a legal opinion against the treaty, which could block the road to ratification if revealed, nor one approving the treaty on the hated Hamiltonian grounds.

After the fact, Jefferson characterized Louisiana as an extraordinary and extraconstitutional action by the executive and Congress that could be ratified by popular acceptance, one that would not stand as precedent for a general practice of broad construction of the Constitution.[43] He was trying to have it both ways. His rationalization for the Louisiana Purchase, taken as a general theory about constitutional interpretation, would allow the two political branches to do almost anything that might earn public approval. The result would be a kind of common law constitution that could be amended as needed by the informal consent of the people. That is a far more radical idea than a practice of broad interpretation of existing constitutional text, however Jefferson might characterize it.

This common law approach does not treat the Constitution as binding law, but it has a seductive lure in times of crisis. Even when a power of extraconstitutional emergency action is not quite asserted, it may lie close to the surface, as it did in the Civil War and has in the war on terrorism. Happily, so far in our history more modest arguments have sufficed to meet the nation's needs.

When Jefferson's protégé James Monroe later became president, he nominated an attorney general who transformed the office.[44] William Wirt was a distinguished Supreme Court advocate who served for twelve years beginning in 1817, the longest tenure to date. Upon his arrival, Wirt was astonished to discover that the office had no system of records whatever.[45] How could he know whether any opinion he might give was consistent with what his predecessors had said? Wirt promptly set up an opinion book and a letter book, and attorneys general have had a continuous body of precedent to draw on ever since. Wirt understood that whether one regards precedent within the executive as normatively binding in the way judges respect the precedents of their own and other courts, consistency is a virtue. Moreover, past executive advisers may have found wise answers to problems. After records were kept, it was natural to treat them as precedents having at least some binding effect. Now the attorney general headed a (small) bureaucracy and was no longer an essentially private lawyer for the executive, one who might care little for what predecessors in that role had done.

JACKSON AND TANEY DEFEAT THE MONSTER

Andrew Jackson's war against the Bank of the United States, the "Monster" as he called it, combined his characteristic aggressiveness with his profound ignorance of economics.[46] The war had two phases. First, Jackson vetoed the bill to recharter the bank; second, he withdrew government deposits from it to speed its demise. In both of these actions, his primary ally and aide was Roger B. Taney.[47] In these episodes, we see how vital an attorney general's advice can be to a president's achievement of his priorities.

As part of a cabinet shakeup in 1831, Jackson chose Taney for attorney general because he knew him and valued his loyalty and his legal and political skills. Taney and others drafted the message vetoing the bank recharter. It was an audacious document. Although all three branches of the federal government had upheld the constitutionality of the bank by this time, the message boldly asserted that Jackson had a right to his own judgment of the issue, and that the bank was unconstitutional.[48] Jackson's veto message gave enduring prominence to the theory first articulated by Attorney General Levi Lincoln that presidents have a power to interpret the Constitution independent of the other branches. In the Senate, Daniel Webster rejoined angrily: "If these positions of the President be maintained, there is an end of all law and all judicial authority. Statutes are but recommendations, judgments no more than opinions."[49]

Webster was overreacting. The president's veto power is plenary—that is, exclusive of the other two branches.[50] No matter how erroneous his constitutional theory for a veto might be, he is entitled to it. Presidents may also veto bills for policy reasons, no matter how baseless, whether or not the bills are constitutional. Thus, Jackson's veto message, although cloaked in constitutional garb, can be understood just as easily as an appeal to the public to agree that the bank was fundamentally inconsistent with U.S. institutions.

Upon receipt of such a message, Congress has the right to override the veto and enact the bill into law on any constitutional theory a court will later accept, but the courts do not review the basis for presidential vetoes of bills that never become law.

Where a president's power is shared with the other two branches, however, there are limits to his or her power of constitutional interpretation. If the president takes an action Congress can overturn with a statute or that a court will enjoin, his or her interpretation is not final in the way that a veto is (if not overridden). It is easy to confuse these two kinds of presidential action, and Webster seemed to do so in his reference to overturning statutes and judgments. The president had, and has, no such power. (Presidents do sometimes decline to enforce statutes they regard as unconstitutional, but such an action is preliminary to a final decision by the courts.) Unfortunately, the eminent Webster was not the last lawyer to make that mistake.

Taney's veto message advanced both the institutional interests of the executive branch and Jackson's political agenda. As we shall see, its theory of independent interpretation haunted Taney many years later, when Abraham Lincoln cited it against him. One never knows what the future uses of precedent will be. As a political statement, it opened the second phase of the battle against the Monster, which proved more difficult than wielding the veto pen, because of resistance within the cabinet. Here too, an important precedent would be set, this time about the nature of a president's power to supervise the cabinet.

President Jackson wanted to withdraw government deposits from the bank as the government needed them, but not all at once. New revenues would go to selected "pet" banks in the states. Taney supported the plan. Treasury Secretary William J. Duane thought it unwise and improper to remove the funds without authorization from Congress.[51] The relevant statute allowed the secretary to withdraw deposits only if he found they were unsafe in the bank, but they were not. No one knew whether the president or the secretary had the power to resolve this issue.[52] Jackson and Duane then argued the withdrawal issue at some length. Jackson instructed Duane to "take the [attorney general's] opinion and pursue it, he being our legal adviser, his opinion of the law, where there were doubts, ought to govern the heads of the Departments as it did the President."[53]

Taney prepared an opinion supporting Jackson, but Duane would not budge. Jackson angrily fired him and replaced him with Taney, who was prepared to withdraw the deposits, and did so.[54] A considerable row with Congress ensued, culminating in a censure resolution in the Senate, which declared that the reasons assigned by Taney for removing the funds were "unsatisfactory and insufficient" and that the president had "assumed upon himself authority and power not conferred by the Constitution and laws, but in derogation of both." Like so many other battles, Jackson won this one, eventually forcing the Senate to expunge the censure resolution. He also nominated Taney to succeed the late John Marshall as chief justice of the Supreme Court, and won his confirmation.[55]

In the battle within the Jackson administration over the bank deposits, everyone seemed to agree that the claim of legal right to withdraw the funds should be made by the officer who was empowered by statute to make the decision. Even so headstrong a president as Andrew Jackson never simply tried to assume the authority the statute had placed in the secretary. Instead, he jawboned the secretary with all of his considerable might. This understanding that presidents may supervise but not displace authority vested in other officers by statute remains dominant today, although it has been vigorously contested at times.[56] An important effect of the understanding is to empower the subordinate officer to enter a dialogue about legal right, as happened with Duane and Jackson, instead of merely awaiting orders. If the two come into agreement, the chances that the rule of law will prevail are enhanced, and the ethical conscience of the officer is honored.

Still, when a president's will is not to be denied, a cabinet officer who cannot acquiesce must resign or be fired. (The president will then have to persuade the Senate to accept a replacement.) This fate would have befallen Taney as well as Duane had he been less than an enthusiastic supporter of withdrawing the deposits. In fact, there is a very persistent—and inaccurate—story that Jackson told Taney that if he could not approve the withdrawals Jackson would find an attorney general who would.[57] The story fits Jackson's temperament, but it does not fit the facts. Taney was always a fierce opponent of the bank. The persistence of the story stems from its power as parable.[58] Every attorney general knows that the day may come when the president will make the blunt point Jackson supposedly made to Taney.

Jackson's attempt to force Duane to defer to the attorney general's opinion of the law appears to have been little more than a tactical move in the dispute. As Duane's recalcitrance shows, a cabinet secretary who is prepared to resist the president on a point of law will certainly ignore the attorney general's opinion. In addition, the secretary will believe that he or she knows the department's statutes better than does the attorney general, and will be buttressed in this opinion by the agency's staff. In consequence, the ultimate power of the attorney general within an administration is to persuade, not to dictate.

LINCOLN SERVES AS HIS OWN LAWYER

When Abraham Lincoln took office, he brought into the cabinet his principal rivals for the Republican presidential nomination.[59] It took strong hands to rein in so headstrong a team of horses. The names now familiar to us all are William Seward at state, Edwin Stanton at war, and Salmon Chase at treasury. All three were eminent lawyers, and all three advised Lincoln generally throughout the Civil War on the mixed issues of military policy and law the war presented. As they came to realize, though, Lincoln himself was a supremely gifted and self-confident lawyer who was quite prepared to rely on his own counsel. Less well known today is Edward Bates, another aspirant for the nomination who served as attorney general.[60] Aged sixty-eight when the administration began, Bates "had neither the desire nor the ability to compete with [Seward, Chase, and Stanton] in attempting to influence the policy of the administration."[61] Nor had he the caliber to engage Lincoln as an intellectual equal. Nevertheless, he was an able man who served honorably and won the respect and affection both of Lincoln and of his other more gifted colleagues.[62]

When news of the firing on Fort Sumter arrived in Washington, Lincoln convened the cabinet to ask its advice on how many militia troops to call up and what date to set for a special session of Congress. This initial meeting typified Lincoln's approach to his cabinet: he had already decided to call up the militia and to delay calling Congress into session until he could devise initial responses to the rebellion, and wanted advice only on the details.[63] Among the myriad decisions he made during the war, many of which were controversial from both legal and policy standpoints, I discuss two here.[64] One is the suspension of the writ of habeas corpus early in the war; the other is issuance of the Emancipation Proclamation at the height of the conflict. These two examples reveal Lincoln's willingness to act as his own lawyer, but to consider the views of Bates and others in the cabinet.

After Fort Sumter fell and a mob in Baltimore blocked the passage of federal troops toward Washington, Lincoln ordered federal troops to seize rail and telegraph lines between Baltimore and Washington to prevent the loss of the capital at the outset of the war. The emergency was grave. A single rail line connected Washington to the northern states, and if troops could not transit Baltimore to make their rail connections, only seaborne relief could arrive with any speed.[65] Lincoln also considered whether to suspend the writ of habeas corpus in Maryland. The Constitution authorizes suspension of the writ "when in cases of rebellion or invasion the public safety require[s] it," but does not say whether it is Congress or the president who takes the action.[66] Before deciding, Lincoln consulted Bates, who provided an answer that was "not encouraging."[67] Nevertheless, Lincoln ordered suspension of the writ in the endangered areas.

A legal challenge soon followed. Military officers arrested John Merryman, a secessionist Marylander, for aiding the rebellion. Merryman sought and obtained a writ of habeas corpus from Chief Justice Taney in his role as circuit judge. (In those days the justices "rode circuit," sitting in the lower federal courts; in that capacity their orders did not carry the force of a Supreme Court opinion.) Taney's opinion asserted that only Congress and not the president could suspend the writ.[68] When the military refused to deliver up Merryman, the frustrated Taney sent the record to Lincoln, who bore ultimate responsibility for the refusal.[69] Normally, the president's next step would have been to appeal Taney's order to the full Supreme Court. The Court was dominated by southerners in 1861 (it had not long ago decided the infamous *Dred Scott* case), however, and could be expected to uphold Taney and rebuke the president. Refusing to yield to Taney, Lincoln took another tack by appealing the *Merryman* order to Congress rather than to the Supreme Court.

In his message to Congress as it convened in July 1861, the president sought ratification for all of his emergency actions since the war began.[70] After reciting the course of events through the firing on Fort Sumter, Lincoln presaged words he would utter one cold November day two years later, saying the question was "whether a constitutional republic, or a democracy—a government of the people, by the same people—can, or cannot, maintain its territorial integrity, against its own domestic foes." Hence, he had resisted force by force. Regarding the suspension, he denied that he had failed to meet his constitutional duty faithfully to execute the laws, as Taney's supporters had charged. Instead, he argued he possessed constitutional power to suspend the writ and had done so "very sparingly." After noting that the Constitution did not specify which branch could suspend the writ, he stressed that a third of the states were in rebellion and that Congress could well have been prevented from assembling. He concluded the nature of the emergency gave him authority to act. The facts were on his side, and like any good lawyer, he built his argument around them. Because of the depth of the crisis in early 1861, I think Lincoln's suspension orders were supported by both right and conscience.

Lincoln then included a famous rhetorical flourish that has misled its readers ever since about the argument he was making: "Are all the laws, *but one,* to go unexecuted, and the government itself go to pieces, lest that one be violated?"[71] But Lincoln had not conceded that he had violated any law, and had clearly and persuasively claimed legal right for his suspension of habeas corpus. Here he was really arguing in the alternative—if Congress thought he had lacked authority for the suspension, it should recognize a residual emergency power in the president to preserve the nation and its Constitution.

This argument from necessity has both its seductions and its dangers. For example, Jefferson had once expressed a view similar to Lincoln's. After his retirement, in a letter responding to an inquiry when officers might "assume authorities beyond the law," Jefferson said that the question

> is easy of solution in principle, but sometimes embarrassing in practice. A strict observance of the written laws is doubtless *one* of the high duties of a good citizen, but it is not *the highest.* The laws of necessity, of self-preservation, of saving our country when in danger, are of a higher obligation. To lose our country by a scrupulous adherence to written law, would be to lose the law itself, with life, liberty, property . . . thus absurdly sacrificing the end to the means.[72]

Although Lincoln would doubtless have agreed with these sentiments during the Civil War emergency, Jefferson's original utterance of them was, indeed, "embarrassing in practice." The context was his unseemly defense of corrupt General James Wilkinson for the general's high-handed and illegal actions in New Orleans in the wake of the unraveling of the Burr conspiracy. In an effort to cover his own tracks, Wilkinson had arrested those who might know too much, jailed them without due process, and exiled them from the territory.[73] This was an occasion for enforcing the laws of the land, not for excusing their flouting.

Justice Robert Jackson, aware of the problems, once argued that inherent emergency power "either has no beginning or it has no end."[74] Yet the crisis at the beginning of the Civil War *was* without precedent in its severity, and if a president's ultimate sources of authority were ever to be invoked, that was the time. The difficulty is that later presidents have been lamentably fond of arguing that if Lincoln could do what he did, they may take less drastic actions that seem necessary to them. The difference, as Lincoln could have told them, lies in the facts.

While preparing his address to Congress, Lincoln had called on Bates to provide an opinion "to present the argument for the suspension."[75] Clearly, the attorney general was being asked to provide a brief for actions that had already been taken, not a more balanced opinion about the legality of prospective actions. Bates complied, producing a tendentious opinion that, in the words of a future chief justice, "would persuade only those who were already true believers."[76] Whatever his former doubts, Bates was in no position to concede that the suspension had violated the Constitution.[77] This time, Bates said the president "must, of necessity, be the sole judge" of how to suppress the rebellion; he admitted, though, that the president's suspension power was "temporary and exceptional."[78] Both Lincoln and Bates recognized congressional power to regulate suspensions of the writ.

As Congress convened, Lincoln was calling on it to share in the responsibility for his actions. By asking Congress for a retroactive grant of authority, Lincoln was implicitly conceding something he never denied, that Congress held the ultimate power to set the course for the Civil War. Congress responded by ratifying Lincoln's actions generally.[79] Yet it was not until 1863 that Congress addressed habeas corpus specifically, passing legislation worded ambiguously as to whether Congress was approving the president's actions or exercising its own suspension powers.[80] This outcome left the power to suspend habeas corpus, like the opinion of Chief Justice Taney in *Merryman*, in limbo.

Lincoln made the most important legal decision of his presidency, and the one for which he is most revered, essentially on his own. The idea of issuing an Emancipation Proclamation grew in Lincoln's mind during the difficult summer of 1862. In July, he brought the cabinet together and read them his draft of a proclamation. He told them that he "had resolved upon this step, and had not called them together to ask their advice," although he welcomed suggestions.[81] The conservative Bates then surprised his colleagues by expressing enthusiastic approval of the proclamation—he hoped it might end the war speedily.[82] After general discussion, which did not alter Lincoln's mind on the essentials, the president accepted Seward's suggestion that promulgation should follow a victory on the battlefield, and withheld it until after the battle of Antietam in September.

In the final Emancipation Proclamation, the president freed all slaves who were held in areas still in rebellion within the Confederate states. By restricting emancipation to regions not yet controlled by the Union Army, Lincoln crafted his proclamation as a military order. The proclamation described itself as "an act of justice, warranted by the Constitution upon military necessity," and resting on Lincoln's power "as commander-in-chief . . . as a fit and necessary war measure for suppressing . . . rebellion."[83] As the war proceeded, escaping slaves trailed the Union Army as it swept across the South, depriving their former masters of their services and seeking redemption of Lincoln's promise.[84] Against objections that the proclamation was an unauthorized taking of private property without just compensation, supporters urged that the powers of the government as a belligerent in war included the right to free an enemy's slaves.[85] The proclamation also had some statutory support.[86]

Lincoln was always prepared to defend his actions as justified by the overriding need to preserve the Union and the Constitution.[87] Lincoln's views of constitutional power generally aligned with what was called the "adequacy of the Constitution" theory at the time.[88] This theory held that the antebellum South's arguments had distorted constitutional analysis by discussing only the rights protected by the Constitution, obscuring its implied commands to maintain the government to protect the general welfare. Proponents of the theory noted the president's duty to ensure faithful execution of the laws and his oath to preserve, protect, and defend the Constitution. Lincoln surely agreed with all this. His more cautious attorney general found himself employing the adequacy theory to defend Lincoln's suspension of habeas corpus after the fact, whether or not he was comfortable with it.[89]

Toward the end of his time as attorney general, Bates asserted that the office "is not properly *political,* but strictly *legal;* and it is my duty . . . to uphold the Law, and to resist all encroachments . . . of mere will and power, upon the province of the law."[90] This quotation is often offered as an aspirational guide to attorneys general. A moment's reflection, however, might have reminded Bates himself that his service could not accurately be so characterized, and that he might not have served his president well if it could. Lincoln's critical actions to save the Union blended some law with large amounts of statesmanship and vision. Although the marks of a lawyer's tools could be seen upon each of the two great decisions discussed above, other imperatives drove them. The attorney general was confined to sounding a note of initial caution regarding suspension of habeas corpus, and a welcome note of acclaim for emancipation.

The ultimate question about the legality of the Emancipation Proclamation is difficult to think about today, repelled as we are by claims of constitutional rights to property in human beings.[91] Yet we know that the original Constitution conferred just such rights, leading the abolitionist William Lloyd Garrison to condemn it as a "Covenant with Death and Agreement with Hell."[92] Perhaps *this* is the place for Lincoln's argument for a residual power to ignore one part of the Constitution to save the rest—and the soul of the nation.[93] Lincoln made just that argument in a letter he wrote in 1864. After reviewing his own moral opposition to slavery and asserting that as president, he could not use his powers of office merely to implement his private values, he continued:

I did understand however, that my oath to preserve the Constitution to the best of my ability, imposed upon me the duty of preserving, by every indispensable means, that government—that nation—of which that Constitution was the organic law. Was it possible to lose the nation, and yet preserve the Constitution? By general law life *and* limb must be protected; yet often a limb must be amputated to save a life; but a life is never wisely given to save a limb. I felt that measures otherwise unconstitutional, might become lawful, by becoming indispensable to the preservation of the constitution, through the preservation of the nation. Right or wrong, I assumed this ground, and now avow it. I could not feel that, to the best of my ability, I had even tried to preserve the Constitution, if, to save slavery, or any minor matter, I should permit the wreck of government, country, and Constitution all together.[94]

Nothing short of the cauldron of the Civil War and the desperate need to win it could have justified the proclamation in law.[95] To us, emancipation is easier to justify as a matter of conscience. In the concluding passage of William Safire's fine historical novel about the first two years of the Civil War, *Freedom,* we discover the exact point at which legal right and moral conscience meet, as Lincoln signs the final version of the proclamation: "Slowly, he did his best to lay across the parchment a bold and clear signature, his whole first name reflecting solemnity. He looked at the freshly inked name, not completely satisfied—it seemed to quaver a little, but there were no second chances—then allowed a smile to light his face. 'That will do.' "[96]

By the time of Lincoln's death, he had given a "bloody and absolute . . . rebirth to his nation."[97] Not long afterward, adoption of the Thirteenth Amendment ratified the Emancipation Proclamation by ending slavery in the United States.

3

The President's Lawyers in the Institutional Presidency

During his long tenure as president, Franklin Delano Roosevelt (FDR) transformed the executive branch. As the administrative agencies of the New Deal proliferated first to address the Depression and then to fight World War II, the president's own bureaucracy expanded as well in an effort to control the emerging "administrative state."[1] Instead of the small cadre of direct advisers that had formerly sufficed for presidents, there would henceforth be an "institutional presidency" that has grown ever since.[2] These bureaucratic developments have somewhat altered the nature of the president's relationships with his legal advisers.

Over the course of U.S. history, the attorney general has evolved from a private lawyer with the United States as one client to the head of a major and complex executive department. One of the original duties of the attorney general, to conduct litigation for the United States in the Supreme Court, evolved into a general supervisory responsibility for most government litigation in all of the federal courts. Since 1870, the attorney general has headed the Department of Justice and has gradually acquired various major administrative responsibilities, for example to investigate crimes through the Federal Bureau of Investigation (FBI) and to administer the federal prisons.[3]

In the twentieth century, the need became apparent to delegate routine advice-giving to subordinate officers. In 1933, Congress created what is now the Office of Legal Counsel (OLC), headed by an assistant attorney general, to write most formal opinions to the president and other executive officers.[4] During the Roosevelt administration, however, the attorneys general did not willingly delegate their responsibility to advise the president on the most important matters to OLC or to anyone else.

As president, FDR encountered many questions of law. Although trained as a lawyer, he did not think like one.[5] His mind ran in broad channels of right and wrong; political opportunity and feasibility were always prominent in his calculations. FDR's casual disdain for what he called "legalisms" did not harm him "because the law governing presidential authority during his era was largely a *political* rather than a *judicial* constraint on presidential power."[6] When treading the edge of the law, he did not worry about being sued or prosecuted, but rather about the reactions of Congress and the people. As we shall see, he took steps to ensure the political legitimacy of his actions, thereby preventing successful assaults on their legal legitimacy.

I recount three episodes that reveal the nature of FDR's legal judgments and the range of his relationships with his attorneys general. The first, the destroyers for bases deal in 1940, featured the central involvement and support of his gifted attorney general Robert Jackson, who was as close to FDR personally as anyone was allowed to come.[7] Here, Jackson contributed to FDR's skillful—and risky—management of public policy as he moved toward supporting Great Britain on the eve of World War II. In the second episode, the internment of Japanese Americans in 1942, the doubts of Attorney General Francis Biddle, who was neither a force in the cabinet nor one of FDR's confidants, were kept in the shadows. Unfortunately, Biddle was unable to prevent the decision that remains the worst blot on Roosevelt's presidency. In the third episode, Biddle was an enthusiastic supporter of military trials for captured Nazi saboteurs. This time, the attorney general should have displayed more restraint.

PRESIDENT ROOSEVELT AND ATTORNEY GENERAL JACKSON SKIRT THE NEUTRALITY LAWS

In 1935, FDR concluded the United States needed to counter the rising strength of the dictators in Europe, but "just as the president's internationalist convictions began to deepen, the isolationist mood of his countrymen started to congeal all the more stubbornly."[8] A series of neutrality acts from 1935 to 1939 were the result. They forbade aid to any belligerent nation; FDR wanted to be able to embargo arms against aggressors only. After World War II began in Europe, Roosevelt began the delicate task of moving U.S. public opinion toward his own position.

In May 1940, Great Britain stood alone against Hitler's surging forces. Prime Minister Winston Churchill, newly installed, began his extended effort to bring the United States to Britain's side. The Royal Navy, protecting Britain against Nazi submarines and invasion forces, had lost about half of its destroyers in home waters. The prime minister, styling himself a "former naval person" to charm Roosevelt by appealing to their shared naval background, sent a message to Roosevelt with a list of "immediate needs," including "the loan of forty or fifty of your older destroyers to bridge the gap" until new naval construction in Britain could provide adequate defense.[9] FDR replied that he would need statutory authority to provide them.

The wily Churchill may have been less interested in the ships themselves than in entangling the two nations "beyond possibility of separation and divorce."[10] In fact, both Roosevelt and Churchill knew that the destroyers "had more psychological and political utility than they had naval value."[11] They were "four-funneled World War I–era heirlooms" that would take months to refit for action. But sending them "would bolster British spirits, signal Hitler that the patience of the neutral Americans was wearing thin, and most significant, help drive home to those same Americans their stake in the struggle against Nazism." Hence, large issues of statesmanship rather than mundane ones of military supply lay at the heart of the destroyer proposal.

For a number of reasons, however, FDR could not simply accede to the proposal, no matter how much he favored helping the British. First, existing neutrality legislation appeared to stand in the way. Second, U.S. national security could not be disregarded—sending warships to an ally would undermine our own defense capacity in a time of danger. Third, the mood of the country was still isolationist. Although sympathy for embattled Britain and rising fear of Hitler were softening the strength of isolationism by 1940, it would remain a potent force until the moment that news of the Pearl Harbor attack arrived in late 1941. Finally, FDR was entering a tense reelection campaign for an unprecedented third term.

Despite these strong reasons to proceed cautiously, the president forged ahead. Robert Jackson later recalled that the summer of 1940 "saw a change in the Roosevelt internal policy. Originally it was to submit any proposal to Congress for specific authorization. It shifted to one of independent executive action."[12] Jackson would aid this transition. Although he would always give the president "the benefit of a reasonable doubt as to the law," he also knew how to put on the brakes when he thought it necessary.[13] The president began clumsily by attempting to send Britain twenty-three new antisubmarine boats without congressional approval: "When the Navy's Judge Advocate General (J.A.G.) declared that such a sale would be illegal, Roosevelt branded him 'a sea lawyer' and 'an old admiral whose mental capacity I know personally.' He advised Navy Secretary Charles Edison to send the J.A.G. on vacation and find a more compliant replacement. In response to Edison's repeated objections, Roosevelt told him to forget legality and follow orders."[14]

The initiative collapsed when Senator David Walsh of Massachusetts heard of the deal and confronted the navy. He then attached the Walsh Amendment to pending legislation on naval shipbuilding, forbidding transfer of any ships unless the navy certified that they were "not essential to the defense of the United States."[15]

In full but temporary retreat, Roosevelt said that he had received an informal opinion from Attorney General Jackson that the sale of ships to a belligerent would violate existing statutory restrictions, and that he now "concurred" in that opinion.[16] Throughout this period, Jackson held the view that selling new warships to a belligerent could not be justified under either the Walsh Amendment or earlier legislation, but he would come to the conclusion that transfers of older vessels presented different problems.[17]

As summer 1940 passed, communications from London rose to a high pitch of Churchillian dramatics: "Mr. President, with great respect I must tell you that in the long history of the world, this is a thing to do now."[18] Sympathetic to Churchill's appeals, the administration shifted ground. Roosevelt had reshuffled his cabinet to include two internationalist Republicans, Secretary of War Henry Stimson and Secretary of the Navy Frank Knox. The cabinet met in August, agreeing that the destroyers would help Britain survive, and that it would advance U.S. interests to supply them. Jackson, however, had informally advised the president that statutory authorization would be necessary for any gift, loan, or sale of warships to Britain. Knox then broached the idea of trading old destroyers for some British naval bases. This proposal broke the logjam. Unlike a cash sale, a trade would leave U.S. defenses not only unimpaired but strengthened, since new bases would have more immediate value than old destroyers. "An exchange that would add strength to our own defenses would stand in very different legal light," Jackson now argued.[19]

At an August 13 meeting in the Oval Office, FDR said he had decided to make the destroyer deal without a statute.[20] He had tried and failed to persuade the Republicans, and Senator Claude Pepper had told him a bill had "no chance of passing." No one demurred, although Stimson later recorded that "everyone felt it was a desperate situation and a very serious step to take." In making the decision, "Roosevelt was fortified by a lengthy legal brief which attorney Dean Acheson had published in the *New York Times* on August 11. Acheson argued that the commander-in-chief had the authority to exchange destroyers for bases without congressional approval so long as the net result of the deal produced an increase in America's national security." Jackson confirmed this opinion, arguing that the combination of the commander in chief powers and the foreign affairs powers sufficed. "On the basis of this advice, which is what Roosevelt wanted to hear, he decided to complete the deal, and then and only then tell Congress."

One obstacle remained. Churchill wanted the destroyers as a gift to Britain, thinking that his nation would approve a "grand gesture of generosity" but not a one-sided trade.[21] Jackson, however, stood firm against the legality of a gift, and so did Roosevelt. He told Churchill: "The trouble is that I have an Attorney General—and he says I have got to make a bargain." To this Churchill rejoined, "Maybe you ought to trade these destroyers for a new Attorney General!"[22] Eventually, Churchill receded and the deal was complete.

On September 3, 1940, President Roosevelt announced that he had made an executive agreement to send Great Britain fifty destroyers built in the World War I era in return for long-term leases on some British bases in the western Atlantic and the Caribbean. Before doing so, he grumbled that "he might get impeached for what he was about to do."[23] He called in the press and said this was the "most important event" in our defense since the Louisiana Purchase. He explained the deal, and when asked if the Senate's ratification would be needed, replied no, "It is done." As he expected, there was criticism—the word "dictator" was heard, but FDR thought it was a risk worth taking for Britain. The risk was considerable: Churchill later wrote that Germany would have been justified in declaring war in response to the deal.

Although the destroyer deal was "unilateral in form, it was accompanied by extensive and vigilant consultation—within the executive branch, between the executive and legislative branches, among leaders of both parties and with the press."[24] As the value of the bases became clear, the criticism abated. An increase in public support for embattled Britain eased the political climate. Once the war came, with the United States and Britain locked in a death struggle with the Axis, history crowned Roosevelt and Jackson the victors in the debate.

The legal technique used to effect the destroyer deal promised fast action and seemed "politically safe" to Attorney General Jackson. It was an "executive agreement," which is a nontreaty agreement between the president and another nation. All U.S. presidents have entered executive agreements. They provide a simple way to make a wide variety of arrangements, some of them quite minor, with other nations. For example, it would make no sense to require the full dignity and cumbersomeness of the treaty process every time the State Department wants to create a utility easement in an overseas embassy or wants to alter the number of accredited personnel in a foreign embassy here. Instead, such decisions are handled by various forms of correspondence between the nations involved.

Because executive agreements bypass the Senate, however, they are both politically and legally sensitive when used for nonroutine matters such as the destroyer deal. An important precedent, well known to both FDR and Jackson, provided encouragement. It involved the recognition of the Soviet

Union in the 1930s. President Roosevelt had employed an executive agreement to settle international claims as part of his effort to normalize relations between the two nations. The Supreme Court had upheld his action in
an opinion by Justice George Sutherland broadly supportive of presidential
power to enter executive agreements.[25] Although the context of the destroyer
deal was different from the Soviet recognition, Roosevelt and Jackson could
anticipate a sympathetic understanding of the interests of the executive in
the foreign policy context if litigation occurred.

Jackson provided an official opinion supporting the use of an executive
agreement to trade destroyers for bases.[26] He later responded to objections
that he had supplied "a made-to-order legal opinion to justify" the action
by arguing that his opinion was made in advance of the decision and that
"far from being the result of the President's decision, [it] was a contributing
factor in reaching it, as may be inferred from the fact that the opinion was
sent to Congress and the country to accompany the message announcing the
exchange."[27] With the expectation that Jackson's *Destroyers* opinion would
become the public explanation for the deal, the president went over it with
Jackson, suggesting minor changes, and Jackson then edited it to make it less
technical and more understandable to the people.[28] FDR remarked cheer-
fully and correctly to Jackson that criticism would focus on the attorney
general's opinion rather than on the president's deal.[29]

Now that emotions have cooled, we can assess the arguments of Jackson
and his critics. His *Destroyers* opinion considered only questions of constitutional and statutory authority. (It omitted any consideration of international
law because the State Department was considering those issues.) To Jackson, the question of whether the deal could be done by executive agreement
rather than by treaty depended on two of the president's constitutional powers. First, his role as commander in chief carried a "responsibility to use all
constitutional authority which he may possess to provide adequate bases"
for the military. In addition, world conditions "forbid him to risk any delay
that is constitutionally avoidable." Jackson was explicitly reluctant to put
much weight on the commander in chief power. He was no doubt aware that
Congress had clear constitutional power to supply the military. Therefore,
this preliminary and inconclusive discussion served to remind everyone that
the president had his own constitutional duty to consider military requisites,
and that he needed to be able to respond speedily to emergent conditions.

Jackson then turned to "that control of foreign relations which the Constitution vests in the President as a part of the Executive function." He asserted that the "nature and extent of this power had recently been explicitly
and authoritatively defined" by the Supreme Court's decision in *United*

States v. Curtiss-Wright Export Corp.[30] Jackson, like some later executive advisers, lifted from its context a quotation that broadly endorsed executive authority. This was the Court's reference to "the very delicate, plenary, and exclusive power of the President as the sole organ of the Federal Government in the field of international relations—a power which does not require as a basis for its exercise an act of Congress, but which, of course, like every other governmental power, must be exercised in subordination to the applicable provisions of the Constitution."[31]

I will have much more to say later about the uses of *Curtiss-Wright*. For present purposes, it is important to note that Jackson relied on it in only a limited and tentative way. Conceding that the president's foreign affairs powers are "not unlimited," he distinguished presidential agreements that create future commitments involving legislation, which would ordinarily require a treaty, from those that do not create any commitments, such as the destroyer deal. "It is not necessary for the Senate to ratify an opportunity that entails no obligation." Quoting *Curtiss-Wright* added little to this line of argument except rhetorical emphasis.

The attorney general then found "ample statutory authority" for the deal. He mentioned some statutes that were rather remote from that context, including an old provision for disposing of vessels found unfit for further use. Jackson asserted that this provision recognized a "right of the President to dispose of vessels of the Navy," and argued that it did not limit his "plenary powers" to vessels already deemed unfit. Here, Jackson surely knew he was on thin ice, since the whole point of the deal was to provide Britain with ships it considered valuable. Turning to the Walsh Amendment, Jackson argued it "clearly recognizes the authority to make transfers and seeks only to impose certain restrictions thereon." He recited the age of the destroyers and the fact that many of their sister ships had been scrapped. He summarized the legislative history of the amendment, which showed that the words "not essential" included ships having more than scrap value. Jackson concluded that the amendment left the Navy free to decide the destroyers would not be essential to our defense if trading them for the British bases "will strengthen rather than impair the total defense of the United States." He also claimed the Walsh Amendment "was enacted by the Congress in full contemplation of transfers for ultimate delivery to foreign belligerent nations."

There was one more statutory restriction to consider: the Espionage Act of 1917 forbade exportation of warships to belligerent nations while the United States remained neutral.[32] Jackson read this provision as inapplicable to the destroyers because they were not originally built for export to a belligerent, but for our own use. Anticipating the obvious objection that the original use of a warship is irrelevant to whether exporting it threatens neutrality, Jackson cited a companion provision in the statute that implied that some warships could be sent to belligerents' ports. Also, he had found some scholarly statements about the international law of neutrality that supported a distinction between selling warships and making them for a belligerent nation. Following this logic, he opined that some newly built ships that were to be sent along with the destroyers could not legally be transferred. Thus, although he approved the central element of the deal, he was able to show that he was honoring statutory limits by disapproving an ancillary feature.

The constitutional analysis in Jackson's *Destroyers* opinion is not troubling. He discussed the president's war and foreign affairs powers broadly, as attorneys general normally have done. Although he hinted in places that some statutes limiting these powers could be unconstitutional, he made no serious assertion that Congress could not limit or forbid the destroyer deal. Instead, Jackson argued the deal was consistent with both the president's needs for military flexibility and the traditional uses of executive agreements.

What is troubling, though, is Jackson's statutory analysis. He strained to find authority for disposing of vessels in an old statute that had little relevance to the deal, because the destroyers were not unfit for service. His argument about the Walsh Amendment was better. It was appropriately creative in arguing for a broad reading of the term "essential," and Jackson was correct that the statute did necessarily contemplate transferring some surplus ships. His concluding argument about the Espionage Act, although also creative, was more strained. His interpretation of the act is crabbed because it omits attention to the act's apparent purpose of protecting neutrality by stopping the flow of warships to belligerent nations. In Jackson's defense, though, is the fact that he had held this view of the act for some time before writing the *Destroyers* opinion and did not craft it for the occasion.[33]

Some legal scholars, including the eminent Edward Corwin, denounced Jackson's opinion. Corwin argued the transaction "was directly violative of at least two statutes" and exercised a power the Constitution "specifically assigned" to Congress (the treaty ratification power, presumably).[34] Both of these assertions are questionable. First, the Espionage Act was the main obstacle, and Jackson had offered a strained but not wholly untenable interpretation of it. Second, the formation of executive agreements had been upheld by the Supreme Court. Dripping with sarcasm, Corwin said Jackson relied on the commander in chief power to "dispose" the armed forces, which he "ingeniously, if not quite ingenuously, construed as the power to *dispose of* them." This was unfair. As Jackson's opinion argued, disposing of weapons can aid our defense if sufficient compensation is present. Other scholars echoed the statutory objection and argued that his analysis of international law was incorrect as it related to his Espionage Act argument.[35]

The international law scholars also thought Jackson should have analyzed the international law of neutrality, which the deal may have contravened. Here they identified a large issue lurking just beneath the surface of Jackson's opinion. Both he and FDR surely knew the destroyer deal would be extremely provocative to Germany, which could quite reasonably regard it as an act of war. The whole point of the neutrality laws was to prevent such provocations with their risk of entanglement in war. FDR and Jackson threaded their way though the letter of the statutory restrictions with mixed success. What they ignored was the spirit of the statutes. The president had decided to skirt the edges of the neutrality laws in an effort to aid the British.[36] That was his responsibility, and it lay in the realm of statesmanship and at the edge of law. His action found much more justification in moral conscience than in legal right.

Jackson's *Destroyers* opinion serves as an example of an attorney general's use of the best set of available arguments for an action that, as both the president and his attorney general well knew, stood at the very edge of executive power. The two of them had thought about the problem together and had adopted arguments they were prepared to share with Congress and the nation. Their knowledge that their analysis would be made public importantly constrained the claims they advanced. Throughout, FDR was fully engaged in working through the legal problems with his attorney general. At the end, this process placed Jackson in the position of an advocate for the president's position, but there had been ample opportunity to serve as counselor and to shape the final nature of the deal with Britain.

After reviewing Jackson's opinion and its critics, historian Arthur Schlesinger, Jr., supported it because of the depth of the emergency (second only to Lincoln's in the Civil War), the use of wide consultation, and congressional ratification by funding for improvements to the bases. He concluded it was a "rather circumspect application of the Locke-Jefferson-Lincoln doctrine" of emergency power.[37]

A curious footnote to the destroyer episode, and one that is also revelatory of the relationship between President Roosevelt and Attorney General Jackson, occurred the next year after passage of the Lend-Lease Act.[38] The act showed Congress's increasing readiness to support future U.S. wartime allies by allowing the president to send them war supplies. Roosevelt was succeeding in his project to bring the people and Congress toward his commitment to aiding Britain. Still, Congress was cautious: it included a provision terminating the president's authorities upon the passage of a concurrent resolution of the two houses of Congress. Roosevelt believed this provision was unconstitutional because it would allow Congress to alter or repeal the act without presenting its action to him for his signature or veto.[39] Jackson was less sure: perhaps this was not a statutory repeal but "a reservation or limitation by which the granted power would expire or terminate."[40] FDR disagreed, and in a role reversal he wrote his attorney general a legal opinion concluding that he "felt constrained to sign the measure, in spite of the fact that it contained a provision which, in my opinion, is clearly unconstitutional."

The president instructed Jackson to keep the opinion in the Justice Department's files to forestall the use of his approval of the act "as a precedent for any future legislation comprising provisions of a similar nature."[41] Roosevelt's legal opinion was the better one—four decades later, the Supreme Court issued a landmark opinion invalidating all provisions like the one Congress appended to the Lend-Lease Act.[42] And Jackson was at fault in this case for unduly focusing on finding a rationale to justify approving this vital legislation at the expense of the long-term institutional interests of the executive branch, to which FDR was more alert.

FDR INTERNS JAPANESE AMERICANS
WITHOUT HIS ATTORNEY GENERAL'S SUPPORT

In contrast to his active role in steering the nation away from strict neutrality and toward outright support of Great Britain, President Roosevelt played a passive role in approving internment of Japanese Americans living on the West Coast in 1942. Nevertheless, he did approve it and bears full responsibility for it.[43]

Perhaps surprisingly, in the immediate aftermath of Pearl Harbor the West Coast was relatively calm. In early 1942, however, a potent mix of factors jeopardized the Japanese American community. War news was very bad, as the Japanese Empire brutally overran the Philippines and other U.S. and Allied territory in the Pacific. Long-standing racial hostility against the Japanese population on the West Coast, fueled by greed for their property and hysterical press coverage of false reports of sabotage and espionage, put pressure on the western congressional delegations and the military to remove the threat by relocating the people.

Neither military nor civilian officers sufficiently resisted this pressure or carefully probed its factual basis. General John DeWitt, a small-minded man who commanded the Western Defense Command, was "near the end of a long and undistinguished career."[44] DeWitt deeply imbibed the hysteria rising on the West Coast, crediting every crazy rumor of impending sabotage. Secretary of War Henry Stimson was a distinguished public servant with a long record in government and a reputation for sound judgment. For a while he demurred to a mass evacuation on constitutional grounds. Those grounds were obvious. Although some of the Japanese were aliens, most were U.S. citizens, born in this country. Both citizens and aliens were persons entitled to equal protection, due process of law, and the writ of habeas corpus.

Attorney General Francis Biddle also objected to evacuations as unconstitutional.[45] As hysteria mounted, Biddle resisted internment as "ill-advised, unnecessary, and unnecessarily cruel."[46] Reports from J. Edgar Hoover at the FBI cast serious doubt on the military necessity arguments. The FBI had arrested about 2,000 Japanese aliens soon after Pearl Harbor; these were the known threats to security. Biddle told Stimson there was no evidence of any plans for attacks or sabotage. Yet as time went by, subordinate officers in the War Department, including DeWitt and Assistant Secretary John McCloy, put increasing pressure on Stimson and Biddle to approve some form of evacuation and relocation of the Japanese Americans. In early 1942, DeWitt's *Final Report* called for mass evacuation, laid out various unsupported scenarios of sabotage and espionage, said that "the Japanese race is an enemy race," and even asserted that "the very fact that no sabotage has taken place to date is a disturbing and confirming indication that such action will be taken."[47] As Stimson swung toward supporting evacuation, Biddle resisted for a time, but he was intimidated by the far more experienced and prestigious Stimson and would not press him hard. Biddle was buttressed somewhat, though, by the persistent objections to evacuation of some of his subordinates in the Justice Department.[48] This pressure from below exemplifies a traditional role of career civil servants throughout the executive—ensuring that the political appointees are aware of departures from the long-term practices of the government.

Temporizing, Biddle asked three prominent New Deal attorneys not in the Justice Department for their views about evacuations; they stated the obvious by supporting action if "reasonably related to a genuine war need" and not disguised discrimination (which it in fact was).[49] On February 9, Biddle wrote Stimson, still resisting mass evacuations. Two days later, Stimson sent President Roosevelt a memo asking whether he supported various options, including extensive evacuations. Stimson tried to make an appointment with FDR, who was "too busy" to see him.[50] Rarely if ever was the president too busy to see his secretary of war in wartime—he was either stalling or evading responsibility for the decision. FDR eventually responded by telephone to

Stimson to "go ahead in the line [he] thought best," but to "be as reasonable as you can." By the time the decision was made, Biddle was "the only significant hold-out, and because he was new to the Cabinet, his opinion held little weight."[51] The President wanted to regard the evacuation question as one of military necessity, not one of fundamental rights of citizens and others. Biddle later reflected:

> I do not think [Roosevelt] was much concerned with the gravity or implications of this step. He was never theoretical about things. What must be done to defend the country must be done. The decision was for the Secretary of War, not for the Attorney General. . . . Nor do I think that the constitutional difficulty plagued him—the Constitution has never greatly bothered any wartime President. . . . Once, he emphasized to me, when I was expressing my belief that the evacuation was unnecessary, that this must be a military decision.[52]

Biddle's last effort to stop evacuations was a memo to the president on February 17.[53] In a follow-up telephone conversation, Biddle agreed to resist no more, having "decided that further opposition was pointless, the President had made up his mind." The War Department drafted a proposed executive order to authorize evacuations, the Justice Department approved it, and Roosevelt signed it.[54] The order was not discussed in the cabinet "except in a desultory fashion."[55] FDR thought that in wartime he could take any action he thought necessary to defend the nation.[56] Yet he never probed the factual basis for the order, nor did he consult General George Marshall or other senior military officers. Aside from DeWitt, most advocates of evacuation were civilians.

Congress soon ratified the order by enacting a brief and thinly deliberated statute that made violating military relocation orders a crime.[57] Neither the executive order nor the statute mentioned Japanese Americans. Both simply allowed the War Department to control the movement of individuals within designated military zones. Nor did they mention internment, although the program evolved into long-term incarceration after inland western governors heatedly refused to resettle the Japanese in their states.[58] Eventually, the Supreme Court upheld the evacuation and internment orders.[59] The majority opinions accepted the executive's claims of military necessity at face value despite some clear signals in the record that they were baseless. For that reason, the internment cases have frequently been cited for the proposition that the Supreme Court will not challenge the executive during a war, although the Court sometimes finds more courage afterward.[60]

The president never expressed any regret about his approval of the program, although his shadowy role, like the lack of explicitness in the order and statute, may signal a certain sense of shame. Roosevelt had long considered the Japanese unsuited to assimilation in the United States and was receptive to baseless claims about the threat they posed to security.[61] This moral blind spot haunts his legacy still. His cabinet officers showed more sensitivity to the legal issues and to the bad precedent being set than he did, but without assistance from the president they did not hold out against strong and persistent forces calling for removal of the Japanese Americans.[62]

Roosevelt, Stimson, and McCloy, all lawyers, should have known that the Constitution forbade mass evacuations without any showing of actual military necessity. Yet within the cabinet it was particularly the duty of the attorney general to assert the rights of U.S. citizens against arbitrary treatment. The War Department could be expected to pursue national security without much attention to civil liberties. Francis Biddle knew that the internment was unconstitutional, but he lacked the fortitude, the power within the cabinet, and the support from his president to prevent it. At least he never told the president these actions would be supported by right and conscience, for he knew they would not.

ROOSEVELT AND BIDDLE PURSUE THE NAZI SABOTEURS

In a third instance of legal advice within the Roosevelt administration, Biddle was an aggressive supporter of a proposal that raised serious ethical concerns about both his behavior and that of the president. This is the tragicomic episode of the Nazi saboteurs.[63] Their trial by military commission in 1942 later served as precedent for the Bush administration's order concerning military trials of suspected terrorists. It was, nevertheless, not a precedent that should have been a model for anyone.

In June 1942, eight German soldiers (one of them a naturalized U.S. citizen) were landed off Long Island, New York, and Jacksonville, Florida, by submarines. They buried their uniforms and entered the country bent on sabotaging industrial facilities. Their blundering came to the FBI's attention, but they were captured only after one of them turned himself in to authorities and named the others. What to do with them? Along with their uniforms, they had shed the legal protections of prisoner of war status. They could be tried as ordinary criminals, but Attorney General Biddle concluded their actions were too preliminary to satisfy criminal law requisites for proving attempted sabotage.[64] It appeared that minor crimes carrying a couple of years in jail might be proved. This seemed far too weak a response to wartime sabotage.

An alternative offered itself: trial by military commission (that is, a tribunal composed of military officers who try violations of the law of war by informal procedures). Spies and saboteurs had suffered that fate ever since General Washington hanged British Major Andre for spying in the Revolutionary War. The advantages of a military tribunal were that "it could act in secret, move swiftly, adopt rules that favored the prosecution, and mete out the death penalty."[65] Secrecy would preserve the false impression (promoted by J. Edgar Hoover) that the FBI had rounded up the saboteurs on its own and would hide the ease with which they had penetrated the mainland. Biddle soon pressed Secretary of War Stimson to convene a special military commission.

On June 30, the president revealed his own hand by sending Biddle a note expressing his belief in the guilt of the saboteurs and saying the death penalty was "almost obligatory."[66] "Without splitting hairs" he could see no difference between this case and the hanging of Major Andre, and concluded "don't split hairs, Mr. Attorney General." A memo to FDR from Biddle that day summarized the advantages of a tribunal: espionage and treason carried the death penalty but probably could not be proved in court, and the president's order could forbid judicial review. Excluding the courts would not, he advised, suspend the writ of habeas corpus, since it was "traditional to deny our enemies access to the courts in time of war."[67]

Both men were happily prejudging the case and manipulating the process to ensure their favored outcome. Ordinary federal criminal trials are well insulated against these sins by the executive; military commissions are not. In *Ex Parte Milligan*, decided just after the Civil War, the Supreme Court had shown that it understood the difference by refusing to allow trial by military commission of a civilian in Indiana, where the courts were open and functioning.[68] Biddle thought *Milligan* was inapplicable to enemy aliens.[69]

The press was soon informed that the president would create a seven-member military commission, and that prosecution would be conducted jointly by Biddle and by the judge advocate general (JAG) of the U.S. Army (who would normally review, not prosecute, such a case). Less than a week after the arrests, FDR issued a proclamation creating the tribunal.[70] The preamble declared that national security demanded that enemies who enter the United States "to commit sabotage, espionage, or other hostile or warlike acts" should be tried under the law of war. The order forbade those subject to it to "seek any remedy or maintain any proceeding" in the federal or state courts unless permitted by the attorney general. Because the attorney general was serving as prosecutor, permission was not likely to occur. The president felt strongly about denying judicial review: "I won't give them up. . . . I won't hand them over to any United States marshal armed with a writ of habeas corpus. Understand?"[71] The long shadow of *Merryman* had fallen over the case.

Roosevelt issued another order appointing seven generals to constitute the court; five experienced military lawyers would be defense counsel. FDR ordered the tribunal to try offenses against the traditional law of war and the statutory Articles of War, and gave it power to make such rules of procedure "consistent with the powers of military commissions under the Articles of War, as it shall deem necessary for a full and fair trial." This grant of discretion to the commission to make procedural rules for the particular case stood in fundamental tension with the admonition to provide a fair trial. An essential guarantee of fair procedure is that it be crafted in advance of its application to a particular defendant to prevent manipulation.

The order went on to provide that evidence could be admitted if it would "have probative value to a reasonable man." This would allow admitting hearsay evidence, which would be inadmissible in regular criminal trials. The concurrence of two-thirds of the members of the court would suffice for conviction and sentence, even to death; courts-martial required unanimity for the death penalty. There would be no jury; courts-martial have military officers appointed as a jury. At the end, the record was to be transmitted directly to the president for his final review, bypassing the normal channels of review within the military, including the JAG's office.

The tribunal met for about three weeks. On the eve of the trial, it adopted some vague procedural rules. As proceedings began, defense counsel immediately objected on constitutional grounds because the courts were open. They were rebuffed. There were four crimes charged: first, violation of the law of war by entering the United States out of uniform to commit sabotage and espionage; second, violation of Article of War 81 by "relieving the enemy" with arms and information; third, violation of Article of War 82 by lurking or spying near military facilities; fourth, conspiracy to commit the first three offenses.

As the trial proceeded, defense counsel tried to get a federal court hearing on a writ of habeas corpus. Relying on Roosevelt's order, a district court refused the initial application. The Supreme Court immediately set oral arguments on an appeal. Both sides submitted briefs to the Supreme Court on the day of oral argument, and the poorly prepared justices heard oral argument for nine hours over the next two days in an effort to understand the issues. The defense emphasized the jurisdictional issue, with the civilian courts in full operation and capable of hearing the main charges of espionage and sabotage. They also objected to the common law nature of some of the charges, saying that a statutory basis was necessary, as it usually is for federal crimes. They also claimed the executive order was ex post facto, because it increased the penalty after the crimes had occurred.

In response, Attorney General Biddle's brief said the courts had never been open to enemy invaders. He pointed out correctly that the actual ruling in *Milligan* was only that a statute required freeing Milligan, and that the Court's discussion of a general duty to resort to civilian courts was unnecessary "dictum" that need not be followed. He may also have sent word to Justice Owen Roberts that the president might execute the saboteurs whatever the Court might do.[72] Roosevelt surely knew that such a threat would be grossly unethical; Biddle surely knew that communicating it would be the same.

On July 30, the justices held their conference to decide the case, and the next day Chief Justice Stone issued a short opinion upholding the jurisdiction of the military tribunal. He promised a full opinion to follow; meanwhile the tribunal could proceed. The trial concluded on August 1 with eight death sentences. The record of 3,000 pages went to Roosevelt, who cannot have studied it in detail. The president approved six of the sentences and reduced the other two to prison terms. Executions took place on August 8.

It took three months for the justices to craft an opinion that could be unanimous. Because six of the saboteurs were already dead, dissents would have been most unseemly. The Supreme Court's full opinion in *Ex Parte Quirin* found statutory authority to use a military tribunal in an oblique reference in the Articles of War and approved the prosecution of common law offenses against the law of war.[73] It decided that the defendants were "unlawful combatants" subject to military jurisdiction. That was all the Court had to decide, since the saboteurs' challenge had been purely jurisdictional. Chief Justice Stone was able to avoid discussing the procedures actually followed by the tribunal, about which he held serious doubts.[74]

None of the participants in this rush to judgment merited praise. The Supreme Court found itself writing an opinion that had to gloss over serious issues in order to approve a fait accompli.[75] The attorney general blessed substantial legal irregularities in his ad hoc response to the presence of the saboteurs. He also stepped out of his role as adviser and overseer of the process to take on a partisan role as prosecutor.[76] He evinced no detachment or caution in addressing the tricky legal issues surrounding the case. Instead, he was an unrestrained advocate throughout. President Roosevelt could claim neither right nor conscience for his actions, only the necessities of war, which did not justify what he did. No one was left to ensure that the rule of law would be maintained. Unfortunately, the case of the Nazi saboteurs would cast its own long shadow, as bad precedents so often do.

PRESIDENT TRUMAN FOLLOWS BAD ADVICE AND THE SUPREME COURT REBUKES HIM

In a landmark decision, the Supreme Court rebuffed President Harry Truman when he took control of the nation's steel mills to avert a strike during the Korean War.[77] Because the *Steel Seizure* case sets the modern parameters for the limits of executive power, and hence guides advice given by today's executive advisers, I discuss it fully in a later chapter. Here I review the curious history of the legal advice Truman received that encouraged him to make the illegal seizure. The story shows the perils of casual reliance on undefined but extensive "inherent" constitutional powers of the president.

April 1952 was a highly stressful time for President Truman. He fired Attorney General J. Howard McGrath, who "had appeared to be obstructing the investigations Truman ordered into corruption in the Bureau of Internal Revenue."[78] He was overburdened with the cares of wartime. There was a military stalemate in Korea. Telephone and telegraph strikes were ongoing, and a steel strike loomed. He quickly nominated a replacement for the disgraced McGrath, but confirmation delays in the Senate left him without an attorney general throughout the period of the steel seizure and the resulting litigation. Solicitor General Philip Perlman served as acting attorney general, and various official and unofficial advisers rushed in to fill the void caused by the vacancy. They did not serve Truman well.

The dispute concerned union demands for a wage increase and management demands for a compensating price increase. President Truman favored higher wages but opposed substantial price increases as inflationary. After various efforts at mediation, a strike loomed. Truman could have invoked the Taft-Hartley Act to stop the strike for eighty days, but declined to do so. He claimed that the act's "cooling-off period" would provide no permanent solution.[79] The act, which had passed over his veto in 1947, was anathema to Truman. Hence, the president faced more of a political than a legal emergency.[80] Some other statutory provisions authorized seizing industries under certain conditions, but they were consistently rejected by Truman's advisers as too cumbersome for use in the steel crisis.[81] Reluctance to use any of the available statutory powers to stop the strike brought Truman and his advisers quickly—and prematurely—to constitutional grounds.

As the strike deadline approached, discussions among staff in the White House, the Defense Department, and the Justice Department reviewed both statutory and constitutional law. The lawyers, none of them having the heft of cabinet secretaries, concluded that dependence on constitutional power was preferable.[82] "It would be less vulnerable to attack in court, involve less complicated administrative operations, and take much less time."[83] The Justice Department does not seem to have received much deference in the discussions, perhaps because it was in bad odor at the time. In addition to the tribulations that had unseated the attorney general, some in the White House thought the department "tended to be evasive, sometimes downright unresponsive, in providing the Executive Office with forthright legal guidance."[84]

In this fluid situation, the views of President Truman took primacy along with those of the chief justice, who should never have offered advice on a case that would come before him:

> From his reading of history, Truman was convinced his action fell within his powers as President and Commander in Chief. In a state of national emergency, Lincoln had suspended the right to *habeas corpus,* he would point out. Tom Clark, now on the Supreme Court, had once, as Attorney General, advised him that a President, faced with a calamitous strike, had the "inherent" power to prevent a paralysis of the national economy. Truman's legal advisers supported his views. And so, significantly, did Fred Vinson. . . . The Chief Justice had confidentially advised the President that, on legal grounds, he could go ahead and seize the mills. . . . Out of friendship and loyalty, Vinson offered advice that was taken quite to heart. The path was clear, Truman told the ever cautious [Treasury Secretary John] Snyder, who opposed seizing the mills. "The President has the power to keep the country from going to hell," Truman would assure his staff. [85]

President Truman's breezy confidence was probably reinforced by his experience of having sent U.S. troops into Korea without statutory authority and without suffering any subsequent penalty from either Congress or the courts. After North Korea suddenly invaded South Korea, Secretary of State Dean Acheson, whom Truman greatly respected, advised him that given the need for a speedy response to the invasion, he should not seek congressional authority to support South Korea but should rely on his constitutional powers.[86] Truman was receptive to this advice. He did not want to slow his military response in a fluid and dangerous situation, and was wary of his enemies in the Senate. The State Department generated a list of precedents of unilateral presidential use of the military. "Truman, impressed by the appearance of precedent and concerned not to squander the power of his office," accepted the recommendation.[87] Congress later ratified his action by voting appropriations and extending the draft.

To the extent that President Truman relied on his unilateral warmaking to justify the more modest action of the steel seizure, he failed to see that the courts would be on firmer ground in reviewing a domestic seizure of industry than they would have been in assessing the need for a military response to an overseas invasion. On April 8, 1952, Truman announced in a nationwide radio address that he was seizing the steel mills to stop the strike. His executive order placed the mills under government supervision and directed them to continue production. The companies immediately sought and obtained an injunction against the order. After the Supreme Court upheld the injunction, the president returned the mills to the custody of the owners. A strike followed and was settled after fifty-three days, before any disruption to the wartime supply of steel occurred.

In the end, then, all survived: the president, the steel companies, the unions, the troops, and the rule of law. President Truman, a competent amateur historian but not a lawyer, made a plausible enough claim of legal right to meet the demands of good conscience. He did seek and receive varying kinds of legal advice, including the inappropriate counsel of the chief justice. And after making his decision, he submitted it both to Congress and to the nation for the support he expected.

The president's own legal conclusion suffered from two defects, however. First, having successfully engaged in unilateral warmaking in Korea, he seems to have succumbed to the seductive lure of the common legal argument that a greater power always includes a lesser one. (No, context counts, and each action needs its own sufficient justification.) Second, he read too much into Lincoln's habeas precedent in the Civil War. The crisis he faced, although substantial, was not so dire as Lincoln's, and Truman had time to seek advance authority from Congress.

The president's lawyers spent too little time assessing whether the Taft-Hartley Act barred the seizure, the ground upon which they would lose before the Supreme Court. Instead of assuring themselves that a statutory amendment need not be sought because the sum of available statutory authorities sufficed, they shifted precipitately to constitutional ground, and unstable ground at that. They compounded their legal jeopardy by claiming executive power without limit and received the negative judicial reaction that they should have anticipated. Their advice does not seem to have been sufficiently independent of presidential desires to satisfy the dictates of good conscience, and it was fatally thin in legal right.

THE REAGAN ADMINISTRATION EVADES THE LAW AND THE LAWYERS

Ronald Reagan entered the presidency with a deep suspicion of the Soviet Union and a strong propensity to detect Soviet influence in leftist movements around the world.[88] Both Reagan and Central Intelligence Agency (CIA) Director William J. Casey abhorred the Sandinista Liberation Front, which had recently taken power in Nicaragua, both for its own politics and for its support for rebels in neighboring El Salvador. Casey was a "charming scoundrel" whose talent lay in "bending rules to the breaking point."[89] Both Reagan and Casey saw the Sandinistas as part of a Soviet and Cuban threat to the security of the Western Hemisphere, not as minor opponents to the United States who were ruling a tropical backwater.

By the end of 1981, Reagan had approved covert actions against the Sandinistas, including training Nicaraguan "Contras" to oppose them. Congress, however, did not share the administration's alarm about the Sandinistas, and in 1982 it began enacting a series of funding restrictions, the Boland Amendments, each of which forbade the use of U.S. funds to overthrow the Sandinistas. Nevertheless, covert action continued under the guise that it was directed to interdicting arms shipments from Nicaragua to El Salvador rather than regime change.[90] In early 1984, with the president's approval, the CIA mined Nicaraguan harbors, and Casey gave a perfunctory and misleading briefing about the operation to the congressional intelligence committees, suggesting that the Contras were doing the mining. When the press revealed that this was actually a CIA operation, Congress reacted angrily.[91] The House attached a new Boland Amendment to an appropriations bill, which Reagan signed to avoid losing the funds. It prohibited military or paramilitary support for the Contras by the CIA, the Defense Department, "or any other agency or entity involved in intelligence activities."[92] Representative Boland explained in the House that this provision "clearly ends U.S. support for the war in Nicaragua" with "no exceptions."[93]

With the president and Congress in fundamental disagreement about policy toward the Contras, the administration adopted a new approach completely hidden from Congress. National Security Adviser Robert M. McFarlane understood that President Reagan wanted the Contras kept together "body and soul."[94] Since the agencies that normally performed intelligence activities were disabled by the Boland Amendment, the initiative passed to the staff of the National Security Council (NSC), which is supposed to be an agency for interpreting intelligence and recommending policy, not for covert action.[95] Within the NSC, the responsibility for keeping the bodies and souls of the Contras attached fell to McFarlane's deputy (and successor), Admiral John M. Poindexter, and to the egregious Lt. Col. Oliver L. North of the Marine Corps. North, lacking experience in either covert operations or Latin America, did possess unquenchable optimism, total devotion to the president's desires as he understood them, indefatigable energy, and atrocious judgment. Thus, with the intelligence professionals sidelined by the Boland Amendment, an amateur operation was cobbled together by officers trained for other duties.

North and Poindexter began finding secret sources of support for the Contras that did not involve expending federal funds. They obtained "donations" to support the Contras from private U.S. citizens and from foreign governments, prominently Saudi Arabia. Perhaps the U.S. donors expected nothing in return except the president's gratitude, but it stretches credulity to say the same of the Saudis. Hence, even if off-the-books private fund-raising was in technical compliance with the Boland Amendments because it did not disburse federal funds, there was surely an expenditure of a less tangible, but no less important, form of the nation's capital. Nonetheless, at a meeting Attorney General William French Smith informally approved the fund-raising as long as federal funds were not used either in the initial overtures or to repay donations.[96] CIA General Counsel Stanley Sporkin agreed.

As the fund-raising efforts went on, North felt the need for a bit more legal buttressing. He turned to an odd source—not the Department of Justice or the CIA or the NSC's staff counsel but the counsel for the obscure Intelligence Oversight Board. This was one Bretton Sciaroni, who possessed more doggedness than brilliance, having passed his bar examination on the fifth try.[97] On the basis of some misleading facts given him by North, Sciaroni gave such blessings as he could command. Now North was prepared to claim that his actions had received full legal review. To him, this was a matter of finding someone who would provide a satisfactory conclusion to cover his flank, not a matter of seeking actual guidance from the executive branch's far more expert lawyers in the regular advising offices.

Meanwhile, a hostage crisis in Lebanon took center stage in the president's mind. By early 1985, Hezbollah, a pro-Iranian terrorist group firmly entrenched in Lebanon, had kidnapped five Americans including the CIA station chief in Beirut. Reagan clearly and constantly communicated to his staff his deep desire to see the hostages freed. The NSC staff responded by concocting a scheme to sell U.S. antitank missiles to Iran in return for which Iran would press Hezbollah to release the hostages. After McFarlane informed President Reagan of the proposal, he gave initial approval and then discussed it with some members of the cabinet, not including the attorney general. Secretary of State George Shultz and Secretary of Defense Caspar Weinberger stated strenuous objections reflecting the traditional reluctance of their departments to arm rogue regimes. Reagan appeared to reserve decision, but arms were already flowing toward Iran.[98]

There were serious legal obstacles to the plan to trade arms for hostages. Iran, for good reason, was listed as a supporter of international terrorism, with the result that it could not buy U.S. arms. In fact, official U.S. policy was to press nations around the world to deny arms to Iran. Hence the plan, in fundamental tension with U.S. law and policy, would have to be both indirect and secret. Israel was asked to sell the arms to Iran, whereupon the United States would replenish the Israeli arsenal. With Reagan's approval and active interest, a series of amateurish and often farcical negotiations ensued. The NSC staff drew on some help from the CIA and employed some extremely dubious private arms dealers. No one ever knew who could or would speak for Iran on the other end. Iran eventually received more than 2,000 antitank missiles and some spare parts for its antiaircraft missiles. In return, three Americans were released, but during the negotiations more than that many new hostages were taken in Lebanon.[99]

The sale of arms to Iran implicated various statutes that controlled international arms sales pursuant to Congress's power to regulate foreign trade. The statutory scheme was complex, with multiple substantive limits on arms sales. Each statute also contained one or both of two common techniques for making the executive conform to the legislative will. First, Congress required the president to make specified findings of the importance of a particular action to our national security. Second, Congress required notification of each action, typically by reporting to the intelligence committees of the two houses. The purpose shared by these two control techniques was political responsibility. If the president approved an action personally and explicitly, his accountability to the law (and to history) was ensured. And if Congress was notified of an action, it would be accountable for acquiescing in or challenging the action. In the ever-changing realm of foreign affairs, these simple control techniques often replace detailed substantive prescription of policy, which is usually difficult or counterproductive to formulate. In Iran-Contra, the Reagan administration would evade both kinds of limits, triggering a scandal.

Here is a brief tour of the statutory horizon. The Arms Export Control Act (1976) required presidential consent to the retransfer of arms initially exported to Israel and notice to Congress if the sale exceeded a stated dollar amount.[100] The second possible authority for arms transfers to Iran was pursuant to intelligence operations conducted under the National Security Act, the CIA's principal (and sublimely vague) charter. The act required that the CIA director and the heads of other intelligence agencies keep the two congressional intelligence committees "fully and currently informed" of all intelligence activities under their responsibility.[101] Where prior notice of significant intelligence activities was not given, the intelligence committees were to be informed "in a timely fashion." In addition, the Hughes-Ryan Amendment to the Foreign Assistance Act (1974) required that "significant anticipated intelligence activities" could not be conducted by the CIA unless and until the president found that "each such operation is important to the national security of the United States."[102]

Thus, whether the arms sales were legal "depends fundamentally upon whether the President approved the transactions before they occurred."[103] Some early sales occurred before the president signed the necessary finding to approve them. The participation of some CIA officers in the deals eventually raised legal concerns. The CIA was well aware of the law governing foreign arms sales and covert actions. Indeed, the president had issued a national security decision directive in early 1985 detailing the requisites for findings—in particular, that they be in writing and subject to congressional reporting.[104] Accordingly, in late 1985 CIA counsel Sporkin quickly drafted a finding for the president to sign.[105] The finding declared that the hostage release efforts were "important to the national security," attempted to ratify prior actions, and directed the CIA not to brief Congress "until such time as I may direct otherwise."[106] It would not be reported for almost a year.

The Sporkin finding was not vetted by the Justice Department. President Reagan's second attorney general, Edwin Meese III, would later say that the retroactivity feature was "of questionable legality."[107] Actually, it was simply illegal, because the whole point of the statutory requirement for a finding is to have the president make the initial decision and take responsibility for it. Had Meese been asked to approve the retroactive finding in advance, he would have had the opportunity to delete it or to consider whether he could approve it as a "second-best" compliance with the statute. In any event, the finding was put before Reagan, who signed it. Later, the president signed two more findings similar to this first one.

Attorney General Meese was consulted about the final finding. Concerned about the notification requirement, he was prepared to opine that the arms sales could be conducted via the National Security Act's provisions regarding covert operations, which he understood to allow delaying reporting for a month or two.[108] He was very concerned about leaks from Congress that might endanger the hostages and thought that a brief delay would allow the operation to be completed, whereupon Congress would be notified.

The secretive, convoluted, and confused decisionmaking concerning the arms sales led to violations of both primary congressional controls on covert action. It was later claimed that Reagan had made an "oral finding" approving the initial sales, so that they were legal from the outset.[109] Whether he actually did so is lost in the mists of history. He gave three answers to the question of whether he had approved them: that he had, that he had not, and that he could not remember. In retrospect, charity suggests accepting the third version. A respect for law suggests that only a written finding should suffice, precisely to avoid the mire in which President Reagan found himself. Moreover, since the Arms Export Control Act and the Hughes-Ryan Amendment required somewhat different kinds of findings to support the sales, the president's lawyers should have researched which was appropriate in a given case and should have put the findings in the terms required by the pertinent statute.[110] Attorney General Meese would later argue that reliance on an oral finding, although "a substantive and procedural error," was legally sufficient because the statutes did not specifically require a written one and because he believed that the president did in fact make the decision to authorize the sales.[111] This rather tortured reasoning confirms the need for the procedural regularity written findings ensure.

The National Security Act required that notification to Congress of covert intelligence activities, if not made in advance, must be "in a timely fashion." After the first written presidential finding directed that congressional notification be withheld, no one ever seems to have revisited the issue. Even if emergency conditions justified a delay in notification, the statute surely required it "where, as in the Iran case, a pattern of relative inactivity occurs over an extended period. To do otherwise prevents the Congress from fulfilling its proper oversight responsibilities."[112] Attorney General Meese later conceded that the delay that occurred was a "policy error." Still, he was prepared to defend a general approach that relied on after-the-fact notice for sensitive operations, because of the danger of leaks by Congress.[113]

In 1985, while deeply embroiled with the Iranian negotiations, North evolved a plan to divert profits from the arms sales to the Contras. It was, he later testified proudly, "a neat idea."[114] Poindexter, having become national security adviser, concurred that it was "a very good idea"[115] and approved it. Both men were by then accustomed to finding nonappropriated funds to support the Contras; perhaps this seemed just another instance of that activity to them. They consulted no lawyers, however, and thus were not reminded of the substantial argument that the proceeds of sales of U.S. arms are federal funds in a way Saudi cash is not.[116] Poindexter then made the extraordinary decision not to inform the president about the plan. His rationale both reveals his own sense of guilt about the diversion and confirms a usurpation of the president's authority that any admiral must have known was improper: "So although I was convinced that we could properly do it and that the President would approve it if asked, I made a very deliberate decision not to ask the President so that I could insulate him from the decision and provide some future deniability for the President if it ever leaked out."[117]

By insulating the president from political responsibility for this reckless scheme, Poindexter made national policy without the participation of any elected official from either branch of government.

By late 1986, both the Iranian and the Contra sides of the operation stood revealed. President Reagan never admitted, possibly even to himself, that arms had been traded for hostages (instead, he claimed that the effort was to empower Iranian "moderates"). As the revelations spread, Reagan initially assigned Attorney General Meese to determine the facts. Not having been asked to approve the initial legality of either part of the Iran-Contra operation, Meese found himself at sea. He had head of OLC Charles Cooper review the legality of the arms sales from the first finding on, and Cooper approved them.[118] He was not asked about the earlier and more dubious sales, which were beginning to be revealed. As Meese and Cooper tried to find out what had occurred, they met a classic stonewall response from Poindexter and Casey. It took threats from Sofaer and Cooper to resign to forestall Casey from giving false testimony to Congress. Poindexter and North responded by conducting a "shredding party," destroying all the documents they could find.

Soon Poindexter and North were dismissed, and a season of more formal investigations commenced: the president's own "Tower Commission,"[119] separate investigations by the two houses of Congress,[120] and an endless criminal inquiry by independent counsel Lawrence Walsh.[121] All of these investigations confronted the substantial political obstacles that the president's second term was winding down, and his popularity was still strong.

President Reagan defended himself by stressing his good intentions and his ignorance of many of the details of the actions of his subordinates. Implausibly, he told the Tower Commission he did not know the NSC staff was supporting the Contras. The commission never could determine whether Reagan had approved the arms sales. The commission also reviewed the involvement of the administration's lawyers in decisions about the arms sales. Understating the fact that "significant questions of law do not appear to have been adequately addressed," the commission concluded the "lack of

legal vigilance markedly increased the chances that the initiative would proceed contrary to law."[122]

This is too tame. If lawyers are not consulted about actions that implicate
complex legal questions, there is little prospect for maintaining the rule of
law. President Reagan's White House Counsel Arthur Culvahouse later recalled: "One of the real problems with the entire Iran-Contra episode was that
not only was it not well-lawyered, but it was *not lawyered* in most respects."[123]
Attorney General Meese "was even asked at times to render off-the-cuff oral
advice on complex legal situations. The obvious desire was to be able to claim
that the Attorney General had given a legal seal of approval to various proposals without permitting them to undergo real legal scrutiny."[124]

At the end of the day, independent counsel Walsh correctly assigned overall responsibility for Iran-Contra to the president: "The tone in Iran/contra
was set by President Reagan. He directed that the contras be supported, despite a ban on contra aid imposed on him by Congress. And he was willing
to trade arms to Iran for the release of Americans held hostage in the Middle
East, even if doing so was contrary to the nation's stated policy and possibly
in violation of the law."[125]

Reagan is said to have told Secretary of State Shultz that "the American
people will never forgive me if I fail to get these hostages out over this legal
question."[126] The president's attitude that law must be subordinated to results, once communicated to willing subordinates, explains much about the
Iran-Contra scandal.

Regarding the Contra operation, I believe using National Security Council
staff to support the Contras violated the Boland Amendment's prohibition
of using any agency "involved in intelligence activities" to support military
operations in Nicaragua.[127] Although the NSC staff is not ordinarily an operational intelligence agency, it so acted during Iran-Contra with the clear
intention of evading the Boland Amendment.[128] The majorities of the House
and Senate committees investigating the Iran-Contra affair concluded that
the administration had engaged in "an evasion of the letter and the spirit" of
the law, and laid blame partially with President Reagan, whose solicitation
of foreign donations for the Contras "set the stage" for his subordinates'
view of the law "not as setting boundaries for their actions, but raising im-
pediments to their goals."[129] All of this is correct. The president did not take
the actions his obligation to execute the laws faithfully would have required
if the executive's actions in Iran-Contra were to be supported by right and
conscience.

The minority report of the Iran-Contra committees contended the Boland Amendments were unconstitutional because they unduly restricted

the president's executive authority in foreign affairs. The House report was written by Representative Richard Cheney of Wyoming, the future vice president. His theory of extremely broad executive power, which would take center stage in the war on terrorism, was incorrect then and is incorrect now, as I will explain in subsequent chapters.

The criminal prosecutions of Poindexter and North ultimately came to little. An appeals court overturned jury convictions of both men for lying to Congress about their activities.[130] The court concluded that insufficient steps had been taken to ensure that the defendants' compelled testimony to Congress during the Iran-Contra hearings, for which they had been granted immunity from prosecution, did not taint their criminal trials. Also, the Justice Department had been very uncooperative with Independent Counsel Walsh, further hampering successful prosecution. The absence of any serious criminal penalty for North and Poindexter was very unfortunate. Both men did all they could to deceive and mislead Congress in its attempts to get at the truth; North in particular was obtusely proud of what he had done.[131] The underlying assumption was that Congress had no business asking about national security.[132]

The Iran-Contra operation created secret national policies supported by funds not appropriated by Congress.[133] This technique evaded the primal constitutional control that underlies the usual statutory requirements that presidents make findings and notify Congress about their activities. The appropriations process "provides the link between government operations and the democratic mandate by requiring that all funding take place by statutes, that is, by the actions of persons who can be turned out by the voters every biennium."[134] Circumventing this process by using unappropriated funds, "no matter how noble the purpose and no matter how beneficent the source, is to strike at the heart of this idea." The official investigations of Iran-Contra, consumed by the effort to discover who did what, failed to make this point about the fundamental unconstitutionality of the secret policies and operations in a way the public could understand.

Thus the scandal ended with a legal whimper, having besmirched President Reagan's second term but not having destroyed the esteem Americans held for him. Without grave political and criminal penalties for the follies and crimes of Iran-Contra, the prospect remained that future administrations would fail to learn clear lessons from the episode. The Reagan administration's evasion of both statutes and lawyers did not draw fierce condemnation from the U.S. public. It should have been clear to everyone, though, that ordinary bureaucratic processes of asking the Justice Department for its advice concerning sensitive executive initiatives could have forestalled the scandal.[135] In any event, the official remonstrances of the various investigating bodies were left to carry the freight of calling future executives to their duties under law.[136]

CONCLUSION: PRESIDENTS, LAWYERS, AND ADVICE

The stories in this and the preceding chapter are not the only ones that could be told about U.S. presidents and their legal advisers, but they are especially rich examples of the varying relationships between deciders and advisers. George Washington made two critical and difficult legal decisions after fully considering the best advice available. Thomas Jefferson irresponsibly attempted to suppress legal discussion of the Louisiana Purchase, and tried to suppress his own conscience as well. Andrew Jackson used his lawyers like shock troops in the battle with the "Monster." Abraham Lincoln made his own legal decisions on matters of the highest sensitivity. Franklin Roosevelt had quite a mixed record, engaging fully with his attorney general in the neutrality controversies, avoiding legal engagement in the Japanese American internments, and spurring his attorney general forward in the case of the Nazi saboteurs. Harry Truman let his own rough notions of presidential power be ratified by lawyers who should have known better. And Ronald Reagan subordinated law to policy, making both bad law and bad policy.

Other prominent presidents have shown varying devotion to matters of legal right and conscience. Theodore Roosevelt could push for effective enforcement of law on the domestic scene, yet snatch Panama from Colombia to build his canal. Woodrow Wilson could send two punitive expeditions to Mexico, yet ask the world to accept his vision of international order in 1919. After World War II, the Vietnam War wrecked two presidencies over issues of policy, not law. Watergate brought down Richard Nixon because he committed felonies or urged their commission. Jimmy Carter's long ordeal in the Iranian hostage crisis showed fidelity to law, but cost him his office. William Clinton's efforts to hide his personal infidelities led him to commit perjury and subjected him to the humiliation of a failed impeachment.

Reviewing all this, one cannot say that more than two centuries of the U.S. government have produced any clear legal or traditional definition of the necessary relationship of presidents to their legal advisers or any effective method of binding presidents to the dictates of right and conscience. Alas, no magical formula is likely to appear in our rowdy democracy. There is more to be said, nevertheless, about both legal right and professional conscience, and those are the topics of the next two chapters.

4

The Professional Responsibility of the President's Lawyers

QUESTIONS OF CONSCIENCE HAUNT US ALL. Lawyers are bound by a set of principles that state their professional responsibility to their clients—codifying the profession's collective conscience, if you will. Government lawyers are subject to these generally applicable principles, although their roles are distinct from private practice in some ways that I will explore.[1] Government lawyers also differ from policy aides, although it would be shallow to suggest that policy advisers routinely abandon their personal consciences when they consider what options and arguments to advance.

The president's lawyers encounter two primary kinds of forces, which tug them in opposite directions. First, powerful incentives to provide supportive advice result from the structure and culture of the executive branch. The counterforce that encourages more independent and perhaps unwelcome advice comes from a combination of the ethical standards that bind all lawyers and the felt obligation of the oath of office executive advisers take. In other words, the lawyers experience conflicting imperatives of duty because they serve both the president and the law. These influences play on the personal character each lawyer brings to the role, with variable effects depending on the content of that character. We shall see that no bright lines illuminate the limits of permissible behavior. Consequently, a legal problem may present a mix of substantive and ethical questions, with no easy answer to any of them. There is no escaping the need for good judgment.

Even the brief tour of U.S. history in previous chapters reveals substantial variations in the behavior of the president's lawyers. Sometimes they are advocates for the president's policy position, evincing little sign of professional restraint. Roger Taney was Andrew Jackson's fierce lieutenant in the war against the "Monster." Sometimes they show enough independence to imperil their continued employment. Francis Biddle opposed the Japanese internment as best he could and as long as he seemed to be having some effect. A skilled lawyer who holds the president's confidence may be able to work in partnership with him or her when they agree and still disagree when that seems necessary. Robert Jackson had that kind of relationship with Franklin Roosevelt (FDR).

A story from Jackson's memoir illustrates his method of guiding FDR toward a correct legal outcome.[2] Jackson reported that the president "did not require [his subordinates] to do things that in their opinions they ought not to do." An example was a 1938 request of the German government, after the burning of the airship Hindenburg, for helium (which is not flammable). The statute "was very clear. The approval of the Secretary of the Interior was indispensable to any exportation of helium. I so advised the President." Yet Interior Secretary Harold Ickes was adamantly opposed to any export to the Nazis, although the State Department favored it. FDR put Jackson on the spot:

> The President turned to me and said, "Now what can I do about this?" The situation was rather tense. . . . I said, "Well, Mr. President, I don't see that you can do anything about helium unless you do something about your Secretary of Interior first. As long as you have such a stubborn one, I don't see how you can transfer helium under the statute." The President laughed heartily, as did all the rest, but that ended the matter—the President would not give a preemptory order to his Secretary that went against the latter's judgment.

Jackson had prevailed; no helium was sent.

Recall that at the outset of the destroyers episode, FDR is said to have bullied subordinates in the navy, demanding legal support for his plans to aid Britain.[3] Assuming that the story is true, the difference in the president's behavior toward his subordinates in the helium episode may be due to the personal respect he held for Jackson and Ickes. By employing a nonconfrontational, indirect approach, Jackson was able to thwart his president's desires while at the same time serving as a buffer between FDR and the ever-prickly Ickes. As we shall see throughout this book, the personality and character of both the president and his advisers determine their relationship—and the executive's adherence to law—in a way that is impossible for outsiders to control.

The helium episode shares a vital characteristic with a much earlier controversy, Andrew Jackson's struggle with his treasury secretary over withdrawal of the national bank deposits. In both cases, the pertinent statute delegated power directly to a cabinet secretary, not to the president. Most statutes creating administrative regimes address subordinate administrators and do not mention the president. What is the president's supervisory power in that case? This is a long-controverted and unsettled question of constitutional and administrative law.[4] I discuss it fully later; for now, notice that once again, everyone assumed that the president could not simply take the statutory decision into his own hands and render it. Instead, presidents need to persuade balky administrators to comply with their wishes. This enduring feature of life in the executive complicates the provision of legal advice, which is often directed to an administrator operating in the shadow of presidential supervision.

THE STRUCTURE AND CULTURE OF THE EXECUTIVE BRANCH

Each of the three constitutional branches has its own distinct culture, which it transmits to new employees through training, peer pressure, and daily exposure to arguments favoring that branch in the contests of the moment. Officers of the two political branches soon form loyalties to their own branch and absorb its values; they readily believe their branch is right and the other is wrong about the enduring issues. All lawyers experience this kind of effect when they act in adversarial contexts. (Indeed, many workers in all fields generate loyalty to their employers, at least if the company treats them decently.)

The president and his cabinet see themselves as representing the nation in a way local politicians in Congress do not, and they usually consider themselves quite open to outside influences from many quarters, including Congress and the general public. From the White House and its environs, Congress appears meddlesome, suspicious, and fractured. In contrast, members of Congress and their staffs see Congress as the "first branch," tied closely to the people and exercising the primal function of legislation.[5] From Capitol Hill, the executive branch appears arrogant, secretive, dangerous in its capacity for sudden action, and strangely unresponsive to the people's will as embodied in Congress. Both of the branches tend to descend into self-righteousness in relating to each other.[6]

This tension between the branches was created intentionally by the framers of the Constitution. In *Federalist Paper 51*, James Madison said the purpose of creating two partly separated political branches was to forestall tyrannical concentrations of power: "Ambition must be made to counteract ambition." Madison envisioned a healthy friction between the branches, with each restraining the other. He was too optimistic in two ways, however. First, when it occurs, interbranch competition for power tends to implode both of the political branches, turning each within itself in a defensive reaction to the other. Then they talk past, and not to, each other. Thus, there is a tendency to impair working relationships. Second, the rise of the party system in the United States, which the framers did not anticipate, has created a second set of loyalties that often submerge institutional interests. This latter phenomenon will be much in evidence when we consider the war on terrorism.

Lawyers for a branch of government are immersed in a long-standing legal tradition of shared views about their branch's powers and perquisites. The body of precedents their predecessors have generated is known to them and is self-perpetuating because no one wants to waive or undermine traditional institutional arguments. (Any concession of authority is eventually punished by the other branch or by the courts, which will cite it as an embarrassing precedent the next time the underlying issue arises.) In addition, career advancement within a branch is more likely for those who strongly champion its interests. Finally, there is never an absence of competing views from the other branch and private parties, which to the government lawyer seem to be skewed by self-interest and clearly erroneous on the merits.

These competing arguments usually spur compensatory aggressiveness in interpretation and argument (although at times they force a retreat from extreme positions). Hence, government lawyers are more likely to display an excess of zeal than a lack of it on behalf of their branch. The substantive legal positions they take are systematically skewed toward the institutional position of the branch they inhabit, whether or not the lawyers have the self-awareness to know that.

THE PRESIDENT'S LEGAL ADVISERS

The president's cabinet, as we have seen, often contains competitors for the president's ear when legal issues arise. There is no formal mechanism to reconcile the clash of views. The president hears the various opinions (or those he or she cares to consider) and decides among them. He or she usually feels quite free to pick and choose, as history has demonstrated, instead of simply deferring to whatever the attorney general says. The cabinet has never served as a real deliberative body that would thrash out proposed decisions for the president to review.[7] Instead, the cabinet is really a staff entity, in the sense that it is a sounding board for advice on major issues occupying the president's mind. As the cabinet has grown over the years, its size has hampered group discussion and debate. In modern times, it often serves largely ceremonial functions. Of course, the president can always call on its members singly or in smaller groups.

The game of influencing the president is played without rules. The insights of game theory are useful in analyzing this unstructured contest. For example, because the cabinet is composed of a group of people who share devotion to the president and who usually serve for a period of years, an incentive to cooperate flows from the knowledge that the help of colleagues may be needed on future issues.[8] Ambition often casts aside cooperation, however. The president always has desirable nominations in his favor—to other cabinet posts, to the Supreme Court. Hence it is very likely that pleasing the president will be the order of the day: "Personalities change when the President is present, and frequently even strong [people] make recommendations on the basis of what they believe the President wishes to hear."[9]

In the rough-and-tumble of the cabinet, the attorney general may be uniquely vulnerable due to the presence of other lawyers who may regard themselves as having equal or superior legal skills.[10] Also, a single legal issue can have multiple policy applications, triggering pressure from several secretaries. But the attorney general has several weapons for fighting back. One is the duty of providing legal advice to the other departments, which they are expected to follow.[11] Another is the Justice Department's control of litigation involving the other departments, which enforces the advising role. And for some presidential decisions, there is a formal requirement that the Justice Department be consulted.[12] History shows, though, that the character and capacity of the attorney general matters most. A strong one is rarely ignored; a weak one is rarely influential. Robert Jackson was strong enough to disagree both with his colleagues and (carefully) with his president; his successor Francis Biddle was weak enough to let his conscience be overborne by a more distinguished colleague, at least when the president would not come to his aid.

When the talking is done and a final presidential decision impends, there is a traditional process for formalizing the decision. In modern times, White House staff or agency officials have usually prepared a decision memorandum for the president, presenting policy options together with outlines of the arguments favoring and disfavoring each one.[13] Legal analysis from the Department of Justice and the department that will administer the policy may be attached or summarized. The president reads the memorandum, perhaps discusses it with some advisers, and decides, usually marking the options memorandum to indicate the choice.

The second President Bush, unlike his predecessors, preferred oral briefings. He considered what he heard and conveyed his decision orally to his staff. This departure from precedent was not trivial. The traditional, routinized paper process fosters bureaucratic regularity by helping to ensure that legal issues have been considered and that the voices of affected departments have been heard. As we learned from Iran-Contra, an oral process can short-circuit these constraints and can imperil the rule of law. At the least, oral advice-giving forfeits the benefits that come from having to write advice down.

Writing imposes an inherent discipline: lawyers and judges say that some opinions just "won't write." A written opinion invites collaboration and considered revision, in part because it may sometime see the light of day. Oral advice can too easily be altered or lost in the mists of time and memory. President Bush's informal style was especially hazardous in crisis times, when pressure and distraction sometimes led his advisers to neglect best practices in favor of horseback decisions.

The modern attorney general has a primary competitor for primacy in providing legal advice to the president. Since World War II, the office of White House Counsel has existed as part of the president's immediate staff, within steps of the Oval Office.[14] FDR created the position in his characteristic organizational style of proliferating advisers with overlapping portfolios, allowing him to dominate them all. Not all of his successors have possessed his bureaucratic skills, but all of them have inherited the structural competition between legal advisers. The opportunity for an aggressive counsel to displace the attorney general is always present, although the counsel has never enjoyed formal primacy.

Compared to the attorney general, the counsel exists in the shadows. He or she is appointed by the president without confirmation by the Senate, is traditionally immune from compelled congressional testimony, has no statutory duties, maintains few records, and has a staff of about a dozen lawyers that changes completely with each new administration. The existence of this "in-house" lawyer's office reduces the president's dependence on the attorney general and, as FDR surely intended, renders the president more independent from both of his primary lawyers, because he or she can play them off against each other.

Over the years, White House counsels have given presidents both legal and policy advice. Some superb lawyers have served in the post: Clark Clifford for Truman, Theodore Sorenson for Kennedy, Harry McPherson for Johnson, Lloyd Cutler for Carter, Boyden Gray for the first President Bush. None of these men were easily ignored. Nixon's counsel, John Dean, brought the office the wrong kind of public attention in Watergate by demonstrating that legal skills and ethical sensitivities did not necessarily coexist.[15] And many less luminous but capable lawyers have served as counsel, threatening neither to dominate nor to destroy the administration. Since Watergate, the counsel's office has been occupied—and sometimes consumed—by ethical issues, in an attempt to prevent the development of scandals within the White House or to contain them after discovery.

The Watergate scandal inflicted a serious injury on the Justice Department, as Attorneys General John Mitchell and Richard Kleindienst were both convicted of serious crimes. In the aftermath, there were even proposals to make the department independent of direct presidential supervision.[16] To defuse suspicion, President Ford nominated the eminent outsider Edward Levi to be attorney general, and President Carter followed with Judge Griffin Bell, both of whom kept a substantial distance from White House staff, and sometimes even from the president.[17] Watergate memories dimmed, though, and since the Reagan administration the president and the attorney general have usually had a close relationship, with the exception of President Clinton's estrangement from Janet Reno. A single presidency can feature the entire spectrum of independence in the attorney general.[18] George W. Bush chose a stranger who pleased his political base (John Ashcroft), an insider whose loyalty was uncontested (Alberto Gonzales), and a distinguished outsider who might repair a tarnished Justice Department (Michael Mukasey).

Delegation of power within the Justice Department has created a specialized entity for the provision of legal advice to the president and the executive agencies, the Office of Legal Counsel (OLC). The office is a group of about twenty lawyers headed by a smaller group of political appointees: an assistant attorney general and (nowadays) four deputies.[19] Since the 1960s, most of the department's formal legal opinions to the president and the heads of departments have been written and signed by OLC.[20] The office plays a very prominent role in this book.

Sometimes called "the attorney general's lawyer," OLC attracts an elite mix of career government attorneys and young lawyers with strong credentials who serve for a few years along their way to other careers.[21] Opinions are generated within OLC by a collaborative process that features initial drafting by the line attorneys and editing by the deputies and the assistant attorney general. The opinions read like judicial ones.[22] They state the facts as given to OLC by the requesting agency and proceed to review the statutory and constitutional issues presented. They rely on standard legal materials such as legislative history and court opinions, and present a conclusion that does not always accord with the desires of the requester.

OLC's bureaucratic detachment from the political offices it advises and its heavy reliance on lawyers who are not selected for their political credentials give it a measure of independence and credibility.[23] Except in the second Bush administration, OLC usually has not shared drafts of its opinions with anyone outside the Justice Department, although it will often indicate informally what its likely answer would be to an opinion request if one were made.[24] OLC opinions are submitted confidentially to the requester. Selected ones are later published, but most are not readily available.[25]

Like the attorney general, OLC experiences competition with the White House Counsel's office in providing advice to the president. In this competition, OLC has important bureaucratic advantages. It has about twice as many lawyers, some of whom are career lawyers with deep knowledge of the law and lore of the separation of powers. It has an impressive internal database of its past opinions, which cannot be assembled anywhere else. In short, it has institutional capacity and memory.[26] The counsel's office has propinquity and political reliability. White House lawyers, living in a superheated political atmosphere, are usually more attuned to the administration's political goals than are the lawyers in OLC, who occupy a separate building several long blocks down Pennsylvania Avenue. Former OLC head Charles Cooper once complained about the absence of any long-term institutional perspective in the counsel's office: "Preserving presidential prerogatives, protecting the office itself, was not viewed as that important. Far more important was getting a good political result or avoiding a bad one."[27]

Career attorneys in OLC are especially apt to see themselves as protectors of the long-run interests of the executive branch, whatever the desires of its temporary leaders.[28] The political appointees in OLC may encounter a challenge from the line attorneys when unusual claims of executive power emerge from the White House. For example, President Nixon's political advisers urged him to make sweeping claims of constitutional power to "impound" federal funds (that is, to refuse to spend them), whether or not Congress had mandated the expenditures. After OLC refused to accede to this untenable position, Nixon fired Assistant Attorney General Roger Cramton and found a successor who would support his claims.[29] (Nevertheless, the department's career attorneys continued a policy of quiet resistance by leaving these arguments out of briefs they filed.) OLC lost the battle and won the war. Nixon's impoundment claims collapsed along with his presidency and have hardly been heard from since.[30]

OLC's power within an administration depends on the attorney general's willingness to rise to its defense. For example, in the Carter administration the Department of Labor once asked OLC whether federal employment training funds could be provided to church schools.[31] OLC replied that the funds could not be provided to most kinds of workers in the schools. The Catholic Church objected and found the ear of Vice President Walter Mondale, who asked Attorney General Griffin Bell to reverse the opinion. Bell asked Assistant Attorney General John Harmon to explain the opinion to

Mondale and others. Then, according to Bell, "President Carter, in a two-paragraph letter to me, flatly overruled our decision."

Furious, Bell responded to Carter, objecting to any "notion that the proper way to proceed was for you to direct . . . the conclusion I would reach in my legal opinion. . . . I was asked for my opinion on a question of law. I was under the professional obligation as your attorney general to state my frank and candid legal opinion on this question." The crusty Bell acknowledged Carter's authority to overrule his opinion, but objected to the idea that White House staff could order a particular conclusion in advance or engineer the president's intervention without discussion with his attorney general.

As Attorney General Bell's sharp rebuke to his president illustrates, legal advisers regard their professional roles as distinct from the policy process. A crucial question is how independent they should try to be. It may be helpful to approach this question by conceiving of a spectrum of independence, running from the cold neutrality we expect of federal judges on one end to the dependency of a mere mouthpiece for the president on the other. Attorneys general and their staff have thought about this question. Griffin Bell's earlier life as a federal judge was in evidence when he described the tension between the "duty to define the legal limits of executive action in a *neutral manner* and the president's desire to receive legal advice that helps him to do what he wants."[32]

In the same vein, former OLC head Randolph Moss has argued that OLC must provide "the *best* view of the law," taking "the obligation neutrally to interpret the law as seriously as a court."[33] He explains that since the executive lacks authority to act except as the Constitution and statutes allow, only that approach can legitimate executive action. He would, however, accord "due respect" to existing practice and precedent within the executive.

I find Moss's approach a bit too strict for two reasons. First, the law concerning proposed executive actions is often quite unclear. If the executive cannot take actions for which there is a reasonable basis when OLC thinks the better view forbids them, there may never be a chance to find out whether OLC was right. A foregone action cannot be tested either in court or in the more informal fora of Congress and public opinion.

Second, even with the deference Moss suggests, OLC might find itself a bit marooned—in but not of the executive branch. Agencies that did not expect a sympathetic hearing from OLC might look for ways to avoid asking the office for opinions, for example by relying on memos from their general counsels. And as we have seen, even great presidents such as Thomas Jefferson and Franklin Roosevelt have been known to avoid asking questions when they anticipated unpalatable answers.

Robert Jackson did not claim a neutral stance. He would give the president "the benefit of a *reasonable doubt* as to the law."[34] I think this is the right general approach. Jackson's position assumed some distance between lawyer and client. It also assumed—correctly—that the officer charged with final legal judgment is the president, not the attorney general. Jackson's core insight was that "the value of legal counsel is in the *detachment* of the adviser from the advised."[35] This perception is an ancient one—recall Shakespeare's Henry V warning his adviser not to "fashion, wrest, or bow your reading," for serious consequences would ensue.

A thoughtful analysis of OLC's role comes from Jack Goldsmith, who headed the office during the administration of the second President Bush.[36] He reports that OLC views itself as the "frontline institution responsible for ensuring that the executive branch . . . is itself bound by law." To ensure that outcome, OLC "has developed powerful cultural norms about the importance of providing the President with detached, apolitical legal advice." In his confirmation hearings, Goldsmith promised to "continue the extraordinary traditions of the office in providing objective legal advice, independent of any political considerations." While in office, though, he learned that OLC is "not entirely neutral" about the President's agenda. He would "work hard to find a way for the President to achieve his ends," including suggesting alternatives. OLC advice, he says, is neither like a private attorney's nor a neutral court's: "It is something inevitably, and uncomfortably, in between."

Goldsmith concedes that OLC always has a "robust" view of executive power, one more supportive of the president than any approved by the Supreme Court or widely accepted in the legal academy or Congress. That is why the cultural norms of detachment and professional integrity are crucial, he says. Goldsmith believes the oath of office and a "powerful professional concern to 'do the right thing'" help OLC resist pressure. His predecessor from the Clinton administration, Walter Dellinger, told him: "You won't be doing your job well, and you won't be serving your client's interests, if you rubber-stamp everything the client wants to do." Goldsmith concludes that "OLC's success over the years has depended on its ability to balance these competing considerations—to preserve its fidelity to law while at the same time finding a way, if possible, to approve presidential actions."[37]

Goldsmith, like Jackson, does not try to be neutral, but does try to be independent of the policy process. Both men appear to understand that their opinions will be skewed toward the president's agenda as compared with those an outsider might generate. Still, both are determined to maintain professional detachment as the way to adhere to law. I think they make the correct accommodation of principle to reality. An important component of this stance is to understand that traditional advice within the executive is already friendlier to executive power than are many outsiders. A lawyer who is aware of the frame of reference within which prior advice has been formulated can more reliably appraise whether a new proposal fits within tolerable limits.

As Goldsmith emphasizes, attorneys in OLC know that the reputation of the office for high-quality legal advice is crucial to its power both within and outside the government. Inside the executive branch, the ability of OLC to attract clients who are under no obligation to seek its advice depends on offering reliable and persuasive opinions. Outside the executive, deference from congressional and judicial officers must be earned. And because outside readers of OLC opinions often assume the advice is self-serving, it is not easy to demonstrate that deference is due.

Congress has made clear that it values independent legal judgment in the Justice Department. Ever since Watergate, Congress has used confirmation hearings for a new attorney general or a head of OLC to obtain promises of independent legal judgment from the nominees. Some examples will show the typical tenor of the dialogue. Edwin Meese, asked whether he could reconcile his duties to the president with those to the people, said that he had "no doubt whatsoever as to my ability to exercise independent judgment" in situations of potential conflict.[38]

Nominees for OLC make statements similar to those quoted above from Jack Goldsmith. His predecessor, Jay Bybee, said that the purpose of the office is "to provide objective legal advice, free from other political constraints or influences."[39] Walter Dellinger promised that his primary goal would be "to give the best independent legal analysis possible" and "to give the President detached, objective advice even if what turns out to be the best legal answer is not what the President was hoping to hear."[40]

Consider the influences on the behavior of executive advisers I have reviewed so far. An aggregate of powerful forces fosters cooperative responses from the president's lawyers: political loyalty, personal ambition, competition for influence, peer pressure, the felt need to resist competition from Congress and elsewhere. Given these forces, it is most unlikely the president will often receive legal advice insufficiently sympathetic to his policy goals. Instead, as experienced legal advisers know, maintaining enough independence of judgment is the typical difficulty. Let us turn to the twin bulwarks of detachment.

THE ETHICAL LIMITS TO ZEALOUS ADVOCACY

A government attorney is governed by the ethics rules of the state bar to which he or she belongs. Because the states usually codify the American Bar Association's *Model Rules of Professional Conduct,* the rules are essentially the same for everyone. Also, all new lawyers have had some ethics instruction. U.S. law schools reacted to Watergate by making professional responsibility courses mandatory for all students. State bar examinations also contain an ethics test. There is no excuse for ignorance.

Ethical precepts that instruct lawyers about the limits to the enthusiasm they should display for the interests of their clients must necessarily be put generally. Life and law are too various and messy for a precise code of conduct. Any general principle, though, risks ineffectiveness precisely when it is most needed. A lawyer who is determined to skirt the edge of acceptable conduct can squeeze most facts into any flexible abstraction. We are left, then, with a characteristic common to moral codes of most kinds: we can seek principles that seem obviously right, remaining prepared to argue their application when doubts arise.

The standard traditional conception of the lawyer's role is quite simple—too simple, unfortunately. The lawyer is to serve as an "amoral gladiator," aggressively advancing the client's interests within the outer bounds of the law, without responsibility for the morality of the means and ends involved.[41] This rather "ruthless" conception rests on twin judgments: that adversary processes will produce good outcomes at the end of the battle, and that clients are entitled to the maximum realization of their interests.[42] In the context of ethical standards for executive advisers, two complications appear. First, discussions of ethics do not always cleanly distinguish the function of advising in litigation, where a judge will rule after open debate, from the provision of advice within the executive, where it may never be tested or even known to the outside world. (Consider a sports analogy. In team sports, players are expected to be aggressive, letting the referee call the fouls. Golf, however, presents subtle problems of self-monitoring.) Second, ethics rules do not usually attempt to incorporate the special concerns surrounding advice-giving within government as opposed to other large organizations.

Some lawyers and scholars have addressed both of these special problems and have initiated an interesting (if inconclusive) debate about them. Let us begin with the traditional view as articulated by a former Justice Department officer:

The discovery by a government attorney of precedent that seemingly would condemn a Presidential policy does not ordain the conclusion that no responsible legal argument can be assembled to vindicate the policy. To the contrary, in most such situations, rational reasons can be adduced for modifying or reversing the adverse precedent, or distinguishing it, in order to effectuate the President's policy goal. The government attorney is ethically bound to develop when necessary plausible arguments for altering or overturning existing law. This duty is comparable to the ethical norm governing private attorneys that endorses advocacy of any nonfrivolous constructions dependent on modification or reversal of existing law, without regard to the attorney's professional opinion as to the likelihood that the construction will ultimately prevail. If a government attorney cannot ungrudgingly adhere to the ethical imperative requiring promotion of the President's policies through legal advocacy, then he might seriously consider voluntary resignation from the Executive Branch.[43]

This argument embodies the traditional rule that when appearing in court, a lawyer may advance claims that are "not frivolous, which includes a good faith argument" for altering existing law.[44] Because a frivolous argument should have little chance of success in court and tends to attract negative publicity, not much constraint attends instructing trial lawyers to do better than that. Yet if the same stance is applied to the provision of confidential counseling to the executive, the incentive to craft responsible arguments that stems from the presence of a neutral arbiter disappears. The contexts are fundamentally different.

Therefore, the counseling function is governed by a different rule: the lawyer is expected to "exercise independent professional judgment and render candid advice."[45] The rule continues: "In rendering advice, a lawyer may refer not only to law but to other considerations such as moral, economic, social, and political factors that may be relevant to the client's situation." An accompanying comment explains that although "a lawyer is not a moral advisor as such, moral and ethical considerations impinge upon most legal questions and may decisively influence how the law will be applied." Thus, the consequences of conduct the law might allow should be considered and explained to the client. Another comment cautions that "a client is entitled to straightforward advice expressing the lawyer's honest assessment. Legal advice often involves unpleasant facts and alternatives that a client may be disinclined to confront."

Sometimes comparisons of government and corporate attorneys are made explicitly. Still, these two roles are not identical. Attorney General Elliott Richardson of the Nixon administration supported Robert Jackson's *Destroyers* opinion by saying that the president "needed a legal rationale for what he was doing. He needed somebody to defend his action. Jackson was like a general counsel of a corporation who says to the CEO, 'This is not free of doubt, boss, and we may get taken to court, but I think we have a strong foundation of justification for taking this position.' " [46]

Richardson's analogy was flawed, however. In the case of the destroyer deal, there was no obvious way to mount a judicial challenge to the president's decision, and none ever appeared. (Instead, as both FDR and Jackson knew at the time, the opinion would be tested in another critical forum, the court of public opinion.)

As in corporate counseling, advice to the executive branch is usually rendered confidentially. In the performance of confidential counseling, whether the client is a private or public entity, the ethical stress on independent judgment and candor reflects the lawyer's responsibility for ensuring that the client adheres to the law. Also, several considerations affect all lawyers as they provide counseling. Lawyers try to avoid writing legal opinions so baseless that they will do more harm than good if ever revealed. All are aware, nonetheless, that if they are not generally supportive of a client's proposals, the client will seek other lawyers who are more compliant. Good lawyers engage in this delicate balancing act with an eye toward their personal reputation and a sense that not everything goes.

Lawyers for the executive differ from other counselors in some important ways. [47] First, rule of law concerns are far more central to their tasks than they are for private lawyers, who may face questions about a government regulatory regime but not the basic issues about the Constitution and statutes that are daily challenges for many executive advisers. [48] Justice Department lawyers also want to display the same fidelity to the law that every attorney general pledges in response to the people's expectations. As former OLC head Douglas Kmiec observed, citizens want their government to "act on a plane higher than the minimum of what the law requires." [49] The Federal Bar Association reflects these differences by saying that a government lawyer "has a responsibility to question the conduct of agency officials more extensively than a lawyer for a private organization would in similar circumstances." [50]

Many OLC opinions approximate the stance Elliott Richardson attributed to Robert Jackson. That is, the best available arguments to support the proposed action are marshaled and endorsed. [51] This is an acceptable

characteristic of an opinion if an exercise of independent judgment has preceded it, and if any serious difficulties in reaching the conclusions are admitted. A need for self-discipline suffuses the advising process. Although OLC
always hears the client's arguments favoring executive power, there is no
mechanism for presenting the other side except the ingenuity and honor
of OLC lawyers. It is OLC's very supportiveness, though, that allows it to
draw a line somewhere, as in the impoundment controversy. Everyone in
OLC knows that if its opinions garner a reputation as naked briefs for the
executive, the influence of the office will evaporate.[52]

Searching for ethical boundaries, some analysts ask: "Who is a government lawyer's client?" The client, after being identified, would be owed the
duty of the attorney's loyalty. Does a Justice Department attorney advising
the White House on a matter of presidential authority represent the United
States, the president, the presidency, the Department of Justice, or the people? One can construct arguments for any of these candidates.[53] The standard
claim by attorneys general that they represent the people is incoherent as a
guideline.[54] Since the great mass of the people cannot readily transmit instructions to their attorneys general, this appears to mean that they owe ultimate
fidelity to the law. For example, Griffin Bell said, "The people are your client.
At the same time, the president is your client. But if there's a conflict, the
people prevail."[55] He then explained this meant he would refuse an illegal
request from the White House, and if pressed would resign.

A competing argument is that government attorneys solely represent the
executive branch and the president as its head.[56] In his 1971 confirmation
hearing for the Supreme Court, William Rehnquist asserted this position to
Senator Edward Kennedy:

> Kennedy: I thought that your client was the public as well.
> Rehnquist: My client, in my position as the assistant attorney general for
> the Office of Legal Counsel, is the attorney general and the president.
> Kennedy: Where does that put the rest of the Constitution?
> Rehnquist: Well, that puts the rest of the Constitution in the position
> of having someone advising them as to what his interpretation of the
> Constitution is.[57]

In other words, OLC advises the executive and the other branches have
plenty of lawyers of their own. This position conforms to the cultural biases
of lawyers for the three branches I have outlined previously. It also provides
relative clarity of role definition. There is a remaining ambiguity lurking in
former assistant attorney general Rehnquist's testimony. He referred to his

client, in the singular, as the attorney general and the president. We have seen by now that these are two different people who may disagree. If they do, the head of OLC is an assistant to the attorney general, not the president, and presumably owes the most immediate duty of loyalty to the former.

General ethical precepts about representation of organizations stress the lawyer's obligation to respond to officers authorized to decide on the organization's behalf.[58] As I noted above, ambiguities about the president's supervisory power over subordinates complicate this determination for the executive branch. Every government lawyer, though, knows who his or her immediate supervisor is. I think it best to regard the chain-of-command problem as one element of the substantive law that may enter into advice in a particular case. This means that a lawyer may need to consider both "who decides?" issues and "what decision?" ones to provide complete advice. Separating these two strands of law should allow the individual adviser to address ethical questions in an orderly way, as part of providing advice to the immediate superior.

The traditional view of the lawyer as amoral gladiator has suffered some direct assaults in recent years.[59] Since the critics call for lawyers to use more discretion in how they represent clients than tradition would allow, their formulations may be of special interest to government lawyers, who encounter difficult discretionary problems about their role constantly. The strongest assault on tradition comes from David Luban, who argues forthrightly that lawyers should be "moral activists" when counseling clients:

> The morally activist lawyer shares and aims to share with her client responsibility for the ends she is promoting in her representation; she also cares more about the means used than the bare fact that they are legal. As a result, the morally activist lawyer will challenge her client if the representation seems to her morally unworthy; she may cajole or negotiate with the client to change the ends or means; she may find herself compelled to initiate action that the client will view as betrayal; and she will not fear to quit.[60]

I think this is too uncompromising for application to executive advisers, although some elements of it can prove beneficial as reminders that a lawyer must be prepared to probe both the means and ends a government client is pursuing. Although Luban's approach probably describes the behavior of some lawyers who promote political causes through their practice, an executive adviser should avoid the loss of detachment it implies and the associated confusion of roles with the policymakers.

Notice that a lawyer's moral qualms about a client's plans are a matter of degree. There is a level of moral objection at which an executive adviser can no longer serve. Consider an example. Americans remain deeply conflicted about the Supreme Court's decision in *Roe v. Wade* and the right to abortion it created.[61] Recent Republican administrations have favored overruling *Roe;* Democratic ones, confirming it.[62] A Justice Department lawyer might have a deep personal commitment to either point of view. Upon a change of administrations, what should the lawyer do when asked to support the new administration's view of the constitutional issues involved if it contradicts his or her own values? The problem is one of private conscience, and a lawyer deeply opposed to a new administration's debatable view of the Constitution should request other work or return to the private sector.[63] Trickier problems arise if some versions of an administration's proposed actions implicate a lawyer's moral values and others do not.

Another refinement of the traditional view of the lawyer's role comes from William Simon, who argues that lawyers should base discretionary judgment on competing legal (not moral) values.[64] This "contextual" formulation holds intrinsic appeal for executive advisers, who find that the legal materials pertinent to formulating advice may include the Constitution, treaties, statutes, past executive opinions, court decisions, and various documents associated with any or all of these sources. If the formulation is to serve as more than tautology, however, it must provide a way to organize the lawyer's approach to these materials. Simon emphasizes that he wants lawyers to maximize the legal merits of the outcomes they promote.[65] He sees good lawyers neither as judges nor as gladiators, but somewhere in between, in the manner of thoughtful executive advisers such as Robert Jackson and Jack Goldsmith.[66]

In the end, general ethical principles like "independent judgment" and "candid advice" are not self-defining in application. Executive advisers striving to understand them must also consider the obligation of the oath.

THE OBLIGATION OF THE OATH

At the moment of taking office, each president takes an oath, one prescribed in terms by the Constitution to "preserve, protect, and defend the Constitution."[67] Each of the president's lawyers, upon entering the federal service, also pledges to defend the Constitution.[68] What does the oath add to the general ethical obligations all lawyers already have? One obvious answer is that it invokes a particular legal text, the Constitution, and requires the lawyer to abide its commands.[69]

Perhaps the oath means somewhat different things to the president and to subordinate officers. In Theodore Roosevelt's phrase, the president is our nation's ultimate "steward of the people."[70] This might mean, as Roosevelt seemed to say, only that a president can take action not clearly forbidden when the nation seems to need it. But it could also mean what Lincoln once argued—that there is a higher obligation still, to preserve the nation even at the cost of constitutional violation.[71] The president's lawyers, who are not themselves constitutional officers, surely have more modest obligations and powers. Their oath should be understood to confine their advice to the parameters of actions allowed by the Constitution. If the president chooses to invoke a higher law, that is a matter for his or her own conscience, and continuation in office will be at stake.

For the president's lawyers, the oath provides at minimum a justification for attempts to hold the executive to law in the face of expedient pressures to deviate from it. In other words, no one should have to ask why the lawyers care about the rule of law, or why they feel obligated to enforce it. More important, the oath serves as a daily reminder to those who take it that they must defend the Constitution even when it is not easy to do so. The oath contains no escape clauses; the obligation is unqualified.

A SYNTHESIS

An effort to combine the general ethical duties of lawyers with the special obligations of the executive adviser occurred in the wake of a controversy over one of the Bush administration's advice memoranda concerning the interrogation of detainees, which I discuss later in this book. A group of former officers and line attorneys in OLC formulated and published ten principles to guide lawyers in the office.[72] The most important of these *OLC Guidelines* are the first five:

    1. "When providing legal advice to guide contemplated executive branch action, OLC should provide an accurate and honest appraisal of applicable law, even if that advice will constrain the administration's pursuit of desired policies. The advocacy model of lawyering, in which lawyers craft merely plausible legal arguments to support their clients' desired actions, inadequately promotes the President's constitutional obligation to ensure the legality of executive action." The authors

explain this as requiring that "OLC must provide advice based on its best understanding of what the law requires. OLC should not simply provide an advocate's best defense of contemplated action that OLC actually believes is best viewed as unlawful. To do so would deprive the President and other executive branch decisionmakers of critical information and, worse, mislead them regarding the legality of contemplated action."

2. "OLC's advice should be thorough and forthright, and it should reflect all legal constraints, including the constitutional authorities of the coordinate branches of the federal government—the courts and Congress—and constitutional limits on the exercise of governmental power." The authors explain that "regardless of OLC's ultimate legal conclusions concerning whether proposed executive branch action lawfully may proceed, OLC's analysis should disclose, and candidly and fairly address, the relevant range of legal sources and substantial arguments on all sides of the question."

3. "OLC's obligation to counsel compliance with the law, and the insufficiency of the advocacy model, pertain with special force in circumstances where OLC's advice is unlikely to be subject to review by the courts."

4. "OLC's legal analyses, and its processes for reaching legal determinations, should not simply mirror those of the federal courts, but also should reflect the institutional traditions and competencies of the executive branch as well as the views of the President who currently holds office." The authors explain that "OLC routinely, and appropriately, considers sources and understandings of law and fact that the courts often ignore, such as previous Attorney General and OLC opinions that themselves reflect the traditions, knowledge, and expertise of the executive branch. Finally, OLC differs from a court in that its responsibilities include facilitating the work of the executive branch and the objectives of the President, consistent with the requirements of the law. OLC therefore, where possible and appropriate, should recommend lawful alternatives to legally impermissible executive branch proposals."

5. "OLC advice should reflect due respect for the constitutional views of the courts and Congress (as well as the President). On the very rare occasion when the executive branch—usually on the advice of OLC—declines fully to follow a federal statutory requirement, it typically should publicly disclose its justification."[73]

The *OLC Guidelines*, crafted by experienced and very thoughtful lawyers, contain much wisdom. I am in general, but not complete, agreement with them. The *Guidelines'* call for a "best understanding" of the law suggests an attitude akin to judicial neutrality, although the later reference to executive traditions may soften that a bit. Robert Jackson's emphasis on the obligation to provide independent judgment should be the core idea. It can combine some detachment with sympathy for the administration's policy goals in a professional relationship. It is not quite the same thing as the neutral judgment of a stranger.

Independent judgment is a professional's usual core responsibility to a client. The judgment can be sympathetic, and should be, but as we have seen, the incentives and culture within the executive branch certainly ensure that much. The problem is to preserve the independence. Since political advisers will reliably be advocates, only the lawyers are likely to intrude the voices of the other two branches, to which the politicians are naturally hostile. (That is why they do not like the lawyers very much.) Part of independent judgment is advice about consequences and alternatives. The overlap with policy can deter giving needed advice. It should not do so, however, because the politicians too often do not give balanced assessments of these matters. In particular, long-run consequences need to be pressed in ways the election cycle will ignore. Moreover, knowledge of the traditions of the branch and access to the past opinions of its advisers provide a store of bottled knowledge.

Some related considerations about the process of advising can also help executive advisers provide relatively neutral, law-based advice. These are "rules enforced on oneself," like Odysseus binding himself to the mast.[74] First, lawyers should sharply distinguish between providing advice before action is taken, when independent judgment is still possible, and after the fact, when the pressure to justify an action that might not have been approved beforehand is enormous. Of course, insist as they might, lawyers are sometimes presented with faits accompli, but the effort to maintain a practice of prior review is worthwhile.

The Cuban Missile Crisis of 1962 provides a vivid example of the value of advice that is rendered before the pressure of events becomes compelling. The crisis brought Attorney General Robert Kennedy deeply into an active role as a general adviser on crisis management, and even as a direct negotiator with Soviet Ambassador Dobrynin.[75] Months earlier, the administration's concern about Soviet intentions to place missiles in Cuba had led to the preparation of "extensive legal memoranda" by the Departments of Justice, State, and Defense on the issues involved.[76] "When the missiles were discovered, the . . . legal arguments were there, available for whatever use might be made of them . . . grist for the mill of decision."[77] Within the Justice

Department, Robert Kennedy asked OLC to write an opinion on options if missile bases were constructed.

On August 30, 1962, Assistant Attorney General Norbert Schlei responded with a memo discussing a "total blockade or . . . 'visit and search' procedures [for offensive weapons] as appropriate reactions . . . to meet a threat to install missile bases in Cuba."[78] The president coined the term "quarantine" and successfully imposed one. Schlei later said that when the crisis came, "the legal spade work that was done far in advance was very helpful."[79] In this case, OLC's prior advice both identified the legal option that was eventually selected and provided some assurance that the option was not just a product of political pressure.

Second, official advisers such as OLC should publish their opinions whenever possible. This tends strongly to ensure that the opinions are fit for the light of day. Here it is important to note that immediate publication is not necessarily needed to obtain the benefits of the discipline that comes from knowledge that an opinion will eventually be critiqued. Confidentiality of advice is always most important while a decision pends, because it allows those deciding to maintain control of the discussion, without outside interference. Afterward, the time soon comes when the advice becomes part of history and precedent.

Third, and related to the second point, advisers should follow a practice of adhering to prior executive branch opinions whenever possible—and they do. This reliance on the judicial principle of stare decisis constrains decision and gives opinions a life beyond the political administration in which they are generated, creating a body of law within the executive branch that endures. In the chapter on interrogation, we will encounter a prominent example of a rare event, the disavowal of an OLC opinion by the administration that had generated it. More commonly, an administration will quietly supersede opinions from earlier ones by issuing new opinions with the distinct inflection of the incumbents, modifying but not repudiating the older opinions.

Now let us draw together much of what precedes in this chapter, in search of an archetype of the modern executive adviser. Role models are always helpful, even if dire reality makes their existence all too rare. In an influential book, Anthony Kronman laments the demise of what he calls the "lawyer-statesman," a person such as Robert Jackson or Dean Acheson.[80] More recent examples might include James Baker and Warren Christopher; the archetype emphatically includes women also. The central characteristic of the lawyer-statesman is "practical wisdom," a developed character trait involving "the attainment of a wisdom that lies beyond technique—a wisdom about human beings and their tangled affairs that anyone who wishes to provide real deliberative counsel must possess."[81] His or her help is not just instrumental, it includes advice about ends, helping clients to understand "their own ambitions, interests, and ideals and to guide their choice among alternative goals."[82] This includes "a balanced sympathy toward the various concerns of which . . . the situation of his client . . . requires that he take account." Kronman notes that sympathy and detachment are both ingredients of a lawyer's advice, and that they are in tension, because compassion generates feelings and detachment moderates or confines them.[83]

Kronman explains that there are narrow and broad views of the counseling role; not surprisingly, he endorses the latter.[84] The narrow view "assumes that the client comes to his lawyer with a fixed objective in mind." That leaves the lawyer two jobs: to supply "information concerning the legal consequences" of proposed actions and to "implement whatever decision the client makes, so long as it is lawful." This is a neat division between means and ends—too neat, he thinks. Instead, Kronman urges the broad view that responsibility goes "beyond the preliminary clarification of [the client's] goals and includes helping him to make a deliberatively wise choice among them." Kronman sees this as a process of "cooperative deliberation." This is much like the "lawyer as friend" conception, he says. We seek both sympathy and detachment from our friends, and need both qualities if their advice is to be welcome and helpful. Kronman concludes that a lawyer cannot be "the mere minister to ambition" that the narrow view entails.[85]

Kronman ties development of practical wisdom to traditional law school teaching: "The common lawyer instinctively mistrusts abstract speculation. He believes that general principles have a role to play in the law but doubts that most serious disputes can be decided by reference to them alone." The lawyer therefore insists on applying a "subtle and discriminating sense" of how "generalities of doctrine should be applied in concrete disputes."[86] Thus the case method of instruction induces a "pragmatic gradualism" that is skeptical about abstract ideas as best guides to real problems.[87] It trains students to be suspicious of broad generalizations and "to insist on the importance of details." (This technique also tends to makes one a gradualist in politics.) Anyone having a fact-based and fact-hungry outlook will resist a priori theorizing as the best way to answer legal problems. This means that an effective executive adviser must possess sensitivity to the facts and must be prepared to defer to those who have kinds of factual experience that an executive law office such as OLC does not contain.

Alas, Robert Jackson is no longer with us, although any young executive branch lawyer would do well to emulate him in a personal search for practical wisdom. With time, experience, and innate good judgment, a lawyer-statesman may emerge from the chrysalis. We must concede, however, that statesmen of all sorts are always in short supply. Never in short supply, unfortunately, are claimants to that status. Washington, D.C., fairly brims with them. Consequently, what matters most is that the president and his or her principal personnel advisers themselves possess enough practical wisdom to select the real lawyer-statesmen available. If, instead, ideology is the talisman, bad advice will very likely follow. Unfortunately, the administration of George W. Bush epitomized the latter tendency.

5

Competing Visions of Executive Power

SOME CLAIMS OF LEGAL RIGHT ARE BEYOND THE PALE. How do we tell which ones? This chapter reviews available approaches to analyzing separation of powers issues in search of boundaries. I conclude that like questions of conscience, claims of right should be tested against some simple, enduring principles that are not easy to apply, but that merit general acceptance within the executive branch.

Traditional constitutional analysis distinguishes between domestic matters, for which the allocation of power between Congress and the executive is relatively well understood, and the external realm of foreign policy and war, for which the allocation is notoriously uncertain. Of course, the boundary between these spheres has always been blurry, and in an era of increasing globalization, it is often evanescent. Still, for two related reasons this chapter focuses mostly on the constitutional law of U.S. foreign relations.[1] First, existing precedents tracking the distinction recognize broader executive power there. Second, in the war on terrorism, the Bush administration relied heavily on foreign relations law in an effort to maximize its discretion and to minimize the participation of Congress and the courts. Like other constitutional law topics, foreign relations law has produced a vast literature. I cannot plumb the depths here. Instead, this chapter summarizes and critiques the main lines of analysis that have dominated the discussion to date.

No one has improved on the characterization by the great separation of powers scholar of the early twentieth century, Edward Corwin, that in foreign affairs the Constitution provides the two political branches an "invitation to struggle" for supremacy.[2] The courts, diffident of their own authority to enter this area and of their competence within it, have often declined to resolve interbranch controversies. Accordingly, firm legal precedents in the form of Supreme Court opinions have been scarce. Into the doctrinal gap have rushed executive and congressional advisers, along with scholars of varying erudition. Analysts and advocates—they are often hard to tell apart—rely on the sparse constitutional text, snippets of constitutional history, practice since the framing by each of the branches, and the institutional advantages each branch holds.

From this eclectic mix flow opinions, often displaying more certainty than persuasiveness, that one branch or another should decide a contested issue. Some apparently respectable support can be mustered for almost any position. To the extent that the courts then provide no definitive answer, each controversy receives some form of political resolution and the debate is left for resumption in the future.

This chapter considers what approach executive advisers *should* take to these indeterminate questions. I will seek to distinguish positions about which disagreement is legitimate from those not supported by a good claim of legal right. This is not easy to do, but each executive adviser must undertake the task, both in forming his or her frame of reference for deciding particular issues and in applying it to construct sound advice.

THE CONSTITUTION AND ITS EARLY IMPLEMENTATION

The text of the Constitution gives each of the three branches some explicit powers relating to foreign affairs and war, but says little about the ways these powers interrelate.[3] Article I authorizes Congress to tax and spend for the "common defense and general welfare," to regulate "commerce with foreign nations," to define "offenses against the law of nations," to "declare war" (and to conduct quasiwars by outfitting privateers), to maintain an army and a navy, to make rules for regulating the military, and to make laws "necessary and proper" to implement these powers and those of the other two branches. This is an impressive list. No one can plausibly claim that Congress is a stranger to the external affairs of the nation.[4] In addition, of course, Congress enjoys "the sole charge of an indispensable and ample purse."[5] Its plenary authority to grant or deny appropriations to the executive is Congress's great check on the president, just as his qualified power to veto legislation is the great check on Congress.[6]

Article II vests the "executive power" in a president without defining the term. The president is designated "commander in chief of the army and navy." He or she also receives foreign ambassadors, enters into treaties subject to senatorial ratification, and is charged to "take care that the laws be faithfully executed." This is a very rough sketch of an office with contours that were cloudy to the Constitution's framers.

Article III extends the federal judicial power to cases arising under the Constitution, federal statutes, and treaties (the "federal question" jurisdiction), to cases involving foreign ambassadors, to maritime cases, and to cases between U.S. states or citizens and foreign states or their citizens. Plainly, litigation involving foreign affairs can appear routinely in the federal courts, and it does.

On its face, then, the Constitution justifies its reputation for indeterminacy. Ever since the founding, interpreters have filled in the blanks in ways that accord with their own values, experience, and perception of the nation's needs. With only acceptable oversimplification, the main schools of thought can be reduced to three main lines: the adherents of either congressional or executive supremacy and those who seek a middle way. Scholars tend to be congressionalists.[7] Executive advisers consistently (and unsurprisingly) display a presidentialist bias. It will be an argument without end.

Recall the approaches taken by Presidents Washington and Jefferson, members of the founding generation, to the controversies I have recounted. Both men were innately cautious about asserting executive power. (Jefferson's Louisiana adventure expanded *national* power, not that of the executive branch alone.) They knew, as did all their contemporaries, that the framers rejected both extremes of executive power they had experienced. The framers created neither a monarch wielding broad prerogative like George III nor a nearly nonexistent executive as under the Articles of Confederation.

In the episodes involving neutrality and pursuit of the Barbary pirates, these early presidents displayed two basic assumptions about their role. One was that they possessed discretion to take initiative within the bounds of existing statutory authority. The other was that Congress could issue definitive instructions if it chose to do so. This appears to have been the dominant early understanding among the framers who served in government. Many years later, Corwin would assert that it was also the enduring judgment of our history: "Actual *practice* under the Constitution has shown that, while the President is usually in a position to *propose,* the Senate and Congress are often in a technical position at least to *dispose.* The verdict of history, in short, is that the power to determine the substantive content of American foreign policy is a *divided* power, with the lion's share falling usually, though by no means always, to the President."[8]

Corwin's maxim that the president proposes but Congress disposes recognizes substantial power in both of the political branches and does not necessarily exclude the courts from playing a role should litigation arise. Equally important, it does not provide firm answers to too many questions. Politics, rather than law, predominates. Under this general understanding, the new republic was free to evolve along its own historical path, and it busily did so for a century and a half before the Supreme Court decided two cases that have dominated modern discussions of the enduring constitutional issues.

TWO TALISMANS: THE *CURTISS-WRIGHT* AND *STEEL SEIZURE* CASES

The Supreme Court's broadest endorsement of executive power in foreign affairs occurs in some discussion in *United States v. Curtiss-Wright Export Corporation*,[9] a case that actually decided very little of modern importance. *Curtiss-Wright* involved a joint effort by Congress and President Franklin Roosevelt to stop arms sales to belligerents in South America. Congress passed a statute authorizing the president to ban the sales if he thought it would promote peace in the region. He did think so and promptly issued an executive order forbidding the sales and rendering them crimes under the statute. The company, indicted for violating the ban, invoked two recent cases in which the Supreme Court had struck down federal statutes for violating the "delegation doctrine," which limits the amount of discretion Congress may confer on the executive without impermissibly giving its legislative powers away.[10] Hence the issue in the case was simply whether Congress and the president, acting together, could control these arms sales.

Justice George Sutherland explained that the executive branch has a special role in foreign policy.[11] He argued correctly that the executive has traditionally served as the sole representative of the views of the United States in communications with foreign nations. (Note that this conclusion does not determine which branch forms the policies the president communicates.) He went on to say that statutes often need to grant broad latitude to presidential discretion in foreign affairs because the executive has the institutional advantages over Congress of unity, secrecy, and speed. Sutherland cited myriad examples of statutes from the earliest days that granted broad foreign policy authority to the executive, and concluded that the statute at hand was constitutional. All of this was sound and remains good law today.

Justice Sutherland's opinion for the Court also included extensive dicta, which means statements unnecessary to decision of the case at hand. Because dicta are not tested by the need to decide conflicted issues, lawyers conventionally say they have no force of law. They do, however, remain in the official reports of cases for future use by advocates hoping to persuade later courts of their soundness. Sutherland, a former U.S. senator, had generated a very broad theory of executive power for foreign policy.[12] *Curtiss-Wright* gave him an opportunity to expound generally on his pet theory, and he took it. He asserted that the foreign policy powers of the United States do not flow from the Constitution, but preexisted it and were simply recognized by the Constitution. This suggests that a court might detect kinds of national power, or executive power, not supported by the text of the Constitution.

The courts have indeed done just that, but by aggressive interpretation from the sparse text, not by admitted invention.

This part of Sutherland's theory has been thoroughly demolished by scholars.[13] Yet it retains a life of its own because it invites arguments of two quite different kinds. The first is that the executive should enjoy broad power to take action in foreign policy without express statutory authority. The second is that when the president takes such action, Congress may not control him or her, even pursuant to its own explicit powers. Neither of these assertions is supported by anything actually decided by the Court in *Curtiss-Wright*. Nevertheless, the need for broad power of executive initiative in foreign affairs is strongly supported by the institutional advantages of the executive over Congress that the Court summarized. This part of the Court's analysis has few detractors today. But it is a considerable leap from that position to say that when Congress does legislate, the president may overcome its will with his or her own. That argument, by disabling congressional control of executive action, threatens "the equilibrium established by our constitutional system," as Justice Robert Jackson later observed.[14] Recall that as attorney general, Jackson cited Sutherland's broad language in his *Destroyers* opinion, but he put no particular weight on it in concluding that the deal was valid.

Judgments about constitutional power contrary to those in *Curtiss-Wright* flow from the *Steel Seizure* case and were essential to the actual decision in that case. As we have already seen, like many separation of powers cases, *Steel Seizure* was litigated under great time pressure and in the glare of intense national publicity.[15] Such trying circumstances can cloud the judgment of advocates. In the trial court, the federal government erred by suggesting, in tones reminiscent of *Curtiss-Wright*, that presidential power is unlimited.[16] More effectively, the government urged that the seizure was necessary and placed it against the background of other emergency actions by past presidents.

The Supreme Court, in a six-to-three vote, upheld the injunction against the president's order. Justice Hugo Black wrote the majority opinion in his characteristically broad strokes. Five justices wrote concurring opinions to elaborate their views. Black began by noting that the government had argued that the president was acting within "the aggregate of his constitutional powers" and had asserted no statutory authority for the order. He concluded that seizures were not merely unauthorized by statute. Instead, in 1947, Congress had "refused to adopt" that remedy by rejecting an amendment to the Taft-Hartley bill that would have authorized emergency seizures.

Without specifying the consequences of this statutory posture, Justice Black moved on to reject the government's constitutional arguments. First, the Court refused to extend the president's broad powers over troops in combat to domestic seizures of private production facilities. That decision was for Congress, said Justice Black, not for the military. Nor did the constitutional clauses vesting executive power in the president (the Vesting Clause) and charging him to take care that the laws be faithfully executed (the Faithful Execution Clause) provide authority, because "the President's power to see that the laws are faithfully executed refutes the idea that he is to be a lawmaker." Only Congress could authorize the taking of private property for public use. Therefore, the executive order was illegal.[17]

Justice Jackson, who had joined the Court in 1941 after his tenure as attorney general, wrote a brilliant concurrence that has been the most influential opinion in the case. He began by offering a framework for analyzing the relative legal postures of president and Congress in a particular instance:

1. When the President acts pursuant to an express or implied authorization of Congress, his authority is at its maximum, for it includes all that he possesses in his own right plus all that Congress can delegate. . . . If his act is held unconstitutional under these circumstances, it usually means that the Federal Government as an undivided whole lacks power. . . .

2. When the President acts in absence of either a congressional grant or denial of authority, he can only rely upon his own independent powers, but there is a zone of twilight in which he and Congress may have concurrent authority, or in which its distribution is uncertain. Therefore, congressional inertia, indifference, or quiescence may sometimes, at least as a practical matter, enable, if not invite, measures on independent presidential responsibility. In this area, any actual test of power is likely to depend on the imperatives of events and contemporary imponderables rather than on abstract theories of law.

3. When the President takes measures incompatible with the expressed or implied will of Congress, his power is at its lowest ebb, for then he can rely only upon his own constitutional powers minus any constitutional powers of Congress over the matter. Courts can sustain exclusive presidential control in such a case only by disabling the Congress from acting upon the subject. Presidential claim to a power at once so conclusive and preclusive must be scrutinized with caution, for what is at stake is the equilibrium established by our constitutional system.[18]

Jackson concluded that the case at hand fell into the third category. Therefore, he inquired whether the executive possessed any constitutional power sufficient to override congressional denial of seizure authority. He could find none. The government's argument that the Vesting Clause granted broad powers was inconsistent with the framers' caution about executive prerogative. Instead, the clause seemed to be "an allocation to the presidential office of the generic powers thereafter stated." The president's military functions did not mean that he could "vastly enlarge his mastery over the internal affairs of the country by his own commitment of the Nation's armed forces to some foreign venture." Such a view would be inconsistent with congressional war powers. And the Faithful Execution Clause must be balanced against the Due Process Clause's protection for private property, to ensure the rule of law.

Jackson went on to disparage arguments for broad and vague presidential powers of an "inherent" nature. Congress could grant and later retract emergency authority, and had often done so in time of war or domestic crisis. Experience suggested that "emergency powers are consistent with free government only when their control is lodged elsewhere than in the Executive who exercises them." The framers had included only one emergency power, to suspend the writ of habeas corpus in times of rebellion or invasion. Jackson would not imply others. He closed by noting "the gap that exists between the President's paper powers and his real powers." As the federal government had grown, the presidential office had expanded to the point that "by his prestige as head of state and his influence upon public opinion, he exerts a leverage upon those who are supposed to check and balance his power which often cancels their effectiveness." Party loyalties increased this leverage. Jackson could not believe "that this country will suffer if the Court refuses further to aggrandize the presidential office, already so potent and so relatively immune from judicial review, at the expense of Congress."

Chief Justice Fred Vinson, joined by Justices Stanley Reed and Sherman Minton, dissented. He emphasized the exigencies of modern wars, both cold and hot. He thought that a review of history demonstrated that "with or without explicit statutory authorization, Presidents have . . . dealt with national emergencies by acting promptly and resolutely to enforce legislative programs, at least to save those programs until Congress could act."[19] Vinson argued that Truman's action was necessary to preserve an opportunity for Congress to act. Congress had legislated in numerous ways to support the Korean War, for example by drafting troops, appropriating funds, and authorizing inflation controls. Here, the president had acted to reconcile two statutory programs, for military procurement and inflation control: "Unlike an administrative commission confined to the enforcement of the statute under which it was created, or the head of a department when administering a particular statute, the President is a constitutional officer charged with taking care that a 'mass of legislation' be executed."[20] Moreover, Truman had sent two messages to Congress reporting his action and offering to abide by any congressional instructions.

The opinions in the *Steel Seizure* case provide much guidance for separation of powers analysis. First, a correction: Justice Black's assertion that the executive never legislates was simplistic. He ignored the large number of executive orders that rest on no clear statutory authority. When these orders have a sufficient constitutional basis, they have the force of law.[21] Still, the majority opinion shared some salutary elements with the concurrences. All of the majority justices were unwilling to imply broad, "inherent" presidential powers to respond to domestic emergencies in a context in which Congress had recently legislated. As Justice Jackson trenchantly noted, such powers "tend to kindle emergencies." Similarly, the justices were unwilling to transform the president's broad power to commit troops to combat into control over the domestic economy and the rights of private citizens. Their caution in these respects was encouraged by living in a world where Stalin and Mao ruled and Hitler and Mussolini were not long dead. The justices did not see Harry Truman as a potential dictator, but they did not want to spawn a precedent with great potential for future misuse.[22]

The majority justices were also willing to imply legislative intent from rejection of a proposed amendment to a bill. The courts should be willing to enforce implied statutory restrictions in appropriate circumstances. Knowing when to do so, however, is tricky. The justices concluded that both houses of Congress had actively considered and had rejected proposals to authorize presidential seizures of the kind that Truman ordered. In that situation it is important for courts to enforce the congressional policy rather than to expect Congress to write everything into text. It would be impractical to expect every statutory policy to be explicit. Most controversies over statutory restrictions on the executive concern implied statutory meaning. It is most unlikely, for example, that President Truman would have seized the mills if a statute had forbidden the action explicitly.

It is fortunate for the rule of law in the United States that the Court did not avail itself of some ready means of avoiding the merits in *Steel Seizure*.[23] The decision has created a vital principle within the executive branch: the president may not contravene statutes setting domestic policy even when there seems a need to do so. (Claims of necessity are readily credited in the White House.)[24] The decision warns against executive overreaching, whether in action or in argument.

Chief Justice Vinson's dissent, which tracked the more restrained parts of the government's position, outlines the best arguments for the seizure, as follows.[25] The president should have the power temporarily to harmonize emerging conflicts in statutory programs until Congress can act.[26] In addition, presidents need some latitude to act in the nation's interests without positive statutory authority. But all of this leaves out the fact that President Truman simply did not need to seize the mills when he did. After exhausting the Taft-Hartley procedures, he would have had a far stronger case.

Steel Seizure illustrates the range of possible interpretations of the three primary constitutional provisions relied upon by the government in this case. The broadest view of the Commander in Chief Clause, one clearly rejected by the majority, is that a state of war makes the president commander in chief not merely of the military but of the nation. Thus, a president who has committed troops unilaterally (as had Truman in Korea) would obtain the legal authority to support them as he or she deemed necessary. The narrowest view, one ill-suited to modern conditions, would be that the president is merely the "first general and admiral," the senior administrator awaiting instructions from Congress on warmaking.[27] An intermediate view would be that the president's wartime powers within the United States follow the facts—that Lincoln possessed the extraordinary powers he employed at the outset of the Civil War because the situation called for them, but that Truman possessed no comparable powers in the lesser crisis of the Korean War.

The broadest view of the clause vesting executive power in the president has always been that it includes everything of an "executive" nature, with the outer boundaries in the eye of the beholder. This position, famously articulated by Alexander Hamilton, is very persistent. Pressed to its limits, it would make the Vesting Clause an exclusive grant of power to the president that would sharply curtail congressional power.[28] Such a view was advanced and rejected in *Steel Seizure*.[29] The narrowest view, espoused by Justice Jackson, is that it serves merely as a cross-reference to the specific kinds of executive power Article II includes. An intermediate position would find some constitutional "executive" power to meet emergencies and would be based on actual necessity rather than an expansive categorical definition of discretion.

The broadest view of the Faithful Execution Clause is an extension of Vinson's position: discretion exists to harmonize conflicting policies in the welter of statutes that touch upon a national problem. The narrowest view is that the president must make do with the tools Congress provides, without trying to adapt them to changing times.[30] In between would be a recognition that Congress cannot foresee all circumstances to which its policies will apply, so that the president needs some flexibility, coupled with a readiness to treat recent and considered statutory policy judgments as binding without modification.

The intermediate readings of all three constitutional provisions converge on a conception of the president as the nation's guardian in a limited sense. They recognize executive power—and responsibility—to respond to emergencies but not to manufacture them, and to honor statutory policies while meeting the practical needs of governance. The courts retain a role in monitoring the president, assessing the actual existence of necessity but deferring when appropriate to executive judgments.

Executive advisers should not lightly advance broad claims of inherent presidential powers in court, where they can produce a Newtonian counterreaction. In *Steel Seizure,* Justice Jackson, who as attorney general had "claimed everything" in the way of executive power, seemed a bit chastened by the robe.[31] He noted that there is usually a wide gap between executive assertions of "inherent" power made in the press for public and political consumption and claims advanced seriously in court.[32] In *Steel Seizure,* that gap closed temporarily, resulting in a precedent that has confined the executive ever since.

Although it is often said that *Curtiss-Wright* is a foreign policy case and *Steel Seizure* a domestic one, close comparison reveals a more mixed picture. Truman's seizure of the mills involved essential supplies for a foreign war in Korea, as his messages to Congress emphasized. Roosevelt's order blocked the export of bombers manufactured in the United States, and the prosecutions occurred in the homeland. Neither case can be located comfortably on one side or the other of the water's edge. A more discriminating analysis is needed.

TWO VIEWS AT THE APEX OF THE AMERICAN CENTURY

Two eminent twentieth-century scholars sought to advance a view of balanced powers between the branches for foreign affairs and war. Edward Corwin of Princeton put his magisterial *The President: Office and Powers* through four editions by 1957. Louis Henkin of Columbia wrote *Foreign Affairs and the Constitution* in 1972.[33] Both men were influenced by the great events of two world wars, another war in Korea, and the Depression. During these times the political branches, although not operating in quiet harmony, reached acceptable accommodations in forming policy.

I have already described Corwin's central judgment that in foreign affairs, "the President proposes, Congress disposes." Since Corwin's thought was never simplistic, though, there is more to be said. The nature of his approach emerges from his treatment of one of the few zones of exclusive presidential power he identified, the right to act as "sole organ of the nation" in the sense of being the sole representative who communicates with foreign governments. The "sole organ" phrase comes from a speech John Marshall made as a member of the House of Representatives, before he became chief justice of the U.S. Supreme Court. Marshall was arguing that the president alone could communicate with Britain in an extradition controversy. Note that this is quite different from being the sole organ of the nation in the sense of defining the policy to be transmitted, for example, forming the law of extradition.[34]

The two kinds of power are often conflated, as Justice Sutherland may have done in *Curtiss-Wright*.[35] Corwin, like other sensitive observers, kept them clearly distinct, to avoid disabling the legislative power of Congress for foreign affairs. He concluded that as "sole organ" of the nation for foreign policy, the president "is entitled to shape the foreign policies of the United States so far as he is actually able to do so within the conditions imposed by the acts of Congress" (including appropriations).[36]

Like Corwin, Louis Henkin perceived at least as much politics as law in the operation of U.S. foreign policy. His main conclusions about the constitutional distribution of power paralleled those of Corwin.[37] Henkin also stressed the simple practical point that the president, in daily command of the apparatus of foreign policy through his or her supervision of the personnel who conduct it, is constantly making new foreign policy without a murmur of objection from Congress. Near the end of a long and distinguished career, Henkin sounded a note of optimism:

> Uncertainty in the constitutional law of foreign relations should not be exaggerated. Much is clear, and the relations of the United States are conducted every minute of every day with respectable efficiency within the framework of the Constitution. The President conducts foreign relations, and no one challenges his authority and responsibility. . . . The President largely makes foreign policy, even if Congresses and members of Congress do not refrain from telling him what it ought to be. . . . At the other end of the constitutional axis, Congress alone clearly adopts domestic legislation, regulates foreign commerce, authorizes spending and appropriates money, and—happily not often—makes war.[38]

Henkin's valediction is worth keeping in mind as our story takes a darker turn.

VIETNAM AND WATERGATE IMPLODE THE IMPERIAL PRESIDENCY

The twin disasters of the Vietnam War and Watergate wrecked the presidencies of Lyndon Johnson and Richard Nixon and left widespread perceptions of a fundamental breakdown in the relations of the branches. In 1973, Arthur Schlesinger, Jr.'s *The Imperial Presidency* was an initial—and powerful—shot in a salvo of criticism. Schlesinger wrote his book "out of a double concern":

> The first concern is that the pivotal institution of the American government, the Presidency, has got out of control and badly needs new definition and restraint. The second concern is that revulsion against inordinate theories of presidential power may produce an inordinate swing against the Presidency and thereby do essential damage to our national capacity to handle the problems of the future. . . . The problem is to devise means of reconciling a strong and purposeful Presidency with equally strong and purposeful forms of democratic control.[39]

Nixon in particular exerted "extraordinary attempts to concentrate power in the executive branch at the expense of other organs of government."[40]

By the end of the 1970s, responding to the concerns expressed by Schlesinger and many others, Congress had made a serious attempt to assert itself in foreign affairs to retrieve "democratic control" of the presidency, as Schlesinger put it. Congress enacted a series of statutes to provide a framework for congressional-executive relations that would ensure a collaborative partnership between the political branches. These statutes ran the gamut: they controlled the introduction of U.S. forces into hostilities, regularized the declaration of national emergencies, rearranged emergency powers to control international trade, and sought to control covert operations and the gathering of national security intelligence.[41] To make clear its seriousness, Congress also created a statutory special prosecutor to pursue high-level misconduct.[42]

In operation, these statutes received at least as much criticism as praise. Hence, both of Schlesinger's concerns (and his overall solution as well) have remained pertinent, because they are perennials. Some observers (notably including future Vice President Dick Cheney) saw the presidency as shackled and in need of rescue.[43] Others saw congressional reforms as ineffectual to ensure control of an incorrigibly imperial executive. Meanwhile, the Supreme Court decided a case that responded to the uncertainty of the times by recognizing needed executive power while sounding constant notes of caution. Importantly, the Court unanimously confirmed that the principle of the *Steel Seizure* case applies to foreign policy.

THE SUPREME COURT INITIATES A LIMITED RESTORATION

In *Dames & Moore v. Regan*,[44] the Court upheld the settlement of the Iranian Hostage Crisis of 1979–1981 by "sole" executive agreement, that is, by an agreement with a foreign nation that is not subjected to the treaty process. (There is a long history of such agreements, and an equally long record of doubts about their legitimacy.) Soon after our diplomatic personnel in Tehran were seized in 1979, President Carter had exercised his emergency statutory authority to freeze assets of foreign nations by blocking Iranian bank accounts worth billions of dollars. To end the crisis, he then entered a claims settlement agreement providing for international arbitration of claims of Americans against Iran. Challenges to both presidential actions were immediate.

Justice William H. Rehnquist's opinion for the Court began with a bow in the direction of Justice Jackson. As a young man, Rehnquist had served as a law clerk to Jackson when *Steel Seizure* was before the Court. Three decades later, he vividly remembered the executive's arguments for essentially unlimited power in that case, and the adverse reaction they sparked in the nation and within the Court.[45] Rehnquist demonstrated the lesson he took from the steel crisis in his approach to the resolution of the hostage crisis. He said he would confine his opinion to questions necessary to decision, avoiding broad analytic strokes that might create an unfortunate precedent ripe for future exploitation by the executive. He echoed Jackson's lament about the difficulty of applying any simple analytic formula to the messy facts and law of a real controversy. Moreover, like *Steel Seizure*, the hostage case had been litigated under great time pressure: making broad statements could invite mistakes.

The Iranian hostage litigation gave Rehnquist an opportunity both to reaffirm the insights of his mentor and to revise and extend them in application to a new context. In *Dames & Moore,* Rehnquist emphasized Jackson's concession that his three categories of power were somewhat oversimplified and suggested that it might be more accurate not to conceive of executive action as falling cleanly into some category, but as existing along "a spectrum running from explicit congressional authorization to explicit congressional prohibition." He thought that this slight reformulation would be especially apt when considering presidential responses "to international crises the nature of which Congress can hardly have been expected to anticipate in any detail."

Having endorsed Jackson's approach, Justice Rehnquist emphasized the danger of excessive reliance on Justice Sutherland's broad dicta in *Curtiss-Wright*. After quoting Sutherland's famous reference to the "very delicate, plenary, and exclusive power of the President" in foreign relations, Rehnquist quoted Jackson's pithy response to the claims of unbounded executive power advanced in *Steel Seizure:* "The example of such unlimited executive power that must have most impressed the forefathers was the prerogative exercised by George III, and the description of its evils in the Declaration of Independence leads me to doubt that they were creating their new Executive in his image."[46]

In *Dames & Moore*, the Court found explicit statutory authority in the president to block the assets of a foreign nation, and then to direct their further disposition. There was, however, no clear statutory authority for the claims settlement portion of the hostage deal. Nevertheless, Justice Rehnquist thought the statutes authorizing the blocking orders were "highly relevant in the looser sense of indicating congressional acceptance of a broad scope for executive action in circumstances such as those presented in this case." He stressed that Congress could not be expected to foresee the nature of future international crises. Therefore, the lack of explicit authority did not "imply 'congressional disapproval'" of executive action.[47] Instead, grants of broad discretion in the vicinity of a particular situation could be considered, in Jackson's formula, to "invite" presidential initiative, at least where no statute exuded contrary implications. This qualification was critically important, for Rehnquist's approach at this point otherwise paralleled the *dissent* in *Steel Seizure*, which had relied on the presence of statutes authorizing conduct of the Korean War to support the validity of President Truman's seizure of the steel mills.[48]

Needing to distance himself from the *Steel Seizure* dissent, Rehnquist flirted with but did not quite embrace an interpretive technique the Court sometimes employs: using long-standing historical practice to support a gloss on the text of the Constitution.[49] The Court began its historical review by noting the long pedigree of international claims settlements as a means for nations to eliminate "sources of friction" between them. From the Federalist Era onward, presidents had settled claims by sole executive agreement in return for lump-sum payments or the establishment of arbitration mechanisms. In doing so, the executive had pursued the interests of the nation, whether or not they coincided with the interests of the claimants. The

Court also cited *United States v. Pink*, describing it as resting on a judgment that settling claims "was integrally connected with normalizing the United States's relations with a foreign state."[50] All of this suggested the presence of a matured and possibly plenary presidential power to settle claims, but the Court would not embrace so sweeping a conclusion.

Instead, Rehnquist argued that for claims settlement there was "a history of congressional acquiescence in conduct of the sort engaged in by the President."[51] This "acquiescence doctrine" is a venerable way for the Court to avoid adjudicating constitutional issues such as those presented in *Dames & Moore* by finding implied statutory support for executive action.[52] Here, Congress had "implicitly approved" the traditional executive practice by creating a special agency to decide claims of Americans against settlement funds. Subsequently, Congress had frequently amended this legislation to address problems surrounding particular agreements without withdrawing the underlying authority to enter them. Thus the Court was able to combine the acquiescence doctrine with apparent deference to the president's independent constitutional powers in foreign affairs in order to justify an executive action—but without having to specify any precise content for either the statutory or constitutional powers!

The Court's approach to these issues has been criticized for having "championed unguided executive activism and congressional acquiescence in foreign affairs over the constitutional principle of balanced institutional participation."[53] This critique reads *Dames & Moore* as allowing the president to prevail in foreign policy whenever he or she does not visibly contravene statutes.[54] It is true that given the power of the president's veto and the executive's natural institutional advantages in foreign policy, a judicial finding that statutory authority exists for an action is extremely difficult for Congress to overturn or modify. The question, then, is whether *Dames & Moore* is far more sweeping in effect than in iteration.[55]

I think *Dames & Moore* is best viewed as a decision that attempts to balance both of the large trade-offs involved, those between executive power and individual rights and between executive and legislative power.[56] The claims of individual right possessed by litigants against Iran were not strong enough to impel the Court to read the president's statutory powers narrowly. And existing Supreme Court precedent suggested that the president might possess a plenary constitutional power to settle claims. The *Dames & Moore* Court was more generous in statutory than constitutional interpretation, leaving the door open to statutory revision if it were to occur.

The Court's animating concern can be traced directly back to *Steel Seizure* and to Justice Rehnquist's memory of the claims of unbounded executive power made and rejected there. The important feature of Justice Jackson's famous three categories of power is that they treat the existence of congressional restrictions on executive action as a real possibility to be examined in the case at hand. Jackson was explicitly cautious about recognizing claims to exclusive executive power, and Rehnquist's opinion shares this attitude. In *Dames & Moore,* the Court extended the principles of *Steel Seizure* to the foreign policy context, upholding executive discretion without writing a blank check for the future.

THE UNITARY EXECUTIVE THEORY ADVANCES AND RETREATS

The Reagan administration began amid the euphoria created by the release of the Iranian hostages. Soon the administration propounded a theory of the "unitary executive" and sought its adoption by the courts.[57] This theory holds that the Constitution creates a unitary executive branch under the plenary control of the president, who may direct his or her subordinates' performance of their statutory duties within the limits of whatever discretion is conferred by statute.[58] The Reagan Justice Department sought to advance the theory wherever it could.[59] Although the theory's direct application is to "vertical" distributions of power within the executive branch, it also created "horizontal" implications for the distribution of power between the executive and Congress.

The attractiveness and endurance of the unitary executive theory stem partly from a powerful normative value underlying it: the need for a strong presidency amid the terrors of the modern world. Until the end of the 1980s, the Soviet Union was a menacing rival superpower in a world stocked with nuclear arsenals. A political value also existed: in the last half of the twentieth century the United States usually had divided government, with mostly Republican presidents and mostly Democratic Congresses. Therefore, conservatives favored a strong executive to advance their political agenda. (In much the same way, liberals in the 1960s had favored executive action to circumvent resistance in Congress to civil rights legislation.) None of this is surprising, for constitutional interpretation never wholly escapes the personal values of the interpreter.

The unitary executive theory was energetically promoted by a group of young law professors who have remained faithful to it ever since.[60] In its primary application to control within the executive, the theory focused on allowing the president to control the independent regulatory agencies. That controversy is not part of the story here. Two aspects of the theory are, however, pertinent to my analysis. First, the doctrinal technique favored by the unitarians, called formalism, emphasizes a strict separation of powers between the branches, with strong autonomy for each within its assigned zone of power. The opposing technique, usually called functionalism, emphasizes the blending of power and the pursuit of an overall balance of power. (As the reader can tell by now, I favor a functional approach to most of the issues this book addresses.)

Both formal and functional approaches have their place, and each has some support in the Constitution's text and history.[61] In terms of the internal organization of the executive, however, an assertion that the framing generation viewed the executive as unitary in the sense modern scholars have favored is "just myth."[62] Perhaps, though, the modern executive branch is so large, disorganized, and unwieldy that a unitarian theory should be recognized as a modern construct.[63] Reasonable minds can differ about that proposition. I want to focus only on two horizontal implications of the theory, one of which is revealed by some episodes I have recounted in prior chapters.

Recall the controversy between Andrew Jackson—surely a strong president—and Treasury Secretary Duane over removal of the bank deposits. Unitarians would argue that Jackson could have given Duane a peremptory order to remove the deposits, and that Duane should have understood that he must abide that command. Neither Jackson nor Duane understood their relationship in that way, however. Jackson could and did fire Duane for rejecting his interpretation, but then he had to persuade the Senate to confirm a replacement, after arguing with Congress about the issue. The understanding Jackson possessed, which was that only the treasury secretary could decide how to implement his statutes, maximized the potential for congressional oversight of administration. Had Jackson and Duane seen the president as the "decider," Congress would have known about the issue only after removal of the funds, when its oversight might have been too late. The twentieth-century helium episode involving President Roosevelt and Attorney General Jackson had the same attributes, although in that case the president desisted after hearing Jackson's advice.

Thus, in operation the unitary executive theory would foster a monolithic executive and risk the exclusion of Congress from effective participation in the policy process. The other horizontal effect of the unitary theory stems from its concentration on formalist approaches to the Constitution. The underlying risk is the same, an excessive concentration of exclusive power in the executive. Fortunately, the Supreme Court, alive to the danger, never explicitly adopted the unitary theory despite efforts by the Reagan administration to persuade it to do so.[64] Instead, the Court followed a wavering path, seeking to maintain an overall balance of power by striking down statutes it concluded had "aggrandized" the power of Congress at the expense of the executive, and upholding others.[65] When the Court upheld the power of Congress to provide for independent prosecutors to pursue high-level executive misconduct, it appeared to have interred the unitary executive theory, at least for the time being.[66] Overall, though, the Court had shown itself prepared to protect the legitimate prerogatives of the executive. Together with *Dames & Moore,* the separation of powers cases of the 1980s rehabilitated the executive from its low estate at the end of the Nixon presidency.

IRAN-CONTRA LEAVES A SURPRISING LEGACY

The Iran-Contra scandal could have derailed the revival of presidential power under way in the Reagan and first Bush presidencies, but its inconclusive legal and political outcome avoided that result. Ironically, two apparently minor episodes sowed seeds of sweeping claims of executive power for the future. The first occurred in the Department of Justice, the second in Congress. Both showed the influence of the unitary executive theory that was then so prevalent in the administration.

Iran-Contra left a bit of unfinished business for Attorney General Meese. He had advised President Reagan that he could lawfully postpone notification to Congress of the Iranian initiative for a month or two. In December 1986, Meese obtained an opinion from his Office of Legal Counsel (OLC) head, Charles Cooper, providing detailed support for Meese's earlier advice.[67] The opinion request put great pressure on Cooper and OLC to justify advice their superior had already given.[68] There were two unpalatable alternatives to a favorable opinion. One was to declare that the attorney general had been in error regarding a very sensitive and politicized issue. The other was to blame the president. In so delicate a situation, one might expect OLC to say as little as possible, support their chief, and retire from the field. That is not what happened, however. Cooper wrote a sweeping opinion prefiguring positions that would be taken fifteen years later in the second Bush administration. His theories are important for that reason, and for their heavy reliance on *Curtiss-Wright.*

Cooper's *Timely Notification* opinion concludes that the statutory requirement to give notice to Congress "in a timely fashion" should be read "to leave the President with virtually unfettered discretion to choose the right moment for making the required notification." The memo explains that "any statutory effort to curtail the President's judgment would raise the most serious constitutional questions" because the president could invoke his "constitutional right to make any decision that is not manifestly and indisputably unreasonable."

This line of analysis invokes the familiar and legitimate "avoidance canon," which we will encounter repeatedly. This is the judicial practice of reading statutes to avoid serious constitutional jeopardy if possible. The courts do that, however, to adjust the powers of the other two branches. When the executive branch invokes the avoidance canon, it aggrandizes its own power.[69] This transforms the canon from a cautious and neutral way to resolve interbranch controversies into an offensive weapon. Thus, the broad reading of the president's constitutional power in *Timely Notification* created an equally wide shadow across a statute. For to the extent that executive power expands, statutes contract under the avoidance doctrine.

The memo recited the president's reason to withhold notice as avoiding disclosure that would threaten the success of sensitive covert operations. Although Cooper did not say so, the executive constantly asserts that Congress leaks secrets regularly. Congress typically responds that it has a long history of successfully keeping sensitive secrets (e.g., the atom bomb project in World War II), and that the executive itself is responsible for many leaks.[70] Both branches can cite examples to support these ritual assertions.

The important issue is to identify the branch that prevails when Congress asserts its claim to notice in a statute. *Timely Notification* repeatedly cites *Curtiss-Wright*'s dicta concerning the special role of the executive in foreign policy. It then minimizes the constitutional powers of Congress over foreign policy by saying that these powers only involve the exercise of authority over U.S. citizens. Even in theory, this is true only of the extraterritorial effects of statutes. Moreover, it ignores the practical effects of U.S. statutes on foreigners. Arguing that secret diplomatic and intelligence missions are at the core of the president's "inherent foreign affairs authority," the opinion says that "almost any congressional attempt to curtail his discretion raises questions of constitutional dimension."

The line of analysis in *Timely Notification* contains two fundamental flaws. First, as a matter of constitutional law, it greatly understates the foreign policy powers of Congress. Moreover, the president's faithful execution duty is conventionally understood as a bar to executive suspension of statutes, whether the statutes be domestic or foreign in application. Second, the opinion brings two quite different arguments dangerously close together.

The president's institutional advantages in the foreign relations realm surely justify recognizing a broad power of executive initiative without special statutory support, but that is a far cry from a power to ignore statutory limits. *Timely Notification* does not quite say that the president may disregard the statute, but the practical outcome is nearly the same if "timely" means whatever the president wants it to mean. And because notice to Congress is a primary tool for legislative control of foreign affairs, the *Timely Notification* stance would threaten many other statutes.

A narrower opinion could have said that Attorney General Meese's original advice that a delay of a month or two in notifying Congress would meet the apparent purpose of the statute. If the much longer delay that occurred thereafter were to be justified, a less broadly phrased opinion could have focused on the need to preserve secrecy in this very sensitive operation, and could have stressed that what is timely varies with the facts. No assertion of nearly uncontrollable executive power would have been needed. Legal opinions generated within the executive branch, like court opinions, can sow harm when they are written more broadly than necessary. At the very least, there is the danger that unsophisticated zealots (like Oliver North) will convert their loose phrases into licenses for action that destabilize our government and injure the nation.

This danger that overbroad arguments for executive power would be offered to justify illegal actions did materialize in the arguments for the defense in the criminal prosecutions of North and Poindexter. The Justice Department, reversing its usual role as prosecutor, filed a brief in support of North's defense to criminal charges.[71] The department claimed: "Congress cannot through its appropriations or other powers invade any sphere of constitutional authority granted exclusively to the President. In particular, the President has plenary power which Congress cannot invade to conduct diplomacy, including covert diplomacy that seeks support (including financial contributions) for the foreign policy he articulates on behalf of the Nation."[72]

The first sentence of this statement is correct; the second is not. The error in the second sentence is its assumption that the president may generate U.S. foreign policy free of the participation of Congress through its legislative or appropriations powers. The consequence of the department's position, if accepted, would be that in Iran-Contra, Congress would have been disabled from requiring either that the president desist from arms sales to Iran or that he stop supporting the Contras.

Presidents are free to initiate activities such as these, whatever their wisdom, unless and until Congress intervenes with a statute.[73] From the earliest days of the nation, the courts have been willing to enforce statutory limits on executive discretion in foreign policy.[74] If the Justice Department's position in defense of North was correct, Congress could not have overridden Washington's Neutrality Proclamation or Roosevelt's destroyer deal. No such claim was made in those times, nor should it be advanced now.[75]

Thus the Justice Department's defense of North took a crucial step beyond the assertions in *Timely Notification*. Instead of arguing that congressional legislation in foreign affairs risks unconstitutionality, as did Cooper, the North brief tried to carve out a broad zone of presidential hegemony for foreign policy. The behavior of all three branches of the federal government since the inception of the nation has been inconsistent with such a theory. All three branches have in fact participated in the development of U.S. foreign policy, and executive advisers must accept that fact and must concede appropriate roles to the other two branches.[76]

The surprising congressional legacy of Iran-Contra involved Dick Cheney, then a U.S. representative from Wyoming.[77] I describe Cheney's rise to prominence in the next chapter. While in Congress, he was an exception to the normal tendency of government officers to show loyalty to the branch in which they serve. Instead, Cheney has always supported broad executive power, wherever he found himself. In the wake of Iran-Contra, Cheney guided preparation of the *Minority Report* of the House investigative committee.[78] He was aided by David Addington, an extraordinary staff lawyer who would become Cheney's right arm in the Bush administration.

The committee's *Majority Report* deplored the violations of law that had occurred in Iran-Contra and sharply criticized the president's own role, as I have described. Given the normal imperatives of partisan politics, it was natural for members of Congress from the president's party to rise to his defense. The *Minority Report* did more than view the facts sympathetically to the administration, however. It articulated a sweeping theory of executive power that Cheney has endorsed ever since as a distillation of his views. Hence, his reaction to Iran-Contra prefigures his later response to the challenges presented by the war on terrorism.

The *Minority Report* begins by acknowledging that "President Reagan and his staff made mistakes" in Iran-Contra. After noting the corrective steps taken, the *Report* insists that the mistakes "were just that—mistakes in judgment and nothing more. There was no constitutional crisis, no systematic disrespect for 'the rule of law,' no grand conspiracy, and no Administration-wide dishonesty or cover-up."[79] This overall conclusion converts widespread illegal conduct into faux pas. It typifies the uncompromising spirit of the *Minority Report*, which rejects every important judgment made by the majority.

Having fired a broadside at the conventional view of the Iran-Contra scandal, the *Minority Report* turns to an extended discussion of the foreign affairs powers in the Constitution. It discovers a broad zone of exclusive executive power:

> Much of what President Reagan did in his actions toward Nicaragua and Iran were constitutionally protected exercises of inherent Presidential powers. . . . It is true that the Constitution also gives substantial foreign policy powers to Congress, including the power of the purse. But the power of the purse—which forms the core of the majority argument—is not and was never intended to be a license for Congress to usurp Presidential powers and functions.[80]

Applying these principles, the report argues that the Boland Amendments were unconstitutional efforts by Congress to interfere with the president's role as "sole organ" of the nation for foreign affairs, in the broad sense *Curtiss-Wright* had claimed for it. For if Congress could not prevent the president himself from negotiating with foreign governments and groups as he chose to, neither could it prevent his staff from doing so. This approach would largely disable Congress from forming the substance of our foreign policy. It comes close to reversing Corwin's famous maxim into "Congress proposes, the President disposes."

POSTMODERN DEBATE: CONGRESSIONALISTS VERSUS NEW REVISIONISTS

Because the executive had sinned grievously in the era of Vietnam, Watergate, and Iran-Contra, a group of influential scholars called for the reinvigoration of congressional power, and for the acceptance of constitutional doctrine that would tie presidents more closely to statutory authority.[81] The congressionalists, emphasizing the U.S. place in the world community, also located constraints on executive discretion in international law.[82] Dean Harold Koh, in an excellent and influential book, called for "balanced institutional participation" by all three branches in forming U.S. foreign relations law.[83]

Eventually, a fin de siècle reaction appeared. Another group of scholars emerged, nationalistic in outlook and disposed to find broad executive authority both necessary and trustworthy.[84] They were the intellectual heirs of the cold war realists, who had emphasized the need to assert U.S. national interests in a chaotic and hostile world.[85] These presidentialists tended to emphasize traditional domestic sources of constitutional law, focusing on the document's text, structure, and original intent.[86] They saw international law as the pursuit of power politics by other means, and therefore not entitled to privileged status. As we shall see, their ideas came to dominate in the administration of George W. Bush.

Between these two extremes, the intellectual heirs of Corwin and Henkin sought to refine their traditional search for a middle way.[87] I think that is the best path to take, although it lacks the dramatic appeal of either of the more extreme positions. As *Dames & Moore* demonstrates, it is possible to allow the president to respond effectively to international crises without disabling either Congress or the courts from participation.

The administration of George W. Bush evinced a decided preference for the *Curtiss-Wright* model of executive power. The intellectual justification for the administration's position was most extensively developed by John Yoo, second in command at OLC, in two books.[88] The brilliant child of Korean immigrants, Yoo had earlier served as law clerk to Justice Clarence Thomas and as counsel to the Senate Judiciary Committee. Justice Thomas, a man known for the certainty of his own views, said of Yoo that he "has a very high level of confidence in views he might reach."[89] Before and after serving in OLC, Yoo has taught at Boalt Hall, the University of California at Berkeley's law school. His theories of executive power in matters of foreign affairs and war suffuse government advice memoranda concerning the war on terrorism.[90] Hence, they are of central importance to this book.

John Yoo admits that his theory "differs, at times sharply, from the conventional academic wisdom," but claims it better reflects both constitutional history and the actual practice of the branches. Yoo has a strong tendency to oversimplify or distort positions with which he disagrees, the better to destroy them. For example, he says that conventional scholars would require prior approval by Congress for uses of force, and that they want a "partnership of equals" between the president, Congress, and the federal courts for most foreign affairs issues.[91] But the conventional scholars whom he cites range from strong congressionalists who would take such a position to those holding more intermediate views such as Henkin. Yoo does note, though, that the traditional view has evolved into a range of opinions placing varying stress on the roles of particular branches.[92]

Yoo also notes correctly that conventional analysis rests heavily on *Steel Seizure* and especially Robert Jackson. He then states, however, that Jackson "hinged the legality of presidential power on explicit congressional authorization." This oversimplifies Justice Jackson's stance. The existence of his "twilight zone" shows that he does not see a need for prior statutory authorization for all executive actions.

Elaborating his own theory, Yoo argues that the Constitution "depends less on fixed legal processes for decisionmaking and more on the political interaction" of the branches.[93] He sees no "single, correct method" for making war and peace. Instead, the branches cooperate or compete "by relying on their unique constitutional powers." Flexible decisionmaking lets the political branches shape their responses to the times. I think there is much truth in this part of his argument, given the variability of actions by the branches through U.S. history. Both Corwin and Henkin would agree with these introductory assertions. What matters, though, is the content of the "unique powers" of the branches.

The error Yoo finds in most scholarship is the imposition of "the template set by our domestic lawmaking system" to foreign affairs and war. This statement strips all the subtlety from the positions of more conventional scholars, who begin with the premise that the Constitution does not treat the domestic and foreign realms as identical. Yoo believes that in foreign affairs the framers drew a sharp distinction between execution (conducting war and entering treaties) and legislation (funding and various specific powers to enact substantive legislation). He thinks the framers "mirrored the British example," which was the traditional system they knew.[94] It is difficult to square this statement with our constitutional history. The framers were not returning to the British model that they had fought a war to reject. Instead, they were creating something new.

The point of Yoo's sharp distinction between execution and legislation emerges after he identifies the consequences. He takes the Hamiltonian view of the Vesting Clause as a broad grant of exclusive power to the executive, which enjoys all power not specifically allocated elsewhere. He does say that the Constitution's allocation of powers left a "gray area" in which each political branch could use its independent powers as it wished, without supervision by the courts. But the gray area he identifies is well within the zone where conventional analysts would say that "Congress disposes." This occurs because Yoo combines his overall attachment to the Vesting Clause with a series of interpretations of other clauses that are skewed to favor the executive. For example, he thinks that the president, not Congress, holds the power to decide between war and peace.[95] In addition, he says, the president, "not Congress or the courts, has the primary initiative to make, interpret, and terminate" treaties.[96]

Funding, says Yoo, was to be the main check on the executive in warmaking, as in Britain (the power in Congress to declare war was to adjust the legal rights war alters).[97] Congress, he thinks, has enough tools through the funding power "to promote or block" warmaking by the executive. In sum, "initiative has been concentrated in the presidency, with Congress usually playing an ex post role of approval through the power of funding or implementing legislation."[98] Yoo reminds us that Congress can stop the president simply by doing nothing, whereupon the money runs out. He never seriously probes the practical utility of this as the central check, although Vietnam certainly proved that defunding is an option Congress selects as a last resort. Noting this problem, he says that we should not "mistake a failure of political will for a violation of the Constitution."[99]

His strategy, then, is to set the courts to one side, to approve a very broad set of inherent and implied powers for the executive, and to restrict Congress to its funding control and its clearly allocated legislative powers, usually exercised reactively. He is not inclined to read the existence of any particular Article I, Section 8 power in Congress as an ex ante restriction on what the president can do. For support, he cites the parts of constitutional history that support broad executive power—the views of Hamilton but not Madison, for example. Of course he relies on a broad view of *Curtiss-Wright*.[100] Yoo's approach is a formula for executive dominance. It is not consistent with the system of carefully divided and balanced power created by the framers of the Constitution.

THE ARSENAL OF INTERPRETIVE APPROACHES

This chapter has touched on a number of ways to interpret constitutional provisions and statutes. Since all of them are deployed daily by analysts and advocates, it is worth pausing to catalog them. There is an enormous literature on this subject; I attempt only an outline here.[101] Let us begin with constitutional interpretation and then move to the statutes.

> 1. Setting the context. Emphasis on the foreign affairs elements of a problem favors executive discretion; emphasis on the domestic elements favors congressional control. When both elements are present, precedents from both realms are pertinent.
>
> 2. Textual arguments. Certain fragments of constitutional text expand indefinitely in the minds of some interpreters: the Vesting Clause for presidentialists; the power to declare war for congressionalists. Advocates often read clauses that seem favorable to their side broadly and clauses that seem opposed narrowly.

3. Constitutional history. The records of the Constitutional Convention and the *Federalist Papers* provide tempting but usually inconclusive sources for interpreting the Constitution's text. Snippets from these sources are regular features in argument. Lawyers tend to use the constitutional history in shallow and manipulative ways that irritate professional historians.[102]

4. Structure. The Constitution's structure invites inferences about its intentions. For example, the separation of powers principle nowhere appears in the text; the document's first three articles, creating and empowering three distinct branches, strongly imply it.

5. Institutional competence. Interpreters argue that the branch best suited to perform a function should exercise it. Hence the famous argument for executive supremacy in foreign affairs drawn from *Curtiss-Wright.*

6. Historical practice. As illustrated by the claims settlement discussion in *Dames & Moore,* a long-continued practice may come to be regarded as a gloss on the Constitution. Few practices have existed without exceptions in our political history, however.

7. Independent interpretation. Assertion of an independent right of the executive to interpret the Constitution is almost as venerable as the Republic. It runs from Levi Lincoln through Roger Taney to Taney's nemesis Abraham Lincoln, and forward to today. Attorney General Edwin Meese sparked a controversy by asserting it.[103] Legal academics have held a debate about the extent to which constitutional interpretation that occurs outside the courts should receive deference from the courts and the people. Some believe that the political branches can make a distinct contribution to our constitutional development.[104] Others defend the special capacity of the courts to enunciate law.[105] None of the scholars, however, "explain in any detail how the executive might police the boundary between constitutional principle and political opportunism."[106]

Consider the historical episodes in previous chapters and the persisting uncertainties about the ethical limits of advocacy. Three primary lessons emerge. First, the actual process of considering constitutional questions varies considerably. Some issues have received high-quality vetting within the executive. Washington's resolution of controversies about the bank and neutrality have had great influence ever since, including in litigation. Some other issues were studiously shielded from legal debate: Jefferson's purchase of Louisiana; Roosevelt's internment of the Japanese Americans. The former was never litigated. The latter received more judicial deference than it was due, to the Court's lasting discredit.

Second, full consideration of constitutional issues within the executive does foster important influences courts cannot readily duplicate. These include complete input on issues of fact and policy from the administrators who will implement a decision, and the rich experience in separation of powers law that exists in OLC and other executive law offices (such as the Legal Adviser to the Department of State). So the answer is, it all depends. When the earmarks of full consideration and debate of legal issues within the executive are present, courts, the people, and history may defer to the president's judgment. When the danger signs of evasion or sloppiness are present, no deference has been earned.

Third, a sharp distinction should be made between claims that the president may employ his or her own view of the Constitution when exercising independent powers (Taney and the bank veto) and claims that the president may defy a court order that rejects his or her interpretation (Lincoln in the *Merryman* case).[107] It is the latter situation that threatens the equilibrium of our system. Appreciating this fact, a comprehensive OLC opinion by former assistant attorney general Walter Dellinger affirmed that "the constitutional structure obligates the executive branch to adhere to settled judicial doctrine that limits executive and legislative power."[108]

To complicate matters further, let us consider the interrelation of constitutional with statutory interpretation. This is the terrain of Justice Jackson's famous three categories of executive action: those supported by statute, those in the twilight zone, and those opposed by statute. Jackson's formula has a major gap, however: it does not specify how either constitutional or statutory provisions should be interpreted to bring them into harmony or conflict. Here the notoriously malleable canons of construction enter the fray. The approaches most pertinent to our topic are:

1. Avoidance canons. We have encountered two of them, both designed to keep statutes from colliding with the Constitution. The main "avoidance canon" is that statutes are to be interpreted, if fairly possible, to avoid constitutional jeopardy. The *Timely Notification* opinion deployed this canon in a particularly aggressive way, narrowing the statute to reconcile it with an expansive view of the executive's constitutional power. A corollary is a call for a "clear statement" from Congress before a statute is read to allow an executive action that may infringe constitutionally protected individual rights.[109] Notice that these two versions of the canon have opposite effects on assertions of executive

power. If the president's constitutional power is to be protected, statutes will be read to allow executive discretion. Yet if citizens' constitutional rights are to be protected, statutes will be read to avoid conferring executive discretion. *Dames & Moore* provides an example of a clear statement issue. Critics have deplored the Court's unwillingness to demand a clear statement from Congress that it was authorizing the president to suspend claims. The clear statement approach, like the avoidance canon, minimizes direct adjudication of constitutional rights. Unlike the avoidance canon in executive hands, it maximizes the participation of all three branches in deciding sensitive issues.

2. The acquiescence doctrine. If all statutes appear to point toward authorizing executive action without explicitly doing so, and especially if they have existed for a long time, congressional acquiescence may be detected. As illustrated by *Dames & Moore*, this doctrine relates closely to historical practice arguments under the Constitution.

3. Deference to executive interpretation of statutes. In administrative law, a well-established doctrine calls for courts to defer to the Executive Branch's interpretation of a statute within the bounds of statutory intent and overall reasonableness. Presidential actions with foreign affairs implications surely deserve this much deference.[110]

Anyone reading the foregoing catalog should be forgiven for concluding that in the hands of a skilled interpreter, the constitutional and statutory materials can be driven to any desired destination. Please resist the temptation. The training of lawyers, whether in law schools or in practice, reflects the assumption that some analyses and conclusions are better than others and deserve more credence. The difference between good advice and bad advice may be subtle, but it is real. To demonstrate this assertion, I turn to the administration of George W. Bush and its record of bad advice.

PART II
Bad Advice

Like Henry V, this president [Bush] has shown a great deal more
mettle than his youthful conduct led the world to expect. . . . Yet his
achievements seem flawed and fragile. . . . He has waged war with too
little regard for the legality of the means and too much confidence in the
sustainability of the ends.
—British historian Niall Ferguson, "The Monarchy of George W. Bush"

I guess those opinions really were as bad as you said.
—Attorney General Alberto Gonzales, in Jack L. Goldsmith,
The Terror Presidency

6

The Bush Administration Declares War on Terrorism

No other U.S. president has reached office via the route taken by former Texas governor George W. Bush.[1] The election of 2000 ended with Vice President Al Gore the winner of the popular vote, but with the outcome in doubt because a statistical tie in the Florida vote prevented a clear victory for either Gore or Bush in the Electoral College, where the Constitution places the initial locus of decision.[2] After more than a month of uncertainty and litigation, the Supreme Court ended the crisis at a stroke in *Bush v. Gore*.[3] As Bush prepared to take the oath of office, questions of the legitimacy of his presidency were posed (mostly by Democrats). These questions were not shared by Bush himself. He instinctively understood that once he became president, the question was how he would behave in office, and how the American people would respond to his leadership.

The Bush administration was far more audacious than anyone expected, in a number of ways. Its governing style included "an appetite for big, visionary ideas, imposed from the top down; an eagerness to centralize decision making in the executive branch; and a tendency to shrug off the advice of experts, be they military experts, intelligence experts or economic experts."[4] These three characteristics are interrelated. A president with a simple, firmly held vision of the world is quite likely to try to impose it on the nation, to use focused executive power as a principal means to that end, and to listen to those who agree with his view of the facts, disregarding others.[5] Ronald Reagan, who has often been identified as a role model for George W. Bush, behaved in these ways (although an acute sense of political possibilities leavened his ideology).[6] Reagan's presidency suffered gravely from the Iran-Contra scandal as a result, but within fifteen years the lesson had dissipated. In fact, some of President Bush's senior advisers took exactly the wrong lesson from Iran-Contra. In addition, the president they served took his ideology straight, undiluted by his intellectual predecessor's political sensitivity.

THE CAST OF CHARACTERS

When President Bush took office in 2001, he was a neophyte in foreign affairs. To compensate for that, he assembled an experienced national security team that would dominate the government in the years after 9/11.[7] These advisers, having experience dating as far back as the Nixon administration and sharing a background of service in the Pentagon, shared a worldview that would shape the administration's responses to terrorism. They were willing to base foreign policy on moral judgments and were inclined to pursue military rather than economic or diplomatic solutions for international problems. They took a unilateral rather than a multinational approach to international action, an outlook that tended to reduce their reliance on and respect for international law.

It was natural for two of the leaders, Dick Cheney and Donald Rumsfeld, to take a didactic approach to the new president—they had first known him as the child of one of their colleagues. One wonders how that fact affected the relationship among these men after 9/11. No one, though, should underestimate President Bush's confidence in his own judgment.[8] His senior advisers offered him counsel that deeply resonated with his own predilections. There are no signs that they had to work very hard to persuade him of the wisdom of their worldview.

The president's unusual method of learning new information reinforced the influence of those closest to him. Most modern presidents, for example Bush's predecessor Bill Clinton, have read widely enough to provide a check on the views held by those in closest daily contact with them. George W. Bush, by contrast, received much of his information orally, by meeting with "a small set of senior advisers."[9] His questions revealed a results-oriented mind, and he looked for the simple solution, toward which he would then drive.[10] This reliance on oral give-and-take with a few people tends to obscure complexity and to diminish the prospects for original thinking, as the period before 9/11 illustrates.[11] In spring 2001, CIA Director George Tenet and counterterrorism coordinator Richard Clarke used one of the president's daily briefings to warn of the Al Qaeda threat, but the swarm of Arab names and places did not focus the president, who said he did not want to be "swatting flies."[12] On September 4, 2001, Clarke finally obtained the meeting of senior officials on counterterror he had sought. He and Tenet again tried to foster a sense of urgency about pursuing Al Qaeda, without much success.[13]

Like Ronald Reagan, George W. Bush tended to evade the massive defense, foreign policy, and intelligence bureaucracies, which both presidents distrusted. Instead, his administration formed and executed policy by means of ad hoc groups of government officials who formed small "shadow governments" within the federal government.[14] Shadow operations have two characteristics that proved to be pernicious in the Bush administration. First, they feature coherence of purpose. That quality was ensured by relying on a group of neoconservatives who distilled the approach of the administration to its essence.[15] There was a resulting descent into "groupthink," a phenomenon that tends to bring out the most extreme views in an isolated and self-reinforcing group.[16] Groupthink, an unattractive word and an even uglier behavior, would be much in evidence in the terror war.

Second, shadow governments stress secrecy, radically reducing the number of officers who know about proposals and placing the nation's demand for wisdom on the shoulders of a relative few. Closed groups exclude competing arguments about facts, policy, and law. Untested conclusions are inherently unreliable. Bureaucratic routines for vetting policy and law are slow and cumbersome because they expose plans to multiple and perhaps conflicting reviews. When shadow governments are created to avoid the costs of these routines, they also forfeit their virtues. It is easy to see and feel the cost of careful consideration of policy and legal issues; it is harder to perceive the benefit of improved judgment from dialogue.

One of the defining features of the Bush administration was the extraordinary role played by Vice President Cheney.[17] His predecessors had suffered one of two fates. Many were simply allowed to molder, at least until the fates intervened (for example, Truman was largely ignored by Roosevelt). Some, however, were granted limited policy portfolios. Lyndon Johnson's volcanic energies were shunted to the space program. Both the senior George Bush and Al Gore supervised federal regulation. Cheney, in contrast, exercised deep and wide-ranging influence throughout the administration. He arrived with the résumé for that role, having served in Congress, as White House chief of staff, and as secretary of defense. After 9/11, a date on which he was "the dominant figure," Cheney became the most powerful vice president in U.S. history.[18] He "preferred to operate largely in the shadows."[19] His understanding of the levers of power within the government and his ability to manipulate them behind the scenes were unsurpassed.

Early in the administration, Cheney's soothing, avuncular manner tended to mask his deeply conservative, ideological nature and his extreme views about executive power, which he had first articulated in the wake of the Iran-Contra scandal. Through the years, his views never wavered. After Iraq invaded Kuwait in 1990, Defense Secretary Cheney tried to persuade the first President Bush that he should respond with military force without seeking congressional authorization.[20] Even in the case of a major commitment of troops to combat, Cheney thought the president needed no authority from Congress. Thus President Truman's unauthorized use of the troops in Korea had ominous precedential effects. Yet Cheney went even further—had Congress declined to grant President Bush's call for authority, Cheney was prepared to argue that the president could go to war anyway, in contravention of the *Steel Seizure* principle.[21]

In the second Bush administration, Vice President Cheney worked to restore executive power after what he saw as the unjustified reverses of Vietnam, Watergate, and Iran-Contra.[22] Instead of treating these three national embarrassments as reasons to cabin executive discretion, he sought to elevate executive power to levels he thought necessary to deal with whatever challenges the modern world might bring. Early in 2002, Cheney talked about his effort to roll back the statutory restraints of the 1970s, which he called "unwise compromises" that had weakened the presidency.[23] He said he had made that case to the second President Bush, who had agreed with it. Neither man seems to have noticed that the powers of the president had rebounded considerably since the dark days of the Ford administration.[24]

Even if the vice president's theory of executive power was unnecessary, however, it proved very powerful. Within the second Bush administration, the theory "had a kind of theological significance that often trumped political consequences."[25] If this blindness to politics within the supremely political realm of the White House seems unlikely, there is a simple explanation for it. The administration was expanding executive power for its own sake. Cheney understood that the executive branch never knows when a need for broad power may arise. Hence all was claimed and nothing conceded, lest a retreat on one issue imperil the overall drive for power.

A corollary to Cheney's general view of executive power was his perception of a need for secrecy. This had two broad components. First, like many executives before him, he feared leaks from Congress, and was accordingly loath to ask it for authority or even to inform it about executive activities. He once argued that having Congress discuss the wisdom of a covert or military operation reduces the likelihood that the operation will occur, so that "the real world effect often turns out . . . not to be a *transfer* of power from the President to Congress, but a *denial* of power to the government as a whole."[26] This view echoes Talleyrand's observation: "To announce too much of what one means to do is the way not to do it at all."[27]

Second, Cheney had a record of tightly restricting the flow of information within the executive branch. As Ford's White House chief of staff, he centralized power and reduced access to the president, preventing leaks to the press and excluding dissenting voices. In 1979, he explained: "There is no question that to the extent that you involve a number of people in the consultative process before you make a decision, you raise the level of noise in the system. You enhance the possibility of premature disclosures and leaks. You also take more time, cut down in efficiency."[28]

Cheney's power was routinely exercised through David S. Addington, his chief of staff and longtime legal counsel.[29] Because everyone knew that Addington was Cheney's "eyes, ears, and voice," much of the vice president's authority accompanied him to meetings.[30] He played a central, if often hidden, role in the administration's decisions after 9/11. After graduating from Georgetown University (summa cum laude) and Duke Law School, he joined the staff of the Central Intelligence Agency. By the mid-1980s, he had allied himself with Cheney, who was then in Congress, and later served as Cheney's general counsel at the Defense Department. On 9/11, few of the principal members of the still-new Bush administration could approach his knowledge of national security law.

David Addington is a fiercely intelligent and aggressive proponent of broad executive power. In the Bush administration, he stopped at little to advance that agenda.[31] Believing that presidential power is "coextensive with presidential responsibility," Addington once asked, "Are you telling me that the Constitution doesn't empower the President to do what he thinks is necessary to prevent an attack?"[32] Like his boss, Addington strongly resisted involving Congress in national security decisions.[33] He dominated debates within the administration by combining hard work, an uncompromising nature, and a willingness to intimidate his adversaries. Associates remarked that "his intensity and emotions and passion for [his] theories are extraordinary," and that "David could go from zero to 150 very quickly. I'm not sure how much is temper and how much is for effect. . . . [He would say sarcastically] 'We could do that, but that would give away *all* of the president's power.' "[34]

The new secretary of defense was Donald Rumsfeld, who had previously held that post in the Ford administration and who had also served in Congress and on Nixon's White House staff. Rumsfeld was a fierce and unyielding bureaucratic infighter who had little patience with the professional military opinions of his generals. Like Cheney, he perceived a need to transform a reluctant military establishment. At Rumsfeld's side stood his deputy, Paul Wolfowitz, an intellectual leader of the neoconservative movement. A "bridge between academia and government," Wolfowitz was "the most influential underling in Washington."[35] The new general counsel at the Defense Department, William J. (Jim) Haynes II, who was a protégé of Addington from the Ford years, would play an important role after 9/11. Together, the civilian team at the Pentagon set out to control the military establishment, and would succeed to an astonishing and unfortunate degree.

Condoleezza Rice, the new national security adviser, quickly became a devoted Bush loyalist.[36] She had been a professor (and later provost) at Stanford, specializing in the Soviet military, and had taken leaves to work in the Pentagon and on the National Security Council staff. She did not share the prevailing neoconservative tendency to think that ideology trumps realpolitick, however, and soon found herself on the sidelines. She was joined there, ironically, by the only two senior members of the administration with combat experience, Colin Powell and Richard Armitage, both at the State Department. In an administration that routinely subordinated diplomatic to military responses, that department could not expect to be at the center of power, and it was not. Increasingly, Cheney and Rumsfeld shouldered Powell and Armitage out of the way.

A group of officials who believe in restoring U.S. power in general and the power of the presidency in particular, and who have great faith in their worldview as well, is quite likely to subordinate law to policy. That is what happened in the Bush administration. Previous chapters of this book have shown how easily policy imperatives can be translated into legal opinions supporting what a president wants to do. The stronger the imperative, the stronger the push to find legal support for it. The rule of law can withstand this pressure only if there is countervailing pressure from somewhere, presumably the Department of Justice. Instead, that department operated to promote rather than to check the most dubious legal initiatives that arose in the administration.

Hence the behavior of the president's principal legal advisers took on special importance in the Bush administration. Attorney General John Ashcroft, Assistant Attorney General Jay Bybee, and White House Counsel Alberto Gonzales had the responsibility to provide the main bulwarks for the rule of law in an exceptionally inward and aggressive administration. Ready to contest them for power were Cheney and Rumsfeld and their aides. As the war on terrorism began, a group of advisers who were prepared to offer a reliable flow of supportive advice emerged and soon achieved dominance.

President Bush's attorney general during his first term was former senator John D. Ashcroft.[37] Educated at Yale and the University of Chicago Law School, Ashcroft had served as Missouri's attorney general, its governor, and as one of its senators for a single term. The child of Christian ministers, Ashcroft had deep religious devotion, strongly conservative political views, and unquestioned personal integrity.[38] Still, Ashcroft seems never to have earned the full personal confidence of the president. (Karl Rove had pressed for his nomination in an effort to please social conservatives.) Ashcroft's interest in social values was not fully shared by the president, and in any event was unrelated to the war that would soon begin. White House Counsel Alberto Gonzales, who was deeply trusted by Bush, soon eclipsed Ashcroft as a legal adviser on the most sensitive post-9/11 issues. Ashcroft then failed the administration's strict tests for loyalty to the president by pursuing policy initiatives without prior White House clearance.[39] No one who committed that sin could expect to hold the president's confidence. After the first term, he was eased out in favor of the more reliable Gonzales.

At the time of Ashcroft's confirmation, which was contested because of his past positions on divisive social issues, he did bow in the ritual manner to the idea that his client would be the people.[40] He did not become a politically deft attorney general, though. He had to absorb the political heat for some of the administration's most controversial decisions. His response to the battering was to become extremely secretive and unresponsive to the news media and to his former colleagues in Congress. That tactic only increased the pressure on him, feeding allegations that he was an enemy of civil liberties.

Those allegations resulted from several legal issues that arose in the aftermath of 9/11.[41] Aside from the topics of surveillance, detention, trial, and interrogation that I discuss later, there was plenty of fodder for controversy. Ashcroft led the administration's battle for the sweeping USA PATRIOT Act, which greatly expanded law enforcement investigative authority.[42] He authorized summary detention of thousands of aliens, many of whom were deported after closed hearings.[43] He took a restrictive approach to the availability of government information under the Freedom of Information Act and other statutes, and under the executive privilege doctrine.[44] Ashcroft's willingness to promote secrecy regarding many kinds of government decisions certainly resonated with the attitude Vice President Cheney had held since the Ford administration.[45] Despite his value as a lightning rod for criticism of administration policies, though, Ashcroft eventually became more of a political liability than an asset, which speeded his departure.

At the Justice Department, OLC was without a Senate-confirmed assistant attorney general for most of President Bush's two terms of office. The effects of this vacuum of power at the top of OLC were to shift effective authority to subordinates in the office and to deprive it of the mature judgment expected of those heading this prestigious group of legal advisers. The consequent damage to the quality of legal advice furnished to President Bush is not easy to calculate, but it was surely severe, as subsequent chapters will reveal. Here is the chronology.

Disagreement over a nominee to head OLC delayed confirmation of the administration's eventual choice, Jay Bybee, until a month after 9/11, and he did not arrive in Washington until after Thanksgiving. Bybee, a law professor from the University of Nevada–Las Vegas who had served in the Justice Department and the White House counsel's office under Reagan and the first President Bush, had to extract himself from his teaching duties before taking the reins at OLC, and by then they were in other hands. In the spring of 2003, Jay Bybee left OLC to become a federal judge. In the fall of 2003, he was replaced by Jack Goldsmith, who had taken leave from teaching law at the University of Chicago in 2002 to work for Defense General Counsel Haynes. After a tumultuous tenure that featured his withdrawal of the notorious "torture memo," Goldsmith resigned in July 2004 to join the Harvard Law School faculty. (An acting replacement, Daniel Levin, issued a replacement memo on interrogation later that year.) In mid-2005, the administration nominated Goldsmith's principal deputy, Stephen Bradbury, as a permanent replacement, but he was never confirmed by the Senate, where displeasure with OLC ran deep. Thus, the office had a permanent head for just over two of the administration's eight years in office.

Within OLC, leadership after 9/11 gravitated to the senior deputy assistant attorney general, the forceful and self-assured John Yoo, whose academic theories are discussed earlier.[46] Yoo had taught foreign relations and international law at Berkeley before joining OLC in 2001. As one of the few political appointees in the administration with this important expertise, he was a natural leader for the OLC group working on terrorism issues. Soon after 9/11, he would have the opportunity to convert his views into national policy, as OLC "went into overdrive" and its lawyers played "a central role in almost every issue raised by the war on terrorism."[47] Yoo left OLC to return to Berkeley in the summer of 2003, by which time the major legal initiatives in the war on terrorism had all been taken.

President Bush's first White House counsel, Alberto Gonzales, has lived a classic realization of the American dream.[48] He was born into a poor family of laborers and raised near Houston in a two-bedroom house with seven siblings and without hot water or a telephone. Nevertheless, he soon displayed the qualities of intelligence, industry, and shrewdness that would carry him to the president's elbow. After high school and a stint in the Air Force, he graduated from Rice University and Harvard Law School. He went on to become a partner in the elite Houston law firm of Vinson and Elkins, doing real estate transactional work. He met and befriended the young George Bush, who made Gonzales his counsel upon becoming the governor of Texas in 1994.

It soon became clear to all that the two men were very close, and that Bush implicitly trusted Gonzales's judgment and loyalty. Gonzales also displayed a lifelong characteristic of discretion to the point of impenetrability.[49] He revealed no confidences about Bush or about himself. He just worked very hard to serve his client, as he had always done at Vinson and Elkins, without any need or desire to parade the story of his astonishing rise from poverty or to put his own advancement ahead of that of his patron. Governor Bush subsequently nominated Gonzales to the Texas Supreme Court, where he served for almost two years.

Upon reaching the presidency, Bush immediately tapped Alberto Gonzales for White House counsel. Well aware that he was a neophyte in Washington, Gonzales assembled a staff of highly credentialed young lawyers, a "feisty, aggressive, neoconservative army" that would press relentlessly for expanded presidential power.[50] They were frequently former law clerks to conservative Supreme Court justices. Several had served in the cottage industry of investigating the Clinton administration. The deputy counsel was Timothy Flanigan, a former head of OLC. He was a law graduate of the University of Virginia, had clerked for Chief Justice Burger, and had headed OLC at the end of the first Bush administration. Others included Brett Kavanaugh and Bradford Berenson. These brilliant young lawyers were neither diffident of their legal judgments nor inclined to defer to their colleagues in the executive departments.

At the first White House counsel staff meeting, the day after the inauguration, Alberto Gonzales told the group to look for opportunities to expand presidential power. Gonzales quoted President Bush as saying that his predecessors had weakened the office and he wanted to restore it, "to make sure that he left the presidency in better shape than he found it."[51] The immediate announcement of this goal, echoing earlier remarks by Dick Cheney, set the tone for legal advice provided in the war on terrorism and revealed that the president's new counsel had been inducted into the fraternity of believers in executive power. To Attorney General Ashcroft's chagrin, it soon appeared that the center of gravity for legal issues had shifted toward the counsel's office.[52] In an uncharacteristic moment of candor, Gonzales remarked that "I will be at [the president's] side. The attorney general is in another building, running another agency."[53]

As White House counsel, Gonzales was expected to be a close confidant of the president, as he was. Their relationship became an issue in Bush's second term, when Gonzales became attorney general. Responding to criticisms that he was too close to the president to give him independent legal advice, Gonzales said: "I think having a good relationship with the president is a good thing for the department. . . . When a friend tells someone, 'No, you can't do that,' you're much more likely to listen to that and to accept it. I've got that kind of relationship with the president. . . . It makes me much more effective as attorney general."[54]

There is certainly force to this argument, but it depends on the adviser's willingness to tell his friend the president that a proposal is illegal. George Bush does not welcome contradiction, and there is no sign that he ever experienced it from Gonzales, either as counsel or as attorney general.

A COALESCENCE OF POWER

Not long into the Bush administration, the traumatic events of 9/11 created a "perfect storm," as the inclinations of the most influential legal advisers toward executive dominance would meet the need for a vigorous response to the worst surprise assault on the United States since Pearl Harbor. Understandably, the crisis atmosphere heightened pressure to support aggressive countermeasures against the terrorists. The result was the immediate formation of an extraordinary bureaucratic arrangement known within the administration as the War Council.

This "secretive five-person group with enormous influence over the administration's antiterrorism policies" was unknown outside the administration.[55] It consisted of White House Counsel Alberto Gonzales, his first deputy Tim Flanigan, Cheney's counsel David Addington, Defense General Counsel Jim Haynes, and John Yoo of OLC. They met every few weeks at the White House or the Pentagon. They would "plot legal strategy," sometimes before meeting with lawyers from the State Department, the National Security Council, and the Pentagon, sometimes excluding them.

Thus the War Council's axis ran through a few people in the offices of the vice president, the White House counsel, the Pentagon, and OLC. A more normal bureaucratic alignment would have featured the president, his counsel, the attorney general, and the assistant attorney general for OLC. The added figure of importance was Addington. The subtracted figures of importance were Ashcroft and Bybee. Addington was integrated into the White House counsel's office in a way that had never happened before. The White House "routed every memo related to national security through Cheney's office, where Addington would review it, and he attended all the important legal . . . meetings, where his aggressive view of executive power dominated the debate."[56] Because he was "always in the room when Gonzales was discussing an important legal issue," he could ensure that the vice president's voice was always heard.[57]

At the Justice Department, John Yoo was able to evade supervision by either of his nominal superiors. He has said that he met with John Ashcroft "at least every few months, and sometimes every few weeks or every few days," to discuss the war on terrorism.[58] Yet bureaucrats who are working together on a crisis would meet far more often than that. Yoo thought that Ashcroft, who led a prayer meeting in his office every morning, seemed "wary of intellectuals." Like Bush, he was an "oral learner" who preferred briefing to long memos. It is unlikely that Yoo would have had much respect for the attorney general's capacities. Nor were Ashcroft and Bybee close. Had they been so, Yoo might have received more supervision. The head of OLC traditionally has met almost daily with the attorney general. Jay Bybee "advised Ashcroft in person only a handful of times during his eighteen months in office."[59] Yoo saw Ashcroft "much more" than did Bybee, but "in practice he worked for Gonzales."[60] After Bybee left OLC, Ashcroft got even for Yoo's circumventions by vetoing suggestions from the White House that Yoo be made head of the office.

Nor did Jay Bybee closely supervise John Yoo. By the time Bybee arrived at OLC, the War Council had formed and had made some important decisions. Yoo had already developed a close working relationship with Addington and others. Having no expertise in national security, Bybee let Yoo and another deputy, Patrick Philbin, lead OLC on terror war issues.[61] Bybee approved Yoo's draft memos with "minimal critical input."[62] Yoo's central role also came from the fact that, at age thirty-four, he had authority to sign legal opinions for OLC.

Further isolating Yoo and the other political appointees working on terrorism issues was the frequent use of high security classifications that not all of the OLC line attorneys would have possessed. The office's normal practices of extensive internal vetting of draft opinions were thus short-circuited. This phenomenon would prove hazardous to the quality of the advice OLC generated. The office found itself giving initial advice that it then would defend to others in the executive branch as final, rather than exchanging views more freely before crafting advice that it would regard as authoritative.[63]

Neither Alberto Gonzales nor John Ashcroft could offer informed opinions to check John Yoo's excesses, and David Addington had "nearly the same characteristics" that made Yoo so "incautious and aggressive."[64] The alliance between Yoo and Addington provoked Ashcroft "to refer privately to Mr. Yoo as 'Dr. Yes' for his seeming eagerness to give the White House whatever legal justifications it desired."[65] Jack Goldsmith concludes that "under pressure to push the envelope, they liked the answers Yoo gave; and lacking relevant expertise, they deferred to his judgment." A former legal adviser to the administration said that after 9/11, a "closed group of like-minded people" took control of legal advice, excluding anyone who seemed "soft" about executive power, including those at the State Department and elsewhere who would usually check extreme positions.[66]

The legal expertise possessed by members of the War Council, who had been working to expand executive power for years, allowed them to dominate meetings. A lot of weight was put on young shoulders. The situation brings to mind Speaker Sam Rayburn's famous remark upon observing a young and arrogant White House staff under Kennedy that he just wished some of them had at least run for sheriff somewhere. In other words, elite legal credentials and political zeal can mask an absence of seasoned political judgment, the kind of judgment the principal officers of the executive branch are expected to possess, and usually do. Unfortunately, as the war on terrorism began, there was not a lawyer-statesman in sight.

A DECLARATION OF WAR AGAINST TERRORISM

Not long into the new administration, 9/11 imposed immense pressure on everyone in the executive branch from the president on down to take strong and effective action in defense of the nation. The term "emergency" was everywhere heard, often to introduce discussion of what responses the Constitution might allow.[67] Amid their own shock, outrage, and pain, the senior officers of the Bush administration began facing these challenges on the morning of 9/11. Experience could not be their primary guide. Existing legal precedents were only tangentially relevant. The starting point for their thinking had to be the need for national security.

In the aftermath of 9/11, fears of two kinds distorted the ordinary thought processes of the president's advisers. Vice President Cheney "was consumed—some would say obsessed—with preventing the next attack."[68] As Jack Goldsmith would later recount, fear of another attack "created enormous pressure to stretch the law to its limits in order to give the President the powers he thought necessary" to prevent one.[69] The day after 9/11, President Bush put heavy pressure on Attorney General Ashcroft, telling him: "Don't ever let this happen again."[70]

Everyone in the administration knew that if another attack did occur, they would be blamed for not doing enough to stop it. Any lawyerly doubts that had hindered executive authority would be judged with "the perfect, and brutally unfair, vision of hindsight."[71] This fear drove much of what OLC later did. Yet countervailing pressure flowed from "elaborate criminal restrictions," causing fear of later prosecution for decisions made as "heat-of-battle judgment calls." Goldsmith concluded that as a result of these twin pressures the war on terrorism was "lawyered to death."[72]

For OLC, the way out of this dilemma was to adopt expansive interpretations of the president's constitutional powers and restrictive interpretations of possibly confining statutes or constitutional rights. Yet this strategy only deferred the need to identify limits to the president's constitutional power and to define the rights of individuals who would be touched by the government's forceful response to terrorist strikes. These questions would demand considered answers eventually. To the extent the administration chose to avoid revealing its actions at all, however, or at least to try to secure deferral of a national debate about them, it risked having the questions answered in cooler times, in the hushed chambers of the courts, with less deference to the administration than might have been expected in the immediate wake of 9/11. Uncharitable hindsight becomes easier as time passes. Yet it is very difficult to take the long view in the midst of a crisis.

Time would prove relevant to the administration's responses to 9/11 in another way as well. Like a medical crisis, the terrorist crisis of 2001 had an acute phase of direct military response in Afghanistan, followed by a chronic one of the homeland security measures and constant worries about the future that we all experience now.[73] Yet as with medicine, measures appropriate in the acute emergency may be needless or harmful for a chronic condition. In law, what is appropriate in a crisis may not be justifiable as "normalcy" returns (in altered form). Law, however, has great difficulty separating an emergency from its aftermath. The needed facts may be unavailable, secret, or disputed. Consider the Civil War: when had the initial rebel threat to the capital, so evident in early 1861, receded enough to justify or require restoring the writ of habeas corpus? (Even in 1864, a rebel army raided in sight of Washington, D.C.)

As time passes without renewed terrorist attacks within the United States, the need for emergency measures seems to diminish. But the best information for judging that threat is necessarily held very secretly within the administration. Congress, the courts, and the public find it very difficult to judge the issue. And we are always no farther from another crisis than the time it takes a news flash to reach us. The law delights in drawing lines, and lines are hard to discern in the shadows of modern security concerns. Notwithstanding this fact, executive advisers must consider the interrelationship of time and emergency measures. An action justifiable today may not be so tomorrow. But how are the president and his legal advisers to judge the tipping points? Later chapters in this book will probe this delicate question in the context of particular presidential initiatives.

An initial question for the president's legal advisers after 9/11 was how legal responses to the attack should characterize it, and what procedural models should govern the responses. Two broad theoretical avenues appeared. The attack could be labeled an ordinary, if heinous, crime and pursued through the criminal process. Or it could be labeled an act of war and pursued under wartime authorities and concepts. A substantial argument was available to support either approach.

Before 9/11, most acts of terrorism were already federal crimes. Prosecutions of the 1993 World Trade Center bombers and the Oklahoma City courthouse bombers had occurred under these statutes.[74] There was also authority to detain dangerous individuals under our immigration and criminal statutes.[75] If gaps remained, Congress could certainly be expected to supplement existing law enforcement authority promptly, as it did with the USA PATRIOT Act. In addition, the Justice Department is full of experienced investigators (the FBI) and prosecutors who stand ready to respond to crimes.

However, comparisons to wartime arose from the scale of the attack (more Americans died than at Pearl Harbor), the rhetoric of *jihad* employed by the terrorists, and the universal reaction in the nation favoring a large-scale response. On 9/11, John Yoo of OLC immediately asserted, "This is war. The law operates differently."[76] There were some problems with the war analogy, though. The legal precedents developed in traditional wars were based on facts unlike those of 9/11 and would require adaptation to our new circumstances. World War II, for example, featured mutual declarations of war by nation-states, extended clashes of arms by soldiers in uniform, and, at the end, formal instruments of surrender. None of these familiar characteristics of war will attend our long twilight struggle with terrorism. Our enemies might include rulers of nations that harbor terrorists, such as the Taliban in Afghanistan, but for the most part they are shifting, shadowy groups of individuals who wear no uniforms, represent no governments, follow none of the conventions that forbid making war against civilians, and cannot be expected to surrender on the deck of the *Missouri*.

Legal responses to terrorism must recognize that terrorists will resort to the ghastliest weapons that they can obtain, and must take an approach devoted to detecting and preventing future attacks rather than obtaining evidence after the fact and jailing any surviving miscreants. Moreover, because the problem is created by a strategy, not a state, it is bounded neither by place nor by time. The challenges this situation poses for the U.S. legal system are obvious and difficult.

The day after 9/11, President Bush announced a war on terrorism.[77] The declaration of a "war" had an effect that should be of special concern to lawyers. In law school we all learn the old Latin maxim that translates, "in war the laws are silent." This statement has an element of truth, but it is greatly oversimplified in two ways. First, the nation's record of protecting civil liberties in wartime is mixed, not empty.[78] Second, since our nation has been engaged in some form of conflict for about 80 percent of its history, one must decide when the maxim bears invoking.[79] It is true, though, that war favors vigor, not constraint.

Throughout U.S. history lawyers and courts have struggled to find an appropriate role for law in wartime, with only limited success. After 9/11, it was the duty of the executive branch's lawyers to ensure that the laws be not silent but heard and followed to the extent necessary. In the pressure cooker of a closed, ideological administration responding to an unprecedented national crisis, however, it was all too easy to ask, as Alberto Gonzales often did, whether proposed legal advice was sufficiently "forward-leaning" and not whether it was adequately considered.[80] Gonzales was surely reflecting the president's own attitude. Bush later explained that he had to demonstrate "the resolve of a commander in chief that was going to do whatever it took to win. No yielding. No equivocation. No lawyering this thing to death."[81] Lawyering there would be, but not of a conventional nature.[82]

Within a week, Congress enacted the Authorization for Use of Military Force (AUMF).[83] This legal equivalent to a declaration of war authorized the president to "use all necessary and appropriate force" against the 9/11 terrorists wherever found and against nations harboring them. The war theory had prevailed from the outset. The facts actually lay somewhere between crime and war, as the presidential commission that investigated the attacks later concluded.[84] The administration's legal response to 9/11, as it developed fully, embraced neither the criminal nor the war model in a straightforward way. Instead, it responded in a way that employed elements of existing approaches but also struck out into uncharted territory.

Within the administration, the War Council, acting entirely in secret, began by drafting what would become the AUMF and then moved on to other issues.[85] It is said that David Addington dominated the meetings, that his overbearing manner deterred debate.[86] Among the participants, he and John Yoo had the most background in national security law, and they would likely have agreed on most points. Even in their absence, though, there might have been little or no debate about the basic approach to take. As Bradford Berenson of the counsel's office recalled, "There was a consensus that we had to move from retribution and punishment to preemption and prevention. Only a warfare model allows that approach."[87] The choice of a war theory, although not generated by Attorney General Ashcroft, was certainly welcomed by him.[88] No one wanted to risk an inadequate response to the new threat to the nation.

A war on terrorism tends to erase the distinction between foreign and domestic affairs, including the boundary between traditional bodies of law that govern these two realms.[89] Recall that in *Steel Seizure,* the government tried to invoke all of the president's war powers because the steel factories the government had seized supplied U.S. troops fighting in Korea. A majority of the Court refused to convert what was predominantly a domestic labor dispute into an unconfined arena for the war powers, even though there was clearly a relationship between any interruption of steel production and military supply. As Justice Jackson said, the Constitution makes the president commander in chief of the army and navy, not of the nation. Declaring a war on terror obscures this distinction. It also invites reliance on the broadest statements the Supreme Court has made in discussing foreign policy and war, even if they do not fit comfortably in the context of efforts to stop terrorist attacks. In particular, judicial statements about the law of war require careful examination before they are transported to the "war" on terror.

CONGRESS IN DISARRAY

The Bush administration's responses to 9/11 would necessarily depend on its relationship with Congress, since congressional cooperation would be needed for various forms of statutory authorization and funding. In fall 2001, Congress found itself in both short-term and long-term disarray.[90] The reasons for the breakdown surely influenced the administration's decisions about what kinds of congressional cooperation to seek and what kinds of intrusions to avoid. Overall, to the extent that Congress lacked internal control of its legislative process, it would be vulnerable to domination by the hierarchically organized executive. And dominated it would be.

A long-term structural problem underlay some of Congress's difficulties in dealing with the Bush administration. Recall that the framers' expectation that there would be a natural tension between the political branches did not take into account the effects of political parties. When the same party holds both the presidency and Congress, as it did during most of Bush's tenure, party discipline fundamentally erodes Madison's plan that ambition would offset ambition.[91] Instead, the dominant party's political program can be formulated by the executive and forced through Congress as long as party discipline holds. The Bush administration often succeeded in doing just that, as we shall see.

Several modern developments within Congress have fostered party dominance. A traditional informal congressional norm has been that "politics stops at the water's edge," that is, policy concerning foreign affairs and wars should be made in a bipartisan manner. This tradition diminished party control. Since about the 1970s, however, Congress has undergone some structural changes that hamper policy coordination in general and bipartisanship in particular. Decentralization of power within Congress was partly responsible, as a reform movement after Watergate broke the power of a handful of committee "barons" who had held tight the reins of power and had dictated the legislative agenda. As power flowed to myriad subcommittee chairs, it became difficult to coordinate policymaking or to reach across the aisle. When the Republicans took control of Congress in 1994, they recentralized power by strengthening the party leadership.[92] That change aided coordination. It could have aided bipartisanship as well, but the new Republican majority in the House was in a mood for confrontation.

In the House, redistricting gerrymanders have produced many safe districts for members of Congress from both parties. The effect of this change has been polarizing: relatively conservative Republicans and relatively liberal Democrats have little in common and little incentive to cooperate with each other. Moreover, the balance of power in both houses has often been on the razor's edge. Both parties have focused more on seeking the electoral victory that would allow them to organize the houses than on compromising with the other party, which might only lead to defeat at the polls.

In this superheated partisan atmosphere, traditional norms of cooperation within Congress had broken down by 2001. Republican leaders, exercising tight control, stifled debate and excluded Democrats from participating in important processes such as conference committees. Memories are long—the Republicans vividly recalled being victims of the same tactics when the Democrats ruled Congress. Former representative Dick Cheney had particularly vivid memories of the decline of civility in Congress—and little doubt about whom to blame.[93] Most recently, the Republican effort in 1998 to impeach President Clinton for lying about his sexual indiscretions did not help relationships within Congress.

In fall 2001, the Bush administration had just suffered a structural setback in Congress. The 2000 election had produced the narrowest margins of party control in Congress in seventy years. The Republicans held the House by 221 to 212 and the Senate only by virtue of the vice president's tie-breaking role, with fifty senators from each party. Then in May, Senator James Jeffords of Vermont switched parties and control of the Senate shifted to the Democrats. (After the 2002 midterm elections, the Republicans had a slightly more comfortable cushion in the House, and the Senate was restored to their control.) The aftermath of 9/11 would produce a temporary surge of national unity and bipartisan action in Congress, but the underlying conditions were not likely to remain suppressed for long. The Bush administration, well aware of that fact, found itself in a hurry to put its responses to 9/11 in place.

From the outset of the Bush administration, its strategy within Congress was to exert tight partisan control over its slim majority in the House and its vanishing majority in the Senate, winning floor votes by demanding unity among Republicans.[94] Democrats could be, and would be, ignored. Partisanship ruled, and traditional separation of powers pressures between the branches were particularly weak.[95] Speaker of the House Dennis Hastert saw his primary responsibility as furthering the president's legislative program rather than asserting the institutional interests of the House. In times past, even congressional leaders of the president's party had been touchy about maintaining the separation of powers.[96]

In the Bush administration, the aggressive congressional oversight of the executive branch that had marked the Clinton years soon evaporated.[97] This phenomenon was plainly visible before 9/11. It encouraged an administration that was already inclined to maximize its institutional perquisites to treat congressional oversight and legislative restriction as threats not worth considering. Nor was extreme secrecy within the executive, which was already evident in a number of contexts, subjected to any meaningful congressional criticism or constraint.[98] The small number of executive officers who generated the administration's responses to 9/11 had little reason to expect congressional prying into their activities. Effectively, they were alone with one another, free of the kinds of sharp and even hostile criticisms that so often improve decisions about policy and law. The result would be the generation of legal advice that poorly withstood its later revelation to the public.

A DECLARATION OF REVERSE LAWFARE

Within the administration, forceful theories calling for executive discretion came from predictable sources: Vice President Cheney, his aide David

Addington, Defense Secretary Rumsfeld, and OLC's John Yoo. These four leaders counted existing law among the threats to national security.

Rumsfeld decried "lawfare," which he defined as "the judicialization of international politics."[99] For some time, the notion of lawfare had been afloat within the Pentagon as shorthand for a perception that a web of international laws and judicial institutions provided a way for weaker nations and groups to retaliate against the United States.[100] For example, there was widespread concern about the operations of the International Criminal Court (ICC), which conducts trials of war crimes and crimes against humanity.[101] President Clinton had signed the treaty creating the ICC. President Bush withdrew U.S. consent to the treaty, preventing U.S. ratification. The effect of the withdrawal was to prevent the ICC from trying U.S. citizens except for their crimes committed in signatory nations.

The ICC reflects a serious and laudable attempt to pursue justice against the world's ogres. Nevertheless, the Bush administration distrusted international organizations generally, fearing they would be dominated by nations resentful of the lone superpower. Hence it was easy for the administration to imagine U.S. officials who had acted in good faith being hauled into a hostile criminal court to answer for actions their own nation had directed them to take.

Criminal jeopardy for U.S. agents could also flow from ordinary criminal courts around the world exercising "universal jurisdiction" to prosecute war criminals. In a famous case, while in Britain for health care the Chilean dictator Augusto Pinochet was arrested on a warrant issued by a Spanish court and held to answer for his crimes against humanity.[102] Although Pinochet was never tried, the Bush administration could draw a parallel. It knew that the world has an ample supply of nations and groups that think ill of the actions of U.S. leaders and might hunger for legal revenge.

There was also domestic jeopardy. The federal War Crimes Act (WCA) imposes penalties for violations of the Geneva Conventions and the laws of war.[103] Military and intelligence professionals who remembered the domestic surveillance scandal in the 1970s and Iran-Contra in the 1980s were ready to believe they could be victims of lawfare "supported in advance and later pursued under different rules in an altered political environment."[104]

The lawfare concern was by no means restricted to the Pentagon. I have mentioned OLC's persistent worries about possible criminal jeopardy for U.S. officers. In addition, a nationalistic strain had recently emerged among U.S. international lawyers.[105] Within the administration, Cheney, Addington, and Yoo embodied a particularly strong version of the new nationalism, combined with concern about lawfare and a devotion to the executive branch as the primary means of wielding national power. At some point, in league with Rumsfeld, they adopted a crucial strategic decision—to conduct reverse lawfare. This consisted of aggressive attempts to disable the forces that might conduct or enable lawfare against the administration: international organizations, international law, courts both foreign and domestic, and lawyers. Such a strategy is fundamentally inconsistent with the rule of law, and much harm would flow from it.

The declaration of reverse lawfare is revealed by the title John Yoo chose for his memoir, *War by Other Means,* a play on Clausewitz's dictum that war is the conduct of politics by other means. In other words, the new dictum would be that law is the conduct of war by other means. Both military force and lawyerly ingenuity would be deployed against terrorists and anyone who might support them. The administration's primary tactic in reverse lawfare was to deny the applicability of potentially restrictive sources of law firmly and clearly, in advance of operations. This tactic appeared in several forms that I explore in succeeding chapters. The technique common to these efforts was the generation of secret legal opinions within the executive, usually by OLC. These opinions articulated a body of law that fit the administration's desires but were unlikely to generate agreement outside its corridors.

For a simple reason, the administration's attempt to conduct reverse lawfare was doomed from the outset: the executive branch does not possess sufficient unilateral authority to change international and domestic law in the ways desired. Since the administration did not ask Congress to enact the legal changes it desired, courts were very likely to adhere to preexisting conceptions of law when litigation arose to test the administration's theories. The Supreme Court did just that, in a series of major cases that removed the legal underpinnings from the war on terrorism. In the wake of these decisions, Congress finally legislated. It did so in ways so sympathetic to claims of need by the executive that the Court struck down a critical portion of the most important statute for going too far in disabling the judiciary. This history suggests that a less unilateral and extreme approach to generating law for the war on terrorism would have been far more effective.

In late September 2001, before either the ashes of the World Trade Center or the nation's emotions had cooled, the initial manifesto of reverse lawfare reached President Bush. John Yoo of OLC signed a memorandum titled *The President's Constitutional Authority to Conduct Military Operations against Terrorists and Nations Supporting Them.*[106] The timing of the opinion was surprising. By enacting the AUMF a few days after 9/11, Congress had already speedily granted the president full authority to strike Al Qaeda and those who harbored it. Therefore, the apparent purpose of Yoo's advice was to stake out the territory—to articulate a maximum claim of power for whatever need might arise. The opinion wrote a blank check for the president to cash at any time.

The *Constitutional Authority* opinion begins by asserting that the president has "broad constitutional power," "plenary authority" to use military force abroad. OLC opinions about presidential war powers normally make such statements. The opinion asserts that it is within the traditions of OLC. With some relish, Yoo cites and quotes a number of opinions from attorneys general and OLC in Democratic administrations to allay any charges that he is taking a partisan stance. Therefore, he quotes opinions by the iconic Robert Jackson and future Supreme Court Justice Frank Murphy that articulate a broad view of the commander in chief power. He then cites OLC opinions from the Clinton administration that supported the use of the military without special statutory authority in the former Yugoslavia and Haiti (and a similar memo from late in the first Bush administration concerning Somalia).

Yoo's memo could easily demonstrate that OLC has never accepted the congressionalist stance that there must usually be a grant of authority from Congress before the president may commit the troops to combat. (Nor is it likely that OLC ever *will* accept such a stance.) All of this is a bit beside the point, though, since Congress *had* granted authority to pursue the terrorists via the AUMF. What seems to animate the *Constitutional Authority* opinion is a concern not directly stated: what if the president wants to take action outside the scope of the AUMF? To anticipate this question, and to reduce congressional power to a minimum, Yoo departs from the Justice Department's precedents and turns to his own constitutional theories, presenting them as if they are standard OLC fare, which they are not.[107]

The structure of Yoo's own theorizing in *Constitutional Authority* is as follows. Again, he begins normally by articulating a broad scope for the commander in chief power. He then introduces his views by sharply distinguishing military action from domestic decisionmaking, where Congress has broad legislative power. The contexts are very different, he argues, because "the Framers expected that the process for warmaking would be far more flexible, and capable of quicker, more decisive action, than the legislative process. Thus, the President may use his Commander-in-Chief and executive powers to use military force to protect the Nation, subject to congressional appropriations and control over domestic legislation."

This framework deprives Congress of legislative powers relating to the conduct of war, despite their manifold presence in the Constitution, and leaves Congress only the power of the purse, which no one can deny but which is notoriously difficult to wield as a control on presidential warmaking. To this, Yoo adds a statement that the constitutional structure "requires that any ambiguities in the allocation of a power that is executive in nature—such as the power to conduct military hostilities—must be resolved in favor of the executive branch." To buttress the notion that warmaking is executive, he makes the Hamiltonian argument, which executive advisers have long admired, that the clause vesting executive power in the president is a broad grant of inherent but unenumerated powers. Therefore, the President has "plenary control over the conduct of foreign relations" as well (citing, of course, *Curtiss-Wright*).

Constitutional Authority then makes a ritual bow in the direction of Justice Jackson's *Steel Seizure* formula, noting that the president is at the "apogee" of his powers in "operating both under his own Article II authority and with the legislative support of Congress." It is the shallowest possible bow, however. For Yoo emphasizes his view that the AUMF and the earlier War Powers Resolution of 1973 "demonstrate Congress's acceptance of the President's unilateral war powers in an emergency." Hence, these are not grants of power but endorsements of preexisting and independent authority. Lest his meaning be mistaken, he uses similar terms throughout the memo: Congress "acknowledged" inherent executive power; presidents have said that authorizing legislation, "although welcome, was not constitutionally necessary."

Finally, Yoo notes that the AUMF "is somewhat narrower than the President's constitutional authority" since it extends only to Al Qaeda and its allies. To forestall the natural argument that the AUMF contained an implied limitation, Yoo concludes the memo with his strongest claim, that Congress cannot "place any limits on the President's determinations as to any terrorist threat, the amount of military force to be used in response, or the method, timing, and nature of the response. These decisions, under our Constitution, are for the President alone to make."

This statement is simply breathtaking. It articulates an extensive zone of exclusive executive power precluding congressional limitation. The memo relegates Congress to a subordinate constitutional role, stripped of any power to command the president except for the power of the purse. Yet Congress was fully supportive of presidential action after 9/11, as was the nation. Discussion of the highly sensitive issue of presidential power to override statutes is entirely unnecessary. Yoo's opinion is detached both from any factual base in particular, well-elaborated options and from any vision that the other two branches of government have any important role to play in the newly declared war on terrorism.[108]

Constitutional Authority is seriously deficient in both right and conscience. Its vision of a hegemonic executive in the foreign realm lies well outside the mainstream of separation of powers analysis. Yoo's attempt to fit the opinion into the body of executive precedents is particularly unpersuasive. It is part of his overall strategy to portray extreme legal positions as routine ones on which the president can safely rely. Essentially, this opinion is John Yoo's opening effort to translate his idiosyncratic and extreme academic theories into the law of the executive and perhaps the nation. No one should doubt the honesty with which Yoo holds these views, but that is not the same thing as the needed moral conscience in advising a client. Self-knowledge is a critical part of that quality, and none appears here. Yoo owed his president a candid assessment of the weight of contrary precedent, however much he might have disagreed with it. The opinion contains no evidence of a spirit of professional detachment. Opinions such as this one badly mislead and ill serve their clients, no matter how supportive they may seem.

The essential strategy of *Constitutional Authority,* one of maximizing presidential power and minimizing congressional and judicial power, would suffuse advice rendered in the particular contexts I next discuss—surveillance, detention, trial, and interrogation of terrorist suspects. The proof of any theory lies in its application, and this one would be tested repeatedly.

7

Surveillance by the National Security Agency

EVER SINCE GEORGE WASHINGTON DISPATCHED NATHAN HALE to spy on the British in New York (Hale's only achievement was immortality), our chief executives have desired information about the capacities and intentions of our enemies.[1] In modern times, much of the spying entails intercepting electronic communications. Whether the technique be the more venerable one of tapping telephones or the twenty-first-century methods of gathering signals in the ether, the purpose and the underlying need remain eternally the same: to forestall another 9/11 or Pearl Harbor or invasion of Long Island. The applicable law, however, has tended to lag behind technological developments to the enduring frustration of presidents, who have repeatedly risked scandal to meet national security needs as they saw them. To provide context for the activities of the Bush administration, a bit of background is in order.

SURVEILLANCE IN THE SHADOWS

The only time President Franklin Roosevelt declined to abide by a Supreme Court decision was after *Nardone v. United States* (1937) forbade federal law enforcement officers to wiretap suspected criminals because a statute barred anyone from intercepting telecommunications.[2] Attorney General Robert Jackson issued an order to comply with the decision. Jackson later reported that as war neared and problems of espionage and sabotage loomed,

> the President discussed the matter with me and said he could not believe that the Supreme Court could mean that the enemies of this country could use its communication system and not be detected. . . . We tried in vain to get legislation to authorize it but Congress bogged down in debate. . . . As the situation grew more desperate, the President's patience failed. On May 21, 1940, after going over the situation carefully and after consultation with me, the President sent a memorandum to me in which he said that . . . he was convinced that the Supreme Court never intended to apply the rule to grave matters involving the defense of the nation.[3]

FDR's memo authorized and directed the attorney general to order wiretaps against "persons suspected of subversive activities against the Government . . . including suspected spies. You are requested furthermore to limit these investigations so conducted to a minimum and to limit them insofar as possible to aliens."[4] Attorney General Jackson believed that FBI Director J. Edgar Hoover was "careful to remain within those bounds."[5] Thus, FDR did not assert presidential power to ignore the Supreme Court's decision in *Nardone* entirely, but he was prepared to interpret it restrictively to allow national security wiretaps, especially of aliens. Moreover, FDR made at least some attempt to gain congressional authorization before he took action on his own responsibility. Later presidents would follow and extend this technique of reading judicial precedent narrowly in the national security context.

A practice begun in the executive branch can take on a bureaucratic life of its own. An action taken by one president, such as FDR's wiretap decision, stands ready for use by later presidents of both parties to defend their own actions.[6] After World War II, as fear of communism rose President Truman yielded to pressure from the Justice Department to authorize wiretapping of suspected subversives and spies. The department's proposal, drafted by J. Edgar Hoover and forwarded by Attorney General Tom Clark, cited FDR's prior use of the activity.[7] This time, although "domestic security" was to be the criterion, there was to be no presumptive focus on aliens, a fact not mentioned by Hoover. Electronic surveillance went on quietly for decades after this authorization, especially in cases involving organized crime and domestic security.[8]

Truman's cold war presidency was marked by the McCarthyite red scare and some capitulations to it on the part of the president (such as the loyalty security program for government employees). Unauthorized domestic surveillance focused on the Communist Party and those suspected of being its fellow travelers. In the 1950s, frustrated by a series of Supreme Court decisions that made it more difficult to prosecute communists, FBI Director Hoover took his efforts underground with COINTELPRO, "a secret infiltration, surveillance, and disinformation program that began with the Communist Party and ultimately targeted even Dr. Martin Luther King, Jr."[9]

More positively, President Truman's legacy includes important structural changes in the nation's intelligence community, with the creation of the Central Intelligence Agency (CIA) and the National Security Agency (NSA). The latter, established in 1952 by a secret presidential directive and charged with signals intelligence, remained unknown to the U.S. public for decades.[10] It was the Vietnam War and the reaction of two presidents to domestic antiwar activities that finally brought NSA into public view, although only partially so.

President Lyndon Johnson trusted his FBI director and was quite responsive to Hoover's tendency to see communist influence on antiwar groups.[11] In 1967, amid demonstrations against the Vietnam War and race riots in U.S. cities and under pressure from President Johnson, CIA Director Richard Helms initiated Operation CHAOS to detect foreign influences on domestic dissent.[12] Both NSA and FBI cooperated, but found little to report. No matter—this began an extended period during which the nation's intelligence agencies conducted surveillance of domestic dissent at the prodding of presidents. The intelligence community was always a reluctant participant (Hoover excepted) and found itself in the uncomfortable position of constantly proving a negative—the absence of significant foreign involvement—to a president who was viscerally convinced it was present.[13]

President Richard Nixon shared his predecessor's tendency to perceive communist involvement in domestic dissent along with his disinclination to accept intelligence reports to the contrary. Consequently, CIA's efforts to show that there were *not* international influences on the antiwar groups drew it ever deeper into domestic surveillance, which was prohibited by its statute.[14] NSA participated by intercepting communications between Americans and foreigners, looking for the same evanescent links. Nixon's suspicious and conspiratorial nature and his distrust for the intelligence community, including eventually the belatedly reluctant Hoover, led him down the path that ended his presidency. By running a multifaceted and amateurish covert operation out of the White House staff to spy on his enemies, Nixon blundered into Watergate, exposure, and ruin. The aftermath produced the statutes the Bush administration would encounter after 9/11.

President Gerald Ford, rightly believing that he needed to clean up Nixon's messes, created the Presidential Commission on CIA Activities within the United States, chaired by Nelson Rockefeller and with Ronald Reagan among its members. The commission, which conducted no witch-hunt, concluded that "the great majority of the CIA's domestic activities comply with its statutory authority," and that some of the illegal activities were "initiated or ordered by Presidents either directly or indirectly."[15] Congress established separate select committees in the two houses to investigate. The House committee was chaired by Democrat Otis Pike of New York, who was prepared to investigate aggressively. The ranking minority member, Dick Cheney of Wyoming, was prepared to defend the prerogatives of the executive equally aggressively. The Senate committee was chaired by Democrat Frank Church of Idaho, who harbored ill-concealed presidential ambitions.[16]

Both committees wound up in disputes with the Ford administration over access to intelligence information, and both became embroiled in political controversy.[17] The Pike committee leaked sensitive information at a critical moment. Senator Church stirred the pot unnecessarily by publicly referring to the CIA as a "rogue elephant."[18] (Besides, he had the wrong elephant.) The Church committee did, however, compile a massive record of the executive's surveillance activities, which has been a primary source for historians ever since.[19]

The president's commission disclosed that NSA had furnished other agencies reports of the foreign communications of U.S. citizens. NSA obtained the intelligence by scanning electronic communications worldwide. Its computers were programmed with "watchlists," words or phrases designed to identify communications of intelligence interest. The use of these words would trigger the interest of yet more computers and analysts. During that period the list surely contained words like Ho Chi Minh, Jane Fonda, and other names familiar to readers of my generation.

NSA established two surveillance operations: MINARET, to intercept foreign communications, and SHAMROCK, to intercept communications entering or leaving the United States. Between 1967 and 1973, NSA added the names of approximately 1,200 Americans to its watchlists under these operations. The acquired communications were disseminated in 2,000 reports to other intelligence agencies. In testimony to the Church committee, NSA Director General Lew Allen struggled to discuss these operations without revealing details of NSA's technological capacities.[20] Allen stressed that all intercepts had involved at least one foreign "terminal," so that none were purely domestic. The Church committee also revealed that the CIA had created a total of 9,944 files on U.S. citizens, including fourteen members of Congress.[21]

President Ford sought to terminate the surveillance controversy by issuing an executive order strengthening executive branch oversight of intelligence, for example by creating an Intelligence Oversight Board that was to report possibly illegal activities to the attorney general.[22] An internal CIA journal questioned the remedy of increased accountability within the executive, since "many of the abuses of the intelligence agencies were caused not by too little, but rather by too much, accountability to the President."[23] Congress set up a standing Select Committee on Intelligence in each house, a structural innovation that still exists. With that, the pot boiled less actively. The Intelligence Oversight Act of 1980 eventually centered oversight in the two select committees and imposed the requirements for notification to Congress of covert activities that became important in Iran-Contra.

After the various investigations revealed the scope of illegal surveillance, a number of lawsuits were filed by persons suspecting they had been its targets. All of the litigation, which went on for some time, eventually foundered because the executive successfully invoked the "state secrets" privilege to bar disclosure of NSA and CIA intercepts and techniques.[24] As the fate of these cases demonstrates, the state secrets privilege provides unqualified protection for the nation's military and foreign policy secrets whatever the cost to private litigants seeking to protect their civil rights. Courts considering claims of the privilege have been prepared to honor claims that particular disclosures might reveal intelligence sources and methods as long as the claims are made by senior executive officers who have personally examined the materials involved. Hence the only real check on abuse of the privilege is the bureaucratic one of ensuring that the reputation and honor of the responsible officer stand behind the claim.

The existence of the state secrets privilege has largely eliminated the courts as overseers of national security surveillance. Judicial oversight would have occurred only after surveillance programs had been in operation long enough for word of them to leak to persons who thought their communications had been intercepted. The fact that oversight through litigation is post hoc does not make it unimportant, however. Litigation challenging an ongoing program could force its alteration or abandonment. And the prospect that litigation will reveal a program someday can affect its initial design. With the courts mostly disabled by the state secrets privilege, these controls have been unavailable for national security surveillance. This consequence puts special pressure on oversight by Congress or from within the executive to assure the legality of the practice.

During the time of the postwar secret surveillance activities but unrelated to them, both Congress and the Supreme Court began extending the warrant requirements of the Fourth Amendment to some, but not all, electronic searches.[25] In *United States v. United States District Court (Keith)*, the Court required a warrant for electronic surveillance that was performed in a domestic law enforcement investigation concerning national security.[26] The case involved the bombing of a CIA office in Michigan. The Court noted that under a recently enacted statute, the Omnibus Crime Control and Safe Streets Act of 1968, warrants were required for electronic surveillance in ordinary law enforcement.[27] The statute contained a disclaimer that it did not limit the constitutional power of the president in either of two ways: to protect the government against attempts to overthrow it by force or "to protect the Nation against actual or potential attack or other hostile acts of a foreign power."[28]

Justice Powell's opinion for the Court began by holding that because the executive branch was claiming constitutional power, the disclaimer made the statute inapplicable. Proceeding onto constitutional ground, the Court held that in domestic security cases, the Fourth Amendment's warrant requirement prevails over the president's executive power. The Court's rationale was the usual one in cases that enforce the warrant requirement: requiring the approval of a neutral magistrate for a search is an effective check on the zeal we expect from law enforcement officers, and the warrant requirement will not unduly interfere with the effectiveness of the investigations. This outcome generated enough doubt about the law concerning foreign intelligence to lead Congress to revisit the subject after the revelations of the 1970s.

REMEDY: THE FOREIGN INTELLIGENCE SURVEILLANCE ACT

In 1978, President Carter signed the Foreign Intelligence Surveillance Act (FISA),[29] conceding at the signing ceremony that FISA required "a prior judicial warrant for *all* electronic surveillance for foreign intelligence or counterintelligence purposes in the United States in which communications of U.S. persons might be intercepted." The Senate committee alertly noted that Carter appeared to have abandoned the claims routinely made by prior administrations that the executive had inherent constitutional power to conduct surveillance without a warrant.[30]

The warrants were to be issued in secret by a special court, the Foreign Intelligence Surveillance Court (FISC), composed of federal judges who had been selected by the chief justice of the United States. The act originally applied only to electronic surveillance.[31] It controlled electronic searches of international communications involving Americans within the United States and communications wholly within the United States, but not wholly foreign surveillance. Warrants were to issue if there was probable cause to believe that the target was a foreign power or the agent of one. This probable cause standard was markedly different from (and weaker than) the one traditionally used in criminal law, which is whether there is probable cause to believe that a crime has been committed. In emergency situations, surveillance could occur for a short period before seeking a warrant.

FISA repealed the disclaimer that had created uncertainty in *Keith*. The legislative history explained emphatically that the statute's recital that it provided the "exclusive means" for conducting electronic surveillance meant that no inherent executive power was being conceded.[32] That assertion by Congress could not negate any actual constitutional power a president might possess, but it had the important effect of removing all implied statutory endorsement of presidential actions not in compliance with FISA. Moreover, if a president did assert residual constitutional authority, that claim would be judged, under Justice Jackson's analytic formula, by the strict test used when a president contravenes the will of Congress.

It is unlikely, though, that President Carter's concession regarding inherent constitutional power had much effect. As we have seen, presidents assert power to interpret the Constitution independently of the positions of other two branches. Although the extent of this power is most unclear when one or both of the other branches has made a clear statement about the limits of executive power, a president is usually entitled to disagree with his or her own predecessors.

Because presidents of both parties have claimed a national security surveillance power for a long time, any incumbent can plausibly assert that the power is real and not merely a figment of political imagination. When at least one president—Jimmy Carter in this case—has seen no need for constitutional authority, the force of arguments drawn from necessity diminishes somewhat. Given these swirling currents of legal considerations, the enactment of FISA could not provide certainty about the relative power of the branches, but it was surely meant to constrain the executive and to eliminate a long-standing pattern of abuse of electronic surveillance.

FISA IN OPERATION

From 1978 until 9/11, the investigative process under FISA worked smoothly, without greatly hampering the executive.[33] Applications for warrants were submitted to the special court by the FBI after two levels of review within the Justice Department, first by the Office of Intelligence Policy and Review (OIPR) and then by the attorney general or deputy attorney general. The FISC granted almost all warrant applications—only one was refused between 1979 and 2002. This nearly automatic approval process may be owed in part to OIPR's role in preventing flawed applications from reaching the court. Also, the court modified some of the applications before granting them.

After 9/11, passage of the USA PATRIOT Act gave the executive branch some amendments to FISA it had long desired.[34] Most important, the original statute required that collecting foreign intelligence be "the purpose" of a warrant; now it needed only to be "a significant" purpose, a phrase the act did not define. This amendment responded to the problem of mixed intelligence and law enforcement purposes in investigations. The Justice Department had erected various internal barriers to cooperation between intelligence and law enforcement personnel, which may have contributed to the failure to apprehend the 9/11 terrorists.[35] Now those barriers were down, and a warrant could serve to authorize a search that might produce both intelligence and evidence of ordinary crime.[36] The PATRIOT Act also allowed "roving wiretaps" of any phone used by a target and eased the obtaining of orders that seek the numbers called from and calling to a telephone.

Controversy has attended dismantling of the Justice Department's "wall" between intelligence and law enforcement. It had originated in post-Watergate concerns about the executive branch's targeting of political enemies and about using intelligence surveillance as a "back door" to ease criminal prosecution.[37] The revelations of the Rockefeller and Church investigations had confirmed that these concerns were justified.[38] Yet it is normal for an intelligence operation to reveal evidence of crime, and the warrant requirement provides some protection for the rights of the target. In the form used in FISA cases, the probable cause standard provides assurance that the investigation is genuinely a foreign intelligence effort. Moreover, the genesis of FISA contains a warning: if an administration chooses to repeat the sins of politicized or backdoor prosecutions of the Vietnam era, it can expect the story to come out eventually, leading to the kinds of punishment that the earlier scandal entailed.

More broadly, FISA is a serious and relatively recent effort to remedy long-standing executive misbehavior. Those characteristics should make it a statute not lightly disregarded by a later president. For not all statutes stand alike in the application of Justice Jackson's formula for considering the interrelation of congressional and executive power. The particular statutory and constitutional context should always drive analysis within Jackson's helpful framework. In the wake of 9/11, the Bush administration would place little emphasis on the pointed message contained in the enactment of FISA. Instead, the executive would stress the preexisting (and shadowy) claims of inherent constitutional power to seek out the nation's enemies.

THE TERRORIST SURVEILLANCE PROGRAM BEGINS

In early 2002, President Bush signed a secret order authorizing NSA to intercept communications within the United States.[39] The "Terrorist Surveillance

Program" (TSP) remained entirely hidden from the U.S. public, and mostly so from Congress, for almost four years, until its existence was revealed by the *New York Times* in December 2005.[40] FISA warrants were not sought, although the statute applied on its face and although the PATRIOT Act had reaffirmed the applicability of FISA to domestic investigations performed by the FBI. Legal opinions supporting the legality of the program generated within the executive branch are still secret. We can infer much of their content, though. The controversy that erupted after revelation of the program led to the immediate issuance of a new administration white paper, a public memorandum issued by the Department of Justice containing the arguments for the TSP, titled *Legal Authorities Supporting the Activities of the National Security Agency Described by the President*.[41]

The genesis of the TSP was as follows. The crucial decisions after 9/11 were rapidly made and closely held. Soon after 9/11, President Bush convened his senior intelligence officials to discuss ways to prevent another attack.[42] The president later remembered asking, "Is there anything more we could be doing, given the current laws?"[43] General Michael Hayden, the NSA's director, responded that more could indeed be done, at least for calls with an international component. He was expressing the agency's ingrained position that FISA allowed it to intercept communications as long as they were not purely domestic. (Of course, the warrant requirement of FISA would apply to those intercepts that were not wholly foreign.)

As options were being explored, Vice President Cheney and his aide David Addington called the NSA's lawyers into Cheney's office and told them that the president had constitutional authority to intercept both foreign and domestic communications without complying with FISA.[44] The NSA lawyers resisted, stressing the agency's view that an international component was essential to the legality of its actions. The press later reported that there was a "very healthy debate" over legal authority—the vice president's office was "pushing and pushing, and it was up to the N.S.A. lawyers to draw a line and say absolutely not."[45] General Hayden recalled the episode differently, testifying that there were "discussions" but "no arguments" and that NSA did insist on a foreign component to all intercepts: "We attempted to make it very clear that that's all we were doing and that's all we were authorized to do."[46] It may be that General Hayden was not present for all of the lawyers' sessions. In any event, NSA did not yield to Cheney's arguments.

The two sides were reflecting positions born of bitter experience. When the press later asked Vice President Cheney about the justification for the TSP, he immediately invoked his view that the post-Watergate statutes such as FISA had impaired the president's constitutional powers:

If you want reference to an obscure text, go look at the minority views that were filed with the Iran-Contra report in about 1987. Nobody's ever read them. [They] are very good at laying out a robust view of the president's prerogatives with respect to the conduct of especially foreign policy and national security matters. . . . In the day and age we live in, the nature of the threats we face . . . the president of the United States needs to have his constitutional powers unimpaired, if you will, in terms of the conduct of national security policy.[47]

For Cheney, here was a chance to shore up the dike. For NSA, institutional memories of the beating it had taken after the revelations of domestic spying in the 1970s remained vivid. NSA's resistance was successful, but only partly so. The tradition that NSA intercepts must have an international component held firm, but compliance with the warrant requirement did not.

Only a few of the administration's lawyers participated in analyzing the issues. The War Council followed a path blazed by John Yoo of the Office of Legal Counsel (OLC), who had suggested warrantless surveillance soon after 9/11.[48] It is said that David Addington was the chief legal architect of the TSP. In any event, it is unlikely that he and Yoo would have disagreed. They dealt with FISA "the way they dealt with other laws they didn't like: they blew through them in secret based on flimsy legal opinions that they guarded closely so no one could question the legal basis for the operations."[49] Revealing his hostility to FISA, Addington once quipped, "We're one bomb away from getting rid of that obnoxious [FISA] court." At the outset of the TSP—and for years afterward—NSA lawyers were not even allowed to see the Justice Department's legal analysis of what NSA was doing.[50]

John Yoo later noted that the press identified him as the author of a classified opinion on the program in 2002.[51] Although the Justice Department forbade him to respond directly to the press reports, he concedes that the department's public white paper "explained the DOJ's legal thinking." The classified opinion, which Yoo wrote with Robert Delahunty, is titled *Authority for Use of Military Force to Combat Terrorist Activities within the United States.*[52] It claims that statutes restricting the use of the military within the United States do not constrain the commander in chief's response to terrorism, because the nation is a battlefield and Congress cannot restrict the president's tactics against the enemy on a battlefield. This sweeping assertion treats ordinary domestic life in the United States as the equivalent of a foreign theater of war. It irresponsibly ignores the fact that the drafters of the Authorization for Use of Military Force (AUMF) were careful not to grant domestic warmaking authority. It also ignores history—the fact that for legal purposes the "homefront" was treated distinctly from foreign fields in two world wars and other major conflicts. The war on terrorism has surely blurred national boundaries, but it has not erased them.

The opinion concludes that if the president decides to use NSA to collect intelligence in domestic communications, Congress cannot intrude. These assertions are far more sweeping than necessary to support a conclusion that FISA need not be followed, as I will explain. As in his September 2001 opinion on conduct of the war on terrorism, Yoo was taking the most aggressive possible stance regarding the extent of executive power rather than the narrowest position that would uphold a planned executive action.

The Yoo opinion on NSA also says that "the government may be justified in taking measures which in less troubled conditions could be seen as infringements of individual liberties."[53] On the surface, this statement is true, as our national history demonstrates. Nevertheless, when it is expressed as part of an attempt to free the executive branch from statutory constraint in a sensitive context involving repeated violations of civil liberties over the years, it is much too facile. It contrasts with a remark once made by Robert Jackson regarding *Merryman:* "The issue between authority and liberty is not between a right and a wrong—that never presents a dilemma. The dilemma is because the conflict is between two rights, each in its own way important."[54] Yoo's essential error was in treating only authority as a right, and subordinating liberty unnecessarily.

After agreement on the TSP was reached, NSA Director Hayden, CIA Director Tenet, and Vice President Cheney brought the proposal to the president, who approved it.[55] Hayden later explained his legal approach, which allowed agency employees to eavesdrop if they had a "reasonable basis" to believe one party to a conversation was a terrorist or part of a terrorist organization. When challenged about the disparity between this standard and the traditional probable cause standard found in the Fourth Amendment (but not in FISA), Hayden responded:

> If there's any amendment to the Constitution that employees of the National Security Agency are familiar with, it's the Fourth. And it is a reasonableness standard in the Fourth Amendment. . . . I am convinced that we are lawful. Because what we're doing is reasonable. . . . The standard of what was relevant and valuable, and therefore what was reasonable, would understandably change, I think, as smoke billowed from two American cities and a Pennsylvania farm field. And we acted accordingly.[56]

This was a plausible legal position, although it left out FISA's warrant requirement and the underlying reason for it—to obtain review by a neutral judge of a determination of need made within the agency. Hayden also offered a distinction regarding warrants: "The president's authorization allows us to track this kind of call more comprehensively and more efficiently. The trigger is quicker and a bit softer than it is for a FISA warrant, but the intrusion into privacy is also limited: only international calls and only those we have a reasonable basis to believe involve Al Qaeda or one of its affiliates."[57]

Alberto Gonzales later explained that the administration's lawyers initially concluded warrantless surveillance could not be squared with FISA, but then decided to "push the envelope."[58] An official who had intimate knowledge of the NSA program explained that working with FISC would have been "logistically challenging," involving initial mass sweeps followed by closer surveillance of those who triggered the watchlists:

> The thinking was that going to the FISA Court, or trying to alter the 1978 Act, would somehow expose, with leaks, or just from questions that we'd have to answer, what our system's capabilities were. Once you take that first step, the rest falls into place—including a fear that if we just talked to FISA about the smaller subset that drew our increased interest they'd feel obligated to trace the legal issues to the huge pool of level-one searches. Either way, we just went ahead.[59]

No more efforts to comply with or to amend the statute occurred for several years.

Two considerations appear to have forestalled pursuit of statutory change. First, perhaps Congress would decline to act. Attorney General Gonzales later explained: "We have had discussions with Congress in the past—certain Members of Congress—as to whether or not FISA could be amended to allow us to adequately deal with this kind of threat, and we were advised that that would be difficult, if not impossible."[60] Here Gonzales conceded that granting authority for surveillance is a sensitive matter in Congress—and had been ever since FDR sought and did not receive it. The underlying dilemma whether to seek statutory authority that might be denied arises frequently. Its importance results from the fact that an administration that has sought and not gained statutory permission for its activities exposes itself to arguments that it occupies Justice Jackson's least favorable category of executive action—in opposition to the will of Congress.

Nevertheless, it is hard to believe that the Congress that rapidly enacted both the AUMF and the PATRIOT Act in the wake of 9/11 would have rejected an urgent appeal from the administration for what it could plausibly have claimed was vital surveillance authority. Hence Gonzales may have revealed the more decisive consideration when he also explained that after some thought was given to seeking legislation, "there was a collective agreement that that process of pursuing legislation would compromise the effectiveness of this program."[61] The Bush administration repeatedly used this fear of leaks from Congress to justify depriving it of a chance to form national security policy or even to know of such a policy's existence.

FISA IN THE TWENTY-FIRST CENTURY

An understanding of the legal and operational issues surrounding the TSP demands acquaintance with some technical facts of daunting complexity.[62] To put the matter succinctly, it is not FISA's phone company anymore. The revolution in telecommunications since 1978 has led some to argue that FISA is so obsolete it may simply be disregarded. Even if that conclusion is not warranted, it should be clear to everyone that adapting the simple assumptions of FISA to twenty-first-century communications is no easy task.

FISA knew a world of telephones connected by networks of wires and long-distance electronic links. It supposed that NSA might be interested in communications over a conventional telephone between someone in Afghanistan, say one O.B. Laden, and someone in the United States. A warrant would issue to tap the conversations between these known persons over the phone line they were using. It was relatively simple to tell whether communications of interest were occurring at least partly in the United States, which was the jurisdictional trigger for FISA. This technological context dwelt close to the comfortable traditions of the criminal law. First a suspect was identified; then the requisite showing was made to intercept his or her communications.

In many situations, the TSP inverts this process. Instead of investigating known suspects, it searches to identify the suspects, whereupon traditional FISA methods become more feasible. This means that the TSP has to give some cursory attention to a vast mass of communications, searching for patterns that might reveal a terrorist plot. For example, before 9/11 it might have been noticed that several Saudi citizens were expressing interest in U.S. flight schools. Asking why could have led into the heart of the plot, yet probable cause in either the Fourth Amendment or the FISA sense would have been present only after the inquiry was well under way.

Today, by contrast to FISA's world, telephones live in cyberspace. That is certainly NSA's home territory, since the agency possesses the world's most powerful computers at its headquarters at Fort Meade, Maryland, and elsewhere. Nevertheless, NSA confronts an overwhelming flood of telecommunications to monitor. Every day, Americans send about 9 trillion e-mails and place about 1 billion cell-phone calls and another billion land-line calls. That could require a lot of warrants. It certainly demands extreme sophistication on the part of NSA to figure out how to detect danger in this overwhelming flood of data. Moreover, old certainties about the points of origin and termination of communications have evaporated. Nowadays, "many purely international communications—telephone calls and e-mail messages from the Middle East to Asia, for example—end up going through telecommunications switches that are physically based in the United States."63 Computers operating the global communications system send messages down the most electronically efficient paths, which have little to do with physical location. In addition, centralization of the Internet's infrastructure in the United States concentrates much of the world's e-mail traffic here. Under President Bush's order, telecommunications companies gave NSA access to the switching systems, sweeping in vast numbers of international and domestic communications together.

How do you find the needles in this haystack? NSA's most difficult job is setting search priorities in the form of its watchlists, which are therefore closely guarded secrets. If the terrorists know where we are looking, it is easy to hide. We (and they) can infer some priorities. Sometimes the destinations of communications matter: if you are making frequent calls to Pakistan not Peoria, you can expect to be monitored. Sometimes the contents trigger interest: if you send a lot of e-mails about best designs for dirty bombs, your addressees might not be the only readers of the e-mails.

It seems likely that the TSP was basically a two-step program. First, there were computer sweeps of vast numbers of communications using the watchlists as a net to capture items of interest. In this stage, no person would read the contents of particular communications. Therefore, it should not be of interest to either FISA or the Fourth Amendment. The next stage, however, would implicate both statutory and constitutional limits. Someone at NSA would look at the catch that the nets had brought in and would decide whether to investigate further. Compliance with FISA would present two serious obstacles. First, often there would be no probable cause as yet to believe the target was a terrorist agent. That is what NSA was trying to determine. Second, in the high-speed world of modern communications, there would be little time to prepare a package justifying a FISA warrant and present it to a judge. Moreover, the numbers of communications triggering some NSA interest via the watchlists might have been so vast that warrants were infeasible in many cases.

The jurisdictional application of FISA was also difficult to determine. It seems nonsensical to sweep messages between or within foreign nations, to which NSA would ordinarily have full access outside of FISA, into the ambit of the statute because of the accident of their transit through the United States. Yet the presence of some of these messages in a computer system should not disable FISA's protection for truly domestic traffic. Obviously, sensitive problems of control and accountability surrounded any attempt to sort these communications, as well as the selection of a legal means of accommodating the brave new world of the cell phone and the Internet to FISA's old world of clunky desk models.

Hence, revisiting FISA after 9/11 to update the statute would have mixed complex technical questions with sensitive political ones. Moreover, ways would have to have been found to address these issues without revealing the nation's intended responses to its adversaries. In the pressured atmosphere after 9/11 any serious attempt to revise FISA was deferred—and never revisited until the existence of the TSP had been revealed.

Under the TSP, decisions to initiate surveillance of particular targets were left to the discretion of NSA. In place of FISA warrants, NSA used an internal checklist to detect a "reasonable basis" to begin surveillance. The fruits of the investigations were probably used to identify suspects and to initiate a subsequent process of full FISA investigation, with warrants sought for surveillance of these individuals. It appears that the program targeted about 7,000 people overseas and about 500 within the United States.

AN INTERNAL DISPUTE OVER LEGALITY

The TSP was subject to recurring legal review. Under the presidential directive creating the program, the attorney general was required to reauthorize it every forty-five days. This was a valuable internal check against "mission creep," although it could not substitute for congressional oversight. Eventually, this requirement led to a crisis within the administration. In March 2004, Deputy Attorney General James B. Comey, standing in for a hospitalized John Ashcroft, refused to reapprove part of the surveillance program.[64] Comey, a graduate of the University of Chicago Law School with two decades of experience as a federal prosecutor, concurred with the new assistant attorney general for OLC, Jack Goldsmith, that there were serious concerns about both oversight within NSA and the overall legality of the program. With second thoughts about surveillance surfacing in the department, Goldsmith had generated a second secret OLC opinion about the program.[65] Its contents remain unknown, but because Goldsmith's purpose was to put the TSP on a "proper legal footing," it must have retreated from the opinion generated at the outset of the program by John Yoo and others.[66] The second OLC memo guided the department's officers in the controversy that soon followed.

Attorney General Ashcroft met with Comey in March 2004; they agreed that the program could not be renewed as it stood.[67] That day Ashcroft was rushed to the hospital for gallbladder surgery and remained in intensive care for more than a week. With surveillance authority about to expire, President Bush sent White House Counsel Alberto Gonzales and Chief of Staff Andrew Card to the hospital to obtain Ashcroft's consent to continuation of the program. When warning of the impending visit reached Comey, he rushed to the hospital with FBI Director Robert Mueller and OLC head Goldsmith, both of whom shared his concerns about the program. Ashcroft, still very sick after his surgery, seemed "pretty bad off" to Comey. When Gonzales and Card entered the room with a form for Ashcroft to sign and explained the purpose of their visit, Ashcroft roused himself and "in very strong terms expressed his view of the matter," refusing his assent and concluding by reminding his visitors that Comey was in temporary charge of the Department. Comey later testified that he "was angry. I thought I just witnessed an effort to take advantage of a very sick man, who did not have the powers of the attorney general because they had been transferred to me. I thought he had conducted himself . . . in a way that demonstrated a strength I had never seen before. But still I thought it was improper."

After the extraordinary meeting at the hospital, Card ordered Comey to come to the White House. Comey insisted on having a witness present and located Solicitor General Ted Olson, who was respected by everyone in the administration. A discussion that included Alberto Gonzales did not resolve the impasse. (At some point both Vice President Cheney and David Addington also told Comey they disagreed with his position.)

Comey testified that the next day, the expiring program was reauthorized without the Justice Department's assent. Comey prepared to resign and soon learned that it was likely that Attorney General Ashcroft, Director Mueller, and OLC head Goldsmith would resign as well. Faced with a set of resignations that would surely have exposed the TSP, President Bush called Comey into a private fifteen-minute meeting in his study. When it became clear that Comey would not abandon his legal conclusion, the president told him sharply, "I decide what the law is for the executive branch." Comey responded, "That's absolutely true, sir, you do. But I decide what the Justice Department can certify to and can't certify to, and despite my absolute best efforts, I simply cannot in the circumstances."[68] After a "very full exchange," as Comey characterized it, the president retreated. He met with Mueller and authorized the Justice Department "to do what [it] thinks is right." With that, the controversy abated.

Although the programmatic changes that followed this crisis remain classified, it appears that they included audits examining selected cases to see how NSA was administering the program, with special attention to agency determinations that sufficient cause existed to initiate surveillance on individuals. This bureaucratic check, although not a full substitute for a warrant approved in advance by a magistrate, had the potential to provide a real constraint on the TSP, at least if it was taken seriously. Still, selection of persons to be targeted remained in the hands of shift supervisors at NSA.

Comey later reflected on the importance of the stand he had taken. In an address to the staff of NSA, he said that the lawyer is

> the custodian of our Constitution and the rule of law. It is the job of a good lawyer to say "yes." It is as much the job of a good lawyer to say "no." "No" is much, much harder. "No" must be spoken into a storm of crisis, with loud voices all around, with lives hanging in the balance. "No" is often the undoing of a career. And often, "no" must be spoken in competition with the voices of other lawyers who do not have the courage to echo it. For all these reasons, it takes far more than a sharp legal mind to say "no" when it matters most. It takes moral character. It takes an ability to see the future. It takes an appreciation of the damage that will flow from an unjustified "yes." It takes an understanding that, in the long run, intelligence under law is the only sustainable intelligence in this country.[69]

In the culminating exchange between President Bush and Deputy Attorney General Comey, both men were right. The president is the final interpreter of the law for the executive branch, as many of Bush's predecessors had established. At the same time, the duty of the deputy attorney general was to give independent and candid legal advice, not to retreat from it under pressure, so that the president's ultimate decision would be fully informed.

The NSA reauthorization controversy reflects well on the Justice Department officers who were involved. Having concluded that the program presented serious legal issues in both design and execution, they held their ground against serious pressure from the president's principal aides and eventually from the president himself. In the end, they prevailed, probably because the president was not willing to risk exposure of the program. The president's own views of the legal arguments made to him are not known, but he listened to them and eventually accepted the Justice Department's position. During and after the episode, those resisting the White House must have known that their ambitions within the administration were at an end. Being called on the White House carpet is rarely a good career move, especially in an administration with an extraordinary focus on personal loyalty to the president. Attorney General Ashcroft was not asked to stay on for the second Bush term. Deputy Attorney General Comey left the administration for private practice in 2005. Assistant Attorney General Goldsmith, whose other clashes with the White House are recounted in later chapters, left for the Harvard Law School faculty in 2004. FBI Director Mueller remained at his post, shielded by his long and virtually guaranteed statutory term.

Any threatened resignation over a matter of principle can be viewed in either of two ways. If one agrees with the subordinate on the merits, this is an act of courage at considerable personal cost. The surveillance controversy certainly involved fortitude. Indeed, it evokes the most famous Justice Department resignations in recent U.S. history—the "Saturday Night Massacre" in 1973. President Nixon ordered Attorney General Elliott Richardson to fire Watergate Special Prosecutor Archibald Cox for investigating Nixon's misdeeds with excessive vigor. Richardson, having promised Congress that he would do no such thing, resigned on the spot rather than execute the president's order. Deputy Attorney General William Ruckelshaus took the same stance, following Richardson into administrative sainthood. Solicitor General Robert Bork, believing that the president could not bargain away his constitutional power to remove subordinates, removed Cox. An enraged public reaction followed, and the road to Nixon's resignation stretched ahead.

Memories of the Saturday Night Massacre and the events that followed it still reverberate in the executive branch. No president wants to be compared to Richard Nixon, as would surely occur in the wake of mass resignations in the Justice Department. This fact gives every attorney general and his or her principal subordinates considerable power to resist a presidential order they consider illegal. Perhaps, though, it gives them *too much* power. If a subordinate official is wrong or at least is not empowered to decide, a threat to resign can wield quite unfair leverage against the president.

For the TSP, the threat combined two powerful elements: exposure of the program and allegations of presidential misbehavior in pressing for an illegal action. President Bush certainly prized the secrecy of the program, which he thought critical to national security. Also he was already beset by critics of his war in Iraq in an election year. Thus, he had little choice but to yield to the pressure placed upon him. Nevertheless, I believe that in this case the Justice Department officers were right to do what they did, for reasons that will be evident some pages from now, after I have analyzed the legal arguments surrounding the surveillance.

MINIMAL NOTICE TO CONGRESS AND THE FISA COURT

Although Congress was not asked to authorize the TSP, a few congressional leaders were briefed in secret as the program began by Vice President Cheney, NSA Director Michael Hayden, and CIA Director George Tenet. With Cheney's "strong encouragement," the initial briefings were limited to four members of Congress, the chairs and ranking minority members of the two intelligence committees.[70] The briefings, which were cursory, said that NSA would hunt terrorists, their supporters, and their financiers.[71] The briefings later expanded to the "gang of eight" that is supposed to receive notice of covert operations: the majority and minority leaders of the two houses along with the four members of the intelligence committees.

After revelation of the TSP in the media in late 2005, the rest of the members of the intelligence committees were eventually included in the secret briefings. This extremely restricted notification to Congress caused considerable resentment after the existence of the program became known to the nation.[72] Members of Congress do not enjoy learning about matters within their legislative and oversight responsibilities from the media rather than from the executive branch. The restricted notification also may have been illegal under the National Security Act's requirement that the intelligence committees be "fully and currently informed of all intelligence activities."[73] Whether illegal or not, it was certainly begrudging and minimal.

The restrictive conditions under which the congressional briefings occurred made it almost impossible for Congress to consider authorizing legislation or to exercise meaningful oversight of the program. At one point in 2004, Cheney asked at a briefing whether "we need to do anything legislatively" and was told to continue without special authorization.[74] No one can know whether this reaction from the gang of eight mirrored the mood of Congress. No members of Congress outside the briefing circle could be told of the existence of the TSP. Congressional staff were excluded from the meetings and were not to be informed about the program. As a result, members of Congress, who rely very heavily on their staff, felt hamstrung. Democratic Senator Jay Rockefeller of West Virginia, the ranking minority member of the Intelligence Committee, raised concerns about the program in a letter to Vice President Cheney. The letter, written by hand to avoid involving any staff personnel, did not receive a response.

The administration also revealed the TSP's existence to the chief judge of the FISA court, District Judge Royce Lamberth, and subsequently to his successor, District Judge Colleen Kollar-Kotelly. Here again, the conditions of notification prevented meaningful oversight. When Judge Lamberth was told of the initiation of the program, "he was ordered to tell no one about it—not even his clerks or his fellow FISA court judges."[75] Hence the administration's provision of information about the TSP to concerned entities in both Congress and the judiciary furnished the shadow but not the substance of interbranch cooperation. When the existence of the program stood revealed, the administration could claim that it had briefed both of the other branches about it, but it had never done so in a way that would empower either other branch to oversee or alter the TSP.

THE TSP AFTER ITS REVELATION

After the existence of the TSP became public knowledge in late 2005, a sharp debate erupted over its legality. In his State of the Union speech the next month, President Bush defended the program, claiming that "previous Presidents have used the same constitutional authority I have." A year earlier, Alberto Gonzales had succeeded John Ashcroft as attorney general.[76] Having endorsed the program at the outset, Gonzales was ill-positioned to abandon it, although he might have reassessed it after four years of implementation. Instead, the administration closed ranks. Charges that the TSP was illegal were coming from many quarters, including some members of Congress and a group of fourteen prominent law professors who wrote an open letter assailing the program.[77] Gonzales responded by defending it without qualification, first in a short letter from the Justice Department's Office of Legislative Affairs and then in the more comprehensive white paper. The Senate Judiciary Committee requested the underlying OLC memoranda and was rebuffed.[78] In addition to the department's usual concerns about protecting executive privilege by shielding legal advice provided to the president, it was surely reluctant to air its internal disagreements over the legality of the program. Instead, it stuck to the ramparts.

Throughout 2006, the administration and Congress gave desultory consideration to various bills designed to authorize the TSP. The administration, having the program in place, had little incentive to press for legislation that might restrict its activities. The Republican Congress, reluctant to give the Democrats an opening in an election year, did not press very hard, notwithstanding bipartisan concerns about the program. The November election, by delivering both houses into the hands of the Democrats, produced marked changes in the behavior of both branches. The incoming congressional leadership made clear its intention to investigate the administration vigorously. The Bush administration soon initiated an attempt to defuse the controversy.

On January 17, 2007, the day before Attorney General Gonzales was due to testify before a hostile Senate Judiciary Committee about the TSP, the administration abruptly reversed course.[79] Gonzales wrote a letter to incoming chair Patrick Leahy and ranking minority member Arlen Specter, both of whom had been thorns in the administration's side regarding the program.[80] The letter announced that "any electronic surveillance that was occurring as part of the Terrorist Surveillance Program will now be conducted subject to the approval of the Foreign Intelligence Surveillance Court." Gonzales went on to explain that an "innovative" arrangement with the FISC had provided the "necessary speed and agility" to accommodate national security needs to court review.

The letter disclosed that in recent days, the Justice Department had obtained several orders "authorizing the Government to target for collection" international communications for which there was probable cause to believe that one of the parties had terrorist connections. Gonzales would not reveal, however, the nature of the new procedures that had made FISC review feasible. The letter's phraseology is consistent with either individual warrants or some form of broad, programmatic approval of the NSA's general approach, such as the review and approval of its watchlists. The Senate Judiciary and Intelligence Committees soon pressed for the documents underlying the new practices described in the attorney general's letter; he promised to provide them in secret.[81] The original presidential order initiating the program and the supporting legal opinions remained undisclosed, however.[82]

In a second major reversal, the Gonzales letter announced that President Bush would not reauthorize the TSP when it reached its next forty-five-day expiration deadline. Henceforth, it appeared, the traditional FISA process would suffice, at least with the modifications recently made by the FISC. The letter said the court orders had followed almost two years of discussions with the FISC regarding how to proceed and were not driven by recent controversy over the program. Those discussions may have been prompted by the period of upheaval within the administration over the legality of the program, which had occurred about three years before Attorney General Gonzales made his announcements to the new Congress. If so, a rather tortuous process of reviewing and refining a hurried initial approval of the TSP had finally produced steps toward executive branch compliance with FISA.

The period after revelation of the surveillance program produced another controversy, one that involved some personal jeopardy for both Attorney General Gonzales and President Bush. Concerned members of Congress asked the Justice Department's Office of Professional Responsibility (OPR) to investigate the role played by government lawyers in approving the TSP. The head of the office, H. Marshall Jarrett, attempted to proceed with an investigation, but was stymied when President Bush refused to grant security clearances to the office's lawyers. The president was reported to believe that there were already sufficient investigations into the program and its inception.[83]

Pressure from Congress continued, and in November 2006, Justice Department Inspector General Glenn Fine announced he would make a full review of the department's role in the TSP.[84] (He had initially deferred to the blocked OPR investigation.) He announced that the necessary security clearances for his staff would be forthcoming. It was not clear, however, whether the investigation would include ethical questions surrounding creation of the program as opposed to oversight of it by the department.

The aspect of this controversy that directly involves the attorney general and the president is their initial denial of security clearances. The two men discussed the issue soon after Gonzales learned that his own conduct while he was White House counsel would be a focus of the investigation.[85] It is unknown whether Gonzales informed the president that his conduct was in question or whether he urged Bush to stop the investigation. If Gonzales either failed to inform Bush of his own jeopardy or pressed the president to protect him, he committed a serious ethical breach. If the president closed the investigation with knowledge that doing so would protect Gonzales, both were culpable. At the very least, after Gonzales knew that the investigation concerned him, he was obligated to recuse himself from further participation in it. His failure to do so was an ethical breach, whether or not a worse one followed. In addition, the attorney general ill served his superior by allowing the propriety of the president's conduct to be brought into question.

In August 2007, the administration and Congress finally reached agreement on a bill amending FISA to authorize the TSP.[86] The statute allowed

NSA to monitor telecommunications without a warrant, even if they were physically intercepted within the United States, as long as the target of the surveillance was "reasonably believed" to be in a foreign nation. The statute also gave the attorney general and the NSA director the power to approve particular instances of international surveillance, with FISC restricted to reviewing and approving the governing procedures adopted by the executive. The sensitivity of the issues and the level of distrust in Congress for the administration remained high, however, and a temporary authorization for six months was the most that could be secured. Still, the administration had won broad authority from a Congress that did not wish to appear unwilling to give the president the tools needed to fight terrorism. When the six-month authorization for the TSP expired in early 2008, the administration and Congress could not agree on a more permanent substitute, mostly because of disagreement over whether the telecommunications companies should receive immunity from lawsuits for cooperating with the program. The TSP then slipped back into the legal limbo where it had dwelt so long before. Yet more months of interbranch wrangling followed, until Congress finally passed another authorization for the program in the summer of 2008.[87]

After revelation of the TSP in late 2005, a series of lawsuits arose to challenge its legality.[88] The plaintiffs usually claimed that they had been subjected to surveillance, which would be a prerequisite to having legal "standing" to bring a lawsuit. The federal government responded by asserting the state secrets privilege to bar the courts from inquiring into the program in any way that would reveal whether the plaintiffs' communications had been intercepted. After a court of appeals dismissed the most prominent case because of the state secrets privilege, the Supreme Court declined to review the decision.[89] Once again the privilege had put the courts on the sidelines as potential overseers of sensitive national security surveillance.

WAS THE TSP LEGAL?

With the known operational details and controversies about the TSP in mind, let us turn to the legal arguments surrounding the program. The centerpiece of the administration's defense of the program is the Justice Department's white paper. This forty-two-page document appears on the department's letterhead but is unsigned by any official. The more conventional practice of issuing a legal opinion by the attorney general or by OLC might have had two perceived disadvantages. First, doing so would have focused political responsibility and criticism on one officer, after the department had suffered serious internal schisms over the program. A memo from the department might have been intended to show unity and to smooth over those difficulties.

Second, as its title implies, the white paper is an advocacy document defending a program that had become bitterly controversial. The paper reads like a litigation brief. It argues for the TSP and expresses few doubts or reservations. It is rather wordy and repetitive—indicia of hurried composition. As an informal document, it could later be abandoned in whole or part with less embarrassment than would attend the retraction of a formal departmental opinion. As we have seen, formal opinions ordinarily adopt a tone of dispassionate analysis and attempt to bind the executive branch as a whole. They are not well suited to a brawl.

The white paper surely reflects the arguments in the secret opinions.[90] It likely differs from those opinions in three ways. First, it carefully avoids giving any details about sensitive operations. This characteristic deprives the paper of much of its potential force, because the department had to assert rather than to show necessity for the program. Consequently, reactions to the paper have tended to reflect the degree of the reader's trust in the Bush administration. Second, the paper smooths over differences between the first OLC opinion by John Yoo and the second by Jack Goldsmith. Because the tone of the paper is not very moderate, however, it may be that it owes more to the original approval of the program than to a modification that may have focused on secret operational details not discussed in the white paper. Third, it may have added new arguments that intervening events suggested. Unlike most formal opinions by the attorney general or the OLC, the paper was the product of an outside testing process that offered an opportunity to refine the department's position.

The testing process began a week after revelation of the TSP in the press, with a five-page letter to the chairs and ranking minority members of the congressional intelligence committees from the Justice Department's Office of Legislative Affairs. (Again, the authorship by the OLA suggested informality as compared to an OLC opinion.) The letter previews most of the arguments the white paper made later at much greater length. Its tone is quite confrontational. It begins by quoting the president's assertions that the TSP is "crucial to our national security," and that leaking classified information "is illegal, alerts our enemies, and endangers our country." After claiming that the president has both constitutional and statutory authority for the TSP (from Article II and the AUMF), the letter concludes that FISA "could not have provided the speed and agility required for the early warning detection system. In addition, any legislative change . . . would have been public and would have tipped off our enemies" about the program.

The department's letter received two immediate responses. First, the fourteen law professors and former government officials wrote their open letter to congressional leaders, refuting the arguments in the OLA letter.[91] Another set of bad grades appeared when the Congressional Research Service (CRS) of the Library of Congress, an entity known for its high-quality and nonpartisan legal analysis, contributed a long memorandum critiquing the OLA letter and the legal basis for the program generally.[92] CRS concluded that "the Administration's legal justification . . . does not seem to be as well-grounded as the tenor of that letter suggests." Hence, there was plenty of grist for the legal mill at the Justice Department, and plenty of warning that the program was under legal assault.

Ironically, both the tone and the analytic strategy of the public white paper closely resemble the confidential advice memoranda that were generated before the fact in the other contexts I explore in this book: detention, interrogation, and trial of terrorist suspects. (It is, however, less extreme than some of the secret opinions, for example John Yoo's early *Constitutional Authority* or the "torture memo" to be reviewed in a later chapter.) Somewhere a blurring of the line between analysis and advocacy had occurred. It is appropriate for a lawyer to say to a client: "Don't do that. . . . What? You've already done it? All right, I'll defend you as best I can." That might explain the white paper, but it does not account for the paper's similarity to the other opinions.

In addressing the principal legal issues concerning the war on terrorism, including those surrounding NSA surveillance, the administration's lawyers followed a four-part strategy. It was designed to maximize executive power at the expense of the other two branches and of individual rights. Here is its architecture:

Step One: set the analytic framework. The memos always emphasize the foreign and wartime aspects of the situation and downplay the domestic or criminal law aspects. The reason for this slant is obvious, because legal precedents involving foreign policy and war are substantially more forgiving to the executive branch than are precedents most lawyers view as primarily domestic. Step Two: interpret the president's constitutional powers *very* broadly, in a way that identifies no limits to them, and interpret possible constitutional restrictions very narrowly. Now the Constitution is on the president's side. Step Three: take the same approach with statutes. That is, interpret statutes that authorize executive action very broadly and statutes that limit executive action very narrowly. And Step Four: fire the canon! That is, invoke the lawyer's "avoidance canon" of construction, which calls for reading statutes in ways that avoid constitutional difficulties.[93] Combining the avoidance canon with a broad interpretation of the executive's constitutional powers casts a wide shadow across the meaning of statutes. Combining all four elements of the strategy makes legal constraints disappear.

This four-part strategy fundamentally lacked the requisites of right and conscience. Its approach to legal doctrine often featured statements of extreme positions with little support in available legal materials. The existence of strong contrary precedents was usually not acknowledged, as the dictates of conscience should have required. The result was consistently bad advice.

The administration's white paper proceeds as follows. First, predictably, it emphasizes the purpose of the TSP "to detect and prevent another catastrophic terrorist attack on the United States." Therefore, the TSP focuses on international communications of persons linked to terrorist organizations. Interception is authorized only if there is a "reasonable basis" to conclude that one party to the communication is affiliated with terrorists. The paper stresses that NSA has to move quickly to identify threats and characterizes FISA as better suited for "long-term monitoring." The paper also notes that Al Qaeda ignores borders, that its members resided in the United States for months before 9/11, and that the organization has explicitly threatened more attacks on the United States.

None of this introductory material is controversial. Its purpose is to invoke the legal authorities for wartime and foreign affairs actions: "The NSA activities are supported by the President's well-recognized inherent constitutional authority as Commander in Chief and sole organ for the Nation in foreign affairs to conduct warrantless surveillance of enemy forces for intelligence purposes to detect and disrupt armed attacks on the United States." This analytic move, however, masks a vitally important question implied by the president's own recognition that the war on terrorism requires a "new paradigm" of analysis. *To what extent* should precedents drawn from traditional wars or wholly foreign activities be used to justify actions taken in a shadowy and long-running "war" of a nontraditional kind, one that flows routinely over international borders traditional legal analysis respected? There is no consensus about the answer to that question; the white paper evades addressing it.

There are several reasons why war and foreign affairs receive relaxed legal scrutiny. Wide executive discretion is often necessary. Congress finds it difficult to legislate intelligently in fluid situations. The courts often lack effective jurisdiction or the facts necessary to exercise review. The civil liberties of U.S. citizens are less frequently involved. Many of these factors pertain to the war on terrorism, but in unusual ways. Consider the TSP. There certainly existed an international component to the program that called for executive discretion. Indeed, in that realm, NSA had traditionally operated under little constraint. Yet there was also a domestic component that implicated the civil liberties of Americans. Spurred by a pattern of abuse of those liberties, Congress had legislated to control electronic surveillance. The courts might find themselves on familiar ground to the extent that criminal law analogies to the program seemed pertinent. Yet the courts also risked entering the swamp of reviewing state secrets and surveillance of foreign communications. Articulating the new paradigm was obviously difficult. The paper should have made some steps, perhaps tentative ones, toward doing so.

In the second step of its analysis, the department argues that Article II of the Constitution grants the president inherent powers of surveillance to detect threats to the nation. The *core* of this idea is surely correct. The Constitution is, as often noted, not a suicide pact.[94] Every U.S. president has believed the duties of his oath extend to protecting the nation, not just its Constitution.[95] (Recall the famous statements to this effect by Jefferson and Lincoln.) Suppose, for example, that in the first week of December 1941, Franklin Roosevelt had asked the navy if it would try to locate the missing Japanese aircraft carriers (they were then steaming toward Hawaii). No one would have asked FDR what his authority was to make that inquiry. Also, the failure of the Bush administration to detect the 9/11 plot has been widely criticized. Where responsibility lies, the power to act must exist as well. But what are the *limits* to this power? Conceding that some inherent executive power exists provides little guidance for answering that question.

The white paper cites *Curtiss-Wright's* endorsement of John Marshall's famous characterization of the president as the "sole organ of the nation" in foreign affairs. The paper does not pause to note the ambiguity in this phrase—whether it means only that the president speaks for the nation, which no one doubts today, or whether it implies exclusive executive power to determine the content of our foreign policy as well. The context of Marshall's remark did not support the latter meaning; nor did any question actually presented for decision in *Curtiss-Wright*.

Having lifted the Marshall quote from its context (as had the Supreme Court), the paper also cites the case for its recognition of the structural advantages of the executive over Congress in foreign affairs: "unity, secrecy, and dispatch," as the Constitution's framers described them. From these advantages the white paper draws the conclusion that the framers "intended that the President would have the primary responsibility and necessary authority as Commander in Chief and Chief Executive to protect the Nation and to conduct the Nation's foreign affairs." That is quite a leap. The structural advantages certainly imply a broad power of initiative for the executive in the foreign realm. They do not necessarily imply "primary responsibility" in the sense that Congress may not control presidential actions involving other nations. Moreover, the Constitution's explicit inclusion of numerous authorities relating to foreign affairs and war among the powers of Congress refutes such an argument.

After invoking *Curtiss-Wright*, the white paper adds a citation to the *Prize Cases*, in which the Supreme Court considered a challenge to Lincoln's naval blockade of the Confederacy.[96] The Court held that whether the rebellion justified the blockade was a question for the president to decide. The paper says that this case confirms that "the Constitution grants the President inherent powers to protect the Nation from foreign attack." Later on, the paper quotes the *Prize Cases* for the proposition that when the nation is attacked, the president is "bound to resist force by force" and "must determine what degree of force the crisis demands" without waiting for Congress to convene and deliberate.

Once again, the paper takes widely accepted principles and extends them to this new context without careful analysis of their applicability. Lincoln's extraordinary actions at the outset of the Civil War, when he confronted a domestic threat on a scale unapproached before or since, should not be treated as automatic precedents for crises less grave in nature. The Supreme Court's endorsement of Lincoln's actions does support the existence of some presidential power to identify and respond to emergent threats, foreign or domestic. But it does not bless everything a president might wish to do. Instead, context always matters.

Having rested its constitutional arguments mainly on two Supreme Court precedents of only indirect relevance, the department sought to bolster its case by asserting that a "consistent understanding" has developed that presidents may conduct warrantless surveillance for foreign intelligence purposes. The paper briefly reviews presidential actions beginning with FDR's approval of wiretaps in 1940, noting that even after the enactment of FISA, presidential advisers were unwilling to concede the absence of any inherent constitutional authority. The president's lawyers rarely make such concessions in any context (although they did so at the time of the enactment of FISA). The paper does not acknowledge that much of the historical surveillance was hidden from both Congress and the people, and that after it was discovered, Congress legislated to control it. This is not a pattern of congressional acquiescence that adds support to the legality of presidential action.

The president's lawyers are usually unwilling to articulate any limits to "inherent" powers, fearing that their words will be cited against them someday. In that tradition, it is unsurprising that the white paper would not state any limits to the constitutional power claimed. (Of course, because the issue concerns an inherent power not based on any constitutional text, it is difficult to articulate limits in any natural way.) The paper does stress that all three branches routinely employ a distinction between foreign and domestic intelligence. It does not discuss the fact, however, that the TSP (and the terrorist threat more generally) blurs that distinction fundamentally. From this part of the paper's analysis, it would be difficult to say what limit to executive power its authors perceive, beyond the need for the president to think an action necessary, and that is no effective limit at all.

The paper considers a specific constitutional constraint: the Fourth Amendment, which protects our rights against unreasonable searches and seizures by the government.[97] Having expanded Article II, the white paper shrinks the Fourth Amendment by understating the force of its warrant requirement. The paper does not contest the settled law that electronic surveillance comes within the ambit of the amendment's protection. Instead, the paper connects arguments based on national security necessity to the amendment's ultimate reasonableness standard and stresses cases allowing exceptions to the warrant requirement where there are "special needs" to do so. Surely national security necessity *does* relate to reasonableness; the question is how far to press the point.

If the TSP were a wide-scale and unconstrained rummaging through the contents of the domestic communications of Americans, it might fail the reasonableness test. Available information about the program, however, does not raise that specter. It appears that contents of communications have been examined by humans only once there is some sign of terrorist affiliation, as detected by NSA's watchlists. The Supreme Court tests reasonableness in part by asking whether a person has a "reasonable expectation of privacy" regarding the subject matter of a challenged search. It has held that we have such expectations for our homes and the content of our electronic communications with others, but not for computerized information we make public in some way, such as our telephone numbers and credit card billing records. NSA appears to have relied on this distinction in constructing the TSP and to have held it within the bounds of general reasonableness. The authors of the white paper would not discuss the details of the program in ways that would have confirmed this conclusion, but it appears they could have done so.

Regarding the general reasonableness standard, the white paper quotes the Supreme Court's usual test, which requires "assessing, on the one hand, the degree to which [a search] intrudes upon an individual's privacy and, on the other, the degree to which it is needed for the promotion of legitimate governmental interests."[98] Conceding that intercepting the contents of communications "implicates a significant privacy interest of the individual," the paper urges that the government's interest "is the most compelling interest possible—securing the Nation from foreign attack in the midst of an armed conflict." Therefore, it is constitutionally reasonable to invade the privacy right when there is, as the TSP requires, a "reasonable basis" to find a terrorist connection to the communication. The paper also mentions the international focus of the program again to buttress its limited nature and the need for effective surveillance. This part of the white paper's argument is on solid ground. The TSP appears to meet the constitutional reasonableness test for the reasons the department advances.

Even if a search is constitutionally reasonable, however, it must have a warrant or must meet an exception to the warrant requirement. The white paper does not pause to ask a question the Supreme Court routinely asks in Fourth Amendment cases: whether authorization by a neutral magistrate— the basis underlying the warrant idea—is a feasible control needed to prevent abuses of executive discretion. To address that issue, let us consider Justice Powell's analysis in the *Keith* case, in which the Supreme Court extended the warrant requirement to domestic national security searches. If one substitutes the words "foreign intelligence" for "national security" in the following passage, a powerful argument for some form of warrant requirement emerges:[99]

Fourth Amendment freedoms cannot properly be guaranteed if domestic security surveillances may be conducted solely within the discretion of the Executive Branch. The Fourth Amendment does not contemplate the executive officers of Government as neutral and disinterested magistrates. Their duty and responsibility are to enforce the laws, to investigate, and to prosecute. But those charged with this investigative and prosecutorial duty should not be the sole judges of when to utilize constitutionally sensitive means in pursuing their tasks. The historical judgment, which the Fourth Amendment accepts, is that unreviewed executive discretion may yield too readily to pressures to obtain incriminating evidence and overlook potential invasions of privacy and protected speech. . . .

It is true that there have been some exceptions to the warrant requirement. But those exceptions are few in number and carefully delineated. . . .

The Government argues that the special circumstances applicable to domestic security surveillances necessitate a further exception to the warrant requirement. It is urged that the requirement of prior judicial review would obstruct the President in the discharge of his constitutional duty to protect domestic security. We are told further that these surveillances are directed primarily to the collecting and maintaining of intelligence with respect to subversive forces, and are not an attempt to gather evidence for specific criminal prosecutions. . . .

The Government further insists that courts "as a practical matter would have neither the knowledge nor the techniques necessary to determine whether there was probable cause to believe that surveillance was necessary to protect national security." These security problems, the Government contends, involve "a large number of complex and subtle factors" beyond the competence of courts to evaluate. As a final reason for exemption from a warrant requirement, the Government believes that disclosure to a magistrate of all or even a significant portion of the information involved in domestic security surveillances "would create serious potential dangers to the national security and to the lives of informants and agents." . . .

The circumstances described do not justify complete exemption of domestic security surveillance from prior judicial scrutiny. Official surveillance, whether its purpose be criminal investigation or ongoing intelligence gathering, risks infringement of constitutionally protected privacy of speech. Security surveillances are especially sensitive because of the inherent vagueness of the domestic security concept, the necessarily broad and continuing nature of intelligence gathering, and the temptation to utilize such surveillances to oversee political dissent. We recognize, as we have before, the constitutional basis of the President's domestic security role, but we think it must be exercised in a manner compatible with the Fourth Amendment. In this case we hold that this requires an appropriate prior warrant procedure.

We cannot accept the Government's argument that internal security matters are too subtle and complex for judicial evaluation. Courts regularly deal with the most difficult issues of our society. . . . Certainly courts can recognize that domestic security surveillance involves different considerations from the surveillance of "ordinary crime." If the threat is too subtle or complex for our senior law enforcement officers to convey its significance to a court, one may question whether there is probable cause for surveillance.

Nor do we believe prior judicial approval will fracture the secrecy essential to official intelligence gathering. The investigation of criminal activity has long involved imparting sensitive information to judicial officers who have respected the confidentialities involved. Judges may be counted upon to be especially conscious of security requirements in national security cases. . . . Moreover, a warrant application involves no public or adversary proceedings: it is an *ex parte* request before a magistrate or judge. . . .

Thus, we conclude that the Government's concerns do not justify departure in this case from the customary Fourth Amendment requirement of judicial approval prior to initiation of a search or surveillance. Although some added burden will be imposed upon the Attorney General, this inconvenience is justified in a free society to protect constitutional values. . . . By no means of least importance will be the reassurance of the public generally that indiscriminate wiretapping and bugging of law-abiding citizens cannot occur.

Application of Justice Powell's traditional and powerful arguments for the warrant requirement to the context of the TSP requires surmounting an obvious objection: foreign intelligence is different from domestic national security investigations. The potential differences are that the government's necessity arguments may be both stronger and harder for a judge to evaluate and that the international component of the targeted communications reduces both the impact on U.S. citizens and their expectations of privacy. To some extent, these are real differences, but they seem unlikely to be dispositive. Domestic terrorism is no slight danger after Oklahoma City. Also, the technological blurring of boundaries in modern communications erodes bright legal lines between domestic and international messages, both of which can easily be caught in the same net.

More important, by enacting FISA, Congress accepted Justice Powell's invitation in *Keith* to legislate concerning the need for warrants in foreign intelligence. The presence of FISA's warrant requirement demonstrates that Congress accepted the Court's basic rationale about the value of a check external to the executive branch. And the altered standard of probable cause for foreign intelligence, that the target be an agent of a foreign power, recognizes the difference from domestic law enforcement. This constitutional compromise gave all three branches a role in foreign intelligence: "The basis for this legislation is the understanding—concurred in by the Attorney General—that even if the President has an 'inherent' constitutional power to authorize warrantless surveillance for foreign intelligence purposes, Congress has the power to regulate the exercise of this authority by legislating a reasonable warrant procedure governing foreign intelligence surveillance."[100]

In 1978, Congress was responding to proven abuses of surveillance authority by NSA.[101] Concerns that the sins of the past will be repeated should never be dismissed—they must be answered.

Instead of grappling with Justice Powell's rationale in *Keith* and its acceptance by Congress in enacting FISA, the white paper discusses the "special needs" exception to the usual criminal law warrant requirement.[102] Where the purpose of a search differs from ordinary crime control, for example inspections in the public schools and by the border patrol, the Court has approved the exception. Since the TSP does not focus on criminal prosecution, the argument for a special needs exception is plausible, and the paper presents it plausibly. Yet this is a straw man. The warrants in controversy are FISA warrants, which do not require probable cause to believe a crime has been committed, the familiar criminal standard. Instead, the relaxed standard of FISA is itself an example of a justifiable special needs exception to the ordinary constitutional standard, but one that modifies warrant requirements rather than discarding them entirely. This part of the paper's argument, then, is simply a minor distraction from the statutory arguments to which I now turn.

The third step in the analysis is statutory authority. The white paper argues that Congress provided statutory authorization for the TSP when it enacted the AUMF in the wake of 9/11.[103] The preamble to the AUMF states that "the President has authority under the Constitution to take action to deter and prevent acts of international terrorism against the United States," and that it is necessary for the United States "to protect its citizens both at home and abroad." Its core provision, section 2(a), provides that the president may "use all necessary and appropriate force against those nations, organizations, or persons he determines planned, authorized, committed, or aided the terrorist attacks that occurred on September 11, 2001, or harbored such organizations or persons, in order to prevent any future acts of international terrorism against the United States by such nations, organizations, or persons."

The AUMF is the legal equivalent of a declaration of war against Al Qaeda and its allies.[104] It certainly provides the necessary authority for the military action in Afghanistan that followed its enactment. Its legal effect within the United States or in the borderland occupied by the TSP, however, is less clear. Neither the AUMF nor its legislative history mentions surveillance, only military action against Al Qaeda and its supporters.[105] Still, there is no geographic limitation in the authorization, and protection of the homeland—the concern shared by all Americans—would have been a clearly implied purpose even if the preamble had not mentioned it. Just before the Senate vote on the AUMF, White House officials tried to insert "in the United States" in the authorizing language to grant internal war powers, but the Senate refused to accept the amendment.[106] From this rather murky history, it seems best to conclude that the AUMF draws no bright line between the domestic and international spheres, but that Congress has not abandoned its traditional caution about granting the executive sweeping domestic powers in wartime.

The white paper argues that surveillance is a "traditional and fundamental incident of war," and hence is among the powers granted by the AUMF. The paper draws this test from *Hamdi v. Rumsfeld*,[107] in which the Supreme Court decided that the AUMF authorized the detention of a U.S. citizen captured in Afghanistan, notwithstanding an earlier statute that forbade the detention of citizens without statutory authority. The possible parallel to the interrelation of AUMF and FISA is evident. If the authority to use military force implies the power to detain prisoners captured on the battlefield, the same authority could easily imply the power to search out the enemy. As the department's initial letter from OLA put it, "we cannot fight a war blind." This argument treats the AUMF as effectively amending FISA and providing the president direct statutory authority, placing him in the strongest legal position he can occupy.

There are two responses to the white paper's reliance on *Hamdi*. First, the Court was careful to restrict its holding to the detention of citizens captured in the theater of war in Afghanistan.[108] It is a long way from there to communications switches in the United States. Second, the statutory pattern in the two contexts differs. Before proceeding to those issues, I speculate that although *Hamdi* was decided years after the TSP was initiated, the department's original justification for the TSP was probably very similar to the way the white paper frames the issue. Asking whether an action is a "fundamental incident" of war, in *Hamdi*'s phrasing, is like asking whether the AUMF implies authority to conduct any war-related activity such as surveillance against the enemy.

Gathering intelligence is closely related to the successful conduct of any war, especially a war against shadowy terrorists. Surely the AUMF authorizes surveillance in the theater of combat in Afghanistan, but how far beyond that? The Congress that speedily enacted the AUMF was focused on pursuing Al Qaeda in the wake of 9/11. Congress does not appear to have given a moment's consideration to how this effort would work with FISA. In the absence of any specific evidence of congressional intent regarding the interrelation of these two statutes, the white paper invokes general principles, the canons of construction.

As we have seen, the canons are principles for interpreting legal texts. Although their use is a standard gambit for lawyers, their manipulability is notorious—often, contradictory canons can be invoked in a given context.[109] The NSA controversy provides fresh proof of the indeterminacy of the canons. The white paper declares: "In the field of foreign affairs, and particularly that of war powers and national security, congressional enactments are to be broadly construed where they indicate support for authority long asserted and exercised by the Executive Branch."[110] This is a perfectly sound principle (for which *Dames & Moore* can be cited), but there are two problems with applying it to the TSP. First, the program intermixed domestic and civil liberties concerns with its international and security purposes. Second, warrantless electronic surveillance had a rather thin and contested legal pedigree even before FISA.[111]

In response to the department's canon, the scholars' letter fires its own: "The DOJ's argument rests on an unstated general 'implication' from the AUMF that directly contradicts *express* and *specific* language in FISA. Specific and 'carefully drawn' statutes prevail over general statutes where there is a conflict."[112] This canon is more closely relevant to the controversy than the one favored by the department. It reflects the sensible conclusion that a statute that addresses a problem should control a later one that addresses a different, but related problem. FISA is certainly a direct attempt to control NSA surveillance in order to stop known executive abuses.

The FISA Congress understood that it was not providing the last word on NSA surveillance. It anticipated future wartime situations by allowing fifteen days of warrantless surveillance after a declaration of war, to give Congress time to adjust the statute as needed.[113] FISA also forbade anyone to conduct electronic surveillance "except as authorized by statute."[114] The scholars think that these provisions require any amendment to FISA to be explicit. The Justice Department argues that the latter provision contemplates that FISA might be amended by any later statute, not solely one that specifically addresses surveillance. I think there is enough interpretive room in these two fragments of the statute to allow a conclusion that a later statute has amended FISA without saying so, but that a stronger case needs to be made for that conclusion than the sketchy history of the AUMF provided.

To summarize the appropriate limit to argument by implication in the presence of a statutory restriction, the scholars quote Justice Frankfurter's opinion in the *Steel Seizure* case:[115]

It is one thing to draw an intention of Congress from general language and to say that Congress would have explicitly written what is inferred, where Congress has not addressed itself to a specific situation. It is quite impossible, however, when Congress did specifically address itself to a problem, as Congress did to that of seizure, to find secreted in the interstices of legislation the very grant of power which Congress consciously withheld. To find authority so explicitly withheld is . . . to disrespect the whole legislative process and the constitutional division of authority between President and Congress.

To this, the scholars added yet another canon, which was really just another way of asserting that relatively specific statutes usually trump relatively general ones:

The DOJ's argument would require the conclusion that Congress implicitly and *sub silentio* repealed the provision that identifies FISA and specific criminal code provisions as "the *exclusive* means by which electronic surveillance . . . may be conducted."[116] Repeals by implication are strongly disfavored; they can be established only by "overwhelming evidence," and " 'the only permissible justification for a repeal by implication is when the earlier and later statutes are irreconcilable.' "[117] The AUMF and [this provision of FISA] are not irreconcilable, and there is *no* evidence, let alone overwhelming evidence, that Congress intended to repeal [FISA].

These are strong arguments. The white paper responds with several undoubtedly important but somewhat indirect considerations: the breadth of the grant of power in the AUMF, the unprecedented nature of the crisis it addressed, the relation of surveillance to the effective conduct of any military campaign, and the use of surveillance by presidents in more conventional wars throughout U.S. history. These factors lead the department to argue that "the absence of any specific reference to signals intelligence activities in the [AUMF] is immaterial." No, not immaterial, but not decisive either.

The paper then argues that Congress, reacting in haste to 9/11, did not feel a need "to attempt to catalog every specific aspect of the use of the forces it was authorizing and every potential preexisting statutory limitation on the Executive Branch." That is correct, and Congress usually does revisit the statutes granting emergency powers when it authorizes military action. After 9/11, it made an effort to adjust the statutes by enacting the PATRIOT Act, which amended FISA without addressing the question of the TSP. At that time, the administration's failure to deal with the authority problem under FISA was not sufficiently respectful of FISA. Congress had done all it could to control electronic surveillance. The white paper's reliance on the ambiguities of the AUMF is not enough to justify the TSP.

But wait! Shoot the canon! In the fourth step of the analysis, the white paper goes on to argue that FISA would be unconstitutional if applied to the TSP. Therefore, FISA should not be read to attempt to constrain the president's inherent constitutional powers to conduct surveillance:

> If an otherwise acceptable construction of a statute would raise serious constitutional problems, and where an alternative interpretation of the statute is "fairly possible," we are obligated to construe the statute to avoid such problems.[118] Moreover, the canon of constitutional avoidance has particular importance in the realm of national security, where the President's constitutional authority is at its highest.[119] Thus, courts and the Executive Branch typically construe a general statute, even one that is written in unqualified terms, to be implicitly limited so as not to infringe on the President's Commander in Chief powers.

The white paper invokes two different versions of the avoidance canon: a stronger one "whether . . . signals intelligence collection . . . is such a core exercise of Commander in Chief [power] that Congress cannot interfere with it at all" and a weaker one "whether the particular restrictions imposed by FISA . . . would impermissibly impede" exercise of the president's constitutional power.[120] The strong version would forbid any version of FISA; the weaker one would invalidate some or all of its core provisions.

The strong canon has potentially breathtaking scope—it might trump almost any statute when national security can plausibly be invoked. Even the weak one presents special dangers when employed by the executive branch.[121] The courts use the canon to minimize resort to their own great power of final constitutional interpretation. By choosing a statutory interpretation that avoids constitutional decisionmaking, they leave power with the political branches, which may then redo the statute if they so desire. But when the executive invokes the canon to support a favored statutory interpretation, the effect is to aggrandize executive power at the expense of congressional power to control it.

The white paper's argument for the strong version of the canon begins with the claim that "the NSA activities lie at the very core of the Commander in Chief power." In contrast, the source and scope of congressional power to restrict this authority is "unclear." Here the paper invokes the extreme *Timely Notification* memorandum from the time of Iran-Contra, arguing that the clause in Article II vesting executive power in the president "has long been held to confer on the President plenary authority to represent the United States and to pursue its interests outside the borders of the country, subject only to limits specifically set forth in the Constitution itself and to such statutory limitations as the Constitution permits Congress to impose by exercising one of its enumerated powers." In other words, executive power is to be interpreted broadly, congressional power narrowly.

Although OLC has sometimes echoed the extreme stance of the *Timely Notification* opinion, it has also taken a more restrained approach that concedes the sharing of powers between the branches for foreign policy and war.[122] The white paper selects the strand of OLC analysis it favors, ignoring rather than answering the strand it disfavors. The Supreme Court is often guilty of shabby treatment of its own precedents, but that does not make such a practice a virtue.

The white paper argues that judicial precedents support the strong version of the avoidance canon. It distinguishes *Steel Seizure* as an essentially domestic case that involved the explicit powers of Congress. After this oversimplification, and following a ritual bow in the direction of *Curtiss-Wright,* the paper goes on to cite a dictum in the one case that had been decided by the special court of review set up by FISA. In a controversy that actually involved the Justice Department's "wall" between intelligence gathering and criminal prosecution, the court said that "the President did have inherent authority to conduct warrantless searches to obtain foreign intelligence information."[123] The court then concluded that, "assuming that is so, FISA could not encroach on the President's constitutional power." Not necessarily—this statement conflates shared with exclusive power.

Proceeding to the weaker version of the canon, the paper relies on the president's determination "that the speed and agility required to carry out the NSA activities successfully could not have been achieved under FISA." The department declined to support this assertion with facts about the program, because it would not reveal them. Hence, it was reduced to noting "certain technological changes" since FISA. As we have seen, enough is known about the technology and the TSP to confirm that the problem of compliance with FISA was serious. The department, unable to defend this part of its position in any detail, could only ask the reader to take its word for the need to invoke the canon.

To these arguments the fourteen scholars make two responses. First, they assert that the statutory scheme is not sufficiently ambiguous to justify invoking the canon in any form.[124] Second, they argue that the canon should be used—if at all—in a fashion opposite to that urged by the department. That is, FISA should be applied in order to avoid a serious constitutional problem posed by the Fourth Amendment! When the smoke clears from all these canon blasts, we are left with two conflicting constitutional arguments and two conflicting statutory arguments. It is preferable to consider them directly rather than to manipulate them with the canons.

Overall, the white paper's strategic approach would bless almost any presidential action, whatever the particular constitutional and statutory context. Although the paper has received sharp criticism since its issuance, the administration has never repudiated it.[125] John Yoo's defense of the TSP in his memoir reflects and amplifies the arguments in the paper.[126] He argues that FISA "does not meet today's challenge," which is not bugging embassies but sorting through billions of innocent communications. He perceives "two distinct legal regimes," crime and war. FISA creates a safe harbor for criminal prosecution, he says, and "if a President chooses to rely on his constitutional authority alone to conduct warrantless searches, then he should use the information only for military purposes."[127] Intercepting the enemy has always been central to military intelligence, he notes. If we agree that the president can respond to attacks with force, why may he not gather intelligence? He cites FDR's precedent and finds authority in the AUMF: if you can kill terrorists, surely you can locate them.

Yoo believes that FISA risks judicial interference "with the operations of an independent and coordinate branch of government." Critics, he argues, "fail to understand that the Constitution grants the President the leading role in foreign affairs." After noting that Congress has "important powers," he concludes that "the Constitution nowhere vests in Congress any explicit authority to dominate national security policy, nor gives it an outright veto over executive decisions in the area." He stresses that "no one seems to doubt that the information gained from the NSA program has led to the prevention of al Qaeda plots against the United States," quoting NSA Director Hayden's statement that "this program has been successful in detecting and preventing attacks inside the United States."[128]

Yoo addresses the reasons why the administration would operate outside FISA after all of its work on drafting the PATRIOT Act. That statute, he says, assumes we know enough to tell when a target is an agent of a terrorist organization. This is a different challenge: we need to cast a wide net, to follow many leads quickly, to move fast on hunches. "In this high-tech world, FISA imposes slow and cumbersome procedures." His example is an Al Qaeda leader captured with a cell phone with U.S. numbers in its memory. Yoo thinks FISA would not give warrants for all those numbers, because we would not know whom they reached. He also notes FISA's lengthy review process, with special FBI and DOJ lawyers preparing a package of up to 100 pages to give the court, with certification of need by a high national security officer and the attorney general. The "real problem" with both FISA and the PATRIOT Act, he says, is that "they depend on individualized suspicion."

Yoo's distinction between criminal and military intelligence gathering undergirds his effort to avoid conceding noncompliance with FISA. But FISA's legislative history does not focus on criminal prosecutions. Rather, the scandal that gave rise to the statute involved repeated privacy violations that never led to criminal charges. The point of FISA was to control executive surveillance for national security purposes rather than to restrict criminal prosecutions. The long-standing controversy over the "wall" separating the two functions reveals that more than the rights of criminal defendants was at stake.

Recall that early in 2007, Attorney General Gonzales first indicated the administration had recently received an order from FISC conforming some of its activities to FISC authorization, and later said that it would operate entirely within the realm of the statute.[129] If the program could eventually be brought within the FISA framework, it is unclear why it could not have been designed initially to comply with the statute. The fifteen-day wartime exception for warrantless surveillance in FISA would have provided the administration some time to seek authority for the program from the FISC, Congress, or both. Even if this very short deadline had been missed, as surely it would have been, the executive would have been in closer compliance with its statutory obligations.[130]

The Bush administration's defenses of the TSP often stress the emergency nature of the program at its inception. An emergency there was, and every benefit of the doubt should be given to the judgments about the initial need to conduct warrantless surveillance. The critical imponderable is *time*— what was at first within any version of the president's inherent constitutional power to protect the nation could not stay so forever. How long? No one can say, but a period of years is too long. Justice Jackson's great opinion in *Steel Seizure* contains some pertinent wisdom:

> The appeal . . . that we declare the existence of inherent powers *ex necessitate* to meet an emergency asks us to do what many think would be wise, although it is something the forefathers omitted. They knew what emergencies were, knew the pressures they engender for authoritative action, knew, too, how they afford a ready pretext for usurpation. We may also suspect that they suspected that emergency powers would tend to kindle emergencies. Aside from suspension of the privilege of the writ of habeas corpus in time of rebellion or invasion, when the public

safety may require it, they made no express provision for exercise of extraordinary authority because of a crisis. I do not think we rightfully may so amend their work, and, if we could, I am not convinced it would be wise to do so. . . . Contemporary foreign experience may be inconclusive as to the wisdom of lodging emergency powers somewhere in a modern government. But it suggests that emergency powers are consistent with free government only when their control is lodged elsewhere than in the Executive who exercises them. That is the safeguard that would be nullified by our adoption of the "inherent powers" formula. Nothing in my experience convinces me that such risks are warranted by any real necessity, although such powers would, of course, be an executive convenience.[131]

The white paper does not adequately justify the TSP. The paper overstates executive power, understates congressional power, and excuses noncompliance with FISA for unpersuasive reasons. It nowhere admits the considerable difficulties with the analysis it employs. Perhaps that is understandable in an advocacy document, but it would not have been responsible in the initial provision of advice about the program.

A SECOND DRAFT

What *should* have been the advice to the president? Here is an outline. I will use the elements of the white paper. Step One: the analytic situation. We *are* in a new paradigm, as President Bush said early in 2002. The war on terrorism has fundamentally blurred comfortable old categories of actions that are foreign versus those that are domestic. To approach this new world, we should reject a simple foreign/domestic distinction and analyze precedents that may be drawn from both contexts, without clean lines to aid our analysis. Related to this perception is the doctrinal assumption I have been urging: that the other two branches, Congress and the courts, have a legitimate claim to participate in deciding what will happen, through their powers as conventionally understood.

Step Two: the Constitution. Neither Congress nor the executive branch has an explicit textual right to control foreign intelligence collection. Although there is a strong claim to some form of inherent executive power to conduct surveillance of the nation's potential enemies, its contours are so cloudy that executive advisers should not readily advance arguments that this power is exclusive of Congress's to regulate it. Hence, FISA is valid on its face, but might not be in some applications. Caution is requisite in extending general wartime precedents, whether from executive practice or judicial decisions, to the war on terrorism. Both the Fourth Amendment and the policy behind the warrant requirement must be accorded their due scope. In the face of constitutional tension between executive authority and civil liberties, a statutory solution is preferable to a raw assertion of power. Fortunately, one is available.

Step Three: the statutes. The AUMF cannot be read fairly to amend FISA, in part because statutes meant specifically to curb executive abuses should not casually be disregarded. Instead, FISA is the governing statute and must be dealt with. How can security needs be accommodated to amending FISA? There are two ways to accomplish that goal.

First, a substantive amendment to FISA need not compromise national security to any appreciable degree. Any terrorist who is smart enough to be dangerous knows that the United States has an agency that tries to intercept threatening communications. What we must conceal from them is *how* we search. Therefore, a bit of statutory ambiguity and obfuscation is needed. In the AUMF or the USA PATRIOT Act or elsewhere, add a vague provision that is styled in public, if mentioned at all, a "technical amendment." It could simply say, as the 2007 statute authorizing the TSP eventually did, that FISA's definition of electronic surveillance subject to the warrant requirement does not include "surveillance directed at a person reasonably believed to be located outside of the United States."[132] Even vaguer language could suffice to notify Congress that FISA was being modified.[133] In secret, inform the intelligence committees of the full scope of the TSP. That would provide substantive authority for the program.

Second, if this approach be thought too dangerous in terms of risking leaks, at least ask Congress to appropriate the necessary funds for the program secretly. The United States has a long history of secret appropriations. In the Jefferson administration, the House voted secret funds in the amount of $2 million for an unspecified "expense" of the mission to France under James Monroe and Robert Livingston. It was to buy New Orleans; instead, they bought all of Louisiana![134] In more recent times, the atom bomb project in World War II involved the expenditure of more than $1 billion— real money in those days—all of it kept secret by distributing the money in smaller amounts in the giant wartime budgets of the War Department. Congress has done that ever since with the intelligence budget.[135] The details of intelligence spending are never publicly announced.[136] We do not know how much is allocated for what, for the obvious reason that there are many unfriendly people around the world who would like to know that also.

If either of these approaches had been taken, Step Four, there is no need to fire the canon. No statute needs be suppressed or disregarded. Instead of a stance that risks confrontation with both other branches, the executive can take one that involves Congress in forming and implementing national policy. And if the courts encounter litigation not barred by the state secrets privilege, they will stand on firm ground as they review fully authorized executive action and avoid the need to answer tricky constitutional questions. I think that this overall outcome would be stable, and that it is the one most consistent with the U.S. scheme of partly separated powers.

8

Indefinite Detention of Enemy Combatants

EVERY WAR PRODUCES PRISONERS; the war on terrorism has been no exception. Unlike most of our nation's prior wars, however, this one has raised a host of fundamental and difficult problems about the treatment of persons captured on the battlefield or elsewhere. The next five chapters consider these problems.

Al Qaeda and other terrorist organizations wear no uniforms—how are we to identify their members as distinguished from innocent bystanders? This shadowy war may last for many decades—how long can we hold our captives? Are they prisoners of war and therefore entitled to the protection of the Geneva Conventions—or are they something else? Al Qaeda's very purpose is to commit acts defined as war crimes, such as murdering civilians—should we prosecute some or all of their members for these crimes? If so, by what process—conventional criminal trial, court-martial, or military commission? An Al Qaeda fighter may have information about terrorist plots and will be unwilling to divulge it—what are the limits of permissible interrogation techniques to forestall future attacks? Prisons are notorious for their abuse of prisoners—how can our military prevent abuse of terrorist suspects?

As the United States began to gather prisoners after its entry into Afghanistan in late 2001, all of these questions urgently demanded answers. Both international and U.S. law offered guidance, although these two legal systems did not always point in the same direction, and neither one had been fully adjusted to deal with the uncertainties attending a war on terrorism. Clearly, our government's policymakers would need to rely on their lawyers for advice, and the lawyers would need all of the creativity and wisdom at their command.

Two of the administration's decisions in the immediate aftermath of 9/11 drove all of its answers to the legal questions about captives. First, President Bush launched a war against terrorism rather than a criminal investigation of murderers. Second, the administration immediately emphasized acquiring intelligence about terrorists and possible future attacks. Ironically, these decisions resulted in putting the civilians at the top of the administration at

odds with some of the nation's professional warriors and intelligence officers. This clash occurred because the civilians broke sharply from a number
of legal and policy traditions the professionals had embraced. The administration would accept only those normal legal consequences of war and
intelligence-gathering it favored, rejecting those it disliked.

The most prominent characteristic of the new paradigm that resulted was
reliance on unilateral executive power. The administration's strategy of reverse lawfare was very much in evidence and suffered several stinging de-
feats in the Supreme Court.

FINDING A LAW-FREE ZONE

An important initial question about prisoners was where to hold them. Both
legal and practical considerations affected the decision. John Yoo reports that
"after weeks of discussion between the Defense, State, and Justice Departments, the CIA, and the National Security Council," many prisoners were
sent to the U.S. Navy base at Guantánamo Bay, Cuba.[1] The base offered
two strong advantages. One was security. Surrounded by Cuba and largely
inaccessible except by navy transport, it would be escape proof and would
provide a difficult target for terrorist attempts to free prisoners or to strike
at their captors. The other advantage was legal status. Because the base was
on Cuban soil and was leased to the United States, it might be beyond the
habeas corpus jurisdiction of the federal courts.[2] If so, the prisoners could be
held indefinitely without legal recourse while the administration figured out
its long-term strategy regarding them. Because the base was not under any
other court system, it would be a law-free zone except for constraints that
apply to executive officers anywhere, such as military law.

By attempting to create a law-free zone, the administration was waging
reverse lawfare. A State Department lawyer working on issues about the legal rights of the prisoners was instructed that the War Council's goal was to
"find the legal equivalent of outer space," a "lawless" universe where prisoners would have no rights and U.S. courts could not intervene.[3] By trying
to avoid the legal hazards of federal court intervention, the administration
created another kind of legal hazard, which it either did not anticipate or did
not value. Law-free zones invite abuse of the weak by the strong. Our military
law strives to keep even theaters of combat from descending into lawless, brutal conditions and has had some impressive successes in that effort.

Conditions at Guantánamo, however, fostered abuse of prisoners in three
ways. First, the "detainees" were assigned an ambiguous legal status that

lacked the familiar rights of prisoners of war.[4] Second, the administration's pressure for intelligence and its willingness to approve harsh interrogation techniques risked systematized abuses, which soon occurred. And third, the absence of any expectation that outside monitors such as the federal courts or the U.S. press would police events at Guantánamo encouraged the captors to behave without restraint.

On December 28, 2001, John Yoo and his colleague Patrick Philbin issued a secret Office of Legal Counsel (OLC) opinion asserting that U.S. courts have no jurisdiction over aliens held at Guantánamo.[5] The *Habeas* opinion begins by noting the stakes involved: "If a federal district court were to take jurisdiction over a habeas petition, it could review the constitutionality of the detention and the use of a military commission, the application of certain treaty provisions, and perhaps even the legal status of Al Qaeda and Taliban members." These were not issues the administration wished any federal court to consider.

The opinion relies principally on *Johnson v. Eisentrager* (1950), in which Justice Jackson wrote an opinion for the Supreme Court holding that federal courts had no habeas corpus jurisdiction over some German soldiers who had been subjected to war crimes trials by military commissions after World War II.[6] Jackson emphasized that the Germans were enemy aliens who had been held and tried overseas and had never entered the territory of the United States. Accordingly, the *Habeas* opinion engages in a careful analysis of the legal status of Guantánamo and concludes that the base is not U.S. territory in any way that is likely to subject activities there to federal jurisdiction.

The *Habeas* opinion's analysis of the jurisdictional issues is quite clear and competent. But in 2004, in *Rasul v. Bush* the Supreme Court distinguished *Eisentrager* and held that Guantánamo is sufficiently controlled by the United States to subject the base to federal habeas corpus jurisdiction. In 2008, in *Boumediene v. Bush* the Court again distinguished *Eisentrager,* holding that Congress could not remove habeas jurisdiction over the base. These developments make the *Habeas* opinion a bad prediction, but it is not a bad opinion just because the Supreme Court later took the other side of a debatable jurisdictional issue. *Habeas* notes the presence of "some litigation risk" of a contrary result. More important, it carefully explains and analyzes the uncertainties that attend its own conclusions. It outlines some paths a court could (and the Supreme Court did) take to reach a contrary conclusion and responds to each one in a considered way. It lacks the tendentiousness and aggressiveness of Yoo's *Constitutional Authority* opinion of September 2001, features that other OLC opinions would soon display.

Reading *Habeas,* a policymaker in the Pentagon could make an informed decision about whether transporting prisoners to Cuba would be likely to bring them within the jurisdiction of the federal courts. There was adequate legal right for the opinion's conclusions at the time it was written. It also demonstrated good conscience in its recognition of and serious attention to contrary precedent.

There was another legal question, though, that OLC should have been asked or that it should have addressed on its own in the *Habeas* opinion. The sanctity of the writ of habeas corpus in Anglo-American law flows from the importance of its core purpose: to ensure that a prisoner can test the legal basis of his or her detention. The federal habeas statute requires the government both to show that detention does not violate the "Constitution or laws or treaties of the United States" and that it has a factual basis.[7] For two obvious reasons, the legality of keeping many of the captives was uncertain. First, because neither Al Qaeda nor Taliban fighters wore uniforms, it was not easy to separate them from the general population of Afghanistan. Second, no neutral process of any kind was being supplied to test the facts underlying their capture. Therefore, federal courts asked to grant habeas petitions for Guantánamo might look for ways to honor the ancient purpose of the writ for those held in U.S. custody. Also, federal due process doctrine might be deployed to test whether a basis existed for detention.

Ultimately, the Supreme Court used both of these techniques to review the basis for detentions. Perhaps it is an unacceptable use of hindsight to criticize OLC in 2001 for failing to anticipate what the Court would do in 2004 and 2008. Nevertheless, for two reasons, close attention to *Eisentrager* should have alerted OLC to the problems. First, the petitioners in that case had been uniformed German soldiers. No one doubted they were enemy combatants. Second, they had enjoyed fair process in their military commission trials. No one doubted that they had had an opportunity to contest the facts alleged against them. Neither of these conditions pertained to the suspected terrorist detainees. The fact that the Supreme Court would distinguish *Eisentrager* on just these grounds is not surprising. It appears that OLC was not explicitly asked the process question. Had the office raised the issue on its own, a detention program that could better withstand the outside scrutiny that eventually occurred might have been devised.

Deciding what process should be used to determine the detainees' status was at least as important as deciding how to prosecute them for war crimes. It was never likely that large numbers of captives—the foot soldiers of Al Qaeda and the Taliban—would be tried for war crimes. A major precedent in everyone's mind, Nuremberg, had prosecuted the politicians and the generals, not privates in the Wehrmacht (unless they personally committed atrocities). Instead, it was quite likely that persons captured and thought to be part of a terrorist organization would be held indefinitely as the "long war" against terrorism continued. Therefore, basic issues of human rights and individual freedom attended the initial decision to detain them. Some appropriate balance needed to be struck with national security. A captive too casually released might go on to strike at the United States; a captive too casually retained might lose his or her liberty for no reason.

When our legal system employs relatively elaborate procedures, as in criminal trials, the effect is to protect individual rights at substantial cost to executive discretion. When it employs relatively modest procedures, as in traffic court, the effect is to protect executive discretion at the cost of individual rights. We cannot have maximum protection for both governmental and individual interests at the same time. The trade-offs can be quite delicate. In making them, some models of overall procedure are more familiar to U.S. lawyers than are others. The common law tradition supposes that a trial featuring a judge, a jury, and the rules of evidence is the norm. Adherence to that norm requires little justification—even when it might be too elaborate—but departures from it engender suspicion. As a result, our legal system is skewed toward maximum procedure.

In a situation that seems to call for *minimum* procedure, a legal architect often finds that appropriate process models are lacking. A temptation may arise to foreswear procedural protections entirely out of fear that recognizing the need to ensure fairness will soon lead to adoption of some variant of the full common law model with its potential to shackle executive discretion. Prisoners in the war on terrorism encountered an administration that had yielded to this temptation and that was unwilling to take basic steps to verify that captives were actually dangerous to the United States.

The exact process due these prisoners held outside the United States would be a subject of controversy for years and the subject of several split decisions by the Supreme Court as well. Hence it would be unfair to say that there was a failure of right or conscience in a decision to furnish one level of process as opposed to another. Whatever the doubtfulness of the legal rights involved, however, it was not consistent with moral conscience to evade the issue entirely.

Two months after 9/11, President Bush issued a military order providing for detention of suspected terrorists and their subsequent trial for war crimes by military commissions.[8] This was an executive order, which is a technique presidents use to instruct their subordinates in the executive branch. Executive orders are based on any combination of constitutional and statutory authority thought to be available, and have been used for many purposes, such as promoting civil rights and fighting inflation.[9] In their sweeping effects, they often resemble statutes, as did Bush's military order. It rested on the president's constitutional power as commander in chief and on authority implied by some statutes including the AUMF. Like other executive orders, it was reviewed for legality by OLC, which approved it.

Most of the order's focus was on trial procedures, which I discuss later. Less prominently, the order also authorized the Defense Department to detain aliens when there was "reason to believe" they were members of Al Qaeda or other terrorist groups, and instructed the secretary to treat them "humanely," with "adequate food, drinking water, shelter, clothing, and medical care." The order did not prescribe any process for deciding who was a terrorist and who was not. Many of the detainees were held incommunicado for several years without any opportunity to challenge the grounds for their detention.[10] Some of them were U.S. citizens.

When habeas corpus petitions were filed to liberate the detainees, the government defended by asserting that the federal courts lacked jurisdiction over "enemy combatants" held outside the United States. The theory of OLC's early *Habeas* opinion, which had considered only aliens, was extended to citizens as well by referring to both as enemy combatants. The term has no significance in international law, but was used by the Supreme Court in *Ex Parte Quirin* (1942) to refer to the Nazi saboteurs, one of whom was a U.S. citizen.[11] The administration used the term both to mine *Quirin* for any support it might give and to steer clear of any terminology that would connote prisoner of war status for the captives.

The first prisoners arrived at Guantánamo in January 2002. The facility eventually held a maximum of about 900, a number that diminished over the years. Although Guantánamo was not the only facility holding U.S. prisoners, it received most of the attention until abuses at the Abu Ghraib prison in Iraq surfaced in 2004. Many of the administration's critical legal and policy decisions about detention were made with Guantánamo in mind. Other prisons were in Afghanistan, in Iraq after that war started, and in undisclosed locations around the world. This last, highly secret category of facilities held prisoners in custody of the Central Intelligence Agency rather than the Defense Department. These were the captives thought to have the most sensitive possible secrets to reveal, and whose identity, location, and treatment the Bush administration was the most anxious to conceal.

Conditions at Guantánamo have been deeply controversial. Most decisions concerning treatment of the detainees were driven by interrogation techniques, which I discuss in a later chapter. I outline the general conditions of captivity here because they inform analysis of the legality of the detention program, no matter what interrogations were performed.[12]

As prisoners first arrived at Guantánamo, they were housed in outdoor cages made of wire, resembling dog runs, at a temporary facility called Camp X-Ray.[13] Conditions were Spartan: a bucket for a toilet, a mat to sleep on, constant lighting, solitary confinement save for two exercise breaks a week. That April, Camp Delta was ready for them. It resembled a U.S. maximum-security prison. The cells, each measuring 6 feet 8 inches by 8 feet, had wire mesh walls, a bunk with a mattress, constant bright lighting, frequent patrols, a hole in the ground for a toilet, a sink, and an arrow painted on the floor pointing toward Mecca. Detainees were kept in their cells except for exercise and shower breaks five days a week. They were clothed in orange jumpsuits and given a few "comfort items" such as toothpaste, blankets, and a Koran. There was no air conditioning, although summer temperatures in Cuba could reach 100 degrees. Later, Camp 4 opened, with dormitories and better conditions for the most cooperative detainees, and then Camps 5 and 6, which were modeled on existing federal prisons. In 2008, as the number of detainees dropped below 300 and military commission trials approached, Camp Justice appeared, with a courthouse for the trials and a tent city for the lawyers.[14]

Who were the detainees? As the war on terrorism began, prisoners were swept up very swiftly in Afghanistan and elsewhere. Several of them were juveniles; several were elderly; some appeared to be insane. The intelligence reports accompanying them were often very thinly based. For three reasons, a dearth of reliable information should not have been surprising. First, chaos is a normal part of military operations. Second, few Americans understand the language and culture of Afghanistan. Third, the U.S. military soon offered cash bounties of thousands of dollars for turning in members of Al Qaeda and the Taliban. Soldiers receiving captives indirectly had no way of knowing for certain who was a terrorist and who was a victim of revenge or cupidity. Uncertain about the threat levels posed by those it held, the military simply continued to hold them.

As lawyers began to challenge the detentions, the administration's strategy of reverse lawfare became evident at Guantánamo. It refused even to identify who was held there until a court ordered disclosure in May 2006.[15] A group of policies hampered effective legal representation for the detainees: "The difficulties the lawyers face include policies designed to reduce their access to their clients; policies that create knotty ethical difficulties for military commission defense lawyers, particularly lawyers in the uniformed services; and practices that, in the words of one lawyer, 'are designed to drive a wedge between lawyers and their clients.'"[16]

A combination of the roadblocks the administration placed in the way of legal representation of the detainees and the difficulty of the legal issues surrounding the program produced years of delay in bringing challenges to the Supreme Court.

THE SUPREME COURT CONSIDERS DETENTION

President Bush's military order authorizing detention and creating military commissions differed in a fundamental way from emergency actions taken by prior presidents: he sought no ratification from Congress for his actions, even though Congress was usually in session and was legislating busily.[17] This omission greatly increased the executive branch's jeopardy in litigation.

As the habeas corpus cases challenging the detentions finally reached the Supreme Court, the question of seeking statutory authorization for the program belatedly arose within the administration. In February 2004, OLC head Jack Goldsmith attended a meeting in White House Counsel Gonzales's office to discuss the Supreme Court's grant of review. Goldsmith asked: "Why don't we just go to Congress and get it to sign off on the whole detention program?" David Addington responded with his usual sarcasm: "Why are you trying to give away the President's power?" He thought asking Congress for its approval would imply a want of unilateral power. Goldsmith found that whenever someone proposed working with Congress, Addington had two questions: "Do we have the legal power to do it ourselves?" and "Might Congress limit our options in ways that jeopardize American lives?" He had a "relentlessly short-term perspective." He would say, "We're going to push and push and push until some larger force makes us stop." He had "no sense of trading constraint for power."[18]

Seeking unilateral power, the administration would suffer constraints not of its own making when the Court acted. There was another way to avoid judicial intervention. If the administration had voluntarily accorded detainees some rudimentary process for determining their status, the Court might not have felt the need to intervene with its own. But this option was rejected as well.[19] The administration's obdurate stand forced its lawyers to argue that no meaningful process need attend indefinite detention. U.S. courts are naturally unreceptive to such claims, even in wartime.

A third kind of negative impact on the government's prospects in the detention litigation stemmed from a combination of excessive secrecy and increasing signs that detainees were being abused. Most facts about the detentions were shrouded in secrecy, unlike the highly visible presidential actions for which past claims of broad constitutional authority had been made. Speculation about abusive conditions of detention became rampant when the first lurid revelations of prisoner abuses at Abu Ghraib in Iraq surfaced in the press on the very day of Supreme Court oral arguments in the detention cases.[20] Even more ominously, the instantly notorious "torture memo" from OLC, approving harsh methods of interrogation for detainees, leaked to the press while the Court was formulating its opinions in the cases.[21] The claims of the executive branch that its actions could not be controlled by courts more urgently required a judicial response after abuses of authority became known.

For two reasons, the posture of the detention cases left the Supreme Court in a quite uncomfortable position. First, there was the intrinsic difficulty of deciding how to protect civil liberties in times of military conflict. The justices were well aware that few of the Court's finest hours had occurred in that context.[22] Particularly poignant was the memory of the Japanese internments during World War II. The Court's decisions upholding them had been a source of embarrassment ever since.[23] In those cases, the Court had been confounded by the difficulty of deciding how (if at all) to review claims of military necessity—even claims as thinly based as those offered to justify the internments.[24] Second, at least the World War II internments had been authorized by statute. After 9/11, Congress, not having been asked to do so, had provided no direct authority for the detention of suspects and therefore no guidance for the courts.

In the post-9/11 detention cases, the executive branch's argument against federal court jurisdiction rested principally on the two primary World War II era precedents.[25] One was *Quirin,* in which the Court rebuffed habeas petitions by the Nazi saboteurs, even though they had been captured and held in the United States. The other was *Eisentrager,* which upheld trials by military commission of German soldiers captured overseas while aiding the Japanese after the fall of the Nazi regime. In 2004, the Court refused to treat these cases as dispositive of issues surrounding the post-9/11 detentions. As a result, the Court confronted serious problems of reconciling the military's needs to conduct secure and secret operations with the basic rights of citizens and aliens held under military authority.

In *Hamdi v. Rumsfeld,*[26] the Court considered the habeas corpus petition of a U.S. citizen captured as an alleged enemy combatant during military operations in Afghanistan. Born in Louisiana, Yasser Hamdi had grown up in Saudi Arabia. Eventually he reached Afghanistan. His petition asserted that he was a relief worker, not an enemy combatant. The government responded that he was a soldier of the Taliban. When the Supreme Court heard his case, he had been imprisoned without a hearing for about two and a half years.

The sole evidentiary basis offered by the government for holding Hamdi was the "Mobbs Declaration." This was a statement by Michael Mobbs, a special advisor to the undersecretary of defense for policy. Mobbs indicated that his position had made him familiar with the facts of Hamdi's capture and detention. Mobbs declared that Hamdi had joined a Taliban military unit in 2001 and was captured in battle while in possession of a weapon by a U.S. ally, the Northern Alliance. Mobbs said Hamdi was labeled an enemy combatant "based upon his interviews and in light of his association with the Taliban." This declaration was hearsay and was probably at several removes from anyone who saw or spoke with Hamdi.[27] Because such a statement cannot be challenged effectively without an opportunity to cross-examine the absent witnesses, it would ordinarily be inadmissible in any U.S. court. In addition, although U.S. military personnel had interviewed Hamdi, he had enjoyed no opportunity to challenge his designation as an enemy combatant in any kind of hearing. Hamdi argued that it could not be fair to hold him on the strength of "an affidavit based on third-hand hearsay."

The government countered that any added process would be both unworkable and "constitutionally intolerable." It even argued that "respect for separation of powers and the limited institutional capabilities of courts in matters of military decision-making in connection with an ongoing conflict" should entirely eliminate any individual process. And if courts did insist on some process, they should review enemy combatant designations under a very deferential "some evidence" standard—which the Mobbs declaration would satisfy.[28]

Eight members of the Supreme Court rejected the executive branch's claim that it could hold a citizen indefinitely without meaningful process. Justice O'Connor wrote an opinion for a plurality of four justices. Justices Souter and Ginsburg concurred in the Court's judgment (making a majority) but dissented from its conclusion that Congress had authorized detentions. Justices Scalia and Stevens dissented on grounds that a citizen could not be held in indefinite military detention when habeas corpus had not been suspended. Only Justice Thomas argued that the detention was within the executive branch's war powers.

The O'Connor quartet decided that Congress had impliedly authorized detaining enemy combatants when it approved using military force against the 9/11 terrorists.[29] The AUMF provided authority for indefinite detention at least while active military operations remained under way in Afghanistan.

Nevertheless, a citizen held under that authority had a due process right to a "meaningful opportunity to contest the factual basis for that detention before a neutral decisionmaker." The Court drew its due process test from the one it uses to assess hearing rights under federal administrative programs. The test weighs private interests against those of the government and considers the adequacy of existing procedures compared with the value of additional safeguards.[30]

Both Hamdi's interest in liberty and the government's interest in detaining enemy warriors were obviously fundamental. The plurality observed that given the nature of the war on terrorism, Hamdi's captivity might become a life sentence if a risk remained that he would return to forces fighting against the United States. The government's interest lay in preventing that possibility. The underlying factual question remained, however: was Hamdi an enemy combatant or an innocent bystander?

Confronted by a clash of basic interests, Justice O'Connor invoked due process fundamentals: the need for notice of the factual basis of a government decision and a "fair opportunity to rebut" it before a neutral decider.[31] Therefore, the Mobbs declaration did not satisfy due process.[32] She was sensitive, however, to the need to avoid burdening military operations. She thought that credible hearsay evidence might need to be accepted and that the burden of proof could be on the prisoner.[33] She concluded that due process standards could be met by "an appropriately authorized and properly constituted military tribunal."[34]

The plurality concluded with a passage much quoted since, cautioning against leaving warmaking solely to the executive: "We have long since made clear that a state of war is not a blank check for the President when it comes to the rights of the Nation's citizens. [citing *Steel Seizure*] Whatever power the United States Constitution envisions for the Executive in its exchanges with other nations or with enemy organizations in times of conflict, it most assuredly envisions a role for all three branches when individual liberties are at stake."[35]

Justice Souter's opinion explained why this is so: "For reasons of inescapable human nature, the branch of government asked to counter a serious threat is not the branch on which to rest the Nation's entire reliance in striking the balance between the will to win and the cost in liberty on the way to victory; the responsibility for security will naturally amplify the claim that security legitimately raises. A reasonable balance is more likely to be reached on the judgment of a different branch."[36]

The *Hamdi* Court's reliance on due process analysis avoided the need to develop these separation of powers overtones in detail. Even so, the quoted passages showed the justices' discomfort with the executive branch's sweeping arguments that it could detain terror suspects on the sole basis of the inherent authority of the president.[37] Justice Scalia's uncompromising dissent was also based on separation of powers analysis in its emphasis that only congressional suspension of the writ of habeas corpus could justify detention of citizens without criminal charges.

Hamdi had two companion cases.[38] In *Rasul v. Bush,*[39] the Court considered petitions brought by aliens captured during hostilities with the Taliban and being detained at Guantánamo. Justice Stevens's opinion for the Court concluded that the captives were not like the World War II prisoners to whom the Court had previously denied habeas corpus in *Eisentrager:* they were not citizens of nations at war with the United States and had been afforded no process to test their claims that they were not enemy combatants. The majority also thought that Guantánamo Bay was not purely foreign territory because the lease from Cuba gave the United States much control over the base.[40] Hence Guantánamo did not provide the safe haven from judicial inquiry the administration had hoped it would be. The Court remanded the case to the district court to address the merits of the prisoners' claims.

Finally, in *Rumsfeld v. Padilla,*[41] the Court considered the petition of a U.S. citizen who had been arrested at O'Hare Airport in Chicago and held for a time as a material witness amid suspicion that he planned to explode a "dirty bomb" in the United States. He was then designated an enemy combatant and transferred to military authority.[42] The Court dismissed Padilla's petition on the technical ground that it had been brought against the wrong custodian. This deferred any resolution of very sensitive issues involving the executive's conversion of a criminal defendant into an enemy combatant and the resulting transfer of jurisdiction from a federal criminal court to a military commission.[43]

The detention cases placed the Court deep in Justice Jackson's "zone of twilight," where Congress has neither clearly authorized nor clearly forbidden executive action. The Court's overall strategy in the three cases was to decide only essential questions, leaving many issues for another day or for Congress to resolve.[44] By focusing on the minimum due process guarantees that must attend detention of a citizen, the *Hamdi* plurality avoided making any direct assessment of the military necessity for the president's order. The plurality also conformed the scope of the detention authority it was approving to the main thrust of the AUMF by emphasizing that Hamdi had been captured on the battlefield in Afghanistan. No blank check for a worldwide war on terrorism was written. Justice Souter's concurrence was stricter: he explicitly invoked the clear statement approach, refusing to imply detention authority because the AUMF was silent regarding it. In *Rasul,* the Court again took a careful approach. It distinguished the war on terrorism from its more conventional predecessors and extended statutory habeas corpus procedures to alien detainees, avoiding any decision on their constitutional rights.[45]

The detention cases left many issues unresolved, including the limits on executive power to designate enemy combatants and the exact nature of required procedures in status hearings and trials by military commission. Instead, the Court invited the executive branch to join Congress to authorize and design fair procedures.[46] Certainly the Court's statement approving the use of military trials in terrorism cases, at least in some circumstances, was a victory for the executive. There were also clear judicial reminders, however, that even when combating terrorism the executive is bound by law and that the constitutional executive power is limited.

Any long-term response to the terrorism threat demands the joint action of the executive and legislative branches, a partnership absent in the detention cases. The Court's decisions finally spurred action from Congress. It enacted the Detainee Treatment Act of 2005 (DTA), regulating some aspects of detention conditions (for example, forbidding cruelty toward detainees) and restricting the jurisdiction of the federal courts to review challenges to the detention program.[47] The DTA forbade habeas corpus for enemy combatants and replaced it with a quite restricted appeal to the District of Columbia Circuit Court of Appeals.

Notice the sequence of events in the detention controversy. Unilateral executive action led to judicial invalidation, which led to statutory resolution of some but not all important issues. This pattern would be repeated for a related issue, the validity of military commission trials. In the *Hamdan* case, discussed in a later chapter, the Court invalidated these trials for lack of statutory authority. Congress then enacted the Military Commissions Act of 2006 (MCA).[48] Along with authorizing the trial of terrorists by military commission, the MCA expanded the DTA's ban on habeas corpus for enemy combatants but preserved the DTA's limited avenue of appeal to the District of Columbia Circuit Court of Appeals.

It surprised no one that an immediate challenge to the MCA appeared. Detainees whose habeas actions had purportedly been squelched by the MCA appealed the validity of the jurisdictional restriction. They claimed that Congress had unconstitutionally suspended the writ of habeas corpus.[49] This litigation raised issues about both congressional control of federal court jurisdiction and the adequacy of procedures the executive had adopted in the wake of the detention cases of 2004 to distinguish terrorist suspects from innocent detainees.

Overall, both the DTA and the MCA are quite friendly to the executive and quite unfriendly to the judiciary. Neither statute specifies, however, the nature of process due the detainees to determine whether they are enemy combatants or not. Another trip to the Supreme Court would be required to address that issue. The journey began in the wake of *Hamdi*.

HOW MUCH PROCESS IS DUE?

Nine days after the Court's decisions in the detention cases, the administration announced that it was creating Combatant Status Review Tribunals (CSRTs) to determine the status of the Guantánamo prisoners.[50] A tribunal would comprise three officers who would consider information provided by the military and the detainee, who could testify in person. The burden of proof was on the detainee to rebut the military's prior determination that he or she was an enemy combatant. The detainee would be assigned a "personal representative," a nonlawyer who could see secret evidence but who could not reveal it to the prisoner. A senior officer would review decisions of the tribunals.

The CSRTs were probably modeled on Geneva Convention Article 5 proceedings.[51] These summary hearings, usually held in combat zones, determine whether a captive is a prisoner of war, a civilian, or an unlawful combatant. The use of summary procedures in the less-pressured context of Guantánamo, where there was more opportunity for careful hearings than a combat zone provides, sparked controversy.[52] Objections to the CSRT procedures focused on the use of secret evidence, to which the prisoner cannot respond effectively, the use of coerced testimony, which is often unreliable, the uncertain neutrality of the deciders, who are military officers but not military judges, and the absence of counsel for the prisoner.[53]

Studies conducted at Guantánamo raised fundamental doubts about the factual basis for holding many of the detainees. One analyst estimated that about a third of the detainees could reasonably be characterized as enemy combatants.[54] Another study of more than 500 cases decided by the CSRTs found that all but 38 prisoners were adjudged to be enemy combatants even though fewer than 10 percent had been alleged to be Al Qaeda fighters and most had been captured by someone other than U.S. forces.[55] This disparity between the likelihood that many detainees were held erroneously and the thin prospects that they would prevail in a CSRT heightened perceptions that the process was fundamentally unfair in operation. A former CSRT member charged that the panels ignored exculpatory evidence and that they were ordered to reconsider cases until they decided that the detainee was actually an enemy combatant.[56]

Over the years, continuing status reviews led to a steadily diminishing number of prisoners held at Guantánamo.[57] Many of them were released or transferred to the custody of their home governments. These developments did not end debate, however, about the dangerousness of many of those still held and about the conditions of their confinement.[58] Court proceedings promised no early end to the disputes.

After enactment of the DTA, the authorized appeals to the District of Columbia Circuit Court concerning status decisions became "mired in a dispute over the kind of evidence the government must supply to enable the appeals court" to exercise its review functions.[59] Congress restricted the court to reviewing whether the Pentagon has followed its own standards and procedures in a particular case and whether those rules are "consistent with the Constitution and laws of the United States."[60] While the circuit court struggled to work out its review responsibilities, the clock continued to tick. By mid-2008, several of the detainees were in their seventh year of incarceration with no end in sight. Meanwhile, the forbidden habeas avenue led to the Supreme Court again.

Section 7 of the MCA reinforced the DTA by banning use of habeas corpus to challenge the legality of detention or to review mistreatment in custody.[61] As lawsuits claiming that this provision was an unconstitutional suspension of the writ headed toward the Supreme Court in spring 2007, a portentous event occurred. The Court at first denied review of one of the challenges, but then took the extraordinary step of reversing itself and granting review after new information about irregularities at Guantánamo surfaced.[62] The administration's decision after the detention cases of 2004 to provide minimal process to the detainees had once again placed it in a bad position before the bar of the Court.

In *Boumediene v. Bush,* a five-to-four majority of the Court held that Section 7 of the MCA was an unconstitutional suspension of the writ of habeas corpus.[63] The petitioners were foreign nationals captured in various parts of the world—Afghanistan, Bosnia, Gambia—and sent to Guantánamo. All denied they were members of Al Qaeda or the Taliban. All had been designated enemy combatants by CSRTs. Some had been seeking habeas since early 2002.

As a preliminary matter, the Court held that the *constitutional* privilege of habeas corpus extended to detainees at Guantánamo. This question had not arisen in *Rasul,* which concerned only the *statutory* implementation of the constitutional right, which was later taken away by Congress. The Court rejected the executive branch's argument that alien enemy combatants detained beyond U.S. borders have no constitutional rights. Justice Kennedy's opinion did not draw bright lines but instead called for a complex analysis of the extraterritorial constitutional availability of habeas.[64] An important factor was "the adequacy of the process" by which a challenged determination had been made. As it had in *Rasul,* the Court distinguished *Eisentrager,* in which the prisoners admitted they were enemy aliens and in which there had been "rigorous adversarial process" in full trials by military commissions. Here, the detainees' status was the core issue, and the CSRTs fell "well short of the procedures and adversarial mechanisms that would eliminate the need for habeas corpus review." The Court disparaged the use of lay personal representatives instead of lawyers for the detainees, the presumption of validity for the military's evidence, the detainees' restricted opportunity to rebut the military's case, and the inability of the DTA's judicial review process to "cure all defects in the earlier proceedings."

The Court upholds procedural alternatives to habeas corpus if they are "adequate and effective" substitutes for the writ, but the DTA's scheme for judicial review failed that test. The Court characterized the scope of review under the DTA as "quite limited." The court of appeals could not "inquire into the legality of the detention generally"; it could only review whether "the CSRT complied with the 'standards and procedures specified by the Secretary of Defense' and whether those standards and procedures are lawful."[65] The fatal omissions were the power to review the application of legal standards to the facts of the case and the power to order release of the detainees.

The Court emphasized that "the writ must be effective. The habeas court must have sufficient authority to conduct a meaningful review of both the cause for detention and the Executive's power to detain." In turn, the efficacy of the required judicial review depended on the nature and adequacy of the proceedings reviewed. This brought the Court back to issues about adequacy of the CSRTs.

The Court reiterated its misgivings about "constraints upon the detainee's ability to rebut the factual basis for the Government's assertion that he is an enemy combatant." In particular, Justice Kennedy emphasized the detainees' lack of counsel and inability to rebut hearsay or classified information. The consequence, he thought, was a "considerable risk of error in the tribunal's findings of fact."

The Court did not hold, however, that CSRT procedures denied due process. Nor would it specify what was necessary to ground effective habeas review. These issues were for the lower courts to determine. The Court did outline some guidance, saying that the court that conducts the habeas proceeding must have the means to correct errors that occurred during the CSRT proceedings. This includes some authority to assess the sufficiency of the Government's evidence against the detainee. It also must have the authority to admit and consider relevant exculpatory evidence that was not introduced during the earlier proceeding. Consistent with the historic function and province of the writ, habeas corpus review may be more circumscribed if the underlying detention proceedings are more thorough than they were here. (p. 2270)

The *Boumediene* decision is an obvious call for the executive branch to reformulate and improve the CSRT procedures. (It does not directly affect military commission trials, unless the accused denies that he or she is even an enemy combatant.) Thus the issue of fair process to determine detainee status, suppressed or ignored by the Bush administration at the outset of the war on terrorism, has haunted it ever since. The Supreme Court has intervened twice, in the detention cases in 2004 and again in *Boumediene*. Congressional efforts to keep the issue away from the courts in the DTA and the MCA proved fruitless.[66]

To the *Boumediene* dissenters, it was the Court, not the other two branches, that had overstepped the bounds of separation of powers. Justice Scalia's impassioned dissent lamented that the decision

will make the war harder on us. It will almost certainly cause more Americans to be killed. . . . At least 30 of those prisoners hitherto released from Guantánamo Bay have returned to the battlefield. . . . These, mind you, were detainees whom *the military* had concluded were not enemy combatants. Their return to the kill illustrates the incredible difficulty of assessing who is and who is not an enemy combatant in a foreign theater of operations where the environment does not lend itself to rigorous evidence collection. Astoundingly, the Court today raises the bar, requiring military officials to appear before civilian courts and defend their decisions under procedural and evidentiary rules that go beyond what Congress has specified. (p. 2294–2295)

Scalia concluded by lamenting that "how to handle enemy prisoners in this war will ultimately lie with the branch that knows least about the national security concerns that the subject entails."

Justice Scalia's central point, that adding process for terrorist suspects risks U.S. lives, deserves a direct response. He is correct, because when the risks of an erroneous determination are shifted away from the detainee and toward the government, more dangerous people will go free than otherwise. This is true of all process guarantees. At the outset of the war on terrorism, the executive placed all risks of error on the detainees by denying all process. As process guarantees have grown, the risks of detaining the innocent have shrunk but the risks of freeing terrorists have increased.

There is a countervailing value that I believe justifies the Supreme Court's approach.[67] The war on terrorism shows every sign of long duration—some call it the "long war." It can be fought effectively only by adhering to the rule of law instead of abandoning law while responding to an acute crisis that evolves into a long-standing one. In the particular case of process for determining detainee status, the Court understands the power of judicial review to legitimize tribunals created by the executive. Legitimacy is a core value to all civilized peoples, and it is worth some risk. The offsetting hope is that a war on terrorism governed by law will be more effective in the long run, and that it will save more lives than might be lost by adhering to the law's constraints. That trade-off is not easy for elected politicians to make. The Bush administration resisted it throughout its tenure in office.

9

Escaping Geneva

AN OVERARCHING LEGAL DECISION that would affect both trials for detainees and the limits of interrogation was made early in 2002: whether the Geneva Conventions applied to the captives, and if so, according to what categorization of their detention. International law concerning the permissible conditions of detaining persons captured in combat is codified in the four Geneva Conventions of 1949. Although based on earlier principles, the conventions responded to the horrific lessons of World War II and tried to ensure decent treatment of people held in any form of modern conflict.

The United States was among the leading sponsors of the conventions and is a signatory to all of them. As ratified treaties, they are binding federal law under the Constitution's Supremacy Clause.[1] Two of them are centrally important to the war on terrorism: the Third Convention Relative to the Treatment of Prisoners of War (POW Convention) and the Fourth Convention Relative to the Protection of Civilian Persons in Time of War (Civilian Convention).[2]

Everyone who is detained in an international conflict enjoys the protection of one of the conventions, but there are important differences in the rights they guarantee. Some provisions, the "common articles," are found in all four of the conventions. Common Article 2 extends the conventions' fullest protections to "all cases of declared war or of any other armed conflict which may arise between two or more of the High Contracting Parties." Common Article 3 requires prisoners to be treated "humanely" and forbids "cruel treatment and torture." It also prohibits the imposition of criminal sentences "without previous judgment pronounced by a regularly constituted court affording all the judicial guarantees which are recognized as indispensable by civilized peoples." The meaning of both of these common articles proved controversial in the war on terrorism.

DEFUSING THE CONVENTIONS

John Yoo reports that in December 2001, the War Council, augmented by representatives from the Department of State and the National Security

Council, met to discuss the application of the Geneva Conventions to the prisoners.[3] The group met repeatedly over the next months. The chair was usually Alberto Gonzales, who tended to foster full discussion and "to keep his own views private." His deputy, Timothy Flanigan, "usually played the role of inquisitor," pressing for explanations and justifications. The State Department was represented by William Howard Taft IV, who had been deputy secretary of defense and general counsel at the Pentagon under Reagan. John Bellinger, counsel for the National Security Council, later succeeded Taft. The confident and combative David Addington was a major presence, but Yoo denies rumors that Addington drafted some OLC opinions that emerged.[4] Surely, however, his influence drove them toward the uncompromising views of executive power he shared with Vice President Cheney.

On January 9, 2002, John Yoo and OLC Special Counsel Robert Delahunty sent a draft opinion to the Pentagon titled *Application of Treaties and Laws to Al Qaeda and Taliban Detainees*.[5] I consider it at length because it appears to have been highly influential in shaping the president's eventual decision about applying the Geneva Conventions to the detainees. In the meantime, the draft triggered sharp controversy within the administration. A final version of the opinion differed only in detail.

The forty-page length and dry, analytic tone of the *Application of Treaties* opinion mask the extraordinary nature of the positions it takes. The opinion adopts John Yoo's extreme views on issues of constitutional and international law. It concludes that the president can either suspend the Geneva Conventions in Afghanistan or, in a lesser step, determine that they do not apply to Al Qaeda and Taliban prisoners.

The particular arguments in *Application of Treaties* flow from two aspects of John Yoo's unusual theories about the law of foreign relations.[6] Both of these positions were readily apparent in the president's decisions about the treaties. First, Yoo believes the treaty power is executive except as specifically stated in the Constitution (as in the Senate's role in ratification). This judgment is based on his belief that the Vesting Clause grants the president vast unenumerated powers in foreign affairs that result in an "independent constitutional obligation to develop and direct foreign policy." I have explained that mainstream foreign relations scholars usually recognize a broad power of executive initiative, conditioned on congressional acquiescence—that the president proposes, but Congress disposes.[7] Yoo finds a much broader set of executive powers that cannot be overridden by Congress, and a more limited role for the courts, than do most others.

Second, and corollary to the first position, Yoo claims that the president enjoys an apparently unlimited power to interpret existing treaties. (An old saying among lawyers is that it matters less who writes the law than who interprets it.) He argues that "treaty interpretation is so tied up in the setting of foreign policy that the power has come to rest with the executive branch." The president can also "interpret, and even violate, international law in the course of executing foreign policy." Yoo is correct that a president's constitutional powers should include some discretion in interpreting our nation's international obligations (presidents do violate international law or suspend treaties on occasion). The question is, how *much* discretion? Yoo states no limits, perhaps believing that the obligation of the president's oath and the existence of his political accountability provide enough of a check on baseless interpretation.

I think a more acceptable limit can be drawn from familiar principles of domestic administrative law. The executive branch's routine interpretation of statutes receives deference from reviewing courts when the statute's text and identifiable purposes command no different result and the interpretation is itself "reasonable."[8] It is difficult to articulate an argument for giving the president more latitude than that, if treaties are to be regarded as binding legal documents.

Somewhat surprisingly, the *Application of Treaties* opinion does not begin with an analysis of the Geneva Conventions themselves. Instead, it focuses on the federal War Crimes Act (WCA), which criminalizes certain violations of the Geneva Conventions and other law of war treaties.[9] There is a reason for this strategy, and it requires a bit of explanation. Our law of foreign relations conventionally divides treaties into two broad categories: those that are self-executing in that they have force domestically without implementing legislation by Congress and those that are not self-executing.[10] For example, an early decision by the Supreme Court held that the treaties ending the Revolutionary War overrode state laws confiscating Tory property without any need for Congress to enact statutes to enforce them.[11] By contrast, a treaty calling for appropriations or other subsequent action by the federal government is not self-executing.

Unlike most scholars of foreign relations law, John Yoo is very reluctant to consider any treaty self-executing absent the clearest evidence of that intention. This is because "treaties exert an impact in the realm of international politics and foreign policy, rather than in constitutional law."[12] This position minimizes the force of the Supremacy Clause, which has long been understood to make self-executing treaty obligations part of federal law, with the same stature as statutes.[13] Instead, Yoo believes the president is ordinarily unconstrained by international law unless it has been codified by Congress.

This background explains why *Application of Treaties* does not analyze the direct force of the Geneva Conventions in U.S. law. Instead, it parses the WCA without stopping to acknowledge that the conventions have been treated as self-executing within the U.S. military ever since their ratification.[14] The opinion does discuss international law at some length, but supposedly always in the context of understanding the WCA's partial codification of it.

This strategy has three crucial interpretive advantages for the executive branch. First, since the WCA is a criminal statute, the opinion invokes the canon of construction called the rule of lenity, which calls for interpreting criminal statutes favorably to defendants—who could be U.S. officials.[15] Therefore, to the extent incorporated treaty provisions could be read to shelter either the detainees from their captors or the captors from prosecution, the captors will receive special solicitation. This stance is difficult to reconcile with the purposes of the Geneva Conventions.

Second and more broadly, the strategy deflects attention from both the international law of war, of which the conventions are a part, and the ingrained traditions in the U.S. military of honoring the law of war even when it may not technically apply. The opinion does mention the option of extending rights to detainees when it is not mandatory to do so and reviews instances of that practice, for example regarding the Viet Cong. The opinion omits any recognition that the military's "voluntary" grant of rights may have been strategic. Following international law without conceding its binding effect prevents any resolution of the question whether the rights are indeed mandatory—even if they are. And that was the central question regarding the Al Qaeda and Taliban detainees.

Third, since the WCA codifies only a few central parts of the conventions, other protections could be left out of the analysis entirely. Of particular importance was Article 5 of the Prisoner of War (POW) Convention, which provides: "Should any doubt arise as to whether persons, having committed a belligerent act and having fallen into the hands of the enemy [merit POW status], such persons shall [be treated as POWs] until such time as their status has been determined by a competent tribunal." On its face, Article 5 appears to have been applicable to the detainees. Having no intention of according them Article 5 hearings, however, the administration simply ignored this provision. The draft OLC opinion encouraged this approach by leaving Article 5 out of its analysis.

The WCA forbids both grave breaches of the Geneva Conventions and certain violations of Common Article 3. The four conventions similarly define grave breaches. Thus, the POW Convention forbids "willful killing, torture, or inhuman treatment, . . . willfully causing great suffering or serious injury to body or health, . . . or willfully depriving a prisoner of war of the rights of fair and regular trial." The Civilian Convention appears to provide residual protections to anyone not covered by the others because it explicitly applies to "those who, at a given moment and in any manner whatsoever, find themselves, in case of a conflict or occupation, in the hands of a Party to the conflict . . . of which they are not nationals." Both the POW Convention and the Civilian Convention forbid coercion to obtain information. Finally, there is the overarching protection of Common Article 3 with its bans on cruel treatment or the use of irregular and unfair courts.

Thus, the portions of the Geneva Conventions the WCA explicitly adopted contain two kinds of essential protections for persons detained in armed conflicts. First, they forbid torture, cruelty, inhumanity, and coercion. Second, they guarantee basic rights to due process. The Bush administration wanted to treat the detainees in ways inconsistent with both these kinds of rights. It wanted to employ harsh interrogation methods, many of which violated Geneva strictures. And it wanted to craft its own procedures for prosecuting war criminals regardless of any prevailing conceptions from international law. Therefore, to meet the administration's goals the detainees would have to fall outside *all* of the Geneva protections codified by the WCA. *Application of Treaties* supports the legality of precisely that conclusion.

Application of Treaties takes an advocate's approach that acknowledges contrary precedent only as a prelude to rejecting its applicability. The opinion's analytic technique combines very broad assertions about presidential power with very narrow, often literal interpretations of Geneva provisions. For example, it eliminates Common Article 3 by noting its applicability to conflicts "not of an international character" and arguing that the war on terrorism *does* involve an international organization, Al Qaeda. This reading is plausible, given the text quoted above. There were at the time, though, widely accepted arguments that the article is meant to be a catchall covering all unconventional conflicts. *Application of Treaties* rejects these arguments by taking the narrow position that as codified in the WCA, the article covers only civil wars.

To buttress this conclusion, the opinion deploys the avoidance canon: "We believe that the Congress must state explicitly its intention to take the constitutionally dubious step of restricting the President's plenary power over military operations (including the treatment of prisoners), and that unless Congress clearly demonstrates such an intent, the WCA must be read to avoid such constitutional problems."[16] This statement exaggerates the president's powers over military operations in general and prisoners in particular. Congress has enacted much valid legislation regarding both.[17] Also, it illustrates the opinion's strategy of bringing international obligations into a domestic framework within which broad views of executive power can be asserted to limit them.

The opinion goes on to argue that because Al Qaeda is not a nation but "merely a violent political movement or organization," Common Article 2 does not protect its members by triggering POW status for them. This too is plausible as a reading of the text, but it does stand in some tension with the administration's declaration of a war on terrorism and its conduct of conventional military operations against Al Qaeda. In any event, the opinion's interpretations of the common articles recognize protections for detainees only in wars between nations and in civil wars. Members of Al Qaeda, falling in neither category, are excluded from the protections the conventions provide.

These initial conclusions suggest, however, that the Taliban would receive protection, since the United States was engaging in armed conflict in Afghanistan. The opinion responds by citing the fact that the Taliban (like Al Qaeda) does not meet the conventions' definition of regular armed forces that merit POW protections because its members are irregulars who do not wear uniforms or obey the laws of war. This is a sound argument, although it is somewhat confounded by the fact that the Taliban was the closest approximation to an army Afghanistan had at the time.

The opinion places greater emphasis on a more strained argument about the Taliban. It relies on various statements by Defense Secretary Rumsfeld that the Taliban was not really the government of Afghanistan. The opinion asserts that it is well within the president's foreign affairs powers to declare Afghanistan a "failed state" with no functioning government. In that case, it would lack capacity to sustain international agreements and would not receive their protection. Therefore, the president can suspend the operation of the Geneva Conventions with regard to Afghanistan.

Presidents do suspend treaties for various reasons, such as a material breach by another nation. Yet the United States had never before characterized a major nation as a failed state, in part because we could not then hold its putative rulers to international obligations. More important, the United States had never before considered suspending the Geneva Conventions for any reason. To do so would be a step of the greatest gravity. The opinion's breezy discussion of suspension omits these major considerations.

The opinion then notes (and rejects) the widely held view that human rights treaties may not be suspended. It concludes that even if suspension violates international law, the president may proceed: "We emphasize that the resolution of that question, however, *has no bearing* on domestic constitutional issues, or on the application of the WCA."[18] The opinion asserts that according the Geneva Conventions domestic legal effect would interfere with the president's constitutional powers in foreign affairs. For the same reason, the "customary" international law of war does not bind the president and cannot supply protections for either group of detainees.[19] Nonetheless, the opinion says that the president's constitutional authority to interpret customary law and to apply it if he chooses to do so allows him to extend protections to either or both groups. It is a matter of discretion, though, not law.

Application of Treaties makes both Al Qaeda and Taliban detainees international outlaws, possessing only those rights the president chooses to grant them. This stance ignores a fundamental purpose of the four Geneva Conventions: to leave no one without some form of international protection, varying with the particular status of the individual. In place of an approach that honors the basic thrust of the conventions, the opinion expends much effort arguing that the detainees fall outside each of several potential categories of protected persons until at the end they are left with nothing.

John Yoo subsequently justified his approach in *Application of Treaties* by asserting that arguments to apply the Geneva Conventions to the detainees make "the basic mistake of treating Al Qaeda as a nation-state which obeys the rules of war."[20] This is an example of his consistent tendency to create straw men that are easily destroyed. To my knowledge, no one has asserted that Al Qaeda resembles, say, Norway. This kind of argument only deflects attention from the real issues. At any rate, Yoo's main conclusion is that the POW Convention applies only to wars between nations that are parties to Geneva and not to more formless entities such as Al Qaeda and the Taliban.[21] Whether or not one accepts that distinction, the Civilian Convention is generally understood to confer basic rights on captives in many other kinds of conflicts.[22]

REPULSING A TRADITIONALIST COUNTERATTACK

The draft *Application of Treaties* opinion created "quite a bit of havoc" among government lawyers.[23] For the State Department, Legal Adviser Taft wrote a forty-page response to the OLC opinion objecting that "the most important factual assumptions on which your draft is based and its legal analysis [are] seriously flawed."[24] In particular, Taft objected to Yoo's "failed state" argument as "without support" and "contrary to the official position of the United States, the United Nations, and all other states that have considered the issue." Taft was right—Yoo had transported the doctrine from the political science literature "without support in international law and without precedent."[25]

It should surprise no one that the State Department would defend the binding effect of treaties. The department daily tries to induce other nations to obey their international obligations and is quite sensitive to the effect of any appearance that the United States is not honoring its own. Therefore, it took the position that Al Qaeda captives were entitled to Common Article 3 protections, and that Taliban prisoners were entitled to POW protections (pending hearings in particular cases of doubt).

From the opposite direction came pressure to allow effective intelligence gathering. As John Yoo put it, if the POW Convention applied, the United States "would be able to ask Osama bin Laden loud questions, and nothing more."[26] "Consensus eluded the group," he reports, although Alberto Gonzales made every effort to achieve it. Someone then decided to override the State Department's objections and issue the opinion. A couple of weeks after its issuance in draft, *Application of Treaties* was edited somewhat and sent to White House Counsel Gonzales as an opinion bearing the same title but over the signature of Assistant Attorney General Jay Bybee.[27] The overall analysis is the same in the two memos. The State Department had been steamrolled.

The final OLC opinion, given the luxury of a bit more time, adds a few points. For example, it observes that even if the basic requirements of Geneva codified in the WCA are regarded as binding, the details of confinement would not have to follow full POW norms because those are found elsewhere in the conventions. This distinction offered the possibility of a middle way between the alternatives of applying the conventions fully to the detainees and denying that they apply at all. This middle way would have honored the fundamental ideas in the grave breach and Common Article 3 formulas and allowed for some flexibility in conditions of confinement. It was not pursued because it would have foreclosed some of the harsh interrogation techniques the administration wanted to employ. In addition, there was probably some distraction from the roiling controversy within the administration. When President Bush finally made his choice, he selected a different compromise that did not succeed in either stilling controversy or protecting the detainees.

A LAST ROUND OF DEBATES

On January 18, 2002, President Bush initially decided against granting POW status to the captives, but that was not the end of the matter. Secretary of State Colin Powell asked for reconsideration of the decision. He was uniquely qualified to do so. Alone among the most senior officers of the administration, he had extensive combat experience. He had reached the military pinnacle of chair of the Joint Chiefs of Staff. In his post at the State Department, he could anticipate the diplomatic effects of the president's decision, and he viscerally understood its military consequences. His objections were met with impatience and with far less respect than they deserved.

Secretary Powell's concerns were shared by General Richard Myers, his successor as chair of the Joint Chiefs of Staff, who had not been consulted regarding the president's initial decision about Geneva.[28] Myers feared that "it would open the door for mistreatment" of U.S. prisoners. During the period of reconsideration initiated by Powell, Myers and Rumsfeld disagreed openly, a rarity. Myers made his point in a National Security Council meeting with Bush and Cheney present, saying "I don't think this is a legal issue." He understood the legal argument against applying Geneva, he said, but stressed that we would be treated as we treated others.

The Pentagon's military lawyers, the judge advocate generals (JAGs), shared Myers's concern about reciprocity under Geneva—if we refused to follow it, others would use the excuse to abuse our troops. They argued that the principles of Geneva "applied to any war and to anyone that the United States fought."[29] John Yoo says these arguments were fully aired, including participation by the uniformed lawyers. The OLC lawyers disagreed with them, arguing that this was a policy issue. Citing history, OLC noted that enemy captors in Korea and Vietnam had abused U.S. troops despite the existence of Geneva. Thus it appears that having characterized reciprocity as a policy issue, OLC nevertheless dove in on one side of the debate, contradicting those who knew far more about it than did the civilian lawyers. OLC also argued that Geneva principles had not become customary international law that bound the United States. The State Department disagreed.

The two kinds of objections that arose over the president's initial decision about the detainees flowed from two sources for which Cheney, Rumsfeld, Addington, and Yoo had little respect: international law and military tradition. The underlying tensions went well beyond issues about the status of the detainees. International law was a primary instrument of lawfare against the United States. And John Yoo had fully imbibed the long-standing hostility of the other three men toward a recalcitrant military bureaucracy.[30] It soon became apparent that their dismissive attitude toward international and military values had found another adherent: White House Counsel Alberto Gonzales.

In late January, Gonzales felt ready to write a memorandum to the president summarizing the debate and preparing Bush for a final decision.[31] The four-page memo avoids detailed legal discussion. Instead, it supplies bulleted points of both law and policy in favor of and against applying Geneva protections to the detainees, and then gives Gonzales's own conclusions. After reciting the earlier OLC conclusion that the POW Convention did not apply to Al Qaeda or the Taliban and summarizing Powell's disagreement with those conclusions, Gonzales stated his view that the president has the constitutional authority to decide that the POW Convention does not apply to either group. He conceded that the Taliban presented a more difficult case, since it was in control of Afghanistan when the United States invaded in late 2001. He passed along OLC's judgment that the president can escape Geneva by determining either that Afghanistan was a "failed state" at the time hostilities commenced or that the Taliban was not a government but a "terrorist-like" group.

Gonzales then asserted that "OLC's interpretation of this legal issue is definitive." Its opinion binds the executive branch, he said, notwithstanding that the legal adviser to the secretary of state "has expressed a different view." This stance that OLC advice is binding on the executive had been asserted frequently in the past—especially by the Justice Department. The difficulty with advancing it in this controversy was that it gave supremacy to the lawyers who had the least actual experience with problems involving war and its prisoners. The Departments of Defense and State had many lawyers who possessed that experience, but they had been shouldered aside.

Gonzales continued by reviewing the consequences of adhering to the earlier decision not to apply the POW Convention to the captives. The first positive consequence would be to preserve "flexibility." Avoiding Geneva would also avoid "foreclosing options," especially regarding "nonstate actors." In the "new kind of war" against terrorism, the need to obtain information from captives and to try some of them for war crimes "renders obsolete Geneva's strict limitations on questioning of enemy prisoners and renders quaint some of its provisions requiring the captured enemy be afforded such things as commissary privileges."

This reference to some Geneva provisions as "obsolete" or "quaint" caused a storm of criticism when the memo was subsequently leaked to the press. There is no sign that it created similar reverberations within the administration.

Gonzales also argued that avoiding Geneva "substantially reduces the threat of domestic criminal prosecution under the War Crimes Act." He noted that the act's prohibition of grave Geneva breaches would include such offenses as "outrages against personal dignity" and "inhuman treatment." These terms are undefined, he said. Moreover, it is "difficult to predict the needs" that might arise in combating terrorism. A presidential determination that Geneva does not apply "would provide a solid defense to any future prosecution."

Turning to the potential negative effects of the earlier decision, Gonzales summarized the objections he had heard. These included arguments that since 1949 the United States had never denied the applicability of the Geneva Conventions and that the first Bush administration stated a policy of applying Geneva "whenever armed hostilities occur with regular foreign armed forces," whatever the technicalities. Gonzales admitted that if the president's decision stood, the United States could not invoke Geneva or the WCA against mistreatment of U.S. forces. The decision would also "likely provoke widespread condemnation" here and abroad and could "undermine U.S. military culture which emphasizes maintaining the highest standards of conduct in combat."

Turning to his own views, Gonzales concluded that the objections to the earlier decision were "unpersuasive." This was a "new type of warfare" not contemplated at the time of Geneva. He believed that the president's "policy of providing humane treatment to enemy detainees" provided the credibility to insist on reciprocity. Of course, terrorists would not follow Geneva in any event. Criticism there would be, but military culture would be preserved by the president's proposed directive to apply the "principles" of Geneva although not the letter.

Colin Powell shot back a response to Gonzales's memorandum urging that the conventions should apply to the conflict. His memo stressed that pursuant to Geneva, the president could still determine that Al Qaeda and some or all of the Taliban do not merit POW status. Even so, all captives should be treated consistently with the principles of the POW Convention. Adhering to the earlier decision would "reverse over a century of U.S. policy and practice" and would "undermine the protections of the law of war for our troops, both in this specific conflict and in general." Not surprisingly, Powell anticipated a "high cost in terms of negative international reaction" if Geneva were not applied. By contrast, following Geneva would provide a "more defensible legal framework" and a "positive international posture" as a result of "taking the high ground." As for OLC, its opinion would likely be rejected by foreign governments or tribunals, whatever its effect might be domestically.

The State Department followed up with a strongly phrased memorandum to Gonzales from Legal Adviser Taft. It argued that a decision to apply Geneva was consistent with both the "plain language" of the conventions and "the unvaried practice of the United States" for more than fifty years.

He reiterated the reciprocity argument and concluded that from a policy standpoint, applying Geneva "provides the best legal basis" for treating the captives "in the way we intend to treat them." Thus, he found the boundary between law and policy blurrier than it seemed to OLC.

Attorney General Ashcroft also weighed in with a letter to the president that he wrote personally rather than relying on his staff.[32] Having been on the sidelines for most of the controversy, he now rushed into the game. His letter argued that a determination against applying Geneva created the least legal jeopardy because courts would not review it. The alternative, applying Geneva but concluding that Al Qaeda and perhaps the Taliban were unlaw-ful combatants not entitled to POW status, might not receive judicial defer-ence. He concluded that rejecting Geneva would minimize "the legal risks of liability, litigation, and criminal prosecution."

OLC followed the attorney general's letter with a substantial memoran-dum regarding the status of the Taliban under Geneva, arguing that its mem-bers could be denied POW status even if the conventions applied generally because they were "unlawful combatants" who wore no uniforms and ig-nored the laws of war.[33] Like the earlier OLC opinions in this extended war of memoranda, the final OLC opinion assured the president he could make categorical determinations that detainees held as members of Al Qaeda and the Taliban were not entitled to Geneva protections because they were un-lawful combatants. That is a justifiable conclusion regarding POW status, but a more dubious one concerning other Geneva protections.

AN EQUIVOCAL ORDER

On February 7, 2002, the president issued an order titled *Humane Treat-ment of Al Qaeda and Taliban Detainees,* modifying his earlier decision.[34] His order accepted "the legal conclusion of the Department of Justice" that no part of the Geneva Conventions applied to Al Qaeda. He decided that Geneva would apply to the Taliban even though he shared the Justice De-partment's legal opinion that this was not mandatory. (He was declining to rely on the dubious "failed state" theory.) Nevertheless, members of the Taliban were unlawful combatants not entitled to POW status. He also ac-cepted the conclusion that Common Article 3 did not apply to either group because this was an international conflict and Article 3 governs internal ones. The president then stressed that "our values as a Nation . . . call for us to treat detainees humanely." He directed that "as a matter of policy, the United States Armed Forces shall continue to treat detainees humanely and, to the extent appropriate and consistent with military necessity, in a manner consistent with the principles of Geneva."

It has been said of General Ulysses Grant that his military orders had such clarity that no subordinate could mistake his directions. The same cannot be said of President Bush's order of February 2002. A lawyer's formulation, it looked in both directions at once: Geneva "principles" applied if "consistent with military necessity." Somewhat more clearly, treatment was to be "humane." John Yoo would later conclude optimistically that "any concerns about a decline in military discipline were cured by President Bush's order that the detainees be treated humanely."[35] That judgment is belied by the reality of the disconnect between the president's order and its execution in the field.[36] Jack Goldsmith noted more accurately that the formula President Bush used in his order was "very vague" and left "all of the hard issues about 'humane' and 'appropriate' treatment to unknown officials."[37]

Even as the president's decision was being debated and formulated, there was obviously a substantial distance between the quiet precincts in which the legal advice was being generated and the turbulent world of the war on terrorism. Lawyers are often distant from the application of their analysis. A way to narrow that gap is to listen to the available voices of experience. They were present—Secretary Powell, the lawyers at the State Department, General Myers, the JAGs—but they were not heard. John Yoo has admitted that the military's legal advice can be seen "as an example of military experts preventing civilians from making serious strategic or tactical mistakes."[38] That is exactly what they were trying to do. Instead, sweeping theories of executive power combined with the extreme self-confidence of the president's lawyers to produce a compromised decision that fostered many misfortunes. The War Council had won most of the battles for the president's ear.

The responsibility for the decisions embodied in President Bush's order rested principally with him, of course. One way or another, the main legal and policy issues were all laid before him, except (perhaps) for the question of process due the detainees. There was a tenable claim of legal right for each of the main positions his order adopted, although the better view was that at least Common Article 3 applied to everyone held captive. The question of conscience raises the issues of statesmanship that have so often surrounded important decisions by presidents. For me, the order lacked a vital presidential quality, wisdom. Some readers will disagree, believing that the president's judgments were correct. If the question is debatable, as I believe it to be, the order is supported by good conscience. History will judge its wisdom.

The president's lawyers deserve very mixed grades. Opinions consistent with traditional U.S. legal interpretation of treaties emanated from the State

Department, but not the Justice Department. The War Council produced overaggressive opinions that presented novel theories as normal ones, for example the "failed state" theory. The *Application of Treaties* opinion, although mostly based on plausible arguments about legal right, failed in the duty imposed by conscience to take an independent and candid look at the issues. Instead, OLC furnished a thinly based, misleading brief for a particular policy position. The effects of this bad advice suffused the president's order.

10

Military Trials for War Crimes

IN FALL 2001, intertwined with questions about the force of the Geneva Conventions were those about the appropriate nature of trials for alleged terrorists. The president's military order provided for trial by military commission of alien terrorists suspected of war crimes.[1] As I have explained, the order relied on the president's constitutional power as commander in chief and on implied authority from some statutes, including the AUMF.

The military order, issued just two months after 9/11, was the product of an intense and pressured process.[2] The War Council became part of an interagency task force chaired by Pierre-Richard Prosper, the State Department's ambassador at large for war crimes issues. Lawyers from the Justice Department initially favored regular criminal trials; uniformed lawyers favored courts-martial. Military commissions were also discussed after former attorney general (and former OLC head) William Barr suggested them to Timothy Flanigan of the White House counsel's office.[3] Flanigan then short-circuited the process, opting for military commissions and drafting a proposed order himself, working with his colleague Brad Berenson and with David Addington. They modeled the draft order on President Roosevelt's order for military trial of the Nazi saboteurs, which the Supreme Court had upheld in *Quirin*.[4] Berenson later explained that "we relied on the same language in FDR's order, the same congressional statute that FDR did, and we had a unanimous Supreme Court decision on point. As a lawyer advising a client, it doesn't get much better than that."[5]

OLC supplied a still-classified opinion by Patrick Philbin concluding that President Bush could convene military commissions without special statutory authority. The opinion, *Legality of the Use of Military Commissions to Try Terrorists,* argued that 9/11 was not a crime but an act of war, and thus had released the president's full war powers. The opinion relied on *Quirin,* but considered neither the defects in *Quirin* itself nor two subsequent changes in the law of war: the adoption of the Geneva Conventions and the Uniform Code of Military Justice (UCMJ).

These omissions would prove fatal to the order when it reached the Supreme Court. In many ways, both the applicable law and the nation's legal culture had evolved since the saboteurs met their fate.[6] Nevertheless, John

Yoo has defended the order as incorporating the "historic compromise" that balances "fair trial for enemies who commit war crimes, and protecting the nation's military and intelligence interests."[7]

In early November 2001, Pentagon General Counsel Jim Haynes told General Tom Romig, U.S. Army JAG, that an order was pending. Haynes stipulated that it could be reviewed by one person, who could take away no copy and no notes. These conditions would allow a rudimentary check for glaring defects, but not full participation in reviewing the order. Romig sent over Colonel Lawrence Morris, who was experienced in the issues. When Morris and Romig discussed the order the next day, they were alarmed that it ignored the changes in law since World War II. Romig feared that the order "was going to be perceived as unfair because it was unnecessarily archaic."[8] Morris gave Haynes some suggested changes, which were ignored.

On November 10, Vice President Cheney convened a meeting to finish the order, inviting Attorney General Ashcroft and Jim Haynes, but no one from the State Department or the National Security Council. (Secretary Powell and National Security Adviser Rice found out about the order by reading about its issuance in the press.) Ashcroft "angrily dissented" from the use of military courts and was overridden. Cheney then took the order to Bush and obtained his signature.

Understanding and appraising the legal basis for the military order requires some background on the differences between military and civilian trials and on the traditional uses of military commissions in the United States. Military commissions differ from civilian courts in several respects. (Their cousins, military courts-martial, are closer to the civilian model, as I will explain.) First, their structure is different. They convene under orders from military authorities, comprise one or more military officers, receive charges from the convening authority, and make decisions that may be appealed within the military (and perhaps ultimately to the president). Federal criminal courts are created by statute, have judges with life tenure, have juries to decide guilt or innocence, receive charges from grand juries or federal prosecutors, and make decisions that may be appealed within the federal courts (and perhaps ultimately to the Supreme Court).

The procedure used in these two kinds of court also differs. The rules of evidence in military commissions are usually less formal than in federal court.[9] For example, hearsay evidence may be admissible.[10] These tribunals might not exclude coerced testimony, as a federal court would do. They might decide guilt by less than a majority; a federal criminal jury must be unanimous. Finally, their sentences may be different. A military commission may impose the death penalty whether or not civilian courts are allowed to do so, and sometimes by a less than unanimous vote of the members.

Thus, the choice between civilian and military trials involves very high stakes. Military commissions have existed for mixed reasons of tradition and military necessity. Their primary uses in the United States have been when martial law has been declared in response to emergency conditions, when military government rules over occupied enemy territory, and when enemies have violated the laws of war.[11] Few would argue that Hermann Goering and his fellow monsters deserved trials in a U.S. district court. At the same time, truncated rights fit very uncomfortably in the U.S. constitutional and criminal law tradition. It is all too easy to imagine rather than demonstrate necessity for summary process. To provide some context for the military order, here is a brief review of the role of military commissions in U.S. history.[12]

MILITARY COMMISSIONS IN AMERICA

In 1775 the Continental Congress enacted Articles of War borrowed from British precedents. When General George Washington heard of British mistreatment of colonial prisoners, he considered retaliating but concluded that "Humanity and Policy forbid the measure. Experience proves, that their wanton Cruelty injures rather than benefits their cause."[13] In the Revolution, both sides used military courts to try spies, most prominently Nathan Hale and John Andre. After the war, the Constitution's assignment to Congress of authority to make rules for the military and to define offenses against the law of nations broke from British practice, which assigned these tasks to the monarch.[14] Early Congresses then adopted and adjusted the British military law framework as U.S. Articles of War. Until the Civil War, all was mostly quiet along this front, except for some high-handed actions by General Andrew Jackson in New Orleans during the War of 1812.[15] During the Mexican War, in the absence of functioning local courts General Winfield Scott issued an order applying martial law both to U.S. soldiers and Mexican citizens. The scheme was fairly administered and caused little complaint.

In the cauldron of the Civil War, military commissions played a more controversial role. These tribunals used court-martial procedures to enforce the customary laws of war and were eventually regularized by an executive order that forbade subjecting prisoners to either cruelty or torture. Controversy about the trials produced an important Supreme Court precedent.

Lambdin Milligan was arrested in Indiana in 1864, was tried before a military tribunal for conspiracy to aid the Confederacy, and was sentenced to hang. In *Ex Parte Milligan,* the Supreme Court, stating that citizens may not be tried by the military when the civilian courts are functioning, held that an 1863 statute regulating habeas corpus required Milligan's release.[16] During Reconstruction, however, the tribunals remained in operation in the South. Henry Wirz, commandant of the infamous Andersonville prison, was tried and condemned by one of them. The Lincoln assassination plotters were also tried and condemned by military commission, although the courts were open in Washington, D.C.—no one was minded to quibble over the rights of the assassins. After the Civil War, Congress gave episodic consideration to revising the Articles of War, but did not do so until the twentieth century.

A MODEL PROCEDURE?

In their modern form, the Articles of War were applied in World War II in a major precedent for the war on terrorism, the case of the Nazi saboteurs. Recall the story of President Roosevelt's order for a military trial of the saboteurs, their speedy execution, and the Supreme Court's awkward opinion in *Ex Parte Quirin* blessing the proceedings.[17] A rudimentary knowledge of the background of *Quirin* should have warned the Bush administration that this was far from a model instance of the rule of law, even in its own time.

Military law has evolved substantially since 1942. In 1950, passage of the UCMJ revised and codified both substantive and procedural military law. The UCMJ provides for courts-martial before military judges with panels of officers as jurors. The law of evidence used in federal criminal trials generally applies. Review of a conviction occurs first within the military, and then by the Court of Appeals for the Armed Forces, a civilian court whose members serve for specified terms. Its decisions can be reviewed by the Supreme Court.

President Bush's order, as had Roosevelt's, called for a "full and fair trial" and attempted to prohibit judicial review. The Bush order itself was quite skeletal; it contemplated that the Defense Department would flesh it out. The order applied to persons who were not U.S. citizens, where there was "reason to believe" that they were members of Al Qaeda or had been involved in acts of international terrorism. The order granted the secretary of defense authority to detain such persons and directed that they be prosecuted for "all offenses triable by military commission." The president recited that the order responded to an "extraordinary emergency." Given the nature of terrorism, he found that it was "not practicable" for the new military commissions to apply the "principles of law and the rules of evidence" used in federal criminal trials. Here he relied on a provision of the UCMJ that authorizes the president to promulgate rules for military commissions, which are to be the same "so far as he considers practicable" as those used in federal criminal trials.[18]

Thus, the president was invoking an exception in the statute. At this point he made an error, however, that would invalidate the order when it reached the Supreme Court.[19] The same section of the UCMJ also provides that the rules for military commissions may not be "contrary or inconsistent with" the UCMJ and that they must be "uniform insofar as practicable" with court-martial procedure. Throughout U.S. history, military commissions and courts-martial have usually followed the same procedures. The Bush order varied substantially from court-martial practice as it had evolved under the UCMJ. Yet the order made no statement that it was impracticable to follow *court-martial* procedures, as the statute required. This was no technical defect, because the Supreme Court would conclude that the order's variations from the court-martial model jeopardized the fairness of the proceedings.

Three controversial features of the order would eventually be criticized sharply by the Court. First, an accused person and his or her civilian counsel could be excluded from proceedings closed to protect "classified or classifiable" information. (Appointed military counsel could be present, but could be forbidden to reveal the evidence to the accused.) Second, evidence could be admitted if it "would have probative value to a reasonable person." This meant that hearsay evidence, ordinarily inadmissible in U.S. criminal trials, including courts-martial, could be admitted if it seemed reliable. It also meant that coerced testimony, also inadmissible in ordinary civilian and military trials, might be allowed. Third, both conviction and sentence (including the death penalty) could occur on a two-thirds vote of the military court. President Bush directed that trial records go to him for final review or to the secretary of defense if so designated.

We have seen that in formulating the order the administration sought little help from the JAG offices in the services, where considerable expertise about military trials resides. Also, the president did not consult Congress. Issuance of the order sparked immediate controversy.[20] Fanning the flames, Vice President Cheney happily mentioned the Nazi saboteurs, who had been "executed in relatively rapid order."[21] Attorney General Ashcroft now rallied to the support of the administration, and even made a statement suggesting that criticism of the order was unpatriotic (his office soon issued a "clarification" that he was not stifling debate but criticizing misinformation).[22] Several hundred law professors and lawyers wrote to Senator Patrick Leahy calling for a statutory basis for the order.[23] Various bills were introduced; none passed. Early in 2002, an American Bar Association Task Force on Terrorism and the Law raised questions and called for use of court-martial procedures and judicial review.[24]

As a result of this controversy, the Department of Defense had the benefit of initial reactions before it drafted detailed trial procedures in *Military Commission Order No. 1*.[25] Along with John Yoo and Patrick Philbin, General Counsel Haynes worked with the JAGs. The political appointees wanted a "draconian system," and the JAGs retorted that some of the rules would be unethical and would risk war crimes prosecution.[26] The final rules ameliorated some points of contention by moving toward the military's preferences.

The tribunals would have jurisdiction over "violations of the laws of war and all other offenses triable by military commission." Presiding officers and prosecuting and defense counsel were to be judge advocates. The accused were presumed innocent and could be convicted on the "reasonable doubt" standard. The accused could obtain witnesses and evidence and could be present at proceedings unless they were closed for security reasons, whereupon military counsel could be present. The two-thirds vote remained sufficient for convictions, but unanimity was now required for death. The secretary was to appoint a new panel to review trials before the secretary's own review. It would be empowered to reverse convictions for "material error of law."

In April 2003, after publishing a draft and receiving comments on it, the Pentagon issued a set of *Crimes and Elements for Trials by Military Commission*.[27] There were twenty-four categories of crimes, including attacks on civilians, taking hostages, and hijacking aircraft. Many of these were also crimes under the federal criminal code. Others, such as aiding the enemy and spying, followed the old Articles of War. By narrowing the set of crimes to those already denounced somewhere in the criminal law or the law of war, the administration hoped to overcome objections that it planned prosecutions for acts not criminal when performed, in violation of constitutional strictures against ex post facto laws.

With substantive and procedural rules in place, the administration appeared to be ready to proceed to trial. The president designated six prisoners at Guantánamo as eligible for trial by military commission. The first trials began in August 2004. Threshold challenges to the proceedings soon began in the federal courts.

Why did it take almost three years to initiate trials for possible war criminals?[28] The decision that the detainees could be tried by military commission put them under the jurisdiction of the Defense Department, but Secretary Donald Rumsfeld "would not start the tribunal process" and was "balking." National Security Adviser Condoleezza Rice engaged an interagency review involving senior lawyers to try to induce President Bush to order Rumsfeld to start the tribunals. Attorney General Ashcroft was pressing for action, saying that if there were no "credible tribunal process up and running, . . . the Justice Department would be dead in the water when they tried to defend the system at the federal appeals courts." At a National Security Council meeting with the president, Rice elaborated the arguments before Bush and Rumsfeld, both of whom seemed inattentive. Bush interrupted to ask Rumsfeld's views, and he responded: "They are bad guys." Americans thought about rights, he said, while he was trying to keep terrorists off the battlefield and get their intelligence. There was a public relations job to do, he said. No decision was made, and time continued to pass. Reverse lawfare had prevailed again.

John Yoo's view of the matter is that the delayed trials were the administration's "most conspicuous policy failure" in the war on terrorism.[29] He attributes it to the "sheer multitude of issues involved in building a working court system from scratch." He says that some military lawyers, trained for courts-martial, resisted use of the more informal commissions—they wanted "a showcase of military justice at its finest." Their position, squarely at odds with that of Secretary Rumsfeld, was part of the struggle between the military professionals and the civilians around Rumsfeld during his tenure.

THE COURT CONSIDERS THE COMMISSIONS

The validity of President Bush's 2001 military order finally reached the Supreme Court in the case of Salim Hamdan, a Yemeni who had served as Osama bin Laden's driver.[30] Captured in Afghanistan and held at Guantánamo, he was clearly an enemy combatant; hence the *Hamdi* issue was not present. Hamdan was charged before a military commission with "conspiracy to commit offenses triable by military commission." The offenses in the conspiracy were attacking civilians and committing acts of terrorism. More specifically the government alleged that Hamdan had aided bin Laden's terror plot by serving as his driver, and had transported and carried weapons. The government characterized him as an Al Qaeda soldier and an unlawful combatant because he had worn no uniform.

Hamdan conceded that a court-martial convened under the UCMJ could try him. (Were he recognized as a POW, that was the procedure he could expect.) He objected, however, that the structure and process of the military commission violated the UCMJ and the Geneva Conventions. Five justices agreed with this contention, making a majority. He also denied that the law of war allowed the offense of conspiracy. A plurality of four justices agreed with this contention. Justice Stevens wrote the plurality opinion, which became a majority opinion in places where Justice Kennedy concurred. The Court's holding was that neither the AUMF nor the Detainee Treatment Act (DTA) authorized use of the military commissions, and the UCMJ and the Geneva Conventions forbade them. The government had conceded that statutory limits were binding in this case—it was not repeating the *Steel Seizure* attempt to rely on sweeping constitutional powers.

As a preliminary matter, the Court held that the DTA did not deprive it of jurisdiction over Hamdan's habeas petition because the statute's limitations on habeas corpus had not been intended to apply to cases already pending at the time of its enactment. The structure of the statute and its legislative history made this a plausible conclusion. More generally, this aspect of the case is an example of the Court's usual readiness to interpret jurisdiction-limiting statutes narrowly so that the judiciary retains some means to consider important constitutional claims.[31] The Court requires Congress to make an "unmistakably clear statement" if it wishes to produce the destabilizing effect of blocking avenues for judicial review of executive action. This is the clear statement approach in its strongest form in a context that involves both individual rights and core judicial powers. (In its later *Boumediene* decision, the Court would hold that Congress had indeed spoken clearly when it again took away habeas jurisdiction in the Military Commissions Act.)[32]

Proceeding to the merits, Justice Stevens summarized the traditional roles of military commissions: they operate under martial law, in occupied territory, and against POWs who violate the law of war. Hamdan's alleged actions, though, were those of a common soldier, not intrinsic violations of the law of war. Moreover, the alleged conspiracy almost entirely predated 9/11. Stevens noted that Congress has never defined conspiracy as a war crime, although it did incorporate the common law of war in the UCMJ. He said that *Quirin* was within that delegation, since espionage and sabotage are central offenses in the law of war. Therefore, the government had to show that it was charging a common law offense. The plurality concluded that it had failed to do so. Justice Kennedy would not have reached this issue.

A majority of the Court also concluded that three aspects of the trial process violated the UCMJ's restrictions on military commissions. First, a "glaring" defect was denial of the right to confront opposing witnesses by allowing closed trials. Second, hearsay evidence was allowed if deemed reliable, even if coerced. Third, a two-thirds vote sufficed for conviction but not for the death penalty. Review then remained within the military, up to the president at the end. All of these elements varied from court-martial procedure. Justice Stevens stressed that military commissions had traditionally followed court-martial procedure. The UCMJ required following federal trial process when practicable, and required court-martial and commission proceedings to be uniform "insofar as practicable." There was no sufficient justification here for the commissions to depart from court-martial procedure; therefore, the court-martial model applied. The Court could see no reason why it would not work acceptably.

Turning to the Geneva Conventions, the Court adopted a minimalist approach that decided no more than necessary. Justice Stevens acknowledged but did not answer the administration's argument that Al Qaeda detainees did not enjoy full POW protection because they were not part of a war between nation-states under Common Article 2. Instead, he decided that "there is at least one provision of the Geneva Conventions that applies," Common Article 3. He rejected the government's argument that this article was for civil wars only. Instead, he adopted the conventional understanding that it was a broad, residual category for conflicts other than traditional wars.

The majority focused on the requirement in Common Article 3 that any trial of persons detained in conflict be by a "regularly constituted" court giving guarantees "recognized as indispensable by civilized peoples." Courts-martial were regularly constituted; special courts were intrinsically more doubtful. The majority concluded that no sufficient justification appeared for departing from regular courts-martial. Justice Stevens then went on to discuss a point that Justice Kennedy did not join. Now writing for a plurality and repeating his earlier analysis, Stevens emphasized that indispensable rights include presence at the proceedings. The Bush military commissions failed at least this part of the test.

Justice Kennedy concurred that Congress had set limits in the UCMJ that the executive had exceeded. He also argued that under Geneva, regularly constituted courts are created in advance of a crisis, not ad hoc by the executive without any checks from elsewhere. He would have confined the analysis to these issues of authorization and would not have decided other issues concerning process and substantive crimes that the plurality had discussed.[33]

Three justices dissented. Justice Scalia would have found no jurisdiction; he concluded that the DTA applied to pending cases. Justice Alito thought that the tribunal was lawfully created and that process issues could be reviewed as they arose. Justice Thomas thought that in this context, the Court should not readily find a lack of authorization. The president should prevail, he argued, and added that the plurality was second-guessing military judgments about process in wartime conditions. He also thought that the alleged conspiracy to murder civilians was triable: it fit the world after 9/11.[34]

Hamdan has evoked a wide range of opinion.[35] John Yoo deplores the decision because it "made the legal system part of the problem, rather than part of the solution to the challenges of the war on terrorism."[36] He thinks that the circus-like trial in federal court of Zacharias Moussaoui shows the effect of "using normal courtroom rules to prosecute terrorists." (Some evidence to the contrary has later emerged in the successful prosecution of Jose Padilla in federal court for terrorism-related crimes.)[37] In any event, the Supreme Court did not say that only full criminal trial procedures would suffice for terrorists. It simply held that existing statutes prohibited the form of trial designed by the administration along the lines of the outdated *Quirin* precedent.

Focusing on what the Court actually did, others have correctly hailed the decision as *Steel Seizure II*, a courageous decision to hold the executive to law in the midst of military conflict.[38] Citing Justice Jackson's famous concurrence, the Court emphasized that "whether or not the President has independent power, absent congressional authorization, to convene military commissions, he may not disregard limitations that Congress has, in proper exercise of its own war powers, placed on his powers."[39] Thus the *Hamdan* Court remanded the question of using military commissions to Congress, which could authorize or prohibit them.

Hamdan fits squarely within a line of Supreme Court cases that resolve wartime tensions by seeking congressional authority for executive action instead of articulating sweeping doctrine about executive authority and civil liberties.[40] In that tradition, "what counts as congressional endorsement of executive action becomes critical."[41] The majority's refusal to find authority for the military order in either the UCMJ or the AUMF employed clear statement principles.[42] This strategy allowed the Court to avoid making binding constitutional decisions about the sensitive procedural issues it identified in the edifice created by the order.

Also, the majority was avoiding any invocation of the opposite canon of construction. The avoidance canon could have been deployed to uphold the order if the Court had thought the president's constitutional authority might otherwise be invaded. Use of that canon would have warned Congress away from participating in forming policy for the war on terrorism. Instead, the Court invited its involvement.

Justice Thomas's dissent must have gratified his former clerk John Yoo, since it began by claiming that the president has "primary responsibility" for protecting national security. Thomas showed how reliance on the avoidance canon could have produced a victory for the administration. He emphasized the presence of the president's constitutional powers and the ambiguities in the relevant statutes and traditions. He was prepared to defer to the president's judgments about the legal regime that should govern trial of the terrorists.

The White House initially reacted to *Hamdan* by reversing the position taken by President Bush in 2002 that the Geneva Conventions did not apply to Al Qaeda or the Taliban.[43] The next day, however, the administration retreated and commenced negotiations with Congress to obtain legislative clarification of the issues.[44] As the administration formulated its legislative position, there resurfaced the long-standing disagreement over appropriate procedure between civilians in the administration, who favored military commissions, and the uniformed lawyers, who favored courts-martial.[45] As before, the civilians won the battle.

A complicated compromise eventually emerged, the Military Commissions Act of 2006 (MCA).[46] Like the earlier DTA, this statute is friendly to the executive branch. The MCA is a quite complicated statute, presenting issues that will take years to resolve. It authorizes military commission trials for suspected terrorists, reinforces the DTA's ban on habeas corpus for enemy combatants, and contains some restrictions on treatment of detainees that I consider in the next chapter.

By providing statutory authority for the military commissions, the MCA shifts the ground for debate to interpretation of its provisions and to overarching issues of constitutional and international law. The MCA authorizes the president to establish military commissions to try "alien unlawful enemy combatants," a category explicitly including members of both Al Qaeda and the Taliban.[47] A provision of disputed effect forbids these combatants "to invoke the Geneva Conventions as a source of rights."[48] Adding to the uncertainty, the MCA authorizes the president "to interpret the meaning and application of the Geneva Conventions."[49]

The procedures for military commission trials allow the use of coerced confessions in the tribunals if the interrogation occurred before the DTA banned "cruel, inhuman, or degrading treatment" of prisoners and if the judge believes the statements are reliable. Evidence obtained by torture may not be used. Classified information will not be disclosed if doing so would harm national security, but the judge will have to provide summaries or redactions of the information to the defense. Convictions may be appealed to a new Court of Military Commission Review and then to the District of Columbia Circuit Court of Appeals and the Supreme Court.

With statutory authority from the MCA in hand, the administration began planning trials. In late 2006, President Bush brought to Guantánamo fourteen "high-profile" terror suspects who had previously been detained in secret CIA facilities.[50] This group included the notorious Khalid Shaikh Mohammed ("KSM"), thought to be the planner of the 9/11 attacks. The administration promulgated an extensive *Manual for Military Commissions* to guide the trials.[51] Preparations began to bring capital charges against KSM and five other high-level prisoners.[52]

Meanwhile, trials of less prominent suspects began as test cases. Australian David Hicks entered a plea bargain. In August 2008, Salim Hamdan was convicted of providing material support for terrorism, but was acquitted of the more serious charge of conspiracy.[53] In a setback for the administration, his sentence was only five and a half years in prison (most of which he had already served) and not the life sentence sought by the prosecution.

When military commission trials finally begin in earnest, trying the leaders of al Qaeda will present special problems. They were held in CIA custody for years and were subjected to the harshest interrogation used for any U.S. prisoners. The Bush administration admitted that KSM was subjected to waterboarding; it may also have employed hypothermia, sleep deprivation, and forced long-term standing.[54] Hence, many of these cases will present extremely unpleasant controversies about whether the interrogations were merely "cruel, inhuman, or degrading" or whether they crossed the line into torture. No one wants to transform defendants into prosecutors and monsters into heroes, but these controversies are a natural consequence of the administration's initial decision to press for information at the possible price of hampering criminal prosecutions.

The Bush administration's choice of procedures for trying terrorists fell short in both right and conscience. Regarding the question of legal right, the president's military order was crafted by a small group of lawyers inexperienced in military law, who relied excessively on the vulnerable *Quirin* precedent. Their second mistake, omitting the needed finding about the impracticability of court-martial procedures, was understandable but unnecessary. Both mistakes were direct consequences of the decision, surely made by high political officers, to exclude the JAGs from any meaningful role in the formulation of the president's order. The JAGs well understood that *Quirin* had been undermined by adoption of the UCMJ and the Geneva Conventions, but no one cared to listen to their correct judgment that the draft order was "archaic."

Regarding moral conscience, greater attention by the president's lawyers to the need to prepare careful and thorough legal advice would have diminished the legal jeopardy attending the order. Also, a lurking issue of great importance was simply evaded: the applicability of the Geneva Conventions, especially Common Article 3. The military order was issued in November 2001, before the controversy within the administration over Geneva reached its peak. Geneva issues were, however, in the air.

In good conscience, Common Article 3's injunction against irregular courts for war crimes trials required a considered response from the administration. It may be that a consequentialist analysis foreclosed such a response. That is, if the detainees were designated POWs, a matter not yet decided in November 2001, Geneva would have required that they be tried for war crimes only by the procedures used by the detaining nation to try its own troops for such crimes—courts-martial. The administration's effort to avoid offering terrorist suspects the full benefit of court-martial procedure breathes from every line of the president's order. Therefore, the applicability of Common Article 3 was bound up in the larger questions about the treatment of the detainees under Geneva. It may be that in the late fall of 2001, the fact that the president had already called for informal trials for terrorist suspects, in clear tension with Geneva requirements, helped drive the administration's final decision not to accord them any Geneva protections whatsoever.

In retrospect, the years of delays in commencing trials for terrorists and the trip to the Supreme Court in *Hamdan* were above all unnecessary. The administration's determination to follow an ad hoc course in selecting trial procedures instead of the proven and clearly legal model of the court-martial proved very shortsighted.

II

Interrogation

OF ALL THE LEGAL ADVICE TENDERED TO PRESIDENT BUSH AFTER 9/11, opinions concerning the limits to permissible interrogation of suspected terrorists proved the most bitterly controversial. The stakes were very high. The administration always understood the importance of gathering information about terrorist plots from those most likely to possess it. Yet charges that U.S. officers were torturing suspects soon surfaced, and torture is deeply inconsistent with the best of our traditions. Part of the controversy has revolved around refined—and intrinsically repellent—efforts to define the boundary between torture and mere cruelty.

Existing law has called for sketching this boundary when necessary, raising difficult issues of legal right. A vital question of moral conscience is how close to the line lawyers responsibly may advise interrogators to go. Some legal judgments, even if supported by credible claims of right, may allow or even encourage unacceptable treatment of prisoners in the war on terrorism. For not every legal question has the same moral dimension. No one need worry much if, to borrow a phrase from Alberto Gonzales, detainees are denied commissary privileges.[1] If, however, detainees are tormented up to or beyond the brink of torture, everyone who values the rule of law should care a great deal.

CONTEMPLATING TORTURE

The torture debate has renewed interest in a very old question: when, if ever, is torture permissible in defense of civilized society?[2] Each of us can attempt a personal answer to this question based on our morality, philosophy, or religion. Democratic societies, however, cannot easily form open policy and law around so sensitive an issue. Torture, like a torturer, is hard to look in the eye.

Two preliminary points may help provide a frame of reference for moral speculation. First, torture has been a common practice throughout human history and remains so today.[3] For centuries, it was openly employed by some continental judicial systems in the search for truth, until it became apparent that the information produced was unreliable.[4] In modern times, supposedly civilized nations have engaged in torture behind closed doors. The French, who yield to no one in their self-regard, fouled their reputation as a high civilization by torturing insurgents in Algeria.[5] Nazi Germany, which generally treated U.S. and British prisoners of war acceptably, visited extreme cruelties on its Russian prisoners, and the overall Nazi record of tormenting and slaughtering innocents gave the whole twentieth century a bad name. Stalin's Soviet Union imposed most of its terror on its own people.[6] The worldwide list of appalling examples is long; recent ones include Argentina and Chile.[7]

Second, hopes for reciprocal kindness provide a weak practical justification for renouncing torture. U.S. prisoners have endured harsh treatment in all recent wars notwithstanding the efforts of international law. In World War II, the Japanese Empire brutalized and sometimes executed Allied prisoners of war.[8] North Korea devised psychological torments for U.S. prisoners that led our military to revise its course of resistance training.[9] North Vietnam tortured captured U.S. airmen, including future Senator John McCain. Nowadays, Al Qaeda chops off the heads of its captives, the better to spread terror. Therefore, reasons other than reciprocity are often advanced to justify banning torture.

Moral values about what kind of nation the United States is may determine our conduct, whatever others might do. Alternatively, renouncing torture can be part of a broader strategy of attempting to articulate and enforce a general regime of international law that can affect some aspects of the behavior of nations, even if not all nations abide every legal stricture. For we can never know how much more torture there would be if the international community did not try to prevent it.

In the twenty-first century, Americans have had to contemplate the morality of torture. The standard hypothetical in debate posits a "ticking bomb."[10] The police capture someone who knows where a bomb on a timer is located. The bomb (nuclear, biological, or chemical) is horrifyingly powerful. Many lives are at stake. May—must—the police torture the suspect to find the bomb before it detonates? "Suppose you had Terry Nichols in custody before the Oklahoma City bombing. You know enough to know that (1) a public building is going to be bombed, and (2) Terry Nichols knows *who, where, and when*. How do you think about torture in such a circumstance?"[11]

The stark ticking bomb scenario is fundamentally misleading as a way to think about the real world. It omits a central, nearly omnipresent factor: uncertainty about the knowledge possessed by a captive. What does he or she know that might be of intelligence value? The usual purpose of interrogation is to find that out; it is rarely available in advance. The answer may well be—nothing. Therefore, the ticking bomb hypothesis must be understood as a rhetorical tactic in the torture debate. Invoking it pressures anyone who is reluctant to countenance torture to concede that there might be *some* circumstance in which it is permissible. At that point, the Kantian categorical imperative falls away, and the argument shifts to a cost-benefit analysis—how many lives must be saved to justify torture? Would not *one* be enough, if that one is innocent and the captive is guilty? Some thoughtful people forthrightly defend torture on these essentially utilitarian grounds.[12]

The difficulty the utilitarians must confront is that torture is extremely difficult to control: "Interrogation presents an elemental challenge: the interrogator wants to learn what the prisoner wants to withhold. The very nature of the enterprise invites abuse, since the obvious temptation is to extract the information by any means necessary. And the temptation to use brute force rises with the perceived cost of failure."[13]

Therefore, torture spreads from the exceptional to the routine.[14] For there are "gravitational laws that govern human behavior when one group of people is given complete control over another in prison. Every impulse tugs downward."[15] In a well-known experiment once conducted at Stanford University, student volunteers were divided into prisoners and guards in a mock prison.[16] The guards soon began abusing the prisoners so badly that the experiment was terminated. Power, it appears, corrupts quickly.

Aware of these problems, some analysts argue legal bans on torture should remain unqualified, with the expectation that an official who yields to perceived necessity and breaks the law can raise a defense of necessity afterward.[17] This position avoids conferring an overbroad license to torture. It also reflects doubt whether law can control executive action in the emergency situations that often induce a temptation to torture. Alternatively, perhaps we should try to "domesticate" torture by authorizing the issuance of warrants for it in carefully controlled circumstances.[18]

The eternal underlying question, whether torture is ever justified in pursuit of the greater good, was posed in 1881 by Fyodor Dostoyevsky in *The Brothers Karamozov.*[19] The intellectually rigorous Ivan presses his more spiritual brother Aloysha:

> "Imagine that you are creating a fabric of human destiny with the object of making men happy in the end, giving them peace and rest at last. Imagine that you are doing this but that it is essential and inevitable to torture to death only one tiny creature—that child beating its

breast with its fist, for instance—in order to found that edifice on its unavenged tears. Would you consent to be the architect on those conditions? Tell me. Tell me the truth."

"No, I wouldn't consent," said Aloysha softly.

And you?

The consequences of torture for nations that perform it must also play a role in any analysis of the practice. An example will show the enduring nature of this problem. Robert Massie's magisterial biography of Peter the Great recounts a great blot on Peter's otherwise impressive record.[20] A traditional warrior class in Moscow, the Streltsy, rose in revolt against Tsar Peter in 1698. Peter crushed the rebellion, and in his anxiety to discover its sources by extracting intelligence, he had the Streltsy brutally tortured by whip and fire (often in his presence). Eventually he slaughtered them, but he did not discover much. Massie ruminates on the episode:

> In Peter's time, as in ours, torture was carried out to gather information, and public execution to deter further crimes. The fact that innocent men have confessed to escape further pain has never stopped torture, nor has the execution of criminals ever stopped crime. Undeniably, the state has a right to defend itself against people who break its laws, and perhaps even a duty to try to deter future infringements, but how far into repression and cruelty can a state or society descend before the means no longer justify the end? It is a question as old as political theory, and it will not be answered here.

Nor here.

Confounding us further is the fact that sometimes torture *works*. Two well-known examples are French claims that torture exposed terrorist plots in Algeria and U.S. claims that torture in the Philippines exposed a 1995 plot to crash eleven commercial airliners into the Pacific.[21] The Bush administration has consistently and emphatically stated that its harsh interrogation methods (whether or not amounting to torture) have produced information that has defeated terrorist plots. I assess that claim below.

The practical counterargument flows from the conventional wisdom that coerced testimony is inherently unreliable (unless it can be verified in some other way). The victim will say what the interrogator wants to hear in hopes the pain will stop. Because torture tests endurance rather than veracity, the error rate is high—and often unknowable.[22] Hence, any utilitarian calculus may depend more on faith than on facts. A more brutal calculus, too often evident in world history, simply values any information gleaned and places no value on the lives or well-being of the victims.

No consensus exists regarding what constitutes torture. For understandable reasons, there is no medical definition of it. Torture is a legal term. It is obvious that such ancient and repellent practices as the rack, the screw, and various burnings, maimings, and flayings constitute torture. Torment has always been their purpose. Proud of their modern sensibilities, nations have now invented "torture lite," techniques such as isolation, stress positions, sleep deprivation, exposure to heat or cold, and exposure to bright lights and constant noise.[23] Analysts often say that duration and combination can convert these techniques into torture pure and simple. Much current controversy surrounds waterboarding, in which the subject is strapped down and taken to the point of drowning by pouring water over his or her nose and mouth. Waterboarding has a bad pedigree—it is a legacy of the Spanish Inquisition. U.S. troops used it against insurgents in the Philippines early in the twentieth century.[24] Its victims call it torture; lawyers are not always so sure.

As we shall see, legal definitions of torture typically focus on the intentional infliction of serious suffering. A central difficulty in line-drawing is the fact that *all* coercive methods of interrogation are meant to overbear the will and induce confession. Some form of discomfort, physical or mental, is always present. How much of what kind is too much? Moreover, although the law has grappled with defining torture for a long time, the kinds of lawyers who advise presidents are usually innocent of any actual experience with the limits of interrogation. Therefore, they lack any "feel" for the issues of fact and policy that underlie legal conclusions. As a result, President Bush's lawyers produced remarkably wooden opinions in a context where the greatest sensitivity was needed.

A HIGH-LEVEL TRIP TO THE DARK SIDE

The events that sent the Bush administration into this quicksand began soon after 9/11. Vice President Cheney set the tone, saying that the United States would soon have to work on the "dark side" of intelligence, using "any means at our disposal."[25] He was not speaking lightly. Cofer Black, head of the CIA's counterterrorism unit, later told Congress that "there was 'before' 9/11 and 'after' 9/11. After 9/11 the gloves come off."[26]

On September 17, 2001, President Bush signed a memorandum authorizing the Central Intelligence Agency (CIA) to capture, detain, and interrogate terrorism suspects.[27] Eventually, the CIA would maintain an entire secret prison system overseas. There were both legal and practical reasons for designating the CIA as the jailer for selected terrorism suspects. Legally, the CIA is exempt from many strictures that bind the other potential jailer, the U.S. military. For example, military law forbids both coercive interrogation and general mistreatment of prisoners. By contrast, the CIA is accustomed to operating on the dark side under a vague statutory charter. Practically, the agency is usually better able to operate in secret than is the military. The administration did not want anyone to know whom it held, what it was doing to them, or what it was learning from them.

President Bush's initial directive to the CIA did not contain guidelines regarding interrogation techniques. This lack of initial legal guidance for interrogations turned out to affect the conduct of the war on terrorism in fundamental ways, because early and unfortunate decisions made within the CIA later migrated to military interrogators and affected the behavior of U.S. agents in many parts of the world. The essential problem was that the CIA did not know how to respond to the president's directive because (unlike the FBI) it had little experience in interrogation and almost no trained interrogators.[28] To fill the gap, the CIA turned to some inapposite sources of guidance.

First, in the 1960s the agency had compiled information gleaned from studying communist practices and from conducting some experiments of its own into its *KUBARK* manual for counterintelligence interrogation.[29] The manual, reflecting judgments still in place on 9/11, catalogs interrogation techniques, many of them coercive, thought to produce reliable information.[30] It gives practical (not moral) advice against inflicting torture, physical brutality, or intense pain because these techniques induce false confessions and increase the hostility of the subject. Instead, the manual suggests techniques such as disorientation, fatigue, humiliation, and sensory deprivation. The purpose is to destroy the psychological will to resist. Success is stated to be common. An update, the *Human Resource Exploitation Training Manual*, came out in 1983 (given the title, 1984 would have been a better date).[31] The new manual elaborates many fine points of the earlier techniques, but mostly stops short of brute force except for remarking that the use of "pain" might be helpful. These limits would not survive the impatience created by the war on terrorism.

Second, as the agency quickly cobbled a program together after receiving the president's directive, it did so "by consulting Egyptian and Saudi intelligence officials and copying Soviet interrogation methods long used in training U.S. servicemen to withstand capture."[32] This training program was called SERE, which stands for "survive, evade, resist, escape."[33] The point of SERE training is to mimic coercion POWs may encounter and to teach resistance to it. It includes humiliation, physical exhaustion, stress positions, and psychological duress. Soon the coercive SERE methods were applied to the detainees. Unfortunately, this understandable step involved a fundamental mistake. As a former head of U.S. Air Force interrogation has observed, the Korean War abuses SERE copied were designed to break the will and make prisoners sign false confessions—producing accurate information was not the goal.[34] For that, noncoercive techniques are conventionally thought to be better. Consequently, "there is strong evidence that the violent interrogation techniques muddied American intelligence files with bad information."

CIA officers in the field soon barraged headquarters at Langley with questions about the limits to approved interrogation methods. They were deeply concerned about lawfare if revelation of their actions broke the rules as later understood. The agency could easily look quite bad. Although it is in the nature of the CIA's mission to consort with unsavory characters around the world and to break numerous local laws wherever it operates, adopting interrogation methods from such notorious sources as the Egyptians and North Koreans might exceed the nation's tolerance. Also, officers who lacked field experience had little practical or legal sense for the boundaries.

It is not surprising that the CIA felt unguided. The part of the president's order of February 7, 2002, that required humane treatment of detainees was addressed to the armed forces, a category that excludes the CIA. In addition, OLC's early *Habeas* and *Application of Treaties* opinions had created large law-free zones outside the United States and had eliminated Geneva protections for the prisoners. Given all that, what law—if any—limited interrogation?

In late 2001, U.S. forces went into Afghanistan and started to gather prisoners. Among them, some "high-value" captives soon began to appear. These were usually assigned to CIA custody; the military held everyone else. The first senior Al Qaeda operative captured was Abu Zubaydah, the group's travel and logistics manager, who was taken in a firefight in early 2002.[35] While Zubaydah recovered from wounds suffered during his capture, he was flown to a secret CIA prison near Bangkok. FBI agents conducted some preliminary interrogations. The FBI is deeply ingrained with the strictures against coercive questioning that suffuse U.S. criminal law. Hence it employed normal noncoercive techniques. Zubaydah revealed some information, including confirmation of the critical fact that the architect of 9/11 was Khalid Sheikh Mohammed ("KSM"), but he also displayed resistance. Impatient CIA agents then intervened, and Zubaydah soon "was stripped, held in an icy room and jarred by ear-splittingly loud music." The shift to coercive techniques had begun, opening a rift between the CIA and the FBI that has never closed during the war on terrorism. Zubaydah was water-boarded, which ended his resistance.[36] He was later transferred to another CIA "black site" in Poland and eventually to Guantánamo.

RENDERING UNTO EGYPT

The CIA did not use its own personnel to conduct all interrogations. Instead, it "outsourced" some of them through one of its most secret activities, the "extraordinary rendition" of prisoners.[37] This practice consists of transporting captives to nations other than the United States, where they are held for interrogation and sometimes tortured.[38] The intelligence obtained is then furnished to the CIA. It appears that about 100–200 prisoners have been rendered in this way, most of them low-level members of Al Qaeda (the CIA prefers to keep high-value captives in its own hands).[39]

In use at times prior to 9/11, rendition has both expanded dramatically and changed its nature since then.[40] The earliest form of the practice is the least controversial. U.S. agents would capture a suspect overseas and spirit him or her back to the United States for trial. A prominent example is Ramzi Yousef, who was rendered to the United States and convicted for his role in the 1993 World Trade Center bombing. (U.S. courts show little interest in the circumstances surrounding the capture of defendants who are otherwise properly before them.)

Before 9/11, there were also some instances of a captive's rendition to his or her home country for trial there. At this point, legal sensitivities intrude. The Convention Against Torture (CAT), which the United States has signed, forbids nations to "return or extradite a person to another state where there are substantial grounds for believing that he would be in danger of being subjected to torture."[41] In addition, under the U.S. torture statute, criminal liability as an accessory can await someone who delivers a victim to a torturer. The federal government has two theories supporting the legality of these renditions. First, it denies that CAT applies when the United States renders someone from another nation, as distinguished from renditions from the United States.[42] Given the comprehensive purposes of CAT, which I review below, this position is too technical to be very persuasive. Hence, a second line of defense has developed: the recipient nation must promise not to torture the prisoner. When the recipient is one of the nations condemned by our State Department for performing torture, such as Egypt, this promise is a fig leaf. At least it can be said, though, that the United States does not gain from torture in this context.

It is the third form of rendition, for interrogation, not trial, that has become prominent and controversial after 9/11. Recipient nations include Egypt, Syria, Jordan, Morocco, and Uzbekistan.[43] As with rendition for trial, the CIA claims that it instructs recipient nations not to torture the captives and has no knowledge that they do so. There are two sufficient answers to any such claim. First, the characteristics common to the recipient nations are: a Muslim population, a government opposed to Al Qaeda, and a notorious devotion to torture. These nations can be in no doubt about the reason for their selection, whatever CIA agents might say upon delivery. Second, the CIA's core duty is to know what occurs within foreign nations. If it does not know whether rendered captives are being tortured, what does it know about anything?

Given the obvious legal jeopardy that attends rendition for interrogation, why did the administration turn to it? The practice offers two strong practical advantages for the CIA. First, foreigners are usually beyond the jurisdiction of U.S. courts. Second, although the CIA's gloves might be off, the agency has too few hands. During the 1990s, budget cuts following the end of the cold war badly eroded the agency's covert action capacities. Also, few CIA personnel have the skills in Arabic and other languages needed to interrogate captives.

In the wake of 9/11, President Bush authorized rendition.[44] The practice is governed by rules set by the National Security Council (NSC) after review by the Department of Justice. Apparently, particular instances of rendition are approved after internal CIA review and consultation with the NSC's lawyers. In March 2002, the Office of Legal Counsel (OLC) issued a still-classified opinion titled *The President's Power as Commander in Chief to Transfer Captured Terrorists to the Control and Custody of Foreign Nations.*[45] One major theme of the opinion is evident in the title: John Yoo's sweeping theory of executive war powers, overriding mere statutes and treaties that might stand in their way. A second argument stemmed from another part of Yoo's basic approach: the minimization of obligations imposed by international law. He later argued in a law review article that CAT has "no extraterritorial effect (except in the case of extradition)" and does not apply to transfers from other countries.[46] Finally, the opinion doubtless asserted that it sufficed for the CIA to extract promises from recipient nations not to torture (the administration made this point publicly whenever rendition was criticized).

Although OLC's opinion supporting rendition remains unavailable, it is hard to believe that it is very persuasive. Rendition for interrogation makes the CIA a direct beneficiary of intelligence obtained by torture. The practice is obviously difficult to square with CAT or with domestic criminal statutes that prohibit torture. I consider these legal strictures below, along with the available OLC opinions.

In addition to these legal difficulties, rendition creates at least two kinds of practical problems. First, information that appears to have been obtained by torture is useless in any U.S. court, including military commissions. It appears that the information leading to Jose Padilla's labeling as a "dirty bomber" came from a prisoner who was transported to Morocco, where he was subjected to extreme torture.[47] Since that information could not be used in the federal criminal court where Padilla was finally tried, he had to be prosecuted for lesser offenses. Second, there is the obvious problem of reliability. In another notorious case, an Al Qaeda agent named Ibn al-Libi was rendered to Egypt, where he provided some of the false intelligence about links between Al Qaeda and Iraq upon which the Bush administration relied in its rush to war with that nation.[48] Egypt, knowing the administration's eagerness to make that link, simply forced the prisoner to confess to it.

After the administration's lawyers approved rendition for interrogation, they had set a problematic baseline for consideration of harsh interrogation techniques performed by Americans. If the CIA could bundle captives off to horrific fates at the hands of some of the world's most repressive regimes, what could it not do itself? Of course, distinctions would be made regarding what U.S. agents could do themselves, but an extreme example had been set. It must have been on the minds of those who reviewed other interrogation issues.

EARLY GUIDANCE FROM THE PRINCIPALS

As prisoners and problems accumulated, CIA Director George Tenet told General Counsel Scott Mueller that standards were needed to guide interrogations. "We need guidance from Justice and the White House on what we're allowed to do," he said.[49] As it happened, there was a high-level structure in place to respond to Tenet's concerns. After 9/11, the National Security Council created a Principals Committee, a cabinet-level group that met frequently to advise President Bush on issues of national security policy.[50] National Security Adviser Rice chaired the committee; its members were

Vice President Cheney, Defense Secretary Rumsfeld, Secretary of State Powell, Attorney General Ashcroft, and CIA Director Tenet.

The Principals Committee met frequently in the small White House situation room. The group began reviewing and approving the use of particular "enhanced interrogation techniques" against individual Al Qaeda captives. (It may have been reviewing renditions as well.) The discussion and instructions were very detailed; for example, the group specified whether a captive could be slapped, deprived of sleep, or waterboarded. A combination of techniques was sometimes approved.

Khalid Sheikh Mohammed was a subject of intense interest for his possible knowledge of terrorist plots. After an informant revealed his location, he was captured and transported first to Afghanistan and then to the CIA black site in Poland.[51] KSM was initially defiant. In response, "a variety of tough techniques were used about 100 times over two weeks" on him, including waterboarding.[52] Interrogators then desisted and asked for advice, fearing they might have crossed the line into torture. He eventually produced a great deal of information, some of it as a result of harsh interrogation and some of it from traditional noncoercive practices. Eventually he was transferred to Guantánamo, where he awaits trial for his crimes.

The urgent desire to forestall future attacks drove these meetings and approvals. Pressure to obtain information from the captives was intense—by summer 2002, "threat reports were pulsing."[53] Eventually, the attorney general demurred. He "was troubled by the discussions. He agreed with the general policy decision to allow aggressive tactics and had repeatedly advised that they were legal. But he argued that senior White House advisers should not be involved in the grim details of interrogations, sources said. According to a top official, Ashcroft asked aloud after one meeting: 'Why are we talking about this in the White House? History will not judge this kindly.' "

Ashcroft's growing discomfort with the operations of the Principals Committee was well-founded. It appears that urgent requests for approvals were flowing from risk-averse CIA officials in the field almost directly to the committee. Missing was the usual bureaucratic process of staff review of policy and legal issues that ordinarily precedes cabinet-level decisions, even urgent ones. Therefore, the committee's decisions always risked being ill-informed. Except for Colin Powell and John Ashcroft, no one in the group had the kind of military or law enforcement experience that might have produced a feel for the issues. Perhaps Ashcroft's discomfort also stemmed from the fact that the committee "took care to insulate President Bush" from its deliberations and decisions.[54] Still, this was not Iran-Contra, which was a rogue operation shielded from the president and almost everyone else. Instead, senior officials gamely tried to manage the war on terrorism on the fly.

It appears that by the time a formal opinion request went to OLC sometime in 2002, the Principals Committee had made a significant number of decisions. The attorney general had given his opinion that the techniques in use were legal. It would have been natural for him to have discussed these matters informally with White House Counsel Gonzales and with his own aides Bybee and Yoo. Whether he did so or not, he certainly knew that the department had already placed the interrogators deep in legal limbo.

In any event, by the time OLC formulated its opinion on interrogation practices, both the administration and the Justice Department were seriously committed to a course of conduct. In essence, OLC was backed into a corner. It would have been extremely difficult for the office to have written an opinion negating the legality of decisions taken by the administration's senior leadership and exposing the CIA to yet another round of retroactive condemnation of its actions. We should not be very surprised that no such opinion emerged. Instead, OLC wrote an opinion meant to remain secret, which tried to navigate its way around some formidable legal obstacles.

A WALL OF LAW AGAINST TORTURE

As they crafted their opinions, the executive's lawyers had to know that both international and domestic law erected formidable barriers to torture and more broadly to most forms of harsh interrogation. Hence the context was quite unlike that in which OLC lawyers commonly find themselves. Many opinion requests place OLC in Justice Jackson's twilight zone, where both constitutional and statutory materials are inconclusive. (For example, the *Habeas* opinion dwelt in that zone.) But not this one. The difficulty of eradicating torture and lesser forms of cruelty has driven the law to state firm prohibitions, not flexible standards that regulate but do not forbid conduct. In practice, these bans may be more aspirational than effective, but they are firmly in place and may not be ignored by lawyers. Here is a brief catalog.

We have seen that the Geneva Conventions require nations to criminalize "grave breaches" of their protections, including "willful killing, torture, or inhuman treatment, . . . [and] willfully causing great suffering or serious injury to body or health." Common Article 3 requires "humane treatment" of prisoners of all kinds and forbids "cruel treatment and torture" or "outrages on personal dignity, in particular humiliating and degrading treatment."

Prisoners of war and civilians cannot be subjected to coercive interrogation of any kind; hence the administration's urgent desire to classify Al Qaeda and Taliban captives as "unlawful enemy combatants" instead.

Domestically, the federal War Crimes Act (WCA) discharged the Geneva obligation by criminalizing both grave breaches of the conventions and violations of Common Article 3.[55] OLC's *Application of Treaties* opinion, however, had already attempted to remove all WCA jeopardy for the war on terrorism by eliminating all Geneva protections for the detainees.[56]

A greater obstacle to harsh interrogation lay in the fact that both international and domestic law contained another explicit and unconditional ban on torture. The international Convention Against Torture and Other Cruel, Inhuman, or Degrading Treatment or Punishment (CAT), which the United States signed, took force in 1987.[57] Although many international agreements have prohibited torture over the years, none had defined it until CAT provided that it is "any act by which severe pain or suffering, whether physical or mental, is intentionally inflicted on a person for such purposes as obtaining . . . information or a confession, [or] punishing him . . . [by a public official]." The ban on torture is unconditional: "No exceptional circumstances whatsoever, whether a state of war or a threat of war, internal political instability or any other public emergency, may be invoked as a justification of torture." Thus, CAT rejects the ticking bomb scenario and all other emergency arguments for torture. The convention also requires state parties to take effective steps to prevent torture, forbids them to send captives to nations where they are likely to face torture, and requires them to "undertake to prevent . . . other acts of cruel, inhuman, or degrading treatment or punishment which do not amount to torture."

The U.S. Senate's 1994 ratification of CAT attached a reservation stating that none of the convention's provisions would be self-executing. To meet its obligations under CAT, Congress then enacted a criminal statute that forbids torture performed outside the United States and closely tracks CAT's definitions of prohibited conduct. Under federal law, torture is "an act committed by a person acting under the color of law specifically intended to inflict severe physical or mental pain or suffering (other than pain or suffering incidental to lawful sanctions) upon another person within his custody or physical control."[58] There are two principal differences between the international and domestic definitions: Congress added the specific intent requirement and narrowed the meaning of mental suffering. I discuss both changes below.

Torture within the United States has long been illegal under general constitutional and statutory provisions. The Constitution's Eighth Amendment forbids the "cruel and unusual" punishment of prisoners. This includes torture, "unnecessary cruelty," and the "wanton infliction of physical pain."[59] The Supreme Court has also held that the Due Process Clauses of the Fifth and Fourteenth Amendments forbid government agents to inflict physical abuse on prisoners. The best-known case is *Rochin v. California* (1952), in which the Court condemned the forced stomach pumping of a criminal suspect, saying that this police conduct "shocks the conscience."[60] Because what shocks the conscience is both subjective and fact-dependent, this constitutional test has proved difficult for the Supreme Court to apply consistently.[61] Therefore, it is also difficult for lawyers to predict what will cross the line into unconstitutional brutality. Equally important, the moral relativity of the "shocks the conscience" test puts domestic constitutional law at odds with the absolute ban on torture in CAT.

In addition, the Fifth Amendment's guarantee against self-incrimination forbids coercive interrogations.[62] Both federal and state criminal laws denounce murder, mayhem, and assault, as does the Uniform Code of Military Justice (UCMJ). There is also a special federal civil remedy for damages for victims of torture in the Torture Victims Protection Act (TVPA).[63]

This barricade of laws against torture should have engendered an attitude of great caution about harsh interrogation in the minds of the president's lawyers. In addition, a few months previously, both the State Department and the uniformed military lawyers had reminded them of the importance of our nation's traditions of complying fully with Geneva protections in all conflicts, whether or not the conventions technically applied. Yet all of this was overborne by the great pressure to approve practices already in use and to produce intelligence no matter the cost.

A GOLDEN SHIELD FOR THE CIA

On August 1, 2002, Assistant Attorney General Jay Bybee sent an opinion to White House Counsel Alberto Gonzales titled *Standards of Conduct for Interrogation under 18 U.S.C. §§2340–2340A*.[64] A still-classified memo listing specific approved techniques of interrogation accompanied it. Some months later, quite similar advice was rendered to the Pentagon, as I discuss in the next chapter.

The prosaic title of the *Interrogation* opinion belies its fate as the centerpiece of legal debate about the war on terrorism—it is commonly condemned as the "torture memo." The principal author of the opinion was John Yoo.[65] He worked closely with David Addington, who ensured that

Vice President Cheney's theories of executive power were reflected.[66] He also shared drafts with the offices of Attorney General Ashcroft and his deputy Larry Thompson, and received suggestions from them.[67] Yoo says that no one suggested significant changes or disagreed with the conclusions in the *Interrogation* memo.[68]

Jack Goldsmith has explained that there may have been a good reason for the lack of opposition: the draft opinion was not shared with the State Department, which would have "strenuously objected."[69] Goldsmith says that "Gonzales made it a practice to limit readership of controversial legal opinions to a very small group of lawyers."[70] This was done "to control outcomes in the opinions and minimize resistance to them." The result of excluding those who might have offered constructive criticism was bad advice that would spark impressive levels of resistance and acrimony after the fact. Unrestrained, *Interrogation*'s authors provided some remarkably creative analysis. The opinion has received sharp criticism for that quality because of the conclusions it supports.

Interrogation is long—just over fifty pages in reprinted form—and is obviously meant to be definitive. It bears the hallmarks of John Yoo's point of view: minimization of obligations imposed by international law, maximization of the executive's constitutional power, highly restrictive interpretation of statutes that might bind the executive, and willingness to compress statutes by invoking the avoidance canon. Its overall purpose is to immunize U.S. agents who employ harsh interrogation tactics from successful prosecution or even the fear of prosecution, as the reader can readily gather from the memo's detailed discussion of available defenses to prosecution. *Interrogation* is designed to comfort the interrogator and not to warn him or her to steer clear of actions that may produce criminal jeopardy. Its basic thrust runs counter to the formidable bodies of law that attempt to eliminate torture and cruelty.

In the usual fashion of OLC opinions, *Interrogation* begins by restating the question asked, in this case by White House Counsel Gonzales. The issue is the "standards of conduct" under CAT "as implemented by" the federal criminal code. Thus, a strategy found in the earlier *Application of Treaties* opinion appears again. International law will be viewed only through the lens of its limited incorporation into domestic law. Consequently, every element of domestic law that tends to confine the substantive reach of international principles can be deployed. Broad concepts of executive power and available materials that suggest narrow statutory interpretation will be especially useful.

Interrogation focuses on the two critical issues about the statutory terminology OLC was asked to address: the meaning of "specifically intended
to inflict" and the meaning of "severe pain or suffering," either physical or
mental. Its overall conclusion is that acts must be "of an extreme nature"—
the opinion repeats the word extreme many times—to constitute crimes.
Actions "may be cruel, inhuman, or degrading, but still not produce pain
and suffering of the requisite intensity" to be criminal. Along the way, the
opinion erects four separate barriers to the successful prosecution of U.S.
interrogators. In its own way, *Interrogation*'s wall against prosecution is as
impressive as the walls against torture it dismantles.

The opinion's first focus is on the specific intent requirement in the torture
statute. OLC opines that a criminal actor "must expressly intend to achieve
the forbidden act. . . . [that is,] the infliction of [severe] pain must be the
defendant's precise objective." It is not enough to know that severe pain will
occur as long as inflicting it is not the interrogator's purpose. It is easy to
understand why this distinction is important in many contexts. For example,
doctors know when their procedures will inflict pain, but they are not torturers because their purpose is to heal and they would eliminate the pain if
they could. In support of its interpretation of specific intent, OLC accurately
cites standard sources at some length, including *Black's Law Dictionary* and
some Supreme Court cases. All of these sources do in fact support a narrow
view of the specific intent requirement under various statutes. The opinion
does warn, however, that proof of a person's knowledge of consequences
allows a jury to infer the intent to produce them.

In the context of harsh interrogation, this analysis of specific intent is
quite artificial. Knowledge and intention are no longer separate, because inflicting pain is the intended means to the end of acquiring intelligence. Cali-
brating the subject's level of distress is central to the interrogator's attempt
to break his or her will, not an unintended by-product of it. Perhaps, then,
Interrogation is aiming at a point it does not mention. Although the opinion
does not quite say so, it suggests strongly that the presence of a purpose to
gather intelligence negates criminal specific intent. If so, an interrogator who
seeks information rather than sadistic pleasure is safe. Given the premises of
the war on terrorism, this would be a very broad shield. Until interrogation
occurs, no one can tell what a detainee knows that might be of value. If an
interrogator were prosecuted and claimed a legitimate purpose, how could
a jury say beyond a reasonable doubt that none had been present?

Interrogation quotes without comment the Senate report that explains the
addition of the specific intent requirement. The report says: "For an act to

be 'torture,' it must . . . be intended to cause severe pain and suffering."[71] The absence of any qualification implies that if the specific intent to cause suffering is present, it does not matter *why* the interrogator inflicts it. This interpretation is consistent with the purposes both of CAT and the torture statute, because they do not recognize a purpose to obtain intelligence as a defense. Any such defense would gut both the convention and the statute. OLC, presumably aware of this problem and having narrowed the intent requirement as much as possible, moves along to the next issue.

Interrogation's substantive definition of "severe pain or suffering" has become notorious for its unpersuasiveness. It says: "Physical pain amounting to torture must be equivalent in intensity to the pain accompanying serious physical injury, such as organ failure, impairment of bodily function, or even death." Mental pain or suffering "must result in significant psychological harm of significant duration, e.g., lasting for months or even years." These definitions are extreme for a reason: they provide a way to negate the specific intent to torture. Since interrogators will routinely intend to inflict suffering, they can escape conviction only if there are significant levels of evident suffering that do not constitute torture. The opinion notes that interrogators can defend themselves on grounds that they held a good faith belief their conduct would not produce the prohibited harm. The more extreme the harm must be, the more effective the defense.

More particularly, these definitions of physical and mental suffering were probably crafted to avoid condemning what the CIA was already doing. Waterboarding was probably on OLC's mind. An inability to breathe combined with apprehension of immediate death from drowning certainly creates impressive levels of physical and mental suffering, as it is intended to do. The procedure can be continued until the subject's resistance is overborne, and repeated as necessary. But there is no clear connection to pain as defined in the opinion or to long-term psychological damage. Similarly, many of the other "enhanced" interrogation techniques do not involve either the intense pain that typifies classic tortures or provable psychological carry-overs. They do seem to be well within anyone's definition of treatment that is "cruel, inhuman, or degrading." Two examples of reported CIA techniques should suffice: "longtime standing" (forcing prisoners to stand, handcuffed and with their feet shackled to the floor, for more than forty hours) and the "cold cell" (forcing prisoners to stand naked in a cell kept at fifty degrees while being continuously doused with cold water).[72]

The opinion's definition of severity has led to much criticism, and fairly so. The language about impending organ failure and death was drawn from a wholly unrelated source, the federal statutes that use similar terms to define indicia of an emergency medical condition for purposes of providing health benefits. Apparently, the OLC lawyers ran a computer word search of the federal statutes, and this is what turned up. Yet the point of the medical definition, which uses the presence of severe pain as one indicator, is to say when it is reasonable for a person in distress to go to an emergency room. The definition may be ungenerous, but it is easy to see that its purpose is to deny benefits to those who respond to minor aches and pains by repairing to the hospital. The context of the federal torture statute is fundamentally different because it concerns the intentional infliction of pain on another person, not the need to endure what nature does to us. There is no reason to think that the level of pain a person should be asked to endure before seeking medical help bears any relation to the level of pain that another person may permissibly inflict on him or her. In addition, there is no small irony in the use of the ameliorative concepts of the medical profession as a way to regulate the intentional infliction of pain. In this respect, as in so many others, the opinion substitutes mere cleverness for practical wisdom.

Interrogation also cites the dictionary definition of severe as "hard to endure." Perhaps this is the common ground between the two kinds of federal statutes that the opinion discusses, but I think that most people find pain hard to endure long before it approaches organ failure or death. (Certainly, we spend a lot of money on palliatives for ordinary levels of pain.) It is easy to see why the opinion seeks to modify the dictionary definition with a more extreme concept of severity. The whole point of using harsh interrogation techniques is to make them hard to endure, and many of them may constitute felonious torture if there is no added element. Therefore, the memo concludes its discussion of definitions by emphasizing that torture "is not the mere infliction of pain or suffering on another, but is instead a step well removed." Citing more dictionary definitions, this time of the term torture, the memo says it must involve "intense pain" or "excruciating pain" caused by "extreme acts."

Interrogation discusses the definition of "severe mental pain or suffering" at some length. The federal torture statute incorporated the Senate's addition of the phrase "prolonged mental harm" to the CAT definition.[73] To OLC, this meant that criminal acts "must cause some lasting, though not necessarily permanent, damage." There was no medical definition of the statutory phrase, but OLC thought that post-traumatic stress disorder might be an example. To limit the reach of this provision, the opinion argues that a defendant must specifically intend the harm, not the actions giving rise to it, and that a good faith defense would be available. Therefore, no matter how intense the mental suffering might be from repeated waterboarding or any other enhanced technique, if lasting damage was uncertain there would be no criminal liability.

Interrogation then turns to the history of CAT, since it is clear the torture statute was enacted to fulfill the obligations of the United States to implement that convention. Here the memo emphasizes CAT's distinction between torture and "other acts of cruel, inhuman, or degrading treatment." The convention requires signatory states to "undertake to prevent" such actions, but does not require their criminalization. Because Congress had taken no action to implement this duty, there was no available statutory definition of cruel, inhuman, or degrading treatment. Had there been one, identifying the border between that treatment and torture would have been easier.

The opinion begins its analysis of the ratification process by asserting the president's responsibility to interpret treaties. Therefore, an executive interpretation that the Senate had accepted would be due special deference. The Reagan administration had told the Senate that it understood torture meant "a deliberate and calculated act of an extremely cruel and inhuman nature, specifically intended to inflict excruciating and agonizing physical or mental pain or suffering."[74] As examples it gave "sustained systematic beatings, application of electric currents to sensitive parts of the body, and tying up or hanging in positions that cause extreme pain."[75] Concerned about the vagueness of the terms "cruel, inhuman, or degrading," the Reagan administration decided it should refer to conduct prohibited by the Fifth, Eighth, and Fourteenth Amendments to the Constitution.[76] That would include the cruel and unusual punishments barred by the Eighth Amendment and the "shocking" mistreatment barred by the Due Process Clauses of the other two amendments.

The ratification process continued into the administration of the first President Bush, which softened the tone of the Reagan interpretation somewhat without seeming to alter its substance.[77] New testimony defined torture as "that barbaric cruelty which lies at the top of the pyramid of human rights misconduct." To OLC, the common ground was "the extraordinary or extreme acts required to constitute torture." OLC thought the Senate understanding at the time of ratification embraced this view, since it referred to torture as "an extreme form of cruel and inhuman treatment."[78] *Interrogation* concludes that the text and history of CAT confirm that the implementing statute meant to prohibit "only the most egregious conduct," "only the most heinous acts."

For two reasons, the OLC reading of the ratification history finds more clarity than the history contains. First, everyone agrees that by definition, torture is an extreme form of cruelty. Therefore, references to that fact do not explain how extreme the conduct must be. Second, no one relishes the explicit drawing of nice distinctions between cruelty and torture. Therefore, attempts to give examples of torture tend to stay well away from mistreatment that might be only cruel. In the end, the administration retreated to a cross-reference. Cruelty would consist of conduct already prohibited by the Constitution. However comforting that strategy was as a way to avoid an ugly subject, it failed to aid in line-drawing, because the Constitution prohibits both torture and various kinds of cruelty.

Interrogation notes that the courts had yet to interpret the federal statute, there having been no prosecutions under it. Hence, OLC sought guidance from cases under the Torture Victims Protection Act. Because the TVPA uses CAT's definition of torture, its caselaw is pertinent. The courts had not performed "any lengthy analysis of what acts constitute torture." OLC, in an appendix to its opinion, summarizes the facts of the cases to provide examples of torture. The appendix reveals why the cases did not search out the border between torture and cruelty: the acts giving rise to the lawsuits were torture in anyone's conception of the term. These included savage beatings, pulling of teeth, death threats, deprivation of food and water, electric shock, and rape. However, there was some evidence of what courts did not consider torture. For example, the European Court of Human Rights had upheld as merely inhuman and degrading the use of wall-standing, hooding, subjection to noise, sleep deprivation, and reduced diets.[79]

The third barrier to prosecution *Interrogation* erects is the president's constitutional power. OLC asserts that the federal torture statute would be unconstitutional "if it impermissibly encroached on the President's constitutional power to conduct a military campaign." The premise is that the interrogation of terrorist suspects is within the "core" of executive war powers. Reciting the history of the 9/11 attacks and the war with Al Qaeda, the opinion stresses the "imperative" need to gain information about future attacks through interrogation. OLC argues that the president's warmaking authority is exclusive, not shared with Congress: "Congress may no more regulate the President's ability to detain and interrogate enemy combatants than it may regulate his ability to direct troop movements on the battlefield."

To forestall a constitutional confrontation, OLC invokes the avoidance canon.[80] "In light of the President's complete authority over the conduct of war, without a clear statement otherwise, we will not read a criminal statute as infringing on the President's ultimate authority in these areas." Arguing that the canon has "special force" for foreign affairs and war, the opinion concludes that the torture statute "must be construed as not applying to interrogations undertaken pursuant to [the president's] Commander-in-Chief authority."

OLC's use of the avoidance canon masks the sweeping implications of its constitutional argument. Everyone agrees that the Commander in Chief Clause gives presidents some power exclusive of congressional direction to command our military in combat. The actual *extent* of that power is, however, quite uncertain.[81] For Congress has a group of explicit war powers, including the raising and regulating of military forces. Statutes control actual military operations in many ways: by determining the number of troops available, procuring their weapons, and even setting or ratifying strategic goals (such as the "Germany first" strategy in World War II). Congress does not, however, try to dictate day-to-day tactics. *Interrogation*, ignoring the actual existence of shared power to control the military, asserts that the zone of exclusive executive power is very broad, extending to interrogation techniques.

Yet interrogation, unlike troop movements, is amenable to general rules set in advance by legislation. The existence of the Geneva Conventions and CAT presuppose this as an international matter; the existence of the federal torture statute presupposes it as a domestic matter. The implication of the OLC opinion is that the torture statute is unconstitutional on its face, because the president may order torture whenever he believes it necessary. Use of the avoidance canon saves the opinion from asserting this astonishing proposition directly, but it is there in the logic, just under the surface of the prose. The opinion's immensely sweeping and unsupported claim of executive authority parallels John Yoo's attempt to free the president from congressional supervision in the war on terrorism in his initial *Constitutional Authority* opinion of September 2001.

In its final section, *Interrogation* erects its fourth barrier to prosecution of interrogators. It reviews "certain justification defenses" that "would potentially eliminate criminal liability." These are necessity and self-defense. Both defenses are recognized in U.S. law, although no federal statute establishes and defines them. The necessity defense allows imposing harm that avoids a greater harm—killing one person to save many others. (Recall the hypothetical posed by Dostoyevsky's Ivan.) OLC could find a Supreme Court case recognizing the necessity defense.[82] The context of that case was rather remote from the torture statute; it involved prison escapees urging the necessity of escape from threats and violence. Also, there appear to be no cases in which the defense has ever prevailed.[83] Nevertheless, OLC argues gamely that the defense could be "successfully maintained" where "any harm that might occur during an interrogation would pale to insignificance" compared to that threatened by a terrorist attack. The facts would matter: the more certain the evidence that a suspect possesses information, the more imminent an attack, and the more grave the feared damage, the sturdier the defense would be.

Interrogation fails to mention a much more fundamental problem with the necessity defense it posits than its thin pedigree in federal law. Both CAT and the federal torture statute ban torture without qualification. The text and history of both reject the notion that torture can be justified. Therefore, whatever the status of the necessity defense generally, this was an inappropriate context in which to claim its applicability.

Interrogation observes that a claim of self-defense is well established in federal law. The doctrine allows the use of force to save either oneself or another person when reasonably believed necessary. From this premise, OLC argues that the defense could also insulate interrogations given a national right of self-defense. This line of argument transports self-defense far from its roots and normal application. (It is really just a recasting of OLC's version of the necessity defense.) The self-defense doctrine ordinarily justifies the use of force against a dangerous assailant, not a helpless prisoner. In the absence of conventional legal support for its new version of the defense, OLC could only cite generalized materials in misleading ways.[84]

Interrogation concludes that even if a government defendant "were to harm" an enemy combatant in interrogation, there would be justification. For both this and the necessity defense, the opinion says euphemistically that "harm" may be justified. It never squarely defends the use of "torture." The delicacy of euphemism is, however, the thinnest of veils for what the opinion really does. It carves out a wide swath of protection for harsh interrogation practices that verge on, but do not quite include, techniques that always and everywhere have been known as torture.

A RETREAT UNDER FIRE

Interrogation could not stand the light of day. Alberto Gonzales disapproved it publicly immediately after its release in June 2004 in the wake of the Abu Ghraib prison abuse scandal. He explained that the memo "explored broad legal theories," and that some of the discussion "quite frankly, is irrelevant and unnecessary to support any action taken by the President."[85] He then said that "overbroad" discussions "that address abstract legal theories, or discussions subject to misinterpretation, but not relied upon by decision-makers are under review, and may be replaced, if appropriate, with more concrete guidance addressing only those issues necessary for the legal analysis of actual practices." (The memorandum was certainly overbroad and certainly not irrelevant.)

In late 2004, a week before Gonzales's confirmation hearings for attorney general, acting OLC head Daniel Levin issued a replacement opinion with a more temperate analysis.[86] Although OLC sometimes qualifies or supersedes one of its prior opinions, this instance of public repudiation is unprecedented, as it would be in most bureaucracies.

The official retraction of *Interrogation* had actually occurred before Gonzales repudiated it, during the tenure at OLC of Jack Goldsmith. When Goldsmith became head of OLC in the fall of 2003, Jay Bybee and John Yoo had both left the office. As he reviewed OLC's recent work, Goldsmith found that two memos "stood out" as problematic, *Interrogation* and its counterpart for military interrogations.[87] *Interrogation* was certainly important. Goldsmith knew it was the basis for what President Bush later called "alternative" interrogation procedures for "key architects" of 9/11 and other attacks: KSM, Zubaydah, and others. A CIA official had called the opinion a "golden shield." It would not be easy to modify or rescind the opinion; obviously there had been considerable reliance on it.

Still, Goldsmith found that *Interrogation* defined torture "too narrowly" using "questionable statutory interpretations." There was an "unusual lack of care and sobriety" in its legal analysis, especially in the assertion that any congressional effort to regulate interrogation would be an unconstitutional interference with the commander in chief power. Goldsmith could find no foundation for this claim in prior OLC opinions or "any other source of law." It would overturn many laws, for example the UCMJ. *Interrogation* "rested on cursory and one-sided legal arguments" that failed to consider congressional power or "the many Supreme Court decisions" in tension with it. Moreover, Goldsmith thought that when a conclusion that Congress is disabled is taken "in secret, respect for separation of powers demands a full consideration of competing congressional and judicial prerogatives," which was not there.

Another problem was the "tendentious tone." "It reads like a bad defense counsel's brief, not an OLC opinion," a senior government lawyer said to Goldsmith. He concluded that the two opinions "lacked the tenor of detachment and caution that usually characterizes OLC work, and that is so central to the legitimacy of OLC." Instead, they appeared "designed to confer immunity for bad acts." They were also "wildly broader than was necessary to support what was actually being done." Usually, he knew, OLC "has precise actions in mind" and conforms its analysis to them. *Interrogation,* however, was "untied to any concrete practices." In December 2003, he concluded he must withdraw and replace the opinion and the military one as well.

The CIA techniques *Interrogation* approved had, however, "been vetted in the highest circles of government." (That would be the Principals Committee.) In early June 2004, the memos started leaking. Within the administration, only David Addington defended them. After Goldsmith decided on withdrawal, Deputy Attorney General James Comey came to his aid. Attorney General Ashcroft was "understandably shaken" to hear the news. When Ashcroft accepted the withdrawal, Goldsmith submitted his resignation to make it "stick." During this period Addington confronted Goldsmith with a list of opinions he had rescinded or modified and said sarcastically that he needed to know which OLC opinions "you still stand by."

Revelation of the OLC opinion led to an impassioned debate. At Gonzales's confirmation hearings, *Interrogation* received bad reviews. OLC veteran and Yale Law Dean Harold Koh called it "perhaps the most clearly erroneous legal opinion I have ever read."[88] Its "absurdly narrow" definition of torture, he said, "flies in the face of the plain meaning of the term." Koh also stated that the opinion's international law positions were erroneous, that it "grossly overreads the inherent power of the President," and that the failure to mention *Steel Seizure* was a "stunning failure of lawyerly craft."

Interrogation has spawned a large legal literature, most of it highly critical.[89] In August 2004, the American Bar Association adopted a resolution condemning "any use of torture or other cruel, inhuman, or degrading treatment or punishment upon persons within the custody or under the physical control of the United States government . . . and any endorsement or authorization of such measures by government lawyers."[90] A group of more than 100 prominent lawyers, retired judges, and law school professors signed a statement condemning *Interrogation,* declaring that it sought to "circumvent long established and universally acknowledged principles of law and common decency."[91]

Characteristically, John Yoo has defended the OLC opinion without reservation.[92] To him, retraction of the *Interrogation* memorandum "was really just politics."[93] The replacement memo "changed little in actual administration policy" but gave political cover by intruding vagueness. It undercut U.S. efforts to prevent attacks by forcing agents in the field "to operate in a vacuum of generalizations. Our intent in the Justice Department's original research was to give clear legal guidance on what constituted 'torture' under the law, so that our agents would know exactly what was prohibited, and what was not." Thus the memorandum's main points, if not some of its legal details, were crafted as field guidance. The specific examples of torture in the appendix would tell agents what not to do.

With Yoo's description in mind, I would summarize the opinion's message to a field agent as follows: "If you are trying to get information, not torturing for its own sake, almost anything goes. Only the most extreme treatment should raise doubt in your mind. And the law and the president's power form your shield rather than a sword to be used against you for what you do." This was a prescription for the abuses soon to follow.

Yoo's discussion of the finer points of the law of interrogation stresses President Bush's order that prisoners be treated humanely as a sufficient guarantee against abuse.[94] Yoo fails to understand, however, that the opinion he wrote looks in the opposite direction, and in many places encourages harsh conduct that threatens to cross the line into outright torture. For example, Yoo notes that U.S. ratification of CAT did require the criminalization of torture, but distinguished "cruel, inhuman, or degrading treatment," for which the convention merely required prevention efforts. Because Congress had not legislated to prohibit cruelty, Yoo converts the distinction from a duty to a license.

Turning the law on its head, Yoo cites the Senate definition of cruelty as incorporating actions already prohibited by the Constitution and then emphasizes that these bans apply to the U.S. criminal justice system, not to enemy aliens outside the country. This line of reasoning removes any barrier to cruelty, even though the Senate had thought that the Constitution provided one. Yoo concludes happily that the opinion allowed U.S. prisons to be rather like boot camps, allowing uncomfortable physical positions, limited sleep, and similar discomforts.

Yoo quotes Anthony Lewis's comparison of the opinion's discussion of defenses to "a mob lawyer to a mafia don on how to skirt the law and stay out of prison."[95] He has said that in response to the CIA's request to know how far interrogators could go, the client needed to know the full range of his options, and to offer any less would have been irresponsible.[96] The advice he provided, however, was misleading to the client in its refusal to discuss or even acknowledge the existence of serious arguments against all of its major positions.

For example, critics have charged that the opinion's assertion that the president's war power could override the torture statute was a breach of professional responsibility because the opinion did not discuss *Steel Seizure*, especially Justice Jackson's famous opinion.[97] That is correct. Yoo asserts that the opinion did not cite Jackson because "earlier OLC opinions, reaching across several administrations, had concluded that it had no application to the President's conduct of foreign affairs and national security." He sees *Steel Seizure* as a case about "labor disputes." Citing an opinion by Walter Dellinger, head of OLC in the Clinton administration, asserting that the president can refuse to enforce unconstitutional statutes (especially when they limit the commander in chief power), Yoo concludes that the Bybee opinion was "really doing little more than following in the footsteps of the Clinton Justice Department and all prior Justice Departments."[98]

Not so. Yoo's apologia misrepresents the traditions of the Justice Department and of U.S. constitutional law. As I argued in an earlier chapter, *Steel Seizure* is a framework decision for separation of powers analysis—it is far from just a case about "labor disputes."[99] Within OLC, *Steel Seizure* is ordinarily regarded as providing fundamental guidance. Jackson's opinion in particular is full of wisdom about emergency powers in wartime, and Yoo would have done well to heed its instruction. His refusal even to cite it is a failure to give candid advice to a client because the case stands in the way of the facile analysis that suffuses *Interrogation*. *Steel Seizure* teaches that statutes should not lightly be set aside even under the pressures of wartime, and that is precisely the point *Interrogation* rejects. It does so without grappling with or even mentioning the primary Supreme Court precedent. Some years after issuance of the *Interrogation* opinion, the Supreme Court would reinforce *Steel Seizure* in *Hamdan*, reminding everyone about separation of powers fundamentals.

Yoo also chides his critics that they do not understand the need to "innovate and take risks." Although Yoo notes the common argument that torture does not work because it produces unreliable information, he asserts that coercive interrogation is effective and has provided much useful intelligence in the war on terrorism. He omits the wide zone of conduct between outright torture and those coercive actions that would bar the admission of evidence in a normal U.S. criminal trial. The *Interrogation* opinion uses advocacy rather than analysis to bring the legal line for permitted conduct as close to torture as possible, never admitting the extraordinary nature of the advice being given.

An OLC opinion that hewed to the lawyer's duty of professional detachment would have outlined the substantial legal and consequential risks created by a very narrow definition of torture. The consequential risks soon appeared at Guantánamo and Abu Ghraib. Above all, there would have been a quality totally absent from the *Interrogation* opinion and from John Yoo's defense of it: a sense of humility and doubt in the face of the great imponderables the torture issue presents. An OLC lawyer asked to opine on mixed issues of constitutional and statutory law is often on firm ground. For example, whether military commissions comport with U.S. law is a question addressed by looking at conventional legal materials.

The question of what constitutes torture is different. Any lawyer asked to address it should feel the need for resources beyond the law books and for the utmost caution in providing an answer. Of course, no ultimate answer is available, as people have known for centuries. Therefore, the lawyer's duty is to look to U.S. history and traditions, to international understandings, and to the views of those who have struggled with the limits to interrogation in the field. This is an issue along the borderline between policy and law. The OLC lawyers should have deferred more than they did to those in the administration who had pertinent experience. In the next chapter, I consider what happened when that deference was both most merited and most lacking—the provision of advice concerning interrogation by the military rather than the CIA.

Of all the legal opinions provided to President Bush during the war on terrorism, *Interrogation* is the most deficient in legal right and moral conscience. Its legal conclusions are almost wholly antithetical to existing bodies of law and their manifest purposes. John Yoo's opinion displays little respect for statutes and treaties in its rush to confirm apparently unlimited executive power over interrogation. In good conscience, the opinion should have admitted the novelty of its positions and their inconsistency with major precedents such as *Steel Seizure*. Instead, the opinion verges on violation of the weakest conception of the advocate's duty—the avoidance of frivolous arguments. In the end, *Interrogation* fails most fundamentally in its absence of a quality lawyers are not required to have but that the president's lawyers should always strive to display, that of wisdom.

HOLDING THE LINE

Jack Goldsmith notes that the replacement opinion by his temporary successor, Dan Levin, took months to complete.[100] It gave the torture law "a much more rigorous and balanced interpretation" than did *Interrogation*. To maintain the golden shield, it stated that none of the conclusions in earlier memos would be different under this one. Goldsmith concludes sadly: "The opinion that had done such enormous harm was completely unnecessary to the tasks at hand."

The imbroglio surrounding the release, retraction, and replacement of *Interrogation* did not end the Bush administration's battles over CIA interrogation techniques. The replacement opinion, sent to Deputy Attorney

General Comey by Daniel Levin at the end of 2004, is *Legal Standards Applicable under 18 U.S.C. §§2340–2340A.*[101] This opinion is a careful retreat, not a capitulation. Running only sixteen pages, it is much shorter and less tendentious than *Interrogation*. It begins with a firm policy statement of the kind that appropriately informs legal analysis: "Torture is abhorrent both to American law and values and to international norms." After noting that "questions" had arisen about the earlier memo, it says the opinion request had asked for a document that could be released to the public. OLC's expectation of a wider audience than the client agency and its knowledge of the furor that had surrounded *Interrogation* are evident throughout the new opinion.

Getting down to business, *Legal Standards* states that it "supersedes" *Interrogation* "in its entirety." Lest the clients in the CIA lose heart, though, the opinion quickly drops the footnote that Jack Goldsmith mentioned and everyone else soon noticed, providing that none of the conclusions in OLC's earlier memos "would be different under the standards set forth in this memorandum." In short, although the supporting analysis was about to change, the authorized behaviors would be the same. The essential strategies of *Legal Standards* are to prune away some of John Yoo's most luxuriant foliage and to adopt a more cautious interpretation of the federal torture statute.

Legal Standards eliminates entirely *Interrogation*'s discussion both of the president's war powers and of the available defenses to prosecution. It finds this analysis "unnecessary" and "inconsistent with the President's unequivocal directive that United States personnel not engage in torture." It is true that OLC, like a court, usually conforms its analysis to the questions raised by the opinion request.[102] For a topic as sensitive as torture, the less said, the better. This opinion takes the president's directive at face value and steers the clients farther away from conduct that might be torture than did *Interrogation*. The earlier opinion had responded to the administration's secret subtext—urgent signals emanating from the Principals Committee calling for approval of harsh interrogation techniques.

By simply eliding these two topics, OLC avoided any need to say which parts of the earlier analysis were defective. It would have been hard to find anything good to say about the fabricated discussion of defenses. The president's war powers were surely overstated as well, but OLC always asserts that there is a zone of exclusive executive power to command the military. Not wishing to make concessions it might regret by paring down Yoo's claims, OLC simply and understandably avoided the topic.

Legal Standards does revisit the statutory definitions of severe pain or suffering and specific intent. The analysis of severity, pulling in both directions, winds up lacking clarity, as do so many attempts to address this issue. First, the opinion disapproves the notorious "organ failure" definition of severe pain. It then parallels *Interrogation* by quoting both dictionary definitions of severity and the ratification history's definition of torture as involving "extreme, deliberate, and unusually cruel practices." However, the new opinion concludes that a definition of severe pain as "excruciating and agonizing" would set too high a threshold. The examples of torture it gives, though, are drawn from the TVPA cases, which all involve extreme brutality (such as severe beatings, pulling of teeth, and cutting off fingers).

Unlike the earlier memo, *Legal Standards* does not conclude that severe suffering must always include severe pain to constitute torture. Admitting the subjectivity of attempts to define pain and suffering, the opinion emphasizes the duration and intensity of mistreatment and the need to distinguish it as beyond cruelty. It may be that adding the durational requirement is a quiet way to endorse waterboarding, which usually breaks its victims quickly.[103] For mental pain and suffering, *Legal Standards* retreats from the earlier, strained interpretation of "prolonged" and defines it to mean "some lasting duration." The examples it gives, however, mostly involve harm lasting several years or more.

Turning to specific intent, the opinion notes inconsistency in the caselaw (knowledge of consequences, not desire to produce them, is sometimes enough to satisfy the requirement). OLC is reluctant to give a precise meaning to the intent element, because the president's directive against torture should not be met by "parsing the specific intent element . . . to approve as lawful conduct that might otherwise amount to torture." This is an implicit rebuke of John Yoo. It would be enough for criminal liability, OLC now says, if there is a "conscious desire" to inflict severe pain or suffering. A good faith defense that such suffering would not occur would be available. Concluding, *Legal Standards* removes an ambiguity left by its predecessor by saying explicitly that a motive to protect national security or any other "good reason" does not justify torture.

Legal Standards is a better and more responsible opinion than *Interrogation*. Both opinions are unsatisfactory in the ways that abstract attempts to define torture usually are. The later opinion's rather muddled discussion of severity is an example of that characteristic. That opinion does, though, set a lower threshold for torture than did *Interrogation* (it would be difficult to set the bar higher). *Legal Standards* also gives clear and restrained advice about the specific intent requirement. Most important, it avoids the strained efforts of its predecessor to erect all conceivable barriers to torture prosecutions.

COUNTERATTACK

Legal Standards is not the Bush administration's last legal opinion on the unhappy subject of torture. Soon after Alberto Gonzales became attorney general, OLC issued a secret opinion said to have been "an expansive endorsement of the harshest interrogation techniques ever used" by the CIA.[104] The opinion authorizes a "combined effects" strategy that allows the CIA to combine several stressful interrogation techniques, including head-slapping, frigid temperatures, and waterboarding. As we have seen, the question of combining techniques had been raised by the CIA from the outset of its program.

Combined Effects was written by Steven Bradbury, who became acting head of OLC in February 2005. Bradbury was the son of poor immigrants, a graduate of the University of Michigan Law School, yet another Thomas clerk, and a former practitioner with Kirkland and Ellis, an elite law firm where he worked with Kenneth Starr. Jack Goldsmith hired him as a deputy at OLC. Bradbury was never confirmed for the permanent position. After rumors appeared about the existence of this opinion, the Senate demanded its release (along with others) as a condition to holding hearings and was rebuffed. Senate Democrats charged that *Combined Effects* both circumvented laws against torture and undermined the public *Legal Standards* opinion.[105] Denying these allegations, the administration continued fruitlessly to press Bradbury's nomination.

The departing deputy attorney general, James Comey, objected to the issuance of *Combined Effects,* telling colleagues that they would be "ashamed" when the memo eventually leaked. After Comey led the 2004 revolt within the administration over NSA surveillance, though, no one who mattered was listening to him. With OLC in rather bad repute after Goldsmith's withdrawal of *Interrogation* and other opinions, incoming Attorney General Gonzales sought to bring the department "back into line with the White House." He kept Bradbury in a kind of probationary status as acting head of OLC for several months until his reliability could be determined.[106]

Former OLC head Charles Cooper said he was "very troubled" by the appearance that legal opinions would be molded to secure a permanent appointment. Bradbury denied that he ever gave anything but his "best judgment" of the law. Of course, he knew that opinions of the sort Jack Goldsmith might write would not be welcome. In any case, Bradbury soon earned such confidence from the attorney general that he was given the public role of arguing for the administration's antiterror policies in congressional hearings and in helping to craft legislation. Another former OLC head, Douglas Kmiec, found this public role a departure from the office's traditional avoidance of advocacy. Thus, Gonzales seemed to place little value on OLC's traditional independence and relative neutrality both within the Justice Department and outside of it. Nor did he evince concern that there might be a gap between the administration's public position regarding torture as articulated in *Legal Standards* and its subsequent secret position contained in *Combined Effects.*

FENDING OFF THE SUPREME COURT AND CONGRESS

In fall 2005, Congress considered what would become the Detainee Treatment Act (DTA).[107] The legislation responded to the Supreme Court's holdings in *Hamdi* and *Rasul* that detainees at Guantánamo had due process rights if citizens and access to habeas corpus if aliens.[108] The existence of these vehicles for judicial review could result in scrutiny and condemnation of CIA practices that OLC had approved. The DTA accepted administration concerns by adopting sharp restrictions on judicial review. Congress also took the occasion to legislate treatment of the detainees.

As the DTA was being formulated, the Bush administration was particularly concerned about the proposed "McCain Amendment" providing that no one in custody of the U.S. government could be subjected to "cruel, inhuman, or degrading" treatment.[109] The amendment defines such conduct ("CID" in common shorthand) by referring to U.S. constitutional barriers to cruel or shocking treatment, as defined in the earlier Senate reservation to CAT.[110] Thus, the purpose of the amendment is to fill the gap in the CAT protections that enactment of the U.S. torture statute had created.

By protecting anyone in U.S. custody, the amendment was designed to reach detainees held outside the United States by the CIA. Less obviously, this jurisdictional provision was crafted to avoid condemning the extremely secret CIA practice of "extraordinary rendition" of captives to countries other than the United States or their home countries for interrogation.

As the DTA moved toward passage, OLC received a request to opine whether the proposed legislation would outlaw any of the CIA's methods. OLC was in a very tight position. Many of the CIA's techniques were so harsh that it would be difficult to write a persuasive opinion that they were not CID. Yet if OLC said the legislation would ban what the CIA was already doing, it would mean that past practices violated international if not domestic law. Also, the CIA would have to abandon some techniques, and OLC would have to draw the difficult line between conduct that was legal and conduct that was CID. (OLC had not previously thought it necessary to opine whether current interrogations failed the international standard because it had not been codified in a federal statute.)

Bradbury responded by writing an opinion that must have had overtones of the repudiated *Interrogation* opinion. The new opinion decided that the DTA would not require any change in the CIA's practices. Apparently the opinion focused on the constitutional "shocks the conscience" test. Because what is shocking depends on the justification for rough treatment, the opinion argued that even waterboarding would not be illegal if there were enough need to gain crucial intelligence about a planned terrorist attack. Then it would not shock the conscience because it would be the necessary choice of a lesser evil. This is just the sort of relativistic analysis *Legal Standards* had foresworn for the stricter test of the torture statute. Employing it for the lesser harm of cruelty reduced the force of the DTA, which would presumably condemn only the sort of wholly gratuitous violence that had surfaced at Abu Ghraib.

The administration vigorously lobbied against the McCain Amendment.[111] President Bush even threatened to veto the entire military budget, to which the DTA was attached, if it were not deleted. Aligned with McCain were various human rights groups, former secretary of state Colin Powell, and a group of retired generals. Vice President Cheney and Senator McCain had several testy exchanges. After tense and protracted negotiations with the administration, Congress persisted in including the amendment, and the president yielded temporarily.[112] He signed the DTA into law, but appended a signing statement claiming the authority to disregard any provision in it that impaired his constitutional powers: "The executive branch shall construe [the DTA] in a manner consistent with the constitutional authority of the President to supervise the unitary executive branch and as Commander in Chief and consistent with constitutional limitations on the judicial power."[113]

Signing statements such as this have been issued for many years by presidents of both parties.[114] They have, however, become bitterly controversial in the Bush administration. There is good reason to acknowledge presidential power to refuse to execute unconstitutional provisions in statutes.[115] The problem is one of limits. The Bush administration has plowed new ground in two ways.[116] First, it issues many more of these statements than have any earlier presidents, and they often contain sweeping boilerplate recitations, said to be written by David Addington, that any provisions conflicting with executive power will be ignored. The DTA statement is an example—it is essentially identical to many others. That makes it very hard to determine which provisions are the subject of real concern and to identify those that actually will not be enforced. Second, the underlying theories of executive power are the extreme formulations characteristic of the reverse lawfare waged by the Cheney/Addington/Yoo group since the outset of the administration. That means that they sweep broadly and without support across statutes of all kinds. Taken seriously, they would disable Congress from legislating meaningful restrictions on the executive branch in many fields, especially foreign affairs and war.

As enacted, the DTA clarifies the defenses to criminal prosecutions and civil suits available to U.S. personnel who commit acts, authorized and determined to be lawful at the time, involving the detention and interrogation of terrorist suspects.[117] To be safe, the defendant need only show that he or she was unaware the actions were unlawful and that a person of "ordinary sense and understanding" would not know to the contrary. This confirms the existence of John Yoo's golden shield. OLC's advice was certainly extreme and shaky, but an agent in the field should not be the one asked to detect its deficiencies or to suffer for its existence.

In the confusion created by President Bush's signature of the bill while issuing a signing statement that read like a veto message, the CIA is said to have reviewed its interrogation techniques and to have discontinued some of them. The president's attempt to comfort the CIA probably would not have eased all concerns in the risk-averse agency. The text of the DTA exposed it to lawfare, whatever partial defenses the statute might have recognized and whatever the president might say. Moreover, there was lingering hostility within Congress, as Senators John McCain and John Warner accused the president of betraying them by renouncing promises they had negotiated with him.[118] In the ensuing atmosphere of distrust, the CIA could expect new levels of outside scrutiny of its activities.

Legal pressure increased again after the Supreme Court's 2006 ruling in *Hamdan* that the detainees enjoyed the protections of Geneva's Common Article 3, which requires prisoners to be treated "humanely" and forbids "cruel treatment and torture" and "outrages upon personal dignity, in particular, humiliating and degrading treatment."[119] Now international standards bound the executive branch, enhancing the risk of lawfare. The administration retreated temporarily. President Bush, acknowledging for the first time that the CIA had detention facilities overseas, transferred some high-value detainees to Guantánamo for trial. The CIA ceased waterboarding for the time being.

In late 2006, Congress enacted the Military Commissions Act (MCA), which alleviated some of the administration's concerns.[120] As the legislation was being drafted, the administration pressured Congress to authorize the CIA's activities. With a congressional election looming, the administration pushed for action before members of Congress adjourned to campaign. President Bush gave a speech confirming that the CIA interrogated high-value prisoners by "an alternative set of procedures," which he characterized as "tough . . . and safe . . . and lawful . . . and necessary."[121] He preferred a bill providing that the DTA satisfied the obligations of Common Article 3 and therefore set the governing standard for U.S. interrogations.[122] The administration's concern centered on Article 3's condemnation of "outrages upon human dignity," which seemed unacceptably vague as guidance in the field. A group of prominent Republican senators, including McCain, Warner, and Lindsay Graham, resisted this strategy. They worried that recasting our Geneva obligations would invite other nations to do the same to the detriment of our interests. They supported the administration's alternative, an effort to amend the federal WCA to specify prohibited abuses of detainees. In the end, this approach prevailed.

As enacted, the MCA both states that the WCA satisfies the U.S. obligation to punish grave breaches of Geneva's Common Article 3 and authorizes the president "to interpret the meaning and application of the Geneva Conventions."[123] It also narrows the substantive scope of the WCA. The MCA lists nine offenses as "grave breaches" of Geneva's Common Article 3 and therefore as war crimes.[124] Along with torture, the list includes "cruel and inhuman treatment," which the WCA now defines complexly as conduct "intended to inflict severe or serious physical or mental pain or suffering." The physical component is limited to "extreme" pain or injury, substantial risk of death, or significant impairment of a body part or mental faculty. For mental pain or suffering, the statute removes the requirement that mental suffering be prolonged, but only for future offenses. The rest of the definition of mental suffering limits it to aggravated situations such as death threats.

The MCA forbids but does not criminalize degrading treatment. The definition refers to existing constitutional limitations. Leftover violations of Common Article 3 are to be addressed by executive regulations. The effort, then, was to make criminal the most serious violations of Article 3 and to condemn the others in some fashion. Congress did not provide much clarity, however, regarding such specifics as whether waterboarding is now illegal.

By 2007, with encouragement provided by the MCA, the administration returned to its characteristic aggressiveness. President Bush signed a secret executive order authorizing "enhanced" interrogation techniques. Like other executive orders, it was reviewed for legality by OLC and approved by Steven Bradbury in a classified opinion. Most of the ground lost in the retreat of 2004 had been regained.

Some indirect light on OLC's position was shed by an exchange of letters between Senator Ron Wyden and the Justice Department. Wyden wrote Bradbury in August 2007 asking for information about the executive order and, in particular, about the administration's definition of the operative terms Congress had brought into domestic law from the Geneva Conventions.[125] These were the commands to ensure "humane" treatment and to avoid "outrages upon personal dignity," including "cruel, inhuman, and degrading treatment." The executive order had taken up the MCA's invitation to the executive branch to interpret these terms. The answer came back not from OLC but from a deputy in the Office of Legislative Affairs (OLA), Brian Benczkowski. Presumably, avoiding an OLC response was meant to negate any implication that the answers bound the executive.

The OLA letter states that the administration had not articulated precise rules for defining permissible techniques for interrogation, but rather would consider the facts of a particular case. For example, it would be relevant that an action was intended to prevent a terrorist attack, not simply to humiliate a detainee. The letter notes that some actions are prohibited entirely, such as the forced performance of sexual acts. The letter is unwilling, though, to be very specific about general limitations. For example, it reminds the senator that CID conduct is defined by the Supreme Court's "shocks the conscience" test, which is relativistic.

Some months later, Senator Wyden tried for clarification and was met with another OLA letter making the same essential points as the first one. With that, the correspondence appears to have subsided. Senator Wyden and some other critics were left to complain about the subjectivity of the administration's position. They argued that Geneva principles should not be subject to a "sliding scale."[126]

CHANGING THE GUARD

The tenure of Alberto Gonzales as attorney general was troubled and brief. Controversy arose from several sources. One, of course, was his role in approving an embattled president's most controversial programs.[127] Many in Congress thought that he had "allowed his intense personal loyalty to President Bush to overwhelm his responsibilities to the law."[128] He was also charged with politicizing the Justice Department in numerous ways, including the use of political tests for career staff attorney positions.[129] He dismissed several U.S. attorneys for reasons that appeared to be political, thereby threatening the integrity of the prosecutorial function. Called to testify before hostile congressional committees, he repeatedly gave evasive and apparently false answers.[130] He was under formal investigation by the department's inspector general regarding the truthfulness of his testimony.[131] He resigned under fire in September 2007 after about two and a half years in his post. He left the Justice Department in substantial disarray.[132] Many senior positions were filled on an acting basis, and portions of the career staff were in open revolt.

Needing a successor of unquestioned integrity, the president settled on retired federal judge Michael Mukasey, who was confirmed in October 2007. Mukasey's confirmation process was contentious. He assured the Senate Judiciary Committee that he would be more independent from the White House than his predecessor.[133] He condemned the *Interrogation* opinion as "a mistake" and "unnecessary." Yet he irritated the committee by holding firm to the Justice Department's traditional view that presidents have some constitutional authority to take actions that conflict with statutory limits, especially in national security matters. The problem was the usual one, that attorneys general will not concede the absence of such authority, but cannot say in advance exactly when it exists.

Most of the controversy attending Mukasey's confirmation resulted from a very unsatisfactory dialogue about torture. The Senate committee repeatedly pressed Mukasey to say whether he considered waterboarding torture.[134] He would not answer the question because he could not do so without making one of two serious errors. If he said waterboarding is not torture, he might not be confirmed; at the least, he would open himself to widespread derision. Besides, he might be lying. If he testified that waterboarding is torture, he would expose the CIA to serious lawfare for actions the Justice Department had approved.[135] Mukasey did say that he found waterboarding "repugnant" and explained his concerns about exposing interrogators to lawfare.[136] Some members of the committee, though, were having too much self-righteous fun to let him off the hook and seek a clear understanding for the future. In the end, Mukasey was confirmed by an unusually close vote of fifty-three to forty.

The new attorney general soon found himself responding to an uproar caused by disclosures that the CIA had taken and later destroyed videotapes of hundreds of hours of interrogations of two senior Al Qaeda captives, Abu Zubaydah and Abd al-Rahim al-Nashiri.[137] The CIA had been warned not to destroy the tapes by White House and Justice Department officials and by members of Congress, but the head of the CIA's directorate of operations ordered the destruction anyway, without informing either the agency's director or its general counsel.[138] It appeared that CIA officials may have lied about the existence of the tapes both to federal judges and to the 9/11 Commission. Investigations of possible obstruction of justice were soon initiated by the CIA inspector general, the Justice Department, and the congressional intelligence committees. Although the golden shield the OLC had originally constructed for the CIA would probably still protect the interrogators themselves, those who covered up the facts would be fully exposed to prosecution.

"Exactly what they feared is what's happening. The winds change, and the recriminations begin," observed Jack Goldsmith.[139] No, not exactly. Both political branches had continued to support the CIA. The executive branch had continued to churn out opinions supporting enhanced interrogations; Congress had twice ratified CIA actions within limits and had erected defenses to prosecution for past interrogations. The CIA's misbehavior concerning destruction of the tapes was its own fault. By the twenty-first century, anyone working in the executive branch should understand the danger of a cover-up.

Some changes were in the wind, though. The new attorney general had an incentive to distance himself from his predecessor by showing the kind of independence the Bush White House had never previously tolerated. Within the Justice Department, the Office of Professional Responsibility initiated an internal review of the OLC opinions concerning harsh interrogation, with a special emphasis on approval of waterboarding.[140] The office was examining "whether the legal advice in these memoranda was consistent with the professional standards that apply to Department of Justice attorneys." After investigating, the office could reprimand miscreant lawyers or even seek their disbarment.

President Bush, however, characteristically refused to yield his ground. In March 2008, he vetoed a bill that would have required the CIA to follow the U.S. Army's field manual for interrogations. The bill would have eliminated most harsh techniques, including waterboarding. "Because the danger remains, we need to ensure our intelligence officials have all the tools they need to stop the terrorists," Bush explained.[141] Even though the administration claimed that it had not resorted to waterboarding since 2003, the president was unwilling to accept a prospective limitation that might tie his hands.

The president's resistance to abandoning harsh interrogation probably reflected his belief in his administration's frequent claims that coercion had elicited information that prevented terrorist attacks. Of course it is impossible to know if there are classified instances supporting these claims. It is true, however, that specific examples that the administration has offered have been discredited.[142] More generally, in 2006 an advisory group reported to the U.S. intelligence agencies that there was no proof that the harsh techniques were effective, and many signs to the contrary.[143] It may be, then, that the Bush administration's decisions to enter the borderlands of torture, like so much that is in the legal opinions supporting them, proved both unnecessary and counterproductive. War entails inhumanity, but it should never be gratuitous.

12

Advice Begets Action: From the Office of Legal Counsel to Abu Ghraib

EVERYONE HAS SEEN THE ICONIC PHOTO FROM ABU GHRAIB PRISON that will feed hatred of the United States for a generation: the hooded man on a box, his arms raised in cruciform style, trailing wires attached to his body.[1] President Bush's lawyers generated advice that led, through some foreseeable intermediate steps, to abuses of this kind. Hence they should share in the blame, whether or not the law ever calls them to account. This chapter tracks the flow of legal advice from the Office of Legal Counsel (OLC) to the Pentagon and thence to the field, where it was translated into operational practices the president and his lawyers never directly blessed but should have anticipated.

At the end of the day, OLC's imprint on the Pentagon's interrogation policy was plain for all to see. Cause and effect is more difficult to gauge for implementation of the policy. Orders had to be translated into actions, and as analysts of war emphasize, the "friction" between the two can be considerable after an operation begins.[2] Considerable it would be in the war on terrorism. Yet good generals know that friction must be anticipated and guarded against. There was insufficient attention to this imperative from the highest levels of the Bush administration to the lowest.

A WARTIME PRESIDENT

The roots of the disconnection between the top and the bottom of the Bush administration that caused scandals at Guantánamo and Abu Ghraib can be traced as far back as the president's own character and his administration's preoccupations from its inception. Both the Afghanistan and Iraq Wars have been conducted in the Bush style. "Character is fate. . . . Bush's [Iraq] war, like his administration, . . . was run with his own absence of curiosity and self-criticism, his projection of absolute confidence, the fierce loyalty he bestowed and demanded."[3] This is not an atmosphere that welcomes or even tolerates arguments about the limits to power or that encourages inquiries to see if abuses are occurring. The wars have reflected all of the administration's neoconservative leaders' main precepts: belief in military power, belief in the United States as a force for good, optimism about U.S. capabilities, reluctance to rely on other nations, and the need to be the dominant superpower.[4]

By fighting two wars simultaneously, the administration stretched the U.S. military in ways that risked a critical loss of control on the ground. The push toward war with Iraq began early. President Bush's first National Security Council meeting in January 2001 discussed the overthrow of Saddam Hussein. In spring and summer 2001, "dozens of reports were generated" at the Defense and State Departments about invading Iraq "as the CIA increasingly warned about the threat from Al Qaeda."[5] Iraq was the war George Bush wanted and eventually got. The war he did not want, in Afghanistan, soon took second place in his priorities.

The signs of distraction were evident immediately after the attacks on 9/11. That night, counterterrorism chief Richard A. Clarke "walked into a series of discussions in the White House about Iraq," not Al Qaeda.[6] He decided that Donald Rumsfeld and Paul Wolfowitz at the Defense Department were using the tragedy to press for war with Iraq, which they had wanted since before the beginning of the administration. Vice President Cheney soon became a leader in the push for war with Iraq.

By fall 2002, it was clear that facts mattered to the Bush administration less than ideology. Analysts throughout the executive branch were being ignored or pressed into an inappropriate role "not to help shape policy, but to affirm it."[7] There was almost no planning for the aftermath of military victory in Iraq. At the Pentagon, "they wanted to focus not on what could go wrong but on what would go right."[8] Clear warnings of impending civil war and chaos were ignored. Intelligence that fit the policy agenda went directly to the president, "bypassing the checks and balances of the intelligence community."[9] Within Iraq, the military and civilian officers clashed. "No one was really in charge of Iraq."[10] Still, after a serious insurgency arose, it was quickly understood that a key tool in counterinsurgency is intelligence. Pressure to produce information from prisoners increased. Conditions were ripe for abuse.

REVERSE LAWFARE CLEARS THE BATTLEFIELD

"On a cold winter morning in January 2002, three months after the United States invaded Afghanistan, we flew through clear skies over sparkling blue-green waters into Cuba," recalls John Yoo.[11] He was there "to see the detention facility where many of [the Al Qaeda and Taliban] fighters would spend the rest of the war." Presumably, although Yoo does not say so, this was not purely an inspection trip or a bit of a boondoggle for a hardworking young bureaucrat. Meetings with the military commanders and their onsite lawyers to discuss interrogations were a more likely purpose of the visit.

As the war on terrorism got under way, three lines of advice that OLC provided to the Defense Department converged. Their synergy heightened the risks that abusive conduct would occur. Thus, we need to consider the various opinions *together* as a set of signals to the field. John Yoo has said he intentionally made a body of law on terrorism. It was applied very aggressively, as he appears to have intended.

The earliest advice was in OLC's *Habeas* opinion to General Counsel William J. Haynes II of the Department of Defense in late 2001.[12] This opinion assured the Pentagon that there was little risk of habeas corpus jurisdiction over Guantánamo (erroneously, as the Supreme Court later decided in *Rasul* and *Boumediene*). Hence, legal scrutiny of what transpired at the base was not expected, and there was doubtless even less expectation of judicial supervision of overseas prisons in Afghanistan and later in Iraq.

The second element of the OLC advice came soon afterward in the *Application of Treaties* opinion, which informed the Pentagon that it need not grant prisoner of war status or other Geneva Convention protections to the detainees. This opinion replaced old certainties with a very indefinite legal environment. Moreover, President Bush's order of early 2002 to treat prisoners "humanely" yet consistent with military necessity could be interpreted to allow almost anything.

By eliminating both fear of the federal courts and guidance from Geneva, these opinions placed all the pressure to assure appropriate restraint on the Pentagon. Yet the military's first and core duty is to protect national security, and the civilian leadership sent very strong messages about the need for effective interrogation down the chain of command. Many of the Pentagon's lawyers did what they could to discharge their duty to ensure the legality of interrogations, but messages they sent about legality were dominated by the civilians' messages about security.

The third line of advice from the OLC concerned interrogation specifically. The administration's tendency to send mixed messages to the field (as in the president's order) made this advice critical to ensuring the legality of operations. Before examining the advice OLC gave the Pentagon, I pause to note some crucial differences between the military and the other agency OLC was also advising about this topic, the Central Intelligence Agency (CIA).

MILITARY LAW AND CULTURE

The U.S. military has long understood the danger that prisoners will be abused and has designed safeguards to prevent it. For example, in the Civil War Lincoln forbade mistreatment of Confederate prisoners. In modern times, the Uniform Code of Military Justice (UCMJ), enacted in 1950, prohibits "cruelty toward, or oppression or maltreatment of" persons subject to a soldier's orders.[13] More generally, it forbids assaults, mayhem, and murder. (Of course, distinctions must be made between combat operations and crimes, as we shall see.)

In 2001, the *Army Field Manual* forbade "acts of violence or intimidation, including physical or mental torture, threats, insults, or exposure to inhumane treatment as a means of or aid to interrogation."[14] "Such illegal acts," the manual emphasized, "are not authorized and will not be condoned by the U.S. Army." Because it was an administrative regulation rather than a statute, the field manual could be altered by the secretary of defense. Its prohibition of abusive interrogation, however, had been in force for almost half a century and was obviously meant to state abiding limits.

Each bureaucracy has its own culture. That of the military is a very powerful one, as it is intended to be. If soldiers are to accept orders that may spell their death, they must first be indoctrinated in traditional ways that begin with the indignities of boot camp. As anyone who has worn the uniform knows, behavior is regulated by thick layers of both internal law and informal norms. Also, there are cultures within cultures. The infantry differs from the military police; both differ from the judge advocate generals (JAGs). Some values, though, are deeply lodged and widely held. After 9/11, both JAGs and line officers would display firm adherence to the Geneva Conventions and all they represent. The leader of this movement was a distinguished former soldier, Secretary of State Colin Powell. Defeat awaited him and his allies at the hands of the arrogant civilian ideologues who drove the administration's policies.

A considerable process of discussion between the Justice and Defense Departments and within the Pentagon preceded the formation of a military interrogation policy and its translation into instructions to the field. Increasingly, the simple clarities of the field manual and the UCMJ were obscured and lost. The process left a long trail of memoranda, like dinosaur tracks in Cretaceous mud.[15] I will analyze OLC's legal advice, then follow the tracks of its acceptance at the Pentagon.

A BRASS SHIELD FOR THE MILITARY

On March 14, 2003, John Yoo signed an opinion incorporating much of the analysis the *Interrogation* opinion had adopted for the CIA. (Jay Bybee was in the process of leaving OLC for the federal bench and probably had his eye on the robe. Yoo was finally free of whatever nominal supervision he had received from Bybee.) Titled *Military Interrogation of Alien Unlawful Combatants Held outside the United States,* this opinion contains eighty-one pages of dense analysis.[16] Issued on the eve of the Iraq War, the opinion is surely intended to supply general guidance for the nation's new military commitment. The opinion also undoubtedly includes much analysis that OLC had provided the Pentagon informally in the preceding months. The *Military Interrogation* opinion was kept secret until the end of March 2008, shielding it from the furor that attended the revelation of *Interrogation* almost four years earlier.

Not surprisingly, *Military Interrogation* begins by stressing the president's constitutional authority as commander in chief. As Yoo had done in earlier memoranda, he characterizes detaining and interrogating the enemy as part of the "core" of that authority. Given the nature of terrorist activity, he says, information "is perhaps the most critical weapon for defeating Al Qaeda." He cites congressional endorsement of the terror war in the Authorization to Use Military Force (AUMF) and other statutes. None of this is controversial.

Yoo then quickly shifts ground to his cherished (and extreme) argument that the clause vesting executive power in the president makes his war powers exclusive. Repeatedly citing OLC's earlier opinions during the war on terrorism, Yoo asserts that Congress has never tried to interfere with the president's interrogation power and implies strongly that it may not do so. Taken seriously, this argument would mean that the prohibitions on abuse of prisoners in the UCMJ and the field manual are unconstitutional, either on their face or whenever the president chooses to contravene them. Presumably, the federal statutes condemning torture and war crimes would suffer the same fate. Yoo may not mean to make so sweeping a claim—at least he does not do so explicitly. But he does not need to do so, because his opinion will find other ways to set these restrictions aside.

The point of the opinion's opening discussion, then, is to identify who is in charge. In this effort, it is seriously incomplete because it neither acknowledges nor analyzes the explicit powers of Congress to regulate the military, which are implemented in many statutes (such as those mentioned above).

The OLC opinion next asserts that the Fifth Amendment's Due Process

Clause does not apply to "interrogations of alien enemy combatants held out-side the United States." First, Yoo denies that the amendment was intended to restrict the commander in chief power. He supports this conclusion by reviewing U.S. attorney general and Supreme Court opinions holding that the Constitution's usual limits on the domestic activities of civilian authorities do not govern extraterritorial actions against aliens by the military in wartime.[17] He does not, however, stop to consider a more precise question: whether the Fifth Amendment's prohibition of official conduct that "shocks the conscience" might apply to military interrogations, even if the full panoply of procedural rights that attend criminal trials does not. The Supreme Court has not had to decide that question, though, because of the various statutory restrictions that control military conduct.

Turning to the statutory issues, Yoo deploys his heavy artillery—several canons of construction that "indicate that ordinary federal criminal statutes do not apply" to interrogation of enemy combatants. He begins with the avoidance canon, which gives his earlier discussion of the commander in chief power operative effect: "In light of the President's complete authority over the conduct of war, in the absence of a clear statement from Congress otherwise, we will not read a criminal statute as infringing on the President's ultimate authority in these areas." He repeats the assertion in *Interrogation* that Congress can "no more regulate" interrogation than it may regulate "troop movements on the battlefield." Therefore, he concludes, general federal criminal prohibitions against "assault, maiming, interstate stalking, and torture" should not be read to constrain the president.

To Yoo, other canons only reinforce this conclusion. He invokes the principle that general criminal laws are not meant to apply to the military in combat, lest it be murder to kill the enemy. He dusts off the hoary principle that laws of general applicability are not read to apply to the sovereign, which means that general laws do not confine executive discretion about treatment of unlawful combatants. (This is a variant of the preceding canon.) Finally, he invokes the rule that specific statutes govern more general ones, so that the UCMJ, not general federal criminal law, controls the military.

This is a blunderbuss approach. Yoo simply takes general interpretive principles found in U.S. law and uses them to sweep away all federal criminal law. A more discriminating approach would have taken seriously the possibility that some interrogation methods could constitute federal crimes even if the government does not apply criminal law to ordinary combat operations. The difference is clearest regarding his cavalier treatment of the torture statute. Yoo concludes that the statute would raise "grave" separation of powers concerns if applied to the executive in wartime, and that it can still reach "other governmental actors in peacetime." This ignores the legislative history of the statute as well as the obvious fact that military personnel under wartime stress are a primary target of international and domestic laws that try to prevent torture.

Yoo leaves the canons after a parting shot for emphasis: if the statutes were "misconstrued" to govern wartime interrogation, no prosecution could be brought because the statutes would be unconstitutional as applied. He then turns to an extended and technical analysis of the possibility that the federal criminal laws could apply to some activities at Guantánamo and other bases because of a statute that governs certain extraterritorial territory of the United States. For example, the statute might expose nonmilitary personnel to jeopardy for their conduct of interrogations. Yoo summarizes the federal statutes that prohibit assault, maiming, and interstate stalking (harassment causing fear of injury).[18] He summarizes the law and notes some ways to avoid applying it to interrogation (for example, "minimal physical contact, such as poking, slapping, or shoving" is unlikely to constitute an assault).

Two criminal statutes remain for Yoo's consideration, and both explicitly apply to conduct of Americans overseas: the War Crimes Act (WCA) and the torture statute. Having picked up the tools of the technician, Yoo finds a way to defuse both of these dangerous statutes. The WCA, he asserts, does not protect Al Qaeda or Taliban detainees because "as illegal belligerents, they do not qualify" for the Geneva protections the WCA enforces. He cites OLC's earlier *Application of Treaties* opinion for this proposition along with the other OLC opinions at the time of the Geneva decision. He concludes firmly that *Application of Treaties* is "the Justice Department's binding interpretation of the War Crimes Act, and it will preclude any prosecution under it for conduct toward members of the Taliban and Al Qaeda."

Yoo concludes that the torture statute "by its terms" does not apply to interrogations conducted within the United States "or on permanent military bases outside the territory of the United States." This is because the statute applies "outside the United States" and then defines the United States to include overseas military bases such as Guantánamo. Still, the statute could apply to some interrogations, he concedes, such as those "conducted at a non-U.S. base in Afghanistan." Accordingly, he repeats the extended analysis from *Interrogation* about the meaning of the torture statute. He reviews the Convention Against Torture (CAT) and asserts that a presidential decision to order interrogation methods inconsistent with it "would amount to a [permissible] suspension or termination" of that convention. He adds a claim that if the convention is considered customary international law, it lacks domestic legal effect "and in any event can be overridden by the

President at his discretion." He does not pause to ask in what sense international law can then be understood as "law," as opposed to bromides.

Because the Senate's ratification of CAT had defined cruel, inhuman, and degrading treatment in terms of existing U.S. constitutional law, Yoo reviews the caselaw at some length. The Eighth Amendment's prohibition of cruel or unusual punishment, he says, does not apply to good faith actions taken to maintain discipline but only to malicious attempts to inflict harm. For conditions of confinement, he quotes the usual judicial inquiry whether there is "deliberate indifference" to the prisoner's well-being. Stressing that "there can be no more compelling government interest than that which is presented here" (that is, basic national security), Yoo concludes that necessity matters and therefore that proving malice or indifference is unlikely even if there is some deprivation and use of force.

The due process stricture against conduct that "shocks the conscience" applies only to "the most egregious official conduct," Yoo says, quoting the cases. He gives examples of specific conduct that has met the test, such as rape, shooting, and beatings. He notes the difficulty of deriving specific guidance from the cases and therefore states some principles. First, justification matters. Second, official negligence is not enough; instead, deliberate indifference might be the test. Third, some physical contact is allowed, perhaps a shove or a slap. Finally, some physical or mental injury must occur to ground a violation.

Military Interrogation closes with the analysis of possible defenses *Interrogation* had provided for the CIA. Yoo adds the canon of construction that criminal laws such as the torture statute are to be "strictly construed in favor of the defendant." This principle suggests to him that it is legitimate to recognize the defenses of necessity and self-defense as OLC had defined them. Never one to avoid threatening a statute, Yoo concludes that criminal laws that did not recognize these defenses might be unconstitutional.

Because *Military Interrogation* is so similar to the *Interrogation* opinion, its deficiencies of right and conscience are similar also. There is one important point to add. The later opinion omits attention to the two most obvious barriers to abusive interrogation in the military: the UCMJ and the field manual. It is not responsible to consider the legal limits to military action without addressing these sources of law. Perhaps the idea was to leave these questions of military law to the military. Yet the opinion purports to be comprehensive. Perhaps John Yoo did not feel comfortable saying what his opinion so strongly implies: that the Pentagon may disregard these limits if it may disregard so many others. It would be extremely difficult to formulate an argument that even passes the frivolity test for the proposition that the

UCMJ does not bind our military. Having no argument to make concerning this central issue, the opinion declines to attempt any. That is a failure of professional responsibility.

COMMAND AND CONTROL

There was a clear need for answers to many of the questions *Military Interrogation* addressed. By the summer of 2002, Guantánamo held about 600 prisoners. Teams of CIA, FBI, and military investigators were seeking intelligence from them. A Defense Department consultant on terrorism captured the overall tone: "This is a war in which intelligence is everything. Winning or losing depends on it."[19]

Tensions soon arose between the FBI agents and other interrogators, probably because of the traditional orientation of the FBI to the constraints of U.S. criminal law.[20] FBI complaints about the techniques used were relayed to General Counsel Haynes at the Pentagon.[21] FBI agents eventually created a "war crimes file" of accusations against military interrogators.[22] Officials at senior levels of the administration were told of the complaints but took no action. There was a powerful incentive to downplay such complaints. In the Bush administration, no one got ahead who seemed soft on suspected terrorists.

As prisoners accumulated at Guantánamo, military interrogators knew that Geneva's POW protections were not to apply, but they did not know what the new limits were. Following the precedent set by the CIA, the military converted the "SERE" training techniques for resisting coercion into methods for performing it.[23] In October 2002, military interrogators at Guantánamo asked for more guidance. As had been the case with CIA interrogations, the presence of a particular prisoner sparked the inquiry. The target was Mohammed al-Qahtani, sometimes known as the "twentieth hijacker" because he tried to enter the United States just before 9/11 after having contact with the hijackers. Interrogators wanted to use techniques the CIA was using: isolation, exposure to cold or water, use of stress positions (such as standing for up to four hours), and waterboarding.[24] They had a memo from a lawyer on the base, Lt. Col. Diane Beaver, concluding that absent Geneva protections, these techniques were legal.[25] Guantánamo's commander, Major General Michael Dunlavey, sent a request for approval up the chain of command to the Pentagon.

The need for advice continued as Major General Geoffrey Miller took command at Guantánamo in November 2002, with no prior experience in managing a prison. He likely felt pressure to produce results from Secretary Rumsfeld, who regarded his senior generals as much too risk-averse and unaggressive.[26] Miller echoed the pending request for more flexibility in interrogations, and the secretary complied.[27]

This began a period of uncharacteristic vacillation on the part of Secretary Rumsfeld, as competing forces within the military and the administration tugged him first one way, then the other. Pressing him toward aggressiveness were Vice President Cheney and the War Council in alliance with interrogators who were frustrated by the resistance of some detainees. Pulling him back were some of his most senior military lawyers and the FBI. Because of his controlling nature, Rumsfeld was never willing to give his subordinates carte blanche to interrogate as they liked. In addition, he showed signs of caution in what he was willing to approve.

Rumsfeld began aggressively by authorizing a "special interrogation plan" for the high-value detainee al-Qahtani.[28] He allowed isolation for up to thirty days, interrogation for up to twenty out of twenty-four hours, and intimidation with dogs. What then happened to al-Qahtani demonstrated what would soon become a frequent pattern of agents stretching their instructions and adding some harsh techniques. The absence of Geneva constraints, it appears, released some unfortunate creative instincts in the interrogators. Al-Qahtani was isolated for five months and interrogated for twenty hours a day on forty-eight out of fifty-four days, until his pulse rate dropped to alarming levels. He was threatened with dogs, subjected to repeated sexual humiliation, and exposed to bright light and earsplitting music. The treatment "destroyed al-Qahtani both physically and psychologically."[29] Years later, his pending military commission trial on terrorism charges was dismissed by the military authorities, perhaps because the interrogation he endured had poisoned the evidence against him.[30]

In December, Rumsfeld approved more restricted techniques for most detainees, such as the use of hooding, exploitation of phobias, forced standing, and deprivation of light and auditory stimuli. These and other practices were ordinarily forbidden by the field manual. Rumsfeld reserved judgment on the most aggressive proposed techniques, including waterboarding. As he initialed his approval of the selected techniques, he added a jocular handwritten inquiry: "However, I stand for 8–10 hours a day. Why is standing limited to 4 hours?"[31] Clearly, he did not think he was approving abusive conduct. Nor was he displaying an understanding of actual conditions in his prisons.

Protests about these methods and their implementation arose within the military. U.S. Navy General Counsel Alberto J. Mora reported allegations of abuse to General Counsel Jim Haynes and others.[32] Mora charged that the policy was "unlawful and unworthy of the military services."[33] He wrote a long memorandum detailing his objections and sent it to Haynes in January 2003. In a meeting with Mora, John Yoo defended himself by saying "that his job was only to state what the law was."[34] Mora, he said, was arguing policy. Certainly the boundary was becoming obscured as other JAGs objected on both grounds. Major General Jack Rives of the U.S. Air Force said several of the techniques were illegal and cautioned: "We need to consider the overall impact of approving extreme interrogation techniques as giving official approval and legal sanction to the application of interrogation techniques that U.S. forces have consistently been trained are unlawful."[35]

The FBI chimed in with its objections to the interrogations, including use of the coercive SERE methods. The FBI warned that the methods in use were "at odds with legally permissible interviewing techniques" for domestic criminal investigations and were being performed by personnel "who have little, if any, experience eliciting information for judicial purposes."[36] In the Pentagon, this probably seemed just the usual FBI focus on ordinary crime, but it did sound a cautionary note about spoiling potential evidence for use in any form of trial.

Meanwhile, interrogators in Afghanistan were employing the methods Rumsfeld had approved, and in some cases were exceeding all limits. At Bagram Air Base, there were at least two homicides caused by "blunt force injuries."[37] These were early warnings of the more extensive abuses still to come. Nevertheless, the drive for intelligence had too much momentum to be thrown abruptly into reverse.

The roiling controversy induced Secretary Rumsfeld to suspend his approval of aggressive techniques. He formed the Pentagon Working Group, which developed policy for a period of months in 2002–2003. The working group, overseen by Haynes, included representatives of the general counsels and judge advocate generals of the uniformed services. Haynes asked OLC for an opinion providing legal guidance, and Yoo supplied *Military Interrogation*.[38] By blessing harsh interrogation techniques, the opinion set the stage for the working group's deliberations and framed its eventual report to the secretary. Jim Haynes instructed the group that Yoo's memo was the "controlling authority" on legal issues, ending the debate with the JAGs. Dissenters were left out as the report was finished. Thus the way to prevent pushback from the uniformed lawyers was simply to exclude them from the process.

The final *Working Group Report* was issued after the onset of the Iraq War.[39] It incorporates much of the OLC analysis from *Interrogation* and

Military Interrogation.[40] The report says that in light of the special needs for intelligence in the war on terrorism and the president's directive calling for balancing military needs with humane treatment, it would be appropriate to authorize interrogations "in a manner beyond that which may be applied" to a POW under Geneva. Having considered domestic and international law, past practices, and diverse policy considerations, the report proceeds to list and evaluate specific approved techniques. The report warns that the purpose of interrogation is to "get the most information from a detainee with the least intrusive method, always applied in a humane and lawful manner with sufficient oversight by trained investigators." Techniques are designed to "manipulate the detainee's emotions and weaknesses to gain his willing cooperation."

Many of the specific techniques on the list are verbal, involving no physical contact "and no threat of pain or harm," such as continuous repetition of questions and deceiving the prisoner about the facts. The report also allows hooding, "mild physical contact," such as light touching or poking, and dietary manipulation, such as changing from hot to cold food. More ominously, it allows techniques that led to abusive treatment in the field: isolation, prolonged interrogation (twenty hours per day), prolonged standing (not to exceed four hours a day), sleep deprivation (for up to four days), light slaps to the face or stomach, removal of clothing, and "use of aversions" such as "simple presence of dog." The report calls for special safeguards in the use of the "exceptional" nonverbal methods, for example on-scene supervision and senior level approval.

The *Working Group Report,* echoing OLC's advice, goes on to say that the Constitution "does not protect" persons held outside the United States. It recites the language of CAT and notes that it forbids cruel, inhuman, or degrading treatment. Because OLC had defined that provision to codify U.S. constitutional law, the report explains that it could mean inflicting pain or harm without a legitimate purpose or for malicious reasons, denying the minimal necessities of civilized life, or use of force so brutal that it shocks the conscience. It also reminds readers that the UCMJ prohibits assaults and other violent crimes.

The report reviews defenses relating to commander in chief authority, necessity, and self-defense. "Where the Commander in Chief authority is being relied upon, a presidential written directive would serve to memorialize this authority." The report warns that the "more aggressive the interrogation technique used, the greater the likelihood" that information it produced would be inadmissible at trial, even by military commission. In addition, the use of techniques beyond those normal for POWs would be a "significant departure from traditional U.S. military norms" with a possibly corrosive effect on our troops.

Secretary of Defense Rumsfeld digested the report for a few days, then issued his instructions to the field.[41] He listed techniques approved for use at Guantánamo, together with specified safeguards. The approved techniques were almost all verbal in nature. Among the "exceptional" measures in the report, he allowed only diet manipulation (switching from hot to cold rations), environmental manipulation (causing "moderate discomfort" from heat or cold), sleep adjustment (changing sleep cycles, not overall deprivation), and isolation (up to thirty days).[42] He reiterated the president's humane treatment/military necessity command. He drew safeguards from the *Working Group Report,* including supervision and adherence to standard operating procedures.

When the chief JAG officers of the military services learned of the *Working Group Report* after it was in draft, they responded furiously.[43] The report's heavy reliance on the OLC opinion particularly aggravated them. From the marines came the observation that "OLC does not represent the services; thus, understandably, concern for servicemembers is not reflected in their opinion."[44] From the air force came the stinging rebuke that "the use of the more extreme interrogation techniques simply is not how the U.S. armed forces have operated in recent history. We have taken the legal and moral 'high road' in the conduct of our military operations regardless of how others may operate."[45] This is "exactly the kind of moral reminder that a good lawyer ought to give clients."[46] It was disregarded.

The formal interrogation policies the Pentagon adopted were substantially tamer than what OLC's *Military Interrogation* opinion would have supported. When Jack Goldsmith took over at OLC and decided to withdraw and replace the opinion because of its "problematic" analysis, it appeared that the Defense Department would not have to alter its approved practices.[47] Attorney General Ashcroft was "not terribly surprised and did not resist" withdrawing the opinion. Goldsmith was sympathetic to Jim Haynes at the Pentagon: "Ever since 9/11, Haynes had been in the middle of a struggle between a White House and Department of Justice bent on pushing the President's war powers to their limits, and the armed forces bent on upholding what Haynes once admiringly described as a 'tradition of restraint' on interrogation and detainee treatment." In the end, the military lawyers had won something of a victory. After they "strenuously objected" to OLC's analysis, Haynes recommended that Rumsfeld approve only the relatively noncontroversial techniques in the *Working Group Report.* Once again, extreme and unsupported analysis emanating from OLC had been unnecessary to meet operational needs.

FRICTION

Had Secretary Rumsfeld's order of April 2003 been followed scrupulously in the field, the scandal that broke a year later would not have occurred. If President Bush's initial order from early 2002 had been posted at the prisons at Guantánamo and elsewhere, "it might have sent a healthy and salutary signal" to treat prisoners humanely even with the accompanying caveats.[48] Instead, because the Bush order remained classified until June 2004, there was "a heavy burden on careful guidance and instruction by the administration, communicating clearly from the top to the field."

What did happen is an object lesson in military friction. A senior Pentagon consultant and former military officer said that President Bush and Secretary Rumsfeld "created the conditions that allowed transgressions to take place. . . . When you live in a world of gray zones, you have to have very clear red lines."[49] A similar analysis came from a Vietnam veteran serving in the administration:

> There's no doubt in my mind as a soldier that part of the responsibility for Abu Ghraib and Afghanistan belongs with the secretary of defense and the president of the United States. There's an old aphorism: Keep it simple, stupid. . . . You always have personalities in uniform—I had them in Vietnam—who will take advantage of any ambiguity, any lack of clarification in the rules of engagement, and kill people, or whatever. . . . You don't have rules for your good people. . . . You need the rules. And when you make any kind of changes in them, any relaxation or even hint of it, you're opening Pandora's box.[50]

The State Department's legal adviser during this period, William H. Taft IV, later reflected that U.S. troops "are trained to comply with the law of war in conducting operations. . . . Discarding familiar rules of conduct and improvising new ones as we go along creates a situation full of temptations to cut corners and adopt practices that seem desirable at the moment but are not well thought through and are bad precedents for other situations that we fail to anticipate."[51]

In particular, he deplored pressure from the administration's lawyers to decide that the Geneva Conventions did not govern the war on terrorism:

"This unsought conclusion unhinged those responsible for the treatment of the detainees in Guantánamo from the legal guidelines for interrogation of detainees reflected in the Conventions and embodied in the *Army Field Manual* for decades. Set adrift in uncharted waters and under pressure from their leaders to develop information on the plans and practices of Al Qaeda, it was predictable that those managing the interrogation would eventually go too far."[52]

Thinking about the interrogation abuses that occurred, a former navy JAG remarked: "I know from the military that if you tell someone they can do a little of this for the country's good, some people will do a lot of it for the country's better."[53] Essentially, that is what occurred. A set of limits that undoubtedly looked humane to Secretary Rumsfeld and his working group became distorted in the field—not beyond recognition, but beyond reason.

In this atmosphere, even traditional techniques from the field manual were reinterpreted in extreme ways. For example, "ego down," which means "attacking the source's sense of personal worth," became a license for degradation, including some of the bizarre sexual humiliations that later shocked the public.[54] "Fear up harsh," as the manual recognizes, can readily become violent if restraint is not exercised. Violence there was. "Environmental manipulation" can be moderate and irritating or so extreme it threatens injury or death. Employed with urgent purpose, it often tended toward the extreme.

Harsh interrogation techniques migrated from Guantánamo to Afghanistan and Iraq. The practices employed, which have been well documented, followed a similar pattern from one place to another.[55] Whether or not this demonstrates a "secret policy" of abuse, as some have alleged, it does at least show that the dangers of harsh interrogation have been systemic.

There are several ways interrogation abuses could have spread in the war on terrorism. First, some of the interrogators and their supervisors were traveling from one detention site to another or observing one another. The presence of CIA interrogators at many Defense Department facilities, including Guantánamo and Abu Ghraib, surely helped to spread harsh interrogation techniques. A military interrogator, witnessing the actions of CIA agents, might well wonder, "If they can do this, why can't I?" Just as legal analysis within OLC migrated from the context of the CIA to the military, practical techniques in the field would have gone through bureaucratic barriers by a kind of osmosis.

Second, it appears that interrogators reacted in similar ways to the dominant signals they received. Read by themselves, Secretary Rumsfeld's authorizations for particular interrogation techniques appeared relatively restrained. But when they were followed by orders such as those issued in Iraq stressing that "the gloves are coming off" and prisoners are to be "broken," interrogators had to understand that results mattered.[56] Nor did it help that Secretary Rumsfeld repeatedly expressed his disdain for the Geneva Conventions.

Third, military lawyers were largely excluded from the process of implementing the interrogation rules.[57] By contrast, in the first Gulf War in 1991, JAG officers had been at all detention facilities where interrogations occurred. In the war on terrorism, there was no one around the prisons on a daily basis whose responsibilities included legal compliance except for the commanders, who were hearing other signals.

A signal *not* sent because it was prevented by the initial OLC advice the president accepted would probably have averted the scandal: a clear message that these are POWs who have the usual protections of the Geneva Conventions. In that way, OLC's theories reached the front lines even if the opinions incorporating them remained stashed away in Washington. As Secretary of State Colin Powell emphasized when the Geneva question was first raised within the administration, the U.S. military has applied Geneva principles successfully in conflicts as stressful as Vietnam. The conventions have historically proved their power to restrain U.S. troops, yet they were cast aside.

Within the military, an important influence on interrogations was the presence of various special forces units operating in the prisons. With President Bush's authorization the Pentagon set up highly secret "special access programs," or SAPS, to capture Al Qaeda leaders anywhere and to form secret interrogation centers in allied countries. (The existence of the SAPs might explain the reference to military necessity in Bush's memo of February 7, 2002.) Information about the activities of the SAPs was very closely held. In June 2002, the administration even objected to a provision in the annual defense appropriations bill that provided for thirty days' advance notice of any new SAP to the House and Senate leaders. The provision remained, but Bush issued a signing statement asserting his constitutional authority over controlling national security information and saying he would construe it "in a manner consistent with the constitutional authority of the President."[58] In other words, congressional oversight would receive minimal response.

In August 2003, Secretary Rumsfeld expanded the SAPs into the Iraq prisons. Now the lines blurred between captured Iraqis, to whom Geneva protections clearly applied, and captured foreign fighters thought to be members of Al Qaeda, who lived in the twilight zone. At OLC, Jack Goldsmith analyzed the problems and concluded that the Fourth Geneva Convention's provisions regarding the duties of an occupying power applied in Iraq to

Iraqi terrorists but not foreigners.[59] Attorney General Ashcroft then asked him to explain the decision, saying that "he had promised the President that the Department of Justice would do everything it could to give the President maximum discretion, within the law, to check Islamist terrorism." After Goldsmith explained his opinion and emphasized that it was widely shared by other government lawyers, Ashcroft assented. On the way to the White House to explain the opinion to White House Counsel Gonzales and David Addington, Goldsmith's deputy Patrick Philbin told him: "They're going to be really mad. They're not going to understand our decision. They've never been told 'no.'" As predicted, Addington was furious: "The President has already decided that terrorists do not receive Geneva Convention protections. You cannot question his decision." Goldsmith replied that this was a different legal question, but Addington, as usual, was in no mood for fine distinctions.

GITMOIZING IRAQ

The prison at Abu Ghraib had been notorious under Saddam Hussein. In June 2003, Brigadier General Janis Karpinski, a reserve officer, came to run it. Like General Miller, she had never run a prison. In mid-2003, signs of insurgency in Iraq became unmistakable and, as U.S. casualties mounted, pressure grew to gather intelligence. In August 2003, General Miller went from Guantánamo to Iraq to review the army program there. He was familiar with the contents of the *Working Group Report*.[60] Wanting to "Gitmoize" the system in Iraq, he briefed the local commanders on methods used in Cuba.[61] He said it was "essential that the guard force be actively engaged in setting the conditions for successful exploitation" of the prisoners.[62] Army Lt. General Ricardo Sanchez, commanding in Iraq, soon issued a directive authorizing interrogation methods beyond those in the field manual, based on Rumsfeld's earlier instructions for Guantánamo.[63] In March 2004, Miller was transferred to command the Iraq prisons. The scandal exploded shortly thereafter.

Several factors made Abu Ghraib a Petri dish for abuse.[64] First, the prison was filled beyond capacity and was understaffed by undertrained personnel. Extensive military sweeps and arrests caused severe sorting problems—who was a combatant? Second, there was a tendency to treat the Iraqi people as the enemy rather than the prize in counterinsurgency warfare.[65] Third, lack of accountability within the executive branch allowed abusive practices to fester. A senior official complained that "the administration simply refused to admit mistakes or to act to correct or remove those who made them."[66] The prison scandal never led to punishment for any high level officers.

An ironic episode occurred just as the prison scandal surfaced. On April 28, 2004, while arguing the *Hamdi* case before the Supreme Court, Deputy Solicitor General Paul Clement, ignorant of actual conditions in the prisons, responded to a question from Justice Stevens about whether the law curtails interrogation. Clement responded that he thought the United States was a signatory to conventions against torture and that it would honor those treaty obligations.[67] At the end of that day, the first pictures from Abu Ghraib reached the U.S. public.

A SPATE OF INVESTIGATIONS

Sometime in January 2004, Secretary of Defense Rumsfeld informed the president that problems had arisen at Abu Ghraib. The first of thirteen high-level investigations conducted by the Pentagon was soon under way.[68] Among these, the best known have been the *Taguba Report,* the *Schlesinger Report,* and the *Fay/Jones Report.*[69] They produced a depressing litany of abuses. The *Taguba Report* uncovered "numerous incidents of sadistic, blatant, and wanton criminal abuse of detainees" at Abu Ghraib.[70] The *Schlesinger Report* condemned "acts of brutality and purposeless sadism" committed by "both military police and military intelligence personnel" at Abu Ghraib and found "a failure of military leadership and discipline."[71] The report found that "techniques effective under carefully controlled conditions at Guantánamo became far more problematic when they migrated and were not adequately safeguarded." The Schlesinger group counted 300 allegations of abuse and 66 substantiated cases. The *Fay/Jones Report* found that although "senior level officers did not commit the abuse at Abu Ghraib they did bear responsibility for lack of oversight of the facility."[72] Unfortunately, the military investigations were not invited to cast their gaze too far up the chain of command, lest ultimate responsibility for the abuses be too clearly assigned.

There have also been multiple investigations by nongovernmental organizations. The International Red Cross, after many battles to obtain access to the detainees, reported that Iraqi captives who were thought to have intelligence value were "at high risk of being subjected to a variety of harsh treatment ranging from insults, threats, and humiliations to both physical and psychological coercion, which in some cases was tantamount to torture."[73] The Red Cross had "regularly brought its concerns to the attention" of the military, with little effect. The American Bar Association, after reviewing the legal advice furnished to the administration, concluded that "the memoranda and the decisions of high U.S. officials at the very least contributed to a culture in which prisoner abuse became widespread."[74] Investigative journalists have probed diligently and effectively by following leads from confidential sources.[75] This diverse collection of nongovernmental investigators, although facing serious difficulties in getting at the facts, has nevertheless uncovered much.

But where was Congress? Sunk in its institutional torpor and still dominated by the Bush administration until the 2006 elections, Congress remained essentially reactive.[76] Eventually it passed some legislation. The DTA and the MCA followed the Supreme Court's calls to action in *Hamdi* and *Hamdan*. Both of these statutes imposed limits on interrogations. But nowhere to be seen was the kind of determined and comprehensive inquiry exemplified by the Church committee of the 1970s and the Iran-Contra committees of the 1980s. Instead, individual members of Congress and some vigilant committees carried the load as best they could. Generally speaking, however, they lacked the clout to force cooperation and response from the administration. Most of the investigative initiative remained with the military and the outsiders.

BOTTOM LINES

The conclusion is inescapable that "systematic military abuse of American prisoners in Iraq, Afghanistan, and at Guantánamo, Cuba, [was] widespread and tolerated."[77] Most estimates of detainee deaths in U.S. custody approximate 100.[78] The interrogations have been intentionally cruel and dehumanizing:

> Detainees in U.S. custody at Guantánamo, in Afghanistan, and in many locations in Iraq have been beaten, menaced by dogs, threatened with infliction of pain, subjected to prolonged periods of solitary confinement, deprived of sleep, subjected to sexual humiliation, exposed to extremes of heat and cold, shackled in painful positions for many hours, and bombarded with bright lights and loud music for extended periods.[79]

The lurid photographs of some of these abuses have increased the impact of the scandal, in part by making the facts undeniable. But was it "torture"?

I think much of it was, in a simple sense. Put away the lawyer's arts for a moment, and ask if our agents imposed "severe pain and suffering" on their prisoners, in the everyday meaning of those words. Much of what happened would qualify, I think. At least it applies to particular actions of extreme abuse that have been repeated all too often. Perhaps more important, the overall pattern of treatment the prisoners received has certainly been "cruel, inhuman, or degrading," in contravention of both international and domestic law. Prisoners have been held incommunicado for years on the basis of very thin and unreliable evidence. The conditions of detention have intentionally been made extremely unpleasant, sometimes in ways reminiscent of the Gulag. Trials of the detainees for war crimes, after years of delay, began only toward the end of the Bush administration. Convictions may be poisoned by the use of coerced testimony. It is a blot on our history.

Who is responsible? The president's legal advisers and the civilians in the Pentagon can accurately say they never approved the harshest interrogation methods that have come to light. President Bush is ultimately responsible for his failure to enforce his command that the captives be treated humanely. Having set aside the reliable legal constraints of Geneva, the administration incurred a special duty to ensure that its own substituted standards be honored. That duty was not discharged. The legal advisers are culpable—they ignored the voices of experience and the counsel of caution and arrogantly propounded overbroad theories of executive power that provided fertile ground for scandal. As it circulated informally, the *Interrogation* memorandum provided an initial license for abuse in its repeated insistence that only "extreme" actions could constitute torture. The subsequent *Military Interrogation* opinion was similarly unrestrained. It should surprise no one that actions ensued which *were* extreme in any ordinary sense of the term. A legal adviser who draws the line of acceptable conduct at the edge of the precipice should know that the client may fall into the abyss.

13

Better Advice

As the Bush administration rode off into the sunset, it left a dismal record of bad legal advice that supported unwise presidential decisions. This chapter traces patterns in the administration's legal errors and evaluates possible remedies for them. Although there is no way to guarantee good advice, following some simple precepts will foster better advice. Every president deserves reliable legal advice, and the nation depends on it.

BAD ADVISERS, BAD ADVICE

Former OLC head Jack Goldsmith, who had found himself trying to correct bad advice his predecessors had given, later reflected on what he had seen.[1] He understood that the tone was set by President Bush himself. Bush relied on "minimal deliberation, unilateral action, and legalistic defense. This approach largely eschews politics: the need to explain, to justify, to convince . . . to compromise." The "unnecessary unilateralism of the Bush years . . . borrowed against the power of future presidencies." Goldsmith explains that the administration "got policies wrong, ironically, because it was excessively legalistic, because it often substituted legal analysis for political judgment, and because it was too committed to expanding the President's constitutional powers." He concludes that questions about what the administration should do collapsed into the lawyers' efforts to define the edges of power. Policy choices then went reflexively right to the legal boundary. It was difficult for anyone to assail the decisions, because OLC opinions could "silence or discipline a recalcitrant bureaucracy."

Goldsmith's perceptions fit the available facts. President Bush was exactly wrong when he promised that the war on terrorism would not be "lawyered to death." His two principal aides, Vice President Cheney and Secretary of Defense Rumsfeld, were fiercely devoted to expanding not just executive power in general but the supremacy of the political appointees at the center of the executive branch in particular. After the diplomatic and military bureaucracies were sidelined, power devolved to the cadre of young lawyers on the War Council. This ideological group, which should have sought the

284

knowledge of those with experience in international and military law, instead concentrated on steamrolling them.

Hence, the War Council's reverse lawfare was partly waged within the executive branch, and quite successfully in terms of achieving domination. It was, however, counterproductive to its larger goals. A baseless legal opinion does more harm than good. That is, extreme advice increases the likelihood that lawfare will overturn it, as the fate of the repudiated opinions implies. Instead, the lawyers should have sought to give ironclad advice that they could defend against all comers. That is where safety from lawfare lies.

Goldsmith's broader point about unnecessary unilateralism is also sound. Presidents who seek ratification from Congress for their emergency actions, for example Abraham Lincoln and Franklin Roosevelt, can build a structure that lasts even longer than the statutes do because it has legitimacy. When President Bush was finally driven by judicial or public pressure to ask Congress for authority, he obtained it. But all the preceding claims of unilateral power left nothing of substance behind. Secret policies based on secret legal theories are not building blocks. The administration's reverse lawfare could not prevail in the long run because it did not engage the other branches in changing the law. Instead, it showed a casual disregard for statutes and international law unmatched by any prior administration. Perhaps the most revealing evidence of this disregard is what the administration did when Congress *did* pass a statute. President Bush's signing statements routinely asserted the power to disregard statutory directives, based on fuzzy but broad claims of executive power.

The Bush administration displayed a basic failure to appreciate the best role of its lawyers.[2] Viewing law as an implement of the war on terrorism rather than a set of constraints upon waging it, the administration employed its lawyers as shock troops of reverse lawfare, not as detached counselors who could anticipate and forestall future legal jeopardy. To their own discredit, many of the lawyers accepted, and even gloried in, this perversion of their role.

All too often, these legal opinions took an oversimplified and selective approach to pertinent legal materials.[3] They neither revealed nor discussed contrary authority. The resulting lack of candor and even of self-awareness fit the administration's style, but not the lawyers' responsibilities. It protected neither the clients nor, in the end, the lawyers themselves. Having read OLC's *Application of Treaties* opinion, an experienced ethicist expressed surprise mixed with dismay:

> When lawyers are asked to provide advice that flirts with the limits of the law, even the most aggressive corporate lawyer will include

significant qualifying language. They will qualify their advice simply as a matter of self-protection and self-respect, anticipating that new corporate managers, a regulator, or a plaintiff may later question the failure adequately to explore risks and contrary arguments.[4]

Executive advisers have a duty of self-knowledge—of knowing that their advice is inherently likely to be quite sympathetic to the client and that the critical question is one of limits. Ignoring the need for detachment and lacking a willingness to consider the legitimate constitutional claims of the other branches, President Bush's lawyers manipulated the law for political ends. Examples abound. They never showed sensitivity to the fact that the canons of construction can lead to any desired result and thus should be used cautiously and responsibly. They were always willing to skate on the thin ice of "inherent" executive power, despite Robert Jackson's long-ago counsel against doing so. Their legal advice, which did not deserve the deference it received within the administration, had grave consequences for the nation. When lawyers remain more in the background, as they should, it is the policymakers who make the most consequential decisions.

The Bush administration's overemphasis on legal theories was a natural consequence of its disregard for facts, especially unwelcome ones. The initiation of the Iraq War is perhaps the best proof of the administration's preference for ideology over fact. What, if anything, should the lawyers have done to counteract this tendency? Their attitude, exemplified by John Yoo, was that they were simply trying to describe the full range of legal options for the policymakers. Ordinarily, that is a good response, one that keeps the lawyers from intruding on policy decisions. In the Bush administration, however, with many of the usual policymakers disabled, the lawyers were operating in a vacuum where policy would gravitate to their articulation of legal limits. In that context, they needed to discharge their professional responsibility as counselors to point out, fully and fairly, the consequences of taking their advice.

It probably takes a lawyer-statesman to have the influence to give unwelcome advice about consequences that will be heard.[5] Robert Jackson could do that; John Ashcroft could not. In the end, the president's own receptivity to disagreement and criticism is crucial. The closed "shadow government" for legal advice that the administration created evaded constructive criticism, forfeiting its contributions. As long ago as the Washington administration, the benefits of legal debate over important issues were demonstrated. To be sure, not every president has taken this lesson to heart. Presidents Thomas Jefferson, Franklin Roosevelt, and Ronald Reagan all suppressed legal debate when it suited their policy ends. Nonetheless, an important element of good conscience in forming legal opinions is consideration of contrary viewpoints and precedents.

The Bush administration structured the provision of legal advice about the war on terrorism to ensure no contrary voice would speak. The two principal policymakers, Dick Cheney and Donald Rumsfeld, relied primarily on two young lawyers whose ideology matched their own, David Addington and John Yoo. White House Counsel Alberto Gonzales was a neophyte in national security and was never known to stand up to his patron the president. Attorney General John Ashcroft was displaced as the primary voice for the Justice Department by Yoo, who was several rungs down the ladder from the top of the department. Nothing in this arrangement promised that a note of caution would be sounded when necessary. The administration received the legal advice it wanted, not the advice it needed.

ACTION, REACTION

"In the eighteenth-century Newtonian universe that is the Constitution, an excessive force in one direction is apt to produce a corresponding counterforce."[6] In the war on terrorism, the Bush administration's lawyers adopted a theory of broadly exclusive executive power to protect national security and tried to minimize the participation of the other two branches. For several years, the other branches left the initiative to the administration. Eventually, counterforces appeared, first in the courts as the Supreme Court repeatedly intervened to cabin executive power and to invite congressional participation in setting antiterror policy. Eventually, Congress also took up its constitutional role by legislating policy for detention, treatment, and trial of terror suspects and for NSA's electronic surveillance program.

Another counterforce emerged as a wide spectrum of the nation's legal and academic community condemned the positions the administration's lawyers had taken. Under pressure from the other branches and the legal community, the administration eventually abandoned much of the theoretical ground it had claimed. The outcome was an object lesson in the dangers of overreaching. Some overall equilibrium in the power of the three branches has returned. In our Newtonian universe, however, equilibrium is always contingent on the next set of forces to arise.

A generation ago, the sins of executive officers during Watergate and Vietnam produced reactions in the courts and Congress that constrained the executive in various ways. After the domestic surveillance scandal of the late 1970s and Iran-Contra in the 1980s, more restrictions were added. Many of these statutes and precedents are still extant. Not a few analysts who are more sober on this topic than Vice President Cheney believe that the post-Watergate reforms have confined the executive branch too much. After all, nothing forces a Newtonian reaction to be just strong enough. The question is: what *should* happen in response to the legal excesses of the Bush administration?

In the battle against terrorism, there seems no need to revise and extend basic concepts of the executive branch's constitutional power. Congress has been prepared to grant the president's requests for statutory authority to investigate, detain, and prosecute suspected terrorists.[7] When the president has not asked for authority, Congress has not had the fortitude to intervene, but the Supreme Court has proved willing to enforce basic requisites of habeas corpus and due process. When future attacks come, as they will, presidents can act on their own authority to stabilize the situation and to respond as they must, invoking traditional judicial precedents that support such actions.[8] After they have responded to the initial crisis, however, presidents must be prepared to seek statutory authority for their actions.

BAD MEDICINE?

Various prescriptions have been advanced to cure the legal ills of the Bush administration. Good doctors, however, avoid the kinds of overenthusiastic and wrongheaded medical interventions that sped an ailing George Washington to his grave. Lawyers, too, must strive to do no more than necessary and to do no harm. This goal is not easy to achieve, for at least two reasons. First, every change in law produces unintended consequences that can offset or negate the intended ones. Second, legal rules tend to induce evasion by people subject to them. In other words, life is unpredictable, and people are unruly. I noted earlier that modern law schools, using the methods of the common law, tend to inculcate habits of caution and incremental analysis in their charges. Those attitudes should guide our inquiry as we try to fit the cure to the disease.

The traditional way for Congress to test the values of individual executive officers is through the Senate's confirmation process. Of course, not all officers go through the process. The principal authors of the administration's legal theories were all exempt from it: Vice President Dick Cheney, his aide David Addington, White House Counsel Alberto Gonzales, and Deputy Assistant Attorney General John Yoo. Obviously, Congress cannot subject an elected vice president to confirmation. It could consider doing so with some or all of the other offices.

It is not clear, however, that separation of powers concepts would allow Congress to impose the confirmation condition on either the White House counsel or the vice president's senior staff.[9] Presidents (and perhaps vice presidents) are entitled to have some "elbow aides" who are selected at their principal's sole discretion. Along with freedom from confirmation scrutiny, these aides usually enjoy immunity from compelled congressional testimony. The testimonial immunity shields their confidential relationship with the president. I think it would be unwise to subject the White House counsel to confirmation. As I have explained, there is a need to give the president a lawyer-confidant to consult, notwithstanding the existence of the attorney general.[10] And because presidents can always find ways to have informal "kitchen cabinets" of confidential advisers, formalizing the counsel's role might simply lead to the "outsourcing" of some advice-giving.

Moreover, I think inquiries in the confirmation process are unlikely to prevent lapses in professional responsibility by the president's lawyers. Questioning would have to be exercised with great skill to detect the sins pertinent here. All nominees for attorney general already assure the Senate they are the "people's lawyer," whatever their actual intentions. Similarly, nominees who wish confirmation are likely to endorse a balanced separation of powers model in testimony. I suspect that even John Yoo, if confronted with his academic writings at the time of his appointment to OLC, would have promised a flexible approach to problems not yet before him. That still leaves plenty of play in the joints in the actual provision of advice, as the role of Congress and the courts is minimized but never denied entirely. Also, at the time of nomination, many important issues are likely unknown. When the Bush administration was assembled in early 2001, no one foresaw the war on terrorism.

Will it be enough, then, to rely on the lessons of history? Will the public beatings Bush administration officials have received deter their successors from repeating their excesses? Recent experience suggests not. It was about a decade from Watergate to Iran-Contra, and another fifteen years to the war on terror. Attempts to aggrandize the executive branch have produced some punishments in each case, but the sting does not seem to last very long. The temptation to pursue grand schemes in the supposed interests of the nation is simply too great to be easily overcome.

Congress ought to become far more vigilant in its oversight of the executive branch than it has been in the war on terrorism. Congress has the "means and motives" (in James Madison's phrase) to oversee executive policy as it is formed and applied. The courts operate too long after the fact and are too diffident in matters of foreign policy and war to provide the essential levels of control. We might have to wait a long time, however, for Congress to pick up its constitutional cudgels. Institutional dysfunction, alas, runs deep. When both the presidency and Congress are in the hands of the same party, as for the first six years of the Bush administration, oversight is not likely to be very vigorous.

Recent congressional efforts to respond to real or perceived executive scandals have shown little promise. At the end of the Clinton presidency, Congress conducted obviously politicized impeachment proceedings over the relatively minor matter of lies about sexual misconduct. At the end of the Bush presidency, Congress showed no appetite to impeach the president and vice president for their far greater sins against the rule of law. A reason for this reluctance may have been that by November 2004, many if not all of the administration's sins stood revealed, and the people reelected the president anyway. Hence the question whether Congress *should* impeach him became moot. Since impeachment has usually proved too blunt an instrument for remedying executive misbehavior, let us turn to other devices.[11]

Because a contributing cause of the bad advice rendered to President Bush was the short-circuiting of normal bureaucratic checks that tend to foster good advice, perhaps Congress should legislate to require adherence to specified checks within the executive. One thoughtful proposal would respond to the Bush practices by setting up "separate and overlapping cabinet offices, mandatory review of government action by different agencies, civil-service protections for agency workers, reporting requirements to Congress, and an impartial decision-maker to resolve interagency conflicts."[12] Because elements of all these checks have been in place since the last century, what animates the proposal is a desire to extend them and enforce them more rigorously. The overall strategy is to employ administrative law techniques to address a separation of powers problem.

Statutory structural changes could easily be overdetermined, however. The deficiency in the Bush administration was not the absence of dissenting voices, but rather a complete unwillingness to listen to them.[13] Normal and long-standing bureaucratic arrangements within the executive branch have successfully vetted legal advice in most modern administrations. It is more important to return to these arrangements than to encumber them with mandated layers of review. As the war on terrorism illustrates, there is often a need for dispatch in providing legal advice and for flexibility in consultation around the bureaucracy. If senior administration officers, most importantly the president and the attorney general, understand and value the need for independent and fully informed legal advice, the errors of the Bush administration will be avoided. If these officers want unreflective, one-sided legal briefs instead, they will find a way to procure them. Then they will march down the rocky trail blazed by the Bush administration.

Some benefits might be realized from the kind of institutional experimentation that does not require a statute and can be altered or abandoned easily if it does not work. For example, perhaps OLC should institute a "devil's advocate" system in which an attorney is assigned to prepare arguments against the prevailing view within the executive branch to test and refine the advice that actually emerges.[14] If independent advice is actually valued by the president, it is easy enough to find and incorporate it.

CRIME AND PUNISHMENT

One way to deter repetition of misconduct is to punish it. Many of the Watergate sinners were (alas) lawyers, including the "unindicted coconspirator" at the top, Richard Nixon. The miscreants were subjected both to prosecutions for their crimes and sanctions by their state bars for their professional irresponsibility. Crimes there have been in the war on terrorism, but it is stretching a long way to ascribe criminal responsibility to the lawyers.

Because the lawyers surveilled no one, detained no one, and interrogated no one, they could be criminals in only two ways. They could be charged either as accessories to those who committed crimes such as torture or as part of a conspiracy to commit those crimes. Both kinds of offense often depend on circumstantial proof of a chain of cause and effect, from which a jury can infer the necessary intention to be an accessory or agreement to be a conspirator.

Criminal liability as an accessory requires that the defendant "has aided or encouraged another to commit a criminal act, with the intent that the person commit the act."[15] Thus, "an attorney who gives advice intended to assist or provide a 'road map' for the client in violating or circumventing the law may be held complicit in the client's criminal conduct."[16]

The easiest way to prove either an accessory or a conspiracy charge would be if any of the legal advice directly endorsed the commission of crimes. Here Nuremberg provides a dark example. The United States successfully prosecuted German government lawyers for writing memos that stripped law of war protections from Russian prisoners, ordered the summary execution of commandos, and authorized the infamous "night and fog" disappearance of political prisoners.[17] (Some German military lawyers courageously resisted the political lawyers who made these decisions and met the fate dissenters to the Nazis could expect.)

Did any of the advice to President Bush meet this test? Under FISA, unauthorized surveillance is a federal crime. Aware of this, the white paper claimed both statutory authority (via the AUMF) and constitutional power for the TSP. Although I find these arguments quite unpersuasive, they have a sufficient basis to avoid criminal jeopardy. In particular, the scope of a constitutional executive power to gather intelligence remains quite unclear.

Even if it was unlawful to detain citizens and aliens without process and to subject them to military trials, as the Supreme Court eventually held it was, the supporting legal advice did not clearly endorse criminal conduct. When advice on detention was initially rendered, it was unclear how long anyone would be held or what the conditions of captivity would be. The order authorizing trials by military commission drew directly from the order the Supreme Court had upheld in *Quirin*. The president's lawyers, operating under time pressure, made an error regarding the UCMJ, but the *Hamdan* Court could have inferred the missing finding. Lawyers make mistakes of that magnitude every day.

The notorious "torture memo," *Interrogation,* does not quite endorse committing the crime of torture. Indeed, it deploys all the lawyer's arts to avoid doing so, albeit very unpersuasively. Ironically, the opinion's urgent effort to immunize CIA personnel for harsh interrogation practices opens the Justice Department lawyers to the very lawfare they were trying to forestall for their clients. When legal advice overreaches as much as this opinion did, it both exposes its authors to jeopardy and strips the clients of claims that they could reasonably rely upon it. Still, the memo is but an extreme example of lawyerly brinksmanship. John Yoo should not be prosecuted for writing it unless a clean distinction from Robert Jackson's *Destroyers* opinion exists. I see such a distinction, but this is a debatable matter of judgment.

True, there is a clear chain of cause and effect between the nature of OLC's legal advice and some of the abuses that ensued. Authorizing action, after all, was the purpose of the advice. But I see no clear evidence of intent to support the criminal activity itself. I believe the president's lawyers were reckless in that regard, and that is bad enough, but it is not criminal. Nor does the agreement between lawyers and interrogators that would be necessary for a conspiracy charge appear to be present. I recall the old French proverb: "It's worse than a crime; it's a blunder."

Perhaps, at the end of his term, President Bush will pardon all of his lawyers. The pardon power is plenary and cannot be challenged in court.[18] Presidents have a lamentable tendency to besmirch their records at the last minute by issuing shady pardons (consider President Clinton in this regard). Pardons or no pardons, criminal prosecution is not the way to discipline President Bush's lawyers.

Criminal jeopardy for the administration's lawyers is not, however, restricted to U.S. courts implementing our domestic law. Part of the lawfare that concerned the administration from the outset of the war on terrorism is conducted by criminal courts around the world exercising "universal jurisdiction" to prosecute war criminals. This fear has been realized. The Center for Constitutional Rights, which has represented many of the detainees, filed a criminal complaint in Germany seeking investigation and prosecution of ten high-level U.S. officials for the torture and inhumane treatment of detainees in Iraq.[19] The defendants included Secretary Rumsfeld, CIA Director George Tenet, and various senior military officers. The charges were brought under a German statute that invokes universal jurisdiction. That jurisdiction exists no matter where in the world the crimes are committed and whether or not there is a local connection to the criminal, the victim, or the crime. German law, like our own, makes torture and grave breaches of Geneva war crimes. The case was dismissed just before a Rumsfeld visit to Germany. It is not likely to be the last.

Civil liability is also possible. Jose Padilla, who was detained under accusation as a dirty bomber and was eventually convicted in federal court of supporting terrorism, has sued John Yoo for participating in the deprivation of his constitutional rights. The suit relies on Yoo's actions as an architect of the administration's legal strategy as a member of the War Council. It will encounter three formidable defenses. First is the problem of proving cause and effect between the opinions and the abuses. Second, the state secrets privilege, as it has so often in the past, may prevent discovery of facts sufficient to support the claim. Many of the facts are available, though. They appear in these pages through Yoo's own memoirs and the writings of many others.

Hence, Yoo may be forced to defend himself on the merits. If so, he will assert the third defense, executive immunity from damages liability. The Supreme Court has articulated the controlling doctrine on this topic.[20] Under it, the lawyers involved in the war on terrorism would be immune from damages if their actions did not violate "clearly established statutory or constitutional rights of which a reasonable person would have known."[21] This is an objective standard that asks about the state of the law, not the state of mind of the official. I think federal judges could find that the lawyers violated clearly established rights in at least two instances: by authorizing surveillance contrary to FISA and by approving detention of "enemy combatants" without calling for any process to determine their status.

John Yoo has complained bitterly about Padilla's suit against him.[22] He deploys the predictable argument that the suit is lawfare threatening the provision of candid legal advice to presidents. Yoo's argument deserves to be taken seriously. As I said earlier, the Bush administration's fear of retroactive lawfare for actions taken in the heat of crisis conditions has some foundation. Newtonian cycles of retribution against executive officers can easily damage the nation. The issue is fact-specific. Watergate deserved punishment; Whitewater did not. Perhaps there is enough play in the immunity defense as the Supreme Court articulates it to prevent overdeterrence of officers. The Supreme Court thinks so; analysts are not so sure.[23] At least the courts are alert to the problem. Nonetheless, I would prefer to avoid both criminal and civil liability for the president's lawyers in the war on terrorism.

LAWYERS PUNISHING LAWYERS

Two more sources of discipline remain: the Justice Department's ethics office and state bar organizations enforcing the rules of professional responsibility that govern all lawyers. We have encountered the Office of Professional Responsibility (OPR), which is empowered to investigate lapses of professional ethics by the Justice Department's lawyers, to recommend disciplinary action, and to conduct liaison with state bar associations regarding misconduct.[24] There is a pending OPR investigation regarding the OLC memos that have caused the greatest controversy, those concerning interrogation. Since the OLC lawyers have left the department, OPR is left to issue rebukes for the record and recommendations to state bar organizations. Neither sanction is meaningless. In the age of the Internet, no lawyer wishes to have the public record of a reprimand trailing along for the balance of his or her career.

After Watergate, state bar organizations produced a rash of disbarments and other penalties. More recently, President Clinton was sanctioned for lying to a federal district court in his tawdry litigation with Paula Jones.[25] President Bush's lawyers should fear bar sanctions, which closely fit the misconduct they have committed. An OPR opinion that misconduct has occurred should be granted deference by the bar authorities because the office has a feel for the nature of executive branch legal advice that state authorities lack.

Let us revisit the rules of professional responsibility all lawyers must follow when they counsel clients. The counseling function is governed by the American Bar Association's (ABA) *Model Rules of Professional Conduct* 2.1, which provides that in representing any client, a lawyer is expected to "exercise independent professional judgment and render candid advice."[26] A leading legal ethics treatise explains that

> a client may consult a lawyer to have her own preconceptions confirmed rather than to seek genuine advice. A lawyer may be tempted to play sycophant to such a client, to ensure continued employment. Rule 2.1 prohibits such an approach, however, first by requiring that a lawyer's advice be candid; and second, by requiring the lawyer to exercise judgment that is both independent and professional.[27]

This comment could have been directly addressed to the Bush administration's lawyers. Recall that this primary ethics rule provides assurance that "a lawyer may refer not only to law but to other considerations such as moral, economic, social, and political factors." The ABA explains that although "a lawyer is not a moral advisor as such, moral and ethical considerations impinge upon most legal questions and may decisively influence how the law will be applied." In other words, legal advice should not be limited to dry descriptions of rules for behavior. The consequences of the client's possible actions must also be considered.

The core duty imposed by these rules is to "exercise independent professional judgment and render candid advice." There are strong grounds to charge some of the Bush administration's lawyers with failure to discharge that duty. The available sanctions are flexible, ranging from rebuke to disbarment. Moreover, since the greatest sins of these lawyers have been against the rule of law, the profession's guardians have a special claim to pursue redress.

Within the White House, former counsel Alberto Gonzales is most clearly culpable of a breach of professional ethics. Whatever the outcome of his legal travails for his conduct as attorney general, he should be sanctioned for his failure to give independent and candid advice. His failures stemmed from a combination of zeal and negligence. Neither is an excuse. He called for "forward-leaning," extreme advice, received it, and endorsed it for the president without seeming ever to question it. Granted, the counsel always has a special and confidential relationship with the president, but it remains a lawyer-client relationship.

The other White House lawyer who should be subject to bar discipline is David Addington. His job as the vice president's voice combined policy and law, but he was characteristically emphatic in making claims about the law and should be held responsible for them. The fact that he believes in unrestrained executive power does not excuse his unwillingness to consider and accord due respect to the competing and well-grounded claims of the other branches.

Within the Justice Department, John Yoo was principally responsible for crafting the administration's extreme legal theories and should be accountable for them. His opinions *Application of Treaties, Interrogation,* and *Military Interrogation* have all caused great damage. All fail the test of independent and candid advice. Of course, Yoo's opinions are candid in one sense—he believes his extreme theories. It is one thing, however, to parade academic theories in print and another to engrave them on the government's legal opinions. The latter activity requires enough self-knowledge to understand and reveal the idiosyncrasy that may attend one's own views.

For John Yoo, there is one more source of legal jeopardy. Some critics of his OLC opinions have called for the University of California–Berkeley to revoke his tenure at its law school, Boalt Hall. The dean has risen dramatically to Yoo's defense, citing traditional principles of academic freedom.[28] In general, these principles should protect a professor's expression of opinion while in temporary government service or otherwise outside the groves of academe. But for me, what counsels most strongly against pursuing revocation of his tenure is simple consistency. Boalt tenured him after he wrote legal scholarship advancing the same arguments that he later tried to write into governmental precedents. If they liked his thinly based views enough to tenure him, they are in no position to recant now. True, "adventurous" and even silly ideas can advance a career in law teaching, even if they should not have that effect elsewhere. (I have seen it done.) The importation of those ideas into the governmental and public realms is the business of the governmental and bar authorities, not that of the university that reviewed and blessed them.

GOOD ADVICE

The executive branch is in need of a restoration project. Former attorney general Alberto Gonzales is under the cloud of investigations into the truthfulness of his congressional testimony and his compliance with federal law in the dismissal of U.S. attorneys. It is clear that he sought to politicize the Justice Department, a place where politics must be closely controlled. The department is resilient, though. After the Watergate scandal, with two attorneys general under criminal prosecution, the department itself rebounded after Edward Levi took its reins.

As for OLC, a senior Justice Department lawyer said of John Yoo, "It will take fifty years to undo the damage that he did to the place."[29] No, not fifty years, but not fifty days either. Ironically, the unhappy events of the Bush administration may buttress OLC's independence in the next administration. The next assistant attorney general for OLC, like the next attorney general, can expect a substantial grilling about independence during confirmation. After the necessary promises are made, the OLC head should be able to succeed in exuding a prickly attitude about that office's need to exercise independent judgment and about the need for the rest of the executive branch to value candor. In return, OLC must display a willingness to consult the rest of the executive branch before purporting to bind it with legal opinions.

Happily, both the Justice Department and OLC possess a proud tradition of providing excellent legal advice. As my selective history of executive advisers over the years revealed, this tradition has not always prevented lapses from the best kind of lawyer's conduct, but it is an important force for training and constraining executive advisers. The president's lawyers need to make a renewed commitment to their craft. The recent effort of former executive advisers to state professional responsibility principles provides a good first step in this process.[30]

In the preceding pages, I have argued that there are two essential requisites to ensure that a president's legal decisions have adequate support. One is a substantive understanding of separation of powers law that follows the *Steel Seizure* model. The other is a style of professional relationship that includes the sympathetic detachment of the lawyer in the mode of Robert Jackson. Neither of these requisites would be easy to legislate in any effective way. Nevertheless, they seek to ensure that the president's decisions are made with right and conscience, as Henry V put it.

Among all the questions that good lawyers should ask, the most important ones are those the lawyers should ask about themselves and their own conduct. Among all the president's advisers, the lawyers have a distinctive role that must be maintained to protect the rule of law and the effective functioning of the executive branch. For it is false that the nation's choice is between adherence to law and defeat at the hands of our enemies. Winning the war on terrorism "requires a scrupulous adherence to the rule of law, and where the law is inadequate, a vigorous and transparent effort at law reform."[31] If this is to be a "long war," as it is sometimes called, we must accommodate our institutions to it, not abandon our principles for temporary and evanescent gains. A strategy that demands compliance with law against a foe that knows no law is difficult but not optional. It demands the best advice our lawyers can give.

At the end of this long story, let us go back near where we began and recall Shakespeare's Chancellor Wolsey, shorn of his power but knowing himself now and possessed of a "still and quiet conscience." That is what matters. A president's legal advisers should never lose sight of the fact that those of their forbears who have distinguished reputations in history are those who maintained a professional detachment that well served their presidents. However difficult it may be to say no, a capacity to insist on the law's requisites is essential to the proper operation of our system of partly separated powers. Understanding this, a lawyer will realize that adhering to professional discipline is in his or her own self-interest as well as the best interests of the president and the nation. In short, professional responsibility is the best guarantee against bad advice.

NOTES

INTRODUCTION

1. *Youngstown Sheet & Tube Co. v. Sawyer*, 343 U.S. 579, 634–635 (1952).

2. Other controversies involving the Bush administration—for example, the justification for invading Iraq in 2003—were more dependent on policy than legal advice and are not considered here.

3. From 1979–1981, I was an attorney-adviser in the Office of Legal Counsel (OLC) of the U.S. Department of Justice. During that time, OLC was led by Assistant Attorneys General John Harmon (Carter administration) and Theodore Olson (Reagan administration). Their deputies were Larry Hammond, Larry Simms, and Leon Ulman. All of these people displayed the highest levels of professional skill, personal integrity, and sensitivity to the nature and limits of the role of executive adviser. They serve as role models for the analysis here.

1. THE DILEMMA OF THE EXECUTIVE ADVISER

1. William Shakespeare, *Henry V,* in *The Complete Works,* ed. Stanley Wells and Gary Taylor (New York: Oxford University Press, 1986), 1.2.13–20. References are to act, scene, and lines.

2. 1.2.29–32.

3. 1.2.96.

4. *A History of the English-Speaking Peoples,* vol. 1, *The Birth of Britain* (New York: Dodd, Mead, 1956), 410.

5. Some writers have done so already. Niall Ferguson, "The Monarchy of George W. Bush," *Vanity Fair* (September 2004): 382.

6. *Henry V,* VHS, directed by Laurence Olivier (Criterion Collection, 1944).

7. *Henry V,* VHS, directed by Kenneth Branagh (Los Angeles: MGM Home Entertainment/Renaissance Films, 1989).

8. A. R. Humphreys, *Introduction, Henry V,* rev. ed. (London: Penguin, 1996).

9. Ibid.

10. Theodor Meron, "Shakespeare's *Henry the Fifth* and the Law of War," *American Journal of International Law* 86 (1992): 1.

11. Henry may also have had reasons of state. See George M. Trevelyan, *History of England,* vol. 1, *From the Earliest Times to the Reformation* (Garden City, N.Y.: Doubleday, 1926), 304: "Henry V, on his accession, revived Edward III's pretensions to the French Crown in order to 'busy giddy minds with foreign quarrels.'"

12. I am not the first former executive adviser to note the relevance of the first act of *Henry V* to modern analysis. See John O. McGinnis, "Models of the Opinion Function of the Attorney General: A Normative, Descriptive, and Historical Prolegomenon," *Cardozo Law Review* 15 (1993): 375, 420–421.

13. *A Man for All Seasons*, DVD, directed by Frank Zinnemann (Culver City, Calif.: Columbia Pictures, 1966).

14. Robert Bolt, *A Man for All Seasons* (New York: Vintage, 1960), 11, 13.

15. Ibid., 37–38.

16. "'His Highness,' as Sir Thomas More put it to Wolsey, 'esteemeth nothing in counsel more perilous than one to persevere in the maintenance of his advice because he hath once given it.'" Winston S. Churchill, *A History of the English-Speaking Peoples,* vol. 2, *The New World* (New York: Dodd, Mead, 1956), 32.

17. Bolt, *Man for All Seasons,* 72.

18. Ibid., xii.

19. Ibid., xi.

20. Shakespeare, *Henry VIII,* 3.2.377–380.

21. 3.2.456–458.

2. THE PRESIDENT'S LAWYERS IN THE FORMATIVE YEARS

1. Harold H. Bruff, *Balance of Forces: Separation of Powers Law in the Administrative State* (Durham, N.C.: Carolina Academic Press, 2006), ch. 2.

2. For a good history of the office of attorney general, see Nancy V. Baker, *Conflicting Loyalties: Law and Politics in the Attorney General's Office, 1789–1990* (Lawrence: University Press of Kansas, 1992). A valuable earlier history by Attorney General Homer Cummings and Special Assistant Carl McFarland is *Federal Justice: Chapters in the History of Justice and the Federal Executive* (New York: Macmillan, 1937). See also Cornell W. Clayton, *The Politics of Justice: The Attorney General and the Making of Legal Policy* (Armonk, N.Y.: M. E. Sharpe, 1992).

3. An Act to Establish the Judicial Courts of the United States, ch. 20, §35, 1 Stat. 73, 92–93 (1789): "And there shall be appointed a meet person, learned in the law, to act as attorney general for the United States, who shall be sworn or affirmed to a faithful execution of the office; whose duty it shall be to prosecute and conduct all suits in the Supreme Court in which the United States shall be concerned, and to give his advice and opinion upon all questions of law when required by the President of the United States, or when requested by the heads of any of the departments, touching any matters that may concern their departments, and shall receive such compensation for his services as shall by law be provided."

4. 28 U.S.C. §511: "The Attorney General shall give his advice and opinion on questions of law when required by the President." Section 512 provides: "The head of an executive department may require the opinion of the Attorney General on questions of law arising in the administration of his department."

5. Attorney General William Wirt, "Duties of the Attorney General," *Opinions of the Attorney General* 1 (1820): 335, reprinted in H. Jefferson Powell, *The Constitution and the Attorneys General* (Durham, N.C.: Carolina Academic Press, 1999), 12–13. There is one known deviation from the practice of refusing opinion requests from members of Congress, by Attorney General Edward Bates of the Lincoln administration. Baker, *Conflicting Loyalties,* 16. Attorneys general do routinely testify before congressional committees, explaining their view of the law as they have presented it to their clients in the executive branch. Congress employs its own lawyers to advise it directly.

6. Susan Low Bloch, "The Early Role of the Attorney General in Our Constitutional Scheme: In the Beginning There Was Pragmatism," *Duke Law Journal* 1989 (1989): 561, 567.

7. The Appointments Clause of the Constitution, art. II, §2, provides that the president "shall nominate, and by and with the advice and consent of the Senate, shall appoint ambassadors, other public ministers and consuls, judges of the Supreme Court, and all other officers of the United States, whose appointments are not herein otherwise provided for, and which shall be established by law. But the Congress may by law vest the appointment of such inferior officers, as they think proper, in the president alone, in the courts of law, or in the heads of departments." See generally Bruff, *Balance of Forces*, ch. 16.

8. *Morrison v. Olson*, 487 U.S. 654, 674–677 (1988) (upholding court appointment of special prosecutors with limited jurisdiction as inferior, not principal, officers).

9. Bruff, *Balance of Forces*, 34–36.

10. Bloch, "Early Role," 576–578.

11. Bruff, *Balance of Forces*, 414–417.

12. For example, Secretary of State William Jennings Bryan could not follow President Woodrow Wilson's drift toward World War I and resigned. This issue of subordination can be quite subtle. Secretary of State Colin Powell slowed the rush of the second President Bush toward war with Iraq, and only departed after the first term was over.

13. Peter M. Shane and Harold H. Bruff, *Separation of Powers Law,* 2d ed. (Durham, N.C.: Carolina Academic Press, 2005), 16–17.

14. For a biography, see John J. Reardon, *Edmund Randolph* (New York: Macmillan, 1974); see also Richard Norton Smith, *Patriarch: George Washington and the New American Nation* (Boston: Houghton Mifflin, 1993), 240–242. Randolph was attorney general from the summer of 1790 until he replaced Jefferson as secretary of state in early 1794.

15. Jefferson once called Randolph "the poorest chameleon I ever saw, having no color of his own and reflecting that nearest him." Smith, *Patriarch,* 173.

16. Baker, *Conflicting Loyalties,* 20–21.

17. Cummings and McFarland, *Federal Justice,* 25–26.

18. See Bruff, *Balance of Forces,* 36–37, for a description of Washington's administrative style.

19. John C. Miller, *The Federalist Era, 1789–1801* (New York: Harper & Row, 1960), 58–59. Thus, Hamilton said that Washington "consulted much, resolved slowly, resolved surely." Ibid., 58.

20. According to Leonard D. White, *The Federalists: A Study in Administrative History* (New York: Macmillan, 1948), 33, Washington "consulted Hamilton and Jefferson on constitutional issues as regularly as he did the Attorney General."

21. Article I, §8 of the Constitution, after enumerating the legislative powers of Congress, provides that Congress may enact laws "necessary and proper" to implement them.

22. White, *Federalists,* 33.

23. Stanley Elkins and Eric McKitrick, *The Age of Federalism: The Early American Republic, 1788–1800* (New York: Oxford University Press, 1993), 232. The opinions are reprinted in Powell, *Attorneys General,* 3–9.

24. Ron Chernow, *Alexander Hamilton* (New York: Penguin, 2004), 352–353. Hamilton's view of broad congressional authority under the Necessary and Proper Clause has dominated our law ever since. Chief Justice Marshall adopted it in *McCulloch v. Maryland,* 17 U.S. (4 Wheat.) 316 (1819).

25. John Marshall later wrote that the debate over the bank led to formation of the two political parties that soon emerged. Jean Edward Smith, *John Marshall: Definer of a Nation* (New York: Henry Holt, 1996), 170.

26. I am indebted to Sanford Levinson for raising the issues considered in this paragraph.

27. Chernow, *Hamilton*, 435. See generally H. Jefferson Powell, *The President's Authority over Foreign Affairs: An Essay in Constitutional Interpretation* (Durham, N.C.: Carolina Academic Press, 2002), 47–54; and David P. Currie, "The Constitution in Congress: The Third Congress, 1793–1795," *University of Chicago Law Review* 63 (1996): 1.

28. Elkins and McKitrick, *Age of Federalism,* 339.

29. John O. McGinnis, "Models of the Opinion Function of the Attorney General: A Normative, Descriptive, and Historical Prolegomenon," *Cardozo Law Review* 15 (1993): 375, 406–419.

30. "Our men of war may repel an attack on individual vessels, but after the repulse, may not proceed to destroy the enemy's vessels generally." Quoted in Noble E. Cunningham, *The Process of Government Under Jefferson* (Princeton, N.J.: Princeton University Press, 1974), 48–49.

31. Powell, *President's Authority,* 91–93.

32. "Restoration under Treaty with France," *Opinions of the Attorney General* 1 (June 17, 1802): 114.

33. *United States v. Schooner Peggy,* 5 U.S. (1 Cranch) 103 (1801).

34. "Restoration under Treaty with France," *Opinions of the Attorney General* 1 (June 25, 1802): 119.

35. In a letter to Abigail Adams (September 11, 1804) he wrote: "You seem to think it devolved on the judges to decide on the validity of the sedition law. But nothing in the Constitution has given them a right to decide for the Executive, more than to the Executive to decide for them. Both magistracies are equally independent in the sphere of action assigned to them. The judges, believing the law constitutional, had a right to pass a sentence of fine or imprisonment; because that power was placed in their hands by the Constitution. But the Executive, believing the law to be unconstitutional, was bound to remit the execution of it; because that power has been confided to him by the Constitution. That instrument meant that its co-ordinate branches should be checks on each other. But the opinion which gives to the judges the right to decide what laws are constitutional, and what not, not only for themselves in their own sphere of action, but for the Legislature & executive also, in their spheres, would make the judiciary a despotic branch." Paul L. Ford, ed., *Writings of Thomas Jefferson,* vol. 8 (New York: Putnam, 1904), 310.

36. Jon Kukla, *A Wilderness So Immense: The Louisiana Purchase and the Destiny of America* (New York: Knopf, 2003), 301. Because the treaty was an act "beyond the Constitution," a constitutional amendment would be a means for "the nation to sanction an act done for its great good, without its previous authority."

37. Cummings and McFarland, *Federal Justice,* 56.

38. McGinnis, "Opinion Function," 416.

39. Paul L. Ford, ed., *Writings of Thomas Jefferson,* vol. 10 (New York: Putnam, 1905) 10–11.

40. Kukla, *Wilderness,* 306.

41. Ibid., 307; Robert V. Remini, *The House: The History of the House of Representatives* (Washington, D.C.: Library of Congress, 2006), 78–79. The Constitution's preamble states its purposes: "To form a more perfect union, establish justice, insure domestic tranquility, provide for the common defense, promote the general welfare, and secure the blessing of liberty to ourselves and our posterity." Perhaps these phrases could provide some authority for the treaty. Also, Article I, §8 begins by empowering Congress to "provide for the common defense and general welfare of the United States." Hence the Federalists argued that Congress had a better claim than the executive to any power to add territory. John Randolph responded for Jefferson by citing the president's function of communication with foreign nations. After "a long and stormy debate," the House approved.

42. It would be most unseemly for an author who is writing this book within the confines of the original Louisiana Purchase to come to any other conclusion.

43. Jefferson's justification is famous. Ford, *Writings,* vol. 8, 244: "The executive in seizing the fugitive occurrence, which so much advances the good of their country, has done an act beyond the Constitution. The Legislature in casting behind them metaphysical subtleties, and risking themselves like faithful servants, must ratify and pay for it, and throw themselves upon their country for doing for them unauthorized, what we know they would have done for themselves had they been in a situation to do it. It is the case of the guardian, investing the money of its ward in purchasing an important adjacent territory; and saying to him when of age, I did this for your good; I pretend to no right to bind you; you may disavow me and I must get out of the scrape as I can; I thought it my duty to risk myself for you. But we shall not be disavowed by the nation, and their act of indemnity will confirm and not weaken the Constitution by more strongly marking out its lines."

44. Baker, *Divided Loyalties,* 55–57, 126–130.

45. Leonard D. White, *The Jeffersonians: A Study in Administrative History, 1801–1829* (New York: Macmillan, 1951), 336–338.

46. Robert V. Remini, *Andrew Jackson and the Bank War: A Study in the Growth of Presidential Power* (New York: Norton, 1967); Arthur M. Schlesinger, Jr., *The Age of Jackson* (Boston: Little, Brown, 1945).

47. Cummings and McFarland, *Federal Justice,* 100–111; Baker, *Divided Loyalties,* 68–71.

48. Congress had chartered and rechartered the bank. Presidents Washington and Madison had signed the bills (recall the Hamilton-Jefferson debate recounted in this chapter). Chief Justice John Marshall upheld the constitutionality of the bank in *McCulloch v. Maryland,* 17 U.S. (4 Wheat.) 316 (1819). Notwithstanding all this, Jackson's veto message explained: "The Congress, the Executive, and the Court must each for itself be guided by its own opinion of the Constitution. Each public officer who takes an oath to support the Constitution swears that he will support it as he understands it, and not as it is understood by others. It is as much the duty of the House of Representatives, of the Senate, and of the President to decide upon the constitutionality of any bill or resolution which may be presented to them for passage or approval as it is for the supreme judges when it may be brought before them for judicial decision. The opinion of the judges has no more authority over Congress than the opinion of Congress has over the judges, and on that point the President is independent of both. The authority of the Supreme Court must not, therefore,

be permitted to control the Congress or the Executive when acting in their legislative capacities, but to have only such influence as the force of their reasoning may deserve." James D. Richardson, ed., *Messages and Papers of the Presidents,* vol. 2 (Washington, D.C.: Bureau of National Literature and Art, 1897), 576–589.

49. Cummings and McFarland, *Federal Justice,* 104.

50. For a discussion of the president's veto power, see Bruff, *Balance of Forces,* ch. 9.

51. The story is told in Daniel W. Howe, *What Hath God Wrought: The Transformation of America, 1815–1848* (New York: Oxford University Press, 2007), 387–389.

52. Robert V. Remini, *The Life of Andrew Jackson* (New York: Perennial Classics, 2001), 262–263.

53. Cummings and McFarland, *Federal Justice,* 108–109.

54. Remini, *Life of Jackson,* 263–264. No one knew whether the president could remove an officer the Senate had confirmed, especially the secretary of the treasury, who had a uniquely direct relationship with Congress because of the duty of handling appropriated funds. See text at note 10 above. Jackson was sure he had the power to remove any cabinet officer, and his actions established that precedent. Jackson sent Duane a curt letter saying his further services were "no longer required."

55. Jackson had earlier nominated Taney for a position as one of the associate justices, but the Senate had refused its consent. The persistent Jackson tried again and succeeded.

56. See generally Peter L. Strauss, "Overseer, or 'The Decider'? The President in Administrative Law," *George Washington Law Review* 75 (2007): 696.

57. Summaries and refutations of the story are in Cummings and McFarland, *Federal Justice,* 109–110; and Baker, *Divided Loyalties,* 23–24.

58. A recent reiteration of the supposed conversation is by Michael Herz, "Imposing Unified Executive Branch Statutory Interpretation," *Cardozo Law Review* 15 (1993): 219, 267 n. 253.

59. Doris Kearns Goodwin, *Team of Rivals: The Political Genius of Abraham Lincoln* (New York: Simon & Schuster, 2005).

60. For a biography, see Marvin Cain, *Lincoln's Attorney General: Edward Bates of Missouri* (Columbia: University of Missouri Press, 1965).

61. William H. Rehnquist, *All The Laws but One: Civil Liberties in Wartime* (New York: Vintage, 2000), 44.

62. Goodwin, *Team of Rivals,* 673–675, notes that Bates's relationship with Lincoln was always "marked by warmth and cordiality." His departure in 1864 to return home to his treasured family produced friendly exchanges with his colleagues in the cabinet. He was a good man, if not a gifted one.

63. In 1863, Lincoln's secretary John Hay recorded of him: "He is managing this war, the draft, foreign relations, and planning a reconstruction of the Union, all at once. I never knew with what tyrannous authority he rules the Cabinet, till now. The most important things he decides & there is no cavil." Ibid., 545.

64. For analysis of Lincoln's legal decisions, see Daniel Farber, *Lincoln's Constitution* (Chicago: University of Chicago Press, 2003); Mark E. Neely, Jr., *The Fate of Liberty: Abraham Lincoln and Civil Liberties* (New York: Oxford University Press, 1991); J. G. Randall, *Constitutional Problems under Lincoln,* rev. ed. (Urbana: University of Illinois Press, 1951); Rehnquist, *All the Laws;* Cummings and McFarland, *Federal Justice,* ch. 10.

65. For a good description and evocation of the crisis, see Nelson D. Lankford, *Cry Havoc! The Crooked Road to Civil War, 1861* (New York: Viking, 2007).

66. The Constitution's text (art. I, §9) does not settle the question. It expresses the suspension power in the passive, not identifying who does the suspending. The power is located in Article I, where the powers of Congress reside. However, the framers knew Congress could be prevented from assembling, since in their memory the Continental Congress had been chased out of Philadelphia by the British, and they knew Congress could not assemble quickly during its long recesses. Paul Finkelman, "Limiting Rights in Times of Crisis: Our Civil War Experience—A History Lesson for a Post-9/11 America," *Cardozo Public Law, Policy, and Ethics Journal* 2 (2003): 25, 31–41.

67. Farber, *Lincoln's Constitution*, 158; Rehnquist, *All the Laws*, 23.

68. *Ex Parte Merryman*, 17 F. Cas. 144 (C.C.D. Md. 1861) (No. 9487). For the full story, see James F. Simon, *Lincoln and Chief Justice Taney: Slavery, Secession, and the President's War Powers* (New York: Simon & Schuster, 2006); see also Richard H. Fallon, Jr., "Executive Power and the Political Constitution," *Utah Law Review* 2007 (2007): 1.

69. Taney said: "It will then remain for that high officer, in fulfillment of his constitutional obligation to 'take care that the laws be faithfully executed,' to determine what measures he will take to cause the civil process of the United States to be respected and enforced." 17 F. Cas. at 153.

70. "Message to Congress in Special Session," July 4, 1861, in Roy P. Basler, ed., *Works of Lincoln*, vol. 4 (New Brunswick, N.J.: Rutgers University Press, 1953), 421.

71. Ibid., 430.

72. Letter to John Colvin, September 20, 1810, in Paul L. Ford, ed., *Writings of Thomas Jefferson*, vol. 11 (New York: Putnam, 1905), 146.

73. Garry Wills, *Henry Adams and the Making of America* (Boston: Houghton Mifflin, 2005), 214.

74. *Youngstown Sheet & Tube Co. v. Sawyer*, 343 U.S. 579, 653 (1952).

75. "Note to Edward Bates," May 30, 1861, in Basler, *Works*, 390.

76. Rehnquist, *All the Laws*, 44. Rehnquist explained: "It essentially argued that each of the three branches of the federal government established by the Constitution was coequal with and independent of the other two." Since the president was not subordinate to the judiciary, it could not order him to free Merryman. (Here Bates found some revenge by invoking Taney's former views as Jackson's spokesman! See note 48 above.) Rehnquist correctly pointed out the inconsistency of this argument with the Supreme Court's foundational opinion in *Marbury v. Madison*.

77. Cummings and McFarland, *Federal Justice*, 190–191, quote an equivocal statement by Bates during this period, which suggested that he had no strong views of his own.

78. "Suspension of the Privilege of the Writ of Habeas Corpus," *Opinions of the Attorney General* 10 (July 5, 1861): 74, reprinted in Powell, *Attorneys General*, 169–178.

79. An Act to Increase the Pay of the Privates in the Regular Army and in the Volunteers in the Service of the United States, and for other Purposes, ch. 63, §3, 12 Stat. 326 (1861), declared Lincoln's actions "hereby approved and in all respects legalized and made valid, to the same intent and with the same effect as if they had been issued and done under the previous express authority of the Congress."

80. Habeas Corpus Act, 12 Stat. 755 (1863).

81. Goodwin, *Team of Rivals,* 464.

82. Goodwin, ibid., 465, speculates that the "terrible division that slavery and the war had wrought upon his family," which he valued "above all else," accounted for the change. His sons fought on both sides.

83. January 1, 1863, reprinted in Shane and Bruff, *Separation of Powers Law,* 1141–1142.

84. This process is vividly evoked in E. L. Doctorow's novel *The March* (New York: Random House, 2005).

85. Randall, *Constitutional Problems,* 371–404.

86. Related statutes allowed confiscation of slaves used in the war, forbade the return of escapees from the rebels and freed them, and freed slaves in the District of Columbia, in the territories, and in military service. Ibid., 364–365.

87. Harold Hyman, *A More Perfect Union* (Boston: Houghton Mifflin, 1975), 127, 139; David H. Donald, *Lincoln* (New York: Simon & Schuster, 1995), 363: "I suppose I have a right to take any measure which may best subdue the enemy." Randall, *Constitutional Problems,* observes: "It would not be easy to state what Lincoln conceived to be the limit of his powers" (513–514). "Neither Congress nor the Supreme Court exercised any very effective restraint upon the President" (517).

88. Jill Elaine Hasday, "Civil War as Paradigm: Reestablishing the Rule of Law at the End of the Cold War," *Kansas Journal of Law and Public Policy* 5 (1996): 129.

89. The strongest arguments in Bates's opinion invoked the adequacy theory and cited the Faithful Execution Clause, the president's oath of office, and the need to put down rebellion to preserve the Constitution.

90. Quoted in Powell, *Attorneys General,* 178.

91. For two laudable attempts to struggle with the issue, see Sanford Levinson, "Was the Emancipation Proclamation Constitutional? Do We/Should We Care What the Answer Is?" *University of Illinois Law Review* 2001 (2001): 1135; Michael Stokes Paulsen, "The Emancipation Proclamation and the Commander in Chief Power," *Georgia Law Review* 40 (2006): 807.

92. Phillip S. Paludan, *A Covenant with Death: The Constitution, Law, and Equality in the Civil War Era* (Urbana: University of Illinois Press, 1975), 3.

93. For reflections on these large issues, see Sanford Levinson, *Constitutional Faith* (Princeton, N.J.: Princeton University Press, 1988), 139–142.

94. "Letter to Albert G. Hodges" (April 4, 1864), in Basler, *Works,* vol. 7, 281.

95. The next year, in the *Prize Cases,* 67 U.S. (2 Black) 635 (1863), the Supreme Court upheld Lincoln's unilateral power to blockade the South, with the effect of making property on blockade runners subject to uncompensated seizure. Although the Court did not mention the Emancipation Proclamation, its opinion implied support for it.

96. William Safire, *Freedom* (New York: Avon, 1987), 1247–1248.

97. These are the concluding words of Gore Vidal's *Lincoln* (New York: Random House, 1984), 657.

3. THE PRESIDENT'S LAWYERS IN THE INSTITUTIONAL PRESIDENCY

1. Stephen Hess, *Organizing the Presidency* (Washington, D.C.: Brookings Institution, 1966), 1–3; Richard E. Neustadt, *Presidential Power and the Modern*

Presidents: The Politics of Leadership from Roosevelt to Reagan (New York: Free Press, 1990).

2. Not until 1857 did Congress provide a private secretary, a steward, and a messenger for the president's personal support (11 Stat. 206). Thus, Lincoln fought the Civil War with a personal staff that would not impress a modern small city mayor.

3. The Department of Justice was created by the Act of June 2, 1870, ch. 150, 16 Stat. 162.

4. Douglas W. Kmiec, "OLC's Opinion Writing Function: The Legal Adhesive for a Unitary Executive," *Cardozo Law Review* 15 (1993): 337.

5. Robert H. Jackson, *That Man: An Insider's Portrait of Franklin D. Roosevelt*, ed. John Q. Barrett (New York: Oxford University Press, 2003), 74: "The President had a tendency to think in terms of right and wrong, instead of terms of legal and illegal. Because he thought his motives were always good for the things that he wanted to do, he found difficulty in thinking that there could be legal limitations on them."

6. Jack Goldsmith, *The Terror Presidency: Law and Judgment inside the Bush Administration* (New York: Norton, 2007), 48–49.

7. For a biography of Jackson, see Eugene C. Gerhart, *America's Advocate: Robert H. Jackson* (Indianapolis, Ind.: Bobbs-Merrill, 1958).

8. David M. Kennedy, *Freedom from Fear: The American People in Depression and War, 1929–1945* (New York: Oxford University Press, 1999), 393; see also Robert Dallek, *Franklin D. Roosevelt and American Foreign Policy, 1932–1945* (New York: Oxford University Press, 1995).

9. Kennedy, *Freedom from Fear*, 445.

10. James MacGregor Burns, *Roosevelt: The Soldier of Freedom, 1940–1945* (New York: Harcourt, Brace, Jovanovich, 1970), 11.

11. The quotations in this paragraph are from Kennedy, *Freedom from Fear*, 453–454.

12. Jackson, *That Man*, 82.

13. Gerhart, *America's Advocate*, 221–222.

14. Aaron X. Fellmeth, "A Divorce Waiting to Happen: Franklin Roosevelt and the Law of Neutrality, 1935–1941," *Buffalo Journal of International Law* 3 (Winter 1996–1997): 413, 467–468.

15. Section 14(a), Act of June 28, 1940, ch. 440, 54 Stat. 681.

16. Fellmeth, "Divorce," 469.

17. Gerhart, *America's Advocate*, 215. Jackson, in *That Man*, said that at a cabinet meeting, "I expressed the view that the shipbuilders would violate a 1917 statute that prohibited fitting out and arming vessels in our country for a belligerent" (94).

18. Roy Jenkins, *Churchill: A Biography* (New York: Plume, 2001), 627.

19. Jackson, *That Man*, 89.

20. The quotations in this paragraph are from Doris Kearns Goodwin, *No Ordinary Time: Franklin and Eleanor Roosevelt—The Home Front in World War II* (New York: Touchstone, 1994), 142.

21. Gerhart, *America's Advocate*, 216.

22. Ibid., 217.

23. Goodwin, *No Ordinary Time*, 147–148.

24. Arthur M. Schlesinger, Jr., *The Imperial Presidency* (Boston: Houghton Mifflin, 1973), 108. Writing during the Nixon presidency, Schlesinger drew a contrast:

"Contrary to the latter-day view that a strong President is one who acts without consultation and without notice, Roosevelt proceeded with careful concern for the process of consent." Ibid., 106.

25. *United States v. Belmont*, 301 U.S. 324 (1937); see also *United States v. Pink*, 315 U.S. 203 (1942). In *Dames & Moore v. Regan*, 453 U.S. 654 (1981), the Court upheld another important executive agreement, one used to settle the Iranian hostage crisis.

26. The opinion is "Acquisition of Naval and Air Bases in Exchange for Over-Age Destroyers," *Opinions of the Attorney General* 39 (1940): 484, reprinted in H. Jefferson Powell, *The Constitution and the Attorneys General* (Durham, N.C.: Carolina Academic Press, 1999), 307–314.

27. Jackson, *That Man*, 91, 93.

28. Ibid., 97–98.

29. Ibid.: "The President said to me, with a chuckle, 'They will get into a terrific row over your opinion instead of over my deal, but after all, Bob, you are not running for office'" (99). Jackson confirms the accuracy of this prediction, noting that the initial political reaction "threatened the Attorney General with everything from immortality to impeachment" (102). He concluded: "The destroyer-bases deal . . . did not last long in the campaign. The people approved the transaction and by and large they did not question the methods much. . . . Roosevelt could have gone much farther in disregarding Congress . . . and could have gotten away with it as far as public sentiment was concerned" (41).

30. 299 U.S. 304 (1935).

31. Ibid., 320.

32. Act of June 15, 1917, ch. 30, 40 Stat. 217, 222. The Walsh Amendment declared that it did not "repeal or modify" this provision.

33. See note 17 above.

34. Edward S. Corwin, *The President: Office and Powers 1787–1984*, 5th rev. ed., ed. Randall W. Bland, Theodore T. Hindson and Jack W. Peltason (New York: New York University Press, 1984), 273 (emphasis in original).

35. "The supplying of these vessels to a belligerent is a violation of our neutral status, a violation of our national law, and a violation of international law." Herbert W. Briggs, "Neglected Aspects of the Destroyer Deal," *American Journal of International Law* 34 (1940): 569. The destroyer deal was a "transaction . . . sustained under statutes which hardly bear the construction placed upon them." Edwin Borchard, "The Attorney General's Opinion on the Exchange of Destroyers for Naval Bases," *American Journal of International Law* 34 (1940): 690. The *Destroyers* opinion relied on the Constitution and "two statutes of dubious relevance." Harold H. Koh, *The National Security Constitution: Sharing Power after the Iran-Contra Affair* (New Haven, Conn.: Yale University Press, 1990), 96.

36. And what about the destroyers themselves? By the end of the year, only nine of them had reached Britain, where they were deemed "even less seaworthy than expected." Kennedy, *Freedom from Fear*, 461.

37. Schlesinger, *Imperial Presidency*, 109.

38. Pub. L. No. 11, 55 Stat. 32 (1941).

39. Article I, §7 of the Constitution requires that bills and other congressional actions that have legal effects be sent to the president for his signature or veto.

40. Robert H. Jackson, "A Presidential Legal Opinion," *Harvard Law Review* 66 (1953): 1353, 1355.

41. Ibid., 1358.

42. *Immigration and Naturalization Service v. Chadha*, 462 U.S. 919 (1983).

43. See generally Peter Irons, *Justice at War* (New York: Oxford University Press, 1983); Greg Robinson, *By Order of the President: FDR and the Internment of Japanese Americans* (Cambridge, Mass.: Harvard University Press, 2001); Page Smith, *Democracy on Trial: The Japanese American Evacuation and Relocation in World War II* (New York: Simon & Schuster, 1995), ch. 8 (ironically titled "The Decision Nobody Made").

44. Smith, *Democracy on Trial*, 103.

45. Biddle was "an Eastern upper-class snob in the grand style." Ibid., 104. A descendant of Edmund Randolph (in more ways than one), he was a liberal civil-libertarian in politics. Biddle's autobiography is *In Brief Authority* (Garden City, N.Y.: Doubleday, 1962).

46. Biddle, *In Brief Authority*, 213.

47. For a summary and refutation of DeWitt's Final Report, see Justice Murphy's impassioned dissent in *Korematsu v. United States*, 323 U.S. 214 (1944).

48. Irons, *Justice at War*, ch. 3.

49. They were Benjamin Cohen, Oscar Cox, and Joseph Rauh. Robinson, *By Order of the President*, 103–104.

50. Ibid., 105–106; Smith, *Democracy on Trial*, 122.

51. Goodwin, *No Ordinary Time*, 322.

52. Biddle, *In Brief Authority*, 219.

53. Geoffrey R. Stone, *Perilous Times: Free Speech in Wartime—From the Sedition Act of 1798 to the War on Terrorism* (New York: Norton, 2004), 294.

54. Executive Order No. 9066, 7 Fed. Reg. 1407 (February 19, 1942).

55. Biddle, *In Brief Authority*, 219.

56. Robinson, *By Order of the President*, 121.

57. Pub. L. No. 503, 56 Stat. 173 (1942). See Irons, *Justice at War*, 66–68, for the legislative history.

58. A notable exception was Republican Governor Ralph Carr of Colorado, who courageously declared that evacuated Japanese Americans would be welcome in Colorado, knowing that his stance would likely end his political career, as it did. Adam Schrager, *The Principled Politician: The Ralph Carr Story* (Golden, Colo.: Fulcrum, 2008).

59. The principal case is *Korematsu v. United States*, 323 U.S. 214 (1944). See generally Irons, *Justice at War*; and *Report of the Commission on Wartime Relocation and Internment of Civilians, Personal Justice Denied* (Washington, D.C.: Government Printing Office, 1983).

60. The war on terrorism will supply important counterexamples, which I consider in later chapters.

61. Robinson, *By Order of the President*, chs. 1–2.

62. Burns, *Soldier of Freedom*, 215–216, observes that federal officials were "divided, irresolute, and not committed against racism" and that "only a strong civil-libertarian President could have faced down all these forces, and Roosevelt was not a strong civil libertarian."

63. My discussion is drawn from Louis Fisher, *Military Tribunals and Presidential Power: American Revolution to the War on Terrorism* (Lawrence: University Press of Kansas, 2005), ch. 5. See also Biddle, *In Brief Authority*, ch. 21; Louis

Fisher, *Nazi Saboteurs on Trial: A Military Tribunal and American Law* (Lawrence: University Press of Kansas, 2003); David Danelski, "The Saboteurs' Case," *Journal of Supreme Court History* 1 (1996): 61; Michael R. Belknap, "The Supreme Court Goes to War: The Meaning and Implications of the Nazi Saboteur Case," *Military Law Review* 89 (1980): 9.

64. Biddle, *In Brief Authority*, 328.

65. Fisher, *Military Tribunals*, 96.

66. Biddle, *In Brief Authority*, 330.

67. Fisher, *Military Tribunals*, 98.

68. 71 U.S. (4 Wall.) 2 (1867).

69. Biddle's inclinations were confirmed by a memo from Oscar Cox of the solicitor general's office, concluding that either a court-martial or a military tribunal could be employed. He thought *Milligan* was inapplicable because these were enemy aliens in disguise intending sabotage. Cox noted courts-martial had to follow procedures in the Articles of War and tribunals had more flexibility, although they generally followed court-martial procedure.

70. Proclamation 2561 (July 2, 1942).

71. Biddle, *In Brief Authority*, 331.

72. John Yoo, *War by Other Means: An Insider's Account of the War on Terror* (Chicago: University of Chicago Press, 2006), 224.

73. *Ex Parte Quirin*, 317 U.S. 1 (1942). See Chapter 10 of this book for a full discussion of the case.

74. Biddle, *In Brief Authority*, 341–342.

75. Edward S. Corwin, *Total War and the Constitution* (New York: Knopf, 1947), 118, called *Quirin* "little more than a ceremonious detour to a predetermined end."

76. A contemporaneous article, Cyrus Bernstein, "The Saboteur Trial: A Case History," *George Washington Law Review* 11 (1943): 131, pointed out that Biddle was authorized to make exceptions to the ban on judicial review, yet was prosecutor, and that making the JAG a prosecutor cut off normal military review.

77. *Youngstown Sheet & Tube Co. v. Sawyer*, 343 U.S. 579 (1952).

78. David McCullough, *Truman* (New York: Simon & Schuster, 1992), 895.

79. Robert J. Donovan, *Tumultuous Years: The Presidency of Harry S Truman, 1949–1953* (New York: Norton, 1982), 385.

80. Maeva Marcus, *Truman and the Steel Seizure Case* (New York: Columbia University Press, 1977), 225–226.

81. Ibid., 76–79.

82. Justice Felix Frankfurter blamed the White House Counsel's office for the bad decision to seize the mills. Letter to Charles Burlingame (January 5, 1953), quoted in Bruce Allen Murphy, *The Brandeis/Frankfurter Connection* (New York: Oxford University Press, 1983), 326.

83. Marcus, *Truman and the Steel Seizure Case*, 78. Future Supreme Court Justice Arthur Goldberg, representing the Steelworkers Union, chimed in with an analysis supporting seizure of the mills on either a statutory or constitutional basis.

84. Ibid., 35–36, quoting future political scientist Richard Neustadt.

85. McCulloch, *Truman*, 896–897.

86. David Halberstam, *The Coldest Winter: America and the Korean War* (New York: Hyperion, 2007), ch. 6.

87. Schlesinger, *Imperial Presidency*, 132.

88. See generally Christopher Andrew, *For the President's Eyes Only: Secret Intelligence and the American Presidency from Washington to Bush* (New York: HarperCollins, 1995), ch. 12.

89. Tim Weiner, *Legacy of Ashes: The History of the CIA* (New York: Doubleday, 2007), 376: " 'By God, we've got to get rid of the lawyers!' [Casey] once muttered to William Webster, Reagan's FBI director."

90. Theodore Draper, *A Very Thin Line: The Iran-Contra Affairs* (New York: Hill and Wang, 1991), 18–19.

91. Ibid., 20–22.

92. During fiscal year 1985, it provided: "No funds available to the Central Intelligence Agency, the Department of Defense, or any other agency or entity of the United States involved in intelligence activities may be obligated or expended for the purpose or which would have the effect of supporting, directly or indirectly, military or paramilitary operations in Nicaragua by any nation, group, organization, movement, or individual." Department of Defense Appropriations Act 1985, §8066, enacted in Further Continuing Appropriations Act, Pub. L. No. 98–473, 98 Stat. 1935 (1984).

93. Draper, *A Very Thin Line*, 24.

94. Ibid., 33.

95. At the time of Iran-Contra, President Reagan's Executive Order No. 12,333 defined the NSC as "the highest Executive Branch entity that provides review of, guidance for, and direction to the conduct of all national foreign intelligence, counterintelligence, and special activities, and attendant policies and programs." Covert actions, or "special activities," were made the responsibility of the CIA "unless the President determines that another agency is more likely to achieve a particular objective." This phrase appeared to mean the armed forces, but could have been stretched to include NSC staff.

96. Draper, *A Very Thin Line*, 78–79. William French Smith's memoir is *Law and Justice in the Reagan Administration: The Memoirs of an Attorney General* (Stanford, Calif.: Hoover Institution Press, 1991).

97. Draper, *A Very Thin Line*, 85–86. Sciaroni's apologia is "Boland in the Wind: The Iran-Contra Affair and the Invitation to Struggle," *Pepperdine Law Review* 17 (1990): 379.

98. Draper, *A Very Thin Line*, 164–169.

99. Draper observes, "So long as the United States was willing to trade arms for hostages, it could be sure that there would be hostages to be traded for arms" Ibid., 389.

100. 22 U.S.C. §2753(a), (d). In addition, the act imposed some restrictions on the countries eligible to receive U.S. arms and on the purposes for which arms could be sold.

101. 50 U.S.C. §413. This provision was from the Intelligence Oversight Act of 1980, Pub. L. No. 96–450, 94 Stat. 1975.

102. 22 U.S.C. §2422.

103. John Tower, Edmund Muskie, and Brent Scowcroft, *The Tower Commission Report: The Full Text of the President's Special Review Board* (New York: Bantam/ Times Books, 1987), 76.

104. Draper, *A Very Thin Line*, 208. If the CIA were not to conduct a covert operation, designation of another agency was to be in a written finding. OLC later

opined that these directives were only for the "internal use" of the executive and were not binding. Koh, *National Security Constitution*, 59.

105. Draper, *A Very Thin Line*, ch. 10.

106. Ibid., 214.

107. Ibid., 215.

108. Edwin Meese III, *With Reagan: The Inside Story* (Washington, D.C.: Regnery/Gateway, 1992), 255.

109. Koh, *National Security Constitution*, 60.

110. The *Tower Commission Report* concluded: "Even if the President in some sense consented to or approved the transactions, a serious question of law remains. It is not clear that the form of the approval was sufficient for purposes of either the Arms Export Control Act or the Hughes-Ryan Amendment. The consent did not meet the conditions of the Arms Export Control Act, especially in the absence of a prior written commitment from the Iranians regarding unauthorized retransfer. Under the National Security Act, it is not clear that mere oral approval by the President would qualify as a Presidential finding that the initiative was vital to the national security interests of the United States. The approval was never reduced to writing. It appears to have been conveyed to only one person. The President himself has no memory of it. . . . In addition, the requirement for Congressional notification was ignored. In these circumstances, even if the President approved of the transactions, it is difficult to conclude that his actions constituted adequate legal authority" (77).

111. Meese, *With Reagan*, 267–268.

112. *Tower Commission Report*, 78.

113. Meese, *With Reagan*, 269–271.

114. Draper, *A Very Thin Line*, 274.

115. Ibid., 275.

116. For cogent arguments that all the Contra evasions were illegal, see William C. Banks and Peter Raven-Hansen, *National Security Law and the Power of the Purse* (New York: Oxford University Press, 1994), ch. 13; Philip Bobbitt, *Constitutional Fate: Theory of the Constitution* (New York: Oxford University Press), ch. 3; and Kate Stith, "Congress' Power of the Purse," *Yale Law Journal* 97 (1988): 1356.

117. Draper, *A Very Thin Line*, 276; Andrew, *For the President's Eyes Only*, 482.

118. Abraham D. Sofaer, "Iran-Contra: Ethical Conduct and Public Policy," *Houston Law Review* 40 (2003): 1081, 1088–1089. Sofaer was legal adviser to the State Department during this period. This paragraph's description of events within the administration is drawn from his account.

119. On August 7, 1987, President Reagan promised specific reforms, including the reduction of all future "findings" pertaining to national security operations to writing, except in cases of "extreme emergency"; forbearance from issuing any retroactive "findings"; and a requirement that agencies designated by the president to perform covert operations comply with all procedures applicable to the president in notifying Congress concerning such operations. See "Letter to the Chairman and Vice Chairman of the Senate Select Committee on Intelligence Regarding Procedures for Presidential Approval and Notification of Congress," *Weekly Compilation of Presidential Documents* 23 (August 7, 1987): 910.

120. Joel Brinkley and Stephen Engelberg, eds., *Report of the Congressional Committees Investigating the Iran-Contra Affair with the Minority Views*, abridged ed.

(New York: Times Books, 1988). The separate reports are S. Rep. No. 216, 100th Cong., 1st Sess. (1987); H.R. Rep. No. 433, 100th Cong., 1st Sess. (1987). See also Peter Kornbluh and Malcolm Byrne, eds., *The Iran-Contra Scandal: The Declassified History* (New York: New Press, 1993); William S. Cohen and George J. Mitchell, *Men of Zeal: A Candid Inside Story of the Iran-Contra Hearings* (New York: Viking, 1988).

121. Lawrence E. Walsh, *Final Report of the Independent Counsel for Iran-Contra Matters* (Washington, D.C.: Government Printing Office, 1994); see also Lawrence E. Walsh, *Firewall: The Iran-Contra Conspiracy and Cover-up* (New York: Norton, 1998).

122. *Tower Commission Report*, 78.

123. Koh, *National Security Constitution*, 162.

124. Ibid., quoting Richard Willard, a former Justice Department officer.

125. Walsh, *Final Report*, vol. 1, 565–566.

126. Koh, *National Security Constitution*, 123.

127. See note 92 above for the full text of the provision.

128. Koh, *National Security Constitution*, ch. 2.

129. *Report of the Congressional Committees*, 30.

130. United States v. North, 910 F.2d 843 (D.C. Cir. 1990), modified, 920 F.2d 940 (D.C. Cir. 1990), cert. denied, 500 U.S. 941 (1991); United States v. Poindexter, 951 F.2d 369 (D.C. Cir. 1991), cert. denied, 113 S. Ct. 656 (1992).

131. Draper, *A Very Thin Line:* North admitted he prepared documents for Congress that were "erroneous, misleading, evasive, and wrong . . . and I make no excuses for what I did" (346). North's memoir is *Under Fire: An American Story* (New York: HarperCollins, 1991).

132. Draper, *A Very Thin Line*, 580–581, 591, describes their views of presidential hegemony in foreign policy.

133. This paragraph reflects the elegant analysis in Bobbitt, *Constitutional Fate*, ch. 3. He quotes Director Casey's gloating remark that there existed a "self-sustaining, stand-alone, off-the-shelf covert action capability" (67).

134. This quotation and the next one are from ibid., 72.

135. Nancy V. Baker, *Conflicting Loyalties: Law and Politics in the Attorney General's Office, 1789–1990* (Lawrence: University Press of Kansas, 1992), 163, quotes Attorney General Griffin Bell: "I bet President Reagan wishes Poindexter and North had asked for a Department of Justice opinion. . . . Just a simple thing like following procedures to get a legal opinion would have avoided that whole problem."

136. For analysis of the legal implications of Iran-Contra, see Koh, *National Security Constitution*, reviewed by Todd D. Peterson, *George Washington Law Review* 59 (1991): 747. See also Jules Lobel, "Emergency Power and the Decline of Liberalism," *Yale Law Journal* 98 (1989): 1385; Frank J. Smist, *Congress Oversees the United States Central Intelligence Agency, 1947–1989* (Knoxville: University of Tennessee Press, 1990); "Symposium: Legal and Policy Issues in the Iran-Contra Affair: Intelligence Oversight in a Democracy," *Houston Journal of International Law* 11 (1988): 1; "Symposium: Foreign Affairs and the Constitution: The Roles of Congress, the President, and the Courts," *University of Miami Law Review* 43(1988): 1; William C. Banks, "While Congress Slept: The Iran-Contra Affair and Institutional Responsibility for Covert Operations," *Syracuse Journal of International Law and Communication* 14 (1988): 291; David E. Colton, "Speaking Truth to Power:

Intelligence Oversight in an Imperfect World," *University of Pennsylvania Law Review* 137 (1988): 571; David Fagelson, "The Constitution and National Security: Covert Action in the Age of Intelligence Oversight," *Journal of Law and Policy* 5 (1989): 275; Louis Fisher, "How to Avoid Iran-Contras," *California Law Review* 76 (1988): 939, reviewing Edmund S. Muskie, Kenneth Rush, and Kenneth W. Thompson, eds., *The President, the Congress, and Foreign Policy* (Lanham, Md.: University Press of America, 1986); Marshall Silverberg, "The Separation of Powers and Control of the CIA's Covert Operations," *Texas Law Review* 68 (1990): 575; and J. Graham Noyes, "Cutting the President Off from Tin Cup Diplomacy," *University of California–Davis Law Review* 24 (1991): 841.

4. THE PROFESSIONAL RESPONSIBILITY OF THE PRESIDENT'S LAWYERS

1. See generally Neal Devins, "Government Lawyering," special ed., *Law and Contemporary Problems* 61, nos. 1–2 (Winter–Spring 1998); Dawn E. Johnsen, "Functional Departmentalism and Nonjudicial Interpretation: Who Determines Constitutional Meaning?" *Law and Contemporary Problems* 67 (Summer 2004): 105; "Symposium: Executive Branch Interpretation of the Law," *Cardozo Law Review* 15 (1993): 21; "Symposium: The Attorney General and the Pursuit of Justice," *John Marshall Law Review* 23 (1990): 151.

2. Robert H. Jackson, *That Man: An Insider's Portrait of Franklin D. Roosevelt,* ed. John Q. Barrett (New York: Oxford University Press, 2003), 116–117.

3. See Chapter 3 of this book, text of note 14.

4. For analyses of the president's supervisory power over administrative officers, see Harold H. Bruff, *Balance of Forces: Separation of Powers Law in the Administrative State* (Durham, N.C.: Carolina Academic Press, 2006), ch. 18; and Peter L. Strauss, "Overseer, or 'The Decider'? The President in Administrative Law," *George Washington Law Review* 75 (2007): 696.

5. See, for example, Abner J. Mikva and Patti B. Saris, *The American Congress: The First Branch* (New York: Watts, 1983).

6. For examples, see Peter M. Shane and Harold H. Bruff, *Separation of Powers Law,* 2d ed. (Durham, N.C.: Carolina Academic Press, 2005), 348–366.

7. Jackson, in *That Man,* observed that the cabinet "was not during my time and, so far as I can learn, never has been a deliberative or collegiate body. It adopts no resolutions and takes no formal actions. Sometimes a consensus of opinion would be reached on some general subject and sometimes disagreement was evident. But the very nature of the body as a gathering of specialists from separate departments makes real debate usually impossible" (28).

8. See generally Robert Axelrod, *The Evolution of Cooperation* (New York: Basic Books, 1984).

9. Robert F. Kennedy, *Thirteen Days: A Memoir of the Cuban Missile Crisis* (New York: Norton, 1969), 11.

10. Jackson, *That Man*: "No department head really has time to master the affairs of his own department, let alone become a critic of another. The one exception was the Department of Justice, because many Cabinet members were lawyers and all had solicitors or counsel who supplied them with legal opinions" (28).

11. Ibid. At a cabinet meeting, Secretary of Commerce Jesse Jones approached

Jackson and "said to me, 'Bob, here's a piece of paper. On it is a question. Here's another piece of paper and on it is the answer that my solicitor says he thinks the Department of Justice should give to this question. If you can give that answer, I want to ask you for a formal opinion. If you can't I just want you to let me know and tear up the other paper.'"

12. An executive order requires proposed executive orders to be submitted to the attorney general for "consideration as to both form and legality." 1 CFR §19.2(b).

13. See Harold H. Bruff, "Judicial Review and the President's Statutory Powers," *Virginia Law Review* 68 (1982): 1, 14–17.

14. See generally Jeremy Rabkin, "At the President's Side: The Role of the White House Counsel in Constitutional Policy," *Law and Contemporary Problems* 56 (1993): 63. Robert Jackson, in *That Man,* recounts that in April 1942, while he was a Supreme Court Justice, he was a weekend guest of President Roosevelt's: "The President asked me what I would think of his appointing a White House Counsel to be his always-on-hand adviser on matters of law. I told him I thought very little of it, because the Attorney General of the United States is by law his responsible legal adviser and to put another lawyer between the President and the Attorney General could not have good administrative results. If there was disagreement between them, the Attorney General would still be the responsible officer, although not the one closest to the President. If they agreed, the post was superfluous" (64–65). FDR had already decided, though, and soon installed Judge Samuel Rosenman in the new post. The president evaded objections from Attorney General Francis Biddle by announcing his decision while Biddle was traveling. Rosenman's memoir is *Working with Roosevelt* (New York: Da Capo, 1952).

15. Dean's aptly titled memoir is *Blind Ambition* (New York: Simon & Schuster, 1976).

16. Hearings before the Subcommittee on Separation of Powers of the Senate Committee on the Judiciary, *Removing Politics from the Administration of Justice,* 93d Cong., 2d Sess. (1974).

17. Rabkin, "At the President's Side," 78–80.

18. For a study comparing many attorneys general, see Nancy V. Baker, *Conflicting Loyalties: Law and Politics in the Attorney General's Office, 1789–1990* (Lawrence: University Press of Kansas, 1992).

19. See generally Douglas W. Kmiec, "OLC's Opinion Writing Function: The Legal Adhesive for a Unitary Executive," *Cardozo Law Review* 15 (1993): 337; John O. McGinnis, "Models of the Opinion Function of the Attorney General: A Normative, Descriptive, and Historical Prolegomenon," *Cardozo Law Review* 15 (1993): 375; Randolph D. Moss, "Executive Branch Legal Interpretation: A Perspective from the Office of Legal Counsel," *Administrative Law Review* 52 (2000): 1303; Cornelia T. L. Pillard, "The Unfulfilled Promise of the Constitution in Executive Hands," *Michigan Law Review* 103 (2005): 676. At times, one of the deputies is a career attorney.

20. Another delegation within the department has given partial independence to the solicitor general's office, which conducts the litigating function. See generally David A. Strauss, "The Solicitor General and the Interests of the United States," *Law and Contemporary Problems* 61 (1998): 165.

21. For a memoir by a former assistant attorney general for OLC, see Douglas W. Kmiec, *The Attorney General's Lawyer: Inside the Meese Justice Department* (New York: Praeger, 1992).

22. Many examples can be found in H. Jefferson Powell, *The Constitution and the Attorneys General* (Durham, N.C.: Carolina Academic Press, 1999).

23. Pillard, "Unfulfilled Promise," Part II.

24. Rabkin, "At the President's Side," 87–88. See also the story told by Robert Jackson in note 11 above.

25. OLC's website is www.usdoj.gov/olc. There are also several volumes of published OLC opinions.

26. Baker, in *Conflicting Loyalties*, quotes President Lyndon Johnson's attorney general Nicholas Katzenbach, who cautioned against relying on the counsel's office for legal advice "because they simply don't have the time and experience and the files on some of this that are absolutely essential to giving good advice to the president. There are files in the Office of Legal Counsel that go back through the years; you know what other presidents have been advised; you know where other presidents have gotten in trouble" (14).

27. Quoted in Terry Eastland, *Energy in the Executive* (New York: Free Press, 1992), 330 n. 24. See generally Nelson Lund, "Lawyers and the Defense of the Presidency," *Brigham Young University Law Review* 1995 (1995): 17.

28. Thomas W. Merrill, "High-Level, 'Tenured' Lawyers," *Law and Contemporary Problems* 61 (1998): 83.

29. Roger C. Cramton, "On the Steadfastness and Courage of Government Lawyers," *John Marshall Law Review* 23 (1990): 165. We need not pine for Cramton. He went on to a widely esteemed career as a law professor at Cornell.

30. Bruff, *Balance of Forces*, 261–266.

31. Baker, *Conflicting Loyalties*, 156–157.

32. Griffin B. Bell with Ronald J. Ostrow, *Taking Care of the Law* (New York: William Morrow, 1982), 185 (emphasis added).

33. Moss, "Perspective," 1306. For a somewhat similar view, see James E. Baker, *In the Common Defense: National Security Law for Perilous Times* (New York: Cambridge University Press, 2007), 325, calling on legal advisers to "dare to argue both sides of every issue . . . [and] ultimately call the legal questions as they believe the Constitution dictates."

34. Eugene C. Gerhart, *America's Advocate: Robert H. Jackson* (Indianapolis, Ind.: Bobbs-Merrill, 1958), 221–222 (emphasis added). Jackson also said that the Attorney General has a dual position, lawyer for the president and "laying down the law for the government as a judge might. I don't think he is quite as free to advocate an untenable position because it happens to be his client's position as he would be if he were in private practice. He has a responsibility to others than the President. He is the legal officer of the United States." Maeva Marcus, *Truman and the* Steel Seizure *Case* (New York: Columbia University Press, 1977), 187.

35. Jackson, *That Man*, 60.

36. The quotations in this and the following paragraph are from Jack Goldsmith, *The Terror Presidency: Law and Judgment inside the Bush Administration* (New York: Norton, 2007), 33–39.

37. See also McGinnis, "Opinion Function," observing that the "central dilemma" for OLC is to provide clients advice "they find generally congenial while at the same time upholding the reputation of the office as an elite institution whose legal advice is independent of the policy and political pressures associated with a particular question" (422).

38. Senate Committee on the Judiciary, *Hearings on the Nomination of Edwin Meese III*, 98th Cong., 2d Sess. 122 (1984).

39. Senate Committee on the Judiciary, *Confirmation Hearings on Federal Appointments* (Part 1), 107th Cong., 1st Sess. 733–734 (2001).

40. Senate Committee on the Judiciary, *Confirmation Hearings for the Department of Justice*, 103d Cong., 1st Sess. 398 (1993).

41. Scott R. Peppet, "Lawyers' Bargaining Ethics, Contract, and Collaboration: The End of the Legal Profession and the Beginning of Professional Pluralism," *Iowa Law Review* 90 (2005): 475: "The standard conception of the lawyer's role has two basic principles or ideals: the principle of nonaccountability and the principle of partisan professionalism. The principle of nonaccountability states that a lawyer is not morally accountable for the means used to advocate for a client, nor for the ends pursued. The principle of partisan professionalism states that while serving as an advocate, a lawyer must, within recognized constraints of legality or professional ethics, seek to maximize the likelihood that a client will prevail. Together, these principles form the basis of how most lawyers view their work and their ethics: a lawyer is a partisan and zealous advocate, dedicated to the client's cause, and absolved of responsibility for that cause and its pursuit, so long as the lawyer acts within the bounds of the law. He or she is an amoral gladiator" (500).

42. See ibid.: "This ruthless conception of lawyering has been defended on various grounds. Such defenses generally share two characteristics: a basic trust in the virtues of the adversary system, and a desire to maximize client autonomy and access to law by restricting a lawyer's ability to impose her own moral judgments on a client's desires and ends" (501).

43. Bruce E. Fein, "Promoting the President's Policies through Legal Advocacy: An Ethical Imperative of the Government Attorney," *Federal Bar News and Journal* 30 (September–October 1983): 406, 408.

44. American Bar Association (ABA), *Model Rules of Professional Conduct* 3.1 (2003).

45. ABA, *Model Rules of Professional Conduct* 2.1.

46. Baker, *Conflicting Loyalties*, 32.

47. See generally Nelson Lund, "The President as Client and the Ethics of the President's Lawyers," *Law and Contemporary Problems* 61 (Spring 1998): 65.

48. Peter M. Shane, "Legal Disagreement and Negotiation in a Government of Laws: The Case of Executive Privilege Claims against Congress," *Minnesota Law Review* 71 (1987): "A government of laws . . . is a government in which officials feel obligated to look to legal points of reference to describe and justify official behavior. This obligation is treated as important, even if not always performed well and even if, because law and political interest may coincide, it is sometimes superfluous. It is deemed important that government officials at least exercise the self-discipline of questioning the legal significance of their acts and, often, of providing explicit justification for those acts in legal terms. It is the habitual commitment to this interpretive regime that perhaps most pervasively differentiates a government of laws from a government of unadorned power" (491–492).

49. Jesselyn Radack, "Tortured Legal Ethics: The Role of the Government Advisor in the War on Terrorism," *University of Colorado Law Review* 77 (2006): 1, 12.

50. Federal Bar Association, *Model Rules of Professional Conduct for Federal Lawyers*, Rule 1.13 (1990) (comment).

51. Nelson Lund, "Rational Choice at the Office of Legal Counsel," *Cardozo Law Review* 15 (1993): 437.

52. Moss, "Perspective."

53. Knowing this, some observers have tried to ask questions more specific to the context in which an ethical issue arises. For example, Robert P. Lawry, "Who Is the Client of the Federal Government Lawyer? An Analysis of the Wrong Question?" *Federal Bar Journal* 47 (1978), argues that a government lawyer has three central ethical concerns: (1) identifying whose directions he or she should take, and on what subjects; (2) identifying whose confidences should be respected, and with whom they may be shared; and (3) determining what role his or her own judgment should play in deciding what to do (61).

54. Baker, *Conflicting Loyalties,* 29–30.

55. Ibid., 153–154.

56. Geoffrey P. Miller, "Government Lawyers' Ethics in a System of Checks and Balances," *University of Chicago Law Review* 54 (1987): 1293. For a critique, see Dennis Thompson, "The Possibility of Administrative Ethics," *Public Administration Review* (September–October 1985): 555.

57. Senate Committee on the Judiciary, *Hearings on the Nomination of William H. Rehnquist and Lewis F. Powell, Jr., to Be Associate Justices of the Supreme Court,* 92nd Cong., 1st Sess. 48 (1971).

58. The American Law Institute's *Restatement (Third) of the Law Governing Lawyers* §96(1)(a)(2000) provides that a lawyer representing an organization "represents the interests of the organization as defined by its responsible agents acting pursuant to the organization's decision-making procedures," and (b) "must follow instructions . . . given by persons authorized so to act on behalf of the organization." Section 97 extends these general principles to government lawyers and adds that the law may impose further duties. By omission, this means that government lawyers do not have a general duty to represent the public interest. They are to follow the directions of their clients, which are usually their employing agencies. See Federal Bar Association, *Model Rules for Federal Lawyers,* Rule 1.13 (a government lawyer represents his or her agency).

59. See generally Peppet, "Lawyers' Ethics," 504–507; and Deborah L. Rhode, *In the Interests of Justice: Reforming the Legal Profession* (New York: Oxford University Press, 2000). For a sensitive defense of the traditional view, see Charles Fried, "The Lawyer as Friend: The Moral Foundations of the Lawyer-Client Relation," *Yale Law Journal* 85 (1976): 1060.

60. David Luban, *Lawyers and Justice: An Ethical Study* (Princeton, N.J.: Princeton University Press, 1988), xxii.

61. 410 U.S. 113 (1973).

62. For the saga of the Reagan administration's response to *Roe,* as seen from within OLC, see Kmiec, *Attorney General's Lawyer,* ch. 4.

63. For a vivid evocation of this dilemma, see Michael Stokes Paulsen, "Hell, Handbaskets, and Government Lawyers: The Duty of Loyalty and Its Limits," *Law and Contemporary Problems* 83 (1998): 61.

64. *The Practice of Justice: A Theory of Lawyers' Ethics* (Cambridge, Mass.: Harvard University Press, 1998).

65. Ibid., 138–139.

66. Some evidence that this intermediate stance is widely shared is provided by an informal study conducted by Patrick J. Butamay, "Causes, Commitments, and Counsels: A Study of Political and Professional Obligations among Bush Administration Lawyers," *Journal of the Legal Profession* 31 (2007): 1.

67. Art. II, §1, cl. 8. The full oath is: "I do solemnly swear (or affirm) that I will faithfully execute the Office of President of the United States, and will to the best of my ability, preserve, protect and defend the Constitution of the United States."

68. 5 U.S.C. §3331. This statute implements the command of Art. VI, cl. 3 of the Constitution that "all executive . . . Officers . . . of the United States . . . shall be bound by Oath or Affirmation, to support this Constitution."

69. For reflections on the meaning of oath-taking, see Sanford Levinson, *Constitutional Faith* (Princeton, N.J.: Princeton University Press, 1988), ch. 4.

70. Theodore Roosevelt, *An Autobiography* (New York: Da Capo, 1988): "[I insisted] upon the theory that the executive power was limited only by specific restrictions and prohibitions appearing in the Constitution or imposed by the Congress under its Constitutional powers. My view was that every executive officer . . . was a steward of the people bound actively and affirmatively to do all he could for the people, and not to content himself with the negative merit of keeping his talents undamaged in a napkin. I declined to adopt the view that what was imperatively necessary for the Nation could not be done by the President unless he could find some specific authorization to do it. My belief was that it was not only his right but his duty to do anything that the needs of the Nation demanded unless such action was forbidden by the Constitution or by the laws. . . . I did not usurp power, but I did greatly broaden the use of executive power" (388).

71. See Chapter 2 of this book.

72. The authors, in the order listed, are: Walter E. Dellinger, Dawn Johnsen, Randolph Moss, Christopher Schroeder, Joseph R. Guerra, Beth Nolan, Todd Peterson, Cornelia T. L. Pillard, H. Jefferson Powell, Teresa Wynn Roseborough, Richard Shiffrin, William Michael Treanor, David Barron, Stuart Benjamin, Lisa Brown, Pamela Harris, Neil Kinkopf, Martin Lederman, and Michael Small. The guidelines are reprinted in *Indiana Law Journal* 81 (2006): 1345, 1348. See also Dawn E. Johnsen, "Faithfully Executing the Laws: Internal Legal Constraints on Executive Power," *UCLA Law Review* 54 (2007): 1559.

73. The second five are: "6. OLC should publicly disclose its written legal opinions in a timely manner, absent strong reasons for delay or nondisclosure. 7. OLC should maintain internal systems and practices to help ensure that OLC's legal advice is of the highest possible quality and represents the best possible view of the law. 8. Whenever time and circumstances permit, OLC should seek the views of all affected agencies and components of the Department of Justice before rendering final advice. 9. OLC should strive to maintain good working relationships with its client agencies, and especially the White House Counsel's Office, to help ensure that OLC is consulted, before the fact, regarding any and all substantial executive branch action of questionable legality. 10. OLC should be clear whenever it intends its advice to fall outside of OLC's typical role as the source of legal determinations that are binding within the executive branch."

74. These process suggestions are adapted from Harold H. Koh, "Protecting the Office of Legal Counsel from Itself," *Cardozo Law Review* 15 (1993): 513.

75. See generally Kennedy's memoir, *Thirteen Days.*

76. Abram Chayes, *The Cuban Missile Crisis* (Oxford, U.K.: Oxford University Press, 1974), 17.

77. Ibid., 24.

78. The memo is reproduced in ibid., 108–116.

79. Baker, *Conflicting Loyalties,* 90.

80. Anthony T. Kronman, *The Lost Lawyer: Failing Ideals of the Legal Profession* (Cambridge, Mass.: Harvard University Press, 1993).

81. Ibid., 2.

82. Ibid., 15–16.

83. Ibid., 66–74. To deliberate well for a client, Kronman says, one needs to "do more than just survey the alternatives under consideration from an external point of view. One must also make an effort to enter, with appreciative feeling, into the different points of view they represent, while at the same time retaining an attitude of detached neutrality toward them" (83).

84. Ibid., 123–134.

85. Ibid., 134.

86. Kronman notes that beyond what is written in law books, the most important part of a lawyer's expertise is the "knowledge of a certain sort of human behavior: the behavior of those who play a role in determining how the law shall be applied. . . . And that in turn requires a knowledge of the ideas, habits, values, precedents, and traditions that belong to the legal order itself" (124).

87. Ibid., 155–159.

5. COMPETING VISIONS OF EXECUTIVE POWER

1. The allocation of powers for *domestic* matters is the topic of Harold H. Bruff, *Balance of Forces: Separation of Powers Law in the Administrative State* (Durham, N.C.: Carolina Academic Press, 2006).

2. Edward S. Corwin, *The President: Office and Powers 1787–1984,* 5th rev. ed., ed. Randall W. Bland, Theodore T. Hindson, and Jack W. Peltason (New York: New York University Press, 1984), 201.

3. For two excellent introductions to the constitutional history, see H. Jefferson Powell, *The President's Authority over Foreign Affairs: An Essay in Constitutional Interpretation* (Durham, N.C.: Carolina Academic Press, 2002); and Abraham D. Sofaer, *War, Foreign Affairs and Constitutional Power: The Origins* (Cambridge, Mass.: Ballinger, 1976). Their overall conclusions are consistent with the positions I take in the text of this chapter. Powell says, "It is the president on whom the Constitution places the duty to formulate and implement the foreign policy of the United States. While the President is dependent on Congress for most of the tools of foreign policy . . . the president needs no authorization to use such tools as may exist. . . . However, the Constitution in no way excludes Congress from using the powerful legislative instruments it does possess . . . to exercise an effective veto on most (though not all) executive policies" (xiv–xv). Sofaer says that "the first forty years of experience under the Constitution present a complex pattern of practices. Anyone seeking precedents that establish areas of exclusive responsibility for either the legislative or executive branch is likely to be sorely disappointed. . . . The legislative and executive branches functioned as separate entities, but with powers over the same matters.

Each was jealous of its authority, [but] neither branch prevailed consistently enough to subordinate the other" (xiv–xv).

4. See generally Arthur Bestor, "Separation of Powers in the Domain of Foreign Affairs: The Original Intent of the Constitution Historically Examined," *Seton Hall Law Review* 5 (1974): 529.

5. Louis Henkin, *Foreign Affairs and the United States Constitution,* 2d ed. (New York: Oxford University Press, 1996), 68. For an overview, see William C. Banks and Peter Raven-Hansen, *National Security Law and the Power of the Purse* (New York: Oxford University Press, 1994).

6. Bruff, *Balance of Forces,* pt. 4.

7. Powell, *President's Authority.* A paradigm example is David Gray Adler and Larry N. George, eds., *The Constitution and the Conduct of American Foreign Policy* (Lawrence: University Press of Kansas, 1996).

8. Corwin, *Office and Powers,* 201 (emphasis in original).

9. *United States v. Curtiss-Wright Export Corporation,* 299 U.S. 304 (1936); see generally H. Jefferson Powell, "The Story of *Curtiss-Wright,*" in *Presidential Power Stories,* eds. Curtis Bradley and Christopher Schroeder (New York: Foundation Press, 2008).

10. Bruff, *Balance of Forces,* ch. 6. The cases were *Panama Refining Company v. Ryan,* 293 U.S. 388 (1935), and *Schechter Poultry Corporation v. United States,* 295 U.S. 495 (1935), the only two Supreme Court decisions ever to overturn federal statutes as overbroad delegations of legislative authority to the executive branch.

11. He said, "It is important to bear in mind that we are here dealing not alone with an authority vested in the President by an exertion of legislative power, but with such an authority plus the very delicate, plenary, and exclusive power of the President as the sole organ of the federal government in the field of international relations—a power which does not require as a basis for its exercise an act of Congress, but which, of course, like every other governmental power, must be exercised in subordination to the applicable provisions of the Constitution. It is quite apparent that if, in the maintenance of our international relations, embarrassment—perhaps serious embarrassment—is to be avoided and success for our aims achieved, congressional legislation which is to be made effective through negotiation and inquiry within the international field must often accord to the President a degree of discretion and freedom from statutory restriction which would not be admissible were domestic affairs alone involved. Moreover, he, not Congress, has the better opportunity of knowing the conditions which prevail in foreign countries, and especially is this true in time of war. He has his confidential sources of information. He has his agents in the form of diplomatic, consular, and other officials. Secrecy in respect of information gathered by them may be highly necessary, and the premature disclosure of it productive of harmful results" (299 U.S. at 319–320).

12. G. Edward White, *The Constitution and the New Deal* (Cambridge, Mass.: Harvard University Press, 2000), chs. 2–3. For domestic matters, Sutherland had a highly constrained theory of executive power that executive advisers have never favored. See Bruff, *Balance of Forces,* 422–426.

13. Charles A. Lofgren, "*United States v. Curtiss-Wright Export Corporation:* An Historical Reassessment," *Yale Law Journal* 83 (1973): 1; David M. Levitan, "The Foreign Relations Power: An Analysis of Mr. Sutherland's Theory," *Yale Law Journal* 55 (1946): 467.

14. The quotation is from *Steel Seizure,* 343 U.S. 579, 638. For a fine discussion of the limits of *Curtiss-Wright,* see Harold H. Koh, *The National Security Constitution: Sharing Power after the Iran-Contra Affair* (New Haven, Conn.: Yale University Press, 1990).

15. See generally Patricia L. Bellia, "The Story of the *Steel Seizure* Case," in *Presidential Power Stories,* ed. Curtis Bradley and Christopher Schroeder (New York: Foundation Press, 2008); "*Youngstown* at Fifty: A Symposium," *Constitutional Commentary* 19 (2002): 1; Christopher Bryant and Carl Tobias, "*Youngstown* Revisited," *Hastings Constitutional Law Quarterly* 29 (2002): 263.

16. The broad claims of power caused an adverse public and judicial reaction. William H. Rehnquist, *The Supreme Court: How It Was, How It Is* (New York: William Morrow, 1987), 47–53. Alan F. Westin, *The Anatomy of a Constitutional Law Case* (New York: Macmillan, 1958), 64, reports a famous colloquy that haunted the government throughout the litigation. It occurred between Assistant Attorney General Baldridge and Judge Pine in the district court: "Mr. Baldridge: 'Section 1, Article II, of the Constitution reposes all of the executive power in the Chief Executive. I think that the distinction that the Constitution itself makes between the powers of the Executive and the powers of the legislative branch of the Government are significant and important. In so far as the Executive is concerned, all executive power is vested in the President. In so far as legislative powers are concerned, the Congress has only those powers that are specifically delegated to it, plus the implied power to carry out the powers specifically enumerated.' The Court: 'So, when the sovereign people adopted the Constitution, it . . . limited the powers of the Congress and limited the powers of the judiciary, but it did not limit the powers of the Executive. Is that what you say?' Mr. Baldridge: 'That is the way we read Article II of the Constitution.' The Court: 'I see.'" Baldridge's argument produced an immediate storm of criticism. President Truman himself issued a disclaimer: "The powers of the President are derived from the Constitution, and they are limited, of course, by the provisions of the Constitution, particularly those that protect the rights of individuals" (67). The government issued another disclaimer in the form of a "Supplemental Memorandum" that it filed in district court, but the damage was done. The steel companies never tired of repeating Baldridge's assertion in their briefs.

17. All of the concurring opinions agreed that Congress had considered presidential seizures and had declined to authorize them. Justice Felix Frankfurter's opinion examined carefully whether Congress had acquiesced in previous presidential seizures that had occurred. He concluded that this was a case of congressional denial of executive power. Justice William O. Douglas characterized the presidential action as an unauthorized taking of property that was legislative in nature and therefore invalid. Justice Harold Burton stated that Congress had specified methods for dealing with this kind of crisis, with which the president had not complied. Justice Tom Clark agreed and went on to say that in the absence of such legislation, "the President's independent power to act depends upon the gravity of the situation confronting the nation."

18. 343 U.S. 579, 635–639.

19. Ibid., 683.

20. Ibid., 702.

21. Bruff, *Balance of Forces,* 154–162.

22. Justice Clark's suggestion that courts can review claims of necessity that the executive makes was especially intriguing. The president's assertion of special institutional competence to assess emergencies persuaded the dissenters, but with the majority it ran afoul of the ready availability of Taft-Hartley procedures.

23. The Court could have denied the injunction on grounds that damages would adequately compensate the companies' losses, or on grounds that Congress could forbid or ratify the seizure but had yet to act.

24. As an example of the kind of executive argument *Steel Seizure* discourages, consider an episode from World War II reported in Frank Freidel, *Franklin D. Roosevelt: A Rendezvous with Destiny* (Boston: Little, Brown, 1990), 437–438: FDR asked the advice of Wayne Morse (then a law school dean) concerning a statutory section governing farm parity pricing the president wished to contravene. To the president's question, "Do you think that stops me?" Morse replied, "No. Congress can pass all the laws it wants to, but if you decide that a certain course of action is essential as a war measure, it supersedes congressional action." FDR initially agreed, but was dissuaded by Justice Black, who heard of the idea and told the president the courts would stop him.

25. For an attempt to rehabilitate Vinson's dissent, which correctly points out that many later cases uphold executive action by following its approach, see Jack Goldsmith and John F. Manning, "The President's Completion Power," *Yale Law Journal* 115 (2006): 2280. For a response, see Harold Koh, "Setting the World Right," *Yale Law Journal* 115 (2006): 2350.

26. President Jefferson had expressed a similar idea in a letter to the governor of Virginia (August 11, 1807) concerning his response to the British attack on the frigate *Chesapeake*. He said: "It often happens that, the Legislature prescribing details of execution, some circumstance arises, unforeseen or unattended to by them, which would totally frustrate their intention, were their details scrupulously adhered to, & deemed exclusive of all others . . . the constitution gives the executive a general power to carry the laws into execution. . . . So if means specified by an act are impracticable, the constitutional power remains, & supplies them." Paul L. Ford, ed., *Writings of Thomas Jefferson*, vol. 10 (New York: Putnam, 1905), 441 n.

27. The quoted phrase is from *Federalist Paper 69*, in which Hamilton distinguishes the president from the English monarch, who could declare war unilaterally. The framers recognized, however, that actual conduct of a war was an executive function.

28. For a review and demolition of these arguments, see Curtis A. Bradley and Martin S. Flaherty, "Executive Power Essentialism and Foreign Affairs," *Michigan Law Review* 102 (2004): 545.

29. Jackson said: "Lest I be thought to exaggerate, I quote the interpretation which [the government's] brief puts upon it: 'In our view, this clause constitutes a grant of all the executive powers of which the Government is capable.' If that be true, it is difficult to see why the forefathers bothered to add several specific items, including some trifling ones" (343 U.S. 579, 640–641).

30. As Justice Frankfurter said: "The nature of that authority has for me been comprehensively indicated by Mr. Justice Holmes. 'The duty of the President to see that the laws be executed is a duty that does not go beyond the laws or require him to achieve more than Congress sees fit to leave within his power.' *Myers v. United States*, 272 U.S. 52, 177" (343 U.S. 579, 610).

31. Jackson's admission that he had "claimed everything" is reported in Rehnquist, *The Supreme Court*, 91.

32. In *Steel Seizure,* Jackson said: "The vagueness and generality of the clauses that set forth presidential powers afford a plausible basis for pressures within and without an administration for presidential action beyond that supported by those whose responsibility it is to defend his actions in court. The claim of inherent and unrestricted presidential powers has long been a persuasive dialectical weapon in political controversy. While it is not surprising that counsel should grasp support from such unadjudicated claims of power, a judge cannot accept self-serving press statements of the attorney for one of the interested parties as authority in answering a constitutional question, even if the advocate was himself. But prudence has counseled that actual reliance on such nebulous claims stops short of provoking a judicial test" (343 U.S. 579, 647).

33. A revision, *Foreign Affairs and the United States Constitution,* appeared in 1996. I cite the later version in this chapter.

34. Powell, *President's Authority,* 23–24, 77–89.

35. Sutherland said: "In this vast external realm, with its important, complicated, delicate, and manifold problems, the President alone has the power to speak or listen as a representative of the nation. He makes treaties with the advice and consent of the Senate; but he alone negotiates. Into the field of negotiation the Senate cannot intrude; and Congress itself is powerless to invade it. As Marshall said in his great argument of March 7, 1800, in the House of Representatives, 'The President is the sole organ of the nation in its external relations, and its sole representative with foreign nations'" (299 U.S. 304, 319).

36. Corwin, *Office and Powers,* 255 (regarding appropriations, 222).

37. Henkin, *Foreign Affairs:* "Both the President and Congress command vast powers in foreign affairs, but the distribution of constitutional authority between them, even as originally conceived, surely as now realized, is not what it is in domestic affairs. The classic separation of executive from legislative functions obtains in some measure in foreign affairs as well, but we have seen also a division of the power to 'legislate' foreign policy between the two political branches, and some concurrent authority. The President makes foreign policy by his conduct of foreign relations generally; by international acts as 'sole organ' or as commander in Chief (including some deployments of U.S. forces); by concluding international agreements; by asserting rights for the United States or responding to claims by others against the United States; by proclaiming 'doctrines' that announce national intentions; by occasional domestic regulation; in a few circumstances even by direction to the courts. Congress makes foreign policy by regulating foreign commerce and intercourse, and by other legislation that impinges on U.S. foreign relations; by spending for the common defense and by some of its spending for the general welfare; by declaring and making war; by adopting statutes or resolutions (such as the War Powers Resolution) defining Executive authority; by authorizing or approving executive agreements. In a sense, there is also a division of executive function: the President carries out the foreign policy that he makes as well as that made by Congress, but Congress 'executes' the President's policies, too, by enacting legislation to implement treaties and by appropriating funds to pay for Executive programs and activities" (83). And speaking of the "invitation to struggle," he said: "In principle as in fact, recurrent competition for power has punctuated relations between President and

Congress, raising the dominant, least tractable constitutional issues of U.S. foreign relations. That the Constitution is especially inarticulate in allocating foreign affairs powers; that a particular power can with equal logic and fair constitutional reading be claimed for the President or for Congress; that the powers of both President and Congress have been described in full, even extravagant adjectives ('vast,' 'plenary'); that instead of a 'natural' separation of 'executive' from 'legislative' functions there has grown an irregular, uncertain division of each—all have served and nurtured political forces inviting struggle. Recurrent disputes have resulted in particular from the separation of power to conduct foreign relations and make foreign policy generally, which the President has acquired, from the power to decide for war or peace, lodged in Congress. Conflict has been compounded also by the blurry bounds of 'Executive power' and the uncertain reach of the authority of the Commander in Chief, in war or in peace. Since, generally, these 'boundary disputes' between Congress and the President have not been resolved in court, they remain unresolved in principle; if the President has succeeded in winning most of them in fact, Congressional 'irredentism' runs deep and erupts in almost every Congressional generation, and Congress has powerful weapons—the power to enact laws and to regulate, its control of the Executive bureaucracy, the 'power of the purse,' political clout" (84).

38. Ibid., 314.

39. Schlesinger, *Imperial Presidency*, x. He explained the rise of the "imperial presidency" as follows: "The assumption of [the war-making] power by the Presidency was gradual and usually under the demand or pretext of emergency. It was as much a matter of congressional abdication as of presidential usurpation. As it took place, there dwindled away checks, both written and unwritten, that had long held the Presidency under control. The written checks were in the Constitution. The unwritten checks were in the forces and institutions a President once had to take into practical account before he made decisions of war and peace—the cabinet and the executive branch itself, the Congress, the judiciary, the press, public opinion at home, and the opinion of the world. By the early 1970s the American President had become on issues of war and peace the most absolute monarch (with the possible exception of Mao Tse-tung of China) among the great powers of the world" (ix).

40. Peter Quint, "The Separation of Powers under Nixon: Reflections on Constitutional Liberties and the Rule of Law," *Duke Law Journal* 1981 (1981): 1, 2.

41. The most prominent statutes were the War Powers Resolution of 1973 (WPR), Pub. L. No. 93–148; The National Emergencies Act (NEA), 50 U.S.C. §1621 et seq.; the International Emergency Economic Powers Act (IEEPA), 50 U.S.C. §1701 et seq.; the Foreign Intelligence Surveillance Act, 50 U.S.C. §1801 et seq.; and the Intelligence Authorization Act of 1980, Pub. L. No. 96–450, 94 Stat. 1975.

42. Ethics in Government Act of 1978, 28 U.S.C. §§49, 591 et seq.

43. L. Gordon Crovitz and Jeremy A. Rabkin, eds., *The Fettered Presidency: Legal Constraints on the Executive Branch* (Washington, D.C.: American Enterprise Institute, 1989).

44. 453 U.S. 654 (1981).

45. Rehnquist, *The Supreme Court*, chs. 1–3.

46. 343 U.S. 579, 641.

47. The Court quoted *Haig v. Agee*, 453 U.S. 280, 291 (1981).

48. Goldsmith and Manning, "Completion Power," 2289–2290; Koh, "Setting," 2372–2373.

49. See Bruff, *Balance of Forces,* 65–66.

50. 315 U.S. 203 (1942).

51. Justice Frankfurter's concurrence in *Steel Seizure* had engaged in an elaborate analysis of congressional acquiescence in wartime industrial seizures and had found it to have been withdrawn in the case at hand.

52. See, for example, *Regan v. Wald,* 468 U.S. 222 (1984), and *Haig v. Agee,* cited by the Court in *Dames & Moore.*

53. Koh, *National Security Constitution,* 140.

54. See also Kevin Stack, "The Statutory President," *Iowa Law Review* 90 (2005): The "most startling aspect of *Dames & Moore* is that the Court aggregated delegations of statutory authority to find a power that it could not trace to any individual authorization, or even to any interlocking set of authorizations" (567).

55. See also Lee R. Marks and John C. Grabow, "The President's Foreign Economic Powers after *Dames & Moore v. Regan:* Legislation by Acquiescence," *Cornell Law Review* 68 (1982): 68.

56. I develop this argument at greater length in "The Story of *Dames & Moore:* Resolution of an International Crisis by Executive Agreement," in *Presidential Power Stories,* ed. Curtis Bradley and Christopher Schroeder (New York: Foundation Press, 2008). See also Samuel Issacharoff and Richard H. Pildes, "Between Civil Libertarianism and Executive Unilateralism: An Institutional Process Approach to Rights during Wartime," in *The Constitution in Wartime: Beyond Alarmism and Complacency,* ed. Mark Tushnet (Durham, N.C.: Duke University Press, 2005), 161: "The courts have developed a process-based, institutionally oriented (as opposed to rights-oriented) framework for examining the legality of governmental action in extreme security contexts. Through this process-based approach, American courts have sought to shift the responsibility of these difficult decisions away from themselves and toward the joint action of the most democratic branches of the government" (162).

57. Charles Fried, *Order and Law: Arguing the Reagan Revolution—A Firsthand Account* (New York: Simon & Schuster, 1991): "The Reagan administration had a vision about the arrangement of government power: the authority and responsibility of the President should be clear and unitary. The Reagan years were distinguished by the fact that that vision was made the subject of legal, rather than simply political, dispute. The battle to rearrange government power was fought in the Supreme Court. As Solicitor General, I was in the front line of this struggle" (133).

58. For excellent overviews and critiques of the theory, see Peter L. Strauss, "Overseer, or 'The Decider'? The President in Administrative Law," *George Washington Law Review* 75 (2007): 696; Martin S. Flaherty, "The Most Dangerous Branch," *Yale Law Journal* 105 (1996): 1725.

59. Douglas W. Kmiec, *The Attorney General's Lawyer: Inside the Meese Justice Department* (New York: Praeger, 1992), ch. 3.

60. Some leading examples are Steven G. Calabresi, "Some Normative Arguments for the Unitary Executive," *Arkansas Law Review* 48 (1995): 23; Steven G. Calabresi and Saikrishna B. Prakash, "The President's Power to Execute the Laws," *Yale Law Journal* 104 (1994): 541; Steven G. Calabresi and Kevin H. Rhodes, "The Structural Constitution: Unitary Executive, Plural Judiciary," *Harvard Law Review* 105 (1992): 1153; and Saikrishna B. Prakash, "Hail to the Chief Administrator: The Framers and the President's Administrative Powers," *Yale Law Journal* 102 (1993): 991.

61. For an introduction to the debate, see Peter L. Strauss, "Formal and Functional Approaches to Separation-of-Powers Questions—A Foolish Inconsistency?" *Cornell Law Review* 72 (1987): 488.

62. Lawrence Lessig and Cass R. Sunstein, "The President and the Administration," *Columbia Law Review* 94 (1994): 1, 4.

63. Ibid., 85–106; Geoffrey P. Miller, "Independent Agencies," *Supreme Court Review* 1986 (1986): 41.

64. See, for example, *Bowsher v. Synar*, 478 U.S. 714 (1986) (White, J., dissenting): 760–761.

65. See generally Harold H. Bruff, "The Incompatibility Principle," *Administrative Law Review* 59 (2007): 225.

66. *Morrison v. Olson*, 487 U.S. 654 (1988). Justice Scalia's impassioned dissent in the case is a classic example of the unitary executive theory.

67. "The President's Compliance with the 'Timely Notification' Requirement of Section 501(B) of the National Security Act," *Opinions of the Office of Legal Counsel* 10 (December 17, 1986): 159, reprinted in H. Jefferson Powell, *The Constitution and the Attorneys General* (Durham, N.C.: Carolina Academic Press, 1999), 483–498.

68. In its footnote 1, the opinion also stressed the "urgent time pressures under which this memorandum has been prepared."

69. H. Jefferson Powell, "The Executive and the Avoidance Canon," *Indiana Law Journal* 81 (2006): 1313.

70. Koh, *National Security Constitution*, 173, concludes that "by any objective standard, the legislative record of keeping secrets has been commendable." As for the executive, it was an aide to President Kennedy who observed: "The Ship of State is the only ship that often leaks from the top." Robert Dallek, *An Unfinished Life: John Fitzgerald Kennedy, 1917–1963* (Boston: Little, Brown, 2003), 313.

71. The brief in the North case was jointly written by OLC and the Criminal Division of the Department. Kmiec, *Attorney General's Lawyer*, 184–185.

72. The brief is quoted in Koh, *National Security Constitution*, 28.

73. The executive branch typically cites references in *Curtiss-Wright* to the delicacy of foreign policy and a concern for secrecy in its implementation to buttress claims of inherent presidential authority to protect national security. For critical assessments of such claims, see Harold Edgar and Benno C. Schmidt, "*Curtiss-Wright* Comes Home: Executive Power and National Security Secrecy," *Harvard Civil Rights–Civil Liberties Law Review* 21 (1986): 349; Jordan J. Paust, "Is the President Bound by the Supreme Law of the Land?—Foreign Affairs and National Security Reexamined," *Hastings Constitutional Law Quarterly* 9 (1982): 719. See also Michael J. Glennon, "Two Views of Presidential Foreign Affairs Power: *Little v. Barreme* or *Curtiss-Wright*?" *Yale Journal of International Law* 13 (1988): 5.

74. See, for example, *Little v. Barreme*, 6 U.S. (2 Cranch; 1804) (Marshall, C.J.), 170.

75. Washington conceded that Congress could alter neutrality policy by legislation. Sofaer, *Origins*, 129; Schlesinger, *Imperial Presidency*, 18–20. Jackson's *Destroyers* opinion, discussed in the previous chapter, makes no claim that the president could ignore statutes; rather, it strains mightily to find compliance with them.

76. Koh, *National Security Constitution*, 4, concludes that the constitutional allocation of powers "rests upon a simple notion: that the power to conduct American

foreign power is not exclusively presidential, but rather, a power shared by the president, the Congress, and the courts." He argues that except for distortions such as Vietnam and Iran-Contra, the decision structure has involved the "balanced institutional participation of all three governmental branches" and that the president has "only limited exclusive powers."

77. My discussion of Cheney's activities in Congress draws on Stephen F. Hayes, *Cheney: The Untold Story of America's Most Powerful and Controversial Vice President* (New York: HarperCollins, 2007), ch. 6.

78. Joel Brinkley and Stephen Engelberg, eds., *Report of the Congressional Committees Investigating the Iran-Contra Affair with the Minority View,* abridged ed. (New York: Times Books, 1988). The full House report is H.R. Rep. No. 433, 100th Cong., 1st Sess. (1987).

79. Brinkley and Engelbery, *Minority View,* 375.

80. Ibid., 397.

81. John Hart Ely, *War and Responsibility* (Princeton, N.J.: Princeton University Press, 1993); Louis Fisher, *Constitutional Conflicts between Congress and the President,* 5th ed. (Lawrence: University Press of Kansas, 2007); Thomas Franck, *Political Questions/Judicial Answers* (Princeton, N.J.: Princeton University Press, 1992); Michael Glennon, *Constitutional Diplomacy* (Princeton, N.J.: Princeton University Press, 1990); David Gray Adler and Larry N. George, eds., *The Constitution and the Conduct of American Foreign Policy* (Lawrence: University Press of Kansas, 1996).

82. See, for example, Myres S. McDougal, *International Law, Power, and Policy: A Contemporary Conception* (Dordrecht, Netherlands: M. Nijhoff, 1954); Myres S. McDougal, Harold D. Lasswell, and W. Michael Reisman, "The World Constitutive Process of Authoritative Decision," *Journal of Legal Education* 19 (Part I [1967]): 253; and *Journal of Legal Education* 19 (Part II [1967]): 403.

83. Koh, *National Security Constitution.*

84. For an introduction, see Curtis A. Bradley, "Symposium Overview: A New American Foreign Affairs Law?" *University of Colorado Law Review* 70 (1999): 1089. Examples include Jack L. Goldsmith and Eric A. Posner, *The Limits of International Law* (New York: Oxford University Press, 2005); Curtis A. Bradley and Jack L. Goldsmith, "Congressional Authorization and the War on Terrorism," *Harvard Law Review* 118 (2005): 2047; Bradley and Goldsmith, "Rejoinder: The War on Terrorism—International Law, Clear Statement Requirements, and Constitutional Design," *Harvard Law Review* 118 (2005): 2683; Eric A. Posner and Adrian Vermeule, *Terror in the Balance: Security, Liberty, and the Courts* (New York: Oxford University Press, 2007); Saikrishna B. Prakash and Michael D. Ramsey, "The Executive Power over Foreign Affairs," *Yale Law Journal* 111 (2001): 231; and Michael D. Ramsey, *The Constitution's Text in Foreign Affairs* (Cambridge, Mass.: Harvard University Press, 2007).

85. See, for example, George F. Kennan, *American Diplomacy 1900–1950* (New York: New American Library, 1951); and Hans J. Morgenthau, *In Defense of the National Interest* (New York: Knopf, 1951).

86. Paul Schiff Berman, "Review Essay: Seeing beyond the Limits of International Law," *Texas Law Review* 84 (2006): 1265.

87. Examples include Flaherty, "Least Dangerous Branch"; Abner S. Greene, "Checks and Balances in an Era of Presidential Lawmaking," *University of Chicago Law Review* 61 (1994): 123; Harold J. Krent, *Presidential Powers* (New York: New

York University Press, 2005); Peter M. Shane, "When Interbranch Norms Break Down: Of Arms-for-Hostages, 'Orderly Shutdowns,' Presidential Impeachments, and Judicial Coups," *Cornell Journal of Law and Public Policy* 12 (2003): 503–542; Peter Spiro, "Treaties, Executive Agreements, and Constitutional Method," *Texas Law Review* 79 (2001): 961; and William Michael Treanor, "The War Powers outside the Courts," in Tushnet, *Constitution in Wartime*, 143.

88. His memoir is *War by Other Means: An Insider's Account of the War on Terror* (Chicago: University of Chicago Press, 2006). For a favorable review, see Robert F. Turner, "An Insider's Look at the War on Terrorism," *Cornell Law Review* 93 (2008): 471. For an unfavorable review, see Stephen F. Rohde, "War by Other Means," *Los Angeles Lawyer* (February 2007): 44. Yoo's theories are fully explained in his *Powers of War and Peace: The Constitution and Foreign Affairs after 9/11* (Chicago: University of Chicago Press, 2005). He says the book's purpose is "to explore the constitutional framework that gave rise to the policies" in the war on terrorism (vii). For a favorable review, see Richard B. Bilder, "Book Review," *American Journal of International Law* 100 (2006): 490. For unfavorable reviews, see Michael D. Ramsey, "Toward a Rule of Law in Foreign Affairs," *Columbia Law Review* 106 (2006): 1450; and David Cole, "What Bush Wants to Hear," *New York Review of Books* (November 17, 2005).

89. Paul M. Barrett, "A Young Lawyer Helps Chart Shift in Foreign Policy," *Wall Street Journal,* September 12, 2005, A1.

90. Ibid., reporting that Yoo was the "primary draftsman of key documents," including those regarding detention and torture of suspected terrorists. Yoo is reported to have told his wife that as a lawyer, he dealt with statutes and treaties, leaving policy to others.

91. Yoo, *Powers* (viii) cites sources for the conventional view: Henkin, *Foreign Affairs*; Koh, *National Security Constitution*, Ely; *War and Responsibility*; Franck, *Political Questions/Judicial Answers;* and Glennon, *Constitutional Diplomacy.*

92. Yoo notes that a new generation of scholars, including Curtis Bradley, Jack Goldsmith, and Michael Ramsey, the revisionists, use the same methods as in other areas of constitutional law, focusing on text, structure, and original intent. He says that they are engaged by others, including Peter Spiro, Martin Flaherty, and William Treanor, who refine the earlier paradigm.

93. Yoo, *Powers,* viii.

94. Ibid., 89.

95. Jide Nzelibe and John Yoo, "Rational War and Constitutional Design," *Yale Law Journal* 115 (2006): 2512.

96. Yoo, *Powers,* 8.

97. Ibid., 141–142.

98. Ibid., 10.

99. Ibid., 159.

100. Peter M. Shane, "Powers of the Crown," *Review of Politics* 68 (2006): 702, reviewing the book, says Yoo's argument is that "so long as Congress provides for the existence of a funded armed service, the president can do with it whatever he wants." Yoo defends this as both faithful to original intent and pragmatic; Professor Shane responds that it is neither. Shane says the key issue is only whether the president needs some form of congressional authority to use force, not a declaration of war, and that most scholars think so. He argues that an ordinary reader of the

constitutional text at the time of the framing could not have thought Congress was limited to defunding and the President in possession of unilateral initiative, given all of Congress's powers. He concludes that anyone who remembered the purpose of the Revolution would have rejected Yoo's claims. All of this is correct.

101. For a good introduction to the theories and the literature, see John H. Garvey, T. Alexander Aleinikoff, and Daniel A. Farber, eds., *Modern Constitutional Theory: A Reader,* 5th ed. (St. Paul, Minn.: West, 2004). For statutory interpretation, begin with William N. Eskridge, Jr., Philip P. Frickey, and Elizabeth Garrett, *Legislation and Statutory Interpretation,* 2d ed. (New York: Foundation Press, 2006); and Peter L. Strauss, *Legislation: Understanding and Using Statutes* (New York: Foundation Press, 2006). See Kevin M. Stack, "The Divergence of Constitutional and Statutory Interpretation," *University of Colorado Law Review* 75 (2004): 1, for an argument that the two fields of interpretation should not be approached similarly.

102. Martin S. Flaherty, "History 'Lite' in Modern American Constitutionalism," *Columbia Law Review* 95 (1995): 523.

103. Edwin Meese III, "The Law of the Constitution," Tulane Law Review 61 (1987): 979.

104. For example, Mark Tushnet, *Taking the Constitution away from the Courts* (Princeton, N.J.: Princeton University Press, 1999) and "Non-Judicial Review," *Harvard Journal on Legislation* 40 (2003): 453, 468–479 (discussing OLC); Larry D. Kramer, "The Supreme Court 2000 Term: Foreword—We the Court," *Harvard Law Review* 115 (2001): 4.

105. For example, Larry Alexander and Frederick Schauer, "On Extrajudicial Constitutional Interpretation," *Harvard Law Review* 110 (1997): 1359.

106. Cornelia T. L. Pillard, "The Unfulfilled Promise of the Constitution in Executive Hands," *Michigan Law Review* 103 (2005): 676, 680.

107. See generally Richard H. Fallon, Jr., "Executive Power and the Political Constitution," *Utah Law Review* 2007 (2007): 1.

108. "The Constitutional Separation of Powers between the President and Congress," reprinted in H. Jefferson Powell, *The Constitution and the Attorneys General* (Durham, N.C.: Carolina Academic Press, 1999), 617, 620.

109. Bradley and Goldsmith, "Congressional Authorization," 2102–2106.

110. Curtis A. Bradley, "*Chevron* Deference and Foreign Affairs," *Virginia Law Review* 86 (2000): 649; Eric A. Posner and Cass R. Sunstein, "*Chevron*izing Foreign Relations Law," *Yale Law Journal* 116 (2007): 1170; Stack, "Statutory President."

6. THE BUSH ADMINISTRATION DECLARES WAR ON TERRORISM

1. The closest analogue is the disputed election of 1876, settled by a special commission in favor of Rutherford Hayes, who lost the popular vote. See generally William H. Rehnquist, *Centennial Crisis: The Disputed Election of 1876* (New York: Knopf, 2004); and Roy Morris, *Fraud of the Century: Rutherford B. Hayes, Samuel Tilden, and the Stolen Election of 1876* (New York: Simon & Schuster, 2004).

2. A balanced assessment of the election controversy is Richard A. Posner, *Breaking the Deadlock: The 2000 Election, the Constitution, and the Courts* (Princeton, N.J.: Princeton University Press, 2001). For citations to the rest of the voluminous literature, see Peter M. Shane and Harold H. Bruff, *Separation of Powers Law,* 2d ed. (Durham, N.C.: Carolina Academic Press, 2005), 1068.

3. 531 U.S. 98 (2000).

4. Michiko Kakutani, "All the President's Books," *New York Times,* May 11, 2006, B1.

5. For praise of these characteristics, see Fred Barnes, *Rebel-in-Chief: Inside the Bold and Controversial Presidency of George W. Bush* (New York: Crown Forum, 2006); and David Frum, *The Right Man* (New York: Random House, 2003). For criticism, see Richard A. Clarke, *Against All Enemies: Inside America's War on Terror* (New York: Free Press, 2004); Robert Draper, *Dead Certain: The Presidency of George W. Bush* (New York: Free Press, 2007); Francis Fukuyama, *America at the Crossroads: Democracy, Power, and the Neoconservative Legacy* (New Haven, Conn.: Yale University Press, 2006); and Jacob Weisberg, *The Bush Tragedy* (New York: Random House, 2008).

6. Lou Cannon and Carl M. Cannon, *Reagan's Disciple: George W. Bush's Troubled Quest for a Presidential Legacy* (New York: PublicAffairs, 2008).

7. James Mann, *Rise of the Vulcans: The History of Bush's War Cabinet* (New York: Viking, 2004).

8. Draper, *Dead Certain,* ch. 5, which begins: "Despite all evidence by those who knew and worked for him that this would be an administration driven by a single willful chief executive, conventional wisdom persisted that George W. Bush would be a puppet—of [Karl] Rove, of Cheney, of his father" (109).

9. Clarke, *Against All Enemies,* 243.

10. George Packer, *The Assassins' Gate: America in Iraq* (New York: Farrar, Straus & Giroux, 2005), calls Bush "the most anti-intellectual President since at least Warren G. Harding" (55).

11. In 2001, Paul Wolfowitz gave the commencement address at West Point. Noting the approaching sixtieth anniversary of the attack on Pearl Harbor, he reminded the audience that the attack was preceded by "an astonishing number of unheeded warnings and missed signals." He called for "an anticipation of the unfamiliar and the unlikely." Mann, *Rise of the Vulcans,* 291. His insight reflected Roberta Wohlstetter's conclusions in her classic *Pearl Harbor: Warning and Decision* (Stanford, Calif.: Stanford University Press, 1962). The foreword to Wohlstetter's book, by Thomas C. Schelling, begins: "It would be reassuring to believe that Pearl Harbor was just a colossal and extraordinary blunder. What is disquieting is that it was a supremely ordinary blunder. . . . It was just a dramatic failure of a remarkably well-informed government to call the next enemy move in a cold-war crisis." Schelling concludes that Wohlstetter demonstrated that "the danger is in a poverty of expectations—a routine obsession with a few dangers that may be familiar rather than likely. . . . The planner should think in subtler and more variegated terms and allow for a wider range of contingencies." That this is easier said than done was proved in December 1941 and again in September 2001.

12. Ron Suskind, *The One Percent Doctrine: Deep inside America's Pursuit of Its Enemies Since 9/11* (New York: Simon & Schuster, 2006), 185.

13. Clarke, *Against All Enemies,* 237–238.

14. James Risen, *State of War: The Secret History of the CIA and the Bush Administration* (New York: Simon & Schuster, 2006); Seymour M. Hersh, *Chain of Command: The Road from 9/11 to Abu Ghraib* (New York: HarperCollins, 2004); Daniel Benjamin and Stephen Simon, *The Next Attack: The Failure of the War on Terror and a Strategy for Getting It Right* (New York: Henry Holt, 2005).

15. Jacob Heilbrunn, *They Knew They Were Right: The Rise of the Neocons* (New York: Doubleday, 2008). Packer, *Assassins' Gate*, notes that many of the neoconservatives were former leftists—their ideological cast of mind sought big ideas to change history, "a characteristic of individuals who migrate from one flock to the other without pausing to graze on tasteless facts under the dull sky of moderation" (56–57).

16. Irving L. Janis, *Victims of Groupthink: A Psychological Study of Foreign-Policy Decisions and Fiascos* (Boston: Houghton Mifflin, 1972).

17. For a sympathetic biography, see Stephen F. Hayes, *Cheney: The Untold Story of America's Most Powerful and Controversial Vice President* (New York: HarperCollins, 2007). See also Barton Gellman, *Angler: The Cheney Vice Presidency* (New York: Penguin, 2008).

18. Mann, *Vulcans*, ch. 18, 296, 370.

19. Ibid., 96.

20. Hayes, *Cheney*, 238–239.

21. Charlie Savage, *Takeover: The Return of the Imperial Presidency and the Subversion of American Democracy* (Boston: Little, Brown, 2007), 60–61. In any event, the Senate voted by a narrow majority, 52–47, to authorize the first Gulf War. Cheney thought that had the vote gone against the president, "from a constitutional standpoint, we had all the authority we needed" to go to war anyway.

22. At a speech in 1996, Cheney said, "I think there have been times in the past, oftentimes in response to events such as Watergate or the war in Vietnam, where Congress has begun to encroach upon the powers and responsibilities of the President; that it was important to go back and try to restore the balance." Ibid., 9.

23. Savage, *Takeover*, 75.

24. Chapter 5 of this book gives numerous examples. The Supreme Court had invalidated the legislative veto. The independent counsel statute had expired. The first Gulf War was successful. President Clinton had asserted independent executive war powers in Kosovo, as had the first President Bush in Panama.

25. Jack Goldsmith, *The Terror Presidency: Law and Judgment inside the Bush Administration* (New York: Norton, 2007), 212.

26. Savage, *Takeover*, 60.

27. Garry Wills, *Henry Adams and the Making of America* (Boston: Houghton Mifflin, 2005), 152.

28. Savage, *Takeover*, 37.

29. "In their first meeting after the inauguration, Cheney told Addington he had one job: restore the power of the presidency." Hayes, *Cheney*, 313.

30. Goldsmith, *Terror Presidency*, 77, quoting Solicitor General Theodore Olson.

31. For profiles, see Jane Mayer, *The Dark Side* (New York: Doubleday, 2008), ch. 4; and "The Hidden Power: The Legal Mind behind the White House's War on Terror," *New Yorker* (July 3, 2006): 44.

32. Goldsmith, *Terror Presidency*, 78–79, first characterizing Addington's views and then quoting him.

33. Ibid., 85.

34. Savage, *Takeover*, 83–84, quoting Colin Powell's chief of staff Lawrence Wilkerson and Associate White House Counsel Timothy Flanigan. "If a situation could be handled through either conciliation or confrontation, [Addington] always seemed to choose the latter." Hayes, *Cheney*, 478.

35. Mann, *Vulcans*, 22.

36. Elisabeth Bumiller, *Condoleezza Rice: A Biography* (New York: Random House, 2007).

37. For a biography, see Nancy V. Baker, *General Ashcroft: Attorney at War* (Lawrence: University Press of Kansas, 2006).

38. There was even a bit of prudery. He ordered draped the seminude art deco statues in the Great Hall of the Department of Justice. The decision was announced by his exquisitely named spokesperson, Ms. Comstock. Ibid., 8.

39. Draper, *Dead Certain*, 281.

40. Baker, *General Ashcroft*, 21.

41. See generally ibid., chs. 6–8.

42. USA PATRIOT ACT of 2001, Pub. L. No. 107–56, 115 Stat. 272. See generally Stephen J. Schulhofer, *The Enemy Within: Intelligence Gathering, Law Enforcement, and Civil Liberties in the Wake of September 11* (New York: Century Foundation Press, 2002).

43. David Cole, *Enemy Aliens: Double Standards and Constitutional Freedoms in the War on Terrorism* (New York: New Press, 2003), 24–25 (giving a figure of more than 5,000 detainees). See Office of the Inspector General, U.S. Department of Justice, *The September 11 Detainees: A Review of the Treatment of Aliens Held on Immigration Charges in Connection with the Investigation of the September 11 Attacks* (Washington, D.C.: Government Printing Office, 2003).

44. Baker, *General Ashcroft*, ch. 8.

45. For analyses of the Bush administration's secrecy policies, see Robert M. Pallitto and William G. Weaver, *Presidential Secrecy and the Law* (Baltimore: Johns Hopkins University Press, 2007); Mark J. Rozell, *Executive Privilege: Presidential Power, Secrecy, and Accountability*, 2d ed. (Lawrence: University Press of Kansas, 2002); Peter M. Shane, "Social Theory Meets Social Policy: Culture, Identity, and Public Information Policy after September 11," *Journal of Law and Policy for the Information Society* 2 (Winter 2005–2006): i.

46. See Chapter 5 of this book. His memoir is John Yoo, *War by Other Means: An Insider's Account of the War on Terror* (Chicago: University of Chicago Press, 2006). Yoo served in OLC from summer 2001 to 2003. He notes that "I was a Bush administration appointee who shared its general constitutional philosophy" (19). Three of the four other deputies had clerked for Justice Thomas or Justice Scalia. Other high positions in the department, he says, were held by "young conservative lawyers in their thirties or forties."

47. Ibid., 20. Yoo argues that the administration's actions were "the result of reasonable decisions, made by thoughtful people in good faith, under one of the most dire challenges our nation has ever faced" (viii). The policies regarding surveillance, detention, and interrogation were "part of a common, unifying approach." Ibid., ix. He says that OLC had to adapt the rules of war to "this new kind of enemy" (21). Prevention of future attacks depended on interrogating suspects and breaking into their communications.

48. For a biography, see Bill Minutaglio, *The President's Counselor: The Rise to Power of Alberto Gonzales* (New York: HarperCollins, 2006).

49. It is possible to read all of Minutaglio's biography of Gonzales, with which Gonzales characteristically did not cooperate, without gaining much of a sense of Gonzales as a person—his innermost dreams, hopes, fears, and opinions. There is just the outer man, serious, careful, endlessly working.

50. Minutaglio, *President's Counselor,* 193–195.

51. Savage, *Takeover,* 73–76.

52. Minutaglio, *President's Counselor,* 209, quoting a senior White House staffer.

53. Ibid., 196.

54. Brian Friel, "Defense Attorney," *National Journal* (March 4, 2006): 18, 20.

55. The description of the War Council comes from Jack Goldsmith's memoir, *Terror Presidency,* 22–25.

56. Savage, *Takeover,* 83. See also Hayes, *Cheney:* "Virtually every legal decision made by the administration after 9/11 that was related to the war on terror had at least crossed Addington's desk" (479).

57. Goldsmith, *Terror Presidency,* 76.

58. Yoo, *Insider's Account,* 100–101.

59. Goldsmith, *Terror Presidency,* 18.

60. Ibid., 24.

61. Ibid., 23; Savage, *Takeover,* 78.

62. Goldsmith, *Terror Presidency,* 169.

63. Tim Golden, "After Terror: A Secret Rewriting of Military Law," *New York Times,* October 24, 2004, A1.

64. Goldsmith, *Terror Presidency,* 169.

65. Scott Shane, David Johnston, and James Risen, "Secret U.S. Endorsement of Severe Interrogations," *New York Times,* October 4, 2007, A1, A22.

66. Savage, *Takeover,* 76.

67. Emergency powers are much discussed in the post-9/11 legal literature. See, for example, Bruce Ackerman, *Before the Next Attack: Preserving Civil Liberties in an Age of Terrorism* (New Haven, Conn.: Yale University Press, 2006); Philip Heymann, *Terrorism, Freedom, and Security: Winning without War* (Cambridge: Massachusetts Institute of Technology Press, 2003); Richard A. Posner, *Not a Suicide Pact: The Constitution in a Time of National Emergency* (New York: Oxford University Press, 2006); Eric A. Posner and Adrian Vermeule, *Terror in the Balance: Security, Liberty, and the Courts* (New York: Oxford University Press, 2007); Bruce Ackerman, "The Emergency Constitution," *Yale Law Journal* 113 (2004): 1029; David Cole, "The Priority of Morality: The Emergency Constitution's Blind Spot," *Yale Law Journal* 113 (2004): 1753; Laurence H. Tribe and Patrick O. Gudridge, "The Anti-Emergency Constitution," *Yale Law Journal* 113 (2004): 1801; Bruce Ackerman, "This Is Not a War," *Yale Law Journal* 113 (2004): 1871.

68. Hayes, *Cheney,* 356.

69. Goldsmith, *Terror Presidency,* 11–12. Chapter 3 of his memoir is titled "Fear and OLC."

70. Ibid., 74.

71. Ibid., 175, quoting Deputy Attorney General James Comey.

72. Ibid., 69.

73. I regard the Iraq war as an essentially unrelated initiative, although some of the legal advice generated at the outset of the 9/11 crisis caused problems there, as I relate in Chapter 12.

74. 18 U.S.C. ch. 113B—Terrorism, §2331 et seq. See generally Gerald Posner, *Why America Slept: The Failure to Prevent 9/11* (New York: Random House, 2003).

75. Antiterrorism and Effective Death Penalty Act of 1996, Pub. L. No. 104–132, 110 Stat. 1214 (codified at 8 U.S.C. §§1531–1537).

76. Paul M. Barrett, "A Young Lawyer Helps Chart Shift in Foreign Policy," *Wall Street Journal*, September 12, 2005, 1. In *Insider's Account*, Yoo says that on September 25, 2001, "I signed an OLC opinion issued to the White House which concluded that a foreign attack had occurred on September 11, the United States was at war, and President Bush had full constitutional authority to launch attacks to destroy the enemy" (10). The memo is discussed later in this chapter.

77. Bob Woodward, *Bush at War* (New York: Simon & Schuster, 2002), 17, 45.

78. Mark A. Graber, "Counter-Stories: Maintaining and Expanding Civil Liberties in Wartime," in *The Constitution in Wartime: Beyond Alarmism and Complacency*, ed. Mark Tushnet (Durham, N.C.: Duke University Press, 2005), 95.

79. Mark E. Brandon, "War and the American Constitutional Order," in ibid., 11.

80. Golden, "After Terror," A12.

81. Woodward, *Bush at War*, 96.

82. Noah Feldman, "Choices of Law, Choices of War," *Harvard Journal of Law and Public Policy* 25 (2002); Kim Lane Scheppele, "Law in a Time of Emergency: States of Exception and the Temptations of 9/11," *University of Pennsylvania Journal of Constitutional Law* 6 (2004): 1023.

83. Pub. L. No. 107–40, 115 Stat. 224 (September 18, 2001). See generally Curtis A. Bradley and Jack L. Goldsmith, "Congressional Authorization and the War on Terrorism," *Harvard Law Review* 118 (2005): 2047.

84. Final Report of the National Commission on Terrorist Attacks upon the United States, *The 9/11 Commission Report* (New York: Norton, 2004): Al Qaeda's "crimes were on a scale approaching acts of war, but they were committed by a loose, far-flung, nebulous conspiracy with no territories or citizens or assets that could be readily threatened, overwhelmed or destroyed" (348).

85. Minutaglio, *President's Counselor*, 228–229.

86. Mayer, "Hidden Power," 50–51.

87. Ibid., 51.

88. Baker, *General Ashcroft*, ch. 4.

89. Vice President Cheney explained that the administration "must look at security in a new way, because our country is a battlefield in the first war of the 21st century." Ibid., 65.

90. See generally Thomas E. Mann and Norman J. Ornstein, *The Broken Branch: How Congress Is Failing America and How to Get It Back on Track* (New York: Oxford University Press, 2006). For a precis of this book, see Norman J. Ornstein and Thomas E. Mann, "When Congress Checks Out," *Foreign Affairs* 85 (November–December 2006): 67.

91. Daryl J. Levinson and Richard H. Pildes, "Separation of Parties, Not Powers," *Harvard Law Review* 119 (2006): 2311.

92. See generally Julian E. Zelizer, *On Capitol Hill: The Struggle to Reform Congress and Its Consequences, 1948–2000* (New York: Cambridge University Press, 2004); E. Scott Adler, *Why Congressional Reforms Fail: Reelection and the House Committee System* (Chicago: University of Chicago Press, 2002); and C. Lawrence Evans and Walter J. Oleszek, *Congress under Fire: Reform Politics and the Republican Majority* (Boston: Houghton Mifflin, 1997).

93. Robert V. Remini, *The House: The History of the House of Representatives* (Washington, D.C.: Library of Congress, 2006), recounts that Speaker Jim Wright took office in 1987, and immediately damaged bipartisan traditions in foreign affairs. "He excluded Republicans from any involvement in House business," and broke an informal norm by delaying a vote on an important budget bill past the fifteen minutes that was usually allowed to gather straggling members, until a vote switched and the bill passed by that margin (472). (Speaker Newt Gingrich would later revise and extend this practice.) Dick Cheney complained that "the degree of partisanship, the strength of feeling, is more than it has been" (473). Republicans found Wright ruthless and eventually hounded him out of office in 1989. Cheney is quoted calling him a "heavy-handed son of a bitch . . . and he will do anything he can to win at any price, including ignoring the rules, bending rules. . . . There's no sense of comity left" (473–474).

94. Mann and Ornstein, *Broken Branch,* ch. 4.

95. Ronald Brownstein, *The Second Civil War: How Extreme Partisanship Has Paralyzed Washington and Polarized America* (New York: Penguin, 2007).

96. Remini, *House,* quotes Speaker Carl Albert to the effect that partisanship "ended at America's shores" (365). Remini recounts that in 1940, Sam Rayburn had taken the Speaker's gavel, "determined to win back the independence of the House and 'not yield to the executive any more of its constitutional prerogatives'" (325). (Court-packing was an example of his concerns.) In a meeting between congressional leaders and President Kennedy in 1961, JFK wished to talk about the role of the Rules Committee, which was then stifling important civil rights legislation. Rayburn angrily rebuked the President: "No, sir, that is House business, and the House of Representatives will decide that. The White House has no business there at all" (384). Kennedy, realizing his mistake, changed the subject.

97. Mann and Ornstein, *Broken Branch,* 151–158.

98. Ibid., 158–162.

99. Goldsmith, *Terror Presidency,* 58–59.

100. The term was brought to prominence in the Bush administration by Charles J. Dunlap, Jr., "Law and Military Interventions: Preserving Humanitarian Values in 21st Century Conflicts" (2001), available at http://www.ksg.harvard.edu/cchrp/Web%20Working%20Papers/Use%20of%20Force/Dunlap2001.pdf.

101. For background on the ICC and the U.S. government's relations with it, see Curtis A. Bradley and Jack L. Goldsmith, *Foreign Relations Law, Cases, and Materials,* 2d ed. (New York: Aspen, 2006), 405–406, 458–459.

102. Michael Ratner and Peter Weiss, "Litigating against Torture: The German Criminal Prosecution," in *The Torture Debate in America,* ed. Karen J. Greenberg (New York: Cambridge University Press, 2006), 261, 263.

103. 18 U.S.C. §2441. At the time, the WCA defined war crimes in general terms, including "grave breaches" of the Geneva Conventions, violations of Common Article 3, and violations of some other law of war treaties. Congress amended the WCA in the Military Commissions Act of 2006 to narrow and specify its prohibitions, as I discuss in Chapter 10.

104. Goldsmith, *Terror Presidency,* 91.

105. See Chapter 5 of this book.

106. The memo is reprinted in Karen J. Greenberg and Joshua L. Dratel, eds., *The Torture Papers: The Road to Abu Ghraib* (New York: Cambridge University Press,

2005), 3, and is available on the Office of Legal Counsel's homepage, at www.usdoj
.gov/olc/warpowers925.htm.

107. In this regard, the memo is quite self-referential: Yoo cites his own work six
times in thirty-two footnotes. Law professors are, however, prone to this sin. I confess to committing it many times in these notes.

108. Regarding the courts, the memo cited the usual Supreme Court decisions
that endorse broad presidential power in foreign relations (*Curtiss-Wright*) and war
(*Prize Cases*) without suggesting that they confine the president in any way.

7. SURVEILLANCE BY THE NATIONAL SECURITY AGENCY

1. See generally Christopher Andrew, *For the President's Eyes Only: Secret Intelligence and the American Presidency from Washington to Bush* (New York: HarperCollins, 1995).

2. 302 U.S. 379 (1937).

3. Robert H. Jackson, *That Man: An Insider's Portrait of Franklin D. Roosevelt*,
ed. John Q. Barrett (New York: Oxford University Press, 2003), 68.

4. President Roosevelt's memo is reproduced in Appendix A to the opinion in
United States v. U.S. District Court, 444 F.2d 651, 669 (6th Cir. 1971). The Supreme
Court affirmed the case in *Keith*, an important decision I discuss later in this chapter.
In defense of his position, the president argued: "It is too late to do anything about
it after sabotage, assassinations, and 'fifth column' activities are completed." At
the time, wiretaps were not usually regarded as searches for Fourth Amendment
purposes.

5. Jackson, *That Man*, 69. Until his death in the 1970s, Hoover was a figure in
all the domestic surveillance controversies. He entered the Justice Department during
the Red Scare after World War I, when for the first time federal intelligence personnel
tried to suppress domestic subversion in peacetime. See generally Robert K. Murray,
Red Scare: A Study in National Hysteria, 1919–1920 (Minneapolis: University of
Minnesota Press, 1955); and Curt Gentry, *J. Edgar Hoover: The Man and the Secrets*
(New York: Norton, 1991), ch. 6.

6. George W. Bush also took advantage of this precedent. Neal Katyal and Richard Caplan, "The Surprisingly Stronger Case for the Legality of the NSA Surveillance
Program: The FDR Precedent," *Stanford Law Review* 60 (2008): 1023.

7. The memo is reproduced in *U.S. District Court*, Appendix A. After quoting
FDR's earlier memo, it argued: "It seems to me that in the present troubled period in
international affairs, accompanied as it is by an increase in subversive activity here at
home, it is as necessary as it was in 1940 to take the investigative measures referred to
in President Roosevelt's memorandum. At the same time, the country is threatened by
a very substantial increase in crime. While I am reluctant to suggest any use whatever
of these special investigative measures in domestic cases, it seems to me imperative
to use them in cases vitally affecting the domestic security, or where human life is in
jeopardy. As so modified, I believe the outstanding directive should be continued in
force. . . . In my opinion, the measures proposed are within the authority of law, and
I have in the files of the Department materials indicating to me that my two most
recent predecessors as Attorney General would concur in this view."

8. *United States v. U.S. District Court* (*Keith*), 407 U.S. 297 (1972), 310 n.10.
Appendix A to the lower court's opinion contains a 1965 memo from President

Johnson continuing national security wiretaps and constraining them by requiring prior approval by the attorney general.

9. David Cole, *Enemy Aliens: Double Standards and Constitutional Freedoms in the War on Terrorism* (New York: New Press, 2003), 116 and ch. 11.

10. Andrew, *President's Eyes,* 197. For histories of the NSA, see James Bamford, *The Puzzle Palace* (Boston: Houghton Mifflin, 1982) and *Body of Secrets* (New York: Doubleday, 2001).

11. Andrew, *President's Eyes,* 322–323.

12. Ibid., 336–338.

13. Helms said that "the only manner in which the CIA could support its conclusion that there was no significant foreign influence on the domestic dissent, in the face of incredulity from the White House, was to continually expand the coverage of CHAOS." Ibid., 348. See also Thomas Powers, *The Man Who Kept the Secrets: Richard Helms and the CIA* (New York: Knopf, 1979).

14. Andrew, *President's Eyes,* 354–355. The National Security Act provides that the CIA "shall have no police, subpoena, law enforcement powers or internal security functions." 50 U.S.C. §403-3.

15. Commission on CIA Activities within the United States, *Report to the President* (Washington, D.C.: Government Printing Office, 1975).

16. See generally Loch K. Johnson, *A Season of Inquiry: The Senate Intelligence Investigation* (Lexington: University Press of Kentucky, 1985); Frank J. Smist, Jr., *Congress Oversees the United States Intelligence Community, 1947–1989* (Knoxville: University of Tennessee Press, 1990).

17. Andrew, *President's Eyes,* ch. 10.

18. Perhaps Church was irritated with the CIA because of his discovery that it had opened his mail!

19. See Senate Select Committee to Study Governmental Operations with Respect to Intelligence Activities, *Final Report,* 94th Cong., 2d Sess., 1976.

20. Johnson, *Season of Inquiry,* 72–77; Bamford, *Puzzle Palace,* 297–302.

21. Andrew, *President's Eyes,* 403.

22. Executive Order 11905. Later presidents issued their own executive orders refining Ford's reforms. Peter M. Shane and Harold H. Bruff, *Separation of Powers Law,* 2d ed. (Durham, N.C.: Carolina Academic Press, 2005), 758–760.

23. Quoted in Andrew, *President's Eyes,* 419. The Pike report reached a similar conclusion.

24. Shane and Bruff, *Separation of Powers Law,* 332–340. The privilege was established by *United States v. Reynolds,* 345 U.S. 1 (1952). See generally Louis Fisher, *In the Name of National Security: Unchecked Presidential Power and the Reynolds Case* (Lawrence: University Press of Kansas, 2006); Robert M. Chesney, "Enemy Combatants after *Hamdan v. Rumsfeld:* State Secrets and the Limits of National Security Litigation," *George Washington Law Review* 75 (2007): 1249; and Amanda Frost, "The State Secrets Privilege and Separation of Powers," *Fordham Law Review* 75 (2007): 1931.

25. *Katz v. United States,* 389 U.S. 347 (1967), had required a warrant for domestic electronic surveillance, but did not extend its holding to cases "involving the national security." Prior to *Katz,* wiretaps not involving physical trespass of property were not regarded as searches for Fourth Amendment purposes.

26. 407 U.S. 297 (1972). See generally Trevor W. Morrison, "The Story of *United States v. United States District Court (Keith):* The Surveillance Power," in *Presidential Power Stories,* ed. Curtis Bradley and Christopher Schroeder (New York: Foundation Press, 2008).

27. 18 U.S.C. §§2510–2520.

28. 18 U.S.C. §2511(3). The disclaimer concerning foreign threats went on, "to obtain foreign intelligence deemed essential to the security of the United States, or to protect national security information against foreign intelligence activities."

29. 50 U.S.C. §1801 et seq. See generally Americo Cinquegrana, "The Walls (and Wires) Have Ears: The Background and First Ten Years of the Foreign Intelligence Surveillance Act of 1978," *University of Pennsylvania Law Review* 137 (1989): 793.

30. Andrew, *President's Eyes,* 436.

31. It was later extended to physical searches, Pub. L. No. 103–359, Title VIII, §807(a)(3), 108 Stat. 3444 (1994).

32. Senate Committee on the Judiciary, *Foreign Intelligence Surveillance Act of 1977,* Report no. 604, 95th Cong., 1st Sess. (1977).

33. Nancy V. Baker, *General Ashcroft: Attorney at War* (Lawrence: University Press of Kansas, 2006), 159–160.

34. Pub. L. No. 107–56, 115 Stat. 272 (October 26, 2001).

35. Shane and Bruff, *Separation of Powers Law,* 738–740.

36. *In re Sealed Case,* 310 F.3d 717 (U.S.F.I.C.R. 2002).

37. Jim McGee and Brian Duffy, *Main Justice: The Men and Women Who Enforce the Nation's Criminal Laws and Guard Its Liberties* (New York: Simon & Schuster, 1996), 318.

38. In addition to the summary of illegal electronic surveillance recounted above, there were lurid revelations of other misdeeds including burglaries, mail opening, and infiltration of domestic dissident groups.

39. Eric Lichtblau, *Bush's Law: The Remaking of American Justice* (New York: Pantheon, 2008), ch. 5; James Risen, *State of War: The Secret History of the CIA and the Bush Administration* (New York: Free Press, 2006), ch. 2.

40. The first story was James Risen and Eric Lichtblau, "Bush Lets U.S. Spy on Callers without Courts," *New York Times,* December 16, 2005, 1, 22. The *Times* had held off publishing the story for a year in response to the administration's repeated entreaties to keep the program secret. Lichtblau, *Bush's Law,* ch. 6. Risen and Lichtblau won a Pulitzer Prize for their reporting.

41. The white paper and two other documents discussed in this chapter (letters from the Office of Legal Affairs and the group of scholars) are reprinted in David Cole and Martin S. Lederman, "Documents Relating to the National Security Agency Spying Program: Framing the Debate," *Indiana Law Journal* 81 (2006): 1355.

42. The NSA's Terrorist Surveillance Program was not the only intelligence effort mounted by the administration. In the related "data-mining" program, the NSA obtained from several telephone companies records of all calls made, whether domestic or international, showing the numbers on both sides of the messages, but not the contents of the messages. Matthew B. Stannard, "Data-Mining Methods Differ, but Goal Same," *Denver Post,* May 15, 2006, 6C. Also, soon after 9/11, FBI agents began working at First Data's processing center in Omaha, which dealt with almost

half of U.S. credit card charges and had links to many others. At first, the agents were trying to track the hijackers' movements and associates through their purchases. The data could also be used to identify new suspects. Especially after passage of the PATRIOT Act, the FBI used national security letters for this purpose. Ron Suskind, *The One Percent Doctrine: Deep inside America's Pursuit of Its Enemies since 9/11* (New York: Simon & Schuster, 2006), 34–36. "Over the years," CIA Director Tenet had made agreements with telecommunications and financial companies to have access to telephone, Internet, and financial records related to secret operations. Bob Woodward, *State of Denial* (New York: Simon & Schuster, 2006), 323–325. Tenet had made the deals directly with the CEOs of the companies, often very informally. After 9/11, the FBI intruded with subpoenas for some of the same material, and the companies resisted. The White House mediated the resulting FBI/CIA tensions, coordinating requests to reduce burdens on the companies. Because the CIA was forbidden by law to gather intelligence in the United States, Tenet asked only for access to passive databanks, not for information on individuals.

43. Scott Shane and Eric Lindblau, "Cheney Pushed U.S. to Widen Eavesdropping," *New York Times*, May 14, 2006, A16.

44. Jane Mayer, "The Hidden Power: The Legal Mind behind the White House's War on Terror," *New Yorker* (July 3, 2006): 54.

45. Shane and Lindblau, "Cheney Pushed," A16, quoting "an intelligence official."

46. Senate Select Intelligence Committee, *Hearing on the Nomination of General Michael Hayden to Be Director of the Central Intelligence Agency,* 109th Cong., 2d Sess., May 18, 2006.

47. Stephen F. Hayes, *Cheney: The Untold Story of America's Most Powerful and Controversial Vice President* (New York: HarperCollins, 2007), 490.

48. Risen, *State of War,* 57.

49. Jack Goldsmith, *The Terror Presidency: Law and Judgment Inside the Bush Administration* (New York: Norton, 2007). The statements and quotes in this paragraph are from 181–182.

50. Jane Mayer, *The Dark Side* (New York: Doubleday, 2008), 68.

51. John Yoo, *War by Other Means: An Insider's Account of the War on Terror* (Chicago: University of Chicago Press, 2006), 99–104.

52. Charlie Savage, *Takeover: The Return of the Imperial Presidency and the Subversion of American Democracy* (Boston: Little, Brown, 2007), 130–131.

53. Risen and Lichtblau, "Bush Lets U.S. Spy."

54. Robert H. Jackson, "Wartime Security and Liberty under Law," *Buffalo Law Review* 55 (2008): 1089, 1106 (reprinting an address given in May 1951).

55. Hayes, *Cheney,* 486.

56. Shane Harris, "More Than Meets the Ear," *National Journal* (March 18, 2006): 28, 32.

57. Press Briefing by Attorney General Alberto Gonzales and General Michael V. Hayden, Principal Deputy Director for National Intelligence (December 19, 2005), available at http://www.whitehouse.gov/news/releases/2005/12/20051219-1.html.

58. Hearing Before the Senate Committee on the Judiciary, *Department of Justice Oversight,* 110th Cong., 1st Sess., January 18, 2007, 12.

59. Suskind, *One Percent Doctrine,* 38.

60. Press Briefing by Gonzales and Hayden.

61. Hearing Before the House Judiciary Committee, *Department of Justice Oversight,* 109th Cong., 2d Sess., April 6, 2006.

62. For a clear explanation of telecommunications technology, including wire, cellular, and Internet, see Jonathan E. Nuechterlein and Philip J. Weiser, *Digital Crossroads: American Telecommunications Policy in the Internet Age* (Cambridge: Massachusetts Institute of Technology Press, 2005).

63. Risen, *State of War,* 49.

64. There is some difficulty in identifying the part of the surveillance program that sparked controversy. It may have been the data-mining program described in note 42 above, not the electronic interception of communications. In any event, the parts of the program were related, and concerns about FISA in one application would have had implications for the others. See Scott Shane and David Johnston, "Mining of Data Prompted Fight over U.S. Spying," *New York Times,* July 29, 2007, A1.

65. Eric Lichtblau, "Senate Panel Rebuffed on Documents on U.S. Spying," *New York Times,* February 2, 2006, A1.

66. Goldsmith, *Terror Presidency,* 182.

67. My account of this controversy is based on similar versions told by David Johnson, "Bush Intervened in Dispute over N.S.A. Wiretapping," *New York Times,* May 16, 2007, A1; Eric Lichtblau and James Risen, "Justice Deputy Resisted Parts of Spy Program," *New York Times,* January 1, 2006, 11; and Daniel Klaidman, Stuart Taylor, Jr., and Evan Thomas, "Palace Revolt," *Newsweek* (February 6, 2006): 34. The quotations are from James Comey's testimony before the Senate Judiciary Committee, May 15, 2007, which is available at http://gulcfac.typepad.com/georgetown_university_law/files/comey.transcript.pdf. Comey's version of events was corroborated by FBI Director Robert Mueller; see David Johnston and Scott Shane, "Notes Confirm Pressure on Ashcroft over Spying," *New York Times,* August 17, 2007, A12. It was also corroborated by Jack Goldsmith; see Neil A. Lewis, "Professor Tells of 'Mess' over Eavesdropping," *New York Times,* October 3, 2007, A21. Attorney General Gonzales took issue with some parts of Comey's story in testimony that caused sharp controversy about his own truthfulness, and that was one factor in his eventual resignation. See David Johnston and Scott Shane, "Gonzales Denies Improper Pressure on Ashcroft on Spying," *New York Times,* July 25, 2007, A10; David Johnston and Scott Shane, "Gonzales Dealt Blow in Account by F.B.I. Director," *New York Times,* July 27, 2007, A1.

68. Barton Gellman, *Angler: The Cheney Vice Presidency* (New York: Penguin, 2008), 318.

69. James B. Comey, "Intelligence under the Law," *Green Bag 2d* 10 (Summer 2007): 439, 444.

70. Hayes, *Cheney,* 488.

71. Norman J. Ornstein and Thomas E. Mann, "When Congress Checks Out," 85 *Foreign Affairs* 67 (November–December 2006): "The NSA surveillance initiatives were shared with a bipartisan group of only eight top party and committee members—all of whom were sworn to secrecy and could reveal nothing to their colleagues—rather than with the full congressional intelligence committees. Members of both parties have been quite open with us about the dismissive attitude, indeed the contempt, with which President Bush and Vice President Cheney have greeted requests for information."

72. Sheryl Gay Stolberg, "Senators Left Out of Loop Make Their Pique Known," *New York Times,* May 19, 2006, A20.

73. Eric Lichtblau and Scott Shane, "Ally Told Bush Spying Projects Might Be Illegal," *New York Times,* July 8, 2006, A1.

74. Hayes, *Cheney,* 489.

75. James Bamford, "Big Brother Is Listening," *Atlantic Monthly* (April 2006): 65, 66.

76. Gonzales was confirmed by a sixty-to-thirty-six vote in the Senate on February 3, 2005, amid concerns about his close relationship with the president.

77. Charlie Savage, "Specialists Doubt Legality of Wiretaps," *Boston Globe,* February 2, 2006.

78. A letter from the Justice Department's Office of Legislative Affairs (March 24, 2006) declining to release unpublished opinions in order to protect "the deliberative process of decisionmaking" within the executive is reprinted in Hearings Before the Senate Judiciary Committee, *Wartime Executive Power and the National Security Agency's Surveillance Authority,* 109th Cong., 2d Sess., 2006 (Ser. No. J-109–59), 147.

79. Hearing Before the Senate Judiciary Committee, *Oversight of the U.S. Department of Justice,* 110th Cong., 1st Sess., January 18, 2007.

80. The letter is available at http://www.fas.org/irp/agency/doj/fisa/ago11707 .pdf.

81. Mark Mazzetti, "Key Lawmakers to Get Files about Surveillance Program," *New York Times,* February 1, 2007, A1.

82. James Risen, "Administration Pulls Back on Surveillance Agreement," *New York Times,* May 2, 2007, A18, reporting that the administration declined to promise it would continue to seek warrants for all NSA surveillance, as it had promised in the attorney general's January letter.

83. Neil A. Lewis, "Bush Blocked Ethics Inquiry, Official Says," *New York Times,* July 19, 2006, A14.

84. Eric Lichtblau, "Justice Official Opens Spying Inquiry," *New York Times,* November 28, 2006, A19.

85. Murray Waas, "Internal Affairs," *National Journal* (March 17, 2007): 34.

86. Protect America Act of 2007, Pub. L. No. 110–55, 121 Stat. 552.

87. FISA Amendments Act of 2008, Pub. L. No. 110-261, 122 Stat. 2466.

88. Joe Palazzolo, "Litigation over Spy Program on Hold," *Legal Times,* October 1, 2007, 8.

89. *American Civil Liberties Union v. National Security Agency,* 493 F.3d 644 (6th Cir. 2007), cert. denied, 128 S.Ct. 1334 (February 18, 2008).

90. "Everything that's in those memos was in the white paper," said a "senior Justice Department official," quoted in Eric Lichtblau, "Senate Panel Rebuffed on Documents on U.S. Spying," *New York Times,* February 2, 2006, A1.

91. Letter to Majority Leader Bill Frist et al. (January 9, 2006) from Curtis A. Bradley (Duke), David Cole (Georgetown), Walter Dellinger (Duke), Ronald Dworkin (N.Y.U.), Richard Epstein (Chicago), Philip B. Heymann (Harvard), Harold H. Koh (Yale), Martin Lederman (Georgetown, visiting), Beth Nolan (formerly of George Washington), William S. Sessions (former FBI director), Geoffrey R. Stone (Chicago), Kathleen M. Sullivan (Stanford), Laurence H. Tribe (Harvard), and William W. Van Alstyne (William and Mary).

92. Elizabeth Bazan and Jennifer K. Elsea, *Presidential Authority to Conduct Warrantless Electronic Surveillance to Gather Foreign Intelligence Information,* January 5, 2006.

93. See generally Trevor W. Morrison, "Constitutional Avoidance in the Executive Branch," *Columbia Law Review* 106 (2006): 1189; and H. Jefferson Powell, "The Executive and the Avoidance Canon," *Indiana Law Journal* 81 (2006): 1313.

94. The phrase comes from (whom else?) Robert Jackson, dissenting in *Terminiello v. City of Chicago,* 337 U.S. 1, 37 (1949). The phrase is also in the title of Judge Richard A. Posner's thoughtful book about the war on terrorism, *Not a Suicide Pact: The Constitution in a Time of National Emergency* (New York: Oxford University Press, 2006).

95. Henry Monaghan, "The Protective Power of the Presidency," *Columbia Law Review* 93 (1993): 1.

96. 67 U.S. (2 Black) 635 (1863). See generally Thomas H. Lee and Michael D. Ramsey, "The *Prize Cases:* Executive Action and Judicial Review in Wartime," in *Presidential Power Stories,* ed. Curtis Bradley and Christopher Schroeder (New York: Foundation Press, 2008).

97. It provides: "The right of the people to be secure in their persons, houses, papers, and effects, against unreasonable searches and seizures, shall not be violated; and no warrants shall issue, but upon probable cause, supported by oath or affirmation, and particularly describing the place to be searched and the persons or things to be seized."

98. *United States v. Knights,* 534 U.S. 112, 118–119 (2001).

99. *Keith,* 407 U.S. 297, 316–321 (1972).

100. Senate Report no. 95-604, vol. 1, 16; 1978 United States Code Congressional and Administrative News (U.S.C.C.A.N.), 3904, 3917.

101. Ibid., vol. 2, 12; 1978 U.S.C.C.A.N., 3909–3910: "Since the 1930s, intelligence agencies have frequently wiretapped and bugged American citizens without the benefit of judicial warrant. . . . Past subjects of these surveillances have included a United States Congressman, Congressional staff member, journalists and newsmen, and numerous individuals and groups who engaged in no criminal activity and who posed no genuine threat to the national security, such as two White House domestic affairs advisers and an anti–Vietnam War protest group."

102. See, for example, *Vernonia School District v. Acton,* 515 U.S. 646 (1995).

103. Pub. L. No. 107-40, 115 Stat. 224 (2001). For a discussion of the legislative history of the AUMF, see Richard F. Grimmett, *Authorization for Use of Military Force in Response to the 9/11 Attacks (Pub. L. 107–40): Legislative History,* CRS Report RS22357.

104. Curtis A. Bradley and Jack L. Goldsmith, "Congressional Authorization and the War on Terrorism," *Harvard Law Review* 118 (2005): 2047.

105. The statute that *did* enable domestic surveillance, the PATRIOT Act, did not address the program despite the existence of an opportunity to seek authorization during its passage.

106. Suskind, *One Percent Doctrine,* 17. On the question of whether the AUMF denied domestic authority, John Yoo, *Insider's Account,* 116, says that in meetings with the congressional leaders, a "statement we had included that the President had the constitutional authority to use force to preempt future terrorist attacks . . . was moved to the statute's findings." He calls this window dressing, and that is true in the sense that the phrase should not be relied on to authorize domestic action, because the statute is not explicit on the point.

107. 542 U.S. 507 (2004). I discuss *Hamdi* in the next chapter.

108. Ibid., 518: "There can be no doubt that individuals who fought against the United States in Afghanistan as part of the Taliban, an organization known to have supported the al Qaeda terrorist network responsible for those attacks, are individuals Congress sought to target in passing the AUMF. We conclude that detention of individuals falling into the limited category we are considering, for the duration of the particular conflict in which they were captured, is so fundamental and accepted an incident to war as to be an exercise of the 'necessary and appropriate force' Congress has authorized the President to use."

109. The classic demonstration of this fact is by Karl Llewellyn, "Remarks on the Theory of Appellate Decisions and the Rules or Canons about How Statutes Are to be Construed," *Vanderbilt Law Review* 3 (1950): 395.

110. The paper cited *Haig v. Agee*, 453 U.S. 280, 293–303 (1981), and other cases.

111. In *Keith*, Justice Powell remarked, 407 U.S. 297, 299 (1972): "Successive Presidents for more than one-quarter of a century have authorized such surveillance in varying degrees, without guidance from the Congress or a definitive decision of this Court."

112. Emphasis in original. The scholars cited *Morales v. TWA, Inc.*, 504 U.S. 374, 384–385 (1992), and other cases.

113. 50 U.S.C. §1811.

114. 50 U.S.C. §1809(a)(1).

115. *Youngstown Sheet & Tube Co. v. Sawyer*, 343 U.S. 579, 609 (1952) (Frankfurter, J., concurring).

116. 18 U.S.C. §2511(2)(f).

117. The scholars cited *J.E.M. Agricultural Supply, Inc. v. Pioneer Hi-Bred International, Inc.*, 534 U.S. 124, 137 (2001), and another case.

118. Citing *Immigration and Naturalization Service v. St. Cyr*, 533 U.S. 289, 299–300 (2001) and *Ashwander v. TVA*, 297 U.S. 288, 345–348 (1936) (Brandeis, J., concurring).

119. The department cites *Department of the Navy v. Egan*, 484 U.S. 518, 527, 530 (1988), and William N. Eskridge, Jr., *Dynamic Statutory Interpretation* (Cambridge, Mass.: Harvard University Press, 1994) (describing "super-strong rule against congressional interference with the President's authority over foreign affairs and national security" [325]).

120. For a strong critique of the administration's use of the canon with FISA, see Morrison, "Constitutional Avoidance," 1250–1258.

121. Powell, "Avoidance Canon."

122. Echoes of *Timely Notification* occur in "Common Legislative Encroachments on Executive Branch Constitutional Authority," an opinion written in 1989 by Assistant Attorney General William Barr for the first President Bush. It is reprinted in H. Jefferson Powell, *The Constitution and the Attorneys General* (Durham, N.C.: Carolina Academic Press, 1999), 523. The Barr memo was superseded by one written in 1996 by Assistant Attorney General Walter Dellinger for President Clinton, titled "The Constitutional Separation of Powers between the President and Congress," reprinted in *The Constitution and the Attorneys General*, 617. The Dellinger memo is much more respectful of the powers of Congress than is the Barr memo; the second Bush administration ignored it.

123. *In re Sealed Case*, 310 F.3d 717, 742 (F.I.S.C.R. 2002).

124. They cite *United States v. Oakland Cannabis Buyers' Coop.*, 532 U.S. 483, 494 (2001) (the "canon of constitutional avoidance has no application in the absence of statutory ambiguity").

125. After the white paper emerged, the scholars sent a follow-up letter to Congress adhering to their earlier position and concluding that "the NSA program lacks any plausible legal foundation." The letter is reproduced in Cole and Lederman, "Documents," 1415.

126. Yoo, *Insider's Account*, ch. 5. He later restated his views in an article, "The Terrorist Surveillance Program and the Constitution," *George Mason Law Review* 14 (2007): 565. For contrasting analyses, see William C. Banks, "The Death of FISA," *Minnesota Law Review* 91 (2007): 1209; John Cary Sims, "What NSA Is Doing . . . and Why It's Illegal," *Hastings Constitutional Law Quarterly* 33 (Winter–Spring 2006): 105, and "How the Bush Administration's Warrantless Surveillance Program Took the Constitution on an Illegal, Unnecessary, and Unrepentant Joyride," *UCLA Journal of International Law and Foreign Affairs* 12 (2007): 163; and Peter P. Swire, "The System of Foreign Intelligence Surveillance Law," *George Washington Law Review* 72 (2004): 1306.

127. Yoo, *Insider's Account*, 112.

128. Ibid., 104.

129. Adam Liptak, "The White House as a Moving Legal Target," *New York Times,* January 19, 2007, A1, notes that the administration often sought "to change the terms of the debate just as a claim of executive authority [was] about to be tested in the courts or in Congress." This avoided accountability and judicial scrutiny. His examples include Attorney General Gonzales's acquisition of FISA authority for surveillance on the eve of oversight hearings and various actions that averted judicial review of the legality of detention of suspected enemy combatants.

130. Modern statutes contain many deadlines for implementing action by the executive, and because many of the deadlines are unrealistic, the executive often misses them, whereupon courts monitor compliance as best they can.

131. *Youngstown,* 343 U.S. 579, 649–652 (1952).

132. 50 U.S.C. §1805a.

133. Morrison, "Constitutional Avoidance," 1256 n. 288, offers another suggestion: to amend the AUMF to authorize "intercepting communications" of international terrorists.

134. Garry Wills, *Henry Adams and the Making of America* (Boston: Houghton Mifflin, 2005), 157. The House later voted a secret $2 million in "expenses" to buy West Florida, with a misleading statement from Congress to justify it (193).

135. Tim Weiner, *Blank Check: The Pentagon's Black Budget* (New York: Warner, 1990).

136. The total nowadays is approaching $50 billion, but the itemization is not revealed.

8. INDEFINITE DETENTION OF ENEMY COMBATANTS

1. John Yoo, *War by Other Means: An Insider's Account of the War on Terror* (Chicago: University of Chicago Press, 2006), 128.

2. Yoo, ibid., says that "the one thing we all agreed on was that any detention facility should be located outside the United States" (142). The underlying concern

was that the federal courts might "substitute familiar peacetime prison standards for military needs and standards."

3. Clive Stafford Smith, *Eight O' Clock Ferry to the Windward Side: Seeking Justice in Guantánamo Bay* (New York: Nation Books, 2007), 242–243.

4. There has been some debate over terminology concerning persons held at Guantánamo and elsewhere. The Bush administration always used and promoted the term "detainees" to emphasize that these people have not been convicted of crime and are not accorded prisoner of war status. This defies the ordinary usages of language, because the captives have been held in secure facilities that were de facto prisons for years, often incommunicado, and often in solitary confinement under very harsh conditions. Having made some introductory remarks concerning these prisoners, I will revert to the more commonly used term for them, detainees.

5. "Possible Habeas Jurisdiction over Aliens Held in Guantánamo Bay, Cuba," reprinted in Karen J. Greenberg and Joshua L. Dratel, eds., *The Torture Papers: The Road to Abu Ghraib* (New York: Cambridge University Press, 2005), 29.

6. 339 U.S. 763 (1950).

7. 18 U.S.C. §§2241, 2243.

8. George W. Bush, *Military Order of November 13, 2001: Detention, Treatment, and Trial of Certain Non-Citizens in the War on Terrorism,* 66 Fed. Reg. 57831, reprinted in Greenberg and Dratel, *Torture Papers,* 25.

9. Harold H. Bruff, *Balance of Forces: Separation of Powers Law in the Administrative State* (Durham, N.C.: Carolina Academic Press, 2006), 154–162.

10. There was also a group of detainees who were aliens residing in the United States. Many were held for a period and then deported for immigration law violations. David Cole, *Enemy Aliens: Double Standards and Constitutional Freedoms in the War on Terrorism* (New York: New Press, 2005), 24–25 (giving a figure of more than 5,000 detainees). See Office of the Inspector General, Department of Justice, *The September 11 Detainees: A Review of the Treatment of Aliens Held on Immigration Charges in Connection with the Investigation of the September 11 Attacks* (2003).

11. Peter Jan Honigsberg, "Chasing 'Enemy Combatants' and Circumventing International Law: A License for Sanctioned Abuse," *UCLA Journal of International Law and Foreign Affairs* 12 (2007): 1. For *Quirin,* see Chapter 3 of this book.

12. My description draws on three books by lawyers who have represented the detainees and who have had personal experience with conditions at Guantánamo: Cole, *Enemy Aliens;* Stafford Smith, *Ferry;* and Joseph Margulies, *Guantánamo and the Abuse of Presidential Power* (New York: Simon & Schuster, 2006).

13. Margulies, *Guantánamo,* ch. 3.

14. Jeffrey Toobin, "Camp Justice," *New Yorker* (April 14, 2008): 32.

15. Stafford Smith, *Ferry,* 151.

16. David Luban, "Lawfare and Legal Ethics in Guantánamo," *Stanford Law Review* 60 (2008): 1981, 2025, quoting Wells Dixon, a lawyer for the detainees and a 1999 graduate of the University of Colorado Law School, who explained: "What we do is completely antithetical to what they are trying to accomplish in Guantánamo. They have three principles: isolation, dependency, and secrecy, and lawyers represent just the opposite principles: transparency and openness. So they always try to drive a wedge between lawyers and their clients" (2025).

17. See Bruff, *Balance of Forces,* 94–102, for a summary of prior actions. In the wake of 9/11, Congress amended or enacted a number of statutes on subjects such as

homeland security and aircraft safety. These are cited in Neal K. Katyal and Laurence H. Tribe, "Waging War, Deciding Guilt: Trying the Military Tribunals," *Yale Law Journal* 111 (2002): 1259, 1276 n. 66.

18. The facts and quotes in this paragraph are from Jack Goldsmith, *The Terror Presidency: Law and Judgment inside the Bush Administration* (New York: Norton, 2007), 122–126.

19. Ibid., 122–123.

20. Jeffrey Toobin, *The Nine: Inside the Secret World of the Supreme Court* (New York: Doubleday, 2007), 231–232. For press reports, see *New York Times*, April 29, 2004, A1 (oral arguments); A15 (prisoner abuses).

21. Toobin, *The Nine*, 232–233. I discuss the "torture memo" in Chapter 11 of this book.

22. See generally Geoffrey R. Stone, *Perilous Times: Free Speech in Wartime from the Sedition Act of 1798 to the War on Terrorism* (New York: Norton, 2004).

23. The detention and internment of Japanese citizens and U.S. citizens of Japanese descent were upheld in *Korematsu v. United States*, 323 U.S. 214 (1944). For the negative reactions of later Justices to *Korematsu*, see David Cole, "The Priority of Morality: The Emergency Constitution's Blind Spot," *Yale Law Journal* 113 (2004): 1029, 1763 n. 34. A less well-known companion case to *Korematsu*, *Ex Parte Endo*, 323 U.S. 283 (1944), held that internees posing no risk of sabotage or espionage must be released, and speeded the end of the camps. Patrick O. Gudridge, "Remember *Endo*?" *Harvard Law Review* 116 (2003): 1933.

24. Justice Jackson's agonized dissent in *Korematsu*, 323 U.S. 214, 242–248 (1944), exemplifies this concern. See Dennis J. Hutchinson, " 'The Achilles Heel' of the Constitution: Justice Jackson and the Japanese Exclusion Cases," *Supreme Court Review* 2002 (2002): 455. For the dismaying background of the litigation, see Peter H. Irons, *Justice at War* (New York: Oxford University Press, 1983).

25. For a comparison of the two eras, see Jack L. Goldsmith and Cass R. Sunstein, "Military Tribunals and Legal Culture: What a Difference Sixty Years Makes," *Constitutional Commentary* 19 (2002): 261.

26. 542 U.S. 507 (2004).

27. The usual definition of hearsay is "a statement made out of court that is offered to prove the matter asserted." Hence, the objection to admitting it is that the person who made the statement is not subject to confrontation by the accused and cross-examination.

28. The government argued: "Under the some evidence standard, the focus is exclusively on the factual basis supplied by the Executive to support its own determination." It cited a prison case stating that the some evidence standard "does not require" a "weighing of the evidence" but rather calls for assessing "whether there is any evidence in the record that could support the conclusion." Under this standard, a court would assume the accuracy of the Mobbs declaration and would ask only whether that articulated basis sufficed. This kind of extremely lenient review of executive action is not typical of federal administrative law, which usually makes substantial inquiries into the actual basis for an agency's action.

29. 18 U.S.C. §4001(a) states that "no citizen shall be imprisoned or otherwise detained by the United States except pursuant to an Act of Congress." As the Court noted, 542 U.S. 507, 517 (2004), this provision was meant to prevent any repeat of the Japanese internment camps of World War II. Its existence forestalled

any argument that inherent executive authority alone supported the detention of citizens.

30. 542 U.S. 507, 529 (2004), citing *Mathews v. Eldridge*, 424 U.S. 319, 335 (1976).

31. The plurality had some statutory help in evaluating procedure. Hamdi had challenged his detention under 28 U.S.C. §2241. The plurality said that "all agree that §2241 and its companion provisions provide at least a skeletal outline of the procedures to be afforded a petitioner in federal habeas review. Most notably, §2243 provides that 'the person detained may, under oath, deny any of the facts set forth in the return or allege any other material facts,' and §2246 allows the taking of evidence in habeas proceedings by deposition, affidavit, or interrogatories."

32. The Court said, 542 U.S. 507, 537 (2004): "Because we conclude that due process demands some system for a citizen-detainee to refute his classification, the proposed 'some evidence' standard is inadequate. Any process in which the Executive's factual assertions go wholly unchallenged or are simply presumed correct without any opportunity for the alleged combatant to demonstrate otherwise falls constitutionally short. As the Government itself has recognized, we have utilized the 'some evidence' standard in the past as a standard of review, not as a standard of proof. . . . This standard therefore is ill suited to the situation in which a habeas petitioner has received no prior proceedings before any tribunal and had no prior opportunity to rebut the Executive's factual assertions before a neutral decisionmaker." The two justices who concurred in the judgment, Souter and Ginsburg, said they would have given a citizen at least as much process as the plurality required.

33. The Court thought that the government could use affidavit evidence "like that contained in the Mobbs declaration, so long as it also permits the alleged combatant to present his own factual case to rebut the Government's return."

34. The Court noted "that military regulations already provide for such process in related instances, dictating that tribunals be made available to determine the status of enemy detainees who assert prisoner-of-war status under the Geneva Convention. See Headquarters, Departments of Army, Navy, Air Force, and Marine Corps, *Enemy Prisoners of War, Retained Personnel, Civilian Internees and Other Detainees,* Army Regulation 190–8, ch. 1, §1–6 (1997)."

35. 542 U.S. 507, 536 (2004).

36. Ibid., 545.

37. Erwin Chemerinsky, "Enemy Combatants and Separation of Powers," *Journal of National Security Law and Policy* 1 (2005): 73.

38. After the Court's decision, the administration agreed to release Hamdi on the condition that he renounce his U.S. citizenship and agree not to return to the United States for at least ten years or take up arms against the United States.

39. 542 U.S. 466 (2004).

40. Three justices dissented on grounds that the habeas corpus statute did not apply to aliens in military detention outside the United States.

41. 542 U.S. 426 (2004).

42. U.S.C. §3144 allows a person's detention without probable cause of having committed a crime on showing that the person has testimony material to a criminal trial or grand jury investigation and poses a risk of flight.

43. Padilla was later transferred back to civilian jurisdiction and convicted of federal conspiracy charges under the criminal code for participation in a terrorism

support cell. The "dirty bomb" allegations made at the time of his arrest were not charged. Abby Goodnough and Scott Shane, "Padilla Is Guilty on All Charges in Terror Trial," *New York Times,* August 17, 2007, A1.

44. Cass R. Sunstein, "Minimalism at War," *Supreme Court Review* 2004 (2004): 47.

45. For an argument that the executive should bear a heavy burden of justification in the habeas proceedings, see Emily Calhoun, "The Accounting: Habeas Corpus and Enemy Combatants," *University of Colorado Law Review* 79 (2008): 77.

46. *Hamdi,* 542 U.S. 507, 538 (2004): "There remains the possibility that the standards we have articulated could be met by an appropriately authorized and properly constituted military tribunal."

47. Pub. L. No. 109–148, 119 Stat. 2739.

48. Pub. L. No. 109–366, 120 Stat. 2600. See generally "Agora: Military Commissions Act of 2006," *American Journal of International Law* 101 (2007): 35, and "Agora (Continued)," *American Journal of International Law* 101 (2007): 322.

49. The Constitution's Suspension Clause, Article I, §9, provides: "The Privilege of the Writ of Habeas Corpus shall not be suspended, unless when in Cases of Rebellion or Invasion the public Safety may require it."

50. The order is available at http://www.defenselink.mil/news/Ju12004/d20040707review.pdf.

51. Geneva's Prisoner of War Convention, 6 U.S.T. 3316, 75 U.N.T.S. 135 (1949), provides in Article 5: "Should any doubt arise as to whether persons, having committed a belligerent act and having fallen into the hands of the enemy [merit POW status], such persons shall enjoy the protection of the present Convention until such time as their status has been determined by a competent tribunal." See note 34 above for a citation to the U.S. military's implementation of this requirement.

52. Margulies, *Guantánamo,* ch. 8.

53. Tim Golden, "For Guantánamo Review Boards, Limits Abound," *New York Times,* December 31, 2006, A11.

54. Benjamin Wittes, *Law and the Long War: The Future of Justice in the Age of Terror* (New York: Penguin, 2008), ch. 3.

55. Margulies, *Guantánamo,* 168–169.

56. Statement of Lt. Col. Stephen Abraham, U.S. Army, available at http://www.scotusblog.com/movabletype/archives/Al%20odah%20reply%206-22-07.pdf. See Ron Suskind, *The Way of the World* (New York: HarperCollins, 2008), ch. 4.

57. By the summer of 2008, about 275 remained at Guantánamo, but many others remained overseas at Bagram and other U.S. bases.

58. William Glaberson, "Pentagon Study Sees Threat in Guantánamo Detainees," *New York Times,* July 26, 2007, A15; Raymond Bonner and Jane Perlez, "British Report Criticizes U.S. Treatment of Terror Suspects," *New York Times,* July 28, 2007, A5; Tim Golden, "U.S. Says It Fears Detainee Abuse in Repatriation," *New York Times,* April 30, 2006, A1.

59. Linda Greenhouse, "Detainees at Guantánamo Fight Further Appeal Delay," *New York Times,* February 22, 2008, A17. In *Boumediene v. Bush,* 128 S.Ct. 2229, 2263 (2008), the Supreme Court summarized the morass as follows: "Although the Court of Appeals has yet to complete a DTA review proceeding, the three-judge panel in *Bismullah* has issued an interim order giving guidance as to what evidence can be made part of the record on review and what access the detainees can have

to counsel and to classified information. See 501 F.3d 178 (C.A.D.C.) (*Bismullah I*), reh'g denied, 503 F.3d 137 (C.A.D.C. 2007) (*Bismullah II*). In that matter the full court denied the Government's motion for rehearing en banc, see *Bismullah v. Gates*, 514 F.3d (C.A.D.C.2008) (*Bismullah III*), 1291."

60. The scope of review of CSRT decisions is in DTA §1005, 28 U.S.C. §2241.

61. 28 U.S.C. §2241(e). See Curtis A. Bradley, "The Military Commissions Act, Habeas Corpus, and the Geneva Conventions," in "Agora (Continued)," 322.

62. *Boumediene v. Bush*, 476 F.3d 981 (D.C. Cir.); cert. granted, 127 S.Ct. 3078 (2007).

63. 128 S.Ct. 2229 (2008). Justice Kennedy's majority opinion was joined by Justices Stevens, Souter, Ginsburg, and Breyer. Chief Justice Roberts dissented along with Justices Scalia, Thomas, and Alito.

64. The Court concluded "that at least three factors are relevant in determining the reach of the Suspension Clause: (1) the citizenship and status of the detainee and the adequacy of the process through which that status determination was made; (2) the nature of the sites where apprehension and then detention took place; and (3) the practical obstacles inherent in resolving the prisoner's entitlement to the writ."

65. DTA §1005(e)(2)(C).

66. The *Boumediene* Court did not reach issues of the application of habeas "to claims of unlawful conditions of treatment or confinement."

67. This paragraph draws on the general thesis of Philip Bobbitt, *Terror and Consent: The Wars for the Twenty-First Century* (New York: Knopf, 2008), especially 269–270.

9. ESCAPING GENEVA

1. Article VI provides: "This Constitution, and the laws of the United States . . . and all treaties . . . which shall be made . . . shall be the supreme law of the land."

2. 6 U.S.T. 3316, 75 U.N.T.S. 135 (POWs); 6 U.S.T. 3516, 75 U.N.T.S. 287 (Civilians).

3. The quotes and facts in this paragraph are from John Yoo, *War by Other Means: An Insider's Account of the War on Terror* (Chicago: University of Chicago Press, 2006), 30–31.

4. It does appear, however, that Addington wrote the critical memo of January 25, 2002, from Alberto Gonzales, then White House counsel, to the president. Yoo's views are also prominent in the memo, which I discuss below. Charlie Savage, *Takeover: The Return of the Imperial Presidency and the Subversion of American Democracy* (Boston: Little, Brown, 2007), 146.

5. The copy reprinted in Karen J. Greenberg and Joshua L. Dratel, eds., *The Torture Papers: The Road to Abu Ghraib* (New York: Cambridge University Press, 2005), 38, is marked "Draft."

6. John Yoo, *The Powers of War and Peace: The Constitution and Foreign Affairs after 9/11* (Chicago: University of Chicago Press, 2005). The quotations in this and the next paragraph are from ch. 6 (revealingly titled "International Politics as Law").

7. See Chapter 5.

8. See Chapter 5. The statement in text is a general one; for more complex analyses, see Curtis A. Bradley, "*Chevron* Deference and Foreign Affairs," *Virginia*

Law Review 86 (2000): 649; Eric A. Posner and Cass R. Sunstein, "*Chevron*izing Foreign Relations Law," *Yale Law Journal* 116 (2007): 1170.

9. 18 U.S.C. §2441.

10. *Foster v. Neilson*, 27 U.S. (2 Pet.) 253 (1829).

11. *Fairfax's Devisee v. Hunter's Lessee*, 11 U.S. (7 Cranch) 603 (1813).

12. Yoo, *Powers*, 165.

13. See generally Derek Jinks and David Sloss, "Is the President Bound by the Geneva Conventions?" *Cornell Law Review* 90 (2004): 97. The Supremacy Clause is quoted in note 1 above.

14. Jinks and Sloss, *President Bound*, 111.

15. Footnote 4 of the opinion explains and invokes the rule of lenity.

16. Greenberg and Dratel, *Torture Papers*, 47.

17. David J. Barron and Martin S. Lederman, "The Commander in Chief at the Lowest Ebb—Framing the Problem, Doctrine, and Original Understanding," *Harvard Law Review* 121 (2008): 689.

18. Greenberg and Dratel, *Torture Papers*, 67 (emphasis in original).

19. Just as Anglo-American courts have generated common law principles through a process of experience and evolution, international law has a "customary" component that includes concepts sufficiently widely recognized to be characterized as law. Controversy surrounds customary international law in part because of problems of indeterminacy.

20. Yoo, *Insider's Account*, 22.

21. Yoo stresses that President Reagan refused to send the Senate a 1977 addition to Geneva that included explicit coverage of nonstate organizations because the provision would protect terrorists. Ibid., 25, 36. (President Carter had signed the addition before he left office.)

22. Jinks and Sloss, *President Bound*, 196–198.

23. Ron Suskind, *The One Percent Doctrine: Deep inside America's Pursuit of Its Enemies since 9/11* (New York: Simon & Schuster, 2006), 111–112.

24. William H. Taft IV, *Your Draft Memorandum of January 9*, January 11, 2002, available at http://www.newyorker.com/online/content/?050214on_onlineonlyo2.

25. David D. Caron, "If Afghanistan Has Failed, Then Afghanistan Is Dead: 'Failed States' and the Inappropriate Substitution of Legal Conclusion for Political Description," in Karen J. Greenberg, ed., *The Torture Debate in America* (New York: Cambridge University Press, 2006), 214, 217.

26. Yoo, *Insider's Account*, 39.

27. Yoo, ibid., 24, says this opinion was again prepared by Yoo and Delahunty. It is reprinted in Greenberg and Dratel, *Torture Papers*, 81.

28. This paragraph is drawn from Bob Woodward, *State of Denial* (New York: Simon & Schuster, 2006), 86–87.

29. Yoo, *Insider's Account*, 35.

30. He would later refer to "a steady pattern of military resistance to civilian decisions since the end of the Cold War [that] shows no signs of receding." Glenn Sulmasy and John Yoo, "Challenges to Civilian Control of the Military: A Rational Choice Approach to the War on Terror," *UCLA Law Review* 54 (2007): 1815, 1845.

31. The memos discussed in text leading up to and including President Bush's order of February 7, 2002, are reprinted in Greenberg and Dratel, *Torture Papers*,

118–143, and in Mark Danner, *Torture and Truth: America, Abu Ghraib, and the War on Terror* (New York: New York Review of Books, 2004), 83–106.

32. Yoo, *Insider's Account,* 42. The letter is reprinted in Greenberg and Dratel, *Torture Papers,* 126, and in Danner, *Torture and Truth,* 92.

33. The opinion is reprinted in Greenberg and Dratel, *Torture Papers,* 136, and in Danner, *Torture and Truth,* 96.

34. The order is reprinted in Greenberg and Dratel, *Torture Papers,* 134, and in Danner, *Torture and Truth,* 105.

35. Yoo, *Insider's Account,* 41.

36. See Chapter 12 of this book.

37. Jack Goldsmith, *The Terror Presidency: Law and Judgment inside the Bush Administration* (New York: Norton, 2007), 120.

38. Sulmasy and Yoo, "Civilian Control," 1821.

10. MILITARY TRIALS FOR WAR CRIMES

1. George W. Bush, *Military Order of November 13, 2001: Detention, Treatment, and Trial of Certain Non-Citizens in the War on Terrorism, Federal Register* 66: 57831, reprinted in Karen J. Greenberg and Joshua L. Dratel, eds., *The Torture Papers: The Road to Abu Ghraib* (New York: Cambridge University Press, 2005), 25.

2. My account of the order's genesis is drawn from Charlie Savage, *Takeover: The Return of the Imperial Presidency and the Subversion of American Democracy* (Boston: Little, Brown, 2007), 135–139.

3. Ibid., 58 n. 1.

4. See Chapter 3 of this book.

5. Jack Goldsmith, *The Terror Presidency: Law and Judgment inside the Bush Administration* (New York: Norton, 2007), 109.

6. See generally Jack L. Goldsmith and Cass R. Sunstein, "Military Tribunals and Legal Culture: What a Difference Sixty Years Makes," *Constitutional Commentary* 19 (2002): 261.

7. John Yoo, *War by Other Means: An Insider's Account of the War on Terror* (Chicago: University of Chicago Press, 2006), ch. 8.

8. Savage, *Takeover,* 138.

9. Nicholas W. Smith, "Evidence and Confrontation in the President's Military Commissions," *Hastings Constitutional Law Quarterly* 33 (2005): 83.

10. The usual definition of hearsay is "a statement made out of court that is offered to prove the matter asserted." Hence, the objection to admitting it is that the person who made the statement is not subject to confrontation by the accused and cross-examination.

11. *Hamdan v. Rumsfeld,* 548 U.S. 557 (2006).

12. The summary that follows is drawn from Louis Fisher, *Military Tribunals and Presidential Power: American Revolution to the War on Terrorism* (Lawrence: University Press of Kansas, 2005); and Detlev F. Vagts, "Military Commissions: A Concise History," *American Journal of International Law* 101 (2007): 35.

13. Fisher, *Military Tribunals,* 8.

14. Justice Story later applauded this change: "The whole power is far more safe in the hands of Congress, than in the executive, since otherwise the most summary

and severe punishments might be inflicted at the mere will of the executive." Joseph Story, *Commentaries on the Constitution of the United States,* ed. Ronald Rotunda and John E. Nowak (Durham, N.C.: Carolina Academic Press, 1987), 418.

15. In late 1814, with the British approaching New Orleans, Jackson declared martial law, and when he continued it past the victory a newspaper article by one Louallier complained that persons accused of crime should be tried in civilian, not military, court. Jackson had him arrested for inciting mutiny, and when U.S. District Judge Dominick Hall issued a writ of habeas corpus on grounds that martial law was no longer justified, Jackson ignored the writ and arrested the judge! After word of the peace treaty arrived, Jackson released Louallier, having already escorted the judge out of the city. On his return, the judge held Jackson in contempt and fined him $1,000, which the general paid. In 1842, Congress remitted the fine to Jackson. Apparently, winning the battle was what mattered. See Daniel W. Howe, *What Hath God Wrought: The Transformation of America, 1815–1848* (New York: Oxford University Press, 2007), 70.

16. 71 U.S. (4 Wall.) 2 (1866). Four justices dissented, arguing that Congress could have authorized use of a military tribunal, although it had not done so. See generally Curtis A. Bradley, "The Story of *Ex Parte Milligan:* Military Trials, Enemy Combatants, and Congressional Authorization," in *Presidential Power Stories,* ed. Curtis Bradley and Christopher Schroeder (New York: Foundation Press, 2008).

17. See Chapter 3 of this book.

18. 10 U.S.C. §836.

19. I discuss this case, *Hamdan v. Rumsfeld,* later in this chapter.

20. Hearing before the Senate Committee on the Judiciary, *Department of Justice Oversight: Preserving Our Freedoms While Defending against Terrorism,* 107th Cong., 1st Sess. (2001) (with testimony for and against the tribunals).

21. Fisher, *Military Tribunals,* 170.

22. Ibid., 175.

23. The letter is reprinted in 147 Cong. Rec. S3277 (daily ed. December 14, 2001).

24. ABA Task Force on Terrorism and the Law, *Report and Recommendations on Military Commissions* (2002). See also Ruth Wedgewood, "Al Qaeda, Terrorism, and Military Commissions," *American Journal of International Law* 96 (2002): 328; Harold Koh, "The Case against Military Commissions," *American Journal of International Law* 96 (2002): 337; and Curtis A. Bradley and Jack L. Goldsmith, "The Constitutional Validity of Military Commissions," *Green Bag 2d* 5 (2002): 249.

25. The order, issued March 21, 2002, is available at http://www.defenselink.mil/news/Mar2002/d20020321ord.pdf.

26. Savage, *Takeover,* 138–139.

27. Military Commission Instruction No. 2 (April 30, 2003), 32 CFR §11.6. At the end of 2003, the department appointed a distinguished group of civilian lawyers to serve as the review panel, including Griffin Bell and William T. Coleman, Jr.

28. The facts and quotations in this paragraph are from Bob Woodward, *State of Denial* (New York: Simon & Schuster, 2006), 276.

29. Yoo, *Insider's Account,* 208.

30. *Hamdan v. Rumsfeld,* 548 U.S. 557 (2006). See generally Jonathan Mahler, *The Challenge:* Hamdan v. Rumsfeld *and the Fight over Presidential Power* (New York: Farrar, Straus & Giroux, 2008); and Dawn Johnsen, "The Story of *Hamdan*

v. Rumsfeld," in *Presidential Power Stories,* ed. Curtis Bradley and Christopher Schroeder (New York: Foundation Press, 2008).

31. For example, *Immigration and Naturalization Service v. St. Cyr,* 533 U.S. 289 (2001); and *Ex Parte Yerger,* 75 U.S. (8 Wall.) 85 (1869).

32. See Chapter 8 of this book.

33. Justice Breyer, also concurring, stressed that the Court's holding concerned the absence of statutory authority and that the president could ask for that.

34. Chief Justice Roberts recused himself because he had written the lower court opinion upholding the order that was on appeal.

35. See "Symposium on the New Face of Armed Conflict: Enemy Combatants after *Hamdan v. Rumsfeld,"* *George Washington Law Review* 75 (2007): 971; "Symposium, A *Hamdan* Quartet: Four Essays on Aspects of *Hamdan v. Rumsfeld,"* *Maryland Law Review* 66 (2007): 750; Neal K. Katyal, *"Hamdan v. Rumsfeld:* The Legal Academy Goes to Practice," *Harvard Law Review* 120 (2006): 65; and Peter J. Spiro, *"Hamdan v. Rumsfeld,"* *American Journal of International Law* 100 (2006): 888.

36. Yoo, *Insider's Account,* x.

37. See Chapter 12, text at note 50.

38. Harold Koh, "Setting the World Right," *Yale Law Journal* 115 (2006): "At bottom, *Hamdan* proves again that Justice Jackson's tripartite structure in *Youngstown* is sufficiently flexible to permit robust executive action when Congress genuinely approves, while constraining executive action against the will of Congress" (2373).

39. 548 U.S. 557, 593 (2006), n. 23.

40. Samuel Issacharoff and Richard H. Pildes, "Between Civil Libertarianism and Executive Unilateralism: An Institutional Process Approach to Rights during Wartime," in *The Constitution in Wartime: Beyond Alarmism and Complacency,* ed. Mark Tushnet (Durham, N.C.: Duke University Press, 2005).

41. Kevin M. Stack, "The Statutory President," *Iowa Law Review* 90 (2005): 539, 569.

42. Cass R. Sunstein, "Clear Statement Principles and National Security: *Hamdan* and Beyond," *Supreme Court Review* 2006 (2006): 1.

43. Mark Mazzetti and Kate Zernike, "White House Says Terror Detainees Hold Basic Rights," *New York Times,* July 12, 2006, A1.

44. Kate Zernike, "Administration Prods Congress to Curb the Rights of Detainees," *New York Times,* July 13, 2006, A1.

45. Kate Zernike, "Military Lawyers Urge Protections for Detainees," *New York Times,* July 14, 2006, A16.

46. Pub. L. No. 109–366, 120 Stat. 2600. See generally "Agora: Military Commissions Act of 2006," *American Journal of International Law* 101 (2007): 35; and "Agora (Continued)," *American Journal of International Law* 101 (2007): 322.

47. 10 U.S.C. §§948c, 948a(1)(A).

48. 10 U.S.C. §948b(g).

49. MCA §§6(a)(2), (a)(3)(a).

50. Sheryl Gay Stolberg, "President Moves 14 Held in Secret to Guantánamo," *New York Times,* September 7, 2006, A1.

51. The manual is available at http://www.defenselink.mil/pubs.

52. William Glaberson, "Hurdles Seen as Capital Charges Are Filed in 9/11 Case," *New York Times,* February 12, 2008, A14.

53. *United States v. Hamdan* (Military Commission, August 7, 2008), available at http://www.defenselink.mil/news/commissionsHamdan.html.

54. Corine Hegland, "How to Court-Martial the Qaeda 14," *National Journal* (September 16, 2006): 59.

11. INTERROGATION

1. See Chapter 9 of this book for Gonzales's use of this example of a Geneva requirement as being "quaint" or "obsolete" in the war on terrorism.

2. For wide-ranging reflections, see Karen J. Greenberg, ed., *The Torture Debate in America* (New York: Cambridge University Press, 2006); Sanford Levinson, ed., *Torture: A Collection* (New York: Oxford University Press, 2004); Rosa Ehrenreich Brooks, "The New Imperialism: Violence, Norms, and the 'Rule of Law,'" *Michigan Law Review* 101 (2003): 2275; Seth F. Kreimer, "Too Close to the Rack and the Screw: Constitutional Constraints on Torture in the War on Terror," *University of Pennsylvania Journal of Constitutional Law* 6 (2003): 278; Levinson, "Precommitment and 'Postcommitment': The Ban on Torture in the Wake of September 11," *Texas Law Review* 81 (2003): 2013; and Jeremy Waldron, "Torture and Positive Law: Jurisprudence for the White House," *Columbia Law Review* 105 (2005): 1681.

3. Oona Hathaway, "The Promise and Limits of the International Law of Torture," in Levinson, *Torture*, 199.

4. John Langbein, "The Legal History of Torture," in ibid., 93. He concludes: "History's most important lesson is that it has not been possible to make coercion compatible with truth" (101).

5. Adam Shatz, "The Torture of Algiers," *New York Review of Books* (November 21, 2002): 53.

6. Simon Sebag Montefiore, *Stalin: The Court of the Red Tsar* (New York: Knopf, 2004).

7. For some harrowing accounts, see Ariel Dorfman, "Foreword: The Tyranny of Terror," in Levinson, *Torture*, 3 (Chile); and Mark Osiel, "The Mental State of Torturers," in ibid., 129 (Argentina).

8. Gavan Daws, *Prisoners of the Japanese* (New York: HarperCollins, 1996).

9. Charlie Savage, *Takeover: The Return of the Imperial Presidency and the Subversion of American Democracy* (Boston: Little, Brown, 2007), 217–219.

10. See, for example, David Luban, "Liberalism, Torture, and the Ticking Bomb," in Greenberg, *Torture Debate*, 35.

11. Jean Bethke Elshtain, "Reflections on the Problem of 'Dirty Hands,'" in Levinson, *Torture*, 77, 85 (emphasis in original).

12. For example, ibid. See also Richard A. Posner, "Torture, Terrorism, and Interrogation," in ibid., 291.

13. Joseph Margulies, *Guantánamo and the Abuse of Presidential Power* (New York: Simon & Schuster, 2006), 29.

14. For vivid testimony on this point, see Anthony Lewis (panelist), "Torture: The Road to Abu Ghraib and Beyond," in Greenberg, *Torture Debate*, 18, recounting that torture victim Jacobo Timmerman once pressed Lewis with the ticking bomb question, and when Lewis guessed he would torture in that case, Timmerman shouted: "No! You cannot start down that road!" He knew where it led.

15. Chris Mackey and Greg Miller, *The Interrogators: Inside the Secret War against Al Qaeda* (Boston: Little, Brown, 2004), 471.

16. David Cole and Jules Lobel, *Less Safe, Less Free: Why America Is Losing the War on Terror* (New York: New Press, 2007), 197.

17. Oren Gross, "The Prohibition on Torture and the Limits of the Law," in Levinson, *Torture*, 229.

18. Alan Dershowitz, "Tortured Reasoning," in ibid., 257.

19. Fyodor Dostoyevsky, *The Brothers Karamazov,* trans. Constance Garnett (New York: Signet, 1957), 226.

20. *Peter the Great: His Life and World* (New York: Random House, 1980), 253.

21. Sanford Levinson, "Contemplating Torture: An Introduction," in Levinson, *Torture*, 34.

22. Langbein, "History of Torture," 93, 96.

23. Seth F. Kreimer, " 'Torture Lite,' 'Full Bodied' Torture, and the Insulation of Legal Conscience," *Journal of National Security Law and Policy* 1 (2005): 187.

24. Paul Kramer, "The Water Cure," *New Yorker* (February 25, 2008): 38.

25. Jane Mayer, *The Dark Side* (New York: Doubleday, 2008), 9–10.

26. House and Senate Intelligence Committees, *Hearing on Pre-9/11 Intelligence Failures,* 107th Cong., 2d Sess. (2002), 6.

27. David Johnston, "At a Secret Interrogation, Dispute Flared over Tactics," *New York Times,* September 10, 2006, A1, A20.

28. Mayer, *Dark Side,* 144.

29. Central Intelligence Agency, *KUBARK Counterintelligence Interrogation* (1963), available at http://www.gwu.edu/~nsarchiv/NSAEBB/NSAEBB122/#kubark.

30. Margulies, *Guantánamo,* 33–39.

31. Central Intelligence Agency, *Human Resource Exploitation Training Manual,* available at http://www.gwu.edu/~nsarchiv/NSAEBB/NSAEBB122/#hre.

32. Scott Shane, David Johnston, and James Risen, "Secret U.S. Endorsement of Severe Interrogations," *New York Times,* October 4, 2007, A1, A22.

33. Mayer, *Dark Side,* 157–165.

34. Savage, *Takeover,* 217–219.

35. The account and quotation in this paragraph are taken from Johnston, "Secret Interrogation," with added details from Scott Shane, "Inside the Interrogation of a 9/11 Mastermind," *New York Times,* June 22, 2008, 1.

36. In addition to Zubaydah, KSM and Ramzi ib al-Shibh were waterboarded. John Yoo says that they provided "much information that prevented future terrorist attacks." *War by Other Means: An Insider's Account of the War on Terror* (Chicago: University of Chicago Press, 2006), 167.

37. Mayer, *Dark Side,* ch. 6.

38. Stephen Grey, *Ghost Plane* (New York: St. Martin's, 2006); Margulies, *Guantánamo,* ch. 9. Terminology varies somewhat, but "ordinary" rendition commonly refers to returning a captive to the United States or to his or her home country for trial. The "extraordinary" version sends the captive to a third country for interrogation. I usually use the term rendition to refer to the latter practice, which is the one at issue here.

39. Margulies, *Guantánamo,* 190.

40. Grey, *Ghost Plane*, ch. 6; Louis Fisher, "Lost Constitutional Moorings: Recovering the War Power," *Indiana Law Journal* 81 (2006): 1199, 1244–1247.

41. I discuss CAT in detail later in this chapter. This provision is in Article 3.

42. David Luban, *Legal Ethics and Human Dignity* (New York: Cambridge University Press, 2007), 171.

43. Grey, *Ghost Plane*, ch. 1.

44. Ibid., ch. 6.

45. Although classified, the memo has been cited in some later OLC opinions. Its contents are described in ibid., 219–227, on the basis of interviews with U.S. officials.

46. John Yoo, "Transferring Terrorists," *Notre Dame Law Review* 79 (2004): 1183, 1229.

47. Grey, *Ghost Plane*, ch. 2.

48. Ibid., 43.

49. Ron Suskind, *The One Percent Doctrine: Deep inside America's Pursuit of Its Enemies since 9/11* (New York: Simon & Schuster, 2006), 56.

50. Except as otherwise cited, the facts and quotations in this and the following two paragraphs are from Jan Crawford Greenburg, Howard L. Rosenberg, and Ariane de Vogue, "Top Bush Advisors Approved 'Enhanced Interrogation': Detailed Discussions Were Held about Techniques to Use on Al Qaeda Suspects," *ABC News*, April 9, 2008, available at http://abcnews.go.com/print?id=4583256.

51. Shane, "9/11 Mastermind," 9.

52. Shane, Johnston, and Risen, "Secret Endorsement," A22.

53. Jack Goldsmith, *The Terror Presidency: Law and Judgment inside the Bush Administration* (New York: Norton, 2007), 165.

54. Lara Jakes Jordan and Pamela Hess, "Bush 'Insulated' from Meeting on Methods," *Boulder Daily Camera*, April 11, 2008, 6A.

55. 18 U.S.C. §2441. At the time of these events, WCA made all grave breaches and violations of Common Article 3 federal war crimes. As I discuss below, after the Supreme Court decided in *Hamdan* that Common Article 3 applies to the detainees, Congress amended WCA in the Military Commissions Act of 2006 (MCA) to decriminalize humiliating and degrading treatment retroactively, so that U.S. interrogators could not be prosecuted for those kinds of treatment of the detainees. See Chapter 10 of this book for more detail on *Hamdan*.

56. See Chapter 9 of this book.

57. 1465 U.N.T.S. 85; see generally Gail H. Miller, *Defining Torture* (New York: Florsheimer Center for Constitutional Democracy, 2005).

58. 18 U.S.C. §§2340–2340A.

59. The quoted phrases are from *Wilkerson v. Utah*, 99 U.S. 130, 136 (1878), and *Hope v. Pelzer*, 536 U.S. 730, 737 (2002).

60. 345 U.S. 165, 172 (1952). See also *County of Sacramento v. Lewis*, 523 U.S. 833 (1998). (The Fifth Amendment applies to the federal government; the Fourteenth, to the states.)

61. Sanford Levinson, "In Quest of a 'Common Conscience': Reflections on the Current Debate about Torture," *Journal of National Security Law and Policy* 1 (2005): 231, 246–251, recounting the Court's struggles in *Chavez v. Martinez*, 538 U.S. 760 (2003).

62. Jerome Skolnick, "American Interrogation: From Torture to Trickery," in Levinson, *Torture,* 105.

63. 28 U.S.C. §1350 note.

64. The memo is reprinted in Mark Danner, *Torture and Truth: America, Abu Ghraib, and the War on Terror* (New York: New York Review of Books, 2004), 115; and Karen J. Greenberg and Joshua L. Dratel, eds., *The Torture Papers: The Road to Abu Ghraib* (New York: Cambridge University Press, 2005), 172.

65. Michael Hirsh et al., "A Tortured Debate," *Newsweek* (June 21, 2004): 50.

66. Yoo's version of events is in *Insider's Account,* ch. 7.

67. Scott Shane, "2 Testify on Their Support for Harsh Interrogation," *New York Times,* June 27, 2008, A15; Yoo, *Insider's Account,* 170.

68. Yoo, *Insider's Account,* 170. Explaining the process within OLC, he says that "career attorneys handle the initial research and drafting of opinions, with editing and review by two political appointees at my level, and then final rewriting and editing by the head of the office."

69. Goldsmith, *Terror Presidency,* 167.

70. Ibid.

71. Senate Committee on Foreign Relations, *Convention against Torture and Other Cruel, Inhuman or Degrading Treatment or Punishment,* Executive Report No. 101-30, 101st Cong., 2d Sess., 1990, 6.

72. Luban, *Ethics and Dignity,* 169 (concluding that these techniques constitute torture and not merely cruelty).

73. Miller, *Defining Torture,* 23–25.

74. Senate Committee on Foreign Relations, *Convention against Torture and Other Cruel, Inhuman or Degrading Treatment or Punishment, Message from the President,* Senate Treaty Document No. 100–20, 100th Cong., 2d Sess. (1988), 4–5.

75. Senate Committee on Foreign Relations, Senate Executive Report No. 101-30, 14.

76. Senate Committee on Foreign Relations, Senate Treaty Document No. 100-20, 15–16.

77. Senate Committee on Foreign Relations, Senate Executive Report No. 101-30, 36.

78. Ibid., 6.

79. *Republic of Ireland v. United Kingdom,* 2 E.H.R.R. 25 (1979–1980).

80. For cogent criticism of this aspect of *Interrogation,* see Trevor W. Morrison, "Constitutional Avoidance in the Executive Branch," *Columbia Law Review* 106 (2006): 1189, 1229–1236. For an argument that the avoidance canon is so subject to abuse by the executive that OLC should foreswear resort to it entirely, see H. Jefferson Powell, "The Executive and the Avoidance Canon," *Indiana Law Journal* 81 (2006): 1313.

81. David J. Barron and Martin S. Lederman, "The Commander in Chief at the Lowest Ebb—Framing the Problem, Doctrine, and Original Understanding," *Harvard Law Review* 121 (2008): 689.

82. *United States v. Bailey,* 444 U.S. 394, 410 (1980).

83. Luban, "Ticking Bomb," 65–66.

84. Luban, *Ethics and Dignity,* 177.

85. Press Briefing by White House Counsel Judge Alberto Gonzales, Department of Defense General Counsel William Haynes, Department of Defense Deputy General Counsel Daniel Dell'Orto, and Army Deputy Chief of Staff for Intelligence General Keith Alexander (June 22, 2004), available at http://www.whitehouse.gov/news/releases/2004/06/20040622–14.html.

86. "Legal Standards Applicable under 18 U.S.C. §§2340–2340A," reprinted in Greenberg, *Torture Debate*, 361.

87. The account and the quotations in this and the next three paragraphs are from Goldsmith, *Terror Presidency*, 142–165.

88. Senate Judiciary Committee, *Hearing on the Nomination of Alberto R. Gonzales to Be Attorney General*, 109th Cong., 1st Sess. (January 7, 2005), 158. See also Harold H. Koh, "A World without Torture," *Columbia Journal of Transnational Law* 43 (2005): 641.

89. See, for example, "Symposium: War, Terrorism, and Torture: Limits on Presidential Power in the 21st Century," *Indiana Law Journal* 81 (2006): 1139; "Symposium: Fighting Terrorism with Torture: Where to Draw the Line?" *Journal of National Security Law and Policy* 1 (2005): 187; Eric A. Posner and Adrian Vermeule, "Should Coercive Interrogation be Legal?" *Michigan Law Review* 104 (2006): 671; Jesselyn Radack, "Tortured Legal Ethics: The Role of the Government Advisor in the War on Terrorism," *University of Colorado Law Review* 77 (2006): 1; Michael D. Ramsey, "Torturing Executive Power," *Georgetown Law Journal* 93 (2005): 1213; and W. Bradley Wendel, "Legal Ethics and the Separation of Law and Morals," *Cornell Law Review* 91 (2005): 67.

90. ABA House of Delegates, *Resolution 10-B* (adopted August 9, 2004), 1.

91. The group included former U.S. attorney general Nicholas Katzenbach, former FBI director William Sessions, seven past presidents of the ABA, former New York governor Mario Cuomo, and former U.S. senator Birch Bayh. Scott Higham, "Law Experts Condemn U.S. Memos on Torture," *Washington Post*, August 5, 2004, A4. It is available at Alliance for Justice, *Lawyers' Statement on Bush Administration's Torture Memos* (August 2004), http://www.afj.org/spotlight/0804statement.pdf.

92. Yoo is not without his defenders. See Eric Posner and Adrian Vermeule, "A 'Torture' Memo and Its Tortuous Critics," *Wall Street Journal*, July 6, 2004, A22, arguing that *Interrogation* is "standard lawyerly fare, routine stuff." No, it is neither.

93. Yoo, *Insider's Account*, Introduction.

94. The summary and quotation of Yoo's views in text are drawn from ibid., ch. 7.

95. The revised opinion deleted discussion of defenses, saying that it would not be consistent with the president's command not to torture.

96. Lincoln Caplan, "Lawyers' Standards in Free Fall," *Los Angles Times*, July 20, 2004, B13.

97. Alliance for Justice, *Lawyers' Statement*.

98. Yoo, *Insider's Account*, 185, citing Walter Dellinger, "Presidential Authority to Decline to Enforce Unconstitutional Statutes" (November 2, 1994), reprinted in H. Jefferson Powell, *The Constitution and the Attorneys General* (Durham, N.C.: Carolina Academic Press, 1999), 577.

99. All constitutional law casebooks for law students treat it as a fundamental precedent and include substantial excerpts from the opinions.

100. Goldsmith, *Terror Presidency,* 164–165.

101. It is reprinted in Greenberg, *Torture Debate,* 361.

102. Some OLC opinions address broad topics and give general guidance; these read like law review articles; see, for example, William P. Barr, "Common Legislative Encroachments on Executive Branch Constitutional Authority" (1989), and Walter Dellinger, "The Constitutional Separation of Powers between the President and Congress" (1996), both reprinted in Powell, *Attorneys General,* 523, 617.

103. Luban, *Ethics and Dignity,* 181–182.

104. Except as otherwise cited, the account and quotations in this and the next three paragraphs are from Shane, Johnston, and Risen, "Secret Endorsement"; see also Lawrence Wright, "The Spymaster," *New Yorker* (January 21, 2008): 42, 52.

105. Philip Shenon and Eric Lichtblau, "White House Renews Battle over Lawyer Who Signed Interrogation Memos," *New York Times,* January 24, 2008, A18.

106. Eric Lichtblau, *Bush's Law: The Remaking of American Justice* (New York: Pantheon, 2008), 281–282.

107. Detainee Treatment Act of 2005, Pub. L. No. 109–148, 119 Stat. 2739, 2740 and Pub. L. No. 109–163, 119 Stat. 3474.

108. See Chapter 8 of this book.

109. As enacted, it is §1003(a) of DTA.

110. As enacted, the definition is §1003(d).

111. Harold Koh, "Can The President Be Torturer in Chief?" *Indiana Law Journal* 81 (2006): 1145, 1153–1154.

112. Vice President Cheney, echoing OLC's view, emphasized that the McCain Amendment only prohibited conduct that "shocks the conscience." Corine Hegland, "Ex-POW versus the Guards," *National Journal* (September 23, 2006): 84.

113. George W. Bush, *President's Statement on Signing of H.R. 2863* (December 30, 2005), available at http://www.whitehouse.gov/news/releases/2005/12/20051230-8 .html.

114. See, for example, Walter Dellinger, "The Legal Significance of Presidential Signing Statements" (1993), reprinted in Powell, *Attorneys General,* 563.

115. Walter Dellinger, "Presidential Authority to Decline to Execute Unconstitutional Statutes" (1994), reprinted in ibid., 577.

116. Savage, *Takeover,* ch. 10. See generally "Symposium: The Last Word? The Constitutional Implications of Presidential Signing Statements," *William and Mary Bill of Rights Journal* 16 (2007): 1.

117. DTA, §1004.

118. See Morrison, "Executive Avoidance," 1248–1250, for a demonstration of the inconsistency of the president's statement with the legislative history of the DTA.

119. See Chapter 10 of this book.

120. Military Commissions Act of 2006, Pub. L. No. 109–366, 120 Stat. 2600.

121. George W. Bush, *President Discusses Creation of Military Commissions to Try Suspected Terrorists* (September 6, 2006), available at http://www.whitehouse .gov/news/releases/2006/09/20060906-3.html.

122. Kate Zernike, "White House Drops a Condition on Interrogation Bill," *New York Times,* September 20, 2006, A21.

123. MCA §§6(a)(2), (a)(3)(a). Section 5 of the MCA makes the Geneva Conventions unenforceable in civil suits against the United States or its agents.

124. Michael J. Matheson, "The Amendment of the War Crimes Act," *American Journal of International Law* 101 (2007): 48.

125. Mark Mazzetti, "Letters Outline Legal Rationale for C.I.A. Tactics," *New York Times*, April 27, 2008, A1. The first of four letters is available at http://graphics8.nytimes.com/packages/pdf/washington/2008042727-INTEL/letter1.pdf. The other three are at the same address, except that the end of the address differs by the letter number, e.g., letter2.pdf.

126. Mazzetti, "Legal Rationale," A12.

127. Eric Lichtblau and Scott Shane, "A Dogged Advocate of Wartime Authority," *New York Times*, August 28, 2007, A1.

128. Philip Shenon and David Johnston, "A Defender of Bush's Power, Gonzales Resigns," *New York Times*, August 28, 2007, A1.

129. Lichtblau, *Bush's Law*, ch. 9.

130. Ibid., 295–296.

131. Philip Shenon, "Inspector General at the Justice Dept. Is Investigating Gonzales's Testimony," *New York Times*, August 31, 2007, A17.

132. Edward T. Pound, Peter H. Stone, Shane Harris, and Corine Hegland, "After Gonzales," *National Journal* (September 1, 2007): 16.

133. Senate Judiciary Committee, *Continuation of Executive Nomination of Michael Mukasey to Be Attorney General of the United States*, 110th Cong., 1st Sess. (October 18, 2007); Philip Shenon, "Attorney General Choice Treads Careful Line at Senate Hearing," *New York Times*, October 18, 2007, A1.

134. Philip Shenon, "Senators Clash with Nominee about Torture," *New York Times*, October 19, 2007, A1.

135. Wright, "Spymaster," 53, quotes Director of National Intelligence Mike McConnell: "If [waterboarding] ever is determined to be torture, there will be a huge penalty to be paid for anyone engaging in it."

136. Scott Shane, "Nominee's Stand Avoiding Tangle of Torture Cases," *New York Times*, November 1, 2007, A1, A16.

137. Eric Lichtblau, "Congress Looks into Obstruction as Calls for Justice Inquiry Rise," *New York Times*, December 8, 2007, A1.

138. Mark Mazzetti, "C.I.A. Was Warned to Keep Interrogation Videotapes," *New York Times*, December 8, 2007, A1.

139. Scott Shane, "The C.I.A. and the Tapes: Sensing Support Shifting Away from Its Methods," *New York Times*, December 13, 2007, A16.

140. Scott Shane, "Waterboarding Focus of Inquiry by Justice Department," *New York Times*, January 23, 2008, A1.

141. Steven Lee Myers, "Bush Vetoes Bill on C.I.A. Tactics, Affirming Legacy," *New York Times*, March 9, 2008, A1.

142. Cole and Lobel, *Less Safe, Less Free*, introduction; and Mayer, *Dark Side*, 175–178.

143. Mayer, *Dark Side*, 331.

12. ADVICE BEGETS ACTION

1. A stylized version of this figure forms the arresting cover of Mark Danner, *Torture and Truth: America, Abu Ghraib, and the War on Terror* (New York: New York Review of Books, 2004).

2. The term "friction" comes from Clausewitz. For an explanation, see John Keegan, *The Second World War* (New York: Viking, 1989), 501–502.

3. George Packer, *The Assassins' Gate: America in Iraq* (New York: Farrar, Straus & Giroux, 2005), 390.

4. James Mann, *Rise of the Vulcans: The History of Bush's War Cabinet* (New York: Viking, 2004), 362–363.

5. Ron Suskind, *The One Percent Doctrine: Deep inside America's Pursuit of Its Enemies since 9/11* (New York: Simon & Schuster, 2006), 22.

6. Richard A. Clarke, *Against All Enemies: Inside America's War on Terror* (New York: Free Press, 2004), 30. The next evening, President Bush pressed Clarke to review everything looking for a connection to Saddam, although Clarke told him Al Qaeda did it. Ibid., 32. Mann, *Vulcans*, 302, reports that in the week after 9/11, "Wolfowitz, joined by Cheney's chief of staff, Scooter Libby, laid out the case for military action against Iraq."

7. Suskind, *One Percent Solution*, 176. Vice President Cheney's office repeatedly manipulated and distorted intelligence data in an attempt to demonstrate Saddam's dangerousness. Ibid., 190. Packer, *Assassins' Gate*, 113, confirms that the advice of experts was unwelcome. All the postwar costs of every kind were absurdly underestimated. For Wolfowitz, "self-righteousness had a dangerous habit of overwhelming inconvenient facts" (117). He made it clear that the "cost of dissent was humiliation and professional suicide" (ibid.).

8. Seymour M. Hersh, *Chain of Command: The Road from 9/11 to Abu Ghraib* (New York: HarperCollins, 2004), 169.

9. Ibid., 222.

10. Packer, *Assassins' Gate*, 303.

11. John Yoo, *War by Other Means: An Insider's Account of the War on Terror* (Chicago: University of Chicago Press, 2006), 18.

12. See Chapter 8 of this book.

13. 10 U.S.C. §893. Military personnel accused of abusing prisoners in Iraq have been charged under this provision.

14. Department of the Army, *Field Manual 34–52, Intelligence Interrogation* (1992), 1–8. The manual was replaced in 2006; the new one still prohibits torture and abuse.

15. The memoranda are reprinted in Danner, *Torture and Truth*, 167–204; and Karen J. Greenberg and Joshua L. Dratel, eds., *The Torture Papers: The Road to Abu Ghraib* (New York: Cambridge University Press, 2005), 223–364.

16. Available at http://graphics8.nytimes.com/packages/pdf/national/OLC_Memo1 .pdf. (In two parts; for the second part, use the same address, but Memo2.pdf.)

17. Yoo relies especially on *Eisentrager*, discussed in Chapter 8, and on *United States v. Verdugo-Urquidez*, 494 U.S. 259 (1990), in which the Court refused to apply the Fourth or Fifth Amendment to limit the rendition of a criminal suspect from Mexico to the United States for trial. Yoo also correctly notes that the Eighth Amendment applies only to persons convicted of crime.

18. 18 U.S.C. §§113, 114, 2261A.

19. Hersh, *Chain of Command*, 2.

20. Explaining why CIA and FBI investigators do not readily cooperate, a CIA official said of the FBI, "They spent their careers trying to catch bank robbers while we spent ours trying to rob banks." Ibid., 102.

21. Ibid., 7.

22. Eric Lichtblau and Scott Shane, "Report Details Dissent on Guantánamo Tactics," *New York Times*, May 21, 2008, A21.

23. See Chapter 11 of this book for a discussion of SERE; for the military, see Senate Armed Services Committee, *The Origins of Aggressive Interrogation Techniques: Part I of the Committee's Inquiry into the Treatment of Detainees in U.S. Custody*, 110th Cong., 2d Sess. (Jun. 17, 2008), available at http://armed-services .senate.gov/hearings.cfm.

24. Department of Defense, Joint Task Force 170, "Request for Approval of Counter-Resistance Strategies" (October 11, 2002), reprinted in Danner, *Torture and Truth*, 167, and in Greenberg and Dratel, *Torture Papers*, 227.

25. Department of Defense, Joint Task Force 170, "Legal Brief on Proposed Counter-Resistance Strategies" (October 11, 2002), reprinted in Danner, *Torture and Truth*, 170, and in Greenberg and Dratel, *Torture Papers*, 229.

26. Hersh, *Chain of Command*, 16.

27. Jane Mayer, "Annals of the Pentagon: The Memo" *New Yorker* (February 27, 2006): 32.

28. The information in this paragraph comes from the U.S. Army's "Schmidt Report," *Army Regulation 15–6 Final Report: Investigation of FBI Allegations of Detainee Abuse at Guantánamo Bay, Cuba Detention Facility* (as amended June 9, 2005), reprinted in Jameel Jaffer and Amrit Singh, eds., *Administration of Torture: A Documentary Record from Washington to Abu Ghraib and Beyond* (New York: Columbia University Press, 2007), A-98, A-110–A-118.

29. Jaffer and Singh, *Administration of Torture*, 7.

30. *United States v. al-Qahtani*, (Military Com'n, May 12, 2008), available at http://www.defenselink.mil/news/commissionsCo-conspirators.html; William Glaberson, "Case against 9/11 Detainee Is Dismissed," *New York Times*, May 14, 2008, A19.

31. Office of the Secretary of Defense, "Counter-Resistance Techniques" (December 2, 2002), reprinted in Danner, *Torture and Truth*, 181, and in Greenberg and Dratel, *Torture Papers*, 236.

32. Mora's chronicle of the events is in a memorandum to the U.S. Navy inspector general titled "Statement for the Record: Office of General Counsel Involvement in Interrogation Issues" (July 7, 2004). His story is told in Jane Mayer, *The Dark Side* (New York: Doubleday, 2008), ch. 9.

33. Charlie Savage, *Takeover: The Return of the Imperial Presidency and the Subversion of American Democracy* (Boston: Little, Brown, 2007), 179.

34. Ibid., 180.

35. Ibid.

36. Federal Bureau of Investigation, "Detainee Interviews (Abusive Interrogation Issues)" (May 6, 2004), reprinted in Jaffer and Singh, *Administration of Torture*, A-130, A-133 (communication of May 30, 2003).

37. Tim Golden, "In U.S. Report, Brutal Details of 2 Afghan Inmates' Deaths," *New York Times*, May 20, 2005, A1.

38. Yoo says that throughout the process, OLC advised the working group on "constitutional and other legal issues." *Insider's Account*, 195.

39. Department of Defense, *Working Group Report on Detainee Interrogations in the Global War on Terrorism: Assessment of Legal, Historical, Policy, and*

Operational Considerations (April 4, 2003), reprinted in Danner, *Torture and Truth,* 187, and in Greenberg and Dratel, *Torture Papers,* 286.

40. For a chart showing the close similarities between *Interrogation* and the report, see Kathleen Clark, "Ethical Issues Raised by the OLC Torture Memorandum," *Journal of National Security Law and Policy* 1 (2005): 455, 472.

41. Secretary of Defense, "Counter-Resistance Techniques in the War on Terrorism" (April 16, 2003), reprinted in Danner, *Torture and Truth,* 199, and in Greenberg and Dratel, *Torture Papers,* 360.

42. Four techniques required advance approval from the secretary: removing privileges, insulting the ego of a prisoner, use of "Mutt and Jeff" interrogators (one harsh, one gentle), and isolation.

43. Luban, *Ethics and Dignity,* 173.

44. Headquarters, U.S. Marine Corps, "Working Group Recommendations on Detainee Interrogations" (February 27, 2003), reprinted in Karen J. Greenberg, ed., *The Torture Debate in America* (New York: Cambridge University Press, 2006), 383.

45. Department of the Air Force, Office of the Judge Advocate General, "Final Report and Recommendations of the Working Group" (February 5, 2003), reprinted in ibid., 377, 378.

46. Luban, *Ethics and Dignity,* 173.

47. The account and the quotations in this paragraph are from Jack Goldsmith, *The Terror Presidency: Law and Judgment inside the Bush Administration* (New York: Norton, 2007). 153–154.

48. The quotations in this paragraph are from Louis Fisher, *Military Tribunals and Presidential Power: American Revolution to the War on Terrorism* (Lawrence: University Press of Kansas, 2005), 195–202.

49. Hersh, *Chain of Command,* 71–72.

50. Packer, *Assassins' Gate,* 326.

51. "War, Not Crime," in Greenberg, *Torture Debate,* 223, 225.

52. Ibid., 227.

53. Scott Shane, David Johnston, and James Risen, "Secret U.S. Endorsement of Severe Interrogations," *New York Times,* October 4, 2007, A1, A23.

54. This paragraph draws on Jaffer and Singh, *Administration of Torture,* 8–9, 26–28.

55. See generally Joseph Margulies, *Guantánamo and the Abuse of Presidential Power* (New York: Simon & Schuster, 2006); Clive Stafford Smith, *Eight O' Clock Ferry to the Windward Side: Seeking Justice in Guantánamo Bay* (New York: Nation Books, 2007); Danner, *Torture and Truth;* Hersh, *Chain of Command.*

56. For the quotation and its source, see Jaffer and Singh, *Administration of Torture,* 31.

57. Fisher, *Military Tribunals,* 202.

58. Hersh, *Chain of Command,* 48.

59. The facts and quotes in this paragraph are from Goldsmith, *Terror Presidency,* 39–41.

60. Savage, *Takeover,* 189–190.

61. Jaffer and Singh, *Administration of Torture,* 23.

62. Major General Geoffrey Miller, "Assessment of DoD Counterterrorism Interrogation and Detention Operations in Iraq" (undated), available at http://www .aclu.org/torturefoia/released/a20.pdf.

63. Jaffer and Singh, *Administration of Torture,* 25–26.

64. Thomas E. Ricks, *Fiasco: The American Military Adventure in Iraq* (New York: Penguin, 2006).

65. Ibid. See also Michael R. Gordon, "Military Hones a New Strategy on Insurgency," *New York Times,* October 5, 2006, A1, reporting the military's absorption of this basic lesson about counterinsurgency.

66. Ricks, *Fiasco,* 408.

67. Hersh, *Chain of Command,* 198.

68. Office of the Inspector General, Department of Defense, "Review of DoD-Directed Investigations of Detainee Abuse" (August 25, 2006), available at http://www.dodig.osd.mil/fo/Foia/ERR/06-INTEL-10-PublicRelease.pdf.

69. These reports are reprinted in Danner, *Torture and Truth,* 279–579, and in Greenberg and Dratel, *Torture Papers,* 405–556, 908–975, and 987–1131.

70. Major General Antonio M. Taguba, *Article 15-6 Investigation of the 800th Military Police Brigade* (March 2004), reprinted in Danner, *Torture and Truth,* 279, and in Greenberg and Dratel, *Torture Papers,* 405.

71. James R. Schlesinger, Harold Brown, Tillie K. Fowler, and Charles A. Horner, *Final Report of the Independent Panel to Review DoD Detention Operations* (August 2004), reprinted in Danner, *Torture and Truth,* 329, and in Greenberg and Dratel, *Torture Papers,* 908.

72. Major General George R. Fay and Lt. General Anthony R. Jones, *Investigation of Intelligence Activities at Abu Ghraib* (August 2004), reprinted in Danner, *Torture and Truth,* 403, and in Greenberg and Dratel, *Torture Papers,* 987.

73. International Committee of the Red Cross, *Report on the Treatment by the Coalition Forces of Prisoners of War and Other Protected Persons by the Geneva Conventions in Iraq during Arrest, Internment, and Interrogation* (February 2004), reprinted in Danner, *Torture and Truth,* 251, and in Greenberg and Dratel, *Torture Papers,* 383.

74. American Bar Association, *Report to the House of Delegates Re: Uses of Torture* (August 2004), reprinted in Greenberg and Dratel, *Torture Papers,* 1132.

75. Some of the most prominent and effective, whose work is cited many times in these pages, have been Mark Danner, Seymour Hersh, Eric Lichtblau, Jane Mayer, George Packer, James Risen, Charlie Savage, and Ron Suskind.

76. Frederick A. O. Schwarz, Jr., and Aziz Z. Huq, *Unchecked and Unbalanced: Presidential Power in a Time of Terror* (New York: New Press, 2007), 93–95.

77. Hersh, *Chain of Command,* 370.

78. Margulies, *Guantánamo,* 136.

79. Kim Lane Schepple, "Hypothetical Torture in the 'War on Terrorism,'" *Journal of National Security Law and Policy* 1 (2005): 285, 300, citing Seth F. Kreimer, "'Torture Lite,' 'Full Bodied' Torture, and the Insulation of Legal Conscience," ibid., 187.

13. BETTER ADVICE

1. Jack Goldsmith, *The Terror Presidency: Law and Judgment inside the Bush Administration* (New York: Norton, 2007). The quotations in this paragraph are from pages 205, 140, 102, and 131.

2. For good general discussions of the ethics of the administration's lawyers, see Kathleen Clark, "Ethical Issues Raised by the OLC Torture Memorandum,"

Journal of National Security Law and Policy 1 (2005): 455; George C. Harris, "The Rule of Law and the War on Terror: The Professional Responsibilities of Executive Branch Lawyers in the Wake of 9/11," *Journal of National Security Law and Policy* 1 (2005): 409; Cornelia Pillard, "Unitariness and Myopia: The Executive Branch, Legal Process, and Torture," *Indiana Law Journal* 81 (2006): 1297; Jesselyn Radack, "Tortured Legal Ethics: The Role of the Government Advisor in the War on Terrorism," *University of Colorado Law Review* 77 (2006): 1; and Jeremy Waldron, "Torture and Positive Law: Jurisprudence for the White House," *Columbia Law Review* 105 (2005): 1681.

3. Frederick A. O. Schwarz, Jr., and Aziz Z. Huq, *Unchecked and Unbalanced: Presidential Power in a Time of Terror* (New York: New Press, 2007), 187–188, assess the performance of the OLC lawyers as follows: "However genuine their beliefs, they breached clear professional obligations in the way they voiced them. They failed even to mention key Supreme Court cases. They failed to identify, let alone respond to, weaknesses in their legal arguments. They failed to consider the expertise of other parts of the federal government such as the military and the State Department. They failed to consider harms to the nation that would flow from following their cramped legal advice. And they failed to note that their legal analysis would handicap America's leadership in the worldwide battle for human rights."

4. Stephen Gillers, "Torture: The Road to Abu Ghraib and Beyond," in Karen J. Greenberg, ed., *The Torture Debate in America* (New York: Cambridge University Press, 2006), 28.

5. See Chapter 4 of this book.

6. Paul Freund, "On Presidential Privilege," *Harvard Law Review* 88 (1974): 13, 20.

7. See, for example, David Cole and James X. Dempsey, *Terrorism and the Constitution*, 2d ed. (New York: New Press, 2002). This book, although highly critical of the executive branch's responses to terrorism, certainly reveals the existence of a full legal toolkit for the government to use in that struggle.

8. Harold H. Bruff, *Balance of Forces: Separation of Powers Law in the Administrative State* (Durham, N.C.: Carolina Academic Press, 2006), ch. 5.

9. Ibid., ch. 16.

10. See Chapter 4 of this book.

11. For an overview of impeachment, see Bruff, *Balance of Forces*, ch. 13.

12. Neal K. Katyal, "Internal Separation of Powers: Checking Today's Most Dangerous Branch from within," *Yale Law Journal* 115 (2006): 2314, 2314.

13. M. Elizabeth Magill, "Can Process Cure Substance: A Response to Neal Katyal's 'Internal Separation of Powers,'" *Yale Law Journal* pocket part (November 2, 2006), available at http://thepocketpart.org/2006/11/2/magill.html.

14. Pillard, "Unitariness and Myopia," 1310.

15. Christopher Kutz, "The Lawyers Know Sin: Complicity in Torture," in Greenberg, *Torture Debate*, 241, makes an argument for criminal liability of the administration's lawyers as accessories.

16. Richard B. Bilder and Detlev F. Vagts, "Speaking Law to Power: Lawyers and Torture," in ibid., 151, 154; see also Geoffrey C. Hazard, Jr., "How Far May a Lawyer Go in Assisting a Client in Unlawful Conduct?" *University of Miami Law Review* 35 (1981): 669.

17. Scott Horton, "Through a Mirror Darkly: Applying the Geneva Conventions to a New Kind of Warfare," in Greenberg, *Torture Debate,* 136. German Field Marshal Keitel derided the laws of war as "obsolete," ibid., 140, a term later echoed unknowingly by Alberto Gonzales.

18. Bruff, *Balance of Forces,* ch. 12.

19. Michael Ratner and Peter Weiss, "Litigating against Torture: The German Criminal Prosecution," in Greenberg, *Torture Debate,* 261, describe the litigation. See also http://www.ccr-ny.org.

20. Ratner and Weiss.

21. *Mitchell v. Forsyth,* 472 U.S. 511, 524 (1985).

22. Scott Horton, "Deconstructing John Yoo," *Harper's,* January, 2008, available at http://harpers.org/archive/2008/01/hbc-90002226.

23. Bruff, *Balance of Forces,* ch. 12.

24. OPR's charter is 28 CFR §0.39. In 0.39a(a)(1), the office may "investigate and refer for appropriate action allegations of misconduct involving Department attorneys that relate to the exercise of their authority to . . . provide legal advice"; (3) report to responsible Department officials the results . . . and, when appropriate, make recommendations for disciplinary and other corrective action"; and (6) engage in liaison with the bar disciplinary authorities of the states . . . with respect to professional misconduct matters."

25. Bruff, *Balance of Forces,* 323.

26. American Bar Association, *Model Rules of Professional Conduct 2.1* (2003).

27. Geoffrey C. Hazard, Jr., and William H. Hodes, *The Law of Lawyering,* 3d ed., vol. 1 (Gaithersburg, Md.: Aspen Law and Business, 2001), §23.2.

28. Christopher Edley, Jr., "The Torture Memos and Academic Freedom," available at http://www.law.berkeley.edu/news/2008/edley041008.html.

29. Eric Lichtblau, *Bush's Law: The Remaking of American Justice* (New York: Pantheon, 2008), 157.

30. See the discussion of OLC guidelines in Chapter 4 of this book. In the spirit of the guidelines, I offer future executive advisers a template for analysis, orderly steps that draw attention to the sources and nature of both powers and limits, that is, disaggregating issues of fact, policy, and law. Every legal issue depends on a set of judgments or hypotheses about underlying facts. What are they here? Are they in dispute? How great is the distance between the White House and the conditions as they exist? Should more questions be asked about the facts before providing advice, or should the advice be made contingent on stated fact assumptions, which might be identified as subject to some doubt? What policy preference is driving the opinion request? Does it reflect a traditional policy position of the executive branch, or is it new? Does the request reflect a perception of emergency, and if so, as determined by whom? Where is the line between policy and law? Regarding identifying and appraising constitutional sources of executive power, what constitutional provisions provide support for the proposed action? What is their constitutional history, and how closely does it relate to the proposal? How have the courts interpreted the provisions? Here it is necessary to distinguish the holdings from the dicta of cases and to be cautious about relying on the latter. What have been the historic interpretations of the executive branch? Are they consistent and persuasive? Concerning identifying

and appraising the statutory context, what constitutional provisions empower Congress in this situation? What is their constitutional history, and how closely does it relate to the proposal? How have the courts interpreted the provisions? Again it is necessary to distinguish the holdings from the dicta of cases and to be cautious about relying on the latter. What have been the historic interpretations of members of Congress and their lawyers? Are they consistent and persuasive? Does the acquiescence doctrine apply to the executive-congressional interrelation in this context and with what persuasive force? Where do we wind up within Justice Jackson's formulation for the intersection of powers? What provisional conclusion about the legality of the proposal emerges? In appraising the prospects for litigation and adverse congressional reaction, if the executive action will be secret from both Congress and the public, a special obligation of sober second thought emerges. This counsels consideration of wider consultation and opportunity for criticism within the executive branch and deference to those having experience with the subject matter involved. Similarly, if the courts are unlikely to review the proposed action, special caution should ensue. The likelihood that Congress and the public will eventually learn about the action, which is always substantial, should lead the lawyer to ask how the action will appear to outsiders and what the consequences for the executive will likely be in the short and long term. This inquiry can naturally include analysis about alternative actions that may achieve the policy goal wholly or partially with less legal and political jeopardy. At the end of the process, the question remains: can the claim of power be advanced with right and conscience? Is the proposed action lawful, in the independent professional judgment of the lawyer? That conclusion is necessary to meet the obligation of the oath to defend the Constitution. And is the lawyer's professional conscience sufficiently satisfied with the answer to allow him or her to sign the opinion, in the expectation that it will someday be made available for all to see? That is a lot of questions, to be sure, but most important executive initiatives raise a lot of issues.

31. Philip Bobbitt, *Terror and Consent: The Wars for the Twenty-First Century* (New York: Knopf, 2008), 288. See also David Cole and Jules Lobel, *Less Safe, Less Free: Why America Is Losing the War on Terror* (New York: New Press, 2007), ch. 12.

BIBLIOGRAPHY

Ackerman, Bruce. "The Emergency Constitution." *Yale Law Journal* 113 (2004): 1029–1092.

———. "This Is Not a War." *Yale Law Journal* 113 (2004): 1871–1908.

———. *Before the Next Attack: Preserving Civil Liberties in an Age of Terrorism.* New Haven, Conn.: Yale University Press, 2006.

Ackerman, Bruce, et al. *Lawyers' Statement on Bush Administration's Torture Memos.* Human Rights Watch, August 2004. Available at http://www.hrw.org/pub/2004/lawyers-statement.pdf.

Adler, David Gray, and Larry N. George, eds. *The Constitution and the Conduct of American Foreign Policy.* Lawrence: University Press of Kansas, 1996.

Adler, E. Scott. *Why Congressional Reforms Fail: Reelection and the House Committee System.* Chicago: University of Chicago Press, 2002.

"Agora: Military Commissions Act of 2006." *American Journal of International Law* 101 (2007): 1 ff.

Alexander, Larry, and Frederick Schauer. "On Extrajudicial Constitutional Interpretation." *Harvard Law Review* 110 (1997): 1359–1387.

American Bar Association. *Report and Recommendations on Military Commissions.* ABA Task Force on Terrorism and the Law, 2002. Available at http://www.abanet.org/leadership/military.pdf.

———. *Model Rules of Professional Conduct.* Chicago: ABA Center for Professional Responsibility, 2003. Available at http://www.abanet.org/cpr/mrpc/mrpc_toc.html.

———. *Resolution 10-B.* August 2004. ABA House of Delegates. Available at http://www.abanet.org/leadership/2003/journal/10b.pdf.

———. "Report to the House of Delegates Re: Uses of Torture." August 2004. In *The Torture Papers: The Road to Abu Ghraib,* edited by Karen J. Greenberg and Joshua L. Dratel, 1132. New York: Cambridge University Press, 2005.

American Law Institute. *Restatement (Third) of the Law Governing Lawyers.* Philadelphia, Pa.: American Law Institute, 2000.

Andrew, Christopher. *For the President's Eyes Only: Secret Intelligence and the American Presidency from Washington to Bush.* New York: HarperCollins, 1995.

Axelrod, Robert. *The Evolution of Cooperation.* New York: BasicBooks, 1984.

Baker, James E. *In the Common Defense: National Security Law for Perilous Times.* New York: Cambridge University Press, 2007.

Baker, Nancy V. *Conflicting Loyalties: Law and Politics in the Attorney General's Office, 1789–1990.* Lawrence: University Press of Kansas, 1992.

———. *General Ashcroft: Attorney at War.* Lawrence: University Press of Kansas, 2006.

Bamford, James. *The Puzzle Palace.* Boston: Houghton Mifflin, 1982.

———. *Body of Secrets.* New York: Doubleday, 2001.

———. "Big Brother Is Listening." *Atlantic Monthly* (April 2006): 65–70.

Banks, William C., and Peter Raven-Hansen. "While Congress Slept: The Iran-Contra Affair and Institutional Responsibility for Covert Operations." *Syracuse Journal of International Law and Commerce* 14 (1988): 291–361.

———. *National Security Law and the Power of the Purse.* New York: Oxford University Press, 1994.

———. "The Death of FISA." *Minnesota Law Review* 91 (2007): 1209–1301.

Barnes, Fred. *Rebel-in-Chief: Inside the Bold and Controversial Presidency of George W. Bush.* New York: Crown Forum, 2006.

Barr, William P. "Common Legislative Encroachments on Executive Branch Constitutional Authority." In *The Constitution and the Attorneys General,* edited by H. Jefferson Powell. Durham, N.C.: Carolina Academic Press, 1999.

Barrett, Paul M. "A Young Lawyer Helps Chart Shift in Foreign Policy." *Wall Street Journal,* September 12, 2005, 1–12.

Barron, David J., and Martin S. Lederman. "The Commander in Chief at the Lowest Ebb—Framing the Problem, Doctrine, and Original Understanding." *Harvard Law Review* 121 (2008): 689–804.

Basler, Roy P., ed. *Works of Lincoln.* Vol. 4. New Brunswick, N.J.: Rutgers University Press, 1953.

Bazan, Elizabeth, and Jennifer K. Elsea. *Presidential Authority to Conduct Warrantless Electronic Surveillance to Gather Foreign Intelligence Information.* Washington, D.C.: Congressional Research Service Report, 2006.

Belknap, Michel R. "The Supreme Court Goes to War: The Meaning and Implications of the *Nazi Saboteur* Case." *Military Law Review* 89 (1980): 59–95.

Bell, Griffin B., with Ronald J. Ostrow. *Taking Care of the Law.* New York: William Morrow, 1982.

Bellia, Patricia L. "The Story of the *Steel Seizure* Case." In *Presidential Power Stories,* edited by Curtis Bradley and Christopher Schroeder. New York: Foundation Press, 2008.

Benjamin, Daniel, and Stephen Simon. *The Next Attack: The Failure of the War on Terror and a Strategy for Getting It Right.* New York: Henry Holt, 2005.

Berman, Paul Schiff. "Review Essay: Seeing beyond the Limits of International Law." *Texas Law Review* 84 (2006): 1265–1306.

Bernstein, Cyrus. "The Saboteur Trial: A Case History." *George Washington Law Review* 11 (1943): 131–190.

Bestor, Arthur. "Separation of Powers in the Domain of Foreign Affairs: The Original Intent of the Constitution Historically Examined." *Seton Hall Law Review* 5 (1974): 527–665.

Biddle, Francis. *In Brief Authority.* Garden City, N.Y.: Doubleday, 1962.

Bilder, Richard B. "Book Review." *American Journal of International Law* 100 (2006): 490 ff.

Bilder, Richard B., and Detlev F. Vagts. "Speaking Law to Power: Lawyers and Torture." In *The Torture Debate in America,* edited by Karen J. Greenberg, 151. New York: Cambridge University Press, 2006.

Bloch, Susan Low. "The Early Role of the Attorney General in Our Constitutional Scheme: In the Beginning There Was Pragmatism." *Duke Law Journal* 1989 (1989): 561–653.

Bobbitt, Philip. *Constitutional Fate: Theory of the Constitution.* New York: Oxford University Press, 1984.

———. *Terror and Consent: The Wars for the Twenty-First Century.* New York: Knopf, 2008.

Bolt, Robert. *A Man for All Seasons.* New York: Vintage, 1960.

Bonner, Raymond, and Jane Perlez. "British Report Criticizes U.S. Treatment of Terror Suspects." *New York Times,* July 28, 2007, A5.

Borchard, Edwin. "The Attorney General's Opinion on the Exchange of Destroyers for Naval Bases." *American Journal of International Law* 34 (1940): 690–697.

Bradley, Curtis A. "*Chevron* Deference and Foreign Affairs." *Virginia Law Review* 86 (2000): 649 ff.

———. "The Military Commissions Act, Habeas Corpus, and the Geneva Conventions." *American Journal of International Law* 101 (2007): 322 ff.

Bradley, Curtis A., and Martin S. Flaherty. "Executive Power Essentialism and Foreign Affairs." *Michigan Law Review* 102 (2004): 545–688.

Bradley, Curtis A., and Jack L. Goldsmith. "The Constitutional Validity of Military Commissions." *Green Bag 2d* 5 (2002): 249 ff.

———. "Congressional Authorization and the War on Terrorism." *Harvard Law Review* 118 (2005): 2047–2133.

———. "Rejoinder: The War on Terrorism: International Law, Clear Statement Requirements, and Constitutional Design." *Harvard Law Review* 118 (2005): 2683–2697.

———. *Foreign Relations Law, Cases, and Materials.* 2d ed. New York: Aspen, 2006.

Bradley, Curtis A., et al. Letter to Bill Frist, Majority Leader, U.S. Senate et al. January 9, 2006. Available at http://www.fas.org/irp/agency/doj/fisa/doj-response.pdf.

Briggs, Herbert W. "Neglected Aspects of the Destroyer Deal." *American Journal of International Law* 34 (1940): 569–587.

Brinkley, Joel, and Stephen Engelberg, eds. *Report of the Congressional Committees Investigating the Iran-Contra Affair with the Minority Views.* Abridged ed. New York: Times Books, 1988.

Brooks, Rosa Ehrenreich. "The New Imperialism: Violence, Norms, and the 'Rule of Law.'" *Michigan Law Review* 101 (2003): 2275–2340.

Brownstein, Ronald. *The Second Civil War: How Extreme Partisanship Has Paralyzed Washington and Polarized America.* New York: Penguin, 2007.

Bruff, Harold H. "Judicial Review and the President's Statutory Powers." *Virginia Law Review* 68 (1982): 1–61.

———. *Balance of Forces: Separation of Powers Law in the Administrative State.* Durham, N.C.: Carolina Academic Press, 2006.

———. "The Incompatibility Principle." *Administrative Law Review* 59 (2007): 225–268.

———. "The Story of *Dames & Moore:* Resolution of an International Crisis by Executive Agreement." In *Presidential Power Stories,* edited by Curtis Bradley and Christopher Schroeder. New York: Foundation Press, 2008.

Bryant, Christopher, and Carl Tobias. "*Youngstown* Revisited." *Hastings Constitutional Law Quarterly* 29 (2002): 373–438.

Bumatay, Patrick J. "Causes, Commitments, and Counsels: A Study of Political and Professional Obligations among Bush Administration Lawyers." *Journal of the Legal Profession* 31 (2007): 1–42.

Bumiller, Elisabeth. *Condoleezza Rice: A Biography.* New York: Random House, 2007.

Burns, James MacGregor. *Roosevelt: The Soldier of Freedom, 1940–1945.* New York: Harcourt Brace Jovanovich, 1970.

Bush, George W. "Military Order of November 13, 2001: Detention, Treatment, and Trial of Certain Non-Citizens in the War on Terrorism." In *The Torture Papers: The Road to Abu Ghraib,* edited by Karen J. Greenberg and Joshua L. Dratel, 29. New York: Cambridge University Press, 2005.

———. "President's Statement on Signing of H.R. 2863." Office of the Press Secretary, December 30, 2005. Available at http://www.whitehouse.gov/news/releases/2005/12/20051230-8.html.

———. "President Discusses Creation of Military Commissions to Try Suspected Terrorists." Office of the Press Secretary, September 6, 2006. Available at http://www.whitehouse.gov/news/releases/2006/09/20060906-3.html.

Cain, Marvin. *Lincoln's Attorney General: Edward Bates of Missouri.* Columbia: University of Missouri Press, 1965.

Calabresi, Steven G. "Some Normative Arguments for the Unitary Executive." *Arkansas Law Review* 48 (1995): 23–104.

Calhoun, Emily. "The Accounting: Habeas Corpus and Enemy Combatants." *University of Colorado Law Review* 79 (2008): 77–136.

Cannon, Lou, and Carl M. Cannon. *Reagan's Disciple: George W. Bush's Troubled Quest for a Presidential Legacy.* New York: PublicAffairs, 2008.

Caplan, Lincoln. "Lawyers' Standards in Free Fall." *Los Angeles Times,* July 20, 2004, B13.

Caron, David D. "If Afghanistan Has Failed, Then Afghanistan Is Dead: 'Failed States' and the Inappropriate Substitution of Legal Conclusion for Political Description." In *The Torture Debate in America,* edited by Karen J. Greenberg. New York: Cambridge University Press, 2006, 214.

Central Intelligence Agency. *KUBARK Counterintelligence Interrogation.* National Security Archive, 1963. Available at http://www.gwu.edu/~nsarchiv/NSAEBB/NSAEBB122/#kubark.

———. *Human Resource Exploitation Training Manual.* National Security Archive, 1983. Available at http://www.gwu.edu/~nsarchiv/NSAEBB/NSAEBB122/#hre.

Chayes, Abram. *The Cuban Missile Crisis.* Oxford, U.K.: Oxford University Press, 1974.

Chemerinsky, Erwin. "Enemy Combatants and Separation of Powers." *Journal of National Security Law and Policy* 1 (2005): 73–87.

Chernow, Ron. *Alexander Hamilton.* New York: Penguin, 2004.

Chesney, Robert M. "Enemy Combatants after *Hamdan v. Rumsfeld:* State Secrets and the Limits of National Security Litigation." *George Washington Law Review* 75 (2007): 1249–1332.

Churchill, Winston. *A History of the English-Speaking Peoples.* 2 vols. New York: Dodd, Mead, 1956.

Cinquegrana, Americo. "The Walls (and Wires) Have Ears: The Background and First Ten Years of the Foreign Intelligence Surveillance Act of 1978." *University of Pennsylvania Law Review* 137 (1989): 793–828.

Clark, Kathleen. "Ethical Issues Raised by the OLC Torture Memorandum." *Journal of National Security Law and Policy* 1 (2005): 455–472.

Clarke, Richard A. *Against All Enemies: Inside America's War on Terror*. New York: Free Press, 2004.

Clayton, Cornell W. *The Politics of Justice: The Attorney General and the Making of Legal Policy*. Armonk, N.Y.: M. E. Sharpe, 1992.

Cohen, William S., and George J. Mitchell. *Men of Zeal: A Candid Inside Story of the Iran-Contra Hearings*. New York: Viking, 1988.

Cole, David. *Enemy Aliens: Double Standards and Constitutional Freedoms in the War on Terrorism*. New York: New Press, 2003.

———. "The Priority of Morality: The Emergency Constitution's Blind Spot." *Yale Law Journal* 113 (2004): 1753–1772.

———. "What Bush Wants to Hear." *New York Review of Books* (November 17, 2005): 18 ff.

Cole, David, and James X. Dempsey. *Terrorism and the Constitution*. 2d ed. New York: New Press, 2002.

Cole, David, and Jules Lobel, *Less Safe, Less Free: Why America Is Losing the War on Terror*. New York: New Press, 2007.

Colton, David E. "Speaking Truth to Power: Intelligence Oversight in an Imperfect World." *University of Pennsylvania Law Review* 137 (1988) 571–613.

Comey, James B. "Intelligence under the Law." *Green Bag 2d* 10 (Summer 2007): 439 ff.

Commission on CIA Activities within the United States. *Report to the President*. Washington, D.C.: U.S. Government Printing Office, 1975.

Commission on Wartime Relocation and Internment of Civilians. *Personal Justice Denied*. Washington, D.C.: U.S. Government Printing Office, 1983.

Corwin, Edward S. *Total War and the Constitution*. New York: Knopf, 1947.

———. *The President: Office and Powers 1787–1984*, edited by Randall W. Bland, Theodore T. Hindson, and Jack W. Peltason. 5th rev. ed. New York: New York University Press, 1984.

Cramton, Roger C. "On the Steadfastness and Courage of Government Lawyers." *John Marshall Law Review* 23 (1990): 165–180.

Crovitz, L. Gordon, and Jeremy A. Rabkin, eds. *The Fettered Presidency: Legal Constraints on the Executive Branch*. Washington, D.C.: American Enterprise Institute, 1989.

Cummings, Homer, and Carl McFarland. *Federal Justice: Chapters in the History of Justice and the Federal Executive*. New York: Macmillan, 1937.

Cunningham, Noble E. *The Process of Government under Jefferson*. Princeton, N.J.: Princeton University Press, 1974.

Currie, David P. "The Constitution in Congress: The Third Congress, 1793–1795." *University of Chicago Law Review* 63 (1996): 1–48.

Dallek, Robert. *Franklin D. Roosevelt and American Foreign Policy, 1932–1945*. New York: Oxford University Press, 1995.

———. *An Unfinished Life: John Fitzgerald Kennedy, 1917–1963*. Boston: Little, Brown, 2003.

Danelski, David. "The Saboteurs' Case." *Journal of Supreme Court History* 1 (1996): 61–82.

Danner, Mark. *Torture and Truth: America, Abu Ghraib, and the War on Terror*. New York: New York Review of Books, 2004.

Daws, Gavan. *Prisoners of the Japanese*. New York: HarperCollins, 1996.

Dean, John. *Blind Ambition*. New York: Simon & Schuster, 1976.

Dellinger, Walter. "The Constitutional Separation of Powers between the President and Congress." In *The Constitution and the Attorneys General*, edited by H. Jefferson Powell, 617. Durham, N.C.: Carolina Academic Press, 1999.

———. "The Legal Significance of Presidential Signing Statements." In *The Constitution and the Attorneys General*, edited by H. Jefferson Powell, 563. Durham, N.C.: Carolina Academic Press, 1999.

———. "Presidential Authority to Decline to Enforce Unconstitutional Statutes." In *The Constitution and the Attorneys General*, edited by H. Jefferson Powell, 577. Durham, N.C.: Carolina Academic Press, 1999.

Dellinger, Walter, et. al. "Ten Principles to Guide the Office of Legal Counsel." *Indiana Law Journal* 81 (2006): 1345–1354.

Dershowitz, Alan. "Tortured Reasoning." In *Torture: A Collection*, edited by Sanford Levinson, 257. New York: Oxford University Press, 2004.

Devins, Neal. "Government Lawyering." Special ed. *Law and Contemporary Problems* 61 (Winter–Spring 1998): 1–190.

Doctorow, E. L. *The March*. New York: Random House, 2005.

Donald, David H. *Lincoln*. New York: Simon & Schuster, 1995.

Donovan, Robert J. *Tumultuous Years: The Presidency of Harry S Truman, 1949–1953*. New York: Norton, 1982.

Dorfman, Ariel. "Foreword: The Tyranny of Terror." In *Torture: A Collection*, edited by Sanford Levinson, 3. New York: Oxford University Press, 2004.

Dostoyevsky, Fyodor. *The Brothers Karamozov*, translated by Constance Garnett. New York: Signet, 1957.

Draper, Robert. *Dead Certain: The Presidency of George W. Bush*. New York: Free Press, 2007.

Draper, Theodore. *A Very Thin Line: The Iran-Contra Affairs*. New York: Hill & Wang, 1991.

Dunlap, Charles J., Jr. "Law and Military Interventions: Preserving Humanitarian Values in 21st-Century Conflicts." Cambridge, Mass.: Harvard University, John F. Kennedy School of Government, Center for Human Rights Policy. Available at http://www.ksg.harvard.edu/cchrp/Web%20Working%20Papers/Use%20of%20Force/Dunlap2001.pdf.

Eastland, Terry. *Energy in the Executive*. New York: Free Press, 1992.

Edgar, Harold, and Benno C. Schmidt. "*Curtiss-Wright* Comes Home: Executive Power and National Security Secrecy." *Harvard Civil Rights–Civil Liberties Law Review* 21 (1986): 349–408.

Edley, Christopher, Jr. *The Torture Memos and Academic Freedom*. Berkeley: University of California at Berkeley School of Law. Available at http://www.law.berkeley.edu/news/2008/edley041008.html.

Elkins, Stanley, and Eric McKitrick. *The Age of Federalism: The Early American Republic, 1788–1800*. New York: Oxford University Press, 1993.

Elshtain, Jean Bethke. "Reflections on the Problem of 'Dirty Hands.'" In *Torture: A Collection*, edited by Sanford Levinson, 77. New York: Oxford University Press, 2004.

Ely, John Hart. *War and Responsibility*. Princeton, N.J.: Princeton University Press, 1993.

Eskridge, William N., Jr. *Dynamic Statutory Interpretation*. Cambridge, Mass.: Harvard University Press, 1994.

Eskridge, William N., Jr., Philip P. Frickey, and Elizabeth Garrett. *Legislation and Statutory Interpretation.* 2d ed. New York: Foundation Press, 2006.

Evans, C. Lawrence, and Walter J. Oleszek. *Congress under Fire: Reform Politics and the Republican Majority.* Boston: Houghton Mifflin, 1997.

Fagelson, David. "The Constitution and National Security: Covert Action in the Age of Intelligence Oversight." *Journal of Law and Policy* 5 (1989): 275–347.

Fallon, Richard H., Jr. "Executive Power and the Political Constitution." *Utah Law Review* 2007 (2007): 1–23.

Farber, Daniel. *Lincoln's Constitution.* Chicago: University of Chicago Press, 2003.

Fay, George R., and Anthony R. Jones. "Investigation of Intelligence Activities at Abu Ghraib." In *The Torture Papers: The Road to Abu Ghraib*, edited by Karen J. Greenberg and Joshua L. Dratel, 987. New York: Cambridge University Press, 2005.

Federal Bar Association. *Model Rules of Professional Conduct for Federal Lawyers.* 1.13. Arlington, Va.: Federal Bar Association, 1990.

Federal Bureau of Investigation. "Detainee Interviews (Abusive Interrogation Issues)." May 6, 2004. In *Administration of Torture: A Documentary Record from Washington to Abu Ghraib and Beyond*, edited by Jameel Jaffer and Amrit Singh, A-130. New York: Columbia University Press, 2007.

Fein, Bruce E. "Promoting the President's Policies through Legal Advocacy: An Ethical Imperative of the Government Attorney." *Federal Bar News and Journal* 30 (September–October 1983): 406 ff.

Feldman, Noah. "Choices of Law, Choices of War." *Harvard Journal of Law and Public Policy* 25 (2002): 457–485.

Fellmeth, Aaron X. "A Divorce Waiting to Happen: Franklin Roosevelt and the Law of Neutrality, 1935–1941." *Buffalo Journal of International Law* 3 (Winter 1996–1997): 413–517.

Ferguson, Niall. "The Monarchy of George W. Bush." *Vanity Fair* (September 2004): 382 ff.

Finkelman, Paul. "Limiting Rights in Times of Crisis: Our Civil War Experience—A History Lesson for a Post-9/11 America." *Cardozo Public Law, Policy, and Ethics Journal* 2 (2003): 25–48.

Fisher, Louis. "How to Avoid Iran-Contras." *California Law Review* 76 (1988): 939–960.

———. *Nazi Saboteurs on Trial: A Military Tribunal and American Law.* Lawrence: University Press of Kansas, 2003.

———. *Military Tribunals and Presidential Power: American Revolution to the War on Terrorism.* Lawrence: University Press of Kansas, 2005.

———. *In the Name of National Security: Unchecked Presidential Power and the Reynolds Case.* Lawrence: University Press of Kansas, 2006.

———. "Lost Constitutional Moorings: Recovering the War Power." *Indiana Law Journal* 81 (2006): 1199–1254.

———. *Constitutional Conflicts between Congress and the President.* 5th ed. Lawrence: University Press of Kansas, 2007.

Flaherty, Martin S. "History 'Lite' in Modern American Constitutionalism." *Columbia Law Review* 95 (1995): 523–590.

———. "The Most Dangerous Branch." *Yale Law Review* 105 (1996): 1725–1839.

Ford, Paul L., ed. *Writings of Thomas Jefferson.* Vol. 8, 10–11. New York: Putnam, 1904.

Franck, Thomas. *Political Questions/Judicial Answers.* Princeton, N.J.: Princeton University Press, 1992.

Freidel, Frank. *Franklin D. Roosevelt: A Rendezvous with Destiny.* Boston: Little, Brown, 1990.

Freund, Paul. "On Presidential Privilege." *Harvard Law Review* 88 (1974): 13–39.

Fried, Charles. "The Lawyer as Friend: The Moral Foundations of the Lawyer-Client Relation." *Yale Law Journal* 85 (1976): 1060–1089.

———. *Order and Law: Arguing the Reagan Revolution—A Firsthand Account.* New York: Simon & Schuster, 1991.

Friel, Brian. "Defense Attorney." *National Journal.* (March 4, 2006): 18 ff.

Frost, Amanda. "The State Secrets Privilege and Separation of Powers." *Fordham Law Review* 75 (2007): 1931–1964.

Frum, David. *The Right Man.* New York: Random House, 2003.

Fukuyama, Francis. *America at the Crossroads: Democracy, Power, and the Neoconservative Legacy.* New Haven, Conn.: Yale University Press, 2006.

Garvey, John H., T. Alexander Aleinikoff, and Daniel A. Farber, eds. *Modern Constitutional Theory: A Reader.* 5th ed. St. Paul, Minn.: West, 2004.

Gellman, Barton. *Angler: The Cheney Vice Presidency.* New York: Penguin, 2008.

Gentry, Curt. *J. Edgar Hoover: The Man and the Secrets.* New York: Norton, 1991.

Gerhart, Eugene C. *America's Advocate: Robert H. Jackson.* Indianapolis, Ind.: Bobbs-Merrill, 1958.

Gillers, Stephen. "Torture: The Road to Abu Ghraib and Beyond." In *The Torture Debate in America,* edited by Karen J. Greenberg, 28. New York: Cambridge University Press, 2006.

Glaberson, William. "Pentagon Study Sees Threat in Guantánamo Detainees." *New York Times,* July 26, 2007, A15.

———. "Hurdles Seen as Capital Charges Are Filed in 9/11 Case." *New York Times,* February 12, 2008, A14.

———. "Case against 9/11 Detainee Is Dismissed." *New York Times,* May 14, 2008, A19.

Glennon, Michael J. "Two Views of Presidential Foreign Affairs Power: *Little v. Barreme* or *Curtiss-Wright?*" *Yale Journal of International Law* 13 (1988): 5 ff.

———. *Constitutional Diplomacy.* Princeton, N.J.: Princeton University Press, 1990.

Golden, Tim. "After Terror, a Secret Rewriting of Military Law." *New York Times,* October 24, 2004, A1.

———. "In U.S. Report, Brutal Details of 2 Afghan Inmates' Deaths." *New York Times,* May 20, 2005, A1.

———. "U.S. Says It Fears Detainee Abuse in Repatriation." *New York Times,* April 30, 2006, A1.

———. "For Guantánamo Review Boards, Limits Abound." *New York Times,* December 31, 2006, A1.

Goldsmith, Jack L. *The Terror Presidency: Law and Judgment inside the Bush Administration.* New York: Norton, 2007.

Goldsmith, Jack L., and John F. Manning. "The President's Completion Power." *Yale Law Journal* 115 (2006): 2280–2313.

Goldsmith, Jack L., and Eric A. Posner. *The Limits of International Law.* New York: Oxford University Press, 2005.

Goldsmith, Jack L., and Cass R. Sunstein. "Military Tribunals and Legal Culture: What a Difference Sixty Years Makes." *Constitutional Commentary* 19 (2002): 261.

Gonzales, Alberto. Letter to Patrick Leahy and Arlen Specter. U.S. Department of Justice, January 17, 2007. Available at http://www.fas.org/irp/agency/doj/fisa/ag011707.pdf.

Gonzales, Alberto, and Michael V. Hayden. Press Briefing by Attorney General Alberto Gonzales and General Michael Hayden, Principal Deputy Director for National Intelligence. U.S. Office of the Press Secretary, December 19, 2005. Available at http://www.whitehouse.gov/news/releases/2005/12/20051219-1.html.

Gonzales, Alberto, et al. Press Briefing. Office of the Press Secretary, June 22, 2004. Available at http://www.whitehouse.gov/news/releases/2004/06/20040622-14.html.

Goodnough, Abby, and Scott Shane. "Padilla Is Guilty on All Charges in Terror Trial." *New York Times,* August 17, 2007, A1.

Goodwin, Doris Kearns. *No Ordinary Time: Franklin and Eleanor Roosevelt—The Home Front in World War II.* New York: Touchstone, 1994.

———. *Team of Rivals: The Political Genius of Abraham Lincoln.* New York: Simon & Schuster, 2005.

Gordon, Michael R. "Military Hones a New Strategy on Insurgency." *New York Times,* October 5, 2006, A1.

Greenberg, Karen J., ed. *The Torture Debate in America.* New York: Cambridge University Press, 2006.

Greenburg, Jan Crawford, Howard L. Rosenberg, and Ariane de Vogue. "Top Bush Advisors Approved 'Enhanced Interrogation': Detailed Discussions Were Held about Techniques to Use on Al Qaeda Suspects." *ABC News,* April 9, 2008. Available at http://abcnews.go.com/print?id=4583256.

Greene, Abner S. "Checks and Balances in an Era of Presidential Lawmaking." *University of Chicago Law Review* 61 (1994): 123–196.

Greenhouse, Linda. "The Supreme Court: The Arguments; Court Hears Case on U.S. Detainees." *New York Times,* April 29, 2004, A1.

———. "Detainees at Guantánamo Fight Further Appeal Delay." *New York Times,* February 22, 2008, A17.

Grey, Stephen. *Ghost Plane.* New York: St. Martin's, 2006.

Grimmett, Richard F. *Authorization for Use of Military Force in Response to the 9/11 Attacks (Pub. L. 107-40): Legislative History.* Washington, D.C.: Congressional Research Service Report No. RS22357.

Gross, Oren. "The Prohibition on Torture and the Limits of the Law." In *Torture: A Collection,* edited by Sanford Levinson, 229. New York: Oxford University Press, 2004.

Gudridge, Patrick O. "Remember *Endo?*" *Harvard Law Review* 116 (2003): 1933.

Halberstam, David. *The Coldest Winter: America and the Korean War.* New York: Hyperion, 2007.

Hamilton, Alexander. *Federalist Paper No. 69.* New Haven, Conn.: Avalon Project, Yale Law School. Available at http://www.yale.edu/lawweb/avalon/federal/fed69.htm.

Harris, George C. "The Rule of Law and the War on Terror: The Professional Responsibilities of Executive Branch Lawyers in the Wake of 9/11." *Journal of National Security Law and Policy* 1 (2005): 409–453.

Harris, Shane. "More Than Meets the Ear." *National Journal* (March 18, 2006): 28 ff.

Hasday, Jill Elaine. "Civil War as Paradigm: Reestablishing the Rule of Law at the End of the Cold War." *Kansas Journal of Law and Public Policy* 5 (1996): 129–152.

Hathaway, Oona. "The Promise and Limits of the International Law of Torture." In *Torture: A Collection*, edited by Sanford Levinson, 199. New York: Oxford University Press, 2004.

Hayes, Stephen F. *Cheney: The Untold Story of America's Most Powerful and Controversial Vice President*. New York: HarperCollins, 2007.

Hazard, Geoffrey C., Jr. "How Far May a Lawyer Go in Assisting a Client in Unlawful Conduct?" *University of Miami Law Review* 35 (1981): 669–683.

Hazard, Geoffrey C., Jr., and William H. Hodes. *The Law of Lawyering*. 3d ed. Vol. 1. Gaithersburg, Md.: Aspen Law and Business, 2001.

Hegland, Corine. "Guantánamo's Grip." *National Journal* (February 3, 2006): 32 ff.

———. "How to Court-Martial the Al Qaeda 14." *National Journal* (September 16, 2006): 59 ff.

———. "Ex-POW versus the Guards." *National Journal* (September 23, 2006): 84–85.

Heilbrunn, Jacob. *They Knew They Were Right: The Rise of the Neocons*. New York: Doubleday, 2008.

Henkin, Louis. *Foreign Affairs and the United States Constitution*. 2d ed. New York: Oxford University Press, 1996.

Henry V. Directed by Sir Laurence Olivier. Criterion Collection, 1944.

Henry V. Directed by Kenneth Branagh. Los Angeles: MGM Home Entertainment/ Renaissance Films, 1989.

Hersh, Seymour M. *Chain of Command: The Road from 9/11 to Abu Ghraib*. New York: HarperCollins, 2004.

Herz, Michael. "Imposing Unified Executive Branch Statutory Interpretation." *Cardozo Law Review* 15 (1993): 219–271.

Hess, Stephen. *Organizing the Presidency*. Washington, D.C.: Brookings Institution, 1966.

Heymann, Philip. *Terrorism, Freedom, and Security: Winning without War*. Cambridge: Massachusetts Institute of Technology Press, 2003.

Higham, Scott. "Law Experts Condemn U.S. Memos on Torture." *Washington Post*, August 5, 2004, A4.

Hirsh, Michael, John Barry, and Daniel Klaidman. "A Tortured Debate." *Newsweek* (June 21, 2004): 50–53.

Honigsberg, Peter Jan. "Chasing 'Enemy Combatants' and Circumventing International Law: A License for Sanctioned Abuse." *UCLA Journal of International Law and Foreign Affairs* 12 (2007): 1–93.

Horton, Scott. "Through a Mirror Darkly: Applying the Geneva Conventions to 'A New Kind of Warfare.'" In *The Torture Debate in America*, edited by Karen J. Greenberg, 136. New York: Cambridge University Press, 2006.

———. "Deconstructing John Yoo." *Harper's* (January 2008). Available at http:// harpers.org/archive/2008/01/hbc-90002226.

Howe, Daniel W. *What Hath God Wrought: The Transformation of America, 1815–1848.* New York: Oxford University Press, 2007.

Humphreys, A. R. "Introduction." In *Henry V,* rev. ed. London: Penguin, 1996.

Hutchinson, Dennis J. "'The Achilles Heel' of the Constitution: Justice Jackson and the Japanese Exclusion Cases." *Supreme Court Review* 2002 (2002): 455 ff.

Hyman, Harold. *A More Perfect Union.* Boston: Houghton Mifflin, 1975.

International Committee of the Red Cross. "Report on the Treatment by the Coalition Forces of Prisoners of War and Other Protected Persons by the Geneva Conventions in Iraq during Arrest, Internment, and Interrogation." February 2004. In *Torture and Truth: America, Abu Ghraib, and the War on Terror,* edited by Mark Danner, 251. New York: New York Review of Books, 2004.

Irons, Peter H. *Justice at War.* New York: Oxford University Press, 1983.

Issacharoff, Samuel, and Richard H. Pildes. "Emergency Contexts without Emergency Powers: The United States' Constitutional Approach to Rights during Wartime." *International Journal of Constitutional Law* 2 (2004): 296–333.

———. "Between Civil Libertarianism and Executive Unilateralism: An Institutional Process Approach to Rights during Wartime." In *The Constitution in Wartime: Beyond Alarmism and Complacency,* edited by Mark Tushnet. Durham, N.C.: Duke University Press, 2005.

Jackson, Robert H. "A Presidential Legal Opinion." *Harvard Law Review* 66 (1953): 1353–1361.

———. *That Man: An Insider's Portrait of Franklin D. Roosevelt,* edited by John Q. Barrett. New York: Oxford University Press, 2003.

———. "Wartime Security and Liberty under Law." *Buffalo Law Review* 55 (2008): 1089 ff.

Janis, Irving L. *Victims of Groupthink: A Psychological Study of Foreign-Policy Decisions and Fiascos.* Boston: Houghton Mifflin, 1972.

Jenkins, Roy. *Churchill: A Biography.* New York: Plume, 2001.

Jinks, Derek, and David Sloss. "Is the President Bound by the Geneva Conventions?" *Cornell Law Review* 90 (2004): 97 ff.

Johnsen, Dawn E. "Functional Departmentalism and Nonjudicial Interpretation: Who Determines Constitutional Meaning?" *Law and Contemporary Problems* 67 (Summer 2004): 105–147.

———. "Faithfully Executing the Laws: Internal Legal Constraints on Executive Power." *UCLA Law Review* 54 (2007): 1559–1611.

———. "The Story of *Hamdan v. Rumsfeld.*" In *Presidential Power Stories,* edited by Curtis Bradley and Christopher Schroeder. New York: Foundation Press, 2008.

Johnson, Loch K. *A Season of Inquiry: The Senate Intelligence Investigation.* Lexington: University Press of Kentucky, 1985.

Johnston, David. "At a Secret Interrogation, Dispute Flared over Tactics." *New York Times,* September 10, 2006, A1.

———. "Bush Intervened in Dispute over N.S.A. Wiretapping." *New York Times,* May 16, 2007, A1.

Johnston, David, and Scott Shane. "Gonzales Denies Improper Pressure on Ashcroft on Spying." *New York Times,* July 25, 2007, A10.

———. "Gonzales Dealt Blow in Account by F.B.I. Director." *New York Times,* July 27, 2007, A1.

———. "Notes Confirm Pressure on Ashcroft over Spying." *New York Times,* August 17, 2007, A12.

Jordan, Lara Jakes, and Pamela Hess. "Bush 'Insulated' from Meeting on Methods." *Boulder Camera,* April 11, 2008, 6A.

Kakutani, Michiko. "All the President's Books." *New York Times,* May 11, 2006, B1.

Katyal, Neal K. "*Hamdan v. Rumsfeld:* The Legal Academy Goes to Practice." *Harvard Law Review* 120 (2006): 65–123.

———. "Internal Separation of Powers: Checking Today's Most Dangerous Branch from Within." *Yale Law Journal* 115 (2006): 2314 ff.

Katyal, Neal K., and Laurence H. Tribe. "Waging War, Deciding Guilt: Trying the Military Tribunals." *Yale Law Journal* 111 (2002): 1259 ff.

Keegan, John. *The Second World War.* New York: Viking, 1989.

Kennan, George F. *American Diplomacy, 1900–1950.* New York: New American Library, 1951.

Kennedy, David M. *Freedom from Fear: The American People in Depression and War, 1929–1945.* New York: Oxford University Press, 1999.

Kennedy, Robert F. *Thirteen Days: A Memoir of the Cuban Missile Crisis.* New York: Norton, 1969.

Klaidman, Daniel, Stuart Taylor, Jr., and Evan Thomas. "Palace Revolt." *Newsweek* (February 6, 2006): 34 ff.

Kmiec, Douglas W. *The Attorney General's Lawyer: Inside the Meese Justice Department.* New York: Praeger, 1992.

———. "OLC's Opinion Writing Function: The Legal Adhesive for a Unitary Executive." *Cardozo Law Review* 15 (1993): 337 ff.

Koh, Harold H. *The National Security Constitution: Sharing Power after the Iran-Contra Affair.* New Haven, Conn.: Yale University Press, 1990.

———. "Protecting the Office of Legal Counsel from Itself." *Cardozo Law Review* 15 (1993): 513–523.

———. "The Case against Military Commissions." *American Journal of International Law* 96 (2002): 337–345.

———. "A World without Torture." *Columbia Journal of Transnational Law* 43 (2005): 641–661.

———. "Can the President Be Torturer in Chief?" *Indiana Law Journal* 81 (2006): 1145–1167.

———. "Setting the World Right." *Yale Law Journal* 115 (2006): 2350–2379.

Kornbluh, Peter, and Malcolm Byrne, eds. *The Iran-Contra Scandal: The Declassified History.* New York: New Press, 1993.

Kramer, Larry D. "The Supreme Court, 2000 Term–Foreword: We the Court." *Harvard Law Review* 4 (2001): 115–169.

Kramer, Paul. "The Water Cure." *New Yorker* (February 25, 2008): 38 ff.

Kreimer, Seth F. "Too Close to the Rack and the Screw: Constitutional Constraints on Torture in the War on Terror." *University of Pennsylvania Journal of Constitutional Law* 6 (2003): 278–374.

———. " 'Torture Lite,' 'Full-Bodied' Torture, and the Insulation of Legal Conscience." *Journal of National Security Law and Policy* 1 (2005): 187–229.

Krent, Harold J. *Presidential Powers.* New York: New York University Press, 2005.

Kronman, Anthony T. *The Lost Lawyer: Failing Ideals of the Legal Profession.* Cambridge, Mass.: Harvard University Press, 1993.

Kukla, Jon. *A Wilderness So Immense: The Louisiana Purchase and the Destiny of America.* New York: Knopf, 2003.

Kutz, Christopher. "The Lawyers Know Sin: Complicity in Torture." In *The Torture Debate in America,* edited by Karen J. Greenberg, 241. New York: Cambridge University Press, 2006.

Langbein, John. "The Legal History of Torture." In *Torture: A Collection,* edited by Sanford Levinson, 93. New York: Oxford University Press, 2004.

Lankford, Nelson D. *Cry Havoc! The Crooked Road to Civil War, 1861.* New York: Viking, 2007.

Lawry, Robert P. "Who Is the Client of the Federal Government Lawyer? An Analysis of the Wrong Question?" *Federal Bar Journal* 47 (1978): 61 ff.

Lee, Thomas H., and Michael D. Ramsey. "The *Prize Cases:* Executive Action and Judicial Review in Wartime." In *Presidential Power Stories,* edited by Curtis Bradley and Christopher Schroeder. New York: Foundation Press, 2008.

Lessig, Lawrence, and Cass R. Sunstein. "The President and the Administration." *Columbia Law Review* 94 (1994): 85–123.

Levinson, Daryl J., and Richard H. Pildes. "Separation of Parties, Not Powers." *Harvard Law Review* 119 (2006): 2311 ff.

Levinson, Sanford. *Constitutional Faith.* Princeton, N.J.: Princeton University Press, 1988.

———. "Was the Emancipation Proclamation Constitutional? Do We/Should We Care What the Answer Is?" *University of Illinois Law Review* 2001 (2001): 1135–1158.

———. "Precommitment and 'Postcommitment': The Ban on Torture in the Wake of September 11." *Texas Law Review* 81 (2003): 2013–2054.

———. "Contemplating Torture: An Introduction." In *Torture: A Collection,* edited by Sanford Levinson, 34. New York: Oxford University Press, 2004.

———. "In Quest of a 'Common Conscience': Reflections on the Current Debate about Torture." *Journal of National Security Law and Policy* 1 (2005): 231–252.

Levinson, Sanford, ed. *Torture: A Collection.* New York: Oxford University Press, 2004.

Levitan, David M. "The Foreign Relations Power: An Analysis of Mr. Sutherland's Theory." *Yale Law Journal* 55 (1946): 467 ff.

Lewis, Anthony. "Torture: The Road to Abu Ghraib and Beyond." In *The Torture Debate in America,* edited by Karen J. Greenberg, 18. New York: Cambridge University Press, 2006.

Lewis, Neil A. "Bush Blocked Ethics Inquiry, Official Says." *New York Times,* July 19, 2006, A14.

———. "Professor Tells of 'Mess' over Eavesdropping." *New York Times,* October 3, 2007, A21.

Lichtblau, Eric. "Senate Panel Rebuffed on Documents on U.S. Spying." *New York Times,* February 2, 2006, A1.

———. "Justice Official Opens Spying Inquiry." *New York Times,* November 28, 2006, A19.

———. "Congress Looks into Obstruction as Calls for Justice Inquiry Rise." *New York Times,* December 8, 2007, A1.

———. *Bush's Law: The Remaking of American Justice.* New York: Pantheon, 2008.

Lichtblau, Eric, and James Risen. "Justice Deputy Resisted Parts of Spy Program." *New York Times,* January 1, 2006, 11.

Lichtblau, Eric, and Scott Shane. "Ally Told Bush Spying Projects Might Be Illegal." *New York Times,* July 8, 2006, A1.

———. "A Dogged Advocate of Wartime Authority." *New York Times,* August 28, 2007, A1.

———. "Report Details Dissent on Guantánamo Tactics." *New York Times,* May 21, 2008, A21.

Liptak, Adam. "The White House as a Moving Legal Target." *New York Times,* January 19, 2007, A1.

Llewellyn, Karl. "Remarks on the Theory of Appellate Decisions and the Rules or Canons about How Statutes Are to Be Construed." *Vanderbilt Law Review* 3 (1950): 395 ff.

Lobel, Jules. "Emergency Power and the Decline of Liberalism." *Yale Law Journal* 98 (1989): 1385–1433.

Lofgren, Charles A. "*United States v. Curtiss-Wright Export Corporation:* An Historical Reassessment." *Yale Law Journal* 83 (1973): 1–32.

Luban, David. *Lawyers and Justice: An Ethical Study.* Princeton, N.J.: Princeton University Press, 1988.

———. "Rational Choice at the Office of Legal Counsel." *Cardozo Law Review* 15 (1993): 437 ff.

———. "Liberalism, Torture, and the Ticking Bomb." In *The Torture Debate in America,* edited by Karen J. Greenberg, 35. New York: Cambridge University Press, 2006.

———. *Legal Ethics and Human Dignity.* New York: Cambridge University Press, 2007.

———. "Lawfare and Legal Ethics in Guantánamo." *Stanford Law Review* 60 (2008): 1981–2026.

Lund, Nelson. "Lawyers and the Defense of the Presidency." *Brigham Young University Law Review* 1995 (1995): 17–98.

———. "The President as Client and the Ethics of the President's Lawyers." *Law and Contemporary Problems* 61 (1998): 65–81.

Mackey, Chris, and Greg Miller. *The Interrogators: Inside the Secret War against Al Qaeda.* Boston: Little, Brown, 2004.

Magill, M. Elizabeth. "Can Process Cure Substance? A Response to Neal Katyal's 'Internal Separation of Powers.'" *Yale Law Journal Pocket Part* (November 2, 2006). Available at http://thepocketpart.org/2006/11/2/magill.html.

Mahler, Jonathan. *The Challenge: Hamdan v. Rumsfeld and the Fight over Presidential Power.* New York: Farrar, Straus & Giroux, 2008.

A Man for All Seasons. Directed by Frank Zinnemann. Culver City, Calif.: Columbia Pictures, 1966.

Mann, James. *Rise of the Vulcans: The History of Bush's War Cabinet*. New York: Viking, 2004.

Mann, Thomas E., and Norman J. Ornstein. *The Broken Branch: How Congress Is Failing America and How to Get It Back on Track*. New York: Oxford University Press, 2006.

Marcus, Maeva. *Truman and the* Steel Seizure *Case*. New York: Columbia University Press, 1977.

Margulies, Joseph. *Guantánamo and the Abuse of Presidential Power*. New York: Simon & Schuster, 2006.

Marks, Lee R., and John C. Grabow. "The President's Foreign Economic Powers after *Dames & Moore v. Regan*: Legislation by Acquiescence." *Cornell Law Review* 68 (1982): 68 ff.

Massie, Robert K. *Peter the Great: His Life and World*. New York: Random House, 1980.

Matheson, Michael J. "The Amendment of the War Crimes Act." *American Journal of International Law* 101 (2007): 48–55.

Mayer, Jane. "Annals of the Pentagon: The Memo." *New Yorker* (February 27, 2006): 32–41.

———. "The Hidden Power: The Legal Mind behind the White House's War on Terror." *New Yorker* (July 3, 2006): 44–55.

———. *The Dark Side*. New York: Doubleday, 2008.

Mazzetti, Mark. "Key Lawmakers to Get Files about Surveillance Program." *New York Times*, February 1, 2007, A1.

———. "C.I.A. Was Warned to Keep Interrogation Videotapes." *New York Times*, December 8, 2007, A1.

———. "Letters Give CIA Tactics a Legal Rationale." *New York Times*, April 27, 2008, A1.

Mazzetti, Mark, and Kate Zernike. "White House Says Terror Detainees Hold Basic Rights." *New York Times*, July 12, 2006, A1.

McCullough, David. *Truman*. New York: Simon & Schuster, 1992.

McDougal, Myres S. *International Law, Power, and Policy: A Contemporary Conception*. Dordrecht, Netherlands: M. Nijhoff, 1954.

McDougal, Myres S., Harold D. Lasswell, and W. Michael Reisman. "The World Constitutive Process of Authoritative Decision (Part I)." *Journal of Legal Education* 19 (1967): 253–300.

———. "The World Constitutive Process of Authoritative Decision (Part II)." *Journal of Legal Education* 19 (1967): 403–437.

McGee, Jim, and Brian Duffy. *Main Justice: The Men and Women Who Enforce the Nation's Criminal Laws and Guard Its Liberties*. New York: Simon & Schuster, 1996.

McGinnis, John O. "Models of the Opinion Function of the Attorney General: A Normative, Descriptive, and Historical Prolegomenon." *Cardozo Law Review* 15 (1993): 375–436.

Meese, Edwin, III. "The Law of the Constitution." *Tulane Law Review* 61 (1987): 979–990.

———. *With Reagan: The Inside Story.* Washington, D.C.: Regnery/Gateway, 1992.

Meron, Theodor. "Shakespeare's *Henry the Fifth* and the Law of War." *American Journal of International Law* 86 (1992): 1–45.

Merrill, Thomas W. "High-Level, 'Tenured' Lawyers." *Law and Contemporary Problems* 61 (1998): 83–108.

Mikva, Abner J., and Patti B. Saris. *The American Congress: The First Branch.* New York: Watts, 1983.

Miller, Gail H. *Defining Torture.* New York: Florsheimer Center for Constitutional Democracy, 2005.

Miller, Geoffrey. "Assessment of DoD Counterterrorism Interrogation and Detention Operations in Iraq." American Civil Liberties Union, 2005. Available at http://www.aclu.org/torturefoia/released/a20.pdf.

Miller, Geoffrey P. "Independent Agencies." *Supreme Court Review* 1986 (1986): 41 ff.

———. "Government Lawyers' Ethics in a System of Checks and Balances." *University of Chicago Law Review* 54 (1987): 1293–1299.

Miller, John C. *The Federalist Era, 1789–1801.* New York: Harper & Row, 1960.

Minutaglio, Bill. *The President's Counselor: The Rise to Power of Alberto Gonzales.* New York: HarperCollins, 2006.

Monaghan, Henry. "The Protective Power of the Presidency." *Columbia Law Review* 93 (1993): 1–74.

Montefiore, Simon Sebag. *Stalin: The Court of the Red Tsar.* New York: Knopf, 2004.

Morgenthau, Hans J. *In Defense of the National Interest.* New York: Knopf, 1951.

Morris, Roy. *Fraud of the Century: Rutherford B. Hayes, Samuel Tilden, and the Stolen Election of 1876.* New York: Simon & Schuster, 2004.

Morrison, Trevor W. "Constitutional Avoidance in the Executive Branch." *Columbia Law Review* 106 (2006): 1189 ff.

———. "The Story of *United States v. United States District Court (Keith)*: The Surveillance Power." In *Presidential Power Stories,* edited by Curtis Bradley and Christopher Schroeder. New York: Foundation Press, 2008.

Moss, Randolph D. "Executive Branch Legal Interpretation: A Perspective from the Office of Legal Counsel." *Administrative Law Review* 52 (2000): 1303–1330.

Murphy, Bruce Allen. *The Brandeis/Frankfurter Connection.* New York: Oxford University Press, 1983.

Murray, Robert K. *Red Scare: A Study in National Hysteria, 1919–1920.* Minneapolis: University of Minnesota Press, 1955.

Muskie, Edmund S., Kenneth Rush, and Kenneth W. Thompson, eds. *The President, the Congress, and Foreign Policy.* Lanham, Md.: University Press of America, 1986.

Myers, Steven Lee. "Bush Vetoes Bill on C.I.A. Tactics, Affirming Legacy." *New York Times,* March 9, 2008, A1.

National Commission on Terrorist Attacks upon the United States. *The 9/11 Commission Report.* New York: Norton, 2004.

Neely, Mark E., Jr. *The Fate of Liberty: Abraham Lincoln and Civil Liberties.* New York: Oxford University Press, 1991.

Neustadt, Richard E. *Presidential Power and the Modern Presidents: The Politics of Leadership from Roosevelt to Reagan.* New York: Free Press, 1990.

North, Oliver L. *Under Fire: An American Story.* New York: HarperCollins, 1991.

Noyes, J. Graham. "Cutting the President Off from Tin Cup Diplomacy." *University of California–Davis Law Review* 24 (1991): 841–877.

Nuechterlein, Jonathan E., and Philip J. Weiser. *Digital Crossroads: American Telecommunications Policy in the Internet Age.* Cambridge: Massachusetts Institute of Technology Press, 2005.

Nzelibe, Jide, and John Yoo. "Rational War and Constitutional Design." *Yale Law Journal* 115 (2006): 2512–2541.

Ornstein, Norman J., and Thomas E. Mann. "When Congress Checks Out." *Foreign Affairs* 85 (November–December 2006): 67–82.

Osiel, Mark. "The Mental State of Torturers." In *Torture: A Collection,* edited by Sanford Levinson, 129. New York: Oxford University Press, 2004.

Packer, George. *The Assassins' Gate: America in Iraq.* New York: Farrar, Straus & Giroux, 2005.

Palazzolo, Joe. "Litigation over Spy Program on Hold." *Legal Times,* October 1, 2007, 8 ff.

Pallitto, Robert M., and William G. Weaver. *Presidential Secrecy and the Law.* Baltimore: Johns Hopkins University Press, 2007.

Paludan, Phillip S. *A Covenant with Death: The Constitution, Law, and Equality in the Civil War Era.* Urbana: University of Illinois Press, 1975.

Paulsen, Michael Stokes. "Hell, Handbaskets, and Government Lawyers: The Duty of Loyalty and Its Limits." *Law and Contemporary Problems* 61 (1998): 83–106.

———. "The Emancipation Proclamation and the Commander in Chief Power." *Georgia Law Review* 40 (2006): 807–834.

Paust, Jordan J. "Is the President Bound by the Supreme Law of the Land? Foreign Affairs and National Security Reexamined." *Hastings Constitutional Law Quarterly* 9 (1982): 719–772.

Peppet, Scott R. "Lawyers' Bargaining Ethics, Contracts, and Collaboration: The End of the Legal Profession and the Beginning of Professional Pluralism." *Iowa Law Review* 90 (2005): 475–538.

Peterson, Todd D. "National Security Constitution." *George Washington Law Review* 59 (1991): 747 ff.

Pillard, Cornelia T. L. "The Unfulfilled Promise of the Constitution in Executive Hands." *Michigan Law Review* 103 (2005): 676–758.

———. "Unitariness and Myopia: The Executive Branch, Legal Process, and Torture." *Indiana Law Journal* 81 (2006): 1297–1312.

Posner, Eric A., and Cass R. Sunstein. "*Chevron*izing Foreign Relations Law." *Yale Law Journal* 116 (2007): 1170–1229.

Posner, Eric A., and Adrian Vermeule. "A 'Torture' Memo and Its Tortuous Critics." *Wall Street Journal,* July 6, 2004, A22.

———. "Should Coercive Interrogation Be Legal?" *Michigan Law Review* 104 (2006): 671 ff.

———. *Terror in the Balance: Security, Liberty, and the Courts.* New York: Oxford University Press, 2007.

Posner, Gerald. *Why America Slept: The Failure to Prevent 9/11.* New York: Random House, 2003.

Posner, Richard A. *Breaking the Deadlock: The 2000 Election, the Constitution, and the Courts.* Princeton, N.J.: Princeton University Press, 2001.

————. "Torture, Terrorism, and Interrogation." In *Torture: A Collection*, edited by Sanford Levinson, 291. New York: Oxford University Press, 2004.

————. *Not a Suicide Pact: The Constitution in a Time of National Emergency*. New York: Oxford University Press, 2006.

Pound, Edward T., Peter H. Stone, Shane Harris, and Corine Hegland. "After Gonzales." *National Journal* (September 1, 2007): 16 ff.

Powell, H. Jefferson. *The Constitution and the Attorneys General*. Durham, N.C.: Carolina Academic Press, 1999.

————. *The President's Authority over Foreign Affairs: An Essay in Constitutional Interpretation*. Durham, N.C.: Carolina Academic Press, 2002.

————. "The Executive and the Avoidance Canon." *Indiana Law Journal* 81 (2006): 1313–1318.

————. "The Story of *Curtiss-Wright*." In *Presidential Power Stories*, edited by Curtis Bradley and Christopher Schroeder. New York: Foundation Press, 2008.

Powers, Thomas. *The Man Who Kept the Secrets: Richard Helms and the CIA*. New York: Knopf, 1979.

Prakash, Saikrishna B. "Hail to the Chief Administrator: The Framers and the President's Administrative Powers." *Yale Law Journal* 102 (1993): 991 ff.

Prakash, Saikrishna B., and Michael D. Ramsey. "The Executive Power over Foreign Affairs." *Yale Law Journal* 111 (2001): 231–356.

Quint, Peter. "The Separation of Powers under Nixon: Reflections on Constitutional Liberties and the Rule of Law." *Duke Law Journal* 1981 (1981): 1–70.

Rabkin, Jeremy. "At the President's Side: The Role of the White House Counsel in Constitutional Policy." *Law and Contemporary Problems* 56 (1993): 63–98.

Radack, Jesselyn. "Tortured Legal Ethics: The Role of the Government Advisor in the War on Terrorism." *University of Colorado Law Review* 77 (2006): 1–48.

Ramsey, Michael D. "Torturing Executive Power." *Georgetown Law Journal* 93 (2005): 1213–1252.

————. "Toward a Rule of Law in Foreign Affairs." *Columbia Law Review* 106 (2006): 1450–1478.

————. *The Constitution's Text in Foreign Affairs*. Cambridge, Mass.: Harvard University Press, 2007.

Randall, J. G. *Constitutional Problems under Lincoln*. Rev. ed. Urbana: University of Illinois Press, 1951.

Ratner, Michael, and Peter Weiss. "Litigating against Torture: The German Criminal Prosecution." In *The Torture Debate in America*, edited by Karen J. Greenberg, 261. New York: Cambridge University Press, 2006.

Reagan, Ronald. Letter to the Chairman and Vice Chairman of the Senate Select Committee on Intelligence Regarding Procedures for Presidential Approval and Notification of Congress. *Weekly Compilation of Presidential Documents* 23 (August 7, 1987): 910.

Reardon, John J. *Edmund Randolph*. New York: Macmillan, 1974.

Rehnquist, William H. *The Supreme Court: How It Was, How It Is*. New York: William Morrow, 1987.

————. *All the Laws but One: Civil Liberties in Wartime*. New York: Vintage, 2000.

————. *Centennial Crisis: The Disputed Election of 1876*. New York: Knopf, 2004.

Remini, Robert V. *Andrew Jackson and the Bank War: A Study in the Growth of Presidential Power*. New York: Norton, 1967.

——. *The Life of Andrew Jackson*. New York: Perennial Classics, 2001.

——. *The House: The History of the House of Representatives*. Washington, D.C.: Library of Congress, 2006.

Rhode, Deborah L. *In the Interests of Justice: Reforming the Legal Profession*. New York: Oxford University Press, 2000.

Richardson, James D., ed. *Messages and Papers of the Presidents*. Vol. 2. Washington, D.C.: Bureau of National Literature and Art, 1897.

Ricks, Thomas E. *Fiasco: The American Military Adventure in Iraq*. New York: Penguin, 2006.

Risen, James. "The Struggle for Iraq: Treatment of Prisoners; G.I.s Are Accused of Abusing Iraqi Captives." *New York Times*, April 29, 2004, A15.

——. *State of War: The Secret History of the CIA and the Bush Administration*. New York: Free Press, 2006.

——. "Administration Pulls Back on Surveillance Agreement." *New York Times*, May 2, 2007, A18.

Risen, James, and Eric Lichtblau. "Bush Lets U.S. Spy on Callers without Courts." *New York Times*, December 16, 2005, 1.

Robinson, Greg. *By Order of the President: FDR and the Internment of Japanese Americans*. Cambridge, Mass.: Harvard University Press, 2001.

Rohde, Stephen F. "War by Other Means." *Los Angeles Lawyer* (February 2007): 44.

Roosevelt, Theodore. *An Autobiography*. New York: Da Capo, 1988.

Rosenman, Samuel. *Working with Roosevelt*. New York: Da Capo, 1952.

Rozell, Mark J. *Executive Privilege: Presidential Power, Secrecy, and Accountability*. 2d ed. Lawrence: University Press of Kansas, 2002.

Safire, William. *Freedom*. New York: Avon, 1987.

Savage, Charlie. "Specialists Doubt Legality of Wiretaps." *Boston Globe*, February 2, 2006.

——. *Takeover: The Return of the Imperial Presidency and the Subversion of American Democracy*. Boston: Little, Brown, 2007.

Scheppele, Kim Lane. "Law in a Time of Emergency: States of Exception and the Temptations of 9/11." *University of Pennsylvania Journal of Constitutional Law* 6 (2004): 1023–1083.

——. "Hypothetical Torture in the 'War on Terrorism.'" *Journal of National Security Law and Policy* 1 (2005): 285–340.

Schlesinger, Arthur M., Jr. *The Age of Jackson*. Boston: Little, Brown, 1945.

——. *The Imperial Presidency*. Boston: Houghton Mifflin, 1973.

Schlesinger, James R., Harold Brown, Tillie K. Fowler, and Charles A. Horner. *Final Report of the Independent Panel to Review DoD Detention Operations*. August 2004. In *Torture and Truth: America, Abu Ghraib, and the War on Terror*, edited by Mark Danner, 329. New York: New York Review of Books, 2004.

Schrager, Adam. *The Principled Politician: The Ralph Carr Story*. Golden, Colo.: Fulcrum, 2008.

Schulhofer, Stephen J. *The Enemy Within: Intelligence Gathering, Law Enforcement, and Civil Liberties in the Wake of September 11*. New York: Century Foundation Press, 2002.

Schwarz, Frederick A. O., Jr., and Aziz Z. Huq. *Unchecked and Unbalanced: Presidential Power in a Time of Terror.* New York: New Press, 2007.

Sciaroni, Bretton. "Boland in the Wind: The Iran-Contra Affair and the Invitation to Struggle." *Pepperdine Law Review* 17 (1990): 379–427.

Shakespeare, William. *The Complete Works,* edited by Stanley Wells and Gary Taylor. New York: Oxford University Press, 1986.

———. *Henry V,* edited by A. R. Humphreys. New York: Penguin, 1996.

Shane, Peter M. "Legal Disagreement and Negotiation in a Government of Laws: The Case of Executive Privilege Claims against Congress." *Minnesota Law Review* 71 (1987): 461–542.

———. "When Interbranch Norms Break Down: Of Arms-for-Hostages, 'Orderly Shutdowns,' Presidential Impeachments, and Judicial Coups." *Cornell Journal of Law and Public Policy* 12 (2003): 503–542.

———. "Social Theory Meets Social Policy: Culture, Identity, and Public Information Policy after September 11." *Information Society Journal of Law and Policy* 2 (Winter 2005–2006): i–xxiii.

———. "Powers of the Crown." *The Review of Politics* 68 (2006): 702–707.

Shane, Peter M., and Harold H. Bruff. *Separation of Powers Law.* 2d ed. Durham, N.C.: Carolina Academic Press, 2005.

Shane, Scott. "Nominee's Stand Avoiding Tangle of Torture Cases." *New York Times,* November 1, 2007, A1.

———. "The C.I.A. and the Tapes: Sensing Support Shifting Away from Its Methods." *New York Times,* December 13, 2007, A16.

———. "Waterboarding Focus of Inquiry by Justice Department." *New York Times,* January 23, 2008, A1.

———. "Inside the Interrogation of a 9/11 Mastermind." *New York Times,* June 22, 2008, 1.

———. "2 Testify on Their Support for Harsh Interrogation." *New York Times,* June 27, 2008, A15.

Shane, Scott, and David Johnston. "Mining of Data Prompted Fight over U.S. Spying." *New York Times,* July 29, 2007, 1.

Shane, Scott, David Johnston, and James Risen. "Secret U.S. Endorsement of Severe Interrogations." *New York Times,* October 4, 2007, A1, A23.

Shane, Scott, and Eric Lindblau. "Cheney Pushed U.S. to Widen Eavesdropping." *New York Times,* May 14, 2006, A16.

Shatz, Adam. "The Torture of Algiers." *New York Review of Books* (November 21, 2002): 53.

Shenon, Philip. "Inspector General at the Justice Dept. Is Investigating Gonzales's Testimony." *New York Times,* August 31, 2007, A17.

———. "Attorney General Choice Treads Careful Line at Senate Hearing." *New York Times,* October 18, 2007, A1.

———. "Senators Clash with Nominee about Torture." *New York Times,* October 19, 2007, A1.

Shenon, Philip, and David Johnston. "A Defender of Bush's Power, Gonzales Resigns." *New York Times,* August 28, 2007, A1.

Shenon, Philip, and Eric Lichtblau. "White House Renews Battle over Lawyer Who Signed Interrogation Memos." *New York Times,* January 24, 2008, A18.

Silverberg, Marshall. "The Separation of Powers and Control of the CIA's Covert Operations." *Texas Law Review* 68 (1990): 575–623.

Simon, James F. *Lincoln and Chief Justice Taney: Slavery, Secession, and the President's War Powers.* New York: Simon & Schuster, 2006.

Simon, William H. *The Practice of Justice: A Theory of Lawyers' Ethics.* Cambridge, Mass.: Harvard University Press, 1998.

Sims, John Cary. "What NSA Is Doing . . . and Why It's Illegal." *Hastings Constitutional Law Quarterly* 33 (Winter–Spring 2006): 105–140.

———. "How the Bush Administration's Warrantless Surveillance Program Took the Constitution on an Illegal, Unnecessary, and Unrepentant Joyride." *UCLA Journal of International and Foreign Affairs* 12 (2007): 163–179.

Skolnick, Jerome. "American Interrogation: From Torture to Trickery." In *Torture: A Collection*, edited by Sanford Levinson, 105. New York: Oxford University Press, 2004.

Smist, Frank J., Jr. *Congress Oversees the United States Intelligence Community, 1947–1989.* Knoxville: University of Tennessee Press, 1990.

Smith, Clive Stafford. *Eight O' Clock Ferry to the Windward Side: Seeking Justice in Guantánamo Bay.* New York: Nation Books, 2007.

Smith, Jean Edward. *John Marshall: Definer of a Nation.* New York: Henry Holt, 1996.

Smith, Nicholas W. "Evidence and Confrontation in the President's Military Commissions." *Hastings Constitutional Law Quarterly* 33 (2005): 83–104.

Smith, Page. *Democracy on Trial: The Japanese American Evacuation and Relocation in World War II.* New York: Simon & Schuster, 1995.

Smith, Richard Norton. *Patriarch: George Washington and the New American Nation.* Boston: Houghton Mifflin, 1993.

Smith, William French. *Law and Justice in the Reagan Administration: The Memoirs of an Attorney General.* Stanford, Calif.: Hoover Institution Press, 1991.

Sofaer, Abraham D. *War, Foreign Affairs, and Constitutional Power: The Origins.* Cambridge, Mass.: Ballinger, 1976.

———. "Iran-Contra: Ethical Conduct and Public Policy." *Houston Law Review* 40 (2003): 1081–1109.

Spiro, Peter J. "Treaties, Executive Agreements, and Constitutional Method." *Texas Law Review* 79 (2001): 961–1033.

———. "*Hamdan v. Rumsfeld.*" *American Journal of International Law* 100 (2006): 888–895.

Stack, Kevin M. "The Divergence of Constitutional and Statutory Interpretation." *University of Colorado Law Review* 75 (2004): 1–52.

———. "The Statutory President." *Iowa Law Review* 90 (2005): 539–600.

Stannard, Matthew B. "Data-Mining Methods Differ, but Goal Same." *Denver Post*, May 15, 2006, 6C.

Stith, Kate. "Congress' Power of the Purse." *Yale Law Journal* 97 (1988): 1343 ff.

Stolberg, Sheryl Gay. "Senators Left Out of Loop Make Their Pique Known." *New York Times*, May 19, 2006, A20.

———. "President Moves 14 Held in Secret to Guantánamo." *New York Times*, September 7, 2006, A1.

Stone, Geoffrey R. *Perilous Times: Free Speech in Wartime from the Sedition Act of 1798 to the War on Terrorism.* New York: Norton, 2004.

Story, Joseph. *Commentaries on the Constitution of the United States,* edited by Ronald Rotunda and John E. Nowak. Durham, N.C.: Carolina Academic Press, 1987.

Strauss, David A. "The Solicitor General and the Interests of the United States." *Law and Contemporary Problems* 61 (1998): 165–177.

Strauss, Peter L. "Formal and Functional Approaches to Separation-of-Powers Questions: A Foolish Inconsistency?" *Cornell Law Review* 72 (1987): 488–526.

———. *Legislation: Understanding and Using Statutes.* New York: Foundation Press, 2006.

———. "Overseer, or 'The Decider'? The President in Administrative Law." *George Washington Law Review* 75 (2007): 696 ff.

Sulmasy, Glenn, and John Yoo. "Challenges to Civilian Control of the Military: A Rational Choice Approach to the War on Terror." *UCLA Law Review* 54 (2007): 1815–1846.

Sunstein, Cass R. "Minimalism at War." *Supreme Court Review* 2004 (2004): 1 ff.

———. "Clear Statement Principles and National Security: *Hamdan* and Beyond." *Supreme Court Review* 2006 (2006) 1 ff.

Suskind, Ron. *The One Percent Doctrine: Deep inside America's Pursuit of Its Enemies since 9/11.* New York: Simon & Schuster, 2006.

———. *The Way of the World.* New York: HarperCollins, 2008.

Swire, Peter P. "The System of Foreign Intelligence Surveillance Law." *George Washington Law Review* 72 (2004): 1306–1374.

"Symposium: A *Hamdan* Quartet: Four Essays on Aspects of *Hamdan v. Rumsfeld.*" *Maryland Law Review* 66 (2007): 750 ff.

"Symposium: Executive Branch Interpretation of the Law." *Cardozo Law Review* 15 (1993): 21 ff.

"Symposium: Fighting Terrorism with Torture: Where to Draw the Line?" *Journal of National Security Law and Policy* 1 (2005): 187 ff.

"Symposium: Foreign Affairs and the Constitution: The Roles of Congress, the President, and the Courts." *University of Miami Law Review* 43 (1988): 1 ff.

"Symposium: Legal and Policy Issues in the Iran-Contra Affair: Intelligence Oversight in a Democracy." *Houston Journal of International Law* 11 (1988): 1 ff.

"Symposium on the New Face of Armed Conflict: Enemy Combatants after *Hamdan v. Rumsfeld.*" *George Washington Law Review* 75 (2007): 971 ff.

"Symposium: The Attorney General and the Pursuit of Justice." *John Marshall Law Review* 23 (1990): 151 ff.

"Symposium: The Last Word? The Constitutional Implications of Presidential Signing Statements." *William and Mary Bill of Rights Journal* 16 (2007): 1 ff.

"Symposium: War, Terrorism, and Torture: Limits on Presidential Power in the 21st Century." *Indiana Law Journal* 81 (2006): 1139 ff.

Taft, William H., IV. "Your Draft Memorandum of January 9." January 11, 2002. Available at http://www.newyorker.com/online/content/?050214on_onlineonly02.

Taguba, Antonio M. "Article 15-6 Investigation of the 800th Military Police Brigade." March 2004. In *The Torture Papers: The Road to Abu Ghraib,* edited by Karen J. Greenberg and Joshua L. Dratel, 405. New York: Cambridge University Press, 2005.

Thompson, Dennis. "The Possibility of Administrative Ethics." *Public Administration Review* 45 (1985): 555 ff.

Toobin, Jeffrey. *The Nine: Inside the Secret World of the Supreme Court*. New York: Doubleday, 2007.

———. "Camp Justice." *New Yorker* (April 14, 2008): 32 ff.

Tower, John, Edmund Muskie, and Brent Scowcroft. *The Tower Commission Report: The Full Text of the President's Special Review Board*. New York: Bantam/ Times Books, 1987.

Trevelyan, George M. *History of England*. Vol. 1: *From the Earliest Times to the Reformation*. Garden City, N.Y.: Doubleday, 1926.

Tribe, Laurence H., and Patrick O. Gudridge. "The Anti-Emergency Constitution." *Yale Law Journal* 113 (2004): 1801–1870.

Turner, Robert F. "An Insider's Look at the War on Terrorism." *Cornell Law Review* 93 (2008): 471–500.

Tushnet, Mark. *Taking the Constitution Away from the Courts*. Princeton, N.J.: Princeton University Press, 1999.

———. "Non-Judicial Review." *Harvard Journal on Legislation* 40 (2003): 453–492.

———. *The Constitution in Wartime: Beyond Alarmism and Complacency*. Durham, N.C.: Duke University Press, 2005.

U.S. Congress. House. H.R. Report No. 433. 100th Cong., 1st Sess., 1987.

———. House and Senate Intelligence Committees. *Hearing on Pre-9/11 Intelligence Failures*. 107th Cong., 2d Sess., 2002.

———. Senate Armed Services Committee. *The Origins of Aggressive Interrogation Techniques: Part I of the Committee's Inquiry into the Treatment of Detainees in U.S. Custody*. 110th Cong., 2d Sess., June 17, 2008. Available at http://armed-services.senate.gov/hearings.cfm.

———. Senate Committee on Foreign Relations. *Convention against Torture and Other Cruel, Inhuman, or Degrading Treatment or Punishment: Message from the President*. Senate Treaty Doc. No. 100-20. 100th Cong., 2d Sess., 1988.

———. Senate Committee on Foreign Relations. *Convention against Torture and Other Cruel, Inhuman, or Degrading Treatment or Punishment*. Executive Report No. 101-30. 101st Cong., 2d Sess., 1990.

———. Senate Committee on the Judiciary. *Hearings before the Senate Committee on the Judiciary on the Nomination of William H. Rehnquist and Lewis F. Powell, Jr., to Be Associate Justices of the Supreme Court*. 92nd Cong., 1st Sess., 1971.

———. Senate Committee on the Judiciary. Subcommittee on Separation of Powers of the Senate Committee on the Judiciary. *Removing Politics from the Administration of Justice: Hearings before the Subcommittee on Separation of Powers of the Senate Committee on the Judiciary*. 93d Cong., 2d Sess., 1974.

———. Senate Committee on the Judiciary. *Foreign Intelligence Surveillance Act of 1977*. Report No. 604. 95th Cong., 1st Sess., 1977.

———. Senate Committee on the Judiciary. *Hearings on the Nomination of Edwin Meese III*. 98th Cong., 2d Sess, 1984.

———. Senate Committee on the Judiciary. Senate Report No. 216. 100th Cong., 1st Sess., 1987.

———. Senate Committee on the Judiciary. *Confirmation Hearings for the Department of Justice*. 103rd Cong., 1st Sess., 1993, 398.

———. Senate Committee on the Judiciary. *Hearings before the Senate Committee on the Judiciary.* 103rd Cong., 1st Sess., 1993.

———. Senate Committee on the Judiciary. *Confirmation Hearings on Federal Appointments (Part 1).* 107th Cong., 1st Sess., 2001, 733–734.

———. Senate Committee on the Judiciary. *Department of Justice Oversight: Preserving Our Freedoms While Defending against Terrorism.* 107th Cong., 1st Sess., 2001.

———. Senate Committee on the Judiciary. *Hearings before the Senate Committee on the Judiciary.* 107th Cong., 1st Sess., 2001.

———. Senate Committee on the Judiciary. *Hearing on the Nomination of Alberto R. Gonzales to Be Attorney General.* 109th Cong., 1st Sess. January 7, 2005.

———. Senate Committee on the Judiciary. *Department of Justice Oversight: Hearing before the Senate Committee on the Judiciary.* 109th Cong., 2d Sess., April 6, 2006.

———. Senate Committee on the Judiciary. *Continuation of Executive Nomination of Michael Mukasey to Be Attorney General of the United States.* 110th Cong., 1st Sess., 2007.

———. Senate Committee on the Judiciary. *Department of Justice Oversight: Hearing before the Senate Committee on the Judiciary.* 110th Cong., 1st Sess., January 18, 2007.

———. Senate Committee on the Judiciary. Testimony of James Comey. *U.S. Senate Judiciary Committee Holds a Hearing on the U.S. Attorney Firings,* May 15, 2007. Available at Georgetown University Law School website, http://gulcfac. typepad.com/georgetown_university_law/files/comey.transcript.pdf.

———. Senate Report No. 95-604. 2 vols. *United States Code Congressional and Administrative News,* 1978.

———. Senate Select Committee to Study Governmental Operations with Respect to Intelligence Activities. *Final Report.* 94th Cong., 2d Sess., 1976.

———. Senate Select Intelligence Committee. *Hearing on the Nomination of General Michael Hayden to Be Director of the Central Intelligence Agency.* 109th Cong., 2d Sess., May 18, 2006.

U.S. Department of Defense. Joint Task Force 170. "Legal Brief on Proposed Counter-Resistance Strategies." October 11, 2002. In *Torture and Truth: America, Abu Ghraib, and the War on Terror,* edited by Mark Danner, 170. New York: New York Review of Books, 2004.

———. Joint Task Force 170. "Request for Approval of Counter-Resistance Strategies." October 11, 2002. In *Torture and Truth: America, Abu Ghraib, and the War on Terror,* edited by Mark Danner, 167. New York: New York Review of Books, 2004.

———. *Manual for Military Commissions.* January 18, 2007. Available at http:// www.defenselink.mil/pubs.

———. "Military Commission Order No. 1." March 21, 2002. Available at http:// www.defenselink.mil/news/Mar2002/d20020321ord.pdf.

———. Office of the Inspector General. "Review of DoD-Directed Investigations of Detainee Abuse." August 25, 2006. Available at http://www.dodig.osd.mil/fo/ Foia/ERR/06-INTEL-10-PublicRelease.pdf.

———. Office of the Secretary of Defense. "Counter-Resistance Techniques."

December 2, 2002. In *Torture and Truth: America, Abu Ghraib, and the War on Terror,* edited by Mark Danner, 181. New York: New York Review of Books, 2004.

———. Office of the Secretary of Defense. "Counter-Resistance Techniques in the War on Terrorism." April 16, 2003. In *Torture and Truth: America, Abu Ghraib, and the War on Terror,* edited by Mark Danner, 199. New York: New York Review of Books, 2004.

———. "Order Establishing Combatant Status Review Tribunal." July 7, 2004. Available at http://www.defenselink.mil/news/Jul2004/d20040707review.pdf.

———. *Working Group Report on Detainee Interrogations in the Global War on Terrorism: Assessment of Legal, Historical, Policy, and Operational Considerations.* April 4, 2003. In *Torture and Truth: America, Abu Ghraib, and the War on Terror,* edited by Mark Danner, 187. New York: New York Review of Books, 2004.

U.S. Department of Justice. Office of the Attorney General. "Restoration under Treaty with France." *Opinions of the Attorney General* 1 (June 17, 1802): 114.

———. Office of the Attorney General. "Restoration under Treaty with France." *Opinions of the Attorney General* 1 (June 25, 1802): 119.

———. Office of the Inspector General. *The September 11 Detainees: A Review of the Treatment of Aliens Held on Immigration Charges in Connection with the Investigation of the September 11 Attacks.* Washington, D.C.: U.S. Government Printing Office, 2003. Available at http://www.usdoj.gov/oig/special/0306/press.pdf.

———. Office of Legal Counsel. "The President's Compliance with the 'Timely Notification' Requirement of Section 501(B) of the National Security Act." In *The Constitution and the Attorneys General,* edited by H. Jefferson Powell, 483. Durham, N.C.: Carolina Academic Press, 1999.

———. Office of Legal Counsel. "Military Interrogation of Alien Unlawful Combatants Held outside the United States." 2003. *New York Times.* Available at http://graphics8.nytimes.com/packages/pdf/national/OLC_Memo1.pdf.

———. Office of Legal Counsel. "The President's Constitutional Authority to Conduct Military Operations against Terrorists and Nations Supporting Them." In *The Torture Papers: The Road to Abu Ghraib,* edited by Karen J. Greenberg and Joshua L. Dratel. New York: Cambridge University Press, 2005.

———. Office of Legal Counsel. "Legal Standards Applicable under 18 U.S.C. §§2340–2340A." In *The Torture Debate in America,* edited by Karen J. Greenberg, 361. New York: Cambridge University Press, 2006.

———. Office of Legislative Affairs. "Letter from the Justice Department's Office of Legislative Affairs." March 24, 2006. In *Wartime Executive Power and the National Security Agency's Surveillance Authority: Hearings before the Senate Judiciary Committee,* 109th Cong., 2d Sess., 2006 (Ser. No. J-109-59), 147.

———. *White Paper.* In "Documents Relating to the National Security Agency Spying Program: Framing the Debate," edited by David Cole and Martin S. Lederman. *Indiana Law Journal* 81 (2006): 1355.

U.S. Department of the Air Force. Office of the Judge Advocate General. *Final Report and Recommendations of the Working Group.* February 5, 2003. In *The Torture Debate in America,* edited by Karen J. Greenberg, 377. New York: Cambridge University Press, 2006.

U.S. Department of the Army. *Field Manual 34-52: Intelligence Interrogation,* 1992. Available at http://www.globalsecurity.org/intell/library/policy/army/fm/fm34-52.

———. "Army Regulation 15-6 Final Report: Investigation of FBI Allegations of Detainee Abuse at Guantánamo Bay, Cuba, Detention Facility (as Amended)." June 9, 2005. In *Administration of Torture: A Documentary Record from Washington to Abu Ghraib and Beyond,* edited by Jameel Jaffer and Amrit Singh, A-98. New York: Columbia University Press, 2007.

U.S. Department of the Navy. General Counsel of the Navy. *Statement for the Record: Office of General Counsel Involvement in Interrogation Issues.* July 7, 2004. Available at http://www.neoprag.com/dcm/moramemo.pdf.

U.S. Departments of Army, Navy, Air Force, and Marine Corps. "Enemy Prisoners of War, Retained Personnel, Civilian Internees, and Other Detainees." *Army Regulation 190-8,* ch. 1, §§1–6 (1997). Available at http://www.au.af.mil/au/awc/awcgate/law/ar190-8.pdf.

U.S. Marine Corps. "Working Group Recommendations on Detainee Interrogations." February 27, 2003. In *The Torture Debate in America,* edited by Karen J. Greenberg, 383. New York: Cambridge University Press, 2006.

Vagts, Detlev F. "Military Commissions: A Concise History." *American Journal of International Law* 101 (2007): 35–48.

Vidal, Gore. *Lincoln.* New York: Random House, 1984.

Waas, Murray. "Internal Affairs." *National Journal* (March 17, 2007): 34 ff.

Waldron, Jeremy. "Torture and Positive Law: Jurisprudence for the White House." *Columbia Law Review* 105 (2005): 1681–1750.

Walsh, Lawrence E. *Final Report of the Independent Counsel for Iran-Contra Matters.* Washington, D.C.: U.S. Government Printing Office, 1994.

———. *Firewall: The Iran-Contra Conspiracy and Cover-up.* New York: Norton, 1998.

Wedgewood, Ruth. "Al Qaeda, Terrorism, and Military Commissions." *American Journal of International Law* 96 (2002): 328 ff.

Weiner, Tim. *Blank Check: The Pentagon's Black Budget.* New York: Warner, 1990.

———. *Legacy of Ashes: The History of the CIA.* New York: Doubleday, 2007.

Weisberg, Jacob. *The Bush Tragedy.* New York: Random House, 2008.

Wendel, W. Bradley. "Legal Ethics and the Separation of Law and Morals." *Cornell Law Review* 91 (2005): 67 ff.

Westin, Alan F. *The Anatomy of a Constitutional Law Case.* New York: Macmillan, 1958.

White, G. Edward. *The Constitution and the New Deal.* Cambridge, Mass.: Harvard University Press, 2000.

White, Leonard D. *The Federalists: A Study in Administrative History.* New York: Macmillan, 1948.

———. *The Jeffersonians: A Study in Administrative History, 1801–1829.* New York: Macmillan, 1951.

Wills, Garry. *Henry Adams and the Making of America.* Boston: Houghton Mifflin, 2005.

Wittes, Benjamin. *Law and the Long War: The Future of Justice in the Age of Terror.* New York: Penguin, 2008.

Wohlstetter, Roberta. *Pearl Harbor: Warning and Decision.* Stanford, Calif.: Stanford University Press, 1962.

Woodward, Bob. *Bush at War.* New York: Simon & Schuster, 2002.

———. *State of Denial.* New York: Simon & Schuster, 2006.

Wright, Lawrence. "The Spymaster." *New Yorker* (January 21, 2008): 42.

Yoo, John. "Transferring Terrorists." *Notre Dame Law Review* 79 (2004): 1183–1235.

———. "Possible Habeas Jurisdiction over Aliens Held in Guantánamo Bay, Cuba." In *The Torture Papers: The Road to Abu Ghraib,* edited by Karen J. Greenberg and Joshua L. Dratel, 29. New York: Cambridge University Press, 2005.

———. *The Powers of War and Peace: The Constitution and Foreign Affairs after 9/11.* Chicago: University of Chicago Press, 2005.

———. *War by Other Means: An Insider's Account of the War on Terror.* Chicago: University of Chicago Press, 2006.

———. "The Terrorist Surveillance Program and the Constitution." *George Mason Law Review* 14 (2007): 565–604.

"*Youngstown* at Fifty: A Symposium." *Constitutional Commentary* 19 (2002): 1.

Zelizer, Julian E. *On Capitol Hill: The Struggle to Reform Congress and Its Consequences, 1948–2000.* New York: Cambridge University Press, 2004.

Zernike, Kate. "Administration Prods Congress to Curb the Rights of Detainees." *New York Times,* July 13, 2006, A1.

———. "Military Lawyers Urge Protections for Detainees." *New York Times,* July 14, 2006, A16.

———. "White House Drops a Condition on Interrogation Bill." *New York Times,* September 20, 2006, A21.

INDEX